LINUX

Second Edition

LINUX

Installation, configuration, and use

Second Edition

Michael Kofler

An imprint of PEARSON EDUCATION

Harlow, England • London • New York • Reading, Massachussetts • San Francisco • Toronto • Don Mills, Ontario • Sydney
Tokyo • Singapore • Hong Kong • Seoul • Taipei • Cape Town • Madrid • Mexico City • Amsterdam • Munich • Paris • Milan

Pearson Education Limited
Head Office:
Edinburgh Gate
Harlow CM20 2JE
Tel: +44 (0) 1279 623623
Fax: +44 (0) 1279 431059

London Office:
128 Long Acre, London WC2E 9AN
Tel: +44 (0) 171 447 2000
Fax: +44 (0) 171 240 5771

and Associated Companies throughout the World.

Visit us on the World Wide Web at:
www.pearsoned-ema.com

First published in this edition by Addison-Wesley
(Deutschland) GmbH 1999

First published in Great Britain 2000

ISBN 0 201 59628 8

British Library Cataloguing-in-Publication Data
A catalogue record for this book is available from the British Library

Translated and typeset by 46
Printed and bound in the United States of America

Preface

The first version of the Linux Kernel (version number 0.01) was put onto the Internet by Linus Torvalds (Helsinki) in September 1991. Since then Linux has been developed at an incredible rate by thousands of programmers world-wide. What at the start had been an inside tip for hackers had, in 1998, an estimated eight million users!

Linux has established itself as a server platform so firmly that by now versions of most commercial database systems have been ported to Linux. Thanks to its increasingly simple installation and its increasingly user-friendly handling, Linux is also more and more becoming an alternative for private users fed up with the insufficient stability and miserable support of commercial suppliers.

What is so special about Linux?

- Linux is free and distributed together with this book! 'Free' refers both to price and the availability of source code. If you are not happy with Linux, you may (if you are familiar enough with programming) try to solve your particular problem yourself.
- Its documentation and support are unbelievable: while printed documentation obviously cannot be provided within a no-charge system, there are numerous online documents which describe nearly every aspect of Linux usage. If, in spite of all this, you still have problems, or discover an error, you can address one of the Linux newsgroups – and chances are you will get an answer back within a couple of days (sometimes hours).

Why this book?

Veritable legends about Linux are roaming through the media – consequently, the expectancy of many new users is quite high. However, the fact is that the installation of Linux may still cause problems (not least depending on your hardware) and that, initially, the utilization of Linux is unfamiliar and often less intuitive than you are accustomed to from a Windows or Macintosh PC. The most important goal of this book is to help you to get past the first obstacles.

The aim of this book is to provide the reader with a competent introduction to the handling of Linux – from installation and configuration to operation of the most important programs. This book should be helpful in getting acquainted with Linux as quickly as possible, without wasting time on installation problems or searching for online documentation. At the same time, it shows the most relevant basic features of Linux and Unix, so that you can understand your Linux system and become capable of configuring it to your own requirements.

I must be careful not to raise too many expectations: this book obviously cannot cover every single aspect of Linux – even ten books of this size would not be up to such a task. However, the matters covered – whether it is how to use the standard shell (`bash`) or how to connect your computer to the Internet – are described in sufficient depth that you can work effectively with Linux and its programs. Rather than being offered a superficial listing of the many programs that run under Linux, you have here a detailed description of the main components.

With Linux into the future!

- If stability and data security are more important to you than advertising slogans,
- if you are looking for a cost-effective entry to the Internet or if you need a stable network server,
- if you no longer wish to be at the mercy of the big software firms for better or for worse (usually the latter),
- if you want to look behind the scenes of your operating system,
- if you want to gather experience with the most varied programming languages (from C++ to SmallTalk),

then Linux is for you. Let yourselves get carried away by my own enthusiasm for Linux!

Michael Kofler `<kofler@ping.at>`, January 1999
`http://www.addison-wesley.de/Service/Kofler/ehome.html`

Acknowledgements

A great deal of recognition is owed in the first place to all of the developers (with Linus Torvalds at their head) who in the course of the past years have made Linux what it is today. Special thanks go to RedHat, Inc. for providing the free part of their excellent distribution for this book.

Contents

Structure of the book

The book is divided into four parts:

- Part I (Chapters 1 to 4) explains installation and first-time use of Linux.
- Part II (Chapters 5 to 8) provides much information on the optimum Linux configuration. It also supplies the necessary basic knowledge.
- Part III (Chapters 9 to 11) is dedicated to Internet access.
- Part IV (Chapters 12 to 20) describes how to apply the Linux system – from entering simple shell commands to image processing with Gimp. (Much of the information in Part IV is also valid for most other Unix systems, not only for Linux.)

Part I first answers some elementary questions about Linux: What is Linux? How did it originate? What is a distribution? Chapter 2 explains the installation of Linux. (Detailed information about how to install the Debian, RedHat, and SuSE distributions follows in the Appendices.) Chapter 3 provides a quick-start guide to running a Linux system: login, logout, shutdown, file handling, displaying and editing files, and so on. Chapter 4 is also very useful when you are taking your first steps with Linux: it describes where you can find online documentation about Linux.

Part II begins with a chapter about the basics of Linux, such as its file system structure, the integration of various hardware components under Linux (for example, mouse, floppy disk drive, streamer), process administration, the boot process, and so on. This chapter is not necessarily a prerequisite for the following chapters about configuration, but it makes their understanding considerably easier. The remaining chapters cover the subjects of basic configuration, elementary network configuration, kernel configuration, and X configuration, including KDE and GNOME.

Part III gives a detailed description if the most important Internet tools of Linux. The emphasis lies on methods which allow effortless and cost-effective utilization of the Internet even with a modem (offline configuration of WWW, email, and news).

Part IV assumes that Linux has been installed and configured to such an extent that you can comfortably work with it. Chapter 12 describes the operation of the `bash`, which is the standard shell for entering commands under Linux. Chapter 14 gives an overview of the most important commands available under Linux (`ls`, `cp`, `find`, `grep`, and so on).

Chapter 15 describes various tools that simplify your everyday work at text consoles or under the X Window System: file managers, programs for conversion of documents between different formats, tools for handling of PostScript files and for image processing, and so forth.

Special chapters have been dedicated to some particularly important programs: the Emacs editor, the LaTeX typesetting program, the LyX word processing program (more precisely, a modern user interface for LaTeX), and the image processing program Gimp, which offers similar functions to the commercial program Adobe Photoshop.

The **Appendices** deal with the special features of some important Linux distributions.

NOTE

Not all of the programs described in this book are supplied with every Linux distribution. If a particular program is missing in your distribution, you will in any case find it on the Internet. If you work with the RedHat distribution, the `contrib` directory of the RedHat FTP server is a good starting point for your search.

TIP

Some sample files pertaining to this book can be found on the Internet, on the author's homepage:

`http://www.addison-wesley.de/Service/Kofler/ehome.html`

New in this edition

The book has been extensively revised and expanded for this edition. The chapters on installation and configuration have once again been adapted to the considerably improved distributions. A new item in the configuration chapter is hard disk access optimization by means of RAID.

Kernel 2.2

This book reflects the new kernel 2.2. Superficially, the new kernel version differs only by a few features visible to the typical Linux user (for instance, easier access to Windows NT partitions, a number of new hardware drivers). Behind the scenes, however, much more has happened; the new functions are mainly to the profit of users who utilize Linux as a server system on high-quality hardware (SMP, RAID, and so on).

KDE and GNOME

Lately, no topic has provided as much material for discussion as the development of the two desktop systems KDE and GNOME, which make the utilization of Linux significantly more user-friendly. While KDE has been available in a stable version for some time, GNOME unfortunately was still in beta status when these lines were written. (This explains why this edition provides more information on KDE than on GNOME.)

Chapter 8 explains installation and configuration of both systems. Furthermore, KDE and GNOME programs are dealt with in the appropriate chapters (the KDE mail program, for example, in Chapter 10 about email).

Internet

The original Internet chapter has now been split into three chapters. New is the treatment of the following tools and programs:

- `kppp`, `linuxconf`, and `yast` for PPP configuration,
- `wwwoffle` for offline Web access,
- `kmail` for reading email,
- `slrn` for reading news articles,
- `leafnode` for offline news access.

LyX and Gimp

One of the most cherished developments of the last year is the development of user-friendly and stable application programs. This is reflected in two new chapters providing detailed descriptions of LyX (a WYSIWYG extension to LaTeX) and Gimp (an image processing program). The chapter on Emacs, which now (at last) takes both versions (GNU Emacs and Xemacs) into account, has also been completely revised.

What you won't find in this book

Linux is too vast to be described in one book. Moreover, it has been a premise since the first edition of this book to describe only a selection of programs, but each one thoroughly. In order to avoid disillusionment, here is a list of topics not to be found in this book.

- This book only describes hardware as far as it could be tested by the author himself. Linux supports countless additional devices and hardware extensions (graphics, network, ISDN, SCSI, and sound cards, scanners, ZIP drives, and so on). When installing and utilizing these, you will probably not be able to avoid a glance into the online documentation.
- The book only touches upon the subject of programming. Consequently, it does not cover kernel internals and the corresponding program code. (It does, however, explain how the kernel can be recompiled. For this, no programming knowledge is required.)
- A further gap concerns networking: the book describes some basics of network configuration (NFS, FTP, Internet access with a modem via PPP or SLIP), but only from the client point of view. If you want to use Linux to run an Internet or Intranet server, you will need some more specific literature.
- Distribution-specific extensions are more or less ignored outside the appendices. This book attempts instead to describe the common denominator of all or at least most Linux distributions. For further information about specific extensions, you will have to consult their accompanying manuals.

- Finally, the book tries to keep clear of commercial programs. However nice the increasing choice of commercial programs may be – ApplixWare, Informix, Oracle, StarOffice, WordPerfect – it would go beyond the scope of this book even to describe only a small selection of these programs.

Part I
Installation

What is LINUX?

1

In order to answer the question 'What is Linux?', this chapter explains some vital concepts which occur frequently throughout the book: operating system, Unix, distribution, Slackware, kernel, and others. A concise overview of the features of Linux and the available programs makes it clear how far-reaching the application possibilities of Linux are.

This section is followed by a brief excursion into the – still short – history of Linux: you get to know how Linux came into being and on which components it is based. A point of central importance is the General Public License (GPL for short), which specifies the conditions under which Linux may be distributed. Only the GPL makes Linux a free system (where 'free' means more than just free of charge).

1.1 What is Linux?

Linux is a Unix-like operating system. The main difference from 'true' Unix systems is that Linux may be copied freely, including the complete source code. (Details of the conditions under which Linux and the associated programs may be distributed are provided on page 15.) There are almost no limitations in functionality – Linux is, in many ways, more complete than some expensive Unix systems. It supports a wider palette of hardware components and, in several areas, it is written in a more efficient code.

An **operating system** is a bundle of programs that realize the most fundamental functions of a computer: the man–machine interface (in practice, the administration of the keyboard, screen, and so on) and the administration of system resources (computing capacity, memory, and so on). You need an operating system in order to be able to start a program and store your own data in a file.

In the course of the history of electronic data processing, various operating systems have emerged. Up until now, your most intensive contact probably will have been with the MS-DOS operating system and the Windows systems built on top of it (Windows 3.1, Windows 95). Furthermore, the basically independent operating systems OS/2 and Windows NT show a fairly close kinship with MS-DOS. Independently of MS-DOS, several other (mostly better) operating systems have been developed, such as those for the NeXT computer, the Apple Macintosh, and the by now nearly forgotten home computers, the Commodore Amiga and the Atari ST.

Long before all these operating systems, there was **Unix**. Thus, historically speaking, Unix is a rather ancient operating system, but in practice, it is more modern than DOS in each and every respect (no 640 Kbytes memory limit, true multitasking, faster, more stable, and so forth). However, its large memory requirements and – at least at first sight – its horrible user interface have made it an operating system employed nearly exclusively on expensive workstations in scientific and technical environments.

NOTE

In this book, Unix is employed as a common denominator of various operating systems derived from it. The names of these operating systems usually end in -ix (Irix, Xenix, and so on) and are mostly registered trademarks of the corresponding manufacturers. UNIX itself is also a registered trademark, which has changed ownership several times during the past few years.

With the free availability of Linux, which does not require a workstation, but only a standard PC, the role of Unix is changing again.

You can install several operating systems in parallel on your PC without any problems. You must simply specify, when starting your computer, whether it should boot under Windows, under Linux or under another operating system. Under Linux, you can even access the file system of DOS or Windows.

The Kernel

The term 'Linux', to be precise, only means the **kernel**: the kernel is the innermost part of an operating system, performing elementary functions, such as memory management, process administration, and control over the hardware. When these words were written, kernel 2.2 had just arrived. Thus, the information given in this book already refers to kernel 2.2.

The version numbers of the kernel need some special attention. We have to distinguish between stable user versions (1.2.*n*, 2.0.*n*, 2.2.*n*) and developer versions (also called hacker kernels, 1.3.*n*, 2.1.*n*, 2.3.*n*). Linux users for whom the stability of the system is important should use a fully developed user kernel. Only those who are interested in participating in the development of the kernel or who have to rely on a new feature of the developer kernel not yet present in the most recent stable user kernel should put up with a hacker kernel. The disadvantages: developer kernels often still contain code that has not been tested thoroughly enough and will probably cause problems. Most distributions are based on stable kernels, but offer the option to install the latest available developer kernel instead.

As Linux is being developed continuously over the Internet, you will find one or more new versions of the developer kernel every week. But do not worry; you do not have to chase after hundreds of updates. Once Linux runs stably on your computer, there is rarely a reason to alter anything. Most modifications of the kernel concern very specific aspects of Linux, such as adaptation of the system to new hardware, correction of errors (which mostly occur only under rare circumstances anyway), or optimization of a function.

> **TIP** Generally speaking, you should not be too puzzled by all these version numbers: not only has the kernel got one number, but so has practically every library, compiler, program, distribution, and so forth, available under Linux. More background information regarding the kernel and its features is given from page 199 onwards, where you can find a description of how to compile an up-to-date kernel optimized for your own computer.

1.2 What does Linux offer?

The question – What is Linux? – has not yet been answered fully. Many users are not interested in the kernel at all – as long as it runs and supports the existing hardware. For these users, the term 'Linux', as used in everyday language, includes, apart from the kernel, the huge bundle of programs that comes with the Linux kernel in the form of distributions (see the following section).

This section gives an overview of the most important features of Linux and the available application programs. Naturally, this overview is not complete – it would make little sense to list every single program that runs under Linux.

Kernel features

- Linux supports multitasking (concurrent execution of several processes), multiuser operation (concurrent usage by several users), paging (swapping of memory to hard disk, if the available RAM is not sufficient), shared libraries (libraries of system functions are loaded only once even when they are needed by several processes), interprocess communication (IPC), and – since version 2.0 – Symmetric Multi Processing (SMP, the use of several processors).
- Linux supports practically all common PC hardware: all Intel 386-compatible processors; ISA, EISA, VLB, and PCI bus systems; most (E)IDE and SCSI hard disk controllers and hard disks, CD-ROM drives and streamers connected to them; most common CD-ROM drives not connected to an IDE or SCSI bus; most network cards, mice, and so on. (A complete list is given in the `Hardware-HOWTO` – see Chapter 4 from page 69 onwards.)
- Linux supports not only Intel processors, but also the DEC Alpha processor, Sun Sparc, Mips, Motorola, and so on. However, the most widely used variation is certainly the Intel one.
- Linux uses its own file system (ext2fs). File names may contain up to 255 characters, files may have sizes up to 2 Gbytes, file systems up to 4 Tbytes. It

is also equipped with a lot of security features. (When Linux is executed on 64-bit processors, file sizes may also be larger than 2 Gbytes.)

- Under Linux, it is possible to access foreign file systems: DOS, Windows 9x (with long file names), NTFS (read only), OS/2 (read only), Minix, NFS (file systems available over the network), and so on. However, it is not possible to access compressed DOS/Windows partitions (except through a long-winded procedure using the DOS emulator).
- Linux supports several binary formats for the execution of binary files: a.out (standard up to version 1.0), ELF (standard since version 1.2), and iBCS2. iBCS2 allows you to use many commercial programs available for SCO Unix without any need for recompilation or porting to Linux. Since more and more software providers offer separate Linux versions of their programs, the iBCS2 emulator is decreasing in importance. (Irony of fate: SCO is now offering an emulator to allow Linux programs to be used under SCO Unix!)
- Under Linux, a range of network protocols is available (TCP/IP, PPP, SLIP, and so on).

Compared with kernel 2.0, kernel 2.2 brings only a few tangible changes for the average user. However, much has happened underneath the surface. For example, SMP support has been significantly improved and memory management has been optimized. A lot of new code can be found in the network functions which, on the one hand, had to become considerably faster and more stable and, on the other hand, were supposed to support additional protocols (including the new IP version, IPnG).

The support of several non-Intel-compatible processors has been integrated in the code better than before. New kernel functions help with dynamic activation/deactivation of modules (instead of leaving this task to the external `kerneld` program). Furthermore, there is a huge number of new or improved hardware drivers for ISDN, network, SCSI, and sound cards.

The minimum requirements for stable execution of Linux in text mode are about 4 Mbytes of RAM for Linux 2.0, and about 5 Mbytes of RAM for Linux 2.2. However, to make the system run reasonably fast, a minimum of 8 Mbytes is a better alternative. If you also wish to use the X Window System, you will need at least 16 Mbytes (better 32 Mbytes). If you want to turn an old 486 PC into a Linux workstation, an older kernel version is probably sufficient. A very stable version is, for example, version 1.2.13. Compared with the 2.n kernels, this version is relatively space-saving.

The X Window System

After booting, Linux initially runs in text mode, with the possibility of switching between several text terminals. (Normally, there are six terminals available which can be accessed via the Alt+F1 to Alt+F6 key combinations).

It is also possible to start the X Window System under Linux. In order to run the X Window System, you need either the free port XFree86 or a commercial X server (for example, XInside or Metro-X). XFree86 supports practically all graphic cards whose producers have released their documentation.

In real terms, the X Window System is just a collection of functions for the graphical display of information on a screen. Built on this base are graphical user interfaces and application programs that greatly facilitate the handling of Linux. Common Linux distributions mostly include the window manager `fvwm`, the desktop systems KDE and GNOME, and a whole range of X programs.

Tools

The input of commands is carried out in a so-called **shell**. A shell is something similar to the DOS command interpreter, only a lot more powerful. Under Linux, several shells are available. The most popular is `bash` (Bourne Again Shell). Anybody who dislikes this can probably get along with `tcsh` (compatible with the C shell).

A large number of **commands** are available for file management and system administration, such as `ls` (corresponds to `DIR` under DOS), `cp` (corresponds to `COPY`), and so on. For handling files there is also a vast choice of file managers which either run in text mode (for example, `mc`, largely compatible with Norton Commander) or even support X.

The range of **editors** varies from simple editors (such as `joe`), to `vi`, an editor which is difficult to handle but available on practically all Unix systems, to huge editors such as Emacs. This program is sometimes ironically called an operating system on its own because it contains such a vast number of functions: Emacs can be used to read and write email and news articles, debug C programs, and so forth. The term editor is no longer really appropriate in this case.

Text processing and formatting

The predominant (free) typesetting program under Linux is LaTeX. To this not-so-easy-to-handle typesetting program, the LyX program provides a modern interface which almost achieves WYSIWYG (what you see is what you get). In addition, Linux provides a variety of tools and utilities to process PostScript files or to convert them into other formats, to display files in different formats on a screen, and so on.

Network software

Linux supports the TCP/IP, PPP, and SLIP protocols. It allows the construction of almost arbitrarily complex local networks. Client and server programs are available for all kinds of connection with the Internet (telnet, rlogin, email, News, ftp, WWW). Thus, under Linux, you can not only use the Internet services, but also establish an Internet server yourself. Samba allows management of networks which Windows PCs can access as clients (access to files, printers, and so on).

Programming

Under Linux you will find a wide range of programming languages: to start with, the GNU C and C++ compilers, for which a whole palette of utilities is available (from `make` to the version control system `rcs` and the debugger `gdb`). Libraries and tool kits allow you to write C programs with graphical user interfaces (such as wxWindows), or with 3-D graphics under OpenGL (mesa). Many other programming languages are also available under Linux, such as Java, Lisp, Oberon, Perl, Python, Sheme, SmallTalk, and Tcl/Tk. Also, the available shells (bash, C shell) are fully programmable.

Emulators

Linux also offers a DOS emulator which allows execution of many DOS programs (but not Windows 3.1). The Wine project is trying to realize the execution of programs for Windows, but this project is still very much under development. The fact that Unix programs which correspond to the iBCS2 standard can be executed has already been mentioned when presenting the kernel features. Emulators for Atari ST, Commodore 64, Commodore Amiga, Sinclair ZX Spectrum, and so on, are primarily targeted at playful characters.

Documentation

There is a huge amount of online documentation for Linux. Information on where to find such documentation and how to view it is provided in Chapter 4 from page 69 onwards.

Others

- Databases: Ingres (relational), Mini SQL (relational, largely SQL compatible), obst (object-oriented), Postgres (object-relational)
- Mathematics: MuPaD (computer algebra system), scilab (largely MathLab compatible)
- Graphics: xv (image processing and conversion), gimp (image processing, similar to Photoshop), POV-Ray (ray tracing)

> **CAUTION** Some of the programs mentioned above are shareware or subject to copyright conditions that differ from those of the GPL. It is permissible to try them out in any case, but in many cases regular or commercial use or commercial distribution are restricted or require registration.

Commercial programs

The components listed so far are immediately available (depending on the extent of the distribution and its installation), and with the increasing diffusion of Linux, more and more commercial programs are being ported to Linux. It is particularly worth noticing that in 1998 nearly all important relational database systems became available for Linux. Thus Linux was recognized as an important server platform by such market giants as Oracle. Commercial software (with very few exceptions) is not free of charge.

The following (incomplete) list includes some important programs that have been ported to Linux: Adabas database, Applixware Office, Common Desktop Environment, Corel WordPerfect, Flagship database, Informix database, JavaWorkshop, LNX-DBMS, Maple, Mathematica, Metro Link Motif, Netscape Navigator/Communicator, Oracle database, Poet, StarOffice, WABI Windows emulator.

Special mention must be made of Motif: many commercial programs are based on Motif, an extension of the X Window System through unified control elements and a wide range of supplementary programs. Several Motif versions are available for Linux; however, none of them is free of charge.

There are two kinds of Motif programs: programs containing the Motif library statically in their program code and programs relying on Motif being installed and linking the library dynamically. The advantage of the first type: Motif need not be installed. The disadvantage: memory consumption is much higher because each motif program loads its own copy of the Motif library into memory.

Motif is sold in two formats: as a package of several libraries sufficient for the execution of Motif programs, or as a development system which also allows you to write your own Motif programs. (The second alternative is obviously the more expensive one.)

NOTE

Efforts are currently being made to produce a free port of Motif. The project is named LessTif, but it is not yet as advanced as the Linux system itself. An extensive list of commercial Linux software can be found in the Commercial HOWTO document (see page 77).

Hardware support

Linux supports nearly all of the common PC hardware. Problems are mostly caused by very recent hardware components (for example, graphics cards) for which no drivers exist as yet under Linux or XFree86. In some (increasingly fewer) cases, new drivers do not fail because of the programmers' lack of motivation, but because the manufacturers involved are not ready to cooperate, do not supply the necessary documentation, or prohibit their use in free code.

Nor is there much hope for owners of so-called GDI printers and other hardware components exclusively designed for use with Microsoft Windows (such as modems whose modem functions are not realized via hardware, but via Windows software).

The outlook for ISA plug-and-play cards is slightly less bleak: they are not yet directly supported by the kernel (or only in very few exceptional cases), but they can be configured via the auxiliary programs `pnpdump` and `isapnp`. In most distributions, the automatic call of `isapnp` is already integrated in the init process. (Prior to this, however, you must create the appropriate configuration files! If needed, cast a glance at the SuSE support database and look for 'PNP.')

```
http://www.suse.de/Support/sdb/
```

Another gap in hardware support is constituted by the USB (Universal Serial Bus). Appropriate modules are already under development, but not yet integrated in kernel 2.2.

General information on currently supported hardware can be found in the Hardware HOWTO (see also page 77). For detailed information Especially on graphic cards and laptops, we recommend the Web site of XFree86 and the Linux Notebook page. In addition, several distributions maintain their own harware compatibility lists:

```
http://metalab.unc.edu/mdw/HOWTO/Hardware-HOWTO.html
http://www.XFree86.org
http://www.cs.utexas.edu/users/kharker/linux-laptop
http://www.redhat.com/support/docs/hardware.html
http://www.suse.de/cdb/
```

Generally speaking, you should ensure *before* buying a new computer or a hardware extension that all components are supported by Linux.

1.3 Distributions

A Linux distribution is a combination of the actual operating system (kernel) and additional programs. A distribution allows a relatively quick and comfortable installation of Linux. All distributions are sold as CD-ROMs. Some distributions are also available on the Internet, but given the huge amount of data (often several hundred Mbytes), copying a whole distribution via the Internet or installing it directly through the network is practically only possible in universities or companies with fast Internet connection.

Distributions differ from each other mainly in the following respects:

- Number, choice, and topicality of the accompanying programs and libraries.
- Programs for installation, configuration, and maintenance of the system: these programs help you to set up hundreds of configuration files of the system correctly and easily. Functioning installation and configuration tools represent an enormous saving of time.
- Adaptation to foreign languages: some distributions still give the impression that English is the only language of this world. Other distributions are specially geared for use in non-English language countries.
- Configuration of the window manager: this configuration determines the visual appearance of the X Window System and has a great influence on the quality of working conditions (function of mouse and keyboard, color settings, and so on). Manual changes of such a configuration often require great effort.
- Package system: administration of Linux application programs is usually carried out via packages. The package system influences the ease of later installation of additional programs and the updating of existing ones. Currently, three

mutually incompatible package systems are in common use: RPM (amongst others, Caldera, DLD, RedHat, TurboLinux, SuSE), TGZ (Slackware), and DEB (Debian).

- Organization of the Init-V boot process: this deals with system start-up, that is, the start of all necessary processes up to the login prompt. The configuration files elaborated in this process bear different names in all distributions and are located in different directories. There is not even a consensus on the assignment of runlevels. All this certainly does not facilitate the task of maintenance.
- Live system: some distributions (increasingly fewer) allow operation of Linux directly from a CD-ROM. Only a minimal base system needs to be installed on the hard disk. Although this is rather slow and inflexible, it allows a relatively easy trying out of Linux.
- Umsdos system: some distributions allow installation of Linux in a directory of a DOS partition. This is slow and has innumerable other disadvantages, but saves (re)partitioning of the hard disk. As with the live system, this variation too is mostly of interest for trying out Linux (in particular if it can be combined with a live system).
- Target platform: many distributions are only available for Intel-compatible processors. However, there are also distributions for DEC Alpha, SUN Sparc, PowerPC (Macintosh), and so on.
- Documentation: some distributions are supplied with manuals (in electronic or in printed form).
- Support: with some distributions you receive free help with the installation (via email and/or phone).

The statement that Linux is free seems to be blatantly contradicted by the price charged for most of the distributions (often over $50 in the US). It is fairly easy to understand why there should be such a charge: although Linux and most application programs can indeed be downloaded free of charge over the Internet, the compilation of an up-to-date distribution requires time and know-how. A good installation program (which also has to be programmed and maintained) is alone often worth the price of a whole distribution! Above all, it will save Linux or Unix novices much time with installation and configuration.

Also, the production of one or more CDs, often accompanied by a substantial manual, costs money, not to mention the availability of personal support in case of installation problems. Also, a distribution becomes expensive when it includes commercial software.

The question of which is the best distribution, which is best suited to whom, and so on, can easily degenerate into a holy war. Somebody who has opted for one distribution and has got used to its peculiarities will not easily switch to a different distribution. Generally, switching distribution can only be done through a complete new installation, which requires a certain amount of effort.

The criteria for choosing a distribution are the topicality of its components (keep an eye on the version numbers of the kernel and important programs, such as the C compiler), the quality of the installation and configuration tools, the available support, accompanying manuals, and so on.

All distributions can be used internationally (assuming a basic knowledge of the English language). Some distributions, however, excel through particular consideration of national language peculiarities, thus saving the user a lot of configuration effort and hassle. Also, the value of a national language manual should not be underestimated.

> **NOTE**
>
> Competition between many distributions may provide a push to their further development, but it also creates upheaval with the installation of programs not supplied together with the distribution (and, in particular, with commercial programs). A missing or obsolete program library is often the cause of a program not running. For Linux novices in particular it is practically impossible to remedy such problems. Some software manufacturers even go so far as to offer support of their products only when it is used together with a specific distribution. (Obviously, each manufacturer chooses a different distribution ...)
>
> To eliminate such problems, the Linux Standard Base (LSB) was called into existence, which is supposed to define the smallest common denominator for future LSB-conformant distributions:
>
> `http://www.linuxbase.org`

Server mirrors on CD-ROM, which are released by many Linux vendors every two or three months, should not be confused with distributions. A server mirror is a copy of all Linux-specific files from Internet servers with Linux software. Many server mirrors do not contain distributions; instead, you will find the most up-to-date versions of all sorts of Linux application programs (normally as single archive files together with their source code).

But don't be hoodwinked by the low cost of server mirrors: installing the programs requires manual work and presumes a certain knowledge of Linux. Beginners are better off with distributions where installation is easily carried out through preconfigured packages. Server mirrors are addressed to experienced Linux users who need the latest versions of Linux programs and online documentation, but have no access to the Internet (or are reluctant to pay all those Telecom charges).

Some current Linux distributions

The following overview of the most important available distributions (in alphabetical order and without claiming to be exhaustive) sets out to provide a general orientation in the field.

Caldera

Caldera Open Linux is a successful attempt to create a Linux distribution for professional users. (Meanwhile, however, many competitors make the same claim.) Depending on the distribution variation, Caldera excels through various commercial add-ons, in particular excellent support of Novell network functions.

Debian

While most distributions are put together by companies whose main aim is to make financial gains out of their distributions, Debian is a true exception: this distribution is put together by committed Linux users who put great emphasis on stability and adherence to the rules of 'free' software. Several concepts of this distribution – such as the professional package administration – have set standards for other distributions and are still at the forefront in several aspects. (Just try to update your distribution without restarting your computer!) During the past years, Debian has become increasingly more user-friendly; however, for Linux novices this distribution is still not suitable because of its difficult package administration program `dselect`.

RedHat

The RedHat distribution is amongst the best maintained Linux distributions currently available. This distribution dominates the American market especially. The package administration on the basis of the `rpm` format (a proprietary development of RedHat) has now been adopted by many other distributions. RedHat Linux is available, in largely uniform outfit, for several processor platforms (Intel, DEC Alpha, SUN Sparc). Besides the original RedHat distribution, there are a number of derived distributions providing various improvements, language adaptations (such as a Spanish distribution), additional components (KDE), and so on.

Slackware

Slackware was (after the SLS distribution which is currently no longer up to date) one of the first available Linux distributions. With regard to maintenance and ease of installation, however, the currently up-to-date Slackware can no longer keep pace with many other distributions.

SuSE

Thanks to its high topicality, the huge number of preconfigured packages, the comprehensive manual, and the excellent maintenance, SuSE Linux (Gesellschaft für Software und Systementwicklung) has become the most widely diffused Linux distribution in Europe. However, SuSE Linux is also available with English-language menus and manuals. The `yast` administration tool not only helps with (nearly) all configuration problems (including ISDN configuration) but, similarly to Debian, also automatically solves dependency problems which may occur during package installation.

TurboLinux

This distribution, put together by Pacific HighTech (PHT), has been specially optimized for use in Japan and has become the market leader there. The distribution is also available in an English version.

Minimal distributions

Besides these large distributions, you will find some collections of miniature systems (down to a complete Linux system on a single diskette!) on the Internet. These distributions are mostly based on old (and therefore smaller) kernel versions. They are particularly designed for special tasks, such as maintenance work (emergency system) or to be able to use a Linux system without a proper installation (straight from one or more diskettes). This is useful if you need to run Linux temporarily on a foreign computer whose hard disk you do not wish (or are not allowed) to repartition.

> **TIP**
>
> A reasonably complete list of the most varied Linux distributions (no matter whether of commercial or other origin) can be found on the Internet:
>
> `http://www.linuxhq.com/dist-index.html`
>
> However, you should also browse through the various computer magazines which frequently carry out comparative tests between distributions and which are obviously more detailed and up to date than this book could hope to be. An overview of some current distributions can also be found in the HOWTO text on distributions – see page 77.

After working on this book, however, I stick to my previous conclusion that life would be wonderful if one could only combine the advantages of all distributions without having to cope with their disadvantages!

1.4 The origin of Linux

This section is concerned not with further details on Linux, but with questions such as: Why does Linux exist at all? How has the system been developed? Why is it free? In this, GNU (GNU is not Unix) and the FSF (Free Software Foundation) play an important role.

Linux is a very young operating system. The very first kernel parts (version 0.01) were developed by Linus Torvalds (Helsinki) on his own. He released the program code in September 1991 over the Internet. Within a very short time, programmers worldwide became interested in the idea and started programming extensions for it: a better file management system, drivers for various hardware components, additional programs, such as the DOS emulator, and so on. All of these components were also made available free of charge, and the entire system grew with breathtaking speed. Such a new operating system would never have been produced in this way without worldwide communication between programmers via the Internet.

One of the main reasons why Linux, although not containing items copyrighted by the big software houses, could nevertheless be developed so quickly, lies in the software which was already freely available at that point in time. Linux has not emerged from nowhere, as is sometimes wrongly assumed, but is based on a broad platform of free software. Minix provided the practical base for the first steps, software which was free though fairly limited in its functionality. Thus, the first Linux versions still used the Minix file system.

Even more important was (and still is) the great number of GNU programs. GNU programs have been around for much longer than Linux. On many Unix systems, GNU programs were already used as better substitutes for various original components – for example, the GNU C compiler, the GNU Emacs (text editor), various GNU utilities, such as `find` and `grep`, and so on. As soon as the Linux kernel was developed to the extent that the GNU C compiler could run on it, practically the whole range of GNU tools became available at a stroke. Thus, the bare kernel suddenly turned into a fairly exhaustive system, which became an attractive environment for an even larger community of developers.

As with Linux, GNU programs can be freely copied, with certain restrictions – and not only as binary programs but with their complete source code. This allows all GNU users to extend or correct the programs themselves in case of problems or errors. These modifications result in ever better and more mature versions of various GNU programs. Especially because of the free availability of the program code, the GNU C compiler has become *the* standard in the Unix world: this compiler is available on practically every Unix system. (There are also ports for DOS/Windows.) In fact, Linux too started with the GNU C compiler.

The combination of the Linux kernel, the numerous GNU components, the networking software of BSD Unix, the likewise freely available X Window System of MIT (Massachusetts Institute of Technology) and its XFree86 port to PCs with Intel processors, as well as several other programs, such as LaTeX, turns Linux distributions into complete Unix systems.

Linux is naturally not simply the brainchild of Linus Torvalds exclusively (even though, without him, there would be no Linux in its current form). Linux is instead the result of very hard work by many committed people, who have been producing free software in their spare time for years (maybe in some cases, as part of their computer studies). Meanwhile, the Linux kernel has exceeded the unbelievable number of one and a half million lines of program code! The most important names are contained in the file `/usr/src/linux/CREDITS`. You can read this file after you have installed your Linux kernel.

Legal matters – the General Public License

Linux is 'free' – but what does this really mean? Often, free is taken to mean free of charge. It is true that Linux is available free of charge (at least, via the Internet); but 'free' also and above all refers to the availability of the complete source code. This brings certain complications. What if a firm uses the Linux code, extends it, and then sells the system? This, too, is permitted, although with one restriction: the program code for the new system must be freely available. This ensures that all users may benefit from extensions to the system.

Thus, the aim of the developers of GNU and Linux was to create a system whose sources are – and remain – freely available. To avoid misuse, software that has been and is being developed as defined by GNU is protected by the General Public License (GPL). The GPL is backed by the Free Software Foundation (FSF, see `www.gnu.org`). This organization was founded by Richard Stallmann (the author of the Emacs editor), with the aim of making high-quality software freely available.

The main tenet of the GPL is that people may modify the code and even sell the resulting programs, but the user/buyer has a right to the complete code, may modify it in his/her turn, and give it away free of charge. Each GNU program must be distributed together with the complete GPL. Software protected by the GPL should therefore not be confused with Public Domain Software which is not protected at all.

Thus, the GPL excludes people from being able to develop and sell a GPL program *without* making the modifications publicly accessible. Each development thus becomes a gain for *all* users.

TIP

You can find the complete GPL on practically every Linux CD, as a text file named `COPYING`.

If you want to read more about the concept of free software, install GNU Emacs and press Ctrl+H, Ctrl+P. Emacs will then display a text that describes the aims of the FSF and provides answers to frequently asked questions (such as: 'Won't programmers starve?').

Besides the GPL, there is the LGPL variation (GNU Library GPL). The essential difference from the GPL is that a library protected in this way may also be used by commercial products whose code is *not* freely available. Without the LGPL, GPL libraries could only be used for GPL programs, which in many cases would be an undue restriction on commercial programmers.

CAUTION

By the way, not all parts of a Linux distribution are protected in the same way. While Linux and many tools are subject to the GPL, other programs available under Linux are shareware (such as the popular graphics program `xv`): private use is free of charge, but any commercial application of the program is only allowed after registration with the author.

Installation

This chapter provides an overview of how to install a Linux system on a PC with an Intel-compatible processor. It does not refer to a particular distribution, but describes the relevant installation steps (such as partitioning the hard disk) in a general way and conveys the necessary basic knowledge (so that you know what you are doing). Specific details of some selected distributions can be found in Appendices A to C.

The most tiresome but in most cases unavoidable step in a first installation of Linux is repartitioning the hard disk. In the course of this chapter, the necessary commands (`FDISK` and `FORMAT` under DOS, `fdisk` under Linux) are described in detail. This chapter also explains the installation of Umsdos, which avoids repartitioning (but has several other disadvantages).

So much for starters: during recent years, installation has become increasingly simple. Many detailed problems described in this chapter refer to older hardware, which by now is only seldom used!

> **NOTE** In this chapter, both DOS and Linux commands appear. Some of these commands even have the same name (`fdisk`!). For this reason, Linux commands are shown in small letters (and under Linux they must be entered this way), whereas DOS commands are given in capitals (although in DOS it does not really matter whether commands are entered in upper or lower case letters).

2.1 Requirements

In order to be able to install Linux, several requirements must be met:

- You need a PC with an Intel 386-compatible processor. (There are Linux distributions for systems with other processors, but this book does not deal with them.)

- You need enough RAM. How much is 'enough' depends on how you want to work with Linux. In text mode, 8 Mbytes are enough for comfortable work. If you want to use the X Window System as your graphical interface, you will need at least 16, or even better 32 Mbytes.
- You need a free partition with sufficient space on your hard disk. Here too, it is difficult to tell how much is 'enough.' A minimum installation without X may fit into 50 Mbytes, if really necessary. If, on the other hand, you carry out a standard installation of a common distribution, 500 Mbytes represents the lower limit. A better value is about 1 Gbyte – this leaves you enough space for testing larger packages, for a private news archive, and so on.

  Some distributions also allow a test installation in which only a minimum of data is actually installed. All other data is read in the framework of a so-called live system from an appropriate CD-ROM. A live installation saves hard disk space, but is slow and inflexible.
- You need hardware components which are recognized and supported by Linux. At present, this is the case for most standard hardware. Problems may be caused by exotic or very recently introduced SCSI, graphic, and network cards. Much hard work is also often required to get (plug & play) sound cards to work properly. No support at all is provided for so-called GDI printers, Windows modems (that is, devices without any intelligence of their own, which have to completely rely on drivers which in turn are only available for Windows), and for USB hardware.
- If you want to work comfortably with the X Window System, you need a mouse with three (!) buttons, as the middle mouse button plays an important role under X. (On a two-button mouse, it is possible to press both buttons together to simulate the missing third button, but this is rather awkward.)
- If hardware problems occur, you need a fairly detailed knowledge of your computer's hardware. Often, installation fails only because the installation program does not recognize particular components. Manual input of hardware data may solve this problem. You will, however, have to know interrupt and I/O addresses.

Buying a computer

As a rule, you will already own a computer when you decide to install Linux – in this case, you will have to live with what you've got and hope that Linux can cope with all of the components. You are in a far better situation if you have not bought your computer yet and are thinking about Linux right now. Then you should consider the following points:

- A frequent source of problems is represented by hardware components that Linux does not know about yet. Old-fashioned hardware may sometimes have its advantages! Before you buy a computer or an expansion, you should check that all of the components are already supported by Linux. To do this, read the `Hardware-HOWTO`, which you will find on the Internet, for example under:

`http://metalab.unc.edu/mdw/HOWTO/Hardware-HOWTO.html`

Additional useful information is also provided by the hardware databases and compatibility lists maintained by RedHat and SuSE:

`http://www.redhat.com/support/docs/hardware.html`
`http://colb.suse.de`

- A particularly vast number of problems is created by very recent graphics cards. Information on which graphics cards are supported by XFree86 can also be found on the Internet. (XFree86 is a free server for the X Window System. XFree86 is supplied with all Linux distributions.)

  `http://www.XFree86.org`

- If the new computer is to be a notebook, cast a glance in the Linux Notebook page:

  `http://www.cs.utexas.edu/users/kharker/linux-laptop`

- Once the hardware obstacles are out of the way, the greatest obstacle for a smooth installation is the operating system pre-installed on the computer (mostly some Windows version) blocking the entire hard disk. Ask your dealer to install the operating system in a small partition (for example 500 Mbytes). Only then can you use the remainder of your hard disk according to your own ideas and create arbitrary additional partitions for Windows, Linux, or other operating systems.
- If the computer is to be equipped with Windows NT, ask your dealer for something like the following configuration:
  - First (primary) partition: about 300 Mbytes of FAT (if possible, with operable MS-DOS or Windows 3.1/9x for maintenance operations, otherwise empty)
  - Second (extended) partition: the entire remaining hard disk
  - Inside this, a logical partition of about 1 Gbyte NTFS with Windows NT.

  This type of partitioning has several advantages: first, the rest of the extended partition is free and can be used later for creation of additional logical partitions for Linux and NT. Second, there is a FAT partition which can be used for data exchange between Windows NT and Linux (including long file names as under Windows 9x). Third, the future LILO installation is easier if the first partition is a FAT partition which can also be modified under Linux.

2.2 Overview of the installation process

A normal Linux installation essentially follows the steps shown below (in the order they are shown). 'Normal' means that your computer already has an operating system installed (DOS, Windows), and that Linux is to be installed for the first time in addition to this operating system. The aim of the installation is that the existing operating system remains usable. After a successful installation, you can choose at start-up time whether you want to boot your computer with Linux or with your former operating system.

'Normal' also refers to the installation medium: this section is based on the assumption that you install Linux from a CD-ROM. Other variations (installation from hard disk, installation via a network connection) are discussed separately (see pages 45 and 46).

- You start up your computer under DOS/Windows. In many Linux distributions, you can at this point read parts of the online documentation, provided it is stored on the CD-ROM in a DOS-compatible format.
- If your current operating system fills the entire hard disk, that is, if you do not have a free partition or hard disk onto which Linux can be installed, you must repartition your hard disk under DOS/Windows (page 23).

  The aim of this step is to free an area on the hard disk so that later on a proper Linux partition can be established to store the Linux file system. Some distributions (Slackware, SuSE) allow you to ignore this step if you carry out a Umsdos installation (page 47) – but this has several disadvantages and is primarily suitable for trial operation to get to know Linux.
- Subsequently, you restart the computer. The Linux installation program is automatically started directly from the CD-ROM. If this does not work (for example, with an old motherboard/BIOS), you need to create one or more installation diskettes (page 30), unless these are not part of the distribution in the first place.
- Whether from CD-ROM or diskette, a minimum Linux system is now started in which the menu-driven installation program is executed. This program looks slightly different in each distribution. For some of the distributions, you will find more detailed instructions for the use of this program in Appendices A to C.
- A fundamental step in the installation process – independently of the distribution you are using – is the generation of Linux partitions on the hard disk (the necessary space for these partitions having been freed in step two).

  Some distributions start the Linux program `fdisk` for this purpose. Other distributions hide the unfriendly handling of this program behind a pretty interface – but this too does not save you the decision about which partition should be created with which size. More information on operation of `fdisk` and sensible hard disk partitioning can be found on page 33.
- In some distributions, the computer must be restarted after partitioning the hard disk. (This measure ensures that the partitioning was indeed modified.)

- In the next step, you specify which parts of the Linux distribution you wish to install. (Installing everything is seldom sensible and usually fails anyway because of space problems.)
- The installed system is now configured by means of various questions (mouse, printer, network settings, and so on).
- One final question still remains unanswered: How should Linux be started in future? There are several possibilities: via a boot diskette (slow), via a diskette with LILO (better), or directly from the hard disk with LILO (ideal). The third variation, however, has the disadvantage that it may under certain circumstances be incompatible with installed operating systems. (By the way, LILO stands for Linux Loader.)

  Therefore, at this point, a piece of advice which will be repeated several times in this book: please *do not* install LILO on your hard disk during the first installation! This procedure may be incompatible with Windows NT (depending on how this has been installed). Once you have a running Linux system, you can still install LILO on your hard disk. This is described in more detail from page 183 onwards. (Installation of LILO on a diskette, in contrast, bears no risk, but booting may take up to two seconds longer.)

Now you can start working with Linux (see Chapter 3 from page 59 onwards for the first steps), or you can manually perform further configuration steps to adapt Linux optimally to your specific requirements.

On the whole, a first installation of Linux (including the basic configuration) will take several hours. Serious problems are normally not to be expected – as long as you do not use hardware components that Linux does not know about.

CAUTION

To summarize again: there are only two critical points in the course of a Linux installation, where you may involuntarily destroy data of other operating systems or make your computer unbootable: hard disk partitioning with `fdisk` and installation of LILO on the hard disk.

TIP

It is highly recommended that Linux novices in particular write down the input values entered during the installation process. Particularly important are the names of partitions, which will probably be needed again later on – and it is easy to forget all those abbreviations, which are often very similar.

Preparation

Before you actually begin, two things need to be done: first, you must make sure that you have an empty diskette – you will need it during installation. Second, you need to find out some details about your hardware. Which SCSI controller are you using? Which network card do you own? Which interrupt and address range are used to address this card? Which port is your mouse connected to? What are the maximum line frequency (in kHz) and vertical refresh rate (in Hz) of your monitor?

You should find the answers to these questions in the documentation supplied together with your computer (I know this is wishful thinking ...). If you have already installed Windows 9x or NT on your computer, you can find most of the information via the Control Panel.

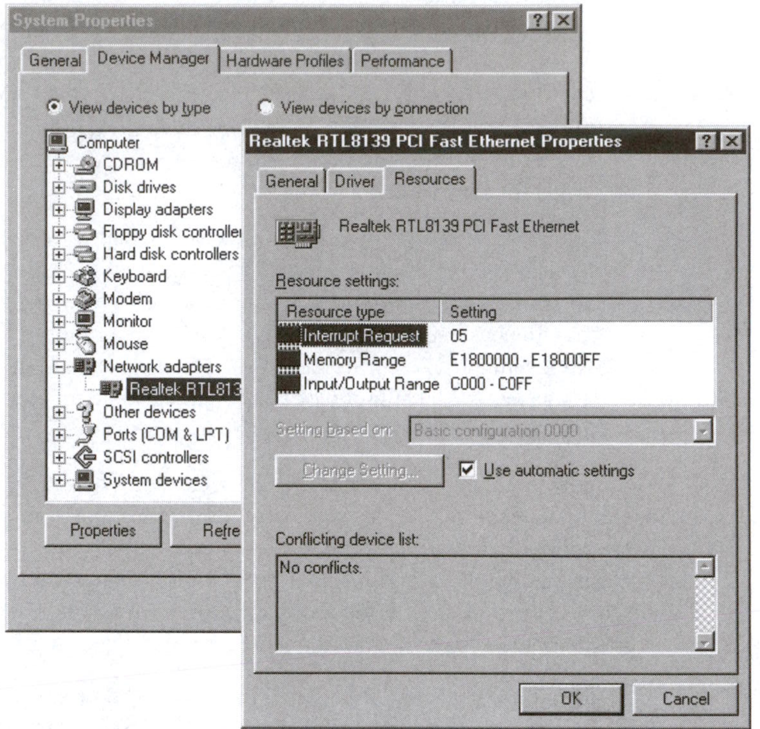

Figure 2.1 The network card is a Realtek Fast Ethernet card and uses interrupt 05 and address range 000-0FF (hexadecimal).

> **TIP** Under Windows 3.1, similar information is supplied by the `MSD.EXE` program (although with a slightly less elegant interface).

If problems arise ...

> **TIP** Before you begin the installation, please read the `README` files on the CD-ROM! These files are always more up to date than the accompanying manuals or this book. Under Windows, you should use `WRITE.EXE` (Windows 3.1) or `WORDPAD.EXE` (Windows 9x and later) to read them. These programs, unlike `NOTEPAD.EXE`, can handle Unix text files that do not have the standard DOS CR/LF linefeed.

A not uncommon, but nevertheless trivial source of error may be the floppy disk drive. If your computer hangs during loading of the boot diskette, try to create a new boot diskette (obviously using a different diskette!).

Linux can cope with many hardware components straight away. However, as new graphics cards, CD-ROM drives, and so on, enter the market every month, there will be many hardware configurations that cause problems. Some cases and possible solutions are discussed at the end of this chapter (page 48). However, in this book I cannot give advice on all likely hardware configurations – simply because I do not possess all this hardware. (On my own computer, Linux runs without problems!)

You may therefore run into a particular installation problem which is not discussed in this book. If this happens, you should study the Linux online documentation first. For this purpose, it is useful if you have access to the Internet via a different operating system (Windows) or a different computer. Nowhere else will you find information more quickly.

A good starting point are the homepages of the individual distributions (for example, `www.debian.org`, `www.redhat.com`, `www.suse.com`). The forum in which you will most likely find a solution in case of hardware problems are the relevant Linux newsgroups (`comp.os.linux.hardware`, and so on). A vast number of Linux links can be found on the author's homepage (see Preface). A useful tool for searching newsgroups is a news search engine (for example `www.dejanews.com`).

Finally, you can always try emailing the author (the address is in the Preface). I will endeavor to help you, but I cannot guarantee an answer to questions about hardware that I do not possess myself.

2.3 Repartitioning your hard disk under DOS/Windows

The aim of this section is to make room for the Linux installation. Repartitioning is required if the partition(s) of your current operating system fill the entire hard disk.

A partition is a self-contained section of a hard disk. Under DOS/Windows, partitions are assigned a specific drive letter (`C:`, `D:`, and so on) and appear to behave like independent hard disks.

If you want to accommodate several operating systems (Windows 9x, Windows NT, OS/2, Linux, and so on) on one hard disk, division into several partitions is essential. Each operating system needs at least one partition. (Thus it is not sufficient that several hundred Mbytes are free on a partition – what you need is a *separate* partition!) The problem is now that most computer dealers, when they sell a computer, fill the hard disk with a single huge DOS/Windows partition. There are several alternatives for repartitioning such a disk.

- You can delete existing partitions and recreate them in a smaller form. This alternative is always possible, but it is not very attractive because all data is lost. Even if you own a streamer, reinstallation of the operating system and restoring of all data will take hours (if not days).

- You can reduce an existing partition by means of the `FIPS` program. This works quite well and without loss of data, provided that the partition to be reduced is a DOS/Windows 3.1/Windows 9x partition (not OS/2, Windows NT, or similar). `FIPS` is a small DOS program which is supplied together with most Linux distributions.
- You can use a commercial utility program for repartitioning (for example Partition Magic). This is an expensive solution, but as with `FIPS` there is no loss of data. Furthermore, it provides a much more user-friendly interface and works also with partitions in other formats.

To start with, this section discusses some basic concepts of partitioning. It describes the `FIPS` program (which is supplied together with practically all Linux distributions), and finally the `FDISK` program (available under DOS, Windows 3.1, and Windows 9x. If you use a different operating system, you must use the appropriate partitioning tool (such as the hard disk manager under Windows NT).

TIP

An even better solution is to avoid all the partitioning hassle: when you buy your computer, insist on the operating system being installed in a small partition (for example 500–1000 Mbytes)! You can then create arbitrary additional partitions for Windows (for installation of application programs) as well as for Linux and other operating systems, and you gain a lot of flexibility. If you already own a computer and do not want to touch the Windows partition, you are obviously free to get yourself a second hard disk for Linux.

REFERENCE

There is a special installation variation of Linux which elegantly circumvents partitioning problems. Here, Linux is not installed in a separate partition, but in a directory of a DOS/Windows partition. This procedure is called Umsdos. It does, however, carry many technical disadvantages and is only supported by a few distributions. Details on this installation variation can be found from page 47 onwards.

Partition types

Before we get into further details of how to apply the `FIPS` and `FDISK` programs, some more background information: in order to increase confusion amongst users, there are three types of hard disk partition – primary, extended, and logical.

On one hard disk, there may exist a maximum of four primary partitions. Furthermore, it is possible to define an extended partition instead of one of the four primary partitions. Within this extended partition, several logical partitions can be created.

An extended partition only serves as a container for logical partitions. The only reason for an extended partition is to circumvent the limit of the four primary partitions. An extended partition without any logical partitions cannot be used under DOS, so that only primary and logical partitions are allowed for the actual storage of data.

To make things even more difficult, the DOS program `FDISK` can only define one primary partition (whereas the homonymous Linux command `fdisk` is capable of creating further primary partitions). In practice, this means that under DOS you can at most define one primary, one extended and, within the latter, several logical partitions.

This bewildering game continues with the naming of partitions in a system with several hard disks. Under DOS/Windows, the drive letters are assigned as follows: `C:` for the primary partition of the first hard disk, `D:` for the primary partition of the second hard disk, and so on. Only after having named all primary partitions can the logical partitions be put into play. (Because no data is stored directly in extended partitions, they are not assigned drive letters.) If you possess three disks with one primary and two logical DOS partitions each, then `C:`, `F:`, and `G:` belong to the first disk, `D:`, `H:`, and `I:` to the second disk, and `E:`, `J:`, and `K:` to the third disk.

By the way, the partitions of foreign file systems cannot be accessed under DOS. These partitions are not assigned a drive letter and are therefore invisible.

NOTE

Finally, one last piece of information: partitioning and formatting a hard disk are two completely different processes. After partitioning a hard disk, you may call up the corresponding disk areas using the letters `C:`, `D:`, and so on, but you cannot yet store any data on them. For use under DOS/Windows, you must first create a file system on each new partition, using the `FORMAT` command.

Subdivision of hard disk space

Before you change the partitioning of your disk, you should think about how much space you want to reserve for each of your operating systems. More precisely, at this point you just want to free enough space on your hard disk, in which you can create new partitions later on. What you will actually be doing with this free space remains open for now. Later, you may even wish to create additional DOS/Windows partitions besides your Linux partitions, if the first one turns out to be too small.

The following guidelines will perhaps be of some help:

- If you work with Windows 9x, 500–1000 Mbytes is a reasonable size for the Windows system partition. If at a later point you install a large number of Windows application programs, you can without problems create a second Windows partition (`D:`).
- Now to Linux: in principle, a minimal Linux system gets by with 50 Mbytes (without the X Window System) – but only few distributions are still capable of generating such a small system. A reasonable value for Linux novices is about 500–1000 Mbytes – this still leaves some space for a couple of commercial application programs. (StarOffice 5.0 alone, for example, requires a stately 160 Mbytes!) More details on this subject can be found on page 38.

- At least one Linux partition should lie entirely within the first 1024 cylinders of a hard disk. The reason: later on, you will probably want to install LILO in order to boot Linux straight from your hard disk. However, LILO can only access the first 1024 cylinders during the boot process.

  Since the cylinder size depends on the BIOS, it is impossible to tell with precision which memory area will be covered by the 1024 cylinders. In the worst case (with very old hardware), the limit already lies at about 500 Mbytes. In the best case (hardware currently on the market), the limit lies at 7.9 Gbytes. The 1024-cylinder limit only applies during the *start-up* of Linux. As soon as the kernel is running, Linux can access the whole hard disk.

REFERENCE

Details regarding cylinders follow on page 33. Do not despair if you cannot find space for a Linux partition within the first 1024 cylinders of your disk. With some clever tricks, the installation of LILO will be successful even in these circumstances (see page 193) – otherwise you can still boot from a diskette.

Reducing a partition using FIPS

In many cases you can use the program `FIPS.EXE`, which is usually located in the `dosutils` directory of Linux CDs, to reduce an existing partition of the operating systems DOS/Windows 3.1/Windows 9x without any loss of data.

CAUTION

Even though `FIPS` is considered to be relatively safe and stable, problems can never be completely ruled out. Therefore, it is highly recommended that you always make a backup of your most important data, even when you use `FIPS`!

Windows 95b, Windows 95 OEM (or OSR2) and Windows 98 use a new file system (FAT32). `FIPS` can cope with this only from version 2.0 onward. Please make sure that you use an up-to-date version!

However, `FIPS` is not able to handle NTFS partitions of Windows NT or the future Windows 2000!

`FIPS` reduces an existing primary partition as far as possible and creates a new, second primary partition in the space it has freed. If you have several hard disks or other partitions, their drive letters may change as a result of this new partition (`D:` may become `E:`). However, things change again as soon as you set up the newly created partition as a Linux partition.

In no case can the reduced primary partition become smaller than the data stored in it (pretty obvious, or ...?). In many cases the partition will be somewhat larger, in particular if non-relocatable files remain in existence during defragmentation.

Thus, `FIPS` divides one primary partition into two smaller primary partitions. This division can only take place in the free area of the partition. (Thus, there must be an area at the end of the partition that is not occupied by any files.) For this reason, it is necessary to defragment the disk beforehand. During this process, the sectors occupied by one file are shifted so that they are contiguous (whereas when the disk is fragmented the sectors of a file may be distributed all over the disk). The first part of the partition is the fully occupied one, the last part is free. Disk access is now somewhat faster than in the fragmented state. (Fragmentation occurs through normal use of the hard disk, that is, through creation and deletion of files of different sizes.)

Before you start defragmenting, you should check the partition for defects (`CHKDSK` under DOS, `SCANDISK` under Windows 9x) and delete any detected sectors that are no longer assigned to a file.

Under DOS 6.0, defragmentation can be carried out with the `DEFRAG` program. Under Windows 95, you click the secondary mouse button on the disk symbol in the Explorer, select the Context menu entry PROPERTIES, dialog tab EXTRAS, and then, in the pop-up dialog, you select the button OPTIMIZE NOW. You can sit back and watch this program working if you click the DETAILS button.

The problem with the use of defragmentation programs is that they consider some system files as not being relocatable. If you are unlucky, and a non-relocatable file lies towards the end of the partition, `FIPS` cannot reduce the partition to its full extent. The `FIPS` documentation gives a couple of hints regarding the origin of such files, but these are valid only for DOS or Windows 3.1.

Unfortunately, it is not known which files are considered as non-relocatable under Windows 9x. (On my own computer, one such file made the application of `FIPS` quite useless. A non-relocatable file was found in the last 5% of a 50% free 300 Mbyte partition. It was impossible to find out which file this was. I cannot tell whether defragmentation programs from other suppliers yield better results.)

> **TIP**
>
> If the defragmentation results are not satisfactory, you can try searching the hard disk for non-relocatable files and manually resetting their system and hidden attributes. The DOS command `ATTRIB /S \*.* > file` writes a list of the attributes of all the files on your hard disk into a text file.
>
> You can now easily read this text file with any editor and subsequently try to change the system and hidden attributes of individual files, either with `ATTRIB` or in the Explorer (secondary mouse button, context menu PROPERTIES). Caution is highly recommended – refrain from modifications in the root directory itself and be careful with the swap file! After this, execute the defragmentation program once more and hope for the best.

Next, you must create a DOS boot diskette (`FORMAT A: /s`) and copy the programs `FIPS` and `RESTORRB` together with the text file `error.txt` onto it. With this diskette, you reboot your computer and then execute `FIPS`. (Do *not* start `FIPS` directly from a running system – by doing so, you run a considerable safety risk).

The usage of `FIPS` is pretty straightforward: the program analyzes the hard disk and displays the result of this analysis. The current partition information (root and boot sectors) can be copied onto the diskette, so that in case of problems the partition can be restored with `RESTORRB`.

Then you can select, using the cursor keys ← and →, at which point the partition should be divided into two smaller partitions. (The partitioning point can obviously only be specified within the unused area of the partition. It is good practice to leave at least a couple of Mbytes free on the partition to be divided, otherwise it will hardly be possible to carry out reasonable work on it later on.) After several safety questions, the partition is permanently divided. (You may abort the program at any time by pressing Ctrl+C if you don't feel completely sure about what you're doing!)

Now, when you reboot your computer, DOS and Windows should work as before. However, the amount of free disk space should be considerably lower. But you have acquired a new empty partition. If you want to use this partition under DOS/Windows, you must format it with the `FORMAT` command. More probably, though, you will want to use this partition under Linux: to do this, you run the DOS program `FDISK` and delete the partition. (During the installation of Linux, you will create a new Linux partition in this area of the hard disk, which is now completely free). Details of how to use `FDISK` follow in the next subsection.

NOTE

`FIPS` also comes with extensive (English) online documentation: `fips.doc` describes the use of the program, `errors.txt` contains a list of possible error messages and a short description, and `techinfo.txt` gives technical background information (for those who are interested). Current information on `FIPS` can also be found on the Internet:

`http://www.igd.fhg.de/~aschaefe/fips/`

Repartitioning your hard disk with `FDISK`

It has already been mentioned that deleting a partition with the `FDISK` program causes a complete loss of all data stored in that partition. Therefore, a backup of all of your data is compulsory!

This is, however, not the only problem: you must also ensure that after the execution of `FDISK` you have the necessary diskettes to reinstall DOS or Windows and then restore the deleted data. (After deleting the partition with `FDISK`, neither DOS nor Windows is available any more!) Frequently, the problem consists in the fact that you have been supplied by your dealer with a preconfigured system. Installation of Windows 9x or Windows NT on a 'naked' computer (without any installed operating system) is at least as complicated as the installation of Linux – except that it is much worse documented.

Since this is a book about Linux (and not a Windows 9x or NT technical reference manual), I must unfortunately leave you to your destiny with your Windows reinstallation. Although I am not a shareholder in any hard disk manufacturing company, I would at least consider buying a second hard disk instead of reinstalling Windows. Not only do you gain more space, but you also have more flexibility and greater safety. Another variation is to ask your dealer for a reinstallation in a reduced partition.

How to use FDISK

There are two `fdisk` commands: the DOS command `FDISK` and the Linux command `fdisk`. In principle, both commands fulfill the same tasks – creation and deletion of partitions. However, they are handled in completely different ways. Furthermore, they have a different degree of functionality: `FDISK` can only create one primary partition, while `fdisk` can create four. Thus, a clear distinction must be made between the DOS and Linux programs. In order to avoid misunderstandings, in this book DOS commands are generally written in upper case. This section refers exclusively to the DOS version; the Linux `fdisk` is described from page 33 onwards.

CAUTION

Yet another hint regarding the duality of the two `fdisk` commands: for the creation and deletion of partitions, please try to use the command that corresponds to the partition – `FDISK` for DOS partitions and `fdisk` for Linux partitions. The only exception to this rule is OS/2. There, you should create Linux partitions with the OS/2 version of `fdisk`. You use the Linux `fdisk` only to modify the labeling of partitions (Linux instead of OS/2). OS/2 may sometimes show an allergy to partitions created by the Linux `fdisk`.

After the start of `FDISK`, you must select the required hard disk with [5]. This point only appears if your system is equipped with more than one hard disk. Switching the active disk is only necessary if you do not want to repartition the first hard disk, but another one. With [4] you can check the partitions of the currently active hard disk.

```
                    MS-DOS Version 6
              Fixed Disk Installation Program
           (C) Copyright Microsoft Corp. 1983-1993

Current fixed disk drive: 1
Choose any of the following:

1. Create a DOS partition or a Logical DOS Drive
2. Set active partition
3. Delete partition or Logical DOS Drive
4. Display partition information
5. Change current fixed disk drive

Enter choice: [1]
```

If there is only one primary partition on your hard disk, you must delete it with command number 3. Then you create a new, smaller primary partition with command number 1.

If you want to create several DOS partitions, you can now create an extended partition which can fill the rest of the hard disk. Within this extended partition, you can create logical partitions (for DOS). Under Linux, you can create further logical partitions (still within the extended partition) for Linux.

You can also wait and create the extended partition under Linux. This has the advantage that with the Linux program `fdisk` you can also create several primary partitions (which is not possible with DOS `FDISK`). Generally, however, it does not matter whether Linux is located in a primary or a logical partition, as far as its use is concerned.

> **CAUTION**
>
> In the main menu item 5 (select hard disk), the `FDISK` program displays logical partitions even if they are not DOS compatible (such as Linux partitions). For this reason, in this menu item (and only there) wrong partition names may occur; for example, `G:` for a DOS partition, which in practice is accessed under `F:`. In the Windows 95 version of `FDISK` this problem has been eliminated – Linux partitions are simply invisible.

2.4 Starting the installation

Now that there is enough space for Linux on the hard disk, the next step is to start the installation. A Linux installation is always carried out with the aid of a minimal Linux system, which essentially consists of a so-called kernel and the installation program itself. (The kernel is, amongst others, responsible for communication with the hardware, such as hard disk access, graphics card addressing, keyboard polling, and so on. Depending on your distribution and your hardware, there are different ways of starting the installation:

- The usual way is to insert the Linux CD into the drive and restart the computer. During this start-up, Linux is executed directly from the CD.
- If this fails (because your old motherboard does not support direct start-up from a CD or because your Linux CD does not envisage this kind of installation) you need to use a boot diskettte. If you are lucky, such a diskette was supplied as part of the distribution. Otherwise, you need to create the boot diskette yourself, which can easily be done in a couple of minutes.
- A further variation consists of starting an installation program located on the CD from within DOS. However, this variation is seldom used today, because the number of computers which can still effectively be used under DOS is getting increasingly small. (A DOS window under Windows is not sufficient for this kind of installation! Starting the Linux installation would result in an uncontrolled termination of Windows which might lead to a loss of data.)

> **TIP**
>
> In order to make booting from a CD-ROM or a diskette possible at all, this option must be enabled in the BIOS of your computer. Often, for reasons of safety, this is not the case (to prevent boot sector viruses).
>
> The BIOS controls your computer at the lowest level. Various configuration data is stored in a small BIOS RAM. This memory is battery-buffered and is therefore maintained even after powering down the computer.

TIP To change the BIOS settings, press Del immediately after switching you computer on. How the settings are changed in detail depends on your BIOS and can therefore not be described in this book. You should find the necessary information in the manual of your computer (more precisely, of your motherboard).

Boot kernel internals

At start-up, the kernel needs to recognize your hardware. Not all of the hardware components will be needed – the sound card plays no role in the installation – but at least access to the hard disks (also in SCSI systems) and to the CD-ROM drive or the network card must function. Unfortunately, there are dozens of SCSI cards and hundreds of network cards, which are mostly incompatible with each other.

For this reason, initially a minimal kernel is loaded which does not recognize much more than EIDE hard disks. All other hardware components are supported via so-called modules. The installation program tries to activate the correct modules automatically – and with many PC configurations, this works fine. Only if this is not the case will you need to supply the required information (via menu-driven dialogs).

Creating installation diskettes

If no installation diskettes are supplied with a distribution, and start-up from the CD-ROM does not work, you must proceed on your own. Basically, you only need to copy a file from the CD-ROM onto an empty diskette. (With some distributions and/or hardware constellations, you may need two or more diskettes.)

It is not possible to use `COPY` or `cp` for copying the so-called image files onto the diskette(s) – `RAWRITE` (DOS/Windows) or `dd` (Linux) must be used instead, the reason being that the file system of the installation diskette does not use the DOS format.

Creating an installation diskette under DOS/Windows

Writing boot diskettes is carried out with `RAWRITE.EXE`. This program transfers the contents of a file, sector by sector, onto a formatted 3.5-inch diskette. This program (or its more recent version `RAWRITE2.EXE`) can usually be found in the `DOSUTILS` directory of any Linux CD.

The following command shows an example of boot diskette creation. You will obviously have to change the drive letter `Z:` of the CD-ROM drive, and adapt the path and directory names according to your Linux CD. `>` is the input prompt and must not be entered.

```
> Z:\DOSUTILS\RAWRITE -f z:\images\boot.img -d a:
```

Creating an installation diskette under Linux

If you already have a Linux system, you can create the installation diskettes from there. Here, `root#` is the input prompt and must not be entered.

```
root#  dd if=/cdrom/images/boot.img of=/dev/fd0
```

The boot process

The boot process runs automatically. The only possibility of influencing it is before the start, where you may simply press [↵] or enter additional parameters. However, this is only required if the boot kernel encounters problems with hardware recognition. (You should therefore try it out first without any additional parameters.) A list of important boot parameters can be found on page 48.

During the loading of the Linux kernel, various messages appear on the screen, regarding the detected hardware. Messages that have been scrolled off the screen can be displayed again with [Shift]+[Page ↑]. Make sure that the messages correspond to your hardware and that your hard disk controller, your hard disks, and your CD-ROM drive are properly recognized. The displayed messages look more or less like the following (they will differ in the details, depending on the detected hardware and the kernel version):

```
Linux version 2.2.0-pre7-ac3 (root@myhost) (gcc version 2.7.2.3)
  #2 Fri Jan 15 17:57:30 MET 1999
Detected 400917748 Hz processor.
Console: colour VGA+ 80x50
Calibrating delay loop... 399.77 BogoMIPS

Memory: 128012k/131008k available (804k kernel code,
  408k reserved, 1748k data, 36k init)
CPU: Intel Pentium II (Deschutes) stepping 01
Checking 386/387 coupling... OK, FPU using exception 16
  error reporting.
Checking 'hlt' instruction... OK.
POSIX conformance testing by UNIFIX
PCI: PCI BIOS revision 2.10 entry at 0xf0550
PCI: Using configuration type 1
PCI: Probing PCI hardware
Linux NET4.0 for Linux 2.2
Based upon Swansea University Computer Society NET3.039
NET4: Unix domain sockets 1.0 for Linux NET4.0.
NET4: Linux TCP/IP 1.0 for NET4.0
IP Protocols: ICMP, UDP, TCP
Starting kswapd v 1.5
pty: 256 Unix98 ptys configured
RAM disk driver initialized:  16 RAM disks of 4096K size
PIIX4: IDE controller on PCI bus 00 dev 21
PIIX4: not 100% native mode: will probe irqs later
    ide0: BM-DMA at 0xc800-0xc807, BIOS settings: hda:DMA, hdb:pio
```

```
    ide1: BM-DMA at 0xc808-0xc80f, BIOS settings: hdc:DMA, hdd:pio
hda: IBM-DHEA-38451, ATA DISK drive
hdc: IBM-DHEA-38451, ATA DISK drive
ide0 at 0x1f0-0x1f7,0x3f6 on irq 14
ide1 at 0x170-0x177,0x376 on irq 15
hda: IBM-DHEA-38451, 8063MB w/472kB Cache, CHS=1027/255/63, UDMA
hdc: IBM-DHEA-38451, 8063MB w/472kB Cache, CHS=16383/16/63, UDMA
Floppy drive(s): fd0 is 1.44M
FDC 0 is a post-1991 82077
Partition check:
 hda: hda1 hda2 < hda5 hda6 hda7 hda8 >
 hdc: [PTBL] [1027/255/63] hdc1 hdc2 < hdc5 hdc6 hdc7 >
VFS: Mounted root (ext2 filesystem) readonly.
Freeing unused kernel memory: 36k freed
Serial driver version 4.27 with no serial options enabled
ttyS00 at 0x03f8 (irq = 4) is a 16550A
ttyS01 at 0x02f8 (irq = 3) is a 16550A
```

Thus Linux has recognized 128 Mbytes of RAM, a Pentium-II processor running at 400 MHz, a PCI bus, a diskette drive, two IDE hard disks, and two serial ports. Further hardware components (if any) can be added later during activation of the modules. (Please note that the clock frequency is not recognized correctly for all processors. However, this does not constitute a problem for the operation of Linux.)

If your computer halts at some point during the message display, there may be difficulties with hardware recognition. If this happens, you must try again with a different kernel or with some additional input of boot parameters.

If all goes well, then, after loading the kernel, the file system with the installation files is loaded, either directly from CD-ROM or from a further diskette (you will be prompted to change diskette). The process ends with the login prompt. What happens now depends entirely on the chosen distribution (see Appendices A to C).

2.5 Creating Linux partitions

One step that no distribution saves you is the creation of new Linux partitions. (This was the reason why we reduced the DOS partition – to free some space for a Linux partition.) There are some differences between distributions with regard to ease of operation. Most of them require that you use the Linux program `fdisk`, which is extensively described in this section. Some distributions shield you from the rather idiosyncratic handling of this program (for example RedHat and SuSE), but the decision of how many and which partitions you want to create remains with you.

About hard disk management

You may skip this basic section if you are not interested in the details of hard disk management. In most cases (in particular with sufficiently modern computers), you will succeed in creating Linux partitions without this knowledge. If, however, problems do occur (for example, with very large hard disks), this section will provide you with a better understanding of the terminology of warnings and error messages.

In theory, Linux supports partitions of up to 4 Tbytes (terabytes, that is, 1024 Gbytes). In practice, you will not be able to exploit this limit to its full extent, as for the time being there are no hard disks that are that big. But, depending on your hardware, you must be prepared to run into difficulties with disks as small as 504 Mbytes. The origin of the problem lies in the not very far-sighted BIOS design. The problems only concern the boot process – once Linux is up and running, it is independent of the BIOS and can address the entire hard disk.

In order to understand the problem better, we need some background information. The size of hard disks is determined by three parameters: cylinders, heads, and sectors. This triplet of numbers is commonly called the CHS geometry of the hard disk (cylinder, head, sector); sometimes you will find the term 3D address (LILO documentation) – it means the same.

For historical reasons, there are various limits for CHS values: the BIOS allows a maximum of 1024 cylinders, 256 heads, and 63 sectors. IDE disks, in turn, provide a maximum of 65536 cylinders, 16 heads, and 255 sectors. The smaller figures thus lead to the magical limit of 504 Mbytes (1024 cylinders, 16 heads, 63 sectors, 512 bytes per sector).

> **NOTE**
>
> CHS values have not related to the physical disposition of a hard disk for a long time. The hard disk has a predetermined CHS triple and behaves as though it really does have that many cylinders, heads, and sectors. In reality, the construction of the disk and the disposition of data look totally different – but this is the responsibility of the hard disk electronics.

BIOS arithmetic

The way out of this dilemma is usually an adapted BIOS version, as is common nowadays with all SCSI and EIDE controllers. The BIOS is still not allowed to signal more than 1024 cylinders (that would not be compatible with DOS/Windows 3.1/Windows 95), but it can manipulate the remaining values: a disk which pretends to have 2100 cylinders and 16 heads (physical CHS value) seemingly becomes one with 525 cylinders and 64 heads (logical CHS value, often called XCHS).

> **TIP**
>
> You can find out what geometry is valid under DOS by calling the program `DPARAM.COM`. This program is started under DOS with the parameter 0x80 (for the first disk) or 0x81 (for the second disk) and yields the number of cylinders, heads, and sectors. You will find the program on some Linux CDs (usually in the `dosutils` directory).

The theoretical maximum (still DOS compatible) is now 7.9 Gbytes (1024 cylinders, 256 heads, 63 sectors), which is nowadays way too small. (When this book reaches the shelves, there will be EIDE hard disks of up to 25 Gbytes around – maybe even larger.)

NOTE

When we talk about DOS, we actually include all operating systems which build on DOS, in particular Windows 3.1 and the first version of Windows 95. Not affected, with regard to hard disk *access*, are Windows 95b, Windows 98, Windows NT, and the future Windows 2000. These operating systems access the hard disk in a similar way to Linux. However, as with Linux, there are problems with the *start-up* of the operating system if it is installed beyond the 1024-cylinder barrier.

For real data access, many BIOS versions distinguish between XCHS and LBA mode (logical block addressing). In the first case, the new (fictitious) CHS geometry is used and the BIOS converts the values into the CHS geometry of the disk. In the second case, the sectors are simply numbered sequentially. The BIOS hands the LBA number directly over to the disk and thus saves a conversion step. (This obviously presumes that the disk, too, understands LBA values; with modern EIDE disks, this is the case.)

Disk managers

The second variation is less elegant than the BIOS solution and has fortunately become less customary: instead of a more modern BIOS, a so-called disk manager is used. This is a small program which is activated immediately after starting the computer and which performs a CHS conversion similar to the BIOS.

Disk managers are unavoidable if the full capacity of a new EIDE disk is to be exploited with an old IDE controller under DOS. Disk managers do not happily coexist with Linux. Try to avoid installing them from the very beginning!

Disk access under Linux

Now to Linux: as Linux does not use the BIOS when it is running, there is no 1024-cylinder limit and therefore no disk size limit. Within Linux, disk access is not carried out using CHS, but through logical block addressing (LBA). Two sectors are combined into a block (1024 bytes), and all blocks are numbered sequentially.

Nevertheless, the inadequacies of DOS and the BIOS create problems even under Linux, for two reasons:

- On the one hand, at Linux start-up the boot kernel is supposed to be loaded from the hard disk. (Theoretically, it is also possible to write the kernel onto a diskette and read it from there – however, this is slower and not particularly elegant). The Linux loader (in short, LILO) is responsible for the start-up, and the loader has to rely on the BIOS. Therefore, in order to be able to start Linux from the hard disk, the kernel must lie within the first 1024 cylinders. (As already stated: with modern hardware, the 1024-cylinder limit corresponds to 7.9 Gbytes. The ancient rule that the kernel must be located within the first 504 Mbytes applies only to very old hardware.)
- On the other hand, it is desirable that disk access is carried out following the same scheme under DOS and under Linux. In particular, all operating systems

should agree on where partitions start. Here, it has become a standard that partitions always begin or end at a cylinder boundary. Therefore, the otherwise antiquated measurement unit of 'cylinder' is still important even under Linux.

TIP

Also, it is not necessary for the whole Linux system to lie in the first 1024 cylinders – only the kernel. Details on LILO configuration can be found from page 183 onwards.

`fdisk`

Finally, some remarks about `fdisk`: because of the above-mentioned BIOS restriction to 1024 cylinders, `fdisk` comes up with the following type of message on hard disks with more than 1024 cylinders: 'The number of cylinders for this disk is set to 1500. This is larger than 1024 and may cause problems with some software.' This warning only refers to the boot process.

`fdisk` generally works with cylinders as units. Thus, partitions always start at cylinder boundaries. As already mentioned, the cylinder size itself depends on the hard disk and the BIOS – and on the fact that the kernel is passed this data correctly.

NOTE

Very old versions of `fdisk` can only handle disks of up to 2 Gbytes. You can find out which version of `fdisk` you are using by calling the command `fdisk -v`. The program should display at least version 2.0d (the current version at the time of writing was version number 2.9).

NOTE

There are lots of online documents available on the subject of hard disk management:

```
/usr/src/linux/Documentation/ide.txt
/usr/doc/packages/util/README.fdisk
/usr/doc/packages/lilo/README
```

A wealth of information is also contained in the HOWTO documents on the subjects of BootPrompt, Large-Disk, and LILO. HOWTO documents can be found, for example, at the following Internet address:

```
http://metalab.unc.edu/mdw/HOWTO
```

TIP

If you are installing Linux on a hard disk larger than 7.9 GBytes, in some cases it is necessary to pass the disk geometry as a kernel option at the beginning of the installation process. For example, to install SuSE Linux 6.1 on a 16 GByte disk, I had to type in `linux hda=2055,255,63` (without spaces!) at the first prompt. This means that the first IDE hard disk has 2055 cylinders, 255 heads and 63 sectors. The same information must also be given in the LILO configuration file (see Section 6.10).

Naming conventions for partitions

DOS partitions are indicated by letters, such as `C:`, `D:`, and so on. Under Linux, device names are used instead. With `fdisk -l` you can obtain a listing of all existing partitions on the first two IDE and the first eight SCSI hard disks. The program displays all partitions (DOS, OS/2, Linux, and so on). On a computer with three SCSI disks, this might look as follows:

```
root#  fdisk -l
Disk /dev/sda: 64 heads, 32 sectors, 116 cylinders
Units = cylinders of 2048 * 512 bytes
   Device Boot  Begin    Start     End  Blocks   Id  System
/dev/sda1    *        1        1     116  118768    6  DOS 16-bit >=32M

Disk /dev/sdb: 64 heads, 32 sectors, 116 cylinders
Units = cylinders of 2048 * 512 bytes
   Device Boot  Begin    Start     End  Blocks   Id  System
/dev/sdb1             1        1     116  118768    6  DOS 16-bit >=32M
The number of cylinders for this disk is set to 1029.
This is larger than 1024, and may cause problems with some software.

Disk /dev/sdc: 64 heads, 32 sectors, 1029 cylinders
Units = cylinders of 2048 * 512 bytes
   Device Boot  Begin    Start     End  Blocks   Id  System
/dev/sdc1             1        1     200  204784    6  DOS 16-bit >=32M
```

The first two disks (116 Mbytes each) are completely filled with one DOS partition each. On the third disk (1.03 Gbytes), only the first 200 Mbytes are reserved for DOS, and the remaining hard disk space is free for Linux partitions.

The above printout also indicates the naming conventions for hard disk partitions: normal hard disks (AT or IDE bus) are named `dev/hd`xy, where x is a letter for the hard disk (`a` for the first disk, `b` for the second disk, and so on), and y a digit for the partition. SCSI hard disks are named analogously, that is, `dev/sd`xy.

The rule for numbering partitions is that figures 1 to 4 are reserved for primary or extended partitions, figures from 5 onwards for logical partitions within the extended partitions. For this reason, there are frequently 'holes' in the numbering (such as `hda1` for a primary, `hda2` for an extended and `hda5` for the first logical partition).

Device names of hard disk partitions	
`/dev/hda`	the entire first IDE disk
`/dev/hda1`	the first primary partition of the first IDE disk
`/dev/hda2`	the second primary partition of the first IDE disk
`/dev/hda5`	the first logical partition of the first IDE disk
`/dev/hda8`	the fourth logical partition of the first IDE disk
`/dev/hdb`	the entire second IDE disk
`/dev/hdb1`	the first primary partition of the second IDE disk

`/dev/sda`	the entire first SCSI disk
`/dev/sda1`	the first primary partition of the first SCSI disk
`/dev/sdd3`	the third primary partition of the fourth SCSI disk

Size and number of Linux partitions

Before you create any partitions with `fdisk`, you should think about how you want to set up Linux. Basically, you can set up Linux in one single large partition or in several smaller partitions. Independently of the above, you should create an additional swap partition into which Linux can transfer blocks of memory in case of insufficient RAM.

The simplest solution is certainly to set up the entire Linux system in one single partition, as large as possible, and only work there. There is, however, a valid reason to separate at least the Linux system proper and the area for your personal data, distributing them into one system and one data partition.

Linux is a system which is still under development. New distributions appear every couple of months. Even if there is no reason to carry out continuous updates, it can from time to time make sense to install a new Linux distribution. In such a case, the partition containing your personal data can remain unaltered, and it can also be used as backup storage for various configuration files. After the reinstallation of Linux, this partition can be linked to the new system without difficulty. If, in contrast, the entire Linux system is located in a single partition, salvaging your personal data is a great deal more difficult.

Some hints on sensible partition size: the size of the system partition depends on which programs you want to install. A reasonable value is about 500–1000 Mbytes – if it is higher, all the better. The size of your data partition (for the home directories) depends on how you (and possibly other users, too) want to work with Linux. Therefore, it is nearly impossible to give any guidelines.

Partitioning recommended for home use	
`/`	Root partition, at least 500–1000 Mbytes
`/home`	Space for users' directories

The division of the hard disk into partitions can be taken a lot further. A more elaborate subdivision might look as follows:

Partitioning recommended for server operation	
`/boot`	Boot partition (for kernel / LILO), 2–10 Mbytes
`/`	Root partition, 80–100 Mbytes
`/usr`	System partition, at least 500–1000 Mbytes
`/usr/local`	Space for additional application programs
`/opt`	Space for additional application programs
`/home`	Space for users' directories
`/var`	Space for temporary data (including news)

This, however, presumes a certain knowledge of the system and makes sense only if Linux is to be used as a network server for a rather large system. As long as there is still free space on your hard disk, it is no problem to extend a running system with further partitions and, if necessary, relocate data from an existing partition to a new one (see page 147).

To sum up: it is not sensible to create one huge partition on the premise that 'It won't hurt.' Reducing a partition without losing data is seldom achieved under DOS and is definitely impossible under Linux.

REFERENCE

As we have stated above, during the boot process `LILO` can only access the first 1024 cylinders of the hard disk. If Linux is to be booted from the hard disk, one hard disk partition (even a small one) should lie completely within this 1024-cylinder limit. Only the kernel and maybe some additional files have to be copied into this partition (space requirement at most 10 Mbytes). You will find further information on this subject from page 183 onwards, where the configuration of LILO is described in detail.

Swap partitions

Independently of the number of partitions for data storage, you will need an additional partition to act as a swap partition. A good indication for the size of this partition is the size of your RAM. The swap partition should have more or less the same size (however, not less than 32 Mbytes). Note that, since kernel 2.2, swap partitions may exceed 128 Mbytes.

Optimization hints

For both speed and safety reasons, it would be optimal to install the Linux partitions on different hard disks (if you are the lucky owner of several hard disks). In this way, continuous movement of the disk head between partitions, which are often physically distant, can be avoided. On some disks, access to the front (outer) part is significantly faster than access to the inner part. This could be a good reason for placing the swap partition in front of the other partitions.

CAUTION

If you have more than two hard disks, you should create the root partition on one of the first two disks. Some hard disk controllers only allow access to the first two disks during the LILO boot process. (Some SCSI and EIDE controllers, however, also allow access to all other disks.)

One last remark: SCSI disks can be divided into a maximum of 15 partitions. In an unfavorable (but fairly frequent) division of the disk into one primary and one extended partition to be used for logical partitions, the number of usable data partitions is reduced to 12 (one primary and a maximum of 11 logical partitions). Thus, it makes no sense to create a great number of small partitions on large disks. (A maximum of 63 partitions is allowed on EIDE disks. The reason for the rather limited number of SCSI partitions is that under Linux you can simultaneously access up to 16 SCSI disks; that is, a total of more than 200 partitions.)

How to use `fdisk`

The `fdisk` program requires different handling than its DOS counterpart. When you start `fdisk`, you must enter the name of the hard disk as a parameter, for example `/dev/had` for the first IDE disk or `/dev/sdb` for the second SCSI disk. The hard disk name must be entered without any partition number (thus, `/dev/sda1` would be wrong).

> **CAUTION** With `fdisk`, you can destroy the contents of your entire hard disk. Please read this information before you use the program! If you start `fdisk` without a parameter, the program automatically works on the first IDE disk, that is, `/dev/had`. This can have fatal consequences if, in fact, you wanted to work on a different disk.

> **NOTE** With Windows 95b and Windows 98, Microsoft has introduced new partition types for partitions in the FAT32 file system. To enable you to recognize and process such partitions correctly, you definitely need an up-to-date version of `fdisk`!

> **NOTE** Some distributions offer the more user-friendly program `cfdisk` for partitioning the hard disk, to be used during the installation process (see page 44). Other distributions use their own partitioning programs (see Appendices A to C).

After starting `fdisk`, you can display a short overview of the available commands by pressing [M] (menu). [P] (print) displays a list of currently existing partitions on the selected hard disk.

With [N] (new), you can create new hard disk partitions. You can create a maximum of four primary partitions. If more than four partitions are to be created, one of the four primary partitions has to be declared as extended. Within the area of the extended partition, you can then create a number of logical partitions (maximum 12 on SCSI disks). If, when creating a new hard disk partition, different types are possible (primary, extended, or logical), `fdisk` prompts for an additional specification of the partition type.

The terms primary, extended, and logical have already been described on page 24. The only substantial difference between the DOS and Linux commands is that under DOS, only one primary and one extended partition can be created, whereas under Linux it is possible to create up to four primary partitions, or up to three primary and one extended partition. The DOS command recognizes the partitions created under Linux, but is not always capable of deleting them. As a general rule, partitions should always be deleted by the same program that created them.

After the type of the new partition has been specified, the program asks where the partition should begin (normally, with the first free cylinder) and how big the partition should be. The unit used for these specifications is 'cylinder.' The cylinder size depends on the hard disk, the BIOS, and the hard disk controller. It is indicated in the second line of the display of the [P] command (on our example disk,

2048 × 512 Bytes = 1 Mbyte). The size can also be specified using the syntax `+nM`, to make a partition *n* Mbytes big.

After the definition of a new partition, the whole partition table can be displayed with [P] (print). After this, further partitions can be defined, existing ones deleted, and so on.

> **TIP** Memorize the names of your newly created partitions, or write them down. During the installation process, you will need to remember these device names (for example, `/dev/sdc2`) more than once.

To create a swap partition, the type of a newly created partition must be changed, using [T] (type), from 'Linux native' (83) to 'Linux swap' (82).

The following printout shows how on the third SCSI disk, which contained only one primary DOS partition, two further primary partitions were created (250 Mbytes for the system and 150 Mbytes for data), plus an extended partition occupying the entire remaining storage area, and within the latter, a logical partition as a small swap partition (16 Mbytes).

```
root# fdisk /dev/sdc
The number of cylinders for this disk is set to 1029.
This is larger than 1024, and may cause problems with some software.

Command (m for help): p
Disk /dev/sdc: 64 heads, 32 sectors, 1029 cylinders
Units = cylinders of 2048 * 512 bytes
   Device Boot  Begin    Start    End  Blocks    Id  System
/dev/sdc1           1        1    200  204784     6  DOS 16-bit >=32M

Command (m for help): m
Command action
   a   toggle a bootable flag
   c   toggle the dos compatiblity flag
   d   delete a partition
   l   list known partition types
   m   print this menu
   n   add a new partition
   p   print the partition table
   q   quit without saving changes
   t   change a partition's system id
   u   change display/entry units
   v   verify the partition table
   w   write table to disk and exit
   x   extra functionality (experts only)

Command (m for help): n
Command action
   e   extended
   p   primary partition (1-4)
 p
```

```
Partition number (1-4): 2
First cylinder (201-1029): 201
Last cylinder or +size or +sizeM or +sizeK (201-1029): +250M

Command (m for help): n
Command action
   e   extended
   p   primary partition (1-4)
 p
Partition number (1-4): 3
First cylinder (452-1029): 452
Last cylinder or +size or +sizeM or +sizeK (452-1029): +150M

Command (m for help): n
Command action
   e   extended
   p   primary partition (1-4)
 e
Partition number (1-4): 4
First cylinder (603-1029): 603
Last cylinder or +size or +sizeM or +sizeK (603-1029): 1029

Command (m for help): n
First cylinder (603-1029): 603
Last cylinder or +size or +sizeM or +sizeK (603-1029): +16M

Command (m for help): p
Disk /dev/sdc: 64 heads, 32 sectors, 1029 cylinders
Units = cylinders of 2048 * 512 bytes
   Device Boot  Begin    Start      End   Blocks   Id  System
/dev/sdc1              1        1      200   204784    6  DOS 16-bit >=32M
/dev/sdc2            201      201      451   257024   83  Linux native
/dev/sdc3            452      452      602   154624   83  Linux native
/dev/sdc4            603      603     1029   437248    5  Extended
/dev/sdc5            603      603      619    17392   83  Linux native

Command (m for help): t
Partition number (1-5): 5
Hex code (type L to list codes): 82
Changed system type of partition 5 to 82 (Linux swap)

Command (m for help): v
839712 unallocated sectors

Command (m for help): w
The partition table has been altered!
Calling ioctl() to re-read partition table.
Syncing disks.
```

Thus, we now have three primary, one extended, and one logical partition on the third SCSI disk. The logical partition is labeled as the swap partition. In the extended partition, cylinders 620 to 1029 are still unused – thus, about 400 Mbytes are free and can later be used for creation of further partitions.

Before you save the new partitioning of your disk with [W] (write), you should execute [V] (verify): this makes `fdisk` check whether its internal information actually corresponds to the disk. This is an additional safety check. Normally, the reaction to [V] is just to display the number of 512-byte sectors not contained in any primary or logical partition (and thus unused).

TIP

As long as you do not terminate `fdisk` with [W], the program does not carry out any modifications to your hard disk! Your input is stored, but not yet executed. If you are not quite sure about what you are doing, you can quit `fdisk` at any time with [Q] (quit) or with [Ctrl]+[C] – your hard disk remains exactly as it is.

CAUTION

With `fdisk` you should never alter partitions which are currently in use (that is, which are registered or 'mounted' under Linux)! If, after [W], `fdisk` displays the warning 'Re-read table failed with error 16: Device or resource busy. Reboot your system to ensure the partition table is updated.', you should take this warning very seriously: it has not been possible to reread the modified partition data (although this data has in fact been altered). In this case, you must reboot your computer with [Ctrl]+[Alt]+[Del]! Then run `fdisk` again and make sure that the partitions have in fact been created as you expected.

As described on page 33, warnings regarding a cylinder number greater than 1024 can normally be ignored. They only concern booting with LILO.

The partitions created with `fdisk` are still empty, that is, no file system is as yet installed. In the same way that under DOS you had to execute the `FORMAT` command after `FDISK`, under Linux you must create a file system using the `mke2fs` command. During installation (after a prompt for confirmation), this command is executed automatically.

`fdisk` **keyboard shortcuts**	
[D]	Delete selected partition (delete)
[M]	Online help (menu)
[N]	Create new partition (new)
[P]	Display list of partitions (print)
[Q]	Quit program (without changing the partition table; quit)
[T]	Change type of partition (for swap partitions; type)
[V]	Verify partition table (verify)
[W]	Change partition table (write)

How to use `cfdisk`

`cfdisk` is a more user-friendly variation of `fdisk`. (It is, however, an independent program of its own, not a user interface for `fdisk`!) It is controlled via cursor keys and a menu. After the start, the program displays all detected partitions together with their sizes. [↑] and [↓] are used to select a partition, [←] and [→] to select a command. In addition, the following keyboard commands are available:

`cfdisk` keyboard shortcuts	
[H]	Online help
[N]	New partition
[D]	Delete selected partition
[T]	Change type of partition (for swap partitions)
[Q]	Quit program (without changing the partition table)
[Shift]+[W]	Change partition table (write)

2.6 Package selection, configuration, system kernel

After having set up the partitions, you will need to carry out the proper installation of the Linux programs. Depending on the distribution, this is carried out by a user-friendly, menu-driven installation program and usually causes no problems at all. It may be difficult to decide which programs to install and which not. (If in doubt, install fewer rather than more. You can always add more software packages later.)

The way the installation program proceeds to configure your computer may be puzzling, in some cases. You may be prompted for details which you might not yet know about. The rule: postpone any installation steps that you do not fully understand (especially LILO). In nearly all distributions, the installation program, or at least similar tools, can also be called up during normal Linux operation to allow necessary configuration steps to be carried out or modified at a later stage.

Chapter 3 presents some basics of Linux usage. Chapter 6 describes the various further configuration possibilities. Details on installation programs of several distributions can be found in Appendices A to C.

Installation of the system kernel

Although the modularized kernel concept has greatly facilitated adaptation of the kernel to the hardware, one point still remains critical: during booting, it is necessary to access the root file system. If special drivers are required for this operation (for example, for a SCSI card), this driver *cannot*, unlike in the installation process, be integrated later as a module – it must be available from the very beginning. Otherwise, the file system (and any modules that might be stored there) cannot be accessed.

Depending on the distribution, there are different procedures to achieve this task, some of which are described by way of example:

- RedHat uses a modularized kernel *without* special modules for SCSI drivers and so on. Instead, a RAM disk file is created (`/boot/initrd`), which can be addressed by LILO in the same way as the kernel. This RAM disk contains the modules used during installation.
- SuSE provides a large number of preconfigured kernels. These kernels, too, are modularized, but in addition, a special module for the required SCSI adapter is directly built in. Selection of the correct system kernel is not carried out on the basis of the first installation, but is left to the user. If you make an error at this point, you might find that what you have done up to this point becomes void!
- Debian sets up a universal kernel. This kernel too is modularized, but it contains drivers for *several* common SCSI cards. (Unfortunately, there is no documentation around to tell which drivers are actually included in this kernel.) Although procedure is simple, it is still not the optimum: on the one hand, the kernel is larger than necessary; on the other hand, the attempt to recognize non-existent SCSI adapters may cause problems. If system start-up fails with such a Debian kernel, all you can do is try to specify additional hardware options during booting. If this fails, too, you definitely have a problem.

2.7 Installation variations

This section summarizes information on several types of installation which, in practice, occur less frequently. As always, the details largely depend on the distribution in question – please check the manual or the online documentation.

Installation from hard disk

An installation from hard disk becomes necessary if neither a CD-ROM drive nor a network connection is accessible during installation. In this case, you need to copy all required data to your hard disk prior to the installation. (This means that at least at this stage – for example in operation under Windows – a CD-ROM drive must be attached or a network connection must be accessible.)

Not all distributions support installation from hard disk. The problem is that, during copying of the installation files from the CD-ROM to the hard disk under DOS/Windows, the file names are destroyed. If the names of the relevant files are not limited to 8+3 characters in the first place, the distribution must also be able to cope with truncated file names. (SuSE uses short file names, and RedHat can cope with mutilated file names.)

A further problem arises from the need for additional space – in most distributions, the installation data take up several hundred Mbytes!

After you have copied the required data to your hard disk, you can start the installation in the same way as your previous attempts, with the difference that you no longer specify a CD-ROM drive as installation source, but the hard disk partition in which the copied installation files can be found (for example, `/dev/hda1` for the first primary partition on the first IDE hard disk). The only point that might cause trouble is the choice of the appropriate hard disk partition. The Linux naming conventions for addressing of hard disks are described on page 37.

Installing Linux via a network connection

The common denominator in this section is that the installation data is neither loaded from a CD-ROM drive nor from the local hard disk, but via a network connection from another computer. Depending on the distribution, there are up to three variations:

- FTP (File Transfer Protocol): the installation data is read from an FTP server. This variation is particularly suitable for universities if the required Linux distribution resides on the local university server.
- NFS (Network File System): the installation data is read from another Unix or Linux computer. The host computer needs to be configured as an NFS server (see page 177); the directory containing the installation data (or the path leading to the CD-ROM drive of the NFS server) must be accessible via NFS.
- SMB (Server Message Block): this variation is comparable with NFS, except that, instead of NFS, the standard Windows SMB protocol is used.

All three variations presume that your computer is equipped with a network card and that it is correctly cabled. Furthermore, the installation kernel must recognize the network card and provide the appropriate module.

During installation, you will be prompted to supply the following information. (Details on the technical terms used in this context can be found from page 171 onwards, in the description of the basics of network configuration).

Network device
The network device to be used – normally `eth0` (the first Ethernet card).

Host and domain name
In principle you can enter any name of your choice, as this name will only be used during the installation. The host name must correspond to the setup of the NFS server. (The server might, for example, be configured in such a way that you can access the directory with the installation data only by giving a certain name defined by the system administrator.)

IP number of the local computer
Here, you are expected to enter a number of the form 192.168.55.37 – the IP number must fit into the local network and should be unique.

Network and broadcast address
These IP numbers describe the extension of the local network (generally, you can use 255.255.255.0 for the network mask; the corresponding broadcast address for this example would be 192.168.55.255).

Name server address

If a name server is running in the local network, you can specify its IP number. This has the advantage that later on you can address the FTP/NFS/SMB server directly via its name. If no name server exists or you do not know its IP number, you need to specify the IP number of the FTP/NFS/SMB server at a later stage.

Name or address of the FTP/NFS/SMB server

This is the computer from which the data is read.

Mount point or FTP directory

this specifies the path leading to the installation data (for example, `/mnt/cdrom` on an NFS server).

User name and password

These specifications may be omitted if the FTP/NFS/SMB server allows access to everybody (unusual).

As soon as access to the installation data is successful, the remaining installation is carried out as from a CD-ROM.

Umsdos – Linux for tasting

The abbreviation Umsdos is a combination of the terms UNIX and MS-DOS and designates an extension of Linux which allows the immediate use of the MS-DOS file system under Linux. Thanks to Umsdos, it is possible to install and execute Linux in a normal DOS partition - the awkward repartitioning of the hard disk is avoided.

In spite of the restrictions of the DOS file system, under Umsdos long file names are available, links can be established, `/` is the path separator instead of `\`, and so on. All Linux-specific file information is stored in each directory in the file `--linux-.---`. This file is invisible from within Linux. When accessing Linux data from within DOS/Windows, this file must in no case be deleted!

At first sight, Umsdos looks like simplicity itself. Unfortunately, Umsdos has several disadvantages that militate against intensive use of this system:

- The file system is based on the MS-DOS file system. Even if you do not notice this when using Umsdos, management of the file system is slower and, above all, much more error prone.
- Under Umsdos, some file types – especially links or very small files – take up a disproportionate amount of disk space (as opposed to the ext2fs file system normally used under Linux).
- The file system is not protected against access by MS-DOS – that is, you can alter or delete Linux files from within MS-DOS or Windows.
- Instead of a swap partition, a swap file has to be used. (This is a further point that makes Umsdos inefficient.)
- While Umsdos used to be quite popular in the past, there are very few distributions left which still support Umsdos installation (Slackware, SuSE).

Umsdos is therefore not a viable alternative for professional use of Linux. But if you just want to try out Linux without turning your whole computer inside out, this variation is quite interesting.

For MS-DOS, Linux simply requires the `linux` directory. For Umsdos, all DOS files can be accessed via the path `/dos`. Both file systems reside on the hard disk in parallel; the more space one file system requires, the less space remains for the other. When you delete Linux files, the space is again available for MS-DOS – and vice versa.

The installation of Umsdos is in principle the same as that of normal Linux, only without the partitioning of the hard disk. You specify an arbitrary DOS partition as the installation partition. The partition is *not* reformatted! (The installation program should not even offer this possibility.)

Although Linux and DOS/Windows share a common file system, switching between the two is only possible through a restart. Under DOS/Windows, all Umsdos files in the `linux` directory are visible and accessible, but only under their abbreviated names (8+3 characters). The opposite case, that is, access of DOS files under Linux, is much easier: the DOS file system is mapped under Umsdos in the directory `/dos`.

2.8 Problems before, during, and after installation

Boot parameters

When Linux breaks down while loading the kernel, the cause is nearly always hardware problems. Problems can arise both during the first boot before installation and after a successful installation (if the installation program installs a different kernel from the one used during the installation itself).

Options which during booting are forwarded via LILO to the kernel may help with hardware recognition. Please note that the options specified at LILO start-up only influence the drivers integrated into the kernel. Drivers which are loaded as modules at a later stage may also be influenced by options, but only if the installation program provides a possibility for entering such options.

In order to enter boot options, press the Shift key during LILO start-up, and an input prompt appears. If you now press Tab, the available kernel names are displayed (if present, also names for booting other operating systems). The syntax for booting with additional options is:

```
kernelname hardware=settings hardware=settings ...
```

`hardware` denotes a hardware component (such as a CD-ROM drive, an Ethernet card, and so on). The settings to be used must be specified without blank spaces (for example, `ether=10,0x300,0,0,eth0`). If settings are to be made for several components, they are separated by spaces (not by commas!).

For most boot options, you need specific knowledge about your hardware. You need to know:

- which hardware components you are using,
- which interrupt is assigned to each of them, and
- which I/O memory area is used for access.

You may be able to find this information in the documentation that comes with your computer. A further source of information is the Control Panel of Windows 9x (see page 21).

The following list shows the most important kernel parameters. Please note that the order of parameters is not consistent (sometimes the I/O address, sometimes the IRQ number is given first). Hexadecimal addresses are shown in the form 0x1234. Without the 0x prefix, the number is interpreted as decimal.

(E)IDE hard disks, ATAPI CD-ROM drives

Parameters for hard disks are specified in the form `hd`*x*`=`*option*. `hda` stands for the first hard disk, `hdb` for the second, and so on. (To be precise, the letters a, b, c, d, and so on denote the first device at the first controller, the second device at the first controller, the first/second device at the second controller, and so on. Depending on whether and how the CD-ROM drive is connected, the second hard disk may also be named `hdc`.)

Parameters for the hard disk controller(s) are specified by means of `iden=`, where, *n* may assume values between 0 and 3. (Each controller controls two disks, thus `ide1` for `hdc` and `hdd`. Most EIDE controllers correspond to two traditional controllers and can therefore handle four disks each.) Several options may be specified in sequence.

`hdx=noprobe`

Do not check whether the disk exists or how large it is. (The disk can still be used if its geometry is explicitly specified by the following option.)

`hdx=1050,32,64`

The hard disk has 1050 cylinders, 32 heads, and 64 sectors. These indications are only necessary in case Linux does not recognize the geometry of the hard disk itself. The values can be taken from the BIOS or from the documentation (if any ...) supplied with the hard disk.

> **TIP** You can find out the geometry valid under DOS by calling the program `DPARAM.COM`. This program is started under DOS with the parameter 0x80 (for the first disk) or 0x81 (for the second disk) and yields the number of cylinders, heads, and sectors. On many Linux CDs, you will find the program in the `dosutils` directory.

`hdx=cdrom`

The drive is an ATAPI CD-ROM drive (this is normally recognized automatically).

`iden=noprobe`

Do not check whether IDE controller n is available or not. (The controller can be used if the addresses are explicitly specified by the following option.)

`iden=0x170,0x376,15`

The controller has the base address 0x170, the controller address 0x376, and is controlled via interrupt 15.

`iden=serialize`

Controllers 0 and 1 are not called simultaneously. (This option prevents data errors and other problems with controllers having a CMD-640 chip.) This option allows only 0 or 1 as values for n.

`iden=dtc2278` or `iden=ht6560b`

Explicit specification of the IDE controller. Both options allow only 0 or 1 as values for n.

SCSI hard disks and controllers

SCSI controllers and their connected hard disks, CD-ROM drives, and streamers are normally recognized straight away and rarely cause difficulties (assuming that cabling and termination are OK). Some SCSI controllers require their BIOS to be activated so that the kernel can detect controller-specific parameters during startup. The following options become necessary if more or less compatible controllers are not recognized correctly or do not have their own BIOS.

> **TIP**
>
> If you still have problems with your SCSI hardware, check the cabling. The SCSI cable must be terminated at both ends, one of which must have an active termination. Termination is carried out via the insertion of termination resistors, via jumpers, or (in modern SCSI controllers) via configuration (which can be called up by pressing a key combination during startup). The bus may not have active terminations at both ends (one must be active, the other one passive), nor may a device between the ends be terminated.

`aha152x=0x330,9,7`

This option is designed for the Adaptec 1505, 1510, 1515, 1520, 1522, and compatible controllers. It must be specified for many sound cards with integrated SCSI controllers (such as Soundblaster-16 SCSI). The Adaptec 2825 controller, too, can be used with the 152x driver in a 152x-compatible mode (a compromise until a proper 2825 driver becomes available). In the above example, the controller is called via I/O address 0x330 and interrupt 9; its SCSI ID number is 7. Further optional parameters exist for reconnect (0/1), parity (0/1), synchronous (0/1), and delay.

`aha1542=0x330,11,4,5`

The Adaptec 1542 controller is called via address 0x330. The values 11 and 4 indicate, in μs, how long the ISA bus is blocked or released by the controller (to allow simultaneous use of several devices on the bus). The last parameter specifies the DMA speed in Mbytes/sec. Values greater than 5 require a fast and reliable motherboard (Warning!).

`aic7xxx=extended`

This option for Adaptec 274x, 284x, and 294x controllers indicates whether the hard disk geometry should be transformed.

`?ncr5380=0x350,5,5` or **`ncr53c400=0x350,5`**

Options valid for NCR 5380 or 53c400 and compatible controllers (such as Trantor T130B). The I/O address is specified first, then the interrupt number, and finally (only for the 5380) the DMA channel. NCR cards require BIOS version 3.06.0 or later.

CD-ROM drives (not ATAPI, not SCSI)

NOTE

The following options only apply to stone-age CD-ROM drives! All common makes – no matter of which manufacturer – are directly connected to the EIDE or SCSI bus and do not cause problems. Only CD-ROM drives of the very first generation, which may still be found in some ancient 486 PC, use their own, manufacturer-specific interfaces whose parameters are controlled via the following options.

`aztcd=0x300`

I/O address for Aztech CDA 268-01, Orchid CD-3110, Okano/Wearnes CDD110 and Conrad TXC. As a second parameter, you may specify `0x79`, in which case the driver will try to handle unknown CD-ROM firmware as well (compatible models).

`cdu31a=0x340,10`

I/O address and interrupt to address Sony CDU31a or 33a. If no interrupt is assigned to the drive, 0 may be specified. As a third parameter, `PAS` can be indicated for Pro Audio Spectrum.

`cm206=0x340,5`

I/O address and interrupt for Philips CM 206.

`gscd=0x300`

I/O address for the Goldstar R-420 drive.

`mcd=0x320,10`

I/O address and interrupt for addressing older Mitsumi CD-ROM drives (FX001, FX001D, LU005, and LU005S; more recent models are addressed via the ATAPI interface). Some Mitsumi drives are preset to interrupt 11. In some kernel versions an optional third parameter can be specified, which increments the maximum reaction time to the CD-ROM drive. (The greater the value (about 5), the longer we wait.) This may help in case of timeout errors.

`mcdx=0x320,10`

As above for the new Mitsumi driver, which is also able to read multi-session CDs.

`sonycd535=0x300,10`
I/O address and interrupt for the Sony CDU 531/535 drive.

`sbpcd=0x300,SoundBlaster`
I/O address for Soundblaster drives. Instead of `SoundBlaster`, `SPEA` or `LaserMate` are also allowed (depending on the drive).

`sjcd=0x300,10`
I/O address and interrupt for Sanyo drives CDR-H94A (often with ISP16 sound card). A third parameter may be indicated to specify the DMA channel.

Miscellaneous

`ether=10,0x300,0,0,eth0`
Specifies that an Ethernet card is to be addressed via I/O address 0x300 and interrupt 10. The meanings of the third and fourth parameters depend on the card (see `Ethernet-HOWTO`); the fifth parameter specifies to which device the card should be assigned. All parameters are optional. The `ether` option is mandatory for many more or less compatible NE-2000 cards. If you have an NE-2000 card and your computer crashes during startup, you should first try using this option.

`mem=97920k`
Specifies that the computer is equipped with 96 Mbytes of RAM. This option is sometimes required for older computers with more than 64 Mbytes of RAM, as their BIOS can detect a maximum of 64 Mbytes. The unit can be Kbytes (as in the above example) or Mbytes (with a capital M). Warning: some systems copy the BIOS into the highest RAM area. Thus, it may be that a system with 96 Mbytes of RAM actually has available a little less than that. In the above example, 384 Kbytes have been left free for this purpose.

`reserve=0x300,0x20`
Specifies that the 32 bytes (hexadecimal 0x20) between 0x300 and 0x31F must not be addressed by any hardware driver to search for components. This option is necessary for some components that are allergic to such tests. Usually, this option goes together with a second option that specifies the exact address of the component that requires this memory area (for example, an Ethernet card, see above).

`root=/dev/hdb3`
Specifies that after loading the kernel, the third primary partition of the second IDE drive is to be used as the root file system. (Similarly, other drives (also SCSI) and partitions can be specified.) This option is useful if an already installed Linux system is to be booted via an installation diskette (for example, after a Windows 9x installation has destroyed the boot sector for LILO).

`vga=-2`
Normally, in text mode, Linux displays 25 lines of 80 characters. If you have a big screen, the above option gives you 80×50 characters and a much better

overview. Instead of `-2`, other values may be specified, depending on the particular VGA card.

`ro` Specifies that the file system is to be mounted as read-only. This is useful if a defective file system has to be repaired manually, used in combination with one of the two following options.

`single` or **`emergency`**
If one of the two above options is used, the computer starts in single-user mode. (To be precise, these options are not evaluated by the kernel itself; they are instead, as is the case with all unknown options, passed on to the first program started by the kernel. This is `/sbin/init`, which is responsible for the initialization of the system. See also page 124.)

Further information

The above listings of kernel parameters are by no means complete. The most easily accessible (but not always completely up-to-date) source of information is the `Bootprompt-HOWTO`. Equally helpful are the HOWTO documents on the subjects of CD-ROM and Ethernet. HOWTO documents can be found on the Internet:

```
http://metalab.unc.edu/mdw/HOWTO/
```

If Linux is already installed, you should take a look at the following files:

```
/usr/src/linux/Documentation/ide.txt
/usr/src/linux/Documentation/*
/usr/src/drivers/*/README.
```

If you have access to a SuSE manual (even an old one), it is well worth reading the *Kernel Parameters* chapter, which contains highly practical information.

As a last resort, it may help to look directly into the kernel code. (The code is – at least in parts – very well documented!) See also page 69 on Linux online documentation and page 454 on the use of `find` and `grep` to search for files.

The computer won't boot any more

Boot diskettes

If the boot diskette created during installation does not lead to the desired effect, most distributions also allow you to try out the installation diskette or CD-ROM. You simply specify `root=/dev/xxx` as an additional boot option, where `xxx` stands for the device name of your root partition.

In addition, many distributions provide a special emergency system. In some of them, this may be a variation of the installation system, while others supply separate image files which you must use to create special boot diskettes for the emergency system (as described on page 31). However, in order to be able to exploit the possibilities of an emergency system, you need a rather comprehensive knowledge of Linux fundamentals.

Booting from hard disk

If after start-up (without a boot diskette, straight from the hard disk) `LILO:` is displayed and nothing more happens, things are probably OK: LILO waits for you to specify under which operating system the computer should be booted. First, press [Shift], then [Tab]. LILO displays the operating systems that can be selected. Use the keyboard to enter a name and press [↵].

Things are worse if LILO does not react to any input, displays lots of zeros or ones, and so on. In this case, something has probably gone wrong with the LILO installation. If you work with DOS or Windows, the simplest solution is to restart the computer with a DOS boot diskette and then execute `FDISK /MBR`. This overwrites the boot sector and at the next restart, DOS/Windows should come up again normally. (Until your next LILO installation attempt, you can start Linux only with a Linux boot diskette.)

If, apart from Linux, you have not installed DOS/Windows, but a different operating system (OS/2, Windows NT, and so on), reconstitution of the boot sector is a bit more difficult. You must start Linux with a boot diskette and reinstall the original boot sector saved during LILO installation. You can read more about this and about a correct (and safe) installation of LILO on page 183.

Memory problems (RAM)

Linux is partly programmed very close to the hardware. It optimally exploits your hardware and in many respects offers better performance than other operating systems. This closeness to the hardware can, however, cause Linux (as opposed, for example, to Windows) to become unstable.

The reason is in most cases an incorrect BIOS configuration of the computer. In the BIOS, you can specify the number of wait states used to access the RAM. In general, the more wait states, the slower. Therefore, the number of wait states is often set to a very low value by users or producers. Depending on the access time and the quality of your RAM chips, the computer may keep running under Windows, but may fail under Linux.

TIP

There are two Linux tools which allow you to perform a memory test. `memtest86` is a mini Linux kernel whose only task is an endless memory test. (You need to boot your computer with this system from a diskette. Then you can run the test over night.) The `memtest` command, in contrast, can be used to test memory during normal operation.

TIP

Unfortunately, both programs are only supplied with very few distributions. (In the Debian distribution, `memtest` can usually be found in the `sysutils` package.) Before you can run `memtest86`, you must even compile it yourself.

```
ftp://sunsite.unc.edu/pub/Linux/system/hardware/
    memtest86-n.tar.gz
ftp://ftp.debian.org/pub/debian/dists/stable/main/
    source/utils/sysutils_n.tar.gz
```

The remedy is a moderate setting of the number of wait states. (When you restart your computer and immediately press [Del], you enter the BIOS setup program.) Information about the correct setting of wait states can be found in the motherboard manual or obtained from your computer vendor.

2.9 System changes and extensions

This section is of interest only to Linux users who already possess a stable and well-configured system. If this is not the case, you should not waste any time with extensions.

Additional installation of packages

Depending on the distribution, different commands and programs are provided which allow additional software packages to be installed, updated, or removed during normal Linux operation:

`rpm` (RedHat, Caldera, DLD, SuSE): page 213
`gnorpm` (RedHat): page 732
`xrpm`: page 219
`tar`: page 220, 483
`yast` (SuSE): page 743
`dselect`, `dpkg` (Debian): page 711

This book does not describe `glint` (old RedHat versions), `setup` and `pkgtool` (both Slackware) and `viper` (DLD).

TIP

For any installation, you should exclusively use the tool provided by the relevant distribution, and you should only install packages that match the distribution. (This advice applies in particular to Linux novices! The recommendation even applies to distributions based on the same package format. If, for example, you extend a SuSE distribution with a RedHat package, problems may occur because of the different installation paths. This applies in particular to packages with system-relevant or distribution-specific contents. *Never* install an `Init-V` package that has been designed for a different distribution!)

Linux updates

First you need to ask yourself what you actually want to update: a specific software package, the kernel, or the whole distribution?

- For a program update, you may get hold of the relevant package via the Internet or from an up-to-date CD-ROM. If possible, the package should be adapted to your distribution – otherwise, incompatibilities are practically built in (different installation paths, and so on). For the installation itself, you need to use the package management program of your distribution (see above).

  The most frequent source of problems is constituted by dependencies from other programs or libraries: the program can only be executed if another program or a program library has previously been updated as well. (Frequently, there are entire chains of dependencies whose manual resolution is quite difficult. For Linux novices, in particular, it is often easier to perform the update within the framework of a distribution update. This is exactly what companies such as RedHat and SuSE live on!)
- The necessary steps for a kernel update are described on page 199 and usually cause no problems. Difficulties may arise if the kernel has changed fundamentally – this will usually require new network and process management commands, an update of the Init-V process, and so on. (In this case, too, a distribution update is often the simpler solution.)
- If you now think that a distribution update is simplicity itself, you will be deluded. No matter how 'intelligent' package management may be (a grandiose solution is the one provided by Debian, which allows updating of the currently running system!) – a distribution update unavoidably means hassle and unexpected loss of time. In any case, you should create backup copies of all configuration files (better, of the entire `/etc` directory and, if possible, also of the `/root` directory). Equally important is a backup of your personal data (not only in the event of a distribution update, but regularly)!

The alternative to a distribution update is a new installation. In this case, however, you will lose all data stored in the system partition. Therefore, it is a good idea to create separate partitions for system and data directly during the very first installation (page 38). By the way, any change of distribution *always* entails a new installation!

TIP

If you have a lot of space on your hard disk, you obviously can install a new Linux system into its own partition and try it out. It is no problem at all to configure LILO in such a way that you can choose to boot with either the old or the new Linux system. You can link the other partition into the file system with `mount` and thus easily exchange data between the two distributions. While working on this book, I had a total of four distributions installed in parallel (besides Windows 95 and NT), selecting the one I needed at boot time.

TIP

Once you have a stable and running Linux system, there are normally very few reasons to perform a complete update. Don't get contaminated by the general version hysteria! Often updating a single package is sufficient to solve a problem.

2.10 Removing Linux

If, at a later time, you want to free the hard disk space occupied by Linux, you must uninstall it. Usually, two steps are necessary: you must delete all Linux partitions, and you must remove LILO from the boot sector of the hard disk.

If LILO was installed in the normal way, the original boot sector can be re-created by Linux without problems during normal operation (see page 183). In most DOS and Windows 9x versions, `FDISK /MBR` too will help to restore the original boot sector. In Windows NT, you need to use the installation program, which is, however, extremely laborious.

Deleting the Linux partitions is a bit more laborious: this must be carried out using the Linux `fdisk` program (and not the DOS program `FDISK` or an `FDISK` version of another operating system). To do this, you must start Linux from an installation diskette, for example, with the diskette you used for your original installation of Linux. You perform the normal installation procedure until you reach `fdisk`, which you use to delete all Linux partitions. Then you simply abort the installation. (If you were to start Linux normally from the hard disk, you would have to use `fdisk` to delete a partition currently in use. This is not possible.)

Linux quick start

This chapter presumes that your installation of Linux has succeeded to the extent that your computer comes up with the login prompt. The aim of this chapter is to describe as briefly as possible how elementary Linux operations can be carried out: how to log in, copy, relocate and delete files, display and edit text files, and so on. With the knowledge acquired in this chapter you will be able to manage any further configuration of your system (Chapters 6 and 7 from page 133 onwards).

The chapter has been kept brief on purpose, without the endless details which for the time being are not relevant. If you want to know more, you can find the basic information about Linux in Chapter 5 from page 85 onwards. At that point, the Linux system is described in detail, so that you will be able to see how and why some commands actually work.

A description of the most important Linux commands and their options in alphabetical order can be found in Chapter 14 from page 437 onwards. Details on the use of the `bash` (Bourne Again Shell) follow in Chapter 12 from page 387 onwards. The `bash` is the command interpreter with which you normally enter and execute commands.

3.1 From DOS to Linux

System start-up

The system start-up up to the login prompt is normally carried out automatically. Depending on your installation of LILO, a few seconds after starting your computer the text 'LILO ...' may appear on your screen; in this case, first press [Shift], then enter the name of your Linux system (in general, 'linux'), followed by [↵] (see also page 182). If LILO does not work, or if you work with Umsdos, you can only start Linux with a boot diskette, where again a LILO input may be required.

Before you can work with Linux, you must log in. This is necessary because Linux distinguishes between different users with different privileges.

Normally, when you log in you enter your user name and the corresponding password. If Linux has just been installed, there is only one user: `root`. After a new installation, `root` often does not even require a password.

> **CAUTION**
>
> With `root`, you are considered to be the system administrator: you can access all files, execute all programs without restrictions and can (unwittingly) cause a lot of damage.
>
> Please only work as `root` if it is really essential!

During the configuration of your system you *must* work as `root`, as otherwise you would not be able to modify the configuration files. One of your first steps as `root` should, however, be to execute the `passwd` command and define a password for `root`.

> **TIP**
>
> How to change the password for root and register new users is described in Chapter 6 from page 133 onwards. Background information about the administration of file access privileges is given on page 96.

Shutdown

> **CAUTION**
>
> A proper shutdown of the system is at least as important as a correct login. Never simply switch the computer off! At worst, you risk the destruction of your file system. In any case, you will be 'punished' with a time-consuming check of the whole file system during the next system start-up.

A proper system shutdown is carried out by executing the command `shutdown now`. As soon as the message 'system halted' appears or the computer restarts (BIOS messages), you can switch it off.

If you wish to reboot the computer, you will need to specify the additional option `-r`, thus `shutdown -r now`. On many Linux systems there is an easier alternative: the key combination Ctrl+Alt+Del. With this, any user (not only `root`) can execute the `shutdown` command. If you work under X, you must switch to a text console beforehand, or terminate X with Ctrl+Alt+←.

> **TIP**
>
> `shutdown` can only be executed by root. If Linux does not react to Ctrl+ Alt +Del (depending on the configuration in `/etc/inittab`) and you do not possess a `root` password, but still need to restart the computer, you should at least execute the `sync` command, which carries out all buffered write accesses to your hard disk. Immediately after this, you can switch your computer off. This is, however, only an emergency solution to minimize the damage.

Handling text consoles

Linux is a multitasking system. This means that you can execute several commands at the same time. To let you exploit the possibilities of multitasking as easily as possible, the standard configuration of Linux offers you a choice of six text consoles. You can switch between these text consoles with Alt+F*n* (thus, Alt+F1 for the first console, Alt+F2 for the second, and so on).

If you work within the X Window System, you change over to a text console by pressing Ctrl+Alt+F*n*. To return to X, you press Alt+F7.

You can log in on any text console (even under different names, if you want). If, on one text console, you have started a time-consuming command, you can switch to a different console and immediately start another command from there. Both commands are now executed – more slowly, but usually still fast enough to allow reasonable work.

Executing commands

Linux is accompanied by countless commands and programs. (The distinction between commands and programs is purely linguistic. All of them are programs. Conventionally, commands are mostly smaller programs necessary for everyday use of Linux.) To execute a command, you simply enter the command name, and sometimes a couple of parameters, followed by ↵. In this book, input of a command (bold) and its results are shown as follows:

```
root# ls -l          # contents of the current directory
lrwxrwxrwx   1 root  root     14 Nov 16 13:08 linux -> /usr/src/linux/
-rw-------   1 root  root   7081 Nov 21 15:50 mbox
-rw-r--r--   1 root  root     46 Nov 21 09:29 setup.prot
```

CAUTION

The # character at the beginning of a line means that here an input has been made by the `root` user. If the first character is $ instead of #, the command can also be executed by other users. Both characters are so-called input prompts which are displayed automatically at the beginning of an input line. You must *not* enter these characters yourself!

On your computer, in front of the # or $ character, the current directory and, perhaps, the name of the computer are displayed. For simplicity's sake, these are generally not shown in this book. The subsequent lines (until another line begins with # or $) are the results of the command.

TIP

Within the command line, you will often find a second #: this character now specifies a comment. When you enter commands, you do not have to enter the comments as well (although it does not hurt). The double meaning of # as `root` prompt and as comment character can sometimes lead to confusion, especially if listings that begin with comments are shown in this book. However, the correct meaning of the character always becomes clear from its context.

Keyboard specials

A special feature of the Linux command interpreter `bash` is the expansion of file names with Tab. You simply enter the first character of a file or program name and press Tab. If the file name can already be uniquely determined at that point, it is expanded completely; otherwise, only up to the point where several possibilities arise. Pressing the Tab key twice yields a display of a list of all file names that begin with the characters already entered.

A further special feature is that with Shift+PgUp and Shift+PgDn you can scroll the screen contents of the text console (only until you change to another console). This allows you to review the results of the last programs executed, even if they have already been scrolled off the screen.

Directories

You can change your current directory with the `cd` command, in the same way as under DOS. `pwd` shows the name of the current directory. A substantial difference between DOS and Linux is that `/` is used as the separation character between directories (instead of `\`). If, by mistake, you use `\`, you will normally receive an error message that the specified file does not exist. This error message is due to the fact that Linux interprets `\` and the subsequent character as a special character.

Also, the concept of home directory is a new one. After logging in, you are automatically in a directory that belongs to you alone. All data and subdirectories contained in it are yours. You may deny access to this data to all users of the system (except for `root`) – even listing the directory with `ls`.

The home directory is abbreviated with the symbol `~`. The home directory of root is `root`. Nearly all other Linux users have their home directories in `/home/name`. With `cd` – without specifying further parameters – you change back to your home directory.

The file system starts with the root directory `/`. Even if the file system includes several hard disks or a CD-ROM drive, all these drives constitute one unique directory tree. The CD-ROM data is normally accessed under `/cdrom` or `/mnt/cdrom`. Therefore, under Linux, there is no need for drive names, such as `A:`, `C:`, and so on, as used in DOS.

> **TIP** An overview of the widely ramified Linux directory tree is shown on page 91. The principal question concerns the criteria used to distribute files within this directory tree.

Files

A listing of the current directory can be displayed with `ls`. More information is shown with `ls -l`. With this option, `ls` largely corresponds to the DOS command `DIR`. File names that start with a dot (full stop) are normally not displayed by `ls`; they are invisible. For this reason, this kind of name is often used for configuration files. To make `ls` show these files as well, the additional option `-a` must be used.

Please note that Linux is case sensitive and distinguishes between upper and lower case letters in file names. Thus, `readme`, `Readme`, and `README` are three different files. In the Linux standard file system, file names can be up to 255 characters long.

With `cp` you can copy files, with `mv` you can rename them, and with `rm` you can delete them. The use of wildcard characters is allowed; they work similarly, but not exactly, as under DOS. For now, the most important difference is that `*` comprises all files, whereas `*.*` comprises only those files that have a dot in their file name. Be careful when using wildcards, particularly in combination with `rm`! If, instead of `rm`, you use the `echo` command, all directories and files included in a combination of wildcard characters are displayed on screen (for example, `echo *.tex`).

When looking for a file, it is best to use the command `find -name '*name*'`. Linux will then search the directory tree, starting with the current directory, for a file name that contains `name`. If you change to the root directory `/` beforehand, the entire file system is searched. This can take a while, especially if a CD-ROM is linked.

TIP Wildcard characters and their function are described from page 87 onwards. A complete file management command reference is given in Chapter 14, starting on page 437.

3.2 Displaying and editing text files

To display a text file on screen, you can use the commands `cat`, `more`, and `less`. `cat` corresponds to the DOS command `TYPE` and displays the file to the end without pausing. `more` and `less` allow you to view the text page by page. With `less`, you can move freely around the text with your cursor keys (even backwards). `more` is terminated automatically when it reaches the end of the file, `less` must be terminated manually by entering Q. `more` and `less` can also be used as filters for pagewise display of other information.

```
user$  cat file      # displays the whole text file
user$  more file     # pagewise display of the file
user$  less file     # pagewise display of the file, also backwards
user$  ls -l | more  # pagewise display of the current directory
```

TIP If you use one of these three programs to display a file that does not contain text, but contains binary data, the terminal emulator may interpret such data as special characters and get confused. In this case, strange characters appear on the screen, because the character set mapping is no longer correct. Remedy: execute the `reset` command.

emacs, jove, and jed

There are as many editors for Linux as you can think of – the only question is which one happens to be installed on your computer. This section summarizes the elementary commands of `emacs` and the more or less compatible editors `xemacs`, `jove`, and `jed`. The subsequent sections describe some more editors.

`emacs` keyboard shortuts	
Ctrl+X, Ctrl+F	loads a new file
Ctrl+X, Ctrl+S	saves the current file
Ctrl+X, Ctrl+W	saves the file under a new name
Ctrl+G	aborts the input of a command
Ctrl+K	deletes one line
Ctrl+X, U	undo (undoes the deletion)
Ctrl+X, Ctrl+C	terminates `emacs` (asking for confirmation to save file)

In `jed`, Del can only be used if an area has been marked beforehand. The first character is marked with Ctrl+Spacebar and the cursor is positioned at the end of the area. Del deletes the area, Ins inserts it (at a different place). In this respect, `jed` differs from the original Emacs.

Emacs is described in detail in Chapter 16 from page 537 onwards. The description refers only to the original Emacs, but all elementary commands work in `jove` and `jed` as well.

TIP When editing configuration files, make sure that the last line too is terminated with ↵. Some Linux programs do not correctly process files if there is no line feed at the end of the last line. (This also applies when you work with a different editor.)

joe

`joe` is a very simple editor. The keyboard shortcuts mostly follow the WordStar text processing program, which is now obsolete. If `joe` is started with the `-asis` option, the program can even handle foreign language special characters.

With `man joe` you obtain a substantial help text for `joe` which describes the remaining commands. `joe` can be configured by means of the file `~/.joerc`. As a point of departure, you may want to use `/usr/lib/joe/joerc`.

`joe` keyboard shortcuts	
Ctrl+K, H	shows/hides the help window
Ctrl+K, E	loads a new file
Ctrl+K, D	saves the file (under a different name, if you so wish)
Ctrl+Y	deletes one line
Ctrl+Shift+-	undo (undoes the deletion)
Ctrl+C	terminates `joe` (asking for confirmation to save file)

pico

`pico` has even fewer commands and is even easier to handle. This editor is only available if you have an installation of the `pine` email program. The advantage of `pico`: the two bottom lines of the screen display an overview of the available commands. A brief description of `pico` is given on page 355.

vi, vim, and elvis

`vim` and `elvis` are two `vi`-compatible editors. For copyright reasons, the original `vi` is not part of Linux. The `vi` command can, however, be executed in most cases, automatically causing the start of `vim` or `elvis`.

The handling of `vi` is unconventional, to put it mildly. (`vi` buffs obstinately claim, however, that there is no better editor. Although this editor will probably not be the first choice of a Linux novice, a short description is nevertheless provided:

- `vi` is relatively compact and will possibly be available if no other editor is running (for example, during system maintenance if Linux was booted from an emergency diskette).
- `vi` is available under practically all Unix systems, and has been taken as a standard. For this reason, various programs call `vi` automatically as editor, if this is not explicitly prevented by an appropriate configuration. In such cases, you need to know at least how you can quit the editor.

Since the author is not a `vi` fan, the introduction to `vi` is limited to the following quotation from a news contribution by Oliver Rembach (with his kind permission, thanks!). This contribution originated from a heated discussion in `de.comp.os.unix.linux.misc`, about whether and to which level of detail `vi` should be described in this book ...

> 'This is the editor. Its name is `vi`. All you need is six functions: with [I] you insert text, with [Esc] you stop doing so, [X] deletes a character, [D] [D] a line. With [:] [W] [Q] *filename* you save, and with [:] [Q] [!] you quit. Got it? Fine. You'll learn the rest later.'

The most important basic difference between `vi` and other editors is that `vi` differentiates between different modes. Text input is only possible in insert mode. Input of most commands is carried out in the complex command mode, which is activated by means of [:]. Previously, the insert mode must have been left by pressing [Esc]. To conclude, a quick reference of the elementary commands:

`vi` keyboard shortcuts	
[I]	change to insert mode
[Esc]	terminate insert mode
[H] / [L]	move cursor left/right
[J] / [K]	move cursor down/up

X	delete one character
D D	delete the current line
P	insert deleted line at cursor position
U	general undo
:	change to complex command mode

Commands in complex command mode

: W *name*	save text under a new name
: W Q	save and quit `vi`
: Q !	quit `vi` without saving
: help	start online help

Editors under X

In the X Window System, you can use all the editors mentioned above in a terminal window. Emacs, in this case, even appears with menus and mouse support. Furthermore, there are several editors specifically designed for X. Most distributions contain one or more of these special X editors (for example, `kedit`, `xjed`, `xedit`, `textedit`).

3.3 The X Window System

CAUTION

Before we start, a warning: the X Window System can only be used if the X server is configured correctly. A wrong configuration of the X server can destroy your monitor! If X has not been configured during the Linux installation (this is not the case with all distributions), X must be configured before it is used for the first time. This process is described in detail from page 221 onwards. (There, the nature of an X server is explained.) Do not start X if you are not sure that the configuration is correct!

Depending on the configuration of your computer, the system starts directly with an X login where you simply have to specify your name and password. If this is not the case, you start X with `startx`.

After the start (and again depending on the configuration) single programs can be started automatically. If this does not happen, you can call up a menu that allows you to start X programs by pressing the left mouse button. The most important program is `xterm`: it corresponds to a text console and allows you to start other programs via the keyboard.

Mouse, input focus

The functioning of the mouse is highly dependent on the settings of the window manager, and you can configure it to a large extent yourself. Therefore, we cannot describe in detail which mouse button does what on your computer.

Generally, the middle mouse button plays a big role under X. Thus, in many X programs, you can slide the scroll bar only with the middle mouse button. (On page 246, you will find configuration hints for a two-button mouse and for a mouse whose middle button does not work.)

In many systems, X is configured in such a way that a window receives input only when the mouse cursor is actually placed somewhere inside it. If, until now, you have worked with MS Windows, where the input focus is determined by activating a window with a mouse click on it, this behavior will probably annoy you. (The way to modify such details is described on page 272.)

Terminating X

When you want to exit X, just press the left mouse button and, in the Context menu, select an entry, such as EXIT FVWM or QUIT X. (The text, once again, depends on the installation.) If you do not find any other alternative, Ctrl+Alt+Backspace will work in most cases. (If you want to change to a text console, you do not have to quit X to do so. Simply press Ctrl+Alt+F1 ... +F6. To return to X, press Alt+F7.)

Online documentation

Linux comes not only with a multitude of additional programs, commands, and tools, but also with at least the same amount of documentation and help texts. This chapter gives an overview of existing documentation files, where to find them and how to read them. The chapter begins with a section which describes how some of the texts can be read under DOS/Windows before installation. The remaining sections describe the different forms of online documentation in a running Linux system: `man` and `info` texts, FAQs (Frequently Asked Questions), HOWTOs, and so on.

> **TIP** Information on how to convert online documents into different formats (DVI, PostScript, HTML, and so on) and how to print out your online information is given in Chapter 15, from page 501 onwards.

4.1 `man` – the online manual for all commands

`man` is a program which displays documentation for many programs and C functions. Historically, the layout of `man` pages for the online documentation of Unix systems is rather old. Therefore, `man` pages are usually available for the traditional Unix commands, many C functions and various data formats.

The biggest disadvantage of `man` pages is the lack of structure of the texts, which can be fairly annoying with longer `man` texts. For this reason, the documentation of GNU programs is realized with `info`, which allows cross-references inside the help texts. `info` is described in the next section.

There are several programs for the display of `man` texts: the most frequently used versions are `man` for the text mode, and `xman` for the X Window System. `tkman` is even more user friendly than `xman`; however, this version is not available on many systems and requires an installation of Tcl/Tk. Some distributions also supply HTML versions of the `man` pages (or a program for dynamic conversion), so that the documentation can also be read with a Web browser.

The following sections describe `man`, `xman`, and `tkman`, followed by some information about the internal organization and formatting of `man` files.

TIP

If you have installed KDE or GNOME, you can easily read `man` texts with the related help browsers. (Why none of the two programs in their current version provides the possibility of searching in the text, however, remains a mystery. In this regard, `man` is more functional.) The following examples show how you can display the `man` page for `ls` and a contents list of all `man` pages.

```
user$ gnome-help-browser man:ls
user$ gnome-help-browser whatis:ls
user$ gnome-help-browser toc:man
user$ kdehelp man:ls
user$ kdehelp 'man:(index)'
```

How to use `man`

```
man [options] [range] subject
```

`man` searches for the manual file specified as the subject in all `man` directories known to the system. If, instead of a subject, a file name is specified (for example, `/cdrom/man/man1/abc.1`), the contents of this file are displayed.

`-a` displays all homonymous `man` pages. (Without this option, only the first of several homonymous files from different subject areas would be shown. In some Linux distributions, however, `-a` is set as default.)

`-f` *`keyword`*
displays the meaning of a keyword (one line of text). This option corresponds to `whatis word`.

`-k` *`keyword`*
displays a list of all available `man` texts in which the keyword occurs. However, no full text search is carried out – only the keywords of each `man` text are analyzed. This option corresponds to `apropos word` (or SEARCH APROPOS in `xman`).

`-S` *`area_list`*
searches only the specified subject areas. This option is useful if you have to distinguish between several homonymous `man` texts.

The optional specification of an area limits the search for man texts to a subject area – for example, `man 3 printf`. This becomes necessary if several homonymous `man` texts exist in different subject areas. Otherwise, `man` would only display the first `man` text found.

> **TIP** If the `-f` and `-l` options or the `whatis` and `apropos` commands do not work, it probably means that a database containing `man` contents information is missing. You can remedy this by executing `/usr/sbin/makewhatis`. (This program is fairly CPU-intensive.)

In many Unix and Linux books, commands are shown together with their `man` numbers – for example, `find(1)`. Thus, you know straight away how to call `man`. `man` knows the subject areas 1 to 9 and n. (Sometimes, programming language commands are assigned additional areas with different letters.)

1	user commands
2	system calls
3	C programming language functions
4	file formats, device files
5	configuration files
6	games
7	miscellaneous
8	system administration commands
9	kernel functions
n	new commands

If you want to read all homonymous `man` texts (of all subjects), you have to use `man` with the option `-a`. Then, `man` displays the first `man` text found. As soon as you have read the text and exited `man` with Q, the `man` text for the following subject is displayed.

As soon as a `man` text is displayed on screen, the following keyboard shortcuts, amongst many others, are available to navigate through the text (if `less` has been specified as the default display program in `/usr/lib/man.config`):

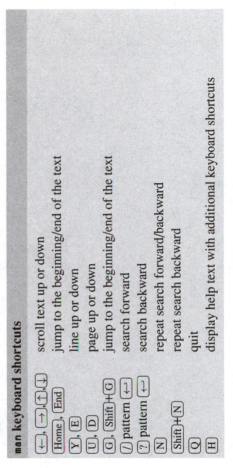

`man` **keyboard shortcuts**	
←, →, ↑, ↓	scroll text up or down
Home, End	jump to the beginning/end of the text
Y, E	line up or down
U, D	page up or down
G, Shift+G	jump to the beginning/end of the text
/ pattern ↵	search forward
? pattern ↵	search backward
N	repeat search forward/backward
Shift+N	repeat search backward
Q	quit
H	display help text with additional keyboard shortcuts

Special features of the X version `xman`

`xman` is normally run as a background program, so that work in the terminal window is not affected. `xman &` – with the coy charm of early X programs – displays a small control window, which shows a help text about the usage of `xman` when you click the HELP button. The MANUAL PAGE button leads to a bigger window in which the required help text can be selected. Unlike `man`, it is not possible to pass `xman` the required help subject as a parameter at calling time.

```
xman [options]
```

`-bothshown`
: divides the main window into two sections (subject list and help text).

`-notopbox`
: starts `xman` without the control window.

In the main window, via the SECTION menu, a list of texts available for each of the nine help subject areas can be viewed. The required subject is selected by clicking on it with the mouse.

The most interesting menu command is SEARCH. It rapidly searches and displays required help subjects. When the search is stopped with the APROPOS button, `xman` displays a list of subjects containing the search item. (However, the Apropos search is not a full text search. Only the keywords of each `man` text are searched through.)

`xman` supports the mouse not only to select subjects and scroll through `man` texts. With [Shift] and the middle mouse button you can quickly toggle between the subject list and the displayed `man` text. [Ctrl] and the left mouse button display the OPTIONS menu, [Ctrl] and the middle mouse button the SECTIONS menu.

The keyboard shortcuts of `xman`, unfortunately, do not correspond to those of `man`. In particular, the cursor keys cannot be used to scroll through the help text. The following table summarizes the available shortcuts:

`xman` keyboard shortcuts	
[F], [B]	one page forward or backward
[Spacebar]	one page forward
[1] to [4]	one to four lines forward
[Ctrl]+[S]	search manual text

`tkman`

Like `xman`, `tkman` provides an X interface for the display of `man` pages. Once the installation of `tkman` has succeeded (it requires the programming languages Tcl and Tk to be installed, amongst others), `tkman` offers the following advantages over `xman`:

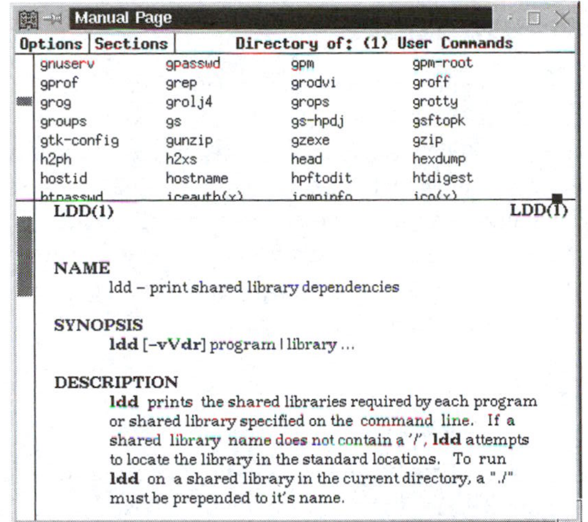

Figure 4.1 Reading `man` texts with `xman`.

- Easy cross-referencing to other `man` pages by simply double-clicking highlighted keywords.
- Management of a list of all recently viewed `man` texts.
- Easy search within a `man` text.
- Possibility of highlighting pieces of text and storing these highlights permanently.
- Extensive configuration possibilities.

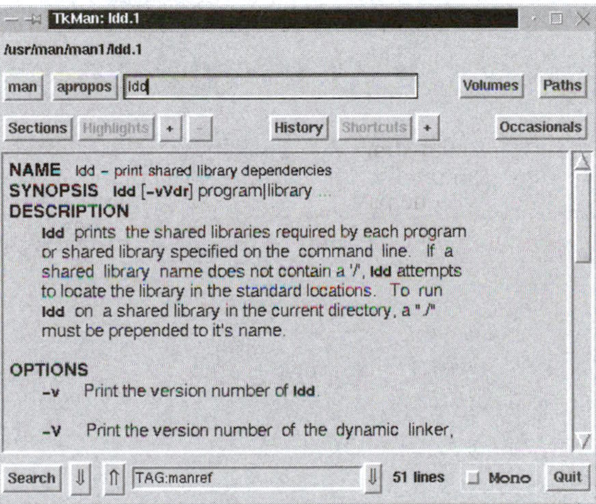

Figure 4.2 Reading `man` texts with `tkman`.

`man` internals

The central control file for `man` is `/etc/man.config`. In this file, the paths for various files are set. This file also contains the specification that the `less` program is used to display the `man` texts. (For this reason, the keyboard commands of `man` and `less` are the same when a text is displayed.)

Generally, there is no need to modify `man.config`. If you want to specify additional directories to be searched by `man`, you can set the `MANPATH` environment variable in `/etc/profile` accordingly. In the standard configuration, `man` searches the following directories for manual texts:

```
/usr/man
/usr/local/man
/usr/X11R6/man
```

Each of these directories has the subdirectories `man1` to `mann` containing the `man` source texts. To be able to display these texts on screen, the `groff` program must be used to convert them into ASCII format. To avoid repeating this conversion for each access to a `man` page, the formatted texts are stored in their own directories (either `cat1` to `catn` in the directories mentioned above, or in a special subdirectory `/var/man` or `/var/catman`). Sometimes, `man` texts are only stored in their formatted form (to save space) – but this is a disadvantage if the texts are to be printed.

The configuration of `xman` can be further modified by entries in the `~/.Xdefaults` or `~/.Xresources` file (see the `xman` manual text).

> **TIP** Information on conversion of `man` source files into readable ASCII documents or PostScript files can be found on page 511.

4.2 `info` – hypertext online help for GNU utilities and Emacs

`info` is a much more powerful program than `man`. It is particularly suitable for displaying voluminous help texts, as it can cope with cross-references across several files. `info` is the preferred documentation format for all GNU tools (such as `find`, `grep`), for the GNU C compiler with all extensions and libraries, and for the Emacs text editor.

> **TIP** Instead of `info`, you can also use `emacs` or `xemacs` and use Alt+X info ↵ or Ctrl+H, I to change into info mode (see also page 546). The main advantage is that you can use the mouse to follow links, which are highlighted in a different color.

Generally, `info` texts are stored in the `/usr/info` directory (depending on the system, also in `/usr/local/info` or `/usr/share/o/info`). Larger help texts are normally distributed across several compressed files whose names end in `.info-nn.gz` or only in `--nn.gz`.

`info [options] [subject]`

`info` is normally called with the parameter `subject`. The subject indicates which info file of the `/usr/info` directory is to be viewed. If `info` is started with no parameters, the program displays an overview of the available help subjects (file `/usr/info/dir`). Subjects not contained in `dir` can only be viewed with the option `-f`. This is, for example, the case for the `elisp` files (documentation about Lisp programming for Emacs). Thus, `info` cannot automatically handle all `info` files contained in `/usr/info`.

`-f` *`file`*
: loads the specified file instead of a file from `/usr/info`. Instead of a subject, the full file name must be given (`jarg300.info.gz`, not just `jarg300`). If the `info` text is distributed across several files, the first file must be specified (for example, `elisp-1.gz`).

`info` keyboard shortcuts	
Spacebar	scroll text down
Backspace	scroll text up
B, E	jump to beginning/end of the info unit
Tab	move cursor to next cross-reference (*)
↵	follow cross-reference to different info unit
N	next info unit of same hierarchy level
P	previous info unit of same hierarchy level
U	one hierarchy level up
L	back to the last text displayed
H	extensive instructions for use (help)
?	command overview
Q	close the help window (quit)

NOTE

`info` comes with a `man` text, which describes the basics of handling the program. Information on the internals of `info` files and on `texinfo` can be found on page 512. With `texi2html`, you can convert `info` files into HTML format – see page 513.

TIP

If you have installed GNOME or KDE you can also read `info` texts very easily by using the corresponding help system. The following examples show how the `info` text on `emacs` and a contents list of all `info` texts is displayed:

```
user$ gnome-help-browser info:emacs
user$ gnome-help-browser toc:info
user$ kdehelp 'info:(emacs)'
user$ kdehelp 'info:(dir)'
```

4.3 Linux-specific online documentation

Reading documentation in other formats

Linux-specific online documentation is available in the most varied formats. The following list gives some hints on the best way such documents can be read.

- ASCII: These texts can be read directly with `less` or any other editor. The programs `a2ps` or `mpage` allow conversion into a PostScript file for subsequent printing.
- PostScript format (extension `*.ps`): These files can be read with the X program `ghostview` or `kghostview`. With `gs`, you can produce a printout even if you do not own a PostScript printer.
- DVI format (`*.dvi`): Such files are the result of a TeX or LaTeX conversion and can be read with `xdvi` or `kdvi`. `dvips` allows their conversion into PostScript files.
- HTML format (`*.html`): These files can be read with any WWW browser (Lynx, Netscape, `kdehelp`).
- Adobe Acrobat format (`*.pdf`): This is a compressed variation of the PostScript format, which has imposed itself particularly for Internet documents with sophisticated layout. The files can be read with `ghostview`, `kghostview`, `xpdf` or `acroread`.

In all versions, except for the last one, files may be compressed. Such files can be recognized by their extension `.gz` or `.bz2`. To decompress them, you execute `gunzip file.gz` or `bunzip2 file.bz2`. This replaces the compressed file with its uncompressed version. Sometimes, several files are combined into one common archive (extension `.tar`), which is usually compressed as well (extension `.tgz`).

REFERENCE

The programs mentioned above are not used only for reading online documentation and are therefore described elsewhere in this book:

`less`:	page 139; same keyboard shortcuts as `man` (page 71)
`ghostview`, `kghostview`:	PostScript viewers, page 518
`xdvi`, `kdvi`:	DVI viewers, page 520
`dvips`:	DVI → PostScript conversion, page 507
Lynx, Netscape, `kdehelp`:	Internet tools, page 326
`acroread`:	PDF viewer, page 522
`bunzip2`, `gunzip`, `tar`:	Standard commands, pages 443, 460, and 483

FAQ – Frequently Asked Questions

Under Linux, FAQs play only a secondary role compared to the HOWTO texts. On the Internet, you will find innumerable FAQs regarding various programming languages, networking questions, and other Unix subjects (security, and so on), but generally only very few FAQs are supplied with Linux distributions (if at all, they can usually be found in the `/usr/doc/FAQ` or `/usr/doc/faq` directory).

The most interesting one is the `Linux FAQ`: this file should be the first resort in case of problems with Linux. It deals with subjects such as installation, compatibility problems, handling the Linux file system, the X Window System, and so on.

HOWTO – how does that work?

HOWTO texts differ from FAQ files mainly in that they are built up more systematically and teach basic knowledge. HOWTO texts are probably the most important source of information for Linux regarding installation, configuration and hardware problems. The only disadvantage is that many of the texts are rather substantial. You will often get more information than you really wanted.

The subjects covered are, amongst others, the handling of special hardware components (SCSI disks, CD-ROM drives, streamers, Ethernet cards, keyboards), and special features of Linux usage (printing, network configuration including UUCP, Term and News, and so on). In ASCII format, the HOWTO texts occupy a total of more than 4 Mbytes – this is far more text than this whole book! (For comparison: the `*.tex` files of this book take up about 2 Mbytes.)

The HOWTO files are normally located in `/usr/doc/HOWTO`. Under Linux there are two forms of HOWTO texts: normal and mini versions. The mini versions are located in the `mini` subdirectory and exist only in ASCII format. The 'big' HOWTOs, on the other hand, are also available in other formats (subdirectory `other-formats`). The most interesting format is certainly the HTML version which can be read with any WWW browser and which is, owing to different type sizes and cross-references, much clearer and easier to read than the ASCII version.

> **TIP** As usual, the most up-to-date version can be found on the Internet:
>
> `http://metalab.unc.edu/LDP/HOWTO`

> **TIP** As a general rule, you should always check the date of last modification of all online files. Occasionally, files are still lurking around whose contents have long become obsolete through more recent versions of the described programs.

Linux HOWTOs

`3Dfx`	`Busmouse`	`DNS`	`Esperanto`
`AX25`	`CD-Writing`	`DOS-Win-to-Linux`	`Ethernet`
`Access`	`CDROM`	`DOS-to-Linux`	`Finnish`
`Alpha`	`Chinese`	`DOSEMU`	`Firewall`
`Assembly`	`Commercial`	`Danish`	`French`
`Benchmarking`	`Config`	`Distribution`	`Ftape`
`BootPrompt`	`Consultants`	`ELF`	`GCC`
`Bootdisk`	`Cyrillic`	`Emacspeak`	`German`

Glibc2	Multi-Disk	RPM	Tips
HAM	Multicast	Reading-List	UMSDOS
Hardware	NET-3	Root-RAID	UPS
Hebrew	NFS	SCSI-Programming	UUCP
INFO-SHEET	NIS	SMB	User-Group
IPX	Networking-Overv	SRM	VAR
ISP-Hookup	Optical-Disk	Security	VME
Installation	Oracle	Serial	VMS-to-Linux
Intranet-Server	PCI	Serial-Programming	VMS2Linux
Italian	PCMCIA	Shadow-Password	Virtual-Services
Java-CGI	PPP	Slovenian	WWW
Kernel	Parallel-Process	Sound	WWW-mSQL
Keyboard-Console	Pilot	Sound-Playing	XFree86
LinuxDoc+Emacs+Is	Polish	Spanish	XFree86-Video-Tim
MGR	PostgreSQL	TeTeX	
MILO	Printing	Text-Terminal	
Mail	Printing-Usage	Thai	

Linux-Mini-HOWTOs

3-Button-Mouse	Firewall-Piercing	Man-Page	Sendmail+UUCP
ADSL	GIS-GRASS	Modules	Small-Memory
ADSM-Backup	GTEK-BBS-550	Multiboot-LILO	Software-Building
AI-Alife	Hard-Disk-Upgrade	NCD-X-Terminal	Software-RAID
Advocacy	IO-Port-Program	NFS-Root	Soundblaster-AWE
Backup-With-MSDOS	IP-Alias	NFS-Root-Client	StarOffice
Battery-Powered	IP-Masquerade	Netscape+Proxy	Term-Firewall
Boca	IP-Subnetworking	News-Leafsite	TkRat
BogoMips	ISP-Connectivity	Offline-Mailing	Token-Ring
Bridge	Install-From-ZIP	Partition	Ultra-DMA
Bridge+Firewall	Kerneld	Partition-Rescue	Update
Bzip2	LBX	Path	Upgrade
Cable-Modem	LILO	Pre-Install-Checkl	VPN
Clock	Large-Disk	Process-Accounting	Visual-Bell
Coffee	Leased-Line	Proxy-ARP-Subnet	Win-Modem-Share
Colour-ls	Linux+DOS+Win95	Public-Web-Browser	WordPerfect
Cyrus-IMAP	Linux+FreeBSD	Qmail+MH	X-Big-Cursor
DHCP	Linux+NT-Loader	Quota	XFree86-XInside
DHCPcd	Linux+Win95	RCS	Xterm-Title
DPT-Hardware-RAID	Loadlin+Win95	README	ZIP-Drive
Diald	Loopback-Root-FS	RPM+Slackware	ZIP-Install
Diskless	Mac-Terminal	Remote-Boot	mini-list
Ext2fs-Undeletion	Mail-Queue	Remote-X-Apps	
Fax-Server	Mail2News	SLIP-PPP-Emulator	

LDP – the Linux Documentation Project

Even longer texts – whole books, indeed – have emerged within the framework of the Linux Documentation Project. These texts, too, were originally available only in electronic form, but at least the *Linux Network Administrators' Guide* has been published as a printed book.

Sven Goldt, Sven van der Meer *et al.*:	*Linux Programmers' Guide*
Larry Greenfield:	*Linux User's Guide*
Michael K. Johnson:	*The Linux Kernel Hackers' Guide*
Olaf Kirch:	*The Linux Network Administrators' Guide*
David A. Rusling:	*The Linux Kernel*
Matt Welsh:	*Linux Installation and Getting Started*
Lars Wirzenius:	*Linux System Administrators' Guide*

NOTE

If these documents were not supplied with your distribution, you may find them (and many more) in different formats on the Internet:

`http://metalab.unc.edu/LDP/linux.html`

Kernel documentation

In the `/usr/src/linux/Documentation` directory you will find much hardware-specific information (only if you have installed the kernel code). This information generally assumes a sound basic knowledge of your computer hardware as well as of programming. But a read through of such documentation is often worthwhile. You will seldom find such excellent information about the internals of your computer. (The kernel code is also well documented; if you have a specific hardware problem, a good read through the corresponding `*.c` files will certainly do you no harm.)

The help texts available for the kernel configuration are very informative too. Even if you do not wish to recompile the kernel, just execute `make xconfig` or `make menuconfig` in the `/usr/src/linux` directory and read the various help texts. (You can also read the ASCII file `Documentation/Configure.help` directly, although the unformatted text is much less readable.)

KDE and GNOME help

Help with KDE programs is obtained by simply pressing F1. In GNOME programs, you need to use the help menu or an appropriate button. In both cases, the documentation is displayed in HTML format, which means that the KDE and GNOME help programs `kdehelp` and `gnome-help-browser` are in reality Web browsers.

As already mentioned in the previous sections, the two help systems can also be used for reading `man` and `info` texts. If the required document has not been specified in the command line, PAGE|CONTENTS in `kdehelp` and the INDEX button in `gnome-help-browser` lead to a start page with a contents list.

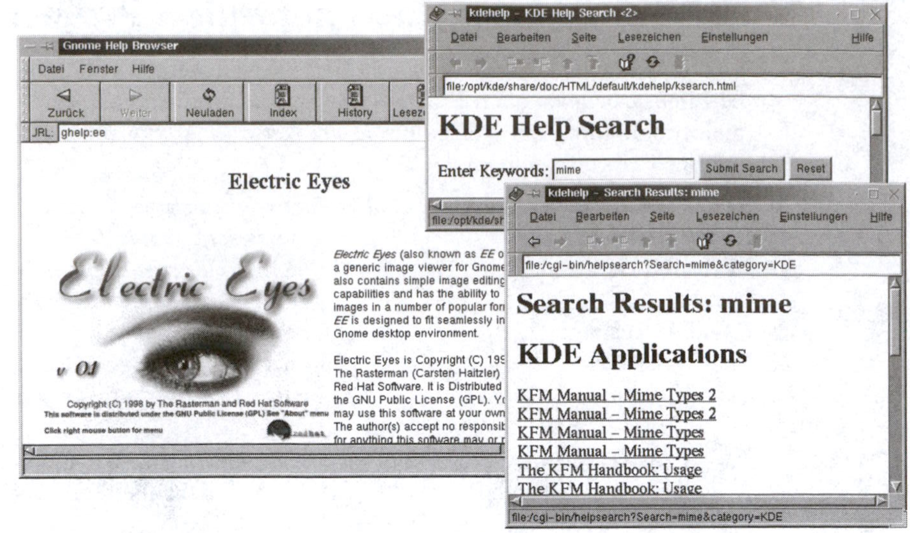

Figure 4.3 GNOME and KDE help systems.

A particularly attractive feature of `kdehelp` is the possibility of performing a full text search in KDE and `man` documents (in future also in `info` texts). Just call `kdehelp` and execute FILE|SEARCH. The search function is, however, relatively slow.

Documentation on individual software packages

Additional documentation on all kinds of software packages (programming languages, tools, and so on) is usually installed in the directory `/usr/doc/`*name*`/` or `/usr/doc/packages/`*name*`/`. The extent and topicality of these files vary greatly. Often, you only find a README file containing the copyright notice and a brief description of where to find the remaining documentation.

Obviously, not all programs adhere to this convention (this would be far too easy). You should in any case also check the installation directories of the programs in question. For example, you will find a large amount of online documentation on LaTeX (teTeX distribution) in the following directory:

```
/usr/lib/teTeX/texmf/doc
```

TIP

With some programs (for example Gimp), the online documentation is so voluminous that it is stored in a package of its own which is not always automatically installed. Thus, it is often worthwhile taking a closer look at the list of packages that have *not* been installed.

TIP

Often you will find late breaking information on security gaps and other problems of various programs on the distributions' homepages. Debian manages information on bug reports and their solution (if there is one) for all packages. SuSe maintains a support database where frequently occurring problems and their solutions are described. Besides a search function, there is also an alphabetic index. If, for example, you have problems with your ISDN configuration, this is the best place to look for a solution.

```
http://www.debian.org
http://www.redhat.com
http://www.suse.com
```

Distribution-dependent documentation

One distinctive feature of different Linux distributions is how online documentation is made available. The following list gives a first overview; further information can be found in Appendices A to C of this book where distribution-specific details are described.

- Several distributions come with an extensive installation manual which is available both in printed form and as an online document in various formats (PostScript, HTML).
- Many distributions make their HTML-formatted documentation more accessible by providing a central start page. (A special mention is deserved by SuSE where, after installation of the appropriate packages, the HTML versions of all `man` texts, numerous `info` texts, all HOWTO texts, all SuSE package descriptions, the entries of the SuSE support database, and many more, can be accessed from one central starting point.)
- Some distributions try to facilitate full text search in the existing online documentation by providing additional tools (such as RedHat's `helptool`).
- Practically all distributions provide daily updated information on their homepages (see above).

Part II
Configuration

Linux fundamentals

The changeover from DOS or any other non Unix-compatible operating system to Linux frequently causes difficulties. Many of these difficulties are due to the fact that, on the surface, Linux has many similarities to other operating systems, although there are substantial differences in its internal structure and administration. This chapter attempts to look behind the scenes, describing the basic Linux features.

The first part of this chapter mainly contains information about several levels of the Linux file system: from handling files and directories (including the use of wild-cards, access privileges, links) to the structure of the Linux directory tree (FSSTND) and the so-called I-nodes which Linux uses internally for data administration.

Subsequent sections deal in more depth with Linux internals, and their contents will probably make full sense only once you have become better acquainted with Linux. They deal with the specifics of process management (Linux being a multi-tasking system), the administration of libraries and the System V Init process (which controls startup and shutdown of your computer).

This chapter is not strictly necessary for the configuration of Linux – since the following chapters describe the procedures step by step. But this chapter will help you understand what you are doing. Such basic understanding of Linux and the way it functions will become necessary at some point when you want to change the configuration of your computer in such a specific way that a description would no longer fit into the framework of this or other books.

TIP If you have never worked with a Unix system before, you should at least read Sections 5.1 and 5.4 (page 116). This will probably save you a lot of frustration when Linux does not react in the way you would have expected from your DOS or Windows experience.

5.1 Fundamentals of file management

This section sheds some light on different aspects of file management under Linux. The range of subjects goes from fairly trivial issues (which file names are allowed) to the internals of file management (I-nodes and so on). This section is intended to help you use the Linux file system as well as understand it. The main subjects are:

- Files and directories (file names, wildcards * and ?, directories).
- Linux directory structure (which files are where, the meaning of abbreviations such as `bin`, `sbin`, `lib`, `usr`, `home`, and so on).
- Ownership and access privileges (who is allowed to read, modify, execute which files, administration of users and groups).
- Links (fixed and symbolic references to other files and directories).
- Access to several data supports (what the `mount` command is used for, how CD-ROMs and floppy disks are linked into the Linux file system).
- Import and export of DOS text files (end-of-line characters (CR+LF under DOS, LF only under Linux), foreign language special characters).
- Different file systems (why different file systems exist, such as `ext2fs` (Linux standard), `msdos`, `iso9660` (CD-ROM), and so on).
- Internals (how the Linux file system is managed internally, what I-nodes are).

Files and directories

If you have been used to working under DOS/Windows, the new freedom for file names will be one of the first things you will like about Linux. Briefly, here are the main facts:

- Under Linux, file names can be up to 255 characters long.
- Linux is case sensitive.
- Special characters are allowed; however, specific rules must be followed when handling such files.
- Files whose names start with a dot (full stop) are considered hidden files (page 90).

This last point needs some additional comments: you may use any number of dots in file names. In Linux file names, the dot is a character like any other, even though it is frequently used to separate parts of names. `README.bootutils.gz` is a completely normal file name which suggests that it is a compressed README file on the subject of boot utilities.

File names which are not immediately recognizable as such when entering commands (such as file names containing spaces) must be enclosed in double quotes (for example, `"a b"`). It is even possible to use foreign language special characters, such as German umlauts or accented letters. You should, however, be aware that these special characters are a potential source of trouble, as the least that can happen is that file names containing special characters are not sorted properly by `ls`.

> **NOTE** Linux supports various file systems, amongst others the MS-DOS file system. The above remarks are only valid for the Linux standard file system `ext2s`. Other file systems have stronger restrictions regarding the maximum number of characters in file names and so on (see also page 105).

Wildcards

In your standard use of files, you will frequently work on whole groups of files – for example, all files ending in `.tex`. In order to make this possible, two wildcards are allowed when entering Linux commands: `?` to specify *one* arbitrary character, and `*` to specify any number (including zero) of characters.

On the surface, this looks exactly the same as under DOS. In reality, however, wildcards under Linux are significantly more flexible than under DOS. The most important difference is that `*` comprises nearly all characters, including dots (as long as they are not the first character of a file name). If you want to include all files, you just specify `*` and not `*.*` as under DOS. (Notes on hidden files follow later.)

A further difference is that even several wildcards do not throw Linux off balance. With `*graph*`, for example, you can search for all files that contain `graph` in their names – such as `graphics.doc`, `applegraph`, and `README.graph`.

If the wildcards `?` and `*` are too general for your purpose, you can achieve stronger restrictions by specifying square brackets. `[abc]` is a placeholder for one of the three letters `a`, `b`, or `c`. If, within square brackets, a hyphen is specified between two letters or digits, then this stands for a character between them: `[a-f]*` thus comprises all files beginning with a letter between `a` and `f`. `*[_.-]*` stands for all files that somewhere in their names contain at least an underscore, a dot, or a hyphen. The expression can be negated using an exclamation mark: `[!a-z]*` means all files that begin with an uppercase letter or a special character. `*.[hc]` comprises all files ending in `.c` or `.h`.

Wildcards can also be used for directories. `*/*.tex` includes all `*.tex` files located in subdirectories of the current directory (only one level, thus no files in sub-subdirectories). `/usr/*bin/*` includes all files in the directories `/usr/bin` and `/usr/sbin`.

When files are copied, another special character is frequently needed – the dot as a placeholder for the current directory. Thus, the command `cp project/*.c .` copies all `*.c` files contained in the `project` directory into the current directory.

Wildcards for file names	
`?`	exactly one arbitrary character
`*`	an arbitrary number (including zero) of arbitrary characters
`[abc]`	exactly one of the specified characters
`[a-f]`	one character out of the specified range

`[!abc]`	none of the specified characters
`[^abc]`	as above
`~`	abbreviation for the home directory

When handling directories, the two files (they are actually links) `.` and `..` are very important. `.` refers to the current directory, `..` to the next higher one.

REFERENCE

Wildcards are not evaluated by the command in which they occur, but by the shell in which the command is called. In addition to the wildcards described above, `bash`, the most frequently used shell under Linux, recognizes a lot more special characters that have a special effect when executing a command (see page 396).

Complications using wildcards

On the surface, handling wildcards looks easier than it actually is. If you experience problems with wildcards, you should simply carry out some experiments with `echo wildcards`. This command displays all file names included in a wildcard combination, without any further effects on files or file names.

One problem is that `*` not only includes files, but also directories. Thus, `ls *` not only shows all files in the current directory, but also the contents of all subdirectories included in `*`. For the `ls` command, this problem can be circumvented by specifying the `-d` option; other commands, however, do not have such an option.

If you want to operate on all directories (but not on normal files), the wildcard combination `*/.` does the trick: this includes all 'files' which contain a reference to themselves as a subdirectory – and this is only the case for directories. (Internally, directories are considered a special form of file – thus the quotes.)

```
user$   echo */.
```

The fact that not the command but the shell is responsible for the evaluation of wildcards has some advantages, but also drawbacks. Thus, with a command such as `ls -R *.tex`, it is impossible to search for `*.tex` files in subdirectories as well. (The option `-R` for the `ls` command causes a recursive search of subdirectories and can be compared with the `/S` option of the DOS command `DIR`.)

The reason is quite simple: the shell expands the pattern `*.tex` for the current directory and passes `ls` the list of files found. If you do not have any directories with the extension `.tex`, `ls` has finished – even the `-R` option cannot do anything about it. Recursive search is only possible in directories that have been passed as parameters.

Linux provides the much more flexible `find` command to search for files. The example below displays a list of all `*.tex` files in the current and all subordinate directories.

```
user$   find . -name '*.tex'
```

The same cause must be attributed to the failure of the attempt to delete `*~` files in all subdirectories. The command `rm -r *~` fails in spite of the `-r` option for recursive elaboration of subdirectories. The reason: `*~` is already expanded by the `bash` – for the current directory. Subdirectories are only considered if they have a name that ends in ~. (But the exact opposite is intended, that is, to delete all files ending in ~ from ordinary directories.)

Deletion of all backup files in subdirectories is only achieved with the following command. Here, the list of all files in question is built with `find` and then passed to `rm` via command substitution (`$(command)`).

```
user$  rm $(find -name '*~')
```

If we are dealing with a *very* large number of files, an error will occur during the execution of the above command: the command line containing all `*~` files becomes so long that it exceeds the maximum command line length. In such cases, find must be used with the `-exec` option – see page 454.

CAUTION

One of the most dangerous Linux commands is `rm -rf *`: this recursively deletes all files and all directories (starting with the current directory)

.

One further difference from MS-DOS comes to light when you try to execute a command of the kind `mv *.x *.y` (for example, to rename all `*.x` files to `*.y` files). Under Linux, this is not possible with one command. The reason for this restriction is the same as above: the shell substitutes `*.x` with the list of all files that correspond to the pattern. For `*.y`, there are no valid file names. The `mv` command is therefore passed a list of several files and the expression `*.y` – and quite understandably, `mv` can do very little with this.

A concrete example: assume that the current directory only contains the files `mark.x`, `peter.x`, and `sandra.x`. When you execute `mv *.x *.y`, the shell substitutes the pattern `*.x` with the above three files. The shell does not find any matching files for `*.y` and passes the pattern as is. Only now is the `mv` command started. It is passed the following parameters:

```
user$  mv mark.x peter.x sandra.x *.y
```

Even if `mv` were passed `mark.x peter.x sandra.x mark.y peter.y sandra.y` as its parameter list, the result would not be the desired one. `mv` is simply unable to rename several files at a time. Either *several* files are moved into another directory, or *one* file is renamed. `mv` may have some superficial resemblance to the DOS command `RENAME`, but nothing more.

Wildcards for advanced users

Unix experts have obviously found a solution to this problem as well: they use the `sed` stream editor. Because of the rather complicated handling of `sed`, examples such as the following should actually only be used for shell programming. Here is a brief description of how this works: `ls` provides the list of files that are to be renamed and passes it on to `sed`. `sed` converts this into a list of `cp` commands, using the `s` command (regular find and replace) and passes this list to a new shell, `sh`, which finally carries out the commands. The line below copies all `*.xxx` files into `*.yyy` files.

```
user$  ls *.xxx | sed 's/\(.*\)\.xxx$/cp & \ 1.yyy/' | sh
```

Another alternative would be the formulation of a small loop (which presumes the use of `bash` and not another shell). The command below makes copies of all `*.tex` files, giving them the extension `.tex~`. (The final character `~` is often used to mark backup files.)

```
user$  for i in *.tex; do cp $i $i~; done
```

NOTE The above examples work, but they are too complicated for standard use. In Chapter 13, which deals with shell programming, the new commands `regmv` and `regcp` are introduced, which can cope with simple regular expressions of the `regcp 'p-*.eps picture*.ps'` type (see page 421).

Hidden files

Under Unix, files whose names begin with a dot are considered hidden files. `*` therefore does not really include all files in a directory: files starting with a dot (frequently, these are configuration files that are meant to be invisible) are ignored.

If you tried to get at hidden files with a `.*` pattern, you would make things even worse: this not only includes hidden files that begin with `.`, but also the `.` and `..` directories (thus, the current directory and the next higher one). If the command in question is capable of handling entire directories, the consequences may prove fatal.

This problem can be circumvented by using the search pattern `.[!.]*`. This searches for all file names whose first character is a dot, and which have at least one more character that is not a dot and an arbitrary number (including zero) of subsequent characters.

```
user$  echo .[!.]*
```

With the `ls` command, the `-a` option can be used. This causes all files (including hidden ones) to be displayed. However, no search patterns (such as `*rc*`) must be specified, as `-a` only functions if `ls` itself searches the files (without the shell intervening in this task).

Again in this case, the only command that really works universally is `find`. The following command finds all hidden files in the current directory and all subdirectories:

```
user$  find . -name '.*'
```

Directories

The Linux directory tree begins with the root directory. Drive specifications, such as `C:`, are neither possible nor make sense under Linux (see also page 100). Within this book, all other directories are considered *subordinate* – thus, the root directory is at the very top of the tree. In some books, the notation convention is exactly the other way round, which may well correspond to the tree image (root down, branches up), but not to the common terminological use.

Two subdirectories exist in every directory: `.` as a reference to the current directory, and `..` as a reference to the next higher one.

One of the biggest problems for newcomers to Unix/Linux is finding a specific file inside the widely branched directory system. A first orientation is given by the following section. The commands `find`, `locate`, and `grep` are also very useful: `find` searches for a specified file name, `grep` for a character string inside a file. By combining these two commands, and with some practice, almost every file can be found (see pages 454 and 459). `locate` functions similarly to find, but uses a previously built database which makes it a great deal faster (page 463).

Linux directory structure (file system hierarchy standard)

A typical Unix system consists of thousands of files. During the development of Unix, certain rules have crystallized concerning which files are typically stored in which directories. These rules have been adapted to Linux peculiarities and are summarized in a special document: the File System Hierarchy Standard (FHS). Most Linux distributions (with very few exceptions) comply with this standard.

NOTE

The precise specification of FHS – current version 2.0 – can be found on the Internet. (In some distributions, the text is also supplied as part of the documentation.)

`http://www.pathname.com/fhs/`

The information summed up in this section is just a first orientation aid (no more!). It reflects not only the FHS, but also the habits of popular Linux distributions.

The file system begins with the root directory. As a rule, it contains only the Linux kernel file and the following directories:

`/bin`

contains elementary Linux commands for system administration which can be executed by all users (not only by `root` as with the files in `/sbin`). Additional programs can be found in `/usr/bin`.

`/boot`

contains files used for booting the system (usually by means of LILO). In some distributions, this directory also contains the kernel; in others, the kernel is located in the `/` directory.

`/dev`

contains all device files. Almost all hardware components – such as the serial interface or a hard disk partition – are accessed via so-called device files (actually, they are not real files). More information about naming conventions for device files can be found on page 114.

`/etc`

contains the configuration files for the entire system. These files control the boot process, the keyboard layout, and the default settings for various Linux components (for example, network configuration) and for various programs (such as `emacs`). Following the FHS rules, X-specific configuration files should be located in the `/etc/X11` subdirectory, however, this convention is not adhered to by all distributions. Many files in `/etc` are described in the chapters dealing with configuration from page 133 onwards. It would also be useful to check the index (under letter E)!

`/home`

contains the home directories of all Linux users. The home directory is defined as the directory in which the user automatically finds him/herself after logging in and for whose files he/she has unrestricted access rights. (Theoretically, the system administrator (`root`) can also create home directories outside of `/home`. This is, however, normally not done. `root` itself has its home directory in `/root`. The reason for this is that user home directories often lie on their own partition or disk. `root`, however, must still be able to work even if these partitions or disks are temporarily not accessible.)

`/lib`

contains several shared libraries or symbolic links to them. These files are needed for the execution of programs. `/lib/modules` contains kernel modules, which are dynamically activated/deactivated in current operation.

`/lost+found`

is the place where lost files are stored. (These are incomplete or corrupted files which can result from an automatic repair of the file system after exiting Linux improperly.)

`/mnt`

contains subdirectories, such as `cdrom` or `floppy`, where external file systems can be linked in. In many systems, the linking of foreign file systems also takes place directly in a root directory (for example, `/cdrom`). This is against the FHS rules, but somewhat easier (it involves less typing).

`/opt`

contains additional packages which can be installed at a later date. In many systems, office packages and other commercial programs are installed in this location. (Another possible place for such programs is `/usr/local`.)

`/proc`

contains subdirectories for all running processes. These are not true files. The `/proc` directory only reflects the Linux-internal process administration (see page 116).

`/sbin`

contains system administration commands. A common feature of all programs stored in this directory is that they can only be executed by `root`.

`/tmp`

contains temporary files. Often, however, temporary files are also stored in `/var/tmp`.

`/usr`

is the most important directory for the typical user. It contains all application programs, the complete X system, the Linux source codes and so on. Ideally, the `/usr` directory should contain only static (invariable) data. The separation of static and dynamic (variable) data becomes very important when Linux is to be run directly from CD-ROM (read-only!): then, the CD-ROM contains all static data and the `/var` directory all corresponding dynamic files. It should also be possible to link the `/usr` directory read-only into the file system in its own partition. This would have the advantage of better security (and the disadvantage of more laborious maintenance).

`/var`

contains variable files. Important subdirectories are `adm` (distribution-specific administration files), `lock` (locking files for access protection of devices), `log` (log files), `mail` (email files, often also stored in `spool/mail`) and `spool` (buffered printer files, news files, and so on).

Thus, the basic structure of directories at root level is fairly easy to understand. The problems come with the subdivision of `/usr` and `/var` into innumerable subdirectories. Generally, many directories are called the same as those at root level – for example, `bin` for executable programs.

Another problem is that there are several groups of executable programs: text-oriented commands, X programs and so on, and an equal number of possibilities to hide these programs. Often, for historical reasons, several parallel paths are managed via links. Thus, `/usr/bin/X11` leads to the same programs as `/usr/X386/bin` and `/usr/X11R6/bin` (and all paths have their logical or historical reasons).

A complete description of the directory structure is impossible *a priori* (and in new versions, it may change again anyway). Thus, we conclude this section with a brief description of the subdirectories of `/usr`:

`/usr` directories	
`/usr/X11`	link to `/usr/X11R6`
`/usr/X11R6`	X
`/usr/bin`	executable programs
`/usr/dict`	dictionaries and related data; occasionally link to `/usr/share/dict`
`/usr/doc`	online documentation, FAQ (frequently asked questions)
`/usr/games`	games; occasionally link to `/usr/share/games`
`/usr/include`	include files for C
`/usr/info`	online documentation for `info`; occasionally link to `/usr/share/info`

`/usr/lib`	various libraries, numerous subdirectories for C compiler, various other programming languages, large program packages, such as `emacs` or LaTeX and so on
`/usr/local`	applications and files which do not directly belong to the Linux distribution or which have been installed later
`/usr/man`	online documentation for `man`; occasionally link to `/usr/share/man`
`/usr/sbin`	programs which can be executed only by `root`
`/usr/share`	architecture-independent data (such as Emacs Lisp files, ghostscript character sets, and so on)
`/usr/spool`	link to `/var/spool` (spool files for printing)
`/usr/src`	source code of Linux (and maybe of additional programs)
`/usr/tmp`	link to `/var/tmp` (temporary files)

Ownership and access privileges

Unix, and therefore Linux too, are designed as multi-user systems – several users can work with the system at the same time. It used to be common practice for several terminals to be connected to one Unix computer, so that in fact several people could use the (at that time very expensive) computer simultaneously and independently of each other.

A typical Linux PC (one keyboard, one screen, no terminals) cannot be used in this way. However, it is not uncommon that different people work with the same computer (at different times). Networked Linux PCs also allow true multi-user operation: via the network, additional users (who use the keyboard and screen of their computers as a terminal) can log in and process data on your computer.

In a multi-user system, it would obviously be grossly negligent to assume that no user modifies data from another user, intentionally or otherwise. For this reason, every Unix system divides all registered users into several user groups. Each user can decide whether his/her files may be read, modified and (if they are programs) executed by other members of his/her group and other users outside his/her group.

In order to allow this kind of management, the following information is stored together with each file and directory:

- The owner of the file.
- The group to which the file is assigned.
- Nine access bits (rwxrwxrwx for read/write/execute by the owner, by members of the group and by the rest of the world).

The owner (user) of a file is generally the person who created the file. The owner can be changed later on with `chown`. Usually, the primary group of the user is used as group. If the user belongs to more than one group, the group membership can be changed with `chgrp`. (You will find more information about users and groups on page 96.)

The state of these bits, the file owner and the group membership can be viewed with `ls -l`. For a typical text file, `ls` supplies the following results: the file can be read and modified by its owner, `michael`. As it is a text file, the first x bit is deactivated, thus the file cannot be executed. All other users, whether members of the `users` group or not, can read this file (but not modify it).

```
michael$  ls -l header.tex
-rw-r--r--    1 michael  users        3529 Oct  4 15:43 header.tex
```

NOTE

`ls -l` not only displays the state of the nine access bits – the very first character of the output line is reserved for the file type (`-` for a normal file, `d` for a directory, `l` for a symbolic link and so on).

If `michael` wants this file to be read only by members of the users group, but not by users outside of this group, he must deactivate the last r bit. This is done by means of the `chmod` command (see page 444). On most systems, the `users` group consists of all 'normal' users.

```
michael$  chmod o-r header.tex
michael$  ls header.tex -l
-rw-r-----    1 michael  users        3529 Oct  4 15:43 header.tex
```

Access to the file `header.tex` may well be limited to two users, `michael` and `cath`. For this purpose, a new group can be created, to which only the two members belong. (If `michael` and `cath` are, for example, the documentation team of a firm, a group name such as `docuteam` would possibly be a good choice. See page 96.)

```
michael$  chgrp docuteam header.tex
michael$  ls header.tex -l
-rw-r-----    1 michael  docuteam     3529 Oct  4 15:43 header.tex
```

NOTE

Files of other users can be copied into one's own directory if the r bit is set for the group or for all other users. This copy is then owned by the user who executed the `cp` command. Now it is possible for this user to change the access bits of the copy and subsequently modify it or (if it is a program) execute it.

Access rights to directories

In principle, the nine access bits are also valid for directories, but with some slight modification of their meaning: the r bit allows other users to view the contents of the directory with `ls`. The x bit allows them to change into this directory with `cd`. If both x and w are set, other users are even allowed to copy foreign files into this directory.

Access rights to devices

Access to various hardware components (floppy disk drives, printers, modems (that is, serial interfaces), streamers) is carried out via devices. In order to be able to control which user may access which device, devices are assigned different user groups. For example, `/dev/ttyS1` (the second serial interface which is normally connected to a modem) is assigned to the group `uucp`.

```
root# ls -l /dev/ttyS1
crw-rw----   1 root    uucp     5,  65 Jul 18  1994 /dev/ttyS1
```

If you want user `hugh` to be able to access the modem, simply add the user name `hugh` to the `uucp` line in the file `/etc/group`. As a result, `hugh` too belongs to the `uucp` group and can access this group's files (and devices).

```
# Change in file /etc/group
uucp::14:uucp,hugh
```

Special rights and privileges

One special user, the system administrator (sometimes called 'superuser'), has greater powers than all other users. Generally, he/she has the name `root` and a top secret password. The system administrator can, independently of ownership and access rights, access all data, register new users, change access rights, ownership, passwords, and so on. He/she is also the only one with access to system administration programs (for example, `shutdown`, `mount`, `fdisk`, and so on). The separation of system administrators and users prevents users endangering the system as a whole.

If you work alone on your own Linux PC, you are obviously your own system administrator. It is always easier to work consistently as `root`. This means not having to worry about access rights, being able to execute all programs at any time, and so on. There is, however, a serious danger that you will unintentionally change data that impacts on the functionality or stability of Linux. Thus, even if you are the sole user of your computer, it makes sense to register at least one user for the day-to-day operation of Linux and use that as well.

TIP

If you do not log in as `root`, you have, amongst others, the disadvantage that you cannot execute `shutdown` or the related commands `halt` and `reboot`. A simple alternative to having to log in as `root` just to switch off the computer is the key combination Ctrl+Alt+Del. This executes the `reboot` command, whether you have `root` privileges or not.

NOTE

The effect of Ctrl+Alt+Del can be specified in `/etc/inittab`. The following setting causes an immediate shutdown:

```
# Setting in /etc/inittab
ca::ctrlaltdel:/sbin/shutdown -t3 -r now
```

User and group administration

The file `/etc/passwd` stores a list of all users (one line per user). Each line contains, amongst other things, the password (in encrypted form), the UID (user identification) number, the GID (group identification) number for group membership, the home directory and the shell. User Kofler thus has UID 501 and belongs to group 100 (`users`, see below).

```
root#  less /etc/passwd
root:o9KzgKPOp1yHk:0:0:root:/root:/bin/bash
bin:*:1:1:bin:/bin:
...
michael:XBGiYtODixV62:501:100:Michael Kofler:/home/michael:/bin/bash
kathrin:sdkfjghsdf89g:502:100:Cath Huber:/home/cath:/bin/bash
```

NOTE If a shadow password system has been installed (by now, default in many distributions), passwords are not stored in `/etc/passwd`, but in a separate file `/etc/shadow`. This improves system security, as access to `shadow` can be restricted more severely than access to `passwd`.

The file `/etc/group` contains a list of all groups. For each group, its GID is stored. Furthermore, in each line additional users can be listed who belong to the group in question. This means that one user may belong to several groups – the primary group stored in `passwd` and an arbitrary number of additional groups. The membership in different groups can be used for an individual setting of access rights. Thus, `michael` not only belongs to the `users` group (see above), but also to the groups `uucp` and `docuteam`.

```
root#  cat /etc/group
root::0:root
bin::1:root,bin,daemon
...
uucp::14:uucp,michael
man::15:man
users::100:games
docuteam::101:cath,michael
```

NOTE Some distributions – for example, RedHat – automatically assign each new user a specific primary group that bears the name of the user. The `users` group is, in this case, just one (of several) additional groups. This can have some advantages as described in the RedHat manual (FAQs).

NOTE Together with each file, UID and GID numbers are stored. The `ls` command (and several other commands) accesses `passwd` and `groups` to display the names corresponding to the numbers. If file systems of foreign computers are linked via NFS, care must be taken that UID and GID numbers on both computers match – otherwise, considerable problems may arise.

In principle, new users can be registered by direct modification of the `/etc/passwd` file (see also page 145). To register new groups, the file `/etc/group` must be extended. One must only be careful that the new group receives an unused GID. However, it is much simpler to use the configuration programs of the distribution in question (for example `usercfg` in RedHat, `yast` in SuSE). Registration of new users and groups can only be carried out by `root`.

Hard links and symbolic links

Links are references to files. Via links, the same file can be accessed from different points within the directory structure without having physically to store the file more than once. Thus, links are an important means to avoid redundancy. In the Linux file system, links occur most frequently in the `/bin` and `/lib` directories. (Take, for example, a closer look at `/usr/bin` or `/usr/lib` using `ls -l`.)

The easiest way to understand links is through an example: assume that in the `test` directory we find the file `abc`; when we execute the command `ln abc xyz`, it appears that a new file `xyz` was created. In practice, however, `abc` and `xyz` are simply two references to the same file. The only way to check this is provided by the `ls` command using the `-l` option. In the second column, it indicates how many links point to a particular file (in this example, 2). If, in addition, the `-I` option is used, `ls` also indicates the I-node of the file which, in the case of links (and only then), is identical.

```
root#  ls -li
 59293 -rw-r--r--    1 root     root     1004 Oct  4 16:40 abc
root#  ln abc xyz
root#  ls -li
 59293 -rw-r--r--    2 root     root     1004 Oct  4 16:40 abc
 59293 -rw-r--r--    2 root     root     1004 Oct  4 16:40 xyz
```

Now, if you modify one of the two files (no matter which one), the other file changes automatically (because actually only one file exists). If you delete one of the files, you just reduce the number of links.

Linux has two forms of links. The above example has introduced hard links, as they are normally created by the `ln` command (see also page 463). If, however, `ln` is used with the `-s` option, the command creates symbolic links. The advantage with symbolic links (sometimes called soft links) is that within the file system they can point from one physical hard disk to another, and they can be applied not only to files, but also to directories. (None of this is normally possible with hard links. Hard links to directories are a special case, inasmuch as they are possible, but can only be created by the superuser.)

With symbolic links, `ls` shows where the original file is located. On the other hand, however, no counter is provided to indicate how many references to the original file there are.

Internally, the difference between hard and symbolic links is that in one case the I-node is stored, and in the other case the file name or (in links outside a directory) the path specification is stored.

```
root#  ln -s abc efg
root#  ls -li
 59293 -rw-r--r--    2 root     root     1004 Oct  4 16:40 abc
 59310 lrwxrwxrwx    1 root     root        3 Oct  4 16:52 efg -> abc
 59293 -rw-r--r--    2 root     root     1004 Oct  4 16:40 xyz
```

Symbolic links behave differently from hard links. Deletion of the original file (that is, `abc`) does not change the link to this file, but now `efg` points to an empty (non-existent) file. If, however, the symbolic link is deleted, this has no effect on the original file.

Symbolic links can be created not only for files but also for directories. This fact can cause some confusion, as it may look as though whole directory trees are doubled via a symbolic link. In practice, the directory link is only an additional path to the same files and subdirectories.

An example: as standard, LaTeX is installed in a fairly jumbled directory structure. If you want to access LaTeX 2_ε files in a simpler way (and without specifying six subdirectories), you define the following link:

```
user$  ln -s /usr/lib/teTeX/texmf/tex/latex latex2e
user$  ls -l latex2e
lrwxrwxrwx   1 user     user           30 Oct  4 17:20 latex2e ->
  /usr/lib/teTeX/texmf/tex/latex
```

Via the link directory `latex2e`, you can now easily access all files contained in `/usr/TeX/lib/texmf/tex/latex2e`. A last hint: if you want to view the contents of `latex2e`, you will need to indicate the subsequent directory separator as well (`latex2e/` instead of `latex2e`).

```
user$  ls -l latex2e/
total 35
drwxr-xr-x   2 root     root         1024 Nov  6 18:09 algorithm
drwxr-xr-x   2 root     root         1024 Nov  6 18:09 amsfonts
....
```

Generally, you should try to specify relative paths in links, not absolute ones. In this way you prevent problems that might arise from mounting directories via NFS or from relocating directories. If the above link command is to be executed by `root` in the home directory, a relative path specification would look like this:

```
root#  cd /root
root#  ln -s ../usr/lib/teTeX/texmf/tex/latex
```

In practice, symbolic links are almost exclusively used – not only because of their more flexible handling, but also because of their greater intelligibility: with `ls -l` you can easily check where a symbolic link points to. With hard links, this is much more difficult.

Links to programs

Under Linux, several commands, which may work in totally different ways, may often point to one and the same program via symbolic or hard links (try to execute `ls -l /usr/bin`!). Although the same program file is executed every time, the program behaves differently according to the link that was used to call it.

The explanation is quite simple: at the design stage, the different ways to call the program were already built in. Each time the program is executed, a check is carried out to see which command name was used to call up the program. If the name is recognized, the program starts the corresponding routines, otherwise it reacts with an error message.

A good example of this way of proceeding is represented by the `mtools` commands for handling MS-DOS diskettes. The commands `mattrib`, `mcd`, and so on point to the same program file, that is, to `mtools`. If you attempt to execute `mtools` directly, the program gives an error message, because the command name `mtools` is not contained in the list of the 13 possible commands.

5.2 File systems and partitions

Access to several hard disks (partitions)

Under DOS/Windows, each data support (hard disks or hard disk partitions, diskettes, CD-ROMs, and so on) is accessed under its own letter, such as `A:` and `B:` for floppy disk drives, `C:`, `D:`, and so on, for hard disks. Under Linux, a different approach is followed: all hard disks (and all other data supports as well) are united into a single file system. Instead of accessing the second hard disk via `D:`, you simply indicate a directory path. Depending on the installation, it could, for example, be the case that data which is physically stored on the second hard disk is accessed via the directories `/home` or `/var`. All other files in the root directory or other directories are (physically) located on the first hard disk.

The typical user thus is not at all aware that his or her data is distributed across several hard disks. (Obviously, it is also possible that Linux will really use only one hard disk (partition).) The organization of the file system occurs at system startup. The point in the directory tree to which the different hard disk(s) (partitions) will be linked is controlled by means of the file `/etc/fstab`. Information about the structure of this file and about correct installation of the file system can be found on page 147.

If you are not sure how your Linux system is currently organized, the simplest thing to do is to execute the `df` command. This command shows at which point in the file system hard disks are linked and how much space is free on each hard disk. In the example below, two partitions of the SCSI hard disk 3 are active. The base file system is located in a 300-Mbyte partition of which 124 Mbytes are still free. Via the path `/mnt/dosi`, a 200-Mbyte partition can be accessed. The path name indicates that this is a DOS partition which under DOS/Windows is accessed with the drive letter `I:`. It makes sense to use descriptive names, but the choice is yours. You can also link a hard disk partition into the path `/asterix/obelix`, if you so wish.

```
root#  df
Filesystem         1024-blocks  Used Available Capacity Mounted on
/dev/sdc7              308223  168861   123951      58%   /
/dev/sdc5              204564   79304   125260      39%   /mnt/dosi
```

You are most likely to come across the above-mentioned hard disk management procedures while working under Linux if you want to access an MS-DOS partition of your hard disk which is currently not linked into your Linux file system. The command for this is called `mount`. With this command, you can link additional data supports into the system (or remove them) while Linux is running. The following example shows a typical application.

CAUTION

You can carry out modifications to the file system only if you are logged in as `root`. If this is not the case, you must change to a free text console and enter `root` when logging in there.

The device names in this section represent the author's system. Each Linux installation is different! For this reason, it is highly likely that you will have to specify a *different* name to access drive `C:` on your computer.

Let us assume that you have a text file on DOS drive `C:` which you want to process under Linux. Currently, this hard disk partition is not accessible under Linux. When executing the `mount` command, you must in principle specify three items: the device name for drive `C:`, the name of a directory into which the hard disk should be linked and the name of the file system.

The device name depends on whether you work with IDE or SCSI disks, and how the hard disk is organized (formatted). Naming conventions for hard disks have already been described on page 37. In case of doubt, `fdisk -l` can help.

The following table summarizes the naming conventions for IDE and SCSI hard disks and partitions. Please note that the numbering of a 'normally' partitioned hard disk shows gaps: an IDE hard disk with one primary data partition, one extended partition (which, internally, is equally handled as a primary partition), and two logical partitions, will have the device names `/dev/hda1`, `-2`, `-5` und `-6`.

Device names of hard disk(s) (partitions)	
`/dev/hda` to `/dev/hdf`	max. 8 IDE hard disks
`/dev/sda` to `/dev/sdp`	max. 16 SCSI hard disks
`/dev/...1` to `/dev/...4`	max. 4 primary partitions
`/dev/hd.5` to `/dev/hd.63`	max. 59 logical partitions (IDE)
`/dev/sd.5` to `/dev/sd.15`	max. 11 logical partitions (SCSI)

In principle, it does not matter which directory you specify with `mount`. If you do not possess a directory created for this purpose during earlier hard disk accesses, simply create a new one with `mkdir`. A common location would be a subdirectory under `/mnt`.

The file system type depends on how the partition or hard disk has been formatted. The most frequent types are `ext2` (Linux file system), `msdos` (MS-DOS, file names with 8+3 characters), `vfat` (Windows 9x, up to 255 characters for file names, only from kernel 1.3.n onwards), and `hpfs` (OS/2, read only).

```
root#  mkdir /dosc
root#  mount -r -t msdos /dev/hda3 /dosc
root#  df
Filesystem         1024-blocks   Used  Available Capacity Mounted on
/dev/sdc7             308223   168887   123925      58%    /
/dev/sdc5             204564    79304   125260      39%    /mnt/dosi
/dev/hda3              45860    44096     1764      96%    /mnt/dosc
```

Now you can read all files on drive `C:` via the path `/mnt/dosc`. For example, `ls /mnt/dosc` displays the contents of the root directory. The mount option `-r` (read only) prevents files on drive `C:` from being modified.

TIP

The input of all `mount` options is a fairly laborious exercise. If you have to access DOS drive `C:` more frequently, you should modify `/etc/fstab`. In this file, all file systems are entered which are to be automatically mounted at system start. `fstab` can also contain drives or partitions which are not yet to be mounted, but whose parameters and options are to be preset. If `fstab` contains the following line, `/mnt/dosc` can be easily linked using `mount /mnt/dosc`. `mount` reads the missing parameters from `fstab`. Further information about the configuration of `fstab` can be found on page 147.

```
# in /etc/fstab
/dev/hda3 /mnt/dosc msdos defaults,noauto 0 2
```

With `umount` you can remove a drive from the file system. As with `mount`, `umount` can only be executed by `root` and only after all accesses to files on the hard disk have been terminated. `umount` must be passed the device name or the point of linkage. Thus, the following commands are equivalent:

```
root#  umount /dev/hda3
root#  umount /mnt/dosc
```

The syntax of the `mount` command is described on page 471. Further examples involving `mount` can be found in the following two sections about access to CD-ROM and floppy disk drives. Mounting of other data supports, such as streamers, optical (changeable) disks and so on, will not be discussed. The handling of printers (which, as peripheral devices, are also linked into the file system) is described in more detail on page 162.

REFERENCE

Data exchange between Linux and DOS/Windows causes problems with text files, because different character set codes are used (this only applies to DOS) and because the end-of-line coding is different (this applies to both DOS and Windows). Information about the handling of text files can be found on page 503.

Access to CD-ROM drives

In principle, CD-ROM drives are managed in the same way as hard disks. There are, however, two essential differences: firstly, in a CD-ROM drive, you can change the CD (whereas you will never be able to change a normal hard disk during operation). Secondly, CD-ROMs have their own standardized file system, named `iso9660`. Depending on the settings in `/etc/fstab`, the CD-ROM drive can be linked into the file system at system start.

If no CD-ROM drive is linked (check using `df`) and you need data from a CD, you must once again use the `mount` command. In the following example, the first drive connected to the second EIDE controller is addressed.

```
root#  mount -t iso9660 -o ro /dev/hdc /cdrom
```

NOTE Depending on the configuration, `mount` can only be executed by `root`, and only if no other CD is currently linked into the file system and the directory `/cdrom` already exists. The device name `/dev/xyz` depends on your CD-ROM drive. Often, `/dev/cdrom` can be used; this is a link to the correct device.

TIP If the CD-ROM drive is registered in `/etc/fstab` with the option `user`, *all* users (and not only `root`) can add and remove the CD with the `mount` and `umount` commands (see also page 154).

Modern CD-ROM drives are connected either to the EIDE or to the SCSI bus. The following list summarizes the corresponding device names:

`/dev/cdrom`	link to the default CD-ROM device
`/dev/hda`	IDE/ATAPI: drive 1, EIDE controller 1
`/dev/hdb`	IDE/ATAPI: drive 2, EIDE controller 1
`/dev/hdc`	IDE/ATAPI: drive 1, EIDE controller 2
`/dev/hdd`	IDE/ATAPI: drive 2, EIDE controller 2
`/dev/scd0`	SCSI drive1
`/dev/scd1`	SCSI drive2

NOTE With the first generation of CD-ROM drives, each and every manufacturer believed in the need for a proprietary interface. This generated a correspondingly large number of kernel modules for each of these interfaces. Today, you will encounter such CD-ROM drives only in stone-age PCs. To be able to access them under Linux, the appropriate kernel modules must be available. Furthermore, you will need to specify the correct device name, such as `/dev/mcd` for primeval Mitsumi drives. Further information can be found in the CD-ROM HOWTO.

Changing a CD is a troublesome procedure. You cannot just open the drive, change the CD and then go on working with the new CD! Several CD-ROM drives with electronic eject do not even allow this – while the CD is mounted, the drive does not react to pressing the eject button.

The procedure is to execute `umount` (which is a way of informing the system that the CD is going to be removed) while the old CD is still in the drive. This causes a check to be carried out to see whether Linux needs any further data from the current CD. If it does, `umount` signals 'device busy', for example if the current directory on any console points to the CD-ROM drive. Execute `cd`!

The CD is released only if no access to the CD is required. Now you can change CD and register the new CD in the same way as the previous one.

```
root#  umount /cdrom
root#  mount -t iso9660 -o ro /dev/hdc /cdrom
```

NOTE If `umount` displays the 'device is busy' message, another program is still using data from the CD-ROM. This is also the case if a directory of the CD-ROM is open in any of the shells. Execute `cd` in all of these shells to return to the home directory. Also, the `fuser` command may help in the search for the process which causes the `umount` problems. Execute `fuser -m /cdrom`.

TIP

The input of `mount` with all its parameters is a fairly laborious exercise. If you enter the CD-ROM device in `/etc/fstab` (see page 147), a simple `mount /cdrom` is sufficient. The command reads the missing information from `fstab`. CD-ROM access can be set up even more easily in the KDE desktop – see page 286.

NOTE

Execution of programs directly from the CD is usually not allowed for reasons of security. If, for example, you want to execute an installation program directly from the CD (without copying it first into a directory on your hard disk) you must call the `mount` command with the additional option `-o exec`.

Long file names on CD-ROMs

Many Linux CDs use long file names which were originally not envisaged in the ISO-9660 standard. To support such file names in spite of that, Linux CDs use the so-called Rockridge extension. This extension of the ISO standard specifies how additional information about the files can be stored. The Rockridge extension is not a Linux-specific peculiarity, but an accepted standard in the Unix world.

Evidently, the Rockridge extension is not the only possibility of storing long file names on CDs. Apple and Microsoft (Joliet) have both defined their own ISO-9660 extensions. Since Linux kernel 2.2, the Joliet extension is supported as well (for kernel 2.0, corresponding patches are available).

Access to floppy disk drives

Access to floppy disk drives can be carried out following the same scheme as for CD-ROMs. The same commands are needed to link a diskette into the file system and to change it.

Under Linux, floppy disk drives are accessed under the device names `/dev/fd0` and `/dev/fd1`. As standard, only `root` can access these devices. If you also want ordinary users to be allowed access, you must add them to the `disk` group and/or change the access bits (see page 94).

The only difference in the execution of `mount` is that now you have to specify the file system of the diskette instead of `iso9660`. (The majority will probably be diskettes in MS-DOS format – thus, option `-t msdos`. In principle, however, diskettes formatted for any other file system supported by Linux are accepted as well.)

The `mount` and `umount` procedure may appear somewhat laborious just to read or write a couple of files (not to mention the fact that these commands can be carried out only by `root`). Thus, it is hardly surprising that a group of commands have been developed which are specially designed to allow easier access to MS-DOS diskettes. All these commands begin with the letter `m` and allow all common operations with MD-DOS diskettes without having to mount them beforehand: formatting (`mformat`), display of disk contents (`mdir`), copying of files in both directions (`mcopy`), and so on. These commands are described in Chapter 14 from page 467 onward.

Access to streamers

Linux supports different streamer types. The two main groups are SCSI streamers and streamers connected via the floppy disk controller (in particular, QIC-80 and QIC-120 streamers). Streamers are *not* linked to the file system with `mount`, because they do not contain a file system (but only one or more archive files).

Instead, data is transferred directly to or from the streamer by means of `tar` or `cpio`. Depending on the streamer, you must specify `/dev/ftape` (floppy streamer), `/dev/nst*` (SCSI streamer) or `/dev/rmt*` (QIC-02 streamer with its own interface card) as the device file. As with `/dev/fd*`, it may be necessary to change the access rights to these devices. With `mt`, tapes can be wound forwards and backwards, see also pages 472 (`mt`) and 483 (`tar`).

TIP: You will find further information about supporting floppy streamers in the Ftape HOWTO, while information about SCSI streamers can be found in the SCSI HOWTO.

5.3 File system types

As we have briefly mentioned in the previous section, Linux supports several types of file system. (To rephrase it in a more positive way, you will hardly find another operating system which can handle such a large number of file systems without problems!) The following paragraphs briefly describe why so many file systems are supported, together with the meaning of individual file system types.

TIP: A list of the file systems which are supported by the current version of Linux can be found in the file `/usr/src/linux/fs/filesystems.c`.

Please note that file system types foreign to Unix are subject to many restrictions compared to the normal Linux file management: thus, in some file systems the length of file names is restricted, no links can be established, and so on.

Which of the above file system types is actually available depends on how the Linux kernel was compiled. Very often, some seldom used file system types are excluded in order to keep the kernel as compact as possible. If, at a later stage, the need arises to access such a file system, the kernel must be recompiled (see page 199).

The rest of this chapter (and with very few exceptions, the rest of this book) refers to the `ext2` file system, which under Linux represents *the* actual standard.

Linux file systems

- The current proprietary Linux file system is called **`ext2`** (extended file system, version 2). It supports file names of up to 255 characters, files of up to 2 Gbytes and can (theoretically) manage data supports of up to 4 Tbytes (terabytes, that is, 1024 Gbytes). For numerous technical management details, it is more reliable and secure than all other file system types available under Linux. Since quota has been integrated into the kernel (version 2), the maximum space requirements of individual users can be limited.

- The predecessor of ext2 was **ext**, which can still be found on older Linux distributions (to about the end of 1993). Today, ext is no longer significant.
- In parallel to ext and ext2, another new file system has been developed for Linux, called **xiafs**. Although it can boast similar features to ext2, it has not succeeded and is of little significance today.

Unix derivatives

- The very first Linux experiments were carried out with the **minix** file system. Minix is designed as a teaching system. It is substantially less powerful and, more important, cannot be copied freely. For this and other reasons the minix file system has been very rapidly superseded by ext and is of little significance for Linux today.
- The **sysv** file system allows access to SCO, Xenix, and Coherent partitions.
- The **ufs** file system allows read-only access to partitions of FreeBSD, NetBSD, NextStep, and SunOS. (Similar to Linux, BSD is a free Unix derivative.) For accessing BSD partitions, the additional BSD disklabel extension is required. An analogous extension also exists for Sun-OS partition tables.

DOS, Windows, and OS/2

- The **msdos** driver allows reading and writing of old MS-DOS and Windows 3.1 partitions (with short file names, 8+3 convention).
- The **umsdos** file system builds on the MS-DOS file system and allows use of long file names with Unix access privileges and links. It is designed to install Linux in an MS-DOS partition. Since this installation variation has a large number of disadvantages, it is practically no longer used.
- With Windows 95, long file names have finally become established in the Microsoft world as well. Linux can read and modify Windows 95 partitions with its **vfat** driver. Since kernel 2.2, it can also be used to read and write vfat32 partitions, used since Windows 95b and Windows 98 for efficient management of large partitions. As the vfat driver can also be used to access normal MS-DOS file systems, the separate msdos driver has only little importance.
- **ntfs** allows read access to Windows NT partitions (Windows NT 4). The ntfs driver also contains experimental write functions which are, however, far from being mature and should only be used after a complete backup of the NT partition has been carried out.
- Similar restrictions also apply to OS/2 partitions. The **hpfs** driver only allows read access.

CD-ROM and network file systems

- The `iso9660` driver allows access to CD-ROMs. ISO 9660 has emerged as the standard for file management on CD-ROMs. Thanks to ISO 9660 it is possible to read the same CD-ROM on the most varied computers and operating systems.

  Originally, ISO 9660 envisaged only short file names. Depending on the operating system, long file names are supported by different and mutually incompatible extensions. Already in version 1, Linux was able to cope with the **Rockridge** extension commonly used under Unix. Since kernel 2.2 (more precisely, since more recent 2.0.n versions), Linux also supports the **Joliet** extension used by Microsoft.
- File systems need not be located on the local hard disk – they can also be mounted through a network. Currently, the Linux kernel supports four network file systems:

  `nfs` (Network File System) is the most important variation under Unix.
  `coda` is best compared with NFS. It provides a large number of additional functions, but is not yet very widely used.
  `ncp` (Netware Core Protocol) is the Novell variation.
  `smb` (Server Message Buffer) is the network file system of Microsoft.

Others

The `proc` file system is not really a file system. It is used for mapping of administrational information of the kernel or of process management. Details can be found on page 117.

Besides the file systems mentioned above, Linux supports a number of other file systems (such as those of the Commodore Amiga, the Apple Macintosh, the Arcon, and so on), which will not be discussed in the framework of this book.

5.4 File system internals

This is not a Unix textbook – thus, a long-winded explanation of how the Linux file system is structured and managed internally is really out of place. On the other hand, some further background knowledge will certainly provide a better understanding of typical Unix and Linux file system features – for example, links.

Internals of the `ext2` file system

Group picture

The following subsections contain many simplifications. For example, for reasons of speed and security, some administration data is stored several times – a fact that, for the sake of simplicity, is ignored. You will find further details (including some very clear illustrations) of the Linux file system in the Linux user manual of LunetIX (see References). General information about the organization of a Unix file system (without consideration of special Linux features) can be found in any Unix or computer science textbook.

The starting point is always a hard disk or a hard disk partition on which normally several hundred Mbytes of linear storage space are available. The first step in managing such an amount of data space efficiently consists in subdividing it into blocks of 1024 bytes (1 Kbyte) each, and numbering these blocks sequentially. Subsequently, the blocks are arranged into several groups, each destined to store a different data type.

The first two groups consist of one block each. The first block (boot block) contains a mini-program to start the operating system. The second block (superblock) specifies how big the four remaining groups are.

Groups three and four consist of several blocks and are organized as bitmaps. Each bit in these bitmaps indicates whether the corresponding I-node (see below) or data block in groups five and six is free or not. The importance of these bitmaps lies in the fact that, when a new file is to be created, they quickly allow the system to determine where on the hard disk free data blocks are available.

`ext2` data block types

Block 1	Group 1	Boot block
Block 2	Group 2	Superblock
Block 3 to n1	Group 3	I-node bitmap (which blocks for I-nodes are free)
Block n1+1 to n2	Group 4	Data bitmaps (which blocks for data are free)
Block n2+1 to n3	Group 5	Storage space for I-nodes (four I-nodes per block)
Block n3+1 to n4	Group 6	Storage space for data (1024 bytes per block)

Group 6 is by far the largest group. It stores the actual contents of the files, whereas the other five groups contain pure management information. (As you will see in the following sections, some blocks in group 6 must also be used for management information: in very large files, for cross-references to further data blocks, and in directories, for the storage of the directory contents.)

I-nodes

I-nodes (information nodes) are the key to data administration. In 128 bytes, the I-nodes store all the management information for a file, except for the file name. (The file name is stored in directories – more about this later.) Information stored in the I-node includes (amongst other things):

- ID numbers of owner and group.
- Access rights.
- File size.
- Number of links.

- Date and time of creation, last modification, last read access and deletion of the file.
- References to the first 12 data blocks of the file.
- Singly, doubly, and triply indirect references to up to 16 million further data blocks. (Linux versions running on 32-bit processors, however, limit the file size to 2 Gbytes.)

TIP

When formatting an `ext2` file system by means of the `mke2fs` command, the density of I-nodes can be specified. Normally, one I-node is assigned to every 4 Kbytes (thus, 25000 I-nodes in a partition of 100 Mbytes). In practice this means that only 25000 files can be stored in this partition, even if the files are very small and would occupy less than 100 Mbytes. If you know that a very large number of very small files (or symbolic links) are to be created on a partition, you can choose a greater I-node density (for example, one I-node for every 1024 bytes). However, since I-nodes themselves take up storage space, the available data area of the partition becomes smaller.

Files

A file consists of an I-node with management information and several data blocks containing the data proper. It is very important that the management information is completely separated from the data and that therefore both can be processed independently. If a file is moved to another directory, only the management information changes, without affecting the data at all.

The number of data blocks required is a function of the file size. One essential piece of information in the I-node is the specification of *where* (that is, in which data blocks) the data of the file is stored. The numbers of the first 12 data blocks are stored directly in the I-node. If the file is bigger than 12 Kbytes, a further I-node points to a block which itself does not contain any data, but references to up to 256 further data blocks (single level of indirection).

For files that are bigger than 268 Kbytes, this is again insufficient: a further I-node value points to a block that points to another 256 blocks of pointers, which finally leads to 256×256 data blocks (doubly indirect). Now, the maximum file size is 65796 Kbytes. For even bigger files, triply indirect addressing becomes necessary, which allows access to further $256 \times 256 \times 256$ data blocks.

Directories

In principle, directories are managed in the same way as files. From a contents point of view, imagine a directory as being a text file which lists all files and subdirectories line by line. Each line contains the name of a file together with its I-node number. Furthermore, this text file contains a reference to itself (`.`) and a reference to the next higher directory (`..`). These two cross-references facilitate and accelerate the management of directories.

This means that the first I-node points to the root directory. The root directory contains all information about the names and I-nodes of the files and subdirectories stored in it. Via the I-nodes of the subdirectories, their files and further subdirectories can be accessed, and so on.

Hard links

Hard links are simply realized by pointing to the same I-node of a file from different locations within directories. This means that a file which is pointed to by several links still has only one I-node. For this reason, all hard links to a file must have the same owners, groups, access rights, and so on.

Part of the I-node data of a file is a counter that increments by 1 with each additional link and decrements by 1 with each deleted link. When this counter reaches 0, there are no more links to the file; the I-node and the data blocks containing the data proper of this file can be released; the file ceases to exist. Hard links are therefore a generalization of normal file management. In principle, one could say that a simple file is a file with only one link.

Symbolic links

Symbolic links are different: both the file name of the link and the entire absolute file name (including all directories) of the file itself are stored. Unlike all other directory entries, no I-node number is stored for symbolic links. (The target file could lie outside the current data support. This may have its own I-node numbering, which could lead to ambiguities. For this reason, the reference must be stored as an absolute file name.)

With symbolic links, the actual link may in fact point nowhere (that is, to a file that no longer exists). This can arise if the file was deleted, or if one of the directories in its access path was renamed, or the data support was not mounted into the file system or it was mounted at a different point, and so on.

A directory with some files, directories, and links might, for example, look like this:

I-node	*File or directory name*	*Path specification for symbolic link*
53	.	
17	..	
63	`file1`	
97	`file2`	
143	`file3`	
	`file4`	`/users/harry/letter.doc`
143	`file5`	

`file3` and `file5` are hard links to the same file (same I-node number). `file4` is a symbolic link (no I-node number, but an absolute path).

Fragmentation of the `ext2` file system

There is no program under Linux for defragmenting the file system, unlike DOS/Windows. Usually, there is no reason to do this, as the file system is managed more intelligently and fragmentation is largely prevented. (Fragmentation is a state of the file system where single files are not stored in contiguous blocks, but scattered all over the partition. This can arise when files are deleted, newly created, extended, or truncated.)

Repairing the `ext2` file system, security aspects

The superblock (group 2) contains a so-called valid bit, which is deleted when the system is started up (more precisely: when the hard disk is linked into the file system via `mount`). This valid bit is set again only after the hard disk has been correctly unlinked (`umount`) at system shutdown and all information temporarily stored in RAM has been saved.

At the next start-up of Linux, this valid bit is checked; if it is 0, that is, if the last Linux session has not been closed properly (power failure, reset key), a file system repair via `e2fsck` is started automatically. In many cases, nothing has happened and/or all files can be reconstructed. Otherwise, the residual pieces of files that cannot be reconstructed are stored in the `/lost+found` directory of the partition in question. In the case of text files, some useful information may still be extracted out of these remains.

> **NOTE** Even if the computer has always been shut down properly, an automatic file system check is nevertheless carried out at regular intervals, after a specific number of boot processes ('/dev/xxx has reached maximal mount count') or a specific time lapse from the last check. This should not worry you (the frequency of the automatic check can be set via `tune2fs` – see page 487).

You may encounter some difficulties if for some reason you want to check or correct the file system manually using `fsck`: this operation should only be performed when the file system is not mounted (or at least mounted as read-only). Data partitions can simply be de-registered with `umount`, but this is not possible with the root partition. In this case, you can start up your computer in single user mode and read-only. In order to do this, you must specify the additional boot options `ro single` in LILO. An alternative is to start the computer using the Linux installation diskettes and execute `e2fsck` from there.

The `ext2` file system was designed with the aim of creating a surefire system. This is reflected in numerous details. Thus, critical information is stored several times (that is, redundantly) in different locations on the hard disk. This is specially useful if your computer comes up with a message of the 'can't read superblock' type. (If this actually happens, quite a lot must have gone wrong. The author has never 'managed' to do this.)

Normally, the superblock, which contains all important information, is stored in the first block of the partition. Copies of this data are stored every 8192 blocks.

Thus, you can try to access the first copy of the superblock with `e2fsck -f -b 8193 device` and reconstruct the file system on this base.

`ext2` restrictions

Although `ext2` is undoubtedly a modern file system, there are still some restrictions or, in other words, there is potential for improvement.

- Currently, the maximum file size (for 32-bit Intel systems) is 2 Gbytes. For some applications, this is no longer sufficient. The easiest solution is to run Linux on a 64-bit system (such as DEC Alpha). Another possibility is to address a partition device directly as a file, which allows the file to grow up to the full partition size. However, this method permits only one file per partition.
- The automatic file system check after a crash or power failure or after exceeding the time or `mount` limit (see `tune2fs`) takes relatively long (proportional to the partition size). A remedy is a so-called *journaling file system*, in which write operations are logged. On the basis of this log information, the file system can be brought back into a consistent state in much less time (although the log operation entails a slight performance overhead in current operation).
- The `ext2` file system lacks the possibility of transparently compressing individual directories (and their contents).

NOTE

Obviously, improvements to the file system are under development. Furthermore, there are a number of unofficial patches, extensions, and even individual approaches to develop an entirely new file system. Unfortunately, there is no central `ext2` Web site. You may, however, find information on the following pages:

```
http://idiom.com/~beverly/reiserfs.html
http://www.netspace.net.au/~reiter/e2compr/
http://narnia.mit.edu/projects/ext2/
http://www.linuxhq.com/
http://www.linuxmama.com/
```

RAID

RAID stands for *Redundant Array of Inexpensive/Independent Disks* (there are two definitions). The basic idea is that of logically linking partitions of several hard disks, with the aim of achieving a more reliable and/or faster overall system:

- RAID can be used to increase data throughput by accessing data almost in parallel: while the system, for example, waits for data from hard disk 1, further data can be requested from hard disk 2, and so on.
- RAID can also be used to increase safety by redundant (multiple) storage of data. This, however, entails a loss of access speed.

The following overview of different RAID levels starts from the idea that partitions of *different* hard disks are to be linked. (Theoretically, it is also possible to link partitions of *one* hard disk; however, this makes no sense – neither from a safety nor from a speed point of view.)

Various RAID levels

Linear concatenation

Here, several physical partitions are combined into one larger virtual partition. The advantage is that very large partitions can be formed which reach across several hard disks. There is no gain in speed, and the risk of failure is higher. (If one hard disk fails, *all* data is lost.)

RAID-0 (striping)

Here too, several partitions are combined into one larger partition. However, the partitions are not linearly written one after the other, but data is distributed almost in parallel across the individual partitions in small blocks (for example, 4Kbytes) so that during access to a larger file data is read alternately from all hard disks. In the best case, this results in a multiplication of the data rate (for example, a triplication in the case of three hard disks). In practice, however, this effect is limited through physical limits (for example, the maximum throughput rate of the SCSI bus) and the additional overhead. As with linear concatenation of partitions, the risk of failure is high (a defective hard disk leads to the loss of *all* data).

RAID-1 (mirroring)

Here, the same data is stored in two partitions. If one hard disk fails, the data is available on the other hard disk. One advantage is the high safety, a disadvantage the halved capacity. The speed depends on the implementation: with hardware RAID, the same speed can be reached for write operations as for a normal access to a partition, while with read and search operations, the speed can even be improved. With software RAID, however, mirroring is significantly slower.

RAID-5 (parity striping)

In principle, RAID-5 functions in the same way as RAID-0, however, in addition, parity information is stored in one of the partitions (a different partition for each data block). Thus, when a hard disk fails, the entire data can be reconstructed. In this way, RAID-5 tries to combine the advantages of RAID-0 and RAID-1, without their disadvantages. If n partitions of equal size are combined into one virtual RAID-5 partition, a space of $n - 1$ times the size of a partition is available for data. The performance overhead for parity information management can at least in part be counterbalanced by striping.

EIDE versus SCSI hard disks

Because of its working principle, the SCSI system offers big advantages for all RAID variations, independently of the software or hardware implementation. The most important one is that, after receiving an appropriate command, hard disks can temporarily 'sign off' from the SCSI bus until data can effectively be supplied. During the remaining time, the SCSI bus is free for transmission of commands or data to other disks. Furthermore, there are very efficient (but also very expensive) RAID controllers for SCSI disks.

If you want (need) to use EIDE disks, the only alternative is software RAID (see below). Optimum performance can only be achieved if the hard disks are connected to different controllers – this means that, in practice, the most widely used and most sensible EIDE configuration is a RAID-0 system with two hard disks and two controllers. Only in this extreme case can the theoretical potential of RAID-0 be almost fully exploited even with EIDE hard disks, that is, the data transfer rate for large files can nearly be doubled.

Hardware versus software RAID

RAID can be implemented either by means of a RAID controller (a SCSI controller with additional RAID functions) or via software. Both variations have their advantages: hardware RAID does not put additional load on the computer (the CPU) and, as a rule, is faster and more stable. In particular, hardware RAID supports changing and restoring of defective disks during current system operation (*hot swap*).

Software RAID, on the other hand, can also cope with EIDE disks and does not cause additional cost. Depending on the RAID level, the same data transfer rate can be reached as with hardware RAID (however, with a higher CPU load).

With hardware RAID, kernel support depends on the actual SCSI card. Software RAID is, in principle, supported since kernel 2.0; with kernel 2.2, the RAID functions were substantially improved and extended. The basic idea, however, is still the same: an intermediate layer is put between the hard disk access driver (IDE/SCSI) and the file system driver (for example, `ext2`). The so-called *multi devices driver support* (in short, `md`) takes several hard disk partitions to construct a new logical device that the file system driver can access (`/dev/md`*n*).

REFERENCE

On page 157 you will find concrete information on how you can create a RAID-0 system (striping) for optimization of hard disk access. This obviously assumes that you have at least two hard disks with Linux partitions. Further information and hints for installation of other RAID levels can be found in the Multi-Disk-HOWTO, the Root-RAID-HOWTO, and the Software-RAID-Mini-HOWTO.

Devices

In the Linux file system, not only is data managed, but also devices and processes (see below). The term device stands for the entire hardware of the computer, such as hard disk, floppy disk drives, serial and parallel interfaces, the working memory (RAM), and so on. Devices are characterized by three items of information: the major device number, the minor device number, and the access type (block or character oriented).

Some explanations: the major device number indicates which driver of the Linux kernel is responsible for its management. Currently, there are about 25 different drivers, listed in `/usr/src/linux/include/linux/major.h`. Many drivers can use the minor device number to distinguish between different (but related) devices. Thus, the driver for diskette drives distinguishes between different drive types (5.25 or 3.5 inch, DD or HD, and so on), the driver for hard disks between different partitions, and so forth. The access type indicates whether the devices are buffered (this is the case for all block-oriented devices, such as hard disks, and so on) or not (character-oriented devices, such as parallel or serial interfaces).

The contents list of `/dev` with `ls -l` displays the device numbers (major and minor) instead of the file size. The first character of the access bits is `b` or `c` (block or character oriented). Additional device files can be created with the `mknod` command (see page 470).

The Linux `/dev` directory only contains I-nodes, but no corresponding files. The entire management information is stored within the I-node. Some devices are realized as links. Thus, `/dev/mouse` points to the device file which is responsible for the interface to which the mouse is actually connected (frequently, the first serial port or `psaux` for PS/2 mice). The following list gives an overview of the most important device names:

`/dev/xxx` names	
`*bm`	various bus mice
`*cd*`	Old CD-ROM drives (Mitsumi, Sony, ...)
`console`	the currently active virtual terminal
`fd*`	floppy disk drives
`ftape*`	link to floppy streamers without rewind
`hd*`	IDE drives (standard hard disks)
`kmem`	memory (RAM) in core format (for debuggers)
`lp*`	parallel interface for printers, and so on
`mem`	memory (RAM)
`modem`	default interface for modem
`mouse`	default interface for mouse
`psaux`	PS/2 mouse
`nftape*`	link to floppy streamers with rewind
`nrft*`	floppy streamers with rewind
`nst*`	SCSI streamers without automatic rewind
`port`	I/O ports
`ptyp*`	terminal masters under X
`ram`	RAM disk
`rft*`	floppy streamers without rewind
`rmt*`	streamers without SCSI
`sd*`	SCSI drives
`scd*`	SCSI CD-ROM drives
`st*`	SCSI streamers with automatic rewind
`tape*`	default streamer

`tty*`	virtual terminals in text mode
`ttyp*`	terminal slaves under X
`ttyS*`	serial interfaces

Some device files have a special function: thus, `/dev/null` serves as a 'black hole' where data can be placed and made to disappear for good (for example, to re-route command output that is not to be displayed). `/dev/zero` is an inexhaustible source of 0-bytes, which is sometimes used to fill files with zeros until they reach a specific size.

TIP

If you can access specific devices only as `root`, a likely cause is that only `root` has write access privileges for the device in question. To allow other users access to these devices, you can register these users in `/etc/group` in the group to which the device belongs (you can determine this group with `ls -l /dev/...`). On single user systems, you can also open up access with `chmod a+rw device` – however, this will create a safety gap!

In older Linux systems, serial interfaces were addressed via the device files `/dev/cua*`. Since kernel version 2.2, these devices no longer exist, and the device name `ttyS*` (which has been around as an alternative for quite some time) must be used.

You will find a complete description of all devices currently known under Linux, together with their device numbers, in the file `/usr/src/linux/Documentation/devices.txt`.

Information about process administration in the `/proc` directory

Information about processes is managed by Linux internally. In order to offer users easy access to such data, the process administration information is mapped in the `/proc` directory: each process is assigned its own subdirectory in `/proc`. This process directory contains some files with various management data.

Important `/proc` files	
`/proc/bus/pci/*`	PCI information (kernel 2.2)
`/proc/cpuinfo`	CPU information
`/proc/ide/*`	IDE drives and controllers
`/proc/interrupts`	interrupt usage
`/proc/ioports`	I/O port usage
`/proc/mdstat`	RAID state
`/proc/modules`	active modules
`/proc/net/*`	network state and usage
`/proc/partitions`	hard disk partitions
`/proc/pci`	PCI informationen (kernel 2.0)
`/proc/scsi/*`	SCSI drives and controllers

`/proc/sys/*`	system and kernel information
`/proc/version`	kernel version

We will not go into detail at this point. But you need to know that the `/proc` directory occupies *no* storage space on the hard disk, since it is simply a mapping of operating system internal data. The same applies to the very large file `/proc/kcore`, which maps the RAM.

`proc` files are partly in text format. These files can be viewed with `cat` or `more`, but not with `less`! (In fact, they are not 'true' files. `less` is, in many respects, far better than `cat` and `more`, but it is also more restrictive about permitted data formats.)

5.5 Process administration

Linux is a multitasking system, that is, several programs (processes, tasks) can be executed almost at the same time. 'Almost', in this context, means that the processes are not actually carried out simultaneously (this would require several parallel computers or at least processors), but that this is the impression given. The programs are each assigned some CPU time (fractions of seconds) in turn. Thus, each program runs more slowly, but still without visible interruptions.

Currently running processes can easily be determined with the `ps` command, using the `-x` option. (To execute this command, you should be logged in as `root` – otherwise, the only displayed processes are the ones you yourself started).

```
root#  ps -x
  PID TTY STAT  TIME COMMAND
    1  ?  S     0:00 init
    7  ?  S     0:00 bdflush (daemon)
    8  ?  S     0:00 update (bdflush)
   38  ?  S     0:00 /usr/sbin/syslogd
   40  ?  S     0:00 /usr/sbin/klogd
   42  ?  S     0:00 /usr/sbin/inetd
   44  ?  S     0:00 /usr/sbin/lpd
   47  ?  S     0:00 /usr/sbin/crond
   52  ?  S     0:00 gpm
   55 v01 S     0:00 -bash
   56 v02 S     0:00 -bash
   57 v03 S     0:00 /sbin/agetty 38400 tty3
   58 v04 S     0:00 /sbin/agetty 38400 tty4
   59 v05 S     0:00 /sbin/agetty 38400 tty5
   60 v06 S     0:00 /sbin/agetty 38400 tty6
   66 v01 S     0:03 emacs grundl.tex
   74 v02 R     0:00 ps -x
```

At the moment when the above command was executed from virtual terminal 2 (`v02`), the `emacs` text editor was active on terminal 1. Furthermore, the Bourne shell (`bash`) was running on both terminals as a command interpreter. The four remaining terminals wait for a login. The remaining processes (ID 1 to 52) are not assigned to any terminal and are used for Linux internal hardware management (keyboard, mouse, printer and so on).

The value in the PID column indicates the process number. Knowledge of this number can be used to terminate programs or background processes that have got out of control by means of the `kill` command.

Processes can assume different states. The most frequent states are R (running) and S (sleeping, the program has nothing to do at the moment and is waiting for input). Programs can also be temporarily interrupted, in which case they show state T (stopped). (The `emacs` editor, for example, can be put into this state with Ctrl+Z). `%program_name` resumes execution of an interrupted process.

The processes managed by Linux are mapped to the `/proc` directory of the file system. The entries in this directory do not, however, correspond to actual files on the hard disk; instead, they are just items of information that are displayed more clearly by using the file system.

Usually, you are only made aware that you are working on a multitasking system when, for the first time, you execute time-consuming commands (for example, to generate an extensive printout or to format a diskette). If you start such a command, you must usually wait until its execution terminates before you can go on working. Under Linux, you can just switch to another terminal and continue working there – practically without delays. (Under X you simply switch to another terminal window. If none is left free, you simply open a new one.)

Background processes

In many cases, there is yet another possibility for executing time-consuming processes. You simply start the program as a background process, by appending an `&` to the command line:

```
root#  fdformat /dev/fd0H1440 > /dev/null &
```

Using the above command, an HD diskette in drive A: is formatted in the background. After entering the command, you can immediately carry on working. As the continuous display of the currently formatted track by `fdformat` would disturb work, all output is re-routed with `>` to the device `/dev/null` (thus, suppressed). Formatting the diskette costs so little CPU time that practically no delay can be felt (as opposed to formatting under MS-DOS, which blocks the whole computer).

Distribution of CPU time

In standard use of Linux – especially when working in text mode – the CPU capacity is normally more than sufficient to satisfy all running processes. In this case, the remaining CPU time is mopped up by an idle process. This process is in principle an endless loop which is executed every time there is no other activity. The situation is different when Linux is overworked (for example, if you are compiling a program while at the same time scrolling a text under X, and so on). In such cases, Linux tries to distribute the available CPU time fairly between all processes.

In some cases, it can make sense intentionally to assign a specific process more or less CPU time. This is done by means of the `nice` command, with which programs can be started with reduced or – only by `root` – augmented priority

A good overview of how much CPU time is currently being used by each program is given by the `top` command. It runs until it is stopped by [Q], displaying a statistical count of all running processes (ordered by CPU time) every five seconds. If possible, this should be started in a terminal (window) of its own.

Daemons

Background processes for system administration are called daemons. These processes are started during the boot process in files of the `/etc/rc.d` directory. The processes are not assigned any terminals, which causes the `ps` command to display only a question mark in the TTY column (see above). Here follows a brief list of the meaning of some of the most important Linux daemons:

`crond` batch daemon (starts other processes at predetermined times); controlled via `/etc/crontab` and user-specific files in `/var/spool/cron/crontabs`

`inetd` starts other network daemons if needed; controlled via `/etc/inetd.conf`

`klogd` stores kernel messages (normally in `/var/adm/*` or `/var/log/*`)

`lpd` print spooler

`syslogd` stores system messages (normally in `/var/adm/*` oder `/var/log/*`); controlled via `/etc/syslog.conf`

Although control of daemons is not specifically dealt with in this book, some additional information may prove useful, even for users with scant system knowledge.

Let us look at `crond` first: if your computer suddenly starts to search through the hard disk, sends you emails and so on, seemingly off its own bat, the cause is nearly always `crond` starting processes automatically. In some distributions, more things are preconfigured than are actually required for Linux on a standalone computer. Check the system-wide file `/etc/crontab` or the user-specific files in `/var/spool/cron/crontabs/*` and comment out any unwanted entries by simply preceding them with a `#`.

The other two log daemons, `klogd` and `syslogd`, store vast amounts of important messages from the kernel and various other programs in log files. If problems arise during the use of Linux, the information contained in these files is essential and often explains the cause of the problem.

These log files, however, have the unpleasant property of seemingly unstoppable growth. Therefore, it becomes necessary to shorten them from time to time. Depending on the configuration, this can be executed automatically by `crond` (for example, once a week), or automatically at each system start, or even manually. The simplest method is simply to delete the files (possibly after having made a backup in a different location). At the next system start, new log files will be created. However, this method has the disadvantage that logging is interrupted until the daemons next start up. The commands of the `prune` package (which usually must be installed separately) allow the log files to be manipulated more easily.

> **REFERENCE** Apart from the above-mentioned daemons, there are several others which provide network services (ftp, http, NFS), load and remove kernel modules dynamically, and so on. You will find more information about various daemons and their configuration in Jochen Hein's book *Linux Companion for System Administrators*.

Pipes

Pipes have nothing to do with process administration, but they represent a rather impressive application of the multitasking system. Pipes are a kind of data transfer mechanism between two processes: the first process supplies data to the second process, which then carries out further processing on that data. Pipes are formed by joining commands with the `|` character.

```
user$  ls -l | more
```

is a simple example of a pipe: `ls` supplies the list of files in the current directory. This list is passed on to `more`, which displays it pagewise on the screen.

```
user$  cat grundl.tex | grep I-node
```

yields all lines of the text file `grundl.tex` that contain the word 'I-node.'

Programs such as `more` or `grep`, which accept data via the standard input and, after processing, forward it to the standard output, are often called filters. Several such filters can be concatenated (separated from each other by `|`).

5.6 Libraries

Practically all Linux programs use the same standard functions, for example for file access, screen display, X support, and so on. Each and every program cannot possibly contain all these functions directly in its code – this would result in huge program files. Most Linux programs build on shared libraries, instead: when a program is executed, the required libraries are automatically loaded as well. The advantage: if several programs use functions from the same library, this library need only be loaded once.

Libraries play a central role in the question as to whether and which programs can be executed on your computer. Libraries caught the attention of a large number of users for the first time during the installation of StarOffice. In versions 3 and 4, StarOffice requested more recent libraries than the ones supplied with the common distributions. To stop you from being helplessly thrown into the dark depths of Linux internals in the event of such and similar problems, the following section provides some basic information on libraries.

Dynamically and statically linked programs

Most Linux programs resort to shared libraries. This saves both hard disk space (because the binary program files are very compact) and RAM (because the same code does not have to be loaded more than once). For MS Windows programmers, the concept of shared libraries can be compared with MS Windows DLLs (Dynamic Link Libraries).

Libraries can, however, also be linked statically, when compiling a program. This means that the library functions are directly integrated into the program code. This makes the program larger, but it also makes it independent of any libraries. This is especially useful for system maintenance (when shared libraries might not be available). For this reason, several elementary programs are also available in a static version.

For legal reasons, statically linked Motif programs are very popular: the Motif library can only be distributed against payment of license fees, but statically linked programs containing the Motif library are free. The most well-known example of a statically linked Motif program is Netscape up to version 4.5. (Statically linked programs are not much appreciated by owners of the corresponding libraries: for them, these programs are a totally unnecessary waste of resources.)

Library formats and versions

During the course of the past few years, two changes to the Linux libraries have taken place, which are as fundamental as they are incompatible.

- First, the libraries changed from a.out to ELF format.
- Some time later, the change took place from the libc 5 library to the glibc 2 library, which is also known as libc 6. (The changes were introduced with RedHat 5.0, Debian 2.0, and SuSE 6.0, just to name the most important distributions.)

In both cases, technical reasons have determined the change of library. The newer formats or versions allow better administration of the libraries, new functions, improved compatibility between the different Linux platforms (Intel, Sun-Sparc, DEC Alpha), and so on.

The problem with library changes lies in the fact that compiled programs can only be executed if the relative libraries are installed and can be found. An attempt to run a glibc program on an old distribution without glibc support ends up with the following cryptic error message:

```
root#  programmxy
bash: /usr/local/bin/programmxy: No such file or directory
```

In such cases, a distribution update is the best solution. In principle, you also have the possibility of installing libc 5 and glibc 2 in parallel – however, this solution is practically limited to professional users (see Glibc-HOWTO). A third alternative for executing the required program is to get hold of an old compiled version which is still linked to the old libraries. (Browse the Internet for programs for older distributions.)

Most of the recent distributions also include the old libc 5 libraries together with the glibc 2 libraries so that at least the opposite case – that is, execution of a libc program on a glibc distribution – should work. Please note, however, that the old libraries are not always installed automatically.

TIP: Additional information can be found in the ELF-HOWTO and in the Glibc-HOWTO. Also, the `man` texts for `ld` and `ldconfig` may be of some help.

Problems with shared libraries

As long as you use Linux as a 'normal' user (and not as a programmer), you will probably only be faced with shared libraries when a library is missing. Normally, such problems occur when you install a new program. When trying to start the program, an error message is displayed which complains about the missing library. (Up-to-date program versions are often linked to the latest version of the corresponding library, which is probably not yet installed on your computer. With older program versions, the opposite may be the case. These might still be linked to an old library type which is no longer supported by your distribution.)

The first step in eliminating the problem is the `ldd` command, which is passed the file name of the program as a parameter. As result, `ldd` lists all the libraries that the program needs. Furthermore, the location of a suitable library is given, as well as information as to which libraries are missing or are only available in an out-of-date version.

```
user$  ldd /bin/ls
        libc.so.6 => /lib/libc.so.6 (0x40003000)
        /lib/ld-linux.so.2 => /lib/ld-linux.so.2 (0x00000000)

user$  ldd /usr/bin/emacs
        libXaw3d.so.6 => /usr/X11R6/lib/libXaw3d.so.6 (0x40000000)
        libXmu.so.6 => /usr/X11R6/lib/libXmu.so.6 (0x4004f000)
        libXt.so.6 => /usr/X11R6/lib/libXt.so.6 (0x4005f000)
        libSM.so.6 => /usr/X11R6/lib/libSM.so.6 (0x400a2000)
        libICE.so.6 => /usr/X11R6/lib/libICE.so.6 (0x400ac000)
        libXext.so.6 => /usr/X11R6/lib/libXext.so.6 (0x400c0000)
        libX11.so.6 => /usr/X11R6/lib/libX11.so.6 (0x400cb000)
        libncurses.so.4 => /usr/lib/libncurses.so.4 (0x40165000)
        libm.so.6 => /lib/libm.so.6 (0x401a3000)
        libc.so.6 => /lib/libc.so.6 (0x401bc000)
        /lib/ld-linux.so.2 => /lib/ld-linux.so.2 (0x00000000)
```

The `ls` command only needs the `libc` library for execution, whereas the Emacs editor needs a whole series of libraries. Here follows some brief information on naming conventions for libraries: the abbreviation `.so` indicates that it is a shared library (as opposed to `.a` for static libraries).

The following digit indicates the main version number. Thus, `ls` requires version 6 of the `libc` library. As you can easily find out with `ls`, `libc.so.6` is in reality a link to the actual library, `libc-2.0.7.so` (thus, glibc 2).

```
user$  ls -lG /lib/libc-* /lib/libc.*
-rwxr-xr-x 1 root 3061550 May 10 1998 /lib/libc-2.0.7.so
lrwxrwxrwx 1 root      13 Jun 12 1998 /lib/libc.so.6 -> libc-2.0.7.so
```

In typical library directories (mostly `/lib`, `/usr/lib`, `/usr/local/lib`, `/usr/X11R6/lib`, and `/opt/lib`) you will find links from the main library version to the actually installed library.

At the start of a program, the matching libraries are found in the following way: `ld.so` is responsible for the links between program and libraries. To prevent this so-called runtime linker from having to search all directories for such libraries, it evaluates the file `/etc/ld.so.cache`, which is a binary file containing all relevant library data (version numbers, access paths, and so on).

In some distributions, the file `/etc/ld.so.cache` is automatically updated at each system start-up by means of the `ldconfig` program. When new libraries are installed, `ldconfig` must be executed manually. If needed, `ld.so.config` must previously be extended with new directories. Depending on the distribution, this is done by the package manager or the setup program.

`ldconfig` in turn evaluates `/etc/ld.so.conf`. This file contains a list of all library directories. In Debian 2.0, for example, this list looks as follows:

```
/usr/X11R6/lib/Xaw3d
/usr/lib/libc5-compat
/lib/libc5-compat
/usr/X11R6/lib
```

The directories `/lib` and `/usr/lib` are searched in any case and are therefore left out in `ld.so.config`.

`libc` updates

Sometimes, an update of the `libc` library becomes necessary to run new programs which require an up-to-date version of this library. This may even be the case when `ldd` does not signal any problems. For example, according to `ldd`, the program only requires `libc` version 5; actually, however, it runs only from 5.4.4 onwards (such as the setup program of StarOffice). If only version 3.12 is installed, there will be problems.

CAUTION

Please note that a `libc` update is a dangerous intervention in the system. On the one hand, new `libc` versions sometimes work only if an up-to-date version of `ld` (and potentially of other programs) is installed as well. On the other hand, during a library update the link from the main number of a library must never (not even temporarily) point into the void! This would completely block the system, because practically no command can be executed without `libc`!

Please avoid using packages of another distribution for such an update, since the administration of library files is largely distribution-dependent.

A manual update to `libc.so.5.4.33` and `libm.so.5.0.9` (responsible for mathematical functions), for example, looks like this:

```
root#  cp /cdrom/directory_xy/libc.so.5.4.33 /lib
root#  cp /cdrom/directory_xy/libm.so.5.0.9  /lib
root#  cd /lib
root#  ln -sf libc.so.5.4.33 libc.so.5
root#  ln -sf libm.so.5.0.9 libm.so.5
root#  ldconfig
```

Do not forget to execute the `ldconfig` command after having installed or updated a library! This program updates a table which allows highly efficient access to all libraries.

Obviously, an update becomes even simpler if you have the appropriate package for your current distribution. Even then, however, it is still a good idea to carry out a backup of your libraries prior to the update.

If things go wrong, you may still resort to the statically linked `sln` command and probably repair an incorrect link. `sln` functions in the same way as `ln`, but does not rely on `libc` (instead, it includes an older version of this library directly in the program file).

5.7 System start (Init-V)

This section describes the processes that occur between switching your computer on and the login prompt. In short, the kernel is loaded and the first program – that is, `init` – is started. `init` then takes care of the basic configuration of the system (linking of file systems) and the start of numerous daemons (for networking functions, printer support and so on).

In most cases, LILO is responsible for the first part, that is, for starting the kernel (see page 183). However, the kernel can also be loaded and executed directly from a boot diskette. LILO can be used to pass various parameters to the kernel (page 48). After the kernel has started, it can, for the moment, only access the root partition in read-only mode.

The way the second part proceeds, that is, the execution of the `/sbin/init` program, depends very much on the configuration of the computer. Although nearly all distributions (with the exception of Slackware) are guided by the System V Init process, as used in many other Unix systems, there are still many differences in detail, in particular, which init files are located in which directories, which numbers or letters are assigned to the different runlevels, and so on.

CAUTION

As a conclusion, there is a further warning: maximum care must be taken if you want to modify files concerning the init process! If you are unlucky, you will no longer be able to boot Linux. This means that you will not even be able to correct your mistake! (Remedy: first, try to start in single user mode by specifying the additional boot parameter `single` or `emergency` in LILO. If that does not help, you must boot your system with an installation diskette, mount the root system manually and then execute the repair. On most installation diskettes, there is no (usable) editor – at least make sure that you have backups of all modified files.)

Never attempt to install an Init-V package of a different distribution! Unfortunately, every Linux distribution uses different configuration files, and for this reason the Init-V packages are more distribution-dependent than any other packages.

The following description is oriented to the RedHat distribution. In principle, a similar procedure also applies to other distributions, but some files are located in different directories or have different names. Also, the sequence in which different processes are started or executed varies with the distributions. To facilitate orientation, you will find some hints on the Init V process of other distributions in the Appendix.

NOTE

In the following text, we constantly talk about scripts. A script is a (usually small) program which is executed by an interpreter. For all scripts discussed in this section, the interpreter is the `bash`. Under Linux, the `bash` is primarily used as command interpreter (comparable with `COMMAND.COM` under DOS). This interactive use of the `bash` is described in Chapter 12. An introduction to `bash` programming can be found in Chapter 13.

Runlevels

The kernel starts `/sbin/init` as the first program. All kernel parameters that have not yet been evaluated are passed on to it. In this way, for example, it can be ensured that Linux starts in single user mode. (Details can be found in the `man` page for `init`.)

Thus, `init` is the first running process. All further processes are started either directly by `init` or indirectly by subprocesses of `init`. (If you execute `pstree` or `ktop`, you will immediately recognize the dominating role of `init`.) In a shutdown, `init` is the last running process which takes care of the orderly termination of all other processes.

The concept of runlevel is central to the understanding of System V mechanisms: you can operate your computer on different runlevels. The normal case is multi-user mode with network (runlevel 3). For computers operated exclusively under X, select the extended runlevel 5 (multi-user, network, automatic start of X via `xdm`). There are restricted modes for maintenance, such as runlevel 2 (multi-user without network) or runlevel 1 (single user). Runlevels 0 (halt) and 6 (reboot) are reserved for shutdown.

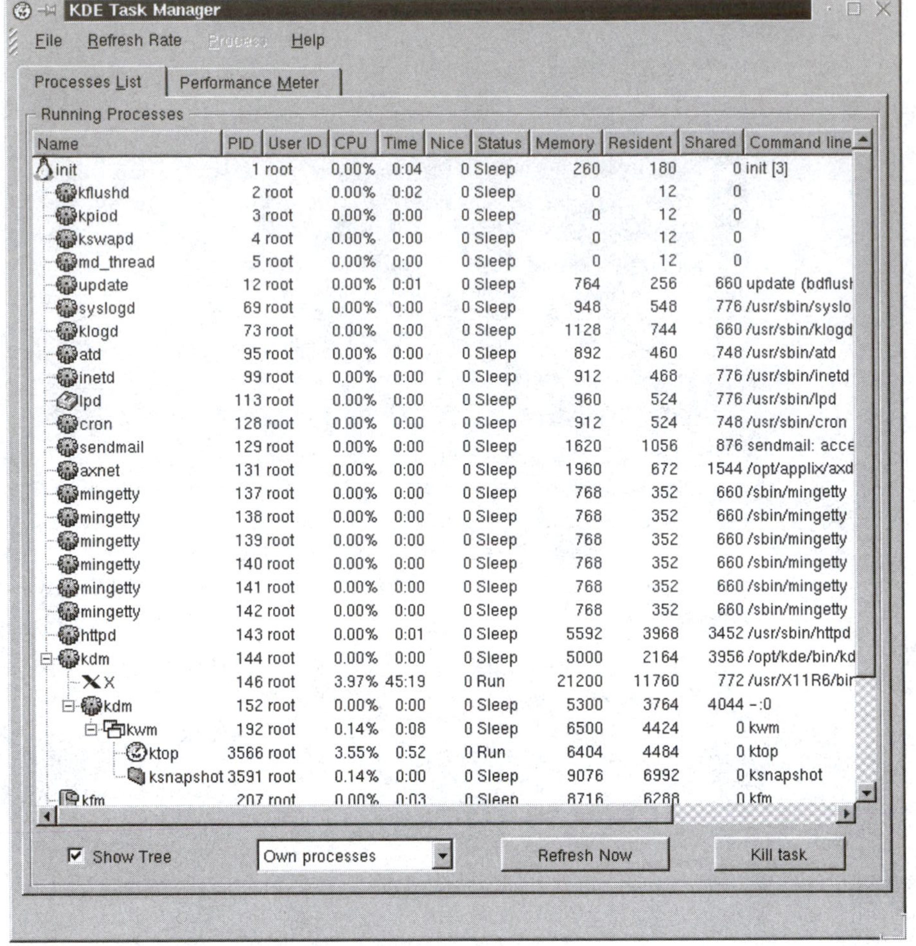

Figure 5.1 The process hierarchy.

> **CAUTION**
>
> Unfortunately, the numbering of runlevels differs between distributions. SuSE and Debian use slightly different runlevels. The meaning of each runlevel is documented in `/etc/inittab`.

At system start-up, the default runlevel is determined by the `initdefault` line in `/etc/inittab`. `root` can also change the runlevel during operation using `init x`. (x must be substituted by a number or letter that specifies the runlevel.) For example, for some maintenance tasks it makes sense to change into single user mode. The runlevel is also changed by `shutdown` and Ctrl+Alt+Del – Linux changes to runlevel 6 for shutting down.

Inittab

At system start, `init` is controlled via the `/etc/inittab` file. `inittab` entries obey the following syntax scheme:

```
id-code:runlevel:action:command
```

`id-code` consists of two characters that uniquely identify the line. The `runlevel` specifies for which runlevel the entry is valid. `action` contains an instruction for `init`. `command` specifies which Linux command or program is to be started.

The following list shows the most important `action` keywords (you will get a full description with `man inittab`):

`ctrlaltdel:` specifies how `init` should react to Ctrl+Alt+Del
`initdefault:` defines the default runlevel for `init`
`once:` `init` starts the specified command when changing to this runlevel
`respawn:` `init` restarts the command after it has terminated
`sysinit:` `init` starts the command once during the boot process
`wait:` `init` waits till the subsequent command has terminated

The following listing represents the slightly shortened `inittab` file from the RedHat distribution. The default runlevel is 3. With a normal system start, `init` executes the scripts `rc.sysinit` and `rc 3`. The `update` daemon is also started. (In some distributions, this command is called `bdflush`. Independently of its name, this daemon ensures that buffered data blocks are regularly written to the hard disk.) Finally, for the text consoles 1 to 6, the `mingetty` program is started for login. (If you require more than six text consoles, this is the right place for changes.)

```
# /etc/inittab for RedHat 6.0
#    0 - halt                        4 - not used
#    1 - single user                 5 - X11
#    2 - multi-user without NFS      6 - reboot
#    3 - multi-user with NFS
# Default runlevel
id:3:initdefault:

# System initialization after reboot
# (check file system, maybe execute fsck, activate swapping,
# mount all file systems listed in fstab)
si::sysinit:/etc/rc.d/rc.sysinit

# Start of specified runlevel
# (Start of network services, printer daemon, activation of
# local keyboard layout, and so on)
l0:0:wait:/etc/rc.d/rc 0
l1:1:wait:/etc/rc.d/rc 1
l2:2:wait:/etc/rc.d/rc 2
l3:3:wait:/etc/rc.d/rc 3
l4:4:wait:/etc/rc.d/rc 4
l5:5:wait:/etc/rc.d/rc 5
l6:6:wait:/etc/rc.d/rc 6
```

```
# The daemon ensures regular saving of
# buffered data blocks to the hard disk
ud::once:/sbin/update

# Reaction to <Ctrl>+<Alt>+<Del>
ca::ctrlaltdel:/sbin/shutdown -t3 -r now

# Allow logins in six text consoles
1:12345:respawn:/sbin/mingetty tty1
2:2345:respawn:/sbin/mingetty tty2
3:2345:respawn:/sbin/mingetty tty3
4:2345:respawn:/sbin/mingetty tty4
5:2345:respawn:/sbin/mingetty tty5
6:2345:respawn:/sbin/mingetty tty6

# only in runlevel 5: start xdm
x:5:respawn:/etc/X11/prefdm -nodaemon
```

System initialization

Even before the `rc` files described in the next subsection start or stop the runlevel-specific services, a system initialization is carried out immediately after computer start-up (`si:` line in `inittab`). In the RedHat distribution, the script `/etc/rc.d/rc.sysinit` is executed (in Debian `/etc/init.d/rcS`, in SuSE `/sbin/init.d/boot`).

`/etc/rc.d/rc.sysinit` tackles the following tasks in the order shown:

- Initialization of the `PATH` variable; the paths in `PATH` will be extended several times at later points. In order to find all relevant files, execute the following command in `/etc`:

  ```
  root# find -type f -exec grep -q PATH {} \; -print
  ```

- Initialization of the `NETWORKING` and `HOSTNAME` variables; for this purpose, the file `/etc/sysconfig/network` is read (if present).
- Mounting of swap partitions (according to `/etc/fstab`).
- Setting of host name (according to the previously initialized variable `HOSTNAME`).
- Setting of NIS domain name: if configured appropriately, the Network Information Service allows centralized administration of a network of computers.
- Checking of the root partition: currently, the partition is mounted in read-only mode.
- Activation of quota for the root partition: the quota system allows limitation of the maximum space request of home directories.
- Initialization of ISA Plug&Play hardware components: `isapnp` configures Plug&Play components on the basis of the file `/etc/isapnp.conf`. This file can be generated by `pnpdump` and probably needs manual editing afterwards.

If you use ISA Plug&Play cards, you should cast a glance at the `man` texts of `isapnp`, `pnpdump`, and `isapnp.conf`.

- Mounting of the root partition in read/write mode.
- Mounting of the `/proc` directory.
- Starting module support for the kernel (only with older distributions with `kerneld`; since kernel 2.2, this task is taken over by the kernel component `kmod`).
- Activation of modules for sound cards and MIDI.
- Activation of RAID support: if `/etc/mdtab` exists, the virtual partitions listed there are created by means of `mdadd`. See also page 157.
- Checking of partitions which, according to `/etc/fstab`, are to be mounted into the file system.
- Mounting of partitions (no NFS partitions, because network services are not yet available).
- Setting of the character set for the text console (`/sbin/setsysfont`).
- Activation of quota for the entire file system.
- Setting of the system time (under consideration of `/etc/sysconfig/clock`).
- Linking of swap files (according to `/etc/fstab`).
- Initialization of the serial interfaces (by means of `/etc/rc.d/rc.serial`, provided this file exists).
- If a SCSI streamer was found, activation of the corresponding kernel module.
- Storing of kernel messages in `/var/log/dmesg`.
- Initialization of the random number generator.

`rc` files

`init` and `inittab` bear responsibility for controlling the `init` process, but the actual work is done by numerous `rc` scripts which are started from within `/etc/rc.d/rc`.

`rc` is passed the new runlevel *n*. `rc` first processes the file `/etc/rc.d/init.d/functions`, where some macros such as `daemon` and `killproc` are defined. Then, all `rcn.d/K*` scripts are executed to end running processes. Finally, all `rcn.d/S*` scripts to start the new processes for the runlevel in question are executed.

The following table shows which script files are executed for some selected runlevels. When switching to single user mode, for example, various network services, `cron` and `syslog` are stopped.

```
rc1.d:  (single user)
K09keytable  K20rwhod     K60atd       K70syslog    S00single
K15gpm       K30sendmail  K60crond     K95nfsfs     S01kerneld
K20nfs       K50inet      K60lpd       K96pcmcia    S20random
K20rusersd   K55routed    K65portmap   K97network

rc3.d:  (multi-user with network)
K20rusersd   S10network   S40atd       S50inet      S80sendmail
```

```
K20rwhod      S15nfsfs      S40crond      S60lpd        S85gpm
K55routed     S20random     S40portmap    S60nfs        S99local
S01kerneld    S30syslog     S45pcmcia     S75keytable

rc6.d:  (reboot)
K09keytable   K20rwhod      K60atd        K70syslog     K96pcmcia
K15gpm        K30sendmail   K60crond      K80random     K97network
K20nfs        K50inet       K60lpd        K90killall    K98kerneld
K20rusersd    K55routed     K65portmap    K95nfsfs      S00reboot
```

To be precise, the script files are not actually located in the `rc`*n*`.d` directories, which merely contain links to them. This has the advantage that some script files (for example, `inet` for the start/stop of Internet daemons) can be used for several runlevels and, if necessary, modified centrally.

The link names are not at all as arbitrary as they look: the initial letter indicates whether it is a start or a kill script. (The S and K links often point to the same file; the script, however, is executed with the `start` or `stop` parameter, according to the initial letter of `rc`.) The subsequent number determines the order in which the scripts are executed. (`sendmail`, for example, can only be started when the network software is already running.)

The script files themselves are stored in `/etc/rc.d/init.d`. These programs first read configuration information from files in `/etc/sysconfig`. Then the corresponding programs – that is, network daemons, mouse drivers, and so on – are started.

Init scripts

To conclude, here is some information about the scripts in `/etc/rc.d/init.d`, where a substantial part of the 'work' is done. The files are described in alphabetical order. The order in which the scripts are executed can be found in the listing above.

`cron`
: starts the `cron` daemon, which is responsible for starting various programs at regular intervals.

`halt`
: terminates all running processes, deactivates swapping and finally deregisters all file systems. Depending on whether the link to `halt` ends with `halt` or `reboot`, the computer is then either halted or rebooted.

`inet`
: starts the TCP/IP services, that is, the base protocol for all Internet services, such as ftp, NFS, http, and so on. The script evaluates `/etc/sysconfig /network` (which contains the host name setting).

`keytable`
: activates the keyboard layout set in `/etc/sysconfig/keyboard`.

`lpd.init`
: starts the printer daemon (responsible for spooling).

`network`
: initializes the network interfaces. On computers without network cards, at least the so-called loopback interface is activated, so that local network services can function, such as, for example, the print spooler. If configured, Ethernet cards and PPP or SLIP connections (via the serial interface) are linked as well.

  The configuration of `network` is rather complex and is carried out via script files in `/etc/sysconfig/network-scripts`: `network` checks whether it contains `ifcgf-`*`type`* files. If this is the case, this configuration file is read, and subsequently `ifup-`*`type`* is executed to set up the interface with `ifconfig` and to insert it into the IP routing table with `route`. (In the same way, to deregister an interface, `ifdown-`*`type`* is executed.) *`type`* can be `lo` (loopback), `eth` (Ethernet), `sl` (SLIP), and `ppp` (PPP). The configuration of these files is best carried out by means of the RedHat-specific program `netcfg`.

`nfs`
: starts the NFS server daemons (so that other computers can access the file system of the local computer).

`nfsfs`
: binds NFS directories of foreign computers into the local file system. The control file is `/etc/fstab`.

`pcmcia`
: loads the kernel modules for the support of PCMCIA cards (only for laptops).

`sendmail.init`
: starts `sendmail`. This program is responsible for sending (not receiving) email. You will find some introductory information about how to configure sendmail on page 359.

`single`
: activates the single user mode: first, all running processes are terminated; then, `init 1` is executed.

`syslog`
: starts the protocol daemons `syslogd` and `klogd`.

The above-mentioned configuration files in `/etc/sysconfig` can easily be adjusted by means of various administration tools.

> **CAUTION**
>
> The System V init scripts are very fault tolerant – if single daemons are not installed, this is accepted without error messages. This is all very good, but it certainly does not facilitate the detection of errors. If a network service does not work, make sure that the necessary programs (such as the packages `nfs-server`, `nfs-server-clients`, `wu-ftp`, and so on) are all installed. Check with `ps -x` which daemons are effectively running. (Some daemons are started by `inetd` only upon the specific request of a network service. `inetd` is controlled via `/etc/inetd.conf`.)

Chronological sequence of system start-up

If you have been overwhelmed by so many `rc` files and have lost the thread, here is a chronological sequence:

`/sbin/init`
: is the program with which the System V process begins. It is started by the kernel and controlled via `/etc/inittab`.

`/etc/rc.d/rc.sysinit`
: cares for system initialization during booting (kernel modules, file systems, swapping).

`/etc/rc.d/rc`
: controls the runlevels. The script is started by `init` with a specification of the required runlevel *n*. It reads `/etc/rc.d/init.d/functions` and subsequently executes all script files for which it finds links in `/etc/rc.d/rc`*n*`.d`.

`/etc/rc.d/init.d/*`
: start and stops various daemons. The script files are started by `rc`, if `/etc/rc.d/rc`*n*`.d` contains links for the corresponding runlevel. Some scripts are controlled via configuration information contained in the `/etc/sysconfig/*` files.

In the RedHat distribution, `/etc/rc.d/rc.local` is designed for additional (personal) modifications. `rc.local` is started after all other `rc` files.

CAUTION

In `rc.local`, no daemons should be started (not even `gpm`) because, in contrast to 'true' `rc` files, there is no distinction between start and kill. Not only are processes started in `rc.local` not terminated at a runlevel change, they are subsequently erroneously started again.

Configuration and administration

After a new installation of Linux, you will find yourself with a system that, in principle, is up and running, but only in very rare cases is it also optimally configured. Most distributions offer their own configuration programs which can also be used after installation during normal operation (`yast` in SuSE, `setup` in Slackware, `control-panel` and `linuxconf` in RedHat, and so on).

This chapter offers a look behind the scenes of these configuration programs. The main aim of this chapter is to make you understand what is controlled and preset where and how. This will free you from the slavery of ready-made tools, so that you can intervene directly if things do not work as expected.

Important subjects are the adaptation of Linux to foreign languages, file system administration, registration of new users, installation of LILO for an easier Linux start-up, kernel configuration, elementary steps of network configuration, and so on.

Tip: Most configuration files are located in the `/etc` directory. You will find references to the files mentioned in this book in the Index, under the letter E.

Reference: The way to configure the X Window System and an offline mail/news system via PPP/SLIP will be described in dedicated chapters from pages 221 and 301 onward. Information about some distribution-specific configuration programs can be found in the appendices. Please do not expect this book to cover all configuration possibilities! The more you want to achieve with Linux (for example, using it as a network server for a major enterprise), the more complex the possibilities of configuration. Jochen Hein has dedicated a whole book to Linux system administration (see References).

6.1 Survival rules

Before you begin to modify any of your system's settings, you should take the time to read this short section. One fundamental problem of this chapter is that many configuration files depend on the particular distribution and interact with the corresponding configuration program.

Survival rule 1

Make yourself familiar with the configuration program belonging to your distribution before directly attempting to modify configuration files. If it is possible to change a setting by means of the originally supplied configuration program, this should be preferred to a manual intervention. (The reason: the distribution-specific configuration conception and manual changes to individual files can easily interfere with each other and, in particular for Linux newcomers, it is almost impossible to keep things under control.) Please read the relevant sections on this subject in Appendices A to C:

Debian: page 711
RedHat (`control-panel`, `linuxconf`): page 727
SuSE (`yast`): page 741

Survival rule 2

Before you start any configuration work, you should definitely make a backup copy of the entire `/etc` directory (where most of the configuration files are located).

```
root# mkdir /etc-backup
root# cp -a /etc/* /etc-backup
```

Survival rule 3

Part of the measures described in this chapter concern the Init-V process, which is also highly distribution-dependent. The functioning of this process is described in Section 5.7, taking the RedHat distribution as an example. Different features of the other distributions can be found in Appendices A and C:

Basics/RedHat: page 124
Debian: page 717
SuSE: page 748

RedHat and SuSE provide for a separate file for simple local adjustments. However, no background processes (daemons) should be started from within these files.

RedHat: `/etc/rc.d/rc.local`. This script file is executed after all runlevel scripts of runlevels 2 (multi-user without network), 3 (multi-user with network), and 5 (multi-user with network and xdm).

SuSE: `/sbin/init.d/boot.local`. The script file is executed at the end of the system initialization (but *before* the runlevel scripts).

Debian does not explicitly envisage a comparable file, but in `/etc/rcS.d`, you can create the file `S99local`, which is then executed, as in SuSE, at the end of the system initialization (but before the runlevel scripts).

Survival rule 4

There may be several reasons why you do not find a particular configuration file in your distribution, one of which being that the underlying program packages have not been installed at all – therefore, make yourself familiar with the package management of your distribution:

`rpm` (Caldera, DLD, RedHat, SuSE, and so on): page 213
`gnorpm` (RedHat): page 732
`dpkg`, `dselect` (Debian): page 711
`yast` (SuSE): page 741

A second alternative is even more probable – the file exists, but is stored in a different location. (Directory paths tend to vary not only from distribution to distribution, but even with virtually every version!) The following commands will help you with your search:

`locate`: page 463
`find`: page 454
`grep`: page 459

This is how you find all files whose name or directory contains `gpm`:

```
root#  locate gpm
```

The following command shows how you can search `/etc` and all subdirectories for files whose content (not the file name) contains the word `gpm`:

```
root#  cd /etc
root#  find -type f -exec grep -q gpm  \; -print
```

Survival rule 5

You would be well advised to check the online documentation (Chapter 4), as it may well be more up-to-date than this chapter!

6.2 Elementary configuration steps

This section deals with the most basic configuration problems: correct support of foreign language keyboards, display of foreign language special characters on screen, setting of system time, and so on.

Keyboard

Many of the problems described in this section emerge from the fact that Unix was developed for American conditions, that is, for a US keyboard and a 7-bit ASCII character set. Very quickly, the necessity arose to allow for additional characters (the special characters for European countries). And even though there is unanimity about the character set – it is called ISO Latin 1 and bears some resemblance to the ANSI character set used in Windows – there is no conformity at all in how this character set is supported.

NOTE

Many useful hints for the adaptation of Linux to foreign languages are contained in the different HOWTO files (for example Chinese, Cyrillic, Danish, Esperanto, Finnish, French, German, Hebrew, Italian, Polish, Portuguese, Slovenian, Spanish, and Thai). General information on the HOWTO documents can be found from page 77 onward.

Significantly greater problems need to be solved in Asian countries where characters are coded in two bytes and special forms of input are required. For lack of personal experience, however, I will not discuss these peculiarities.

Thus, there is no central file in which you simply tell the system that you want to use the ISO Latin 1 character set. One program needs a certain option, the next one requires a system variable to be set, the third program is persuaded to cooperate via a configuration file, and so on. The same can be said for the support of function keys on the keyboard. Therefore within this section you will find several subsections that describe the configuration of various important programs.

A central point for keyboard management is the `loadkeys` program. This program loads a table which controls the mapping between keyboard codes and characters. If, for example, you are configuring your system for a German keyboard, the setting should be `de-latin1.map`. A variation on this is `de-latin1-nodeadkeys.map`. The only difference is that the special characters `, ', ~, and ^ can be entered immediately (without a subsequent space). With the following command, you can try out any keyboard table you like. (Compressed tables are automatically decompressed.)

```
root#  loadkeys /usr/lib/kbd/keymaps/i386/type/name.map
```

If you want your keyboard table to be loaded automatically at system start-up, you must store the setting permanently. Unfortunately, the configuration file has a different name in nearly every distribution (a problem that will arise over and over again in the course of this chapter).

In RedHat, the name of the keyboard table must be entered into the file `/etc/sysconfig/keyboard`:

```
# /etc/sysconfig/keyboard (RedHat)
# line split only for reasons of space
KEYTABLE=
  "/usr/lib/kbd/keymaps/i386/qwertz/de-latin1-nodeadkeys.map.gz"
```

In SuSE, the corresponding file is `/etc/rc.config`. The specified file is searched for in the subdirectories of `/usr/lib/kbd/keymaps`.

```
# /etc/rc.config (SuSE)
KEYTABLE="de-lat1-nd.map.gz"
```

In Debian, the keyboard table is taken from `/etc/kbd/default.map`. If you wish to modify the keyboard table, you need to copy the required table to that location.

TIP

At the moment, `loadkeys` only applies to the text console. Information on keyboard configuration for the X Window System can be found on page 242.

Function keys in the bash

`bash` stands for 'bourne again shell' and denotes the GNU standard shell. The shell essentially corresponds to the command interpreter in DOS. It allows you to execute commands and shell programs (scripts). After logging in, you will normally find yourself in the `bash`.

When working with the shell, you will probably notice that you cannot enter foreign language special characters and that the Del, Home, and End keys do not work as expected.

The keyboard configuration for the bash can be set globally in the file `/etc/inputrc` or individually in `~/.inputrc`. If the file does not yet exist, it must be created.

```
# /etc/inputrc or ~/.inputrc
set meta-flag on
set convert-meta off
set output-meta on
"\e[1~": beginning-of-line
"\e[3~": delete-char
"\e[4~": end-of-line
```

This file controls the `readline` function, which the bash uses internally to process keyboard input. The first three instructions ensure firstly that 8-bit characters are recognized during input, secondly that these are not converted into other characters, and thirdly that they are actually output. The next three lines control the reaction to the Home, Del, and End keys.

In order to make the modifications take effect, you must log out using `logout` or Ctrl+D and log back in at the new login prompt. This automatically loads the configuration file of the bash. To try things out, however, it is easier to execute the `bash` command. Then a new shell is loaded and you can return to your old shell with `exit`. This is particularly useful if the reconfiguration did not lead to the desired result – because in the old shell the old keyboard mapping still applies.

NOTE

Handling of the `bash` is described in a separate chapter from page 387 onward. Further information about the `readline` function and its configuration can be obtained with `info readline`. The handling of the `info` program is described on page 74.

Input and display of foreign language characters

In their default settings, many Linux programs for text processing and display work in 7-bit mode, which means that they have problems representing special characters defined outside the US-ASCII character set. In many cases, this is remedied by the environment variable `LC_TYPE`, which is taken into account by some programs.

```
# Addition to /etc/profile or ~/.bashrc
export LC_TYPE=ISO-8859-1
```

Other programs evaluate the environment variable `LANG`, which can be used to set the country's language (in the following example, the German language):

```
# Addition to /etc/profile or ~/.bashrc
export LANG=de_DE.ISO-8859-1
```

REFERENCE

Many other programs possess their own environment variables or configuration files, which have to be adjusted. Special information on the `less` program (text display) and the Emacs editor can be found on pages 139 and 539.

A remark regarding `profile`: this file is automatically executed by the shell at each login. It is therefore particularly suitable for the definition of system variables and abbreviations. Background information on `profile` can be found on page 425.

NOTE

Unfortunately, Linux does not yet know the Euro symbol. (To be precise, this is not a problem of the Linux kernel, but of the programs running under Linux and of the individual distributions. The kernel supports Unicode.) Until a standard has emerged, you will need to use special character sets and change the keyboard table manually (and this, too, functions only for a very limited number of programs). A package including the required character sets and further information is available on the Internet:

`ftp://ftp.freshmeat.net/pub/euro-patch/`

Time of day

Under DOS, the system time is simply taken from your computer CMOS clock. Under Linux, things are not that easy. Because of their virtually international networking, Unix computers worldwide use one and the same time, GMT. GMT stands for Greenwich Mean Time, which is the measure of all things (at least timewise) on all Unix computers.

When you store a file, the stored time is not the current local time, but a time that is converted to this international standard. When, later on, you look at the file with `ls -l`, that time is reconverted to the local time at the location of the computer. This complicated-looking procedure allows you to determine which file is 'more recent': a file stored in Munich at 18:00 local time, or a file stored in New York at 12:30 local time.

To make all this work, Linux must first know in which time zone the computer is located. Depending on the distribution, setting the time zone is carried out via different files:

Debian: `/etc/timezone`
RedHat: `/etc/localtime`
SuSE: `/etc/rc.config`

To be accurate, `/etc/localtime` is not a normal file, but a link to the time zone file. The following command shows how this link is created (for RedHat).

`/usr/share/zoneinfo` contains hundreds of files with time zone information for all sorts of places in the whole world.

```
root#  ln -sf /usr/share/zoneinfo/Europe/Berlin /etc/localtime
```

Second, Linux must know what time it is in the CMOS clock in your computer. This time is read by means of `clock`. It is either local time or GMT. If you also use your computer under DOS/Windows, it is easier to keep the clock set to local time. You communicate this state of affairs to Linux via the following files:

Debian: `/etc/default/rcS`
RedHat: `/etc/sysconfig/clock`
SuSE: `/etc/rc.config`

Setting the default editor

Some programs – for example, the `elm` mail program – automatically start an editor to view and edit files. These programs take the environment variables `EDITOR` and/or `VISUAL` into account. If these variables have not been set, the `vi` editor, which is probably the worst editor of all, is normally started by default. The two variables are set in the file `/etc/profile`:

```
# Addition to /etc/profile
# to prevent programs from calling vi
export EDITOR=/usr/bin/emacs
# export EDITOR=/usr/X11R6/bin/xemacs
export VISUAL=$EDITOR
```

Setting the input prompt

The shell in which you enter your commands always displays the name of the computer and the name of the current directory (or ~), when you are in your home directory) at the beginning of each input line. Displaying the current directory is fine, but information about the computer's name only makes sense in a networked system. If you work on a single computer and only want to display the directory name, you can simply change the default setting of the environment variable `PS1` in `/etc/profile`:

```
# Modification in /etc/profile
PS1="\w \$ "
```

TIP The background to this setting is explained on page 402, where all environment variables of the `bash` are described. The `bash` is the standard command interpreter under Linux.

Configuration of `less`

`less` is used for a pagewise screen display of text files and is therefore one of the most frequently used Linux commands. In many distributions, the program is also used for display of `man` texts.

Texts with foreign language special characters often cause problems, which can be remedied by assigning the text 'latin1' to the `LESSCHARSET` environment variable. This assignment should be carried out in `/etc/profile`.

```
# Addition to /etc/profile
export LESSCHARSET=latin1
```

But there are additional ways of making `less` much easier to handle. The environment variable `LESS` allows you to set the default options for `less`. A useful one is `-mm`: this displays the current line number in each file. (For very long text files, this takes some time; therefore the option is not active by default.)

The environment variable `LESSOPEN` allows you to specify a shell script (that is, a small program) which is automatically started at each `less` call. This program can, for example, be used to decompress compressed files automatically; that is, `less` can be used to view the contents lists of `tar` archives, and so on. In the Slackware and SuSE distributions, such a script file is installed as a standard; in all other distributions you should make the effort and install the files yourself – it will be worth it.

```
# Addition to /etc/profile
export LESSCHARSET=latin1
export LESS=-MM
export LESSOPEN="|lesspipe.sh %s"
```

`lesspipe.sh` must be located in a `PATH` directory, normally in `/usr/bin`. Depending on the file name extension, this program first calls `tar` (archive files), `rpm` (package files), `gunzip` (compressed text files) or `groff` (`man` texts). The results of these programs are then passed to `less`. In practice, `lesspipe.sh` works as a filter. The file that is being viewed is obviously left unaltered.

```
#!/bin/sh
# file /usr/bin/lesspipe.sh
lesspipe() {
  case "$1" in
  *.tar) tar tvvf $1 2>/dev/null ;;   # contents of .tar and .tgz
  *.tgz) tar tzvvf $1 2>/dev/null ;;
  *.tar.gz) tar tzvvf $1 2>/dev/null ;;
  *.tar.Z) tar tzvvf $1 2>/dev/null ;;
  *.tar.z) tar tzvvf $1 2>/dev/null ;;
  *.rpm) rpm -qpli $1  2>/dev/null ;; # contents of .rpm
  *.Z) gzip -dc $1  2>/dev/null ;;    # contents of compressed files
  *.z) gzip -dc $1  2>/dev/null ;;
  *.gz) gzip -dc $1  2>/dev/null ;;
  *.zip) unzip -l $1 2>/dev/null ;;
                                      # groff
  *.1|*.2|*.3|*.4|*.5|*.6|*.7|*.8|*.9|*.n|*.man) FILE=`file -L $1` ;
  src    FILE=`echo $FILE | cut -d ' ' -f 2`
    if [ "$FILE" = "troff" ]; then
      groff -s -p -t -e -Tascii -mandoc $1
    fi ;;
  esac
  }
lesspipe $1
```

Finally, you can even configure the keyboard shortcuts of `less`. For this purpose, you must use a `lesskey` file (see the homonymous `man` text). In addition, the environment variable `LESSKEY` must contain the name of the `lesskey` file. This mechanism is used by SuSE.

6.3 Text console configuration

Many Linux programs can be executed both in a text console and in the X Window System. If your only text console command is `startx`, you may as well skip this section. If, however, X is not yet configured, or if you use a relatively old, low-performance computer without any X at all, it is worthwhile improving ease of work at the text console by means of some simple measures.

Additional keyboard shortcuts

You can extend the keyboard tables in `/usr/lib/kbd/keymaps` yourself and assign character strings to function keys or special functions to certain key combinations.

CAUTION

However, before you make major modifications, you should familiarize yourself with Linux and application programs such as Emacs and the X Window System. Many alterations to the keyboard table will not be portable, that is, they often work only in text mode and even there only when entering commands in the command interpreter.

If you append the following lines to `de-latin1-nodeadkeys`, you can use Ctrl+← and Ctrl+→ to move the cursor wordwise both in shell (`bash`) command input and in some editors.

```
# Addition to /usr/lib/kbd/keymaps/quertz/de-latin1-nodeadkeys
control keycode 105 = Meta_b  # Shift + <-- gives 'Meta-Back'
control keycode 106 = Meta_f  # Shift + --> gives 'Meta-Forward'
```

NOTE

Configuration of the keyboard under X is described from page 242 onward. The reaction to the Ctrl+Alt+Del key combination is controlled through the file `/etc/inittab`, where shutdown with this key combination can be (de)activated (page 125).

Further information about keyboard management can be obtained through `man loadkeys`, `man keytables`, `man showkey`, and `man dumpkeys`. With the `showkey` program you can determine which codes are assigned to individual keys. `dumpkeys` outputs the current keyboard mapping. Check also the Keyboard-HOWTO text.

Mouse support

Originally, only the X Window System was designed for the mouse. However, the `gpm` program allows limited use of the mouse even in text mode. After starting this program, the mouse can be switched on by pressing the left mouse button. Now the mouse cursor appears on screen and the mouse can be moved. By keeping the left mouse button depressed, a screen area can be selected. A double click selects a word, a triple click a whole line.

By pressing the middle mouse button, the stored characters are inserted at the current insertion point. If `gpm` is called with the option `-B132`, insertion can be carried out with the right mouse button (an important feature for a two-button mouse).

Thus, as a rule, the mouse is only used to facilitate input and to copy text between text consoles. It is not possible to use the mouse to change the position of the insertion point (for example, in an editor). Linux programs that work in text mode ignore the existence of the mouse. Text insertion appears to these programs as a normal keyboard input. The only exceptions are those programs that are specifically oriented towards cooperation with `gpm`, such as Emacs, `lynx`, `mc`, `slrn`, and `tin`.

In the call to `gpm` the type of mouse must be specified after the option `-t`: `mman` for MouseMan compatible mice, `ms` for a Microsoft compatible mouse, `msc` for Mouse Systems, `logi` for Logitech, `bm` for an ATI or bus mouse, or `ps2` for a PS/2 mouse. (`gpm -t help` shows a complete list of all mouse types.) For three-button mice, your chances are best with `msc` or `mman`.

```
root#   gpm -t mman
```

During experimenting, `gpm -k` is very useful to stop a running `gpm`. Only then can `gpm` be restarted with different parameters.

`gpm` assumes that a link points from `/dev/mouse` to the correct interface (usually `/dev/ttyS0` or `/dev/ttyS1` for the serial interface, `/dev/psaux` for PS/2 mice). Tips for handling the serial interface can be found from page 169 onward, in the context of modem configuration.

Nowadays, `gpm` is automatically set up by practically all distributions. Since `gpm` is a background process (a 'daemon' in Unix jargon), it should be automatically started and stopped by the Init-V system when the runlevel is changed (see page 124).

Inverse or colored text display

Generally, text consoles display white text on a black background. This is, however, not very eye-friendly. The screen display can be inverted by means of the `setterm` command. To make all consoles profit from this screen display, the command must be added to `/etc/profile` (`profile` is evaluated at each login).

```
# Addition to /etc/profile
# black characters on white background
setterm -inversescreen
```

Instead of `setterm -inv` (here in its short form) you can also execute `setterm -background white -foreground black -store`. You obtain exactly the same effect, but you can use this notation to set other colors as well (such as blue background and red characters). With the `setterm` options `ulcolor` and `hbcolor` you can furthermore set the colors for underlined and for bold text. (These attributes are, for example, used in the display of `man` texts.)

TIP

As different programs use text console colors in the most varied way (`ls`, `less`, `minicom`, `jed`, and so on), it is difficult to find a setting in which all programs give optimum results. Most programs simply start from the principle that white characters are displayed on a black background. Thus, `setterm -inv` causes comparatively few problems, whereas the setting of other color schemes is occasionally problematic.

Text mode with 80×50 characters

If you have a big screen, 80×25 characters in text mode are not the optimum. With 80×50 characters you can display much more information. You must, however, set this text mode at boot time as a kernel option. For this reason, the configuration depends on how you boot Linux.

If you use a boot diskette, you can modify the kernel image with `rdef -v /dev/fd0 -2` accordingly. If you boot with LILO, you type the option `vga=-2` during booting, or you insert the line `vga=extended` into `/etc/lilo.conf`. Details of the boot process and its configuration can be found in this chapter from page 180 onward.

TIP

In contrast to the information given in the `man` text, more recent versions of `setfont` also change the video mode. Thus `setfont` can be used for a later change of the number of lines.

Since kernel 2.2, activation of special text modes only works if the corresponding option of the *Console Drivers* group is activated.

With the SVGATextMode package, you can use your text console in (nearly) any resolution. The program is supplied with most distributions.

Character sets

When referring to character sets previously, we were discussing problems with foreign language special characters. In this section, we want to touch on another aspect of character sets, that is, the representation of characters on your screen. You can use the `setfont` program to choose between different character sets that are used to display characters in text mode. The available character set files are contained in the `/usr/lib/kbd/consolefonts` directory. However, only the smallest part of these files (`iso01.*`) contains foreign language special characters.

If you want to use a character set other than the default set, you can try it out with `setfont` beforehand. When choosing a suitable character set, you have to consider the necessary size. You need an 8×16 or an 8×8 character set, depending on whether you run Linux in 25- or 50-line mode.

TIP

The `setfont` command is also very useful if a program (in most cases, the X System) has destroyed the current character set. Without the specification of an additional parameter, the program regenerates the standard character set (8×16). If you work in 50-line mode, you need an 8×8 or 8×9 character set which can be regenerated with `setfont -9`.

6.4 Registering users and passwords

After a new installation of Linux you can only log in as `root`. If `root` has not yet been provided with a password, this should be done immediately! This section shows how you can define your own passwords and register new users.

Defining a password for root

After you have logged in as `root`, you execute the `passwd` command. You will be asked to enter a new password twice. The input is not displayed on screen. The new password is only accepted if the two inputs match. From now on, you must use the specified password every time you log in as `root`.

In the same way as `root`, all other users too can change their own passwords. `root`, however, can also change the password of any arbitrary user.

```
root#  passwd kofler
Changing password for kofler
Enter the new password (minimum of 5, maximum of 8 characters)
Please use a combination of upper and lower case letters and numbers.
New password:  ******
Re-enter new password:  ******
Password changed.
```

In older Linux systems, all users' passwords are stored in the file `/etc/passwd`. You can edit this file with a normal editor (only if you are logged in as `root`), but you cannot modify the passwords in this file directly, because they are encrypted. However, a password can be completely deleted by deleting the characters between the first and the second colon in the line that begins with the user name. This is a useful feature, as afterwards you can again log in without having to enter any password at all.

CAUTION

Running Linux without a password for `root` constitutes a major security risk. You should only do this if you are absolutely sure that you and you alone work with your computer. Please note, however, that someone could also log in via the Internet (even if you use only a modem connection with SLIP or PPP).

Apart from `root`, there are quite a number of other users present in `/etc/passwd` (such as `bin`, `adm`, and so on). These users too should be provided with passwords (or * characters instead of the password), if this is not already the case by default. (The * prevents anyone from logging in – practically an unbreakable password.)

In more recent Linux systems, `/etc/passwd` only contains information on the existing accounts; the passwords themselves are stored in `/etc/shadow`. This system is significantly more secure, because `shadow`, as opposed to `passwd`, can only be read by `root`.

TIP

What to do if you forget your `root` password? In this case, you must boot your computer with the installation diskettes. Use `mkdir` to create a new directory (on the RAM disk of the installation directory) and mount the partition on which your Linux system is located into this directory:

```
mount -t ext2 /dev/xxx/dir
```

Now you can access the file `/dir/etc/passwd` or `/dir/etc/shadow` and delete the `root` password. The editor needed to do this must be started with the path specification `/dir/usr/bin`.

If you want to prevent other users from changing the `root` password in the same way, you must set the boot sequence in the BIOS of your computer to C:, A: (thus, booting with a diskette is no longer possible) and secure the BIOS with a password, which this time you must definitely not forget ... .

Registering new users

System maintenance and configuration can only be carried out by `root`. For your normal work, however, you should register one or more users (even if you are the only one to use your computer). The main advantage is that you cannot inadvertently and unintentionally alter or delete system files. Furthermore, your own data is stored in its own directory and can therefore be secured more easily (for example, for a backup or before a system change).

TIP

If you quickly want to execute a command as `root`, but are not logged in as `root`, you can use the `su` command to change the current user to `root`. Obviously, you must know the password. `exit` or Ctrl+D returns to the original user.

Registration of a new user is best carried out through the configuration programs of the current distribution (for example `linuxconf` in RedHat, `yast` in SuSE). In addition, many distributions provide the `adduser` or `useradd` command. If you have installed KDE, you can employ the user-friendly `kuser` program for administration.

Background information

User administration is mainly controlled via the two files `/etc/passwd` and `/etc/group`. For each user, `passwd` contains one line of the following pattern:

```
# Addition in /etc/passwd
kofler:adg897fdajkl897:501:100:Michael Kofler:/home/kofler:/bin/bash
```

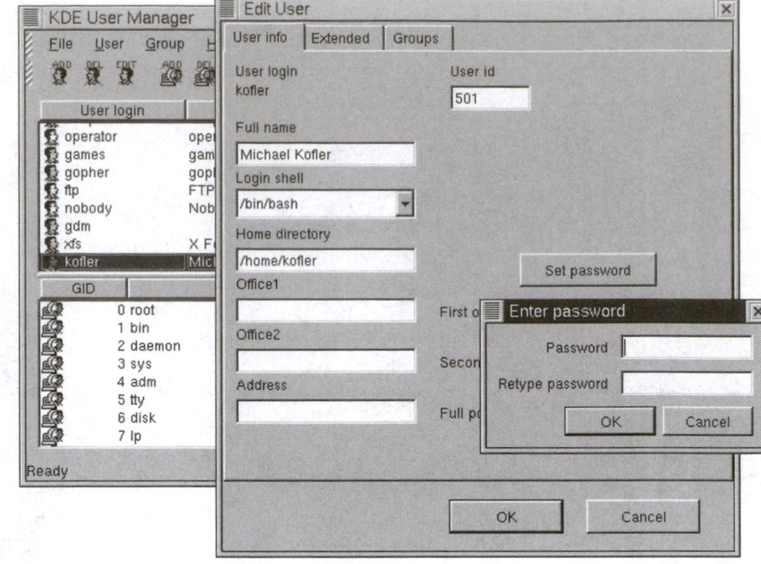

Figure 6.1 KDE user administration.

Here, `kofler` is the login name. The character string `adg897fdajkl897` stands for an encrypted password. If this character string is not specified, the login can be used without a password. If a `*` is present instead of the string, the login is locked. (This is the case with many administrative accounts which are not used by real persons but only by system processes and daemons.)

501 is the UID (user identification number), 100 the GID (identification number of the primary group), `Michael Kofler` the complete name (for email, news, and so on), `/home/kofler` the user's home directory, and `/bin/bash` the user's shell. The UID must be a unique number; this is important for the management of file access rights.

The GID must correspond to a group from `/etc/group`. Normally, the GID of the `users` group is used. It is, however, also possible to create a new group in `/etc/group`. If the new user will belong to other groups as well, his or her UID must be added to the relevant groups in `/etc/group`.

```
# a line from /etc/group
users::100:kofler
```

A different shell can be specified (for example, `tcsh` for lovers of the C shell) instead of the `bash`. The new user can later change this shell without problems by means of the `chsh` command.

As already mentioned, many Linux distributions nowadays use shadow passwords. In this case, `/etc/passwd` does not contain any password information. This is instead stored in `/etc/shadow`.

In its default configuration, RedHat Linux does not use shadow passwords; instead, it uses the so-called PAM (Pluggable Authentication Modules) tools for authentication of users. Configuration of PAM is carried out via the files in `/etc/pam.d`. Comprehensive documentation can be found in `/usr/doc/pam-`*n*.

Access privileges

As `root`, you automatically have access to all system files and devices (devices look like files and allow access to the hardware – such as `/dev/ttyS1` for the second serial interface which is often connected to a modem.) If, instead, you log in as a normal user without `root` privileges, you will find that a number of devices are denied to you: you can no longer access diskette drives, you cannot use the modem, and so on.

On single-user systems this is easily remedied by specifying more liberal settings for the rights to access devices. You simply log in as `root`, change to the `/dev` directory and execute the following `chmod` command for the devices in question:

```
root#  cd /dev
root#  chmod a+rw fd*
```

`/dev/fd*` (all devices that point to floppy disk drives) must be substituted by the relevant device name, such as `ttyS*` for the serial interfaces, `lp*` for the parallel interfaces (printers), and so on.

CAUTION

If you are not the only person to work on your computer, `chmod a+rw` represents a considerable security risk. You can distribute access privileges in a more controlled manner by listing those users in specific groups (for example, `uucp`) in `/etc/group` who are allowed to access files or devices of that group (for example, the serial interface for modem use). Thus you can leave the access bits of the device files unaltered. You will find further information about access privileges from page 94 onward.

6.5 File system administration

If Linux is properly configured, you can access various hard disk partitions, the CD-ROM, and so on, immediately after the system has started up. This section will deal mainly with the `fstab` file, which is responsible for all this. Furthermore, we describe how to create swap partitions and swap files.

TIP

Additional background information about the internals of the file system can be found in Chapter 5 from page 100 onward.

The fstab file

The `/etc/fstab` file specifies which storage devices are to be mounted into the file system. In any case, `fstab` must contain the following two lines (which, depending on your configuration, may look slightly different). Further hard disk partitions, CD-ROMs and diskettes can be mounted manually using the `mount` command.

```
# two sample lines in /etc/fstab
/dev/hda2    /        ext2    defaults 0 1
/proc        /proc    proc    defaults 0 0
```

The first line creates the system directory on the second partition of the first IDE disk. (Depending on which hard disk partition you have installed Linux in, you must specify the device name of your own Linux partition instead of `/hda2`.) The second line mounts the process administration system into the file system. The files and directories of the `/proc` directory do not really exist on the hard disk; they are just an image of the data which is used internally by the kernel for process administration.

The above two lines clearly show the format of `fstab`: in the **first column**, the device name of the storage device must be specified. (A number of examples of the naming conventions for hard disk partitions can be found on page 37.) If remote computers' directories are to be mounted via NFS, the device name is `computer_name:/directory`.

The **second column** specifies at which point the storage device is mounted in the directory tree. Unlike DOS, which administers several hard disks as separate systems (which are accessed under C:, D:, and so on), Linux uses a unique directory tree. The directories specified in the second column must already exist in the root file system. The directories do not need to be empty, but after a successful mount process, you can no longer access the files contained in them (you can only access the files of the mounted storage device).

The **third column** specifies the file system.

File systems supported by Linux	
`ext2`	Linux standard
`hpfs`	OS/2 (read only)
`iso9660`	CD-ROM
`minix`	commonly used for Unix diskettes
`msdos`	DOS partitions or diskettes
`nfs`	access to directories of other computers via network
`ntfs`	Windows NT file system (NT 4, read only, from kernel 2.2 onward)
`proc`	process administration
`swap`	swap partitions or files
`vfat`	Windows 9x file system (FAT32 from kernel 2.2 onward)

The **fourth column** specifies the access options for the storage device. Several options must be separated by commas (no spaces).

`mount` **options**	
`block=`*n*	block size (for example, for CD-ROM drives)
`conv=auto`	automatic conversion of DOS text files (page 504)
`exec`	allow program execution (for CD-ROM drives)
`default`	default setting
`gid=`*n*	group membership of files (for DOS and OS/2)

`noauto`	data support not automatically mounted
`noexec`	no program execution allowed
`ro`	read only (write protection)
`sw`	swap (swap file or partition)
`sync`	no buffering of write accesses (slower, but safer)
`uid=`*n*	user ownership of files (for DOS and OS/2)
`umask=`*m*	inverse access bits of files (for DOS and OS/2)
`user`	every user is allowed to execute (u)mount

The options `gid=`*n*, `uid=`*n*, and `umask=`*m* can be used to preset access privileges for files. This makes sense for file systems in which this information cannot be stored or cannot be evaluated by Linux (DOS, Windows, OS/2). Without the use of this option, DOS files are owned by `root`; the files can be read by all users, but only modified by `root`. The three options allow more liberal access.

Please note that the `umask` value is interpreted firstly as an octal value and secondly as inverse to the value of the `chmod` command (page 444). Thus `umask=0` means that every user is allowed to read, write, and execute all files. `umask=111` sets the execute bit to 0, but still allows read and write access.

The option `noauto` means that the storage device mentioned in this line is not immediately available, but it can be easily mounted with `mount name` without having to specify all further mount options explicitly at each call (all missing specifications are automatically read from `fstab`). This can, for example, be quite useful for CD-ROM drives or infrequently needed data partitions. (Also, a partition not mounted into the system cannot normally be destroyed.)

The `user` option allows normal users to unmount and remount the file system in question with `umount` and `mount`. Normally, only `root` can do this. The `user` option is particularly useful when frequent media changes are needed (diskettes, CD-ROMs).

The `exec` option is intended for CD-ROM drives. For reasons of security, Linux programs on CDs can normally not be executed. `exec` deactivates this protection.

The **fifth column** contains information for the `dumpfs` program and is presently ignored. The **sixth column** specifies whether and how file systems are to be verified. The root directory should be assigned the value 1, all other modifiable file systems 2. File systems that are not to be verified (for example, CD-ROMs, `proc` and `swap`) are assigned 0.

Information similar to `fstab` is stored in the file `mtab`: it contains a list of all storage devices that are *currently* mounted. Thus, `mtab` changes dynamically with every `mount` or `umount` command.

NOTE

Information about `fstab` can be obtained with `man fstab`. Further information that also applies to `fstab` can be found in `man mount`. In particular, about 30 options are described that apply equally to `mount` and `fstab`. (In practice, `fstab` is simply a centralized collection of options that are then passed to `mount`.)

Distributing Linux file systems across several partitions

In the installation chapter (see page 38) we discussed the advantages of installing Linux in two or more partitions. In particular, this is a good way to achieve a fairly strict separation between the Linux system proper and your personal data.

How can a second Linux partition, created with `fdisk` during installation, be mounted into the file system? The first step is to use `mkfs -t ext2` (or briefly `mke2fs`) to create a file system in this so far unformatted partition.

CAUTION

The creation of additional Linux partitions is a far-reaching intervention in the Linux system. If you do not want to follow the present examples blindly, you might first wish to read the fundamental section on file management in Chapter 5 (page 86) and the description of some elementary commands, such as `cp`, `ln`, and `mount`, in Chapter 14 (page 437).

Whatever you do, do not format the partition in which Linux is located! With `fdisk -l` you can find out which partitions are planned to be Linux partitions. `df` displays a list of all partitions that are already mounted into the file system and must under no circumstances be formatted.

```
root#  mkfs -t ext2 /dev/sdc3
mke2fs 0.5a, 5-Apr-94 for EXT2 FS 0.5, 94/03/10
64256 inodes, 257024 blocks
12851 blocks (5.00%) reserved for the super user
First data block=1
Block size=1024 (log=0)
Fragment size=1024 (log=0)
32 block groups
8192 blocks per group, 8192 fragments per group
2008 inodes per group
Superblock backups stored on blocks:
  8193, 16385, 24577, 32769, 40961, 49153, 57345, 65537, 73729,
  ..., 212993, 221185, 229377, 237569, 245761, 253953
Writing inode tables: done
Writing superblocks and filesystem accounting information: done
```

There are several possibilities for carrying on from here: the first variation is to access the new partition via a new directory – for example, `/home1`. If space in the root directory becomes scarce, it is generally best to transfer already existing data – for example, from `/home` – into the new partition. The third variation is slightly more complex and uses symbolic links to allow the transfer of several directories of the root directory into the new partition.

The following examples are geared towards the home directory `/home`. You can, however, proceed in the same way if you want to transfer `/usr/local`, `/var/spool`, or other directories into a new partition.

Please note that in the following examples `/dev/sdc3` will be used as the name for the new partition. On your computer, you must obviously substitute `/dev/sdc3` with the name of your own partition.

Variation 1 – accessing the second partition via a new directory

This variation is particularly recommended to Linux newcomers. It is easy to perform and practically without risk. In order to access the freshly formatted partition, you simply create a new directory with `mkdir` and then use the `mount` command to mount the partition at that point into the directory tree:

```
root#  mkdir /home1
root#  mount -t ext2 /dev/sdc3 /home1
```

All data on the partition `/dev/sdc3` can now be accessed under `/home1`. Now you can, for example, register a new user whose working directory will be located in `/home1`. With this, the data is physically stored on the new hard disk partition.

To make the new partition automatically available at the next Linux start-up, without having to mount it manually with `mount`, an addition to `fstab` is required:

```
# Addition to /etc/fstab
# Mount /dev/sdc3 as /home1 into the file system
/dev/sdc3        /home1      ext2          defaults     0 2
```

TIP

The transfer of the home directories into their own partition has enormous advantages when changing or updating the system. Before a new installation takes place, most frequently only the data contained in `/root` and `/etc` must be saved (with a backup, for example, in a directory of `/home1`). Subsequently, the root partition can be reformatted and a new distribution installed. After the installation, `fstab` is modified as described above to reallow access to the data partition. Now, only the new `/etc/passwd` file remains to be adapted to make all old logins available again.

TIP

If you have a great deal of space on your hard disk, you can create *two* system partitions plus one additional data partition. Then you can install a new Linux distribution into the second system partition. In this way, you can use two Linux versions in parallel (and with a common data partition). You can set up LILO in such a way that you can start up with either the one or the other Linux system (see page 183). (While I was working on this book, I had up to four Linux distributions installed in parallel.)

Variation 2 – accessing the second partition via an already existing directory

The first variation is simple, but not very elegant. Essentially, it has two disadvantages: firstly, there are now two locations for home directories, `/home` and `/home1`. Secondly, it is impossible to free the space occupied up to this point in `/home`. (Very often, the choice of too small a system partition is the reason for distributing the system across two partitions later on.)

It would be better if all users could still find their home directories in `/home`. The assumption here is that all data contained in the already existing `/home` directory is copied into the new partition. Before you execute the commands shown below, you must ensure that nobody is using any of the directories in `/home`; that is, only `root` is logged in.

```
root#  mv /home /home.bak              # rename /home into /home.bak
root#  mkdir /home                     # new empty directory /home
root#  mount -t ext2 /dev/sdc3 /home # mount new partition here
root#  cp -dpR /home.bak/* /home       # copy all data from /home.bak
```

If everything has gone according to plan, you can use `ls /home` to access the `/home` directory as before. Physically, however, the data is now located on its own hard disk partition, that is, on `/dev/sdc3` (third partition of the third SCSI disk). Use `ls -R /home` to make sure that all data has actually been copied. In `/home.bak` you still have a backup copy of the old directory. Once you are sure that all data has been copied, you can delete this copy with `rm -r /home.bak`.

Up to now, the new partition for `/home` has only been mounted with `mount`. To make this partition automatically available at the next system start-up, you must add the following line to `fstab`:

```
# Addition to /etc/fstab
# Mount /dev/sdc3 as /home into the file system
/dev/sdc3        /home      ext2          defaults         0 2
```

In principle, you can transfer any other directory (or subdirectory) to another partition in exactly the same way we transferred `/home` in the above example. However, system data contained in the `/bin`, `/dev`, `/etc`, `/lib`, `/root`, and `/sbin` directories should never be removed from the root directory.

Variation 3 – accessing the second partition via several directories

Variation 2 has the disadvantage that it is not possible to create two directories on the new partition that would be completely independent of each other. It could be useful, for example, to accommodate both `/home` (with the user data) and `/usr/local` (with subsequently installed user programs) in the new partition. As the new partition cannot simultaneously be mounted via `fstab` as `/home` and as `/usr/local`, this seems to be impossible.

In such a situation, symbolic links can help. You mount the new partition in an arbitrary new directory in the file system (for example, `/localpart` for local data partition), copy the required directories into the new partition and then create links from the original directories to the new locations.

```
root#  mkdir /localpart                    # new directory
root#  mount -t ext2 /dev/sdc3 /localpart # mount new partition here
root#  cp -dpR /home /localpart            # copy /home into it
root#  cp -dpR /usr/local /localpart       # copy /usr/local into it
root#  mv /home /home.bak                  # rename /home
root#  mv /usr/local /usr/local.bak        # rename /usr/local
root#  ln -s /localpart/local /usr/local  # link to new partition
root#  ln -s /localpart/home /home         # link to new partition
```

If you now access data in `/usr/local`, the link points to `/localpart/local`, that is, to the new partition. These links are transparent, that is, you will not notice them while working normally. Again, you must make an addition to `fstab` if you want the new partition to be mounted automatically into the file system at the point `/localpart` at every system start-up:

```
# Addition to /etc/fstab
# Mount /dev/sdc3 as /localpart into the file system
/dev/sdc3       /localpart ext2         defaults      0 2
```

In principle, you can transfer any number of directories in this way. You must, however, make sure that the access rights are kept the same. In newly created directories or links, you may have to use `chown` to change owners or `chmod` to change the access bits.

Mounting DOS, Windows, and OS/2 partitions

Under Linux, you can also access DOS, Windows, and OS/2 partitions. For the DOS file system, obviously all restrictions apply (file names with a maximum of 8+3 characters, no links). For Windows, currently – that is, in kernel 2.2 – the file systems of Windows 9x (including FAT32) and of Windows NT 4 are supported. NT file systems can, however, only be read (but not modified). For OS/2 partitions too, access is limited to read-only.

Depending on who is allowed to access the DOS partition, you must use the `gid`, `uid`, and `umask` options in `fstab` (see above). If you need to access DOS partitions only from time to time, you can specify the `noauto` option in the `fstab` entry. This has the advantage that `mount /mnt/dos` can be executed very easily and without specifying any additional options. On the other hand, the DOS partition is not mounted automatically all the time, which is a small safety risk (as with any other partition).

The necessary additions to `fstab` look as follows (again, you must substitute the device names and directories used in your system):

```
# Addition to /etc/fstab
# Mount DOS partition /dev/hda5 as /mnt/dosc into the file system
/dev/hda5       /mnt/dosc      msdos   defaults   0   0
# If read-only (no writing) is required
/dev/hda6       /mnt/dosd      msdos   ro         0   0
# Windows 9x partition
/dev/hda7       /mnt/win95     vfat    defaults   0   0
# Windows 9x partition, free rw access for all users
/dev/hda8       /mnt/win95-rw  vfat    umask=111  0   0
# Windows NT partition
/dev/hda9       /mnt/nt        ntfs    defaults   0   0
# OS/2 partition
/dev/hda10      /mnt/os2       hpfs    defaults   0   0
```

Mounting a CD-ROM drive

There is not much difference between mounting hard disk partitions and mounting CD-ROM drives. The latter are normally mounted into the file system at the points `/mnt/cdrom` or `/cdrom`. Instead of `/dev/hdb`, you must specify the device name of your own CD-ROM drive.

```
# Addition to /etc/fstab
# Mount CD-ROM drive as /cdrom into the file system
/dev/hdb        /cdrom     iso9660        ro,user,noauto  0   0
```

The option `ro` means that no data can be modified on the CD-ROM drive (read only). `user` allows every user (not only `root`) to mount and unmount the CD-ROM drive with `mount` and `umount`. `noauto` ensures that the CD-ROM is not automatically mounted into the file system at system start-up (but only when required by `mount`).

Instead of `/dev/hdb`, you must specify `/dev/hdc` or `/dev/hdd`, if the CD-ROM drive is connected to the second controller.

REFERENCE

The device names for the different types of CD-ROM drive are listed on page 102. When changing CDs, you must execute `umount` and `mount` to make Linux aware of the modified file system (see page 103). You can only access your CD-ROM drive if you use a kernel that has built-in support for your particular type of CD-ROM drive.

Since kernel 2.2 (precisely, since later 2.0.*n* kernels) Linux also recognizes Joliet CDs. These are CD-ROMs for Windows 9x/NT with long file names. Although these CD-ROMs comply with the ISO-9660 standard, they do not employ the Rock-ridge extension commonly used under Unix, but the Joliet extension for representation of long file names introduced by Microsoft. If you are using an older Linux kernel, you can still use Joliet CD-ROMs, but you will only see the short forms of the file names.

TIP

If you want to mount a Linux CD and immediately execute programs contained on it, you need to use the `mount` option `exec`. Normally, execution of programs from a CD-ROM is prohibited for security reasons.

```
root# mount -o exec /cdrom
```

Mounting swap partitions

The creation of a swap partition is usually carried out within the framework of the installation of Linux. If this has not happened, you need a dedicated empty hard disk partition, which can be created using the `fdisk` program. The `fdisk` command `T` must then be used to change the partition type from 83 (Linux) to 82 (Linux swap). After the partition has been formatted with `mkswap` it can be activated with `swapon`.

If the swap partition is to be used automatically at each startup of Linux, the hard disk partition must be entered into `fstab`:

```
# Addition to /etc/fstab
# Mount swap partition
/dev/sdc6       none       swap           sw    0    0
```

Mounting a swap file

The creation of a swap file is, strictly speaking, just an expedient. Accessing a swap file is considerably slower than accessing a swap partition. The only advantage of a swap file is that it can be created without repartitioning the hard disk.

Swap files are normally created in the `/dev` directory. The first step consists of using the `dd` command to create an empty file with a specified size. The data source is `/dev/zero`, a device out of which any number of zero bytes can be read. The size specification is in blocks, with the block size set to 1024. Subsequently, the swap file is formatted with `mkswap` and activated with `swapon`. The following example creates a small swap file of about 1 Mbyte.

```
root#  dd bs=1024 if=/dev/zero of=/dev/swapfile count=1000
1000+0 records in
1000+0 records out
root#  mkswap /dev/swapfile 1000
Setting up swapspace, size = 1019904 bytes
root#  sync
root#  swapon -v /dev/swapfile
swapon on device /dev/swapfile
```

Swap files can also be entered in `fstab`:

```
# Addition to /etc/fstab
# Mount a swap file
/dev/swapfile  none      swap          sw       0  0
```

How much swap space is available and how much of it is actually used can be checked with the `free` command. All indications are in Kbytes.

```
root#  free
              total     used     free   shared  buffers    cached
Mem:         127696    66600    61096    57760     4612     32192
-/+ buffers/cache:     29796    97900
Swap:        144512        0   144512
```

This means that a total of 124 Mbytes of RAM and 141 Mbytes of swap space are available. (It is not clear what has become of the remaining 4 Mbytes of RAM. Note that 1 Mbyte is 1024 Kbytes.)

The swap space is totally unused. 65 Mbytes of the RAM are used, divided into 35 Mbytes used as buffer or cache for files and only 29 Mbytes for running programs and their data. (At that point, KDE 1.0 and XEmacs 20.4 were running. In addition, several shell windows were open.)

6.6 Hard disk tuning

This section is explicitly addressed to advanced Linux users. It shows two ways in which – depending on the hardware – file access speed can be significantly increased. The first variation – use of the so-called bus master DMA mode – is of interest for all users who use a modern mainboard and EIDE hard disks. The second variation – distribution of data across several partitions – assumes several hard disks (and, ideally, a SCSI system).

Bus master DMA mode

The bus master DMA mode allows a particularly efficient data transfer between EIDE hard disks and main memory. Transfer is not carried out byte per byte via the CPU, but via a DMA (*Direct Memory Access*) channel. Thus, a direct temporary connection is established between hard disk and main memory; the transfer is controlled by the DMA controller. The advantages of the bus master DMA mode are obvious: the data transfer rate is significantly higher; at the same time, CPU load for loading/saving of large files is reduced because the DMA controller and not the CPU are looking after this.

For you to be able to use the bus master DMA mode, both your mainboard and your hard disk must support this mode. Nowadays, this is the case with many modern mainboards (for example, with the Inter Triton chip set) and hard disks. With regard to mainboard support, you are advised to read the corresponding manual and check the kernel messages displayed during booting and by the `dmesg` command:

```
root#  dmesg
...
PIIX4: IDE controller on PCI bus 00 dev 21
PIIX4: not 100% native mode: will probe irqs later
    ide0: BM-DMA at 0xc800-0xc807, BIOS settings: hda:DMA, hdb:pio
    ide1: BM-DMA at 0xc808-0xc80f, BIOS settings: hdc:DMA, hdd:pio
...
```

Whether your hard disk supports DMA transfer can easily be found out by calling `hdparm` (`/dev/hda` stands for the first EIDE hard disk):

```
root#  hdparm -i /dev/hda
...
DMA=yes, maxDMA=2(fast)
...
```

A third prerequisite is the availability of the corresponding kernel module. (Kernels supplied with current distributions fulfill this requirement. In older distributions, you may need to recompile the kernel, setting the *Intel 82371 PIIX DMA support* option in the *Floppy, IDE, other block devices* option group to Y or M.)

CAUTION

Even if all three requirements are met, the DMA mode is often *not* activated automatically for safety reasons: depending on the chip set, the length of the hard disk cable (according to the specification, a maximum length of 45 cm is allowed), and so on, the DMA mode may lead to reliability problems. For this reason, DMA mode experiments should be carried out with extreme care: execute `umount` for all partitions that are not needed! Ideally, you should have a separate partition available for your DMA tests which does not contain any valuable or unsaved data.

Whether the DMA mode is already active can be determined with `hdparm -d`:

```
root #  hdparm -d /dev/hda
/dev/hda:
 using_dma    =  0 (off)
```

Activation is carried out separately for each hard disk by means of `hdparm -d1`. (If needed, `-d0` deactivates the mode.)

```
root#  hdparm -d1 /dev/hda
/dev/hda:
 setting using_dma to 1 (on)
 using_dma    =  1 (on)
```

To find out whether everything works properly you can, for example, copy an extensive directory tree in a partition of the hard disk for which the DMA mode has been activated:

```
root#  mkdir /test-partition/test1
root#  cp -a /usr /test-partition/test1
root#  cp -a /test-partition/test1 /test-partition/test2
```

Subsequently, you should take a look into `/var/log/messages`: if you find error messages or warnings with the text 'DMA disabled,' the kernel has automatically deactivated the DMA mode after having encountered one or more problems.

When everything works as desired, you can integrate the `hdparm` command into the Init process, so it is executed automatically at every start-up of the computer. The appropriate file depends on the distribution. In SuSE 5.2, this is `/sbin/init.d/boot.local`, in RedHat `/etc/rc.d/rc.local`.

Obviously, DMA also works with most SCSI controllers, where this feature has been used for a long time, with no need for special activation.

NOTE

Further information on this subject can be found in the `man` text for `hdparm` (which, as well as bus master DMA mode, also offers other possibilities of speed optimization) and in the comments of `drivers/block/ide-dma.c` (2.2.n kernel code). Basic information on the bus master DMA mode (independent of Linux) can be found on Intel's Web server:

`http://developer.intel.com/design/pcisets/busmastr/FAQs.htm`

Prime information on the use of Ultra DMA (development has not stopped with the bus master DMA mode) is available in the Ultra-DMA Mini-HOWTO.

Striping (RAID-0)

RAID stands for *Redundant Array of Inexpensive/Independent Disks* (there are two definitions). The basic idea is to logically connect partitions of several hard disks. As a result, you can obtain a more reliable and/or faster overall system. Basic information on RAID can be found in a separate section from page 112 onward.

At this point, our task is to configure a very simple form of RAID, so-called striping. Our reward will be that some hard disk operations can be executed nearly n times as fast (where n denotes the number of hard disks).

Three essential conditions need to be met for striping:

- You need at least two hard disks (ideally SCSI disks), each of which has enough free space to create a new partition.

- The kernel components *Multiple devices* and *RAID-0* must be available (either directly integrated in the kernel or as modules). This is the case with all current distributions. (If not, the kernel must be recompiled. The corresponding options can be found in the *Block devices* group.)
- Finally, you need the commands `mdadd`, `mdcreate`, `mdrun`, and `mdstop`. Usually the corresponding package will still need to be installed. (In SuSE, the package name is `mdutils` (series `ap`), in RedHat, it is `raidtools`.)

CAUTION

With the current Linux distributions, different versions of the RAID commands are supplied. Up to version 0.4.*n* (used, for example, by SuSE 6.0), the commands are `mdxy` and the configuration file is `/etc/mdtab`. From version 0.5 onward (supplied with RedHat 5.2 and higher), the commands are `raidxy`; the configuration file has a new syntax and is located in `/etc/raidtab`. This section takes both cases into account; you simply need to execute the command that matches your version.

Access to the virtual RAID partitions is carried out via the devices `/dev/md*`. In some older distributions, however, these are not created automatically. This can be remedied by means of the following commands:

```
root#  mknod /dev/md0 b 9 0
root#  mknod /dev/md1 b 9 1
root#  mknod /dev/md2 b 9 2
root#  mknod /dev/md3 b 9 3
root#  chown root.disk /dev/md*
root#  chmod 660 /dev/md*
```

The first step towards the RAID-0 partition is now to combine two (or more) unused partitions (in the following example `/dev/hda10` and `/dev/hdc10`) into one multiple-disk device (`/dev/md0`):

```
root#  mdadd /dev/md0 /dev/hda10 /dev/hdc10    # up to version 0.4
root#  raidadd /dev/md0 /dev/hda10 /dev/hdc10 # since version 0.5
```

The partitions specified in `mdadd` should be of the same size. If this is not the case, striping only works for part of the total capacity of the partitions, that is, the theoretically possible gain in speed can be achieved only partially.

Subsequently, it must be stated that this new device is to be addressed as a RAID-0 partition (option `-p0`). As page size, the default value of 4 Kbytes is used (that is, data is distributed across the hard disks in 4-Kbyte blocks). If required, a different page size can be specified by means of `-cnk`.

```
root#  mdrun -p0 /dev/md0                     # up to version 0.4
root#  raidrun -p0 /dev/md0                   # since version 0.5
```

As the next step, a file system must be created on the new virtual partition `/dev/md0`. (Caution: all data stored in the partitions specified in `mdadd` is lost!)

```
root#  mke2fs /dev/md0
```

Now, the `mount` command can be used to mount the new partition into the Linux file system. The partition is accessed via the `/striped` directory – obviously, you may use another name instead.

```
root#  mkdir /striped
root#  mount -t ext2  /dev/md0 /striped/
```

Now all files stored inside the `/striped` directory use the RAID-0 functions. Management information on all `md` devices can be obtained with the following command:

```
root#  cat /proc/mdstat
Personalities : [1 linear] [2 raid0] [3 raid1] [4 raid5]
read_ahead 128 sectors
md0 : active raid0 hda10 hdc10 2056256 blocks 4k chunks
md1 : inactive
md2 : inactive
md3 : inactive
```

Before you shut down your computer, you need to execute `umount` and `mdstop` or `raidstop`:

```
root#  umount /striped
root#  mdstop /dev/md0                              # up to version 0.4
root#  raidstop /dev/md0                            # since version 0.5
```

Automatic `mount/umount` for RAID partitions

When you start up your computer the next time, you need to execute the above commands again (except for `mke2fs`). It is essential that the commands are executed with the same options and that, above all, the order of partitions remains unchanged. In the long run, this is rather annoying.

To automate the chores, you need either the `/etc/mdtab` or the `/etc/raidtab` file, depending on the version of your RAID commands. These files serve as an equivalent to `/etc/fstab` and contain information on the parameters of the `md` devices.

`/etc/mdtab`

The file is created with `mdcreate`. Make sure that you specify the hard disk devices in the same order as in the original `mdadd` command.

```
root#  mdcreate raid0 /dev/md0 /dev/hda10 /dev/hdc10
```

The resulting file `/etc/mdtab` contains an additional checksum and looks as follows:

```
# /etc/mdtab entry for /dev/md0
/dev/md0        raid0,4k,0,96e7219c     /dev/hda10 /dev/hdc10
```

The device `/dev/md0` can now be activated by a single command without lots of parameters:

```
root#  mdadd -ar                                    # up to version 0.4
```

`/etc/raidtab`

Except for the checksum, the file contains the same information, but is easier to read. It cannot be created by means of a command. (Use an editor.) The syntax is extensively described in the `man` text for `raidtab`.

```
# /etc/raidtab for /dev/md0
raiddev /dev/md0
  raid-level       0
  nr-raid-disks    2
  nr-spare-disks   0
  device           /dev/hda10
  raid-disk        0
  device           /dev/hdc10
  raid-disk        1
```

Obviously, the activation command for the `/dev/md0` device is now `raidadd` instead of `mdadd`:

```
root#  raidadd -a                              # since version 0.5
```

`/etc/fstab`

The following manual addition to `/etc/fstab` provides easier use of `mount`:

```
# Addition to fstab
/dev/md0     /striped   ext2  defaults   0  1
```

With this, `mount` can be executed as follows:

```
root#  mount /striped
```

Init-V process

If you use an up-to-date distribution, the configuration is now terminated. Both RedHat and SuSE take an existing `mdtab` or `raidtab` file into account in the Init process, automatically executing `mdadd` or `raidadd` first and then mounting all partitions contained in `/etc/fstab` by means of `mount`. Correspondingly, `umount` and `mdstop` or `raidstop` are executed during shutdown (`shutdown`, `reboot`). Take a look at the following files:

RedHat: `/etc/rc.d/rc.sysinit`, `/etc/rc.d/init.d/halt`
SuSE: `/sbin/init.d/boot`, `/sbin/init.d/halt`, `/sbin/init.d/reboot`

If you use an older distribution, you need to insert `mdadd` or `raidadd` after the start of the kernel daemon, but before the `mount` commands for file systems into the system initialization file. In the same way, you must execute `mdstop` or `raidstop` after the `umount` commands in the scripts for halt or reboot. (Background information on the Init-V process can be found on page 124.)

RAID for the `/root` partition

RAID cannot readily be for the `/root` partition. The reason is that reading of a RAID partition works only after the corresponding kernel modules are active. For this, however, the kernel and various configuration files must be loaded first (a classical chicken and egg problem).

NOTE

Information on how RAID can be used for the `/root` partition as well is given in the Root-RAID-HOWTO and the Software-RAID-Mini-HOWTO. The procedure described in these two documents will become significantly simplified with kernel version 2.2 thanks to new MD options (see `/usr/src/linux/Documentation/md.txt` in the 2.2 kernel).

Swap partitions

Speed maniacs amongst Linux fans will obviously want to know whether striping is also possible for swap partitions. The answer is obviously 'yes,' and you don't even need elaborate preparations or the multiple device driver. The Linux kernel automatically distributes swap data across all partitions of equal priority before it begins to write to swap partitions of lower priority. (Background information can be found in `man 2 swapon`.)

Thus, you only need to ensure that the swap partitions located on the different hard disks are assigned the same priority. (Normally, this is not the case; instead, swap partitions are given a sequential priority number.) If you want to set the priority number yourself, you need to set the option `pri=`*n* in `/etc/fstab`:

```
# Modification (bold) in /etc/fstab
...
/dev/hda9    swap    swap    pri=1   0   0
/dev/hdc9    swap    swap    pri=1   0   0
...
```

Benchmarks

The effect these measures really have on the working speed depends on a variety of parameters, such as your hardware, frequency and type of data access of your applications, and so on. Often, the `bonnie` program is employed to obtain repeatable indices of disk performance. You can find this program on the Internet, for example, under:

```
ftp://ftp.redhat.com/pub/contrib/i386/bonnie- n.rpm
```

The program creates a test file of pre-determined size and performs different write, read, and search operations in it. At the same time, it also measures the CPU load. To make the results repeatable, the file size must be a multiple of the main memory – otherwise, you do not measure disk performance, but the caching efficiency of Linux (which is fairly good ...).

For the figures shown below, the file size was 400 Mbytes. The tests were carried out on a normal partition with and without DMA transfer and on a RAID-0 partition with DMA. The test system was equipped with a Pentium II 400, Intel BX chip set, 128 Mbytes of RAM, and two IBM 8.4-Gbyte EIDE hard disks on `/dev/hda` and `/dev/hdc`. It may well be possible therefore that on your computer the results are completely different (either better or worse).

```
root# bonnie -s 400
             -------Sequential Output-------- ---Sequential Input-- --Random--
             -Per Char- --Block--- -Rewrite-- -Per Char- --Block--- --Seeks---
             K/sec %CPU K/sec %CPU K/sec %CPU K/sec %CPU K/sec %CPU  /sec %CPU
Without DMA   3318 34.8  3797 27.5  1891 53.4  3571 72.4  4281 70.0  47.9  6.9
With DMA      7387 47.7  6927 12.7  2924  9.3  7402 33.2  7921 10.0  52.5  0.7
DMA+RAID0    12659 81.8 11979 21.9  4558 15.2  9322 43.4 13961 19.3  62.3  0.9
```

A brief comment: with most operations, activation of DMA data transfer nearly doubles the data transfer rate (when reading large data blocks, from 4.3 to 7.9 Mbytes/sec). In all operations except for writing single characters (per char), the CPU load decreases dramatically (when reading large data blocks, from 17 to 10 per cent!). Only the number of random accesses per second remains practically unaltered – here, the limiting factor is the positioning time of the hard disk, which is not altered with DMA transfer.

RAID-0 again considerably accelerates block operations (reading and writing of large contiguous amounts of data). With smaller data blocks, the effect is not as strong, but still perfectly visible. The number of random accesses per second is only marginally improved through striping. The higher speed is achieved at the expense of CPU load. In other words: striping is mainly sensible if you frequently process large files (image processing), but does not help much when accessing smaller files or small data segments of large files (which is, however, the standard case with many applications). Better striping results can probably be achieved with SCSI hard disks; in that case, it would also be sensible to combine more than two hard disks.

6.7 Printer configuration

Generally, printing documents under Linux is a multistage process. The starting point is the file that needs printing. Such a file is first converted into PostScript format. (Most Unix programs only support PostScript for printing.) If a PostScript printer is available, this file can be printed directly. Otherwise, `gs` can be used to convert PostScript into the format of the non-PostScript printer. This and other tools for handling PostScript files are described in a separate section on page 501.

The issue at this point is how a correctly formatted file finds its way to the printer. Your printer will normally be connected to one of the parallel interfaces which under Linux are accessed as `/dev/lp0` (corresponds to `LPT1:` under DOS) and `dev/lp1`.

CAUTION

Up to kernel 2.0, the device names were different: `/dev/lp1` for `LPT1:` and `/dev/lp2` for `LPT2:`, and so on. With kernel 2.2, the default numbering has changed. However, via appropriate options for the `lp` kernel module, an arbitrary numbering can be achieved. This will probably be used by some distributions to maintain, for reasons of compatibility, `/dev/lp1` as the device for the first parallel interface, in spite of kernel 2.2. If you have upgraded an old distribution (one with kernel 2.0) to kernel 2.2 yourself, you should also read the information on page 212!

When you want to send a file to the printer, you simply execute a `cp` command in which you specify the interface device as a target. (The same applies for printers connected to a serial interface. Serial interfaces are administered as `/dev/ttyS0` and `/dev/ttyS1`.) A postfixed `&` causes printing to be carried out in the background.

```
root#  cp file /dev/lp0 &
```

NOTE Direct addressing of the interface is only a makeshift solution. In particular (depending on the printer), problems may arise when files do not end with Ctrl-D. These problems can be solved by proper configuration of `lpd` (see below).

In order for the parallel interface to be available at all, the corresponding option (parallel printer support) must have been set when compiling the kernel. This is always the case with kernels supplied with standard distributions. (Printer support is usually available as a module.) However, please ensure correct setting of the options when you compile the kernel yourself.

Furthermore, you need to have access rights to the device `/dev/lp1`. These are normally restricted to the user `root` and the command `lpr` (no matter who executes it; see below). On single-user systems you can liberalize the access rights through `chmod a+rw /dev/lp0`. Alternatively, you can allow specific users to access `/dev/lp0` by assigning `/dev/lp?` to the `lp` group and indicating the user names in the `lp` group line in `/etc/group` (see also page 94).

The printer daemon `lpd`

In order to avoid each Linux user having to know to which device the printer is connected, whether someone else is printing, and so on, the Unix environment has printer control commands that lie between the user and the printer and thus facilitate printing. These commands also allow printing over the network and administer a spooler that temporarily stores files to be printed. Under Linux, printer control normally conforms to the Berkeley system (BSD). If the `lpd` printer daemon (which is a background process) is configured correctly, a file is simply printed out with `lpr file`.

NOTE The Unix world has a second standard for controlling printing: the one defined by System V. Its functionality is similar to the BSD system, but the commands have different names and there are differences in configuration. Under System V, files are printed out with `lp file`. In this chapter, we only deal with BSD print commands.

Configuring `lpd`

`lpd` is a so-called daemon, that is, a background process which is started when the system is booted. `lpd` represents the interface between the printer and the commands `lpr` (print), `lpq` (show status), `lprm` (delete spool files), and `lpc` (advanced spooler control).

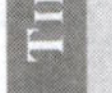

`lpd` can only work when the computer is configured at least to the point that the network protocol is running. (For this purpose, however, there is no need for an actual network of several computers (see page 171).)

At the start of `lpd`, the file `/etc/printcap` is evaluated. This file contains the data used to configure the printer (or printers, if more than one is connected). The minimum definition of a printer in `printcap` looks as follows:

```
# /etc/printcap
lp:lp=/dev/lp0:sd=/usr/spool/lp0:sh
```

The line begins with `lp`. This keyword can be followed, after a `|` character, by the name of the printer. Subsequently, various settings are specified, separated by colons. Do not insert any spaces anywhere in this line!

`lp=` specifies the printer device (`/dev/lp0` corresponds to `LPT1:` under DOS). `sd=` specifies the directory in which spool files are to be stored. `sh` causes `lpd` to suppress the printing of a title page before every print job.

The following `printcap` file has practically the same effect as the one above, but is more clearly formulated and assigns the printer a name. The setting `mx#0` allows an unlimited size of print files. (Without this command the size is limited to 1 Mbyte which is occasionally insufficient. You can, however, circumvent this limit by using `lpr -s` – which causes a symbolic link to be created, instead of the copy that is made when printing a file.)

Please note that the lines that belong together must be separated by a backslash (\) . Single entries must be enclosed by colons on both sides, otherwise `lpd` gets confused by the spaces used for indenting.

```
# /etc/printcap
lp|minoltasp3500:\
  :lp=/dev/lp0:\
  :sd=/usr/spool/lp0:\
  :mx#0:\
  :sh
```

Modification of `printcap` takes effect only after the next start of Linux. As this is annoying in the long run, you can use a little trick: first you use `ps -x` to determine the process number of `lpd`, then `kill -HUP` *n* to ask the process to read the configuration files again.

Spooler management

Files are now printed with `lpr file`. If `lpd` was configured as described above, the files are printed without any modifications. Therefore, before they can be printed, the files must be present in the specific printer format.

`lpr` can also be used as a filter to prevent the creation of huge files: `ls -l | a2ps | lpr` generates a listing of the files in the current directory, converts this listing into PostScript format and sends it to the printer. (`a2ps` and the related `mpage` command are described on page 505.)

For large files, the file to be printed is spooled, that is, `lpd` temporarily stores the data in a directory such as `/var/spool/lp1`. It is possible to execute several print commands in a row before the printing of the first file is terminated.

`lpq` provides you with a list of all spooled files and print jobs. Both the size of the file and its job number are shown. You can specify the job number as a parameter of `lprm` when you want to remove a file from the print spooler. Please note that all spool data is stored on the hard disk and is not changed by a restart of Linux. After the restart, `lpd` detects whether there are files that have not yet been printed and, if this is the case, keeps on trying to send the data to the printer.

The `lpc` command allows more detailed control over the printing process. After you have started this command, you find yourself in a special working environment in which you can execute commands such as `status`, `help`, and so on. With `topq` you can place a print job at the top of the waiting list. You must specify the printer name and the job number as parameters. Some of the commands in `lpc` (for example, `topq`) can only be executed by `root`. `exit`, `bye`, or `quit` terminate `lpc`.

Automatic conversion into printer format

One problem we have not yet looked at is the conversion of documents into the printer format. For this purpose, `lpd` provides a filter concept: in `printcap`, the command `if=` can be used to specify a filter program. When `lpr` is called, the file is processed by the specified filter and the result passed to the printer. (Thus, a 'filter' is simply a program that processes input data and supplies output data.) Depending on the configuration, the filter program performs two tasks:

- It converts files of different formats (ASCII, LaTeX, `*.dvi`, and so on) into PostScript files by calling different translation programs (`a2ps`, `latex`, `dvips`, and so on). It is essential that the filter recognizes the file type.
- It uses `gs` to convert PostScript files into files in the format of the connected printer (if this printer is not a PostScript printer in the first place).

Depending on the distribution, filters of different scopes are provided, two of which will be briefly mentioned:

RedHat/Caldera only supply a filter for the conversion PostScript → printer format or text → printer format, thus presuming that `lpr` is only passed PostScript files for printing. The filter `/var/spool/lpd/lp/filter` can easily be configured with `printtool`.

SuSE uses the more versatile `apsfilter`, which performs both of the conversions mentioned above. It is configured with `yast` (ADMINISTRATION|HARDWARE|PRINTER). This creates three printer interfaces, `lp`, `raw`, and `ascii`. `raw` is suitable for printing files that are already in the printer format straight to the printer without any conversion. `ascii` is for printing ASCII files, `lp` for all other files (which are then converted as needed).

`apsfilter` works transparently when calling `lpr`. If you have configured `apsfilter` for the HP Laserjet, the instruction `lpr file.dvi` translates the DVI file into a PostScript file by means of `dvips`, converts the result into the format of the HP Laserjet, and finally prints it.

By specifying `-P`, `lpr` can forward options to `apsfilter`. `-Praw` prevents the automatic conversion. (This is useful if a file is already in the current printer format.) `-Pascii` treats a file as an ASCII file (even when it contains foreign language special characters and is therefore classified by `file` as a binary file).

```
root#  lpr file.dvi     # automatic conversion into printer format
root#  lpr -Praw file   # printing without conversion
root#  lpr -Pascii file # treat file as ASCII text
```

> **NOTE** Although the filter might look simple because of its easy installation, it is a complex and error-prone tool! If you want to get rid of it again, simply delete the corresponding entries in `/etc/printcap`.

6.8 Modem configuration

The title of this section is perhaps misleading: the main topic is not so much the configuration of the modem (which is usually not required at all), but the correct use of the serial interface for connection between modem and computer.

In the simplest case, you have a modem connected to the first or second parallel port. (Sometimes, the mouse occupies the first serial port.) Under Linux, you address the modem via `/dev/ttyS0` (corresponds to COM1: under DOS/Windows) or via `/dev/ttyS1` (COM2:). No configuration whatsoever is required!

In some distributions, a link is established during modem configuration which points from `/dev/modem` to `/dev/ttyS`n. This link is, however, not mandatory and may cause locking problems (when two programs want to access the serial port at the same time).

```
root#  ls -l /dev/ttyS0,1 /dev/modem
lrwxrwxrwx  1 root root     10  Jan  5  /dev/modem -> /dev/ttyS0
crw-rw----  1 root uucp  4, 64  Jan  5  /dev/ttyS0
crw-rw----  1 root uucp  4, 65  Dec 11  /dev/ttyS1
```

> **NOTE** Up to Linux kernel 2.0.n, the modem could also be addressed via `/dev/cua`n. Since kernel 2.2, this is no longer possible. When you change to kernel 2.2, you will probably need to modify the `/dev/modem` link or the configuration settings of various programs.

The easiest way to try out your modem is to start one of the programs `minicom` or `seyon` (see page 525) and to enter `ATH` followed by ↵. This instructs the modem to break a possibly existing connection (to 'hang up'). The modem answers with `OK`. Now you know that communication between Linux and the modem does work. In some cases, during start of `minicom` or `seyon`, you may need to specify the port through which the modem should be addressed.

Only if this test brings out problems, or if you are under the impression that your modem (after Internet configuration) transmits data at a significantly lower speed than expected, is the information contained in the remainder of this section of interest for you.

NOTE

An important precondition for a connection between modem and computer via the serial interface is that the kernel supports the serial interface or that it is able to load the appropriate module. In all current distributions, this is automatically the case. If you compile a kernel yourself, make sure that the option CHARACTER DEVICES|STANDARD SERIAL SUPPORT is activated.

Also, please note that with some motherboards the serial interfaces need to be activated in the BIOS setup.

Modem fundamentals

A modem connects a computer with a phone line. Several different types exist:

External modems

External modems are peripheral devices with their own power supply which are connected to the serial port of the computer with a cable. They have the disadvantage that they add to the heap of spaghetti behind your desk, but in return cause much fewer problems in getting up and running. A further advantage is that these modems can be easily switched on and off (for example, to carry out a modem reset without having to restart the whole computer).

Internal modems

Internal modems consist only of an expansion card; the serial port is integrated. Problems with these modems result from the fact that they usually need to be configured via plug & play. Linux, however, supports plug & play only very half-heartedly (via the commands of the `isapnp` package). Since I had no opportunity to test a plug & play modem, I cannot speak of own experience in this matter. Further information can be found in the Modem-HOWTO and in the Plug-and-Play-HOWTO.

Windows modems

In these modems, communication is not carried out via hardware, but via software. This software (in the form of appropriate drivers) is, however, only available for Microsoft Windows – hence the name of these modems. Currently (and probably also in the future) it is not possible to use Windows modems under Linux.

ISDN modems

While the above modems are based on analog data modulation, an ISDN phone line can do without this modulation. (In this respect, ISDN modem are not modems in the traditional sense of the word.) However, as I still do not have ISDN access, I had no way of testing ISDN access via Linux. Therefore, I must again refer you to external documentation:

```
/usr/src/linux/Documentation/isdn/*
http://alumni.caltech.edu/~dank/isdn/
```

`http://www.isdn4linux.de/leafsite`
`http://www.suse.de` (look for ISDN in the support database)

All further information in this section refers to traditional (internal and external) modems.

Modem control

The Hayes AT instruction set has established itself as the *de facto* standard for control languages between computer and modem. Practically all current modems understand these commands. For example, the command `ATDT12345` means that the modem should dial the number 12345.

A sample application for AT instructions can be found on page 316 where – in the framework of a script for automatic establishment of a PPP connection – it is shown how the loudspeaker of the modem can be switched off. (This eliminates the annoying beeping during dialing.)

Modem speed

In common language use, there are two 'modem speeds' which are often confused. One speed means the transfer rate to another modem (for example that of an Internet provider) via the phone line; the other speed specifies how fast your computer and your modem communicate via the serial interface.

Transfer rates between two modern modems currently reach up to 56000 bits per second (bps). Whether this rate can effectively be attained depends on how far both modems (yours and the one you dialed up) are compatible and how good the quality of the phone line is. Except for the top transfer rate you pay for when you buy your modem, you have no further influence on the transfer rate. The modem automatically selects the best possible transfer rate; no special configuration is required.

Now to the speed of the serial interface: on a typical PC, this reaches a maximum of 115200 bps (with modern hardware potentially even 230400 bps). You will probably ask yourself why the serial interface should work faster than the modem. The reason: when both modems agree, data can be compressed for transmission. In this case, the effective data flow is higher than the maximum transfer rate.

While you have no influence on the transfer rate, the speed of the serial interface can be manipulated – more about this in the next but one subsection. If the serial interface is configured too slowly in the default setting (which happens with some computers), it represents a bottleneck for the modem. But do not expect any miracles – even at maximum speed the serial interface cannot transfer more data to the computer than the modem can provide!

Accessing the serial interface

Usually, only `root` and all users of the `uucp` group are allowed to access `/dev/ttyS`*n*. To allow other users to access the serial interface, you must either assign them to the `uucp` group (for example by means of `linuxconf`, `kuser` or `yast`) or – even more easily – allow the device to be accessed by all users:

```
root# chmod a+rw /dev/ttySn
```

Most programs that access a serial interface create a lock file. This is used to signal to all other programs that the interface is currently blocked. Lock files are usually stored in `/var/lock`. Here, the problem is again that access to this directory is reserved to `root`. The easiest solution is once again to allow write access to `/var/lock` to all users.

However, in this case too it is more elegant (and more secure) to assign all modem users to the `uucp` group. In SuSE, not even this is sufficient, because even `uucp` group members do not have write access to the `lock` directory. The remedy is to use the following command:

```
root# chmod g+w /var/lock
```

Serial interface detection

On some computers, the serial interface runs too slowly in the default configuration, thus constituting a bottleneck for the modem. If your modem works significantly slower than expected (or the data rates reached under Windows are not attained under Linux), you will need to familiarize yourself with the commands described below.

Initial information on the serial interface is usually displayed at system start-up. This information can be called up again at any time by means of `dmesg`.

```
root# dmesg
...
Serial driver version 4.13p with no serial options enabled
ttyS00 at 0x03f8 (irq = 4) is a 16550A
ttyS01 at 0x02f8 (irq = 3) is a 16550A
```

A second way of obtaining information on the serial interfaces is offered by the `setserial` command:

```
root# setserial -bg /dev/ttyS*
/dev/ttyS0 at 0x03f8 (irq = 4) is a 16550A
/dev/ttyS1 at 0x02f8 (irq = 3) is a 16550A
```

NOTE

On very old PCs (approximately up to the 486 generation) the serial interface is provided by the 8250 or 16450 chips (instead of 16550). In this case, the maximum speed of the serial interface is a meager 9600 bits per second. The simplest solution is to deactivate the built-in serial interfaces and plug in an additional card with two serial interfaces.

The speed of the serial interface is usually determined by the program that communicates with the modem (such as, for example, a terminal emulator). Therefore, the interface speed cannot be set globally, but via configuration files for the individual programs (such as `minirc.dfl` for the `minicom` terminal program).

With `setserial`, it is also possible to set parameters for the serial interface which were not detected automatically. During testing with kernel 2.1.131, for example, we encountered the problem that `setserial` did not recognize the interface chip. (Consequently, subsequent attempts to use the interface were destined to fail. The problem no longer occurred with kernel 2.2.)

```
root#  setserial /dev/ttyS0
/dev/ttyS0, UART: unknown, Port: 0x03f8, IRQ: 4
```

The remedy is to use the following command:

```
root#  setserial /dev/ttyS0 uart 16550A
```

In such a case it is sensible to execute `setserial` in the context of the Init V process. Debian, RedHat, and SuSE already provide the appropriate scripts:

```
/etc/rc.boot/0setserial    Debian
/etc/rc.d/rc.serial        RedHat (executed by rc.sysinit)
/sbin/init.d/serial        SuSE
```

CAUTION

For a correct application of `setserial` you must obviously know the actual data of the serial interface. An attempt to set incorrect data can in the worst case end with the computer grinding to a halt!

Serial interface speed

If you access the serial interface with `pppd` (Internet access), you can set the speed beforehand by means of the `stty` command. Although one might expect the contrary (>), the input redirection character < is correct: `stty` changes the speed by reading data from the interface. Legal speeds are, for example, 38400, 57600, 115200, and 230400 (rare).

```
root#  stty ispeed 115200 < /dev/ttyS1
```

Some programs can only be configured with speeds of up to 38400 bits per second (which in the old days was considered as the absolute maximum). To obtain a higher interface speed with these programs as well, the additional program `setserial` must be used to set the option `spd_hi` or `spd_vhi` for the interface in question. This ensures that when the corresponding interface is accessed, the request for 38400 bps is automatically converted into 57600 bps or 115200 bps.

```
root#  setserial /dev/ttyS1 spd_hi  #  57600 instead of 38400 bps
root#  setserial /dev/ttyS1 spd_vhi # 115200 instead of 38400 bps
```

With more recent models, it is even possible to reach a speed of 230400 bps by employing a little trick (according to the Modem-HOWTO):

```
root#  setserial /dev/ttyS1 spd_cust baud_base 230400 divisor 1
```

TIP

Lots of additional information on handling the serial interface and various modems (including exotic models) can be found in the Modem-HOWTO and Serial-HOWTO texts.

6.9 Network configuration

As we have already mentioned in the introduction to this chapter, the subject of network configuration will be limited to fairly elementary configuration steps:

- configuration of the loopback interface,
- integration of your computer into an existing network of other Linux computers,
- networking of a few Linux computers (NFS and ftp).

One precondition for the network functions to be used at all is the kernel. The network functions must be either permanently integrated or available as modules (which is always the case for kernels supplied with current distributions).

NOTE

A special way of networking – Internet access via a modem using PPP or SLIP – is described in a separate chapter from page 301 onward. In the following chapters, you will also find a description of how to configure email and news systems for offline operation (`sendmail`, `fetchmail`, `leafnode`).

No description will be found in this book on: networking with DOS/Windows/Novell computers (Samba), advanced network services, such as NIS, configuration of your computer as an http, mail, news and printer server, and so on. You will need all these services if you want to use your Linux computer as a network server. Then, however, you will also need another book that is specially dedicated to these subjects.

NOTE

There is a vast amount of online information available on the subjects of networks and the Internet. In addition to the `man` texts for many programs and configuration files, there are also the HOWTO texts about Ethernet, Firewall, NET-2, NIS, News, PPP and UUCP, plus the Mini-HOWTO texts about Dip+SLiRP+CSLIP, Multiple Ethernet, PLIP, Proxy ARP, SLIP+proxyARP, Tiny News and Token Ring (see also page 77). Highly recommended is the Network Administrator's Guide by Olaf Kirch, which is available both in printed form and online (Linux Documentation Project, see page 79). Many Internet standards are defined in so-called RFCs (Requests for Comment).

```
http://metalab.unc.edu/mdw/
ftp://ftp.nic.de/pub/doc/rfc
ftp://ftp.gwdg.de/pub/rfc
```

Basics

All distributions include configuration programs that allow you to carry out a basic configuration: `linuxconf` in RedHat, `yast` in SuSE, `netconfig` in Slackware, and so on. The problem in using these programs is that the technical terms that occur (IP address, host name, and so on) are often not known. This section briefly describes the most important terms that allow the configuration programs to be used.

The subsequent section briefly deals with the files that are modified by the configuration programs, thus opening the way to manual configuration (if it should become necessary).

TCP/IP

The data transmission protocol TCP/IP, together with the associated programs, accomplishes two essential tasks: it identifies each computer through a unique number (address) and takes care that data sent to a given address effectively arrives at its destination. Data is transmitted in the form of small packages.

Host and domain name

If a computer is to make use of network services, it must be uniquely identifiable. Identification is achieved in parallel in two ways: by a name and by a number. The name is intended for human users, the number for internal administration.

The name, composed of host and domain name, identifies the computer within the network – for example, `jupiter.galactic.network`. The host name identifies a single computer, the domain name the network in which the computer is located. The domain name can be composed of several terms, separated by dots. If you only have one computer (not networked), you can use two arbitrary names of your choice. Inside a true network, it is better to use 'reasonable' names. The host name should uniquely identify the computer, and the domain name should give some information about the network. In a local network without Internet connection, nothing can be said against a host name like `jupiter` and a domain name like `galactic.network`.

TIP

As a host name, you should not use the name of the computer manufacturer, its owner or any other person, a project, and so on – all this can cause confusion. It is better to use short and memorable names of animals, plants, planets, rivers or whatever comes to mind. Names must not contain foreign language special characters.

Please do not use `localhost` as an unimaginative host name! This name occupies a special position because it is considered a 'fully qualified' network name even without a domain name. Thus, if `localhost` is combined with any domain name, this may lead to problems, depending on the current configuration (SuSE!).

NOTE

If you need a domain name and IP number of worldwide validity for connecting a business or any other institution to the Internet, you will get the necessary data through your Internet provider or by arrangement with the NIC (Network Information Center, `http://www.nic.com`).

IP address or IP number

IP numbers consist of four bytes, represented decimally and separated by dots, for example 192.168.1.2. Local networks that are not permanently connected to the Internet or are not connected to the Internet at all should use IP numbers that begin with

192.168. (These are numbers specially reserved for this purpose in order to avoid possible conflicts.)

Interface

Properly speaking, the IP address does not identify a computer but an IP interface. Often, one computer has several interfaces with different IP addresses. Typical interfaces are the loopback interface (127.0.0.1, see below), the Ethernet interface and the PPP or SLIP interface. When we talk about *the* IP address (as though there existed only one), we mean the one through which the computer is accessed from outside (for example, in the local network). Generally, this is the IP number of the Ethernet interface which is associated with the host and domain names and which is unique within the network.

Interface name

Inside Linux, interfaces are assigned not only an IP number, but also an interface name. Typical names are `lo` or `lo0` for the loopback interface, `eth` or `eth0` for the first Ethernet interface and `ppp0` for the first PPP interface.

Loopback interface

This interface plays a particular role: it allows use of the network protocol for local services, that is, for communication inside the computer. Generally, its IP number is 127.0.0.1.

The loopback interface is necessary to make the network protocol function even if no network exists at all. This may seem paradoxical, but it is needed for many elementary Linux commands. The reason: many commands base their communication on the network protocol, regardless of whether the data remains on the local computer or is transferred through a network to a remote computer. An example is the printer daemon `lpd`, which handles the printer spooling and can be used both locally and by remote computers.

Network mask and broadcast address

The extent of a local network is expressed through two masks. (These are again four-byte groups of numbers used internally as bit patterns for IP addresses.) If the local network includes all 192.168.1.n numbers, the corresponding netmask is 255.255.255.0 and the broadcast address 192.168.1.255.

Gateway

A gateway is a computer located at the interface between two networks (often between the local network and the Internet). During configuration, the IP address of the gateway (if present) must be specified in order to know which computer is responsible for forwarding packages that are not processed locally.

Name server

A name server is a computer which carries out the conversion between computer names and IP numbers. In small networks, local IP numbers are generally known by means of a table. In larger networks, and particularly in the Internet, there are dedicated databases to administer this information.

If, for example, you specify the name of an ftp server in Japan, the name server looks up its address in its own database. If the name is not present, the name server contacts other name servers. Thus, address resolution may take some time. In order to store such information locally for further use, it might be useful to configure your own name server. This, however, is not described in this book.

Configuring the loopback interface

If you simply want to set up the loopback interface on your computer, you need only specify the host and domain name during network configuration. As the computer is not networked, you can use any name of your choice. Now your computer recognizes the IP number 127.0.0.1.

> **TIP**
>
> Changes to the network configuration only take effect after you restart the computer. However, if your distribution supports the System V init process, there is an easier way: you use `init 1` to switch to single-user mode. (This terminates all running processes – do not forget to save all open files. The switch will take a few seconds.) Afterwards, you call `init 3` to switch back to multi-user mode with network support. Depending on the distribution, the numbers may differ. In SuSE, you must first execute `init S` and then `init 2`. The runlevel numbers are documented in `/etc/inittab`.

Subsequently, you should check the loopback interface. `ifconfig` shows the state of the current Internet configuration. `route` supplies a list of all known interfaces and information about how these interfaces can be accessed.

```
root#  ifconfig
lo  Link encap:Local Loopback
    inet addr:127.0.0.1  Bcast:127.255.255.255  Mask:255.0.0.0
    UP BROADCAST LOOPBACK RUNNING  MTU:3584  Metric:1
    RX packets:14 errors:0 dropped:0 overruns:0
    TX packets:14 errors:0 dropped:0 overruns:0
root#  route
Kernel routing table
Destination  Gateway  Genmask         Flags  MSS   Window Use  Iface
localnet     *        255.255.255.0   U      1500  0        0  eth0
```

With the `ping` test program, you can send data packets to `localhost` or `127.0.0.1`. These data packets are moved only inside the computer (and not over a real network), but they prove that, in principle, the TCP/IP software is working. `ping` continues to run until it is stopped with Ctrl+C.

```
roog#  ping localhost
PING localhost (127.0.0.1): 56 data bytes
64 bytes from 127.0.0.1: icmp_seq=0 ttl=64 time=0.3 ms
64 bytes from 127.0.0.1: icmp_seq=1 ttl=64 time=0.1 ms
64 bytes from 127.0.0.1: icmp_seq=2 ttl=64 time=0.1 ms
 <Strg>+<C>
--- localhost ping statistics ---
3 packets transmitted, 3 packets received, 0% packet loss
round-trip min/avg/max = 0.1/0.1/0.3 ms
```

Configuring the computer in a local network

If you want to embed your Linux computer into an (already existing) local TCP/IP network, the configuration program asks some more questions. The correct answers now strongly depend on how the existing network is configured. For the following example, the following assumptions are made: local network with addresses 192.169.1.n, domain name `galactic.network`, no gateway, no name server. Then, the following input would be possible (and sensible):

Host name: `jupiter` (if this name is still free to be used)
Domain name: `galactic.network`
IP number: 192.168.1.27 (if this number is still free to be used)
Netmask: 255.255.255.0
Broadcast address: 192.168.1.0

Furthermore, you must specify through which interface (normally the connected Ethernet card) the connection to the network will be made. If a gateway and/or a name server exist, simply specify their IP addresses (if necessary, together with their host and domain names).

TIP

The network connection will only work if the kernel correctly recognizes your Ethernet card. The `dmesg` command displays the corresponding kernel messages.

Configuration files

In most cases, a simple network configuration carried out with the tools supplied by the current distribution will work without problems. If, however, you want to know where you can intervene manually, this section gives you some information. But please, make backup copies of all files you intend to modify – depending on the distribution, cooperation between configuration files is not very fault tolerant!

/etc/HOSTNAME or /etc/hostname

This file just contains the complete Internet name of the computer (for example, `jupiter.galactic.network`).

/etc/hosts

This file contains a list of known IP numbers: 127.0.0.1 is the standard IP number for the loopback device. Additional numbers may designate the Ethernet, PPP or SLIP interfaces.

```
# /etc/hosts
# For loopbacking.
127.0.0.1       localhost
192.168.1.5     jupiter.galactic.network  jupiter
```

If only the loopback device is configured (no local network embedding), `/etc/hosts` looks as follows. (As a domain name, you may for example use `localdomain`, if you have no better idea.)

```
# /etc/hosts
# For loopback
127.0.0.1         localhost computer_name computer_name.domain_name
```

`/etc/networks`

While `hosts` contains a table of known IP addresses of network users, `networks` contains a list of the IP addresses of known networks. 127.0.0.0 indicates the loopback network, whereas 192.168.1.0 indicates the local network.

```
# /etc/networks
loopback        127.0.0.0
localnet        192.168.1.0
```

`/etc/host.conf`

This file specifies how TCP/IP should determine unknown IP numbers. The following sample file specifies first evaluating the `/etc/hosts` file (keyword `hosts`) and then asking the name server specified in `/etc/resolv.conf` (`bind`). The second line allows you to assign more than one IP number to a host name specified in `/etc/hosts`.

```
# /etc/host.conf
order hosts, bind
multi on
```

`/etc/resolv.conf`

First, this file specifies the name server IP address (keyword `nameserver`). The keyword domain ensures that incomplete Internet names (for example, `jupiter`) are extended by their domain name (to `jupiter.galactic.network`). This is mainly intended to improve ease of use, because it allows local Internet names to be specified in abbreviated form.

```
# /etc/resolv.conf
domain galactic.network
search galactic.network
nameserver 192.168.1.2
```

Apart from the files mentioned above, there are countless other `/etc` files that control all sorts of network and Internet services. More important for elementary configuration, however, are some additional configuration files that unfortunately depend on the individual distributions. Some examples follow below.

RedHat

Local network configuration is carried out via script files in `/etc/sysconfig/network-scripts` (see also page 131).

```
#!/bin/sh
# /etc/sysconfig/network-scripts/ifcfg-eth0
#>>>Device type: ethernet
#>>>Variable declarations:
DEVICE=eth0
IPADDR=192.168.1.5
NETMASK=255.255.255.0
```

```
NETWORK=192.168.1.0
BROADCAST=192.168.1.255
GATEWAY=none
ONBOOT=yes
#>>>End of variable declarations
```

SuSE

Configuration is carried out via the central file `/etc/rc.config`. The following listing shows an excerpt:

```
# Excerpt from /etc/rc.config
IPADDR_0=192.168.1.5
NETDEV_0=eth0
IFCONFIG_0="192.168.1.5 broadcast 192.168.1.255 \
  netmask 255.255.255.0"
NETWORK_0="-net 192.168.1.0"
GATEWAY_0=""
FQHOSTNAME=jupiter.galactic.network
NAMESERVER=""
```

Configuring a small network with ftp and NFS

In a way, this section contradicts the intention of this book to limit the subject of networking to the client view. However, as it often occurs in practice that two or three Linux computers are networked to the point that they can at least exchange files, we will deal very briefly with the setup of a fairly simple mini-network. The necessary configuration is quite modest and easy to follow.

A precondition is that the computers are networked and configured as described above. For all computers, the same domain name and broadcast address must be used. Host names and IP numbers must be set individually, for example (with three computers):

IP addresses: 192.168.1.5, 192.168.1.6, 192.168.1.7
Host names: `jupiter`, `uranus`, `saturn`
Common domain name: `galactic.network`
Common netmask: 255.255.255.0
Common broadcast address: 192.168.1.0

The next step consists of inserting into `/etc/hosts` both your own IP address and the IP addresses of the other two computers. Thus, on all three computers, this file looks exactly the same:

```
# /etc/hosts
127.0.0.1       localhost
192.168.1.5     jupiter.galactic.network  jupiter
192.168.1.6     uranus.galactic.network   uranus
192.168.1.7     saturn.galactic.network   saturn
```

This ensures that the computers can reach each other immediately after a reboot or a restart of the network programs. In `ping`, you can specify the IP address, the complete name, or the short form (third column in `/etc/hosts`). If it does not work, check that the cabling is correct, that the Ethernet card is recognized by the kernel on all computers, that the interface of the Ethernet card is active (`ifconfig`) and that the local network is contained in the routing table (`route`).

```
root#  ping uranus
PING uranus.galactic.network (192.168.1.6): 56 data bytes
64 bytes from 192.168.1.1: icmp_seq=0 ttl=255 time=2.0 ms
64 bytes from 192.168.1.1: icmp_seq=1 ttl=255 time=1.2 ms
64 bytes from 192.168.1.1: icmp_seq=2 ttl=255 time=1.2 ms
 <Strg>+<C>
---  uranus.galactic.network ping statistics ---
3 packets transmitted, 3 packets received, 0% packet loss
round-trip min/avg/max = 1.2/1.4/2.0 ms
```

FTP server configuration

`ftp` is a protocol that allows transmission of files between computers. (The usage of `ftp` from the client's side is described on page 335.)

In most distributions, an FTP server is installed automatically (often, this is `wuftpd`). `ftp` should then work immediately – simply try out `ftp localhost`. To transmit the files of a specific user, you need to execute `ftp` *hostname*. Subsequently, you enter login name and password.

If no FTP server is installed, you need to look for the appropriate package in your distribution and install it. To make anonymous FTP work, you need to create the directory `/home/ftp` and fill it with data. For this purpose, it is best to follow the `man` text for `ftpd`, which includes many details regarding security aspects.

For reasons of security, `ftp` cannot be used for logins without a password. (We are talking about the login names on the server side. You yourself can work on a login without a password, but you cannot access the data of a foreign account that is not protected.) In addition, in the file `/etc/ftpusers`, users can be listed that are *not* allowed to use `ftp`. Usually, `root` is listed in this file for safety reasons.

Together with `ftp`, some other network services should work straight away: try `telnet` or `rlogin`. For security reasons, it is normally impossible to log in directly as `root`. Try to log in under a different name first and then execute `su`.

Access control

If you want to have precise control over who is and who is not allowed to use which network services, you can modify the files `/etc/hosts.allow` and `/etc/hosts.deny`. The syntax in these files is `service:user`.

With `in.ftpd: 192.168.1.` in `hosts.allow` you allow all members of the local network to use `ftp`. With `ALL:ALL` in `hosts.deny` you deny all users access to any other network service. `allow` takes precedence over `deny`; therefore, access to network services is now largely protected against unwanted access. (This sample setting is very restrictive as, for example, it allows no access to `telnet` and `rlogin`.)

```
# /etc/hosts.allow
in.ftpd: 192.168.1.

# /etc/hosts.deny
ALL:ALL
```

Internally, access control is carried out through `tcpd`, a daemon that starts other network daemons. `tcpd` itself is started by `inetd`, when a network service is requested. The configuration is stored in `/etc/inetd.conf`. Amongst others, there is a (default) line for `ftp`:

```
# a line from /etc/inetd.conf
ftp   stream  tcp    nowait  root  /usr/sbin/tcpd  in.ftpd -l -a
```

Thus, when the `ftp` service is requested, `inetd` starts `tcpd` with the parameters `in.ftpd -l -a`. `tcpd` first evaluates `hosts.allow` and allows access if the requested service corresponds to a pattern. If nothing is found there, `tcpd` checks the file `hosts.deny` and denies access if a matching line is found. If neither `hosts.allow` nor `hosts.deny` contains a matching entry (thus, also if both files are empty), `tcpd` allows access.

NFS server configuration

If the entire file system (or even just one directory) of a computer is to be available to other computers, the computer must be configured as an NFS server. The NFS configuration is largely independent of the configuration of the other network services.

Most distributions are preconfigured in such a way that the computer can automatically be used as an NFS server. (If not present, the `portmap` and `nfs-server` packages need to be installed.)

To make NFS work, `rpc.portmap`, `rpc.mountd`, and `rpc.nfsd` must be started. These three `rpc` programs are daemons, which together provide the services of the NFS server. With `ps -x | grep rpc` you can make sure that these daemons are running. (On some systems, the more secure `portmap` runs instead of `rpc.portmap`.)

The file `/etc/exports` controls which user is allowed to access which directories and how (read-only or read-write). The following file (which is installed on the `jupiter` computer) allows all network users to access the `cdrom` directory, users of `uranus` to read `/usr/local`, and users of `saturn` to read and write all directories (which obviously constitutes a serious safety risk!).

```
# /etc/exports of the jupiter computer
/cdrom      (ro)
/usr/local  uranus(ro)
/           saturn(rw)
```

On the client side, no special configuration is needed. To mount the NFS file system, a simple `mount` command is sufficient. A corresponding entry can also be prepared in `/etc/fstab` (with the option `noauto`!). The following instruction makes all files in `/usr/local` on `uranus` available on the local computer under `/usr/local`. This can be used to save space (as the programs located in this directory need only be installed on one computer).

```
root#  mount -t nfs jupiter:/usr/local /usr/local
```

TIP

In order to prevent problems with access and ownership rights, you must ensure that `/etc/passwd` and `/etc/group` are synchronized on all computers. On all computers, the same UID and GID numbers must apply. (In large networks, this can be achieved through NIS or `rpc.ugidd`.)

In kernel 2.2, the locking behavior of NFS has changed. If you encounter locking problems, you can remedy them by means of the `nolock` option in `mount` or `fstab`.

6.10 Boot diskettes/LILO

To be precise, in this section, 'boot process' only means the start of the kernel and access to the root partition. Once this has succeeded, the system is initialized. This is the responsibility of the `/sbin/init` program, which is started by the kernel as the very first process to run. (The Init V process too is often considered as part of the boot process. More information on the Init process can be found from page 124 onward.)

For booting, the Linux kernel must be able to be loaded from a diskette or from a hard disk. This kernel must include all drivers needed to access the root partition. (If the root partition is located on a SCSI disk, the kernel must include the appropriate SCSI driver. Other drivers may be loaded as modules at a later stage – but only after access to the root partition is working. The only exception to this rule is to load the SCSI driver into a RAM disk during booting and activate it from there as a module. RedHat uses this booting concept in its default configuration. The advantage of this process is that it can be configured *without* recompiling the kernel.)

There are many ways to boot Linux:

- The easiest but slowest variation is loading the kernel from a boot diskette. (see page 181).
- Using a boot diskette with LILO is already somewhat more elegant. Only the tiny LILO program (that is, the Linux Loader) is loaded from the diskette. Subsequently, it accesses the hard disk and loads the kernel from there. LILO fundamentals are discussed from page 183 onward; LILO installation on a diskette is described on page 189.
- An even more elegant solution is to install LILO itself on the hard disk. This, however, is not entirely without problems, since conflicts with other operating systems may occur. Page 191 describes not only how to install LILO into the MBR (Master Boot Record), but also how to create a backup copy of this sector beforehand.
- Usually, the kernel file loaded by LILO is located in a Linux partition. If this partition starts in a sector that can no longer be reached by the BIOS (1024-cylinder limit), the kernel and the other boot files can also be installed in a DOS partition – see page 193.

- To avoid conflicts with other operating systems, LILO can also be started by a foreign boot manager. On page 194 you will find instructions on how to persuade the Windows NT 4 boot manager to start LILO (and thus Linux).
- An alternative to LILO is constituted by the DOS program `loadlin`. (`loadlin` must only be started from a 'true' DOS system, *not* in a DOS window under Windows or OS/2.) Further details follow on page 196.

NOTE

Once Linux has been correctly installed in a hard disk partition, you can also use the installation diskette or the installation CD-ROM of most distributions for booting. During start-up, you only need to specify the option `root=/dev/hd`*xx* to ensure that, after start-up of the kernel, instead of loading the installation program, your root file system is mounted and its Init process started.

This kind of emergency boot process may cause problems with SCSI disks. Often, the kernel does not include the required SCSI driver. If the corresponding module is only loaded later by the installation program, mounting your root file system is no longer possible. Therefore, some distributions supply pre-configured kernels with the most frequently used SCSI drivers.

TIP

Please make an effort and read the whole section before you install LILO on your hard disk (I know that the section is rather long). In particular, please read the subsections on pages 191 and 192, which deal with the creation of a backup of the boot sector and with restoring the boot sector after a failed LILO installation!

Kernel boot diskette

Even if, in the long run, you plan to use LILO, you still need a boot diskette first! The reason: if something goes wrong with the LILO installation, if during a later installation of Windows 9x LILO is overwritten again, and so on, you need to be able to start Linux in spite of all this.

Usually, you are offered the possibility of creating a boot diskette at some point of the installation procedure. You should definitely take advantage of this possibility. If, at a later stage, you want to create a new boot diskette (for example, with a recompiled kernel), the procedure is as follows:

```
root#  fdformat /dev/fd0            # format diskette (if unformatted)
root#  cp /boot/vmlinuz /dev/fd0    # copy kernel to diskette
root#  rdev /dev/sdc2 /             # determine boot partition
root#  rdev /dev/fd0 /dev/sdc2      # set this partition in the kernel
root#  rdev -v /dev/fd0 -2          # extended VGA mode (50 lines)
root#  rdev -R /dev/fd0 1           # register boot partition as read only
```

The above lines assume that the kernel file has the name `/vmlinuz`. In some distributions, the kernel file is located directly in the root directory (thus, `/vmlinuz`) or it has a different name. If you just have compiled a new kernel (see page 199), the new kernel file will have the name `/usr/src/linux/arch/i386/boot/zImage` or `.../bzImage`.

> **CAUTION**
>
> If you have installed Linux on a SCSI hard disk, you need a kernel in which the required SCSI driver is integrated. With RedHat in particular, this is not the case with the automatically installed kernel. Thus, for the creation of a boot diskette, you *must* recompile the kernel. (If, from RedHat version 4.1 onward, you want to create a boot diskette without recompiling the kernel, you need to create a LILO boot diskette – see page 189.)

Instead of `cp`, you can also use the `dd` command, mentioned in many other Linux books, to transfer the kernel file onto the diskette (see page 450). For this purpose, both commands function in the same way: they transfer the kernel file directly into the first sectors of the diskette. Thus, there is no file system on the diskette, but just a series of data blocks. (If there was a file system before the `cp` or `dd` command was executed, it is overwritten.) On this diskette, no other file can be stored without destroying the first one.

It is essential for the creation of a boot diskette that the correct root partition is specified in `rdev` (otherwise, the kernel will be loaded, but once it is running, it will not find the partition containing the Linux file system). The easiest way to find out the correct name of the root partition (`/dev/sdc2` in the above example) is to call `rdev` without any parameters. Alternatively, `df` shows which file systems are located in which partitions.

The next two `rdev` commands are optional. With the first one, you modify the kernel so that the extended VGA mode is used. The second command causes the file system to be mounted read-only first. Subsequently, Linux checks that the system is error-free and if this is the case it mounts it in read-write mode.

Using LILO

This section describes the usage of LILO during the boot process. Thus it presumes that LILO is already installed. At start-up, LILO attracts our attention with the text `lilo:`.

Normally, LILO is set in such a way that there is a short delay (of some seconds) during the boot process, in which you can press [Shift] if you want to manually choose the operating system that should be started. At the prompt, you type in the name of the operating system and press [↵]. Pressing [Tab] displays a table with the options you can choose from. If a default operating system has been defined and you do not press [Shift] during the delay, LILO automatically starts the default operating system.

A particularly attractive feature of LILO is that you can enter additional kernel options. To do this, you press [Shift] and enter the name of the required operating system, followed by the required options. The most frequently used options are `root=` (selection of a different root partition), `ro` (start Linux read-only) and `single` (start Linux in single-user mode). Kernel options can also mean salvation from various hardware problems. (In this case, however, it makes more sense to specify these options in the `append` line of `lilo.conf`.)

> **NOTE** A table with the most important parameters can be found on page 48. Please note that, during LILO input, the American keyboard layout applies. Some characters will be in different positions.

LILO internals

LILO (Linux Loader) is a tiny program that can be installed in the boot sector (the first sector) of a diskette, of a hard disk or of a hard disk partition. The program allows you to choose between several installed operating systems and, in particular, to start Linux. LILO is the fastest and most popular method for starting Linux. (All information in this section refers to LILO version 0.20.)

> **CAUTION** Installation of LILO is, however, a rather delicate matter, especially when LILO is installed into the MBR (Master Boot Record) of the hard disk. If something goes wrong, you will not be able to boot your computer from your hard disk, either under your old operating system or under Linux.
>
> Particular problems may arise when LILO is installed on computers running Windows NT, if the first hard disk partition is not a DOS or Windows 95 partition (but, for example, an NTFS or Windows 98 partition with FAT32). If in such a constellation you install LILO into the MBR, you may no longer be able to start Windows NT.

> **CAUTION** If you use the EZ-Drive disk manager, you must under no circumstances install LILO in the MBR! This restriction probably applies to other disk managers as well (disk managers allow access to big EIDE disks with old BIOS versions; see page 33). If you still want to use LILO, installation is possible only on a diskette or in the first sector of the Linux partition. This last variation will not be discussed here; it is extensively described in the LILO documentation.

In most distributions, the LILO configuration can be carried out as part of the installation process. Because of the risks mentioned above, however, a manual installation of LILO has its advantages. You have much better control over what really happens, can create a backup diskette of the MBR, and so on. LILO in the MBR is not a precondition for running Linux! During the first few days – until you have familiarized yourself with the handling of Linux – you can always boot from a diskette.

> **NOTE** There is very substantial online documentation about LILO. `man lilo.conf` and `man lilo` describe the installation program and the format of the control file. A detailed description can normally be found in `/usr/doc/lilo` or `/usr/doc/packages/lilo`. (If these directories do not exist in your distribution, use `locate` to find `user.tex`.) Very informative texts are the Mini-HOWTOs about LILO and NT-OS-Loader + Linux.

CAUTION

If you first install LILO and then Windows 9x (or another Microsoft operating system), LILO is overwritten without warning. It is easy to reinstall LILO by calling `lilo` under Linux. However, you need a boot diskette to be able to start Linux at all. Therefore, do not throw away your Linux boot diskette even after a successful LILO installation!

Also, if you update your Linux system (new kernel), please do not forget to update your boot diskette as well.

Functioning

To put it simply, the function of LILO is to load and execute the file containing the Linux kernel. However, this is not as easy as it sounds:

More precisely speaking, the boot sector of the hard disk or diskette contains a tiny program (first stage), whose only task is to load the larger LILO main program (second stage). (The boot sector, that is, the first sector of the hard disk or diskette, would be much too small to store the entire LILO program. Code contained in the boot sector is automatically executed by the BIOS at system start-up – this is why the boot sector plays such an important role in starting a computer.)

The LILO main program (the file `/boot/boot.b`) is located anywhere on the hard disk. The boot sector with the start program also contains the numbers of the sectors where the main program can be found.

As soon as the LILO main program is running, it gives the user the possibility to choose between different operating systems via the keyboard. If the user opts for Linux, LILO must load the kernel file. For this purpose, a table was created during installation of LILO (the file `/boot/map`), which contains the sequence of all sectors in which the kernel file is located.

The reason for this unusual procedure is that while LILO is running, no information is as yet available on DOS, Linux, or other file systems. From LILO's point of view, the hard disk is a huge conglomerate of data sectors. LILO must know at each stage where the data sectors are that are needed next.

On the basis of the above description, it should be clear that LILO can only function as long as the location of the kernel file on the hard disk remains exactly the same. (Each copy command and, in particular, each recompilation of the kernel causes a change even if the file name remains the same. In such cases, LILO needs to be reinstalled by means of the `lilo` command. `lilo` carries out the preparatory work, creating updated versions of `/boot/boot.b` and `/boot/map`, and storing their start sectors and other information in the boot sector.)

LILO is executed before any operating system is running. For this reason – unlike Linux – LILO has to rely on the BIOS. For historical reasons, however, the BIOS only allows access to the first 1024 cylinders of a hard disk. In order to make the startup of Linux work, the kernel file must be located within the first 1024 cylinders of the hard disk. With older BIOS versions or hard disks, the location of the Linux kernel may be limited to the first 508 Mbytes of the hard disk. (Depending on the hard disk geometry and the BIOS version, however, the first 1024 cylinders might comprise up to 7.9 Gbytes – see page 33.)

So long as the first Linux partition lies completely within the 1024-cylinder limit, there are no problems. If this is not the case, the Linux kernel could as a last resort be copied into a DOS or Windows partition below this limit. However, this entails several disadvantages (see page 193).

Apart from the cylinder limit, there is another restriction: during the boot process, most BIOS versions can only access the first two hard disks. On a system with several hard disks, the kernel file must thus be located on one of the first two disks. (Even an IDE/ATAPI CD-ROM drive is counted as a 'hard disk' in this context. Modern BIOS versions are exceptions as they are used, for example, in many SCSI controllers – here, all hard disks can be accessed without restrictions.)

Both the cylinder limit and the limitation to two hard disks apply only to the Linux kernel file. Linux itself (that is, the `root` partition) could also be installed on the fifth disk starting with cylinder 2500. Once the kernel is running, there are no more problems.

Apart from Linux, LILO can currently boot the operating systems DOS, Windows 9x (which corresponds to DOS in its boot process), OS/2 and several versions of Unix. Unfortunately, Windows NT is not officially supported and has to rely on a boot manager of its own. (More about Windows NT on page 194.) It is still unclear how LILO and the forthcoming Windows 2000 will coexist. If Microsoft does not change the boot process, the same information should apply as for Windows NT 4.

LILO configuration

The installation of LILO consists of two steps: first, you create the configuration file `/etc/lilo.conf`, then you execute the `lilo` command. This command evaluates the configuration file, uses this information to create a new boot sector, and writes this to the location specified by `lilo.conf`. Usually, this is the MBR of a hard disk or diskette; it may, however, also be a normal file.

> TIP
> Please note that you must call `lilo` every time the kernel file changes (for example, after a recompilation), even if you do not change `lilo.conf`! For LILO it is not the file name that counts, but the sector number at which the file begins.

The file `lilo.conf` consists of two parts: the first part controls the general behavior of the boot program, the second part (keyword `image` or `other`) lists all operating systems started by LILO (DOS, Windows, OS/2, and Linux). The first operating system in this list is automatically taken as the default system. Comments begin with the hash character (#).

In principle, you can install a different operating system (for example, different Linux distributions) on each hard disk partition and use LILO to select the required partition. You can also use LILO to differentiate between different Linux kernel files within a partition (for example, `vmlinuz`, `vmlinuz.old`). This is of particular interest if you wish to test a new Linux version without throwing away the old one.

Global section

The first part of `/etc/lilo.conf` begins with the instruction `boot=` and specifies where LILO is to be installed. For installation on a diskette, the specification is `/dev/fd0`. To install LILO into the MBR of the first IDE hard disk, you use `/dev/hda`; for the first SCSI disk, `/dev/sda`.

`delay` specifies how many tenths of a second LILO waits for manual input. The shortest delay is 0, but then you must keep [Shift] depressed even before you start LILO if you do not want to use the default operating system.

`prompt` has the opposite effect and forces a user input before the boot process is started. In this case, [↵] causes the default operating system to be booted. All other operating systems can be selected as described above. `prompt` prevents an unintentional reboot.

`compact` allows a particularly fast loading of the kernel (above all, from the diskette), but it does not work on all computers or with all hard disk controllers.

The `map` option allows you to specify the file in which the sector numbers of the kernel files and other files are to be stored. Without this option, `/boot/map` is used, which is usually a sensible default setting.

A further option which is often omitted is `install`: this specifies the file in which the LILO main program (the second stage loader) is stored. The default setting is `/boot/boot.b` and needs to be changed only in rare cases.

The `linear` option causes the sector addresses in `/boot/map` not to be stored as CHS triples (cylinder, head, sector), but as LBA values (Logical Block Addressing, see also page 33). When LILO and the BIOS cannot agree on a common interpretation of the hard disk geometry, using `linear` is often the easiest solution.

> **NOTE**
>
> According to the SuSE support database, the `linear` option reduces the maximum address range depending on the CHS geometry signaled by the BIOS. The reason for this is the 16-bit arithmetic used in the calculation of sector numbers. Under unfavorable circumstances – in particular with a CHS geometry of more than 64 sectors per track as commonly used by current BIOS versions – `linear` allows only a smaller area of the disk to be addressed than it would be possible without this option (which, depending on the BIOS, allows up to 7.9 Gbytes).

```
# /etc/lilo.conf (part 1)
# LILO global section
boot = /dev/fd0          # installation in the MBR of a diskette
delay = 100              # wait 10 seconds
# prompt                 # force input (no automatic start)
# compact                # faster, especially with diskettes; can cause
                         # problems with some hard disks
# map=/boot/map          # default setting in any case
# install=/boot/boot.b   # default setting in any case
# linear                 # required for some hard disks
```

In some cases (big disks, old BIOS, and so on), LILO has problems with the hard disk geometry. As a first solution, you should try the `linear` option. If this does not work, you must use the `disk` option with its suboptions `bios`, `sectors`, `heads`, and `cylinders`. Background information on this subject can be found on page 33 and in the LILO documentation.

```
disk=/dev/hda      # additional iformation for device /dev/hda
  bios=0x80        # 0x80 for the first disk, 0x81 for the second, ...
sectors=63         # number of sectors
heads=255          # number of heads
cylinder=522       # number of cylinders
```

Linux Image

Now to the second part of `lilo.conf`: here, you can specify up to 16 operating system versions that you can choose to run. The first system is used as the default setting. A common feature of all entries is the `label` command which gives each version a name. These names must be entered during the manual selection of the operating system – thus, it is better to choose short and meaningful names without spaces or special characters.

TIP Unless you have specified a special keyboard table during LILO configuration (keyword `keytable`, see LILO documentation), the US keyboard layout applies for entering label names. Some characters may be located in different positions.

To boot Linux, the `image` and `root` commands must be specified in addition to `label`. `image` determines the name of the kernel file, `root` the partition on which the root directory is located.

`vga` specifies the VGA mode: `extended` stands for the extended mode with 50 lines, `normal` for the standard mode, `ask` for confirmation during booting, and an arbitrary number $n > 0$ for the VGA mode n. (Warning! If this VGA mode does not exist or is not correctly supported, you cannot use Linux correctly.) If you want to use a RAM disk, you can specify its size in Kbytes with `ramdisk=`.

`read-only` specifies that the root partition is first mounted read-only. Then, the Init process can check and, if needed, repair the file system, before it is mounted again (and definitely) in read-write mode. This option should always be used!

With `append`, additional kernel options can be specified (for example, to circumvent hardware problems). If you use a kernel adjusted to your hardware or a modularized kernel, kernel options are seldom required. The most important options are described on page 48.

```
# /etc/lilo.conf (part 2)
image = /boot/vmlinuz                  # kernel file
        label = linux
        root = /dev/hda8               # root device
        read-only
        # initrd = /boot/initrd        # in RedHat with SCSI
        # vga = extended               # text mode 80x50 characters
# alternative: 'linuxbak' for booting an older kernel version
image= /boot/vmlinuz.bak               # kernel file
        label = linuxbak
```

```
root = /dev/hda8               # root device
read-only
# initrd = /boot/initrd        # in RedHat with SCSI
# vga = extended               # text mode 80x50 characters
# append = "aic7xxx=extended" # kernel option for SCSI card
```

RedHat Linux on a SCSI hard disk

RedHat Linux handles SCSI disks in a different way than most other distributions. The SCSI driver is normally not integrated into the kernel, but is loaded as a module from a RAM disk. LILO needs to be configured accordingly.

The RAM disk file is created with `mkinitrd`. It contains all modules needed for booting. When executing the command, the correct kernel number must be specified (in order for the appropriate modules to be read). Furthermore, a module for the loopback device needs to be available in the currently running kernel.

```
root#  mkinitrd /boot/initrd 2.2.3
```

The resulting RAM disk must then be specified with `initrd=/boot/initrd` as an additional `image` option in `/etc/lilo.conf`. You can do without this unusual boot concept by recompiling the kernel and integrating the SCSI driver directly (not as a module).

DOS, Windows 3.1, Windows 9x, and OS/2

In DOS and OS/2 versions, `other` is used to select the partition, `table` to specify the partition table, and (for OS/2) `loader` to indicate a system-specific boot program. Windows 3.1 and 9x are treated in the same way as DOS.

```
# /etc/lilo.conf, (part 3)
# alternative: 'dos' for booting DOS/Windows on /dev/hda1
other = /dev/hda1                 # DOS/Windows partition on
        label = dos
        table = /dev/hda          # disk device (without number!)
# alternative: 'os2' for booting OS/2 on /dev/hdb1
other = /dev/hdb1
        label = os2
        table = /dev/hdb
        loader = /boot/os2_d.b
```

For booting of OS/2, it may be necessary to change the order of hard disks. In this case, you need to add the following lines to `lilo.conf`:

```
map-drive = 0x80
    to    = 0x81
map-drive = 0x81
    to    = 0x80
```

NOTE

With the above `dos` variation, you may even boot Windows NT – however, only if LILO was not installed in the boot sector (MBR) of the hard disk. In practice, this results in two possible alternatives: on the one hand, LILO diskettes; on the other hand, LILO installation on a primary partition of the hard disk which is *not* the Windows NT partition and which was made the default partition by means of `fdisk`. The latter variation is in fact fairly uncommon. A better way to start both Windows NT and Linux without a boot diskette is described on page 194.

NOTE

A vast number of additional options is described in the online documentation – for example, `message` to display an informative text. Furthermore, you will find a description of how to use LILO to instigate password protection during the boot process itself.

LILO boot diskette

If you specify `/dev/fd0` in the `boot` option of `lilo.conf`, LILO is installed in the boot sector of the (formatted) diskette in drive A:. This way of installing LILO has the advantage that it poses absolutely no danger to the hard disk. Nevertheless, the boot process is significantly faster than with a normal boot diskette, because only LILO is loaded from the diskette. The kernel file and all other required files are read from the hard disk.

This is at the same time an advantage and a disadvantage: the advantage is the higher speed, the disadvantage the dependency on the fact that the kernel file can be accessed. If the kernel file cannot be found, this kind of LILO boot diskette is of no value at all.

Setting up LILO

To set up LILO, you need a `lilo.conf` file of the following kind. `/boot/vmlinuz` must point to a kernel that contains all drivers needed to access the root partition. Path and device names need to be adjusted to suit your computer. You may need additional options which have been described in the configuration section (such as `initrd` with RedHat on SCSI systems). Once the configuration file is set up correctly, you insert a formatted diskette into the drive and execute `lilo`.

```
# /etc/lilo.conf
boot=/dev/fd0                    # device of the diskette drive
prompt
timeout=100
image = /boot/vmlinuz            # kernel file
        label = linux
        root = /dev/hda8         # root device
        read-only
        # initrd = /boot/initrd  # RedHat with SCSI
other=/dev/hda1
```

```
        label=dos
        table=/dev/hda
```

LILO boot diskette with its own kernel

With some more effort, it is possible to create a LILO boot diskette that has its own kernel. This diskette must contain a file system (minix or ext2), LILO, the kernel file and other files needed for the boot process (usually only `boot.b` and `map`). The preparations are as follows:

```
root#  mkfs -t minix /dev/fd0 1440          # create minix file system
root#  mkdir /mount/floppy                  # if directory does not exist
root#  mount -t minix /dev/fd0 /mnt/floppy/ # mount into file system
root#  mkdir /mnt/floppy/boot
root#  cp /boot/vmlinuz /mnt/floppy/boot    # copy the kernel
root#  cp /boot/boot.b /mnt/floppy/boot/    # copy boot.b
root#  mkinitrd                             # in RedHat with SCSI
root#  cp /boot/initrd /mnt/floppy/boot/    # in RedHat with SCSI
```

The next step is to create a special LILO configuration file for the diskette. The main difference is that `map` and `install` point to the diskette (instead of the usual hard disk). The file `/mnt/floppy/boot/map` has not been forgotten in the above commands; it is only created through the execution of the `lilo` command.

In the example below, three variations are provided. In the default setting, an attempt is made to boot from the hard disk (this is the fastest way). If this fails (for example, because the kernel file is no longer where it belongs), a new attempt can be started, selecting the `linuxfromdisk` variation at the LILO prompt. Please note that in this variation `image` points to the kernel file on the diskette. As a third variation – for the sake of completeness – it is possible to boot DOS/Windows.

```
# /etc/lilo.conf-floppy
boot = /dev/fd0                    # device of the diskette drive
compact                            # fast, but does not always work
delay = 100
install=/mnt/floppy/boot/boot.b    # on the diskette!
map=/mnt/floppy/boot/map           # on the diskette!
image =  /boot/vmlinuz             # kernel from hard disk
         label = linux
         root = /dev/hda8          # enter your root device!
read-only
image =  /mnt/floppy/boot/vmlinuz # kernel from diskette
         label = linuxfromdisk
         root = /dev/hda8          # enter your root device!
read-only
other = /dev/hda1
         label = dos
         table = /dev/hda
```

In order to install this LILO configuration on the diskette, the following commands are required:

```
root#  chmod go-w /etc/lilo.conf-floppy  # otherwise LILO will complain
root#  lilo -C /etc/lilo.conf-floppy     # install LILO
root#  ls -lR /mnt/floppy/
   drwxrwxr-x   2 root     root          80 Jun 16 20:24 boot

   /mnt/floppy/boot:
   total 11
   -rw-rw-r--   1 root     root        3708 Jun 16 19:39 boot.b
   -rw-------   1 root     root        7168 Jun 16 20:24 map
   -rw-rw-r--   1 root     root      403672 Jun 16 19:37 vmlinuz

root#  sync                              # execute buffered operations
root#  umount /mnt/floppy
```

TIP Owners of a RedHat distribution can create a LILO boot diskette in a much simpler way. You just need to execute the following command with the correct kernel number:

```
root# mkbootdisk --device /dev/fd0 2.0.36-0.7
```

NOTE More information about how to create sophisticated boot diskettes that even have their own `root` file system and can therefore be used for maintenance work can be found in the HOWTO text on the subject of boot diskettes. In most distributions, the installation diskettes themselves can be used for this purpose.

LILO installation in the boot sector of the hard disk

CAUTION Once more: of all LILO variations, this is the most dangerous one! Depending on the NT installation, it is incompatible with the Windows NT boot manager and in any case incompatible with disk managers (DOS access of big EIDE disks with a very old BIOS).

Creating a backup copy of the boot sector

During the execution of `lilo` for installation into the MBR of a hard disk, it is automatically checked whether there is already a backup copy of the boot sector in the `/boot` directory. Only if this is not the case (that is, during the first execution of `lilo`), the command saves the current boot sector in the file `/boot/boot.0300` (for IDE disks) or `/boot/boot.0800` (for SCSI disks). If you want to save the boot sector manually, you must execute one of the following commands *before* you execute `lilo` for the first time. The first command applies to the first IDE disk, the second command to the first SCSI disk:

```
root#  dd if=/dev/hda of=/boot/bootsektor.ide  bs=512 count=1
```

```
root#  dd if=/dev/sda of=/boot/bootsektor.scsi bs=512 count=1
```

If you want to transfer the current boot sector to a diskette, you need a formatted diskette (see `fdformat` on page 453). Then, you execute one of the following commands:

```
root#  dd if=/dev/hda of=/dev/fd0 bs=512 count=1  # first IDE disk
root#  dd if=/dev/sda of=/dev/fd0 bs=512 count=1  # first SCSI disk
```

If a diskette generated in this way is present in drive A: when the computer is restarted, the computer boots in exactly the same way as from the boot sector on the hard disk. This is most impressive under Windows 9x.

NOTE

When you create a boot diskette under Windows 95 (CONTROL PANEL | ADD/REMOVE PROGRAMS | STARTUP DISK), you can only use it to start DOS, but not Windows. This may be sufficient to restore a damaged system, but it is not at all elegant. If, on the other hand, you proceed as described above, you can start Windows 95 from a diskette quickly and without problems. (Assuming, that is, that the Windows partition has not been damaged and that all system files are available. In contrast, the 'original' Windows 95 boot diskette is autonomous, because files such as `COMMAND.COM` are loaded directly from the diskette.)

Setting up LILO

To set up LILO, you need a `lilo.conf` file which, except for the `boot` line looks exactly as the diskette version. Path and device names need to be adjusted to suit your computer. You may need additional options which have been described in the configuration section.

```
# file /etc/lilo.conf
boot=/dev/hda                          # device of the first IDE disk
# boot=/dev/sda                        # device of the first SCSI disk
prompt
timeout=100
image = /boot/vmlinuz                  # kernel file
        label = linux
        root = /dev/hda8               # root device on
        read-only
        # initrd = /boot/initrd        # RedHat with SCSI
other=/dev/hda1
        label=dos
        table=/dev/hda
```

Removing LILO from the hard disk

In order to remove LILO from the hard disk, you must restore the boot sector. In the simplest case, you simply execute `lilo -u`. This causes LILO to read the boot sector saved in `/boot` during the first LILO installation and to use it to overwrite the current LILO boot sector.

```
root#  lilo -u
```

If you have made your own backup copy of the boot sector, you can reinstall it with `dd`. The first command applies to the first IDE disk, the second command to the first SCSI disk:

```
root#  dd if=/boot/bootsektor.ide of=/dev/hda bs=512 count=1
root#  dd if=/boot/bootsektor.scsi of=/dev/sda bs=512 count=1
```

If problems occur during the uninstallation of LILO, you can use a boot diskette to start DOS and then execute `FDISK /MBR`. This creates a boot sector for the automatic start of DOS/Windows (and overwrites the LILO boot sector). However, this method does not work for some versions of Windows 9x and not at all for Windows NT.

Installing LILO in a DOS partition (1024-cylinder limit)

If the Linux root partition is situated outside the magic 1024-cylinder limit or on a non-accessible hard disk, the kernel file and other boot information can be copied into a DOS or Windows partition that lies below this limit. (For startup, LILO needs the kernel file, the files `boot.b` and `map` and possible message files if the `message` option is used.)

```
root#  mkdir /dosc                       # if the directory does not exist
root#  mount -t vfat /dev/hda1 /dosc     # device name of Windows partition
root#  mkdir /dosc/lilo
root#  cp /boot/vmlinuz /dosc/lilo       # kernel file
root#  cp /boot/* /dosc/lilo
```

In `/etc/lilo.conf` you must change the path settings for the kernel file and possibly other files accordingly. New in comparison with previous `lilo.conf` files are the options `install` and `map`, which no longer (as in the default setting) point to the Linux directory `/boot`, but to the DOS directory `C:\LILO`.

However, please make sure that the root directory remains unchanged. (The `root` option specifies where the Linux root partition is located. This location has not changed.)

```
# /etc/lilo.conf
boot=/dev/hda
prompt
timeout=100
install=/dosc/lilo/boot.b
map=/dosc/lilo/map
image= /dosc/lilo/vmlinuz
        # use 'root=' to specify your root partition!
        root = /dev/hda8
        label = linux
        read-only
other=/dev/hda1
         label=dos
         table=/dev/hda
```

Now you can execute `lilo`, with the DOS partition still being mounted. During a restart, LILO loads the kernel file from the DOS partition and then starts Linux.

CAUTION

The problem with this kind of LILO installation is that LILO must be able to rely on the fact that the location of the kernel file is not changed. (LILO does not store the file name, but the sector number at which the file starts.) If you defragment the DOS partition or move, copy, or do other things to the `lilo` directory, the location of the file on disk (thus, the start sector) can change. LILO will no longer find the kernel file, and the boot process will fail. Remedy: you must start Linux with a boot diskette, mount the DOS partition and execute `lilo` once again. This will reinstall LILO.

TIP

If you install a new kernel, you must mount the DOS partition again, copy the new kernel file into it and re-execute `lilo`. In contrast to a 'normal' LILO configuration, the file `/boot/vmlinuz` does not play any role at all – the only file that counts is `/dosc/lilo/vmlinuz`.

Starting LILO with the Windows NT boot manager

Windows NT 4.0 uses its owm boot manager which functions in a similar way to LILO and is usually installed in the MBR of the first hard disk or the first partition. With this boot manager, you can start various NT versions and sometimes also an existing Windows 9x.

In version 0.20, LILO is not capable of starting Windows NT itself if the boot sector specified by NT has been overwritten by LILO. Therefore, this section describes the opposite process: the Windows NT boot manager stays where it is, but gets equipped with an additional menu entry for starting LILO. Thus, at computer start-up, you can easily decide between NT and LILO. (Inside LILO you may again have several options to choose from, for example, different Linux kernels.)

In my opinion, this is by far the most elegant way of booting Linux, because even with Windows re-installations and updates (Service Packs, and so on) no problems are to be expected.

NOTE

The NT boot manager and associated files are always installed in the first partition of the first hard disk. This section assumes that this partition is a DOS (or Windows 9x) partition, but not an NTFS partition.

The following procedure should theoretically also work with NTFS partitions – however, due to lack of suitable configuration, this could not be tested. In any case, this would make the LILO set-up more complicated, because currently Linux provides no possibility for writing files to an NTFS partition. You would therefore need to copy the file `bootsec.lin` described below onto a diskette, restart the computer under NT and then copy `bootsec.lin` to the NT partition and edit `BOOT.INI`.

> **TIP** If you have accidentally overwritten the NT boot manager with LILO, you can either try to use `lilo -u` to restore the boot sector, or you need to start the Windows NT setup program with the installation disks and restore the boot sector with the emergency disk. Even if you have the required diskettes, this is a time consuming enterprise.

LILO configuration

The first step is to use `dd` to copy the boot sector of the Linux root partition of your hard disk into a file. Which partition this is can be determined with `rdev` (in the example below, `/dev/hda8`). Please be extremely cautious when entering the `dd` command! With incorrect parameters, `dd` can cause a lot of damage.

```
root#  rdev
/dev/hda8 /
root#  dd if=/dev/hda8 bs=512 count=1 of=/boot/bootsec.lin
```

Now you edit `/etc/lilo.conf` in such a way that `lilo` does not change the boot sector of a hard disk or diskette, but the file `/boot/bootsec.lin` described above. The remaining LILO settings are the same as with a LILO installation in the MBR of a hard disk (see pages 183 and 191). Thus, when you execute `lilo` the next time, only the file `bootsec.lin` is changed.

```
# in /etc/lilo.conf
boot=/boot/bootsec.lin
# ... all other settings as before
```

The next step is to teach the NT start program `NTLDR` that, as well as various Microsoft products, there is something called Linux. All files required for the start-up process are in the first partition of the first hard disk (independently from the hard disk/partition in which NT itself is installed). Therefore, `bootsec.lin` too needs to be copied into that partition.

If this first partition is a FAT partition (that is, a traditional DOS/Windows file system), you can mount this partition into the file system with `mount` and simply copy `bootsec.lin` into its root directory. If, however, this partition is an NTFS partition, you need to copy `bootsec.lin` onto a DOS diskette, start NT, and copy the file from the diskette to the NTFS partition under NT.

Now, you just need to edit the `NTLDR` configuration file `BOOT.INI` (do not forget to create a backup first): this file too is located in the root partition of the first hard disk. (In detail, the file may look different depending on your hardware configuration. For reasons of space, long files have been split across two lines; \ is used as a separator. In `BOOT.INI`, however, these lines must be kept together!)

```
[boot loader]
timeout=60
default=multi(0)disk(0)rdisk(1)partition(2)\WINNT4
[operating systems]
multi(0)disk(0)rdisk(1)partition(2)\WINNT4=\
"Windows NT Workstation, Version 4.0"
```

```
multi(0)disk(0)rdisk(1)partition(2)\WINNT4=\
"Windows NT Workstation, Version 4.0 [VGA Mode]" /basevideo /sos
C:"Microsoft Windows"
```

Now, you append an additional line to the end of the file, namely:

```
C:\bootsec.lin="LILO"
```

If you carry out this modification under Linux, you need to be careful that you are using the correct newline character. (Under DOS/Windows, an additional Ctrl-M character is used. With most Unix editors, input of this character is a long-winded matter (Emacs: Ctrl+Q, Ctrl+M). The easiest solution is to copy an arbitrary line and edit it. During copying, the Ctrl-M at the end of the line is preserved.)

When you now restart your computer, LILO is shown in an additional line besides the operating systems existing so far. When you select this option, `NTLDR` starts LILO. There, you have again all possibilities of LILO, that is, depending on your configuration, you may choose between different Linux kernels.

Starting Linux from DOS (LOADLIN)

With `LOADLIN.EXE` you can start Linux from within DOS. Via an appropriate configuration of `AUTOEXEC.BAT`, DOS can be set up in such a way that after booting you can choose between Linux and DOS. In this respect, `LOADLIN` is a true alternative to LILO.

The biggest advantage of `LOADLIN` is that you do not have to touch your boot sector. The disadvantage is that DOS needs to be available as operating system (a DOS window under Windows is *not* sufficient). `LOADLIN` cannot be used on computers where only Windows NT is installed.

Preparation

The use of `LOADLIN` assumes that you know the device name of your root partition. If you are not sure, execute `df` and write down the name of the file system that is mounted at the mounting point `/` (in the following example, this would be `/dev/sda15`).

```
root#  df
Filesystem         1024-blocks  Used Available Capacity Mounted on
/dev/sda15            303251  261723     25867      91%   /
/dev/scd0             584560  584560         0     100%   /cdrom
/dev/sda12            303251  114286    173304      40%   /home1
/dev/sda11            303251  189963     97627      66%   /usr/local
```

Furthermore, you need a copy of the kernel file that can be read under DOS. You must therefore copy this file into a DOS partition. The easiest way is to mount the DOS partition C: into the Linux file system and to copy the kernel file (generally `/boot/vmlinuz`) into it. A sensible place would be the `C:\LOADLIN` directory which you can, if necessary, create under Linux. In the `mount` command, instead of `/dev/sda1`, you must specify the name of the first DOS partition. If you do not know its name, just execute `fdisk -l`.

```
root#  mkdir /dosc
root#  mount -t msdos /dev/sda1 /dosc  # /dev/sda1: place of
                                       # the DOS partition
root#  mkdir /dosc/loadlin
root#  cp /boot/vmlinuz /dosc/loadlin
root#  cp /cdrom/dosutils/loadlin.exe /dosc/loadlin
root#  umount /dosc
```

Calling `loadlin` manually

The preparations under Linux are now over. Exit Linux with Ctrl+Alt+Del and boot DOS. If you normally work with Windows, exit Windows. (It is not sufficient to open a DOS window under Windows. In Windows 95, you can boot directly under DOS: simply press the F8 key during start-up and select the corresponding option.) Now you can try out `loadlin` under DOS:

```
>  C:
>  CD \LOADLIN
>  SMARTDRV /C                        (only for Windows 3.1)
>  LOADLIN vmlinuz root=/dev/sda15 ro
```

Instead of `/dev/sda15`, you must specify the device name of your own Linux root partition. If you need additional parameters for starting the kernel, you have to specify these as well (see page 48). If you want to work under Linux in text mode with 80×50 characters, the option to be used is `vga=-2`.

CAUTION

Please note that once you have started Linux you can only get back to DOS through a restart. Save all open files, exit Windows properly, and so on. If you use Windows 3.1, the command `SMARTDRV /C` carries out all write operations on the hard disk that might have remained open.

Automatic start of Windows 95 or Linux

Up to this point, starting Linux from DOS still looks rather laborious. A first improvement could be to write a batch file that starts `loadlin` with all parameters. It would be even more elegant if immediately after starting the computer, a menu came up in which you could select between DOS/Windows and Linux. Such a configuration is possible both for DOS 6.0 (to start either DOS or Windows 3.1 or Linux) and for DOS 7.0 (to start either Windows 95 or Linux).

NOTE

This section only describes the version for Windows 95. If you are still running DOS 6.0, please consult `dosutils/LOADLIN.doc/manual.txt` for the necessary steps. The configuration is as easy as the one for Windows 95, though it uses a different syntax.

The Windows 95 boot process is controlled through two text files, `C:\MSDOS.SYS` and `C:\CONFIG.SYS`. Both files are write-protected and generally invisible. If you work with the Explorer, you must use VIEW | OPTIONS to specify that you really want to see all files. The write-protect attribute can be altered with the right mouse button, in the Context menu entry PROPERTIES. Before you modify any of these files, remember to make a backup copy first.

In `MSDOS.SYS` you can specify additional options for the boot process. Very useful are `Logo=0` (no Windows 95 logo, which confuses some graphics cards), `BootGUI=0` (no automatic start of Windows; the computer starts in DOS mode and Windows can be started manually with `win`) and `BootMenuDelay=2` (gives you two seconds of time to activate the system boot menu by pressing F8, but slows down every boot process). The following listing shows the settings on my own computer:

```
; file C:\MSDOS.SYS
[Paths]
WinDir=C:\WINDOWS
WinBootDir=C:\WINDOWS
HostWinBootDrv=C
[Options]
BootMulti=1
BootGUI=0
Network=1
Logo=0
BootMenuDelay=2
;The following lines are required for compatibility with
;other programs.
;Do not remove them (MSDOS.SYS needs to be >1024 bytes).
;xxxxxxxxxxxxxxxxxxxxxxxxxxxxxxxxxxxxxxxxxxxxxxxxxxxxxxxxxxxxxxxxxxxxxa
; ...
```

The `CONFIG.SYS` file is far more interesting. Here you can define a second menu that is automatically displayed after the optional system boot menu (press F8). This menu is defined in the `[menu]` section at the beginning of the file. The syntax is easy: the first word after the keyword `menuitem` serves as an internal identification, the subsequent text is displayed in the menu. `menudefault` selects one of the entries as the default entry and specifies the time (in seconds) during which the user can choose between the other entries.

Next, for each menu ID, a separate section must be defined in order to specify the commands needed for this entry. These commands are similar to the ones found in your `CONFIG.SYS` file. Normally, no device drivers are needed for the Windows start (because Windows uses its own drivers), but they are needed for the DOS start. The line `shell=win` starts Windows and makes sense only if the setting `BootGUI=0` is used in `MSDOS.SYS`. The following file is geared to the peculiarities of the author's computer. Do not copy it blindly, but experiment very carefully with a file of your own.

```
rem file config.sys
[menu]
menuitem=Win95, Windows 95
menuitem=DOS, start in DOS mode
menuitem=Linux, Linux, the better alternative!
menudefault=Linux,10
```

```
[Win95]
shell=win

[DOS]
DEVICE=C:\SCSI\ASPI8DOS.SYS /D
DEVICE=C:\SCSI\ASPICD.SYS /D:ASPICDO
device=C:\WINDOWS\COMMAND\display.sys con=(ega,,1)
Country=043,850,C:\WINDOWS\COMMAND\country.sys

[Linux]
shell=c:\loadlin\loadlin.exe @c:\loadlin\linux1.par
```

The Linux section in `CONFIG.SYS` is limited to a single line which uses `shell` to start the `LOADLIN` program. The parameters for `LOADLIN` cannot be specified directly in `CONFIG.SYS` because, for some unknown reason, DOS converts all parameters into upper case. `LOADLIN`, however, relies on the correct spelling in upper and lower case. On my computer, the parameter file `linux1.par` looks like this:

```
c:/loadlin/vmlinuz root=/dev/sda15 ro vga=-2
```

Obviously, you can extend `CONFIG.SYS` with several entries for different Linux versions, for example if you want to boot alternatively with an old or a new kernel.

TIP

Further information about the structure of `MSDOS.SYS` and `CONFIG.SYS` can be found in good books on Windows 95 administration and in the help file `admin\reskit\helpfile\win95rk.hlp` on the Windows 95 CD-ROM.

6.11 Recompiling the kernel

Essentially, there are three reasons to recompile the kernel:

- You want to show off with your friends and colleagues, boasting your insider knowledge: 'I have compiled the latest Linux kernel myself!'
- You want to optimize the kernel for your hardware and software requirements. Because of the modularized kernel concept, which has by now become a standard with all distributions, this argument has receded very much into the background; however, it has still not lost all its validity. For example, no SCSI drivers are integrated in the RedHat default kernel. Booting on SCSI systems only works by loading the appropriate module as a RAM disk – quite a complicated procedure.
- You want to use a more up-to-date version of the kernel or extend the kernel with a patch.

Thus there is usually no need for average Linux users to compile their own kernels. On the other hand, this is a good way to get to know your system better – and the motto of this book is to allow you to go behind the scenes.

Fear not – compiling does not presume any programming knowledge! You simply need to answer some questions on the configuration of your computer. Then, compilation is carried out fully automatically. Compiling also does not constitute a safety risk – and if you stick to the following instructions you will afterwards be able to start up your computer with both the old and the new kernel.

Preconditions for compiling the kernel are the installation of the kernel code and the installation of an appropriate compiler (see below) together with the associated tools (such as `make`, various libraries). Caution, the kernel code is fairly large! Together with the resulting binary files, it takes up more than 70 Mbytes.

Compiler questions

Today's Linux world knows two popular C compilers, `gcc` (the 'classic' GNU C compiler) and `egcs` (experimental step in the development of GCC). `egcs` is required in particular because of the new libc6 (alias glibc2) (see also page 120).

Further informationen on `egcs` can be found in the egcs-FAQ:

`http://egcs.cygnus.com/faq.html`

For the translation of kernel 2.0.*n* you absolutely need `gcc`, preferably in its version 2.7.*n*. For the new kernel 2.2.*n* it is again recommended that `gcc` is used, however, `egcs` appears to work as well. As the majority of kernel developers uses `gcc`, you would be well advised to do the same.

How do you determine which compiler is used on your system? The easiest way is to find out from which package `gcc` originates:

```
root#  which gcc
/usr/bin/gcc
root#  rpm -qf /usr/bin/gcc
egcs-981208-1
```

In this case, we see that `egcs` is installed. In most distributions, simultaneous installation of `gcc` and `egcs` leads to problems – therefore, you should install `egcs` first, und then `gcc` (probably together with `gccfront`).

Kernel version numbers

There are 'stable' kernel versions (1.0.*n*, 1.2.*n*, 2.0.*n*, 2.2.*n*) and so-called developer or hacker kernels (1.1.*n*, 1.3.*n*, 2.1.*n*, 2.3.*n*, and so on). For the vast majority of Linux users it makes no sense to keep chasing after the latest version of the developer kernel. Developer kernels are only intended for those Linux users who want to participate in the development, test the latest code and maybe correct it. Here, problems must be expected. However, once you have installed an optimized kernel for your computer and it runs without problems, there is hardly any reason for an update.

This section is based on kernel 2.2.*n*. At the time of writing these lines, the most up-to-date version available was 2.2.pre7ac4. Thus, kernel 2.2 was nearly, but not entirely ready. Big changes between the version described here and version 2.2.0 are, in any case, not to be expected. (pre7 means that we are dealing with the seventh pre-release of the anxiously awaited kernel 2.2.0. ac4 means that, in addition, the fourth patch version to 2.2.pre7 by Alan Cox was taken into account. Such patches are extensions which are not yet officially authorized but the majority of them will probably be integrated into 2.2.0.)

Overview

Now, before the real fun begins, here is an overview of the subsections which are to follow:

- Modules: explains what modules are and their advantages.
- Installing/updating the kernel code: explains where to obtain a current kernel code and how to install it (including patches).
- Configuring the kernel: before the compilation begins, hundreds of options can be set.
- Compiling the kernel: explains how to compile and install the kernel.

TIP

Further information about kernel compilation can be found in `/usr/src/linux/README` and in the files in `/usr/src/linux/Documentation`. Please also read the Linux Kernel FAQ!.

`http://www.tux.org/lkml/`

Modules

Many kernel components can be either directly integrated into the kernel or loaded at a later stage in the form of modules. Modules exist since version 1.2, however, it has taken some time for this concept to be used by all distributions. Modules have several advantages:

- Kernel modules can be loaded on demand. If a module is only needed infrequently, this can save memory space, that is, the kernel is not larger than absolutely necessary.
- In case of a hardware change (a new network card, for example) no new kernel needs to be compiled: it is sufficient to load the new module. In most Linux distributions, this happens automatically.
- When a new kernel module is developed, there is no need to recompile the kernel every time. It is sufficient to recompile the module, which can then be tested under normal operating conditions.
- Hardware manufacturers can provide modules as binary files to support their hardware without having to release the source code.

In spite of all the advantages of the module concept, a monolithic kernel which contains exactly the modules required for your hardware is still a viable alternative. A compact kernel is often easier to maintain and does not have to rely on various modules to be installed in the right place and in the required version.

TIP Further details on the handling of modules are contained in the files `/usr/src/linux/Documentation/modules.txt` and `./kmod.txt`.

NOTE With kernel 2.2, module management has fundamentally changed. While up to kernel 2.0 the `kerneld` program was responsible for loading modules, this task is now taken over by the `kmod` component of the kernel. However, only a few changes directly affect the user. On page 203 you can find information on a kernel update in a distribution which is not yet preconfigured for Kernel 2.2.

Using modules

All current distributions are set up so that modules are started automatically – either by the `kerneld` program (up to version 2.0) or directly by the kernel (since version 2.2). An example: you use the `mount` command to mount a CD-ROM into your file system. This automatically activates the `isofs` module, which is needed for reading the ISO-9660 file system of the CD-ROM.

In other words: as a rule, module management is automatic and transparent, without the user having to intervene with the manual module management programs described in the following paragraphs. However, if it does not work (for example, after a not entirely successful kernel update), you should know the module commands that allow you to load modules manually.

```
insmod module_name [option=value ...]
```

Integrates the specified module into the kernel. The module name is specified without path information and without the `.o` extension; thus, for example, `insmod nfs` for the NFS module stored in `/lib/modules/`*n*`/fs/nfs.o`, where *n* is the version of the current kernel. With `insmod`, various options can be passed to the module (in the same way as the kernel options in monolithic kernels; see page 48).

```
modprobe module_name [option=value ...]
```

`modprobe` works in the same way as `insmode`; however, it is checked whether the module to be loaded depends on other modules. This assumes that the `depmod -a` command has been used beforehand to create the dependency file `/lib/modules/`*n*`/modules.dep`. (These dependency files are usually created during installation of the kernel modules, that is, there is hardly any need to execute `depmod` manually.)

```
rmmod module_name
```

Removes the specified module from the kernel and frees the corresponding memory space. The command can only be executed successfully if the module is not currently in use.

lsmod

lsmod supplies a list of all modules presently integrated into the kernel.

kerneld

kerneld is a daemon which automatically recognizes when a particular kernel module is needed. kerneld is only used up to kernel version 2.0.

The daemon loads modules on demand (and removes them when they are no longer used). kerneld is based on the above-mentioned dependency file of depmod and the optional control file /etc/conf.modules. This file can be used to specify options for individual modules. The syntax of conf.modules is described in the man page for depmod.

kmod

kmod is not an independent program, but a kernel component since kernel 2.2. It takes over the task of kerneld, as far as automatic loading of modules is concerned. kmod too takes /etc/conf.modules into account (through a detour via modprobe). In contrast to kerneld, kmod does not bother to remove unused kernel modules.

If you wish unused modules to be removed automatically, you should set up crontab to execute rmmod -a every five minutes.

```
root#  export EDITOR=emacs
root#  crontab -e
```

crontab starts an editor to modify the crontab file for root. There, you enter the following line:

```
0-59/5 * * * * /sbin/rmmod -a
```

In distributions delivered with kernel 2.2, no change of crontab will be needed because a corresponding setting will be preconfigured. (When these lines were written, no distribution yet included kernel 2.2.)

Installing/updating the kernel code

The kernel source code is located in the /usr/src/linux directory. If this directory is empty, you have not installed the kernel code. All distributions offer the installation of the kernel code at least as an option. However, the kernel included in the distribution is more often than not already outdated.

Current kernel versions (in the form of compressed tar archives) can be found on the Internet, for example under the following addresses:

```
ftp://ftp.gwdg.de/pub/linux/kernel/v2.2
ftp://ftp.funet.fi/pub/Linux/PEOPLE/Linus/v2.2
```

On the Internet servers of your distributions, you will also find kernel files of the stable versions in the relevant package format. Developer kernels are seldom found.

In principle, there are two possibilities for updating the kernel code:

- You can use so-called patch files to update from one version to the one immediately following. For example, if you want to update from version 2.2.29 to 2.2.30, you must execute the `patch` command to carry out the kernel patch `patch-2.2.30`. `patch-2.2.30` is a text file that describes at which points the individual files of the version 2.2.29 source code must be modified. (Thus, the complete and correct source code of the immediately preceding version is a necessary precondition for any successful update.) Patch files have the advantage of being relatively small and can be easily obtained via the Internet using FTP.
- In the case of major version changes – for example, from 2.2.3 to 2.2.30 – you would have to carry out dozens of patches in a row. This is not very practical and it may become a source of errors. For this reason, the kernel code is also available as a complete package. Typical file names look something like `linux-2.2.30.tar.bz2`. Such compressed archive files (about 11 Mbytes in size) must be installed in the `/usr/src` directory using `tar`.

Now to the details: new kernels are usually installed in `/usr/src/linux`. If this directory contains an existing kernel, there will be chaos. Therefore it is sensible either to delete the old kernel code (`rm -rf /usr/src/linux`) or, if you have enough disk space available, to rename it. (The following discussion assumes that currently kernel 2.2.29 is installed and an update to version 2.2.30 is to be carried out.)

```
root#  cd /usr/src
root#  mv linux linux-2.2.29  # backup of the current kernel code
```

Sometimes, `/usr/src/linux` is only a link to the directory in which the currently installed Linux code is located:

```
root#  cd /usr/src
root#  ls -l linux
lrwxrwxrwx   1 root  root    11 Apr 30 16:58 linux -> linux-2.2.29
```

In this case, you only need to delete the link before you install the new kernel code:

```
root#  rm linux
```

Now unpack the new kernel code into the `linux` directory. Kernel archives are always compressed, either with `gzip` or (ever more frequently) with `bzip2`. In the following lines, the `tar` options for both variations are indicated.

```
root#  cd /usr/src
root#  tar -xIvf linux-2.2.30.tar.bz2
root#  tar -xzvf linux-2.2.30.tar.gz
```

If you want to update this kernel to the next version, you must get hold of the patch file `patch-2.2.31.gz` (for example, via FTP). Subsequently, you change to the `./linux` directory, decompress the patch, and apply it to the kernel code with `patch -p1`.

```
root#  cd /usr/src/linux
root#  bunzip2 -cd patch-2.2.31.bz2 | patch -p1
```

If the patch file is present in uncompressed form, the patch command is:

```
root#  patch -p1 < patch-2.2.31
```

With the following command, you can undo a patch:

```
root#  patch -R -p1 < patch-2.2.31
```

NOTE

Kernel patches always apply to the official kernel code released by Linus Torvalds. Many distributions, however, use modified kernels into which various, 'unofficial' patches have been built in. Before you modify any kernel code yourself by means of a patch, you should always make sure that you have a correct basis from which to start.

Information on the current kernel code and a collection of unofficial patches which confer additional functionality to the kernel (but which have not yet been fully tested or are not generally desired) can be found at the following addresses:

http://www.linuxhq.com/
http://www.linuxmama.com/

Configuring the kernel

Before you can compile the kernel, you must edit the `.config` in the `/usr/src/linux` directory by entering all options that apply to the new kernel (which SCSI card, which Ethernet card, which network functions, and so on). `.config` is not edited manually, but by means of a special configuration program which is started via `make`. Since kernel version 2.0, three different variations of this program have been available. (You must choose one of the three `make` versions listed below.)

```
root#  cd /usr/src/linux
root#  make config          or
root#  make menuconfig      or
root#  make xconfig
```

`make config` is the least elegant version. You must answer an endless list of questions one after the other. The advantage of this variation is that there is no need to install any additional program.

`make menuconfig` is much easier to handle: the configuration is still carried out in text mode, but you can now choose the individual configuration points from a menu. It is therefore possible to change a single point very quickly without having to repeat all other settings. `make menuconfig` only works if the ncurses library containing the necessary screen control functions is installed.

`make xconfig` is even more sophisticated: this variation only runs under X and only if Tcl/Tk is installed. The configuration is now carried out via mouse clicks and in a very well-designed program.

Independently of the variation you choose, you will still have to answer a number of questions about the kernel configuration. Do not rely on seemingly reasonable default settings – even though they are all right with many options. If you have any

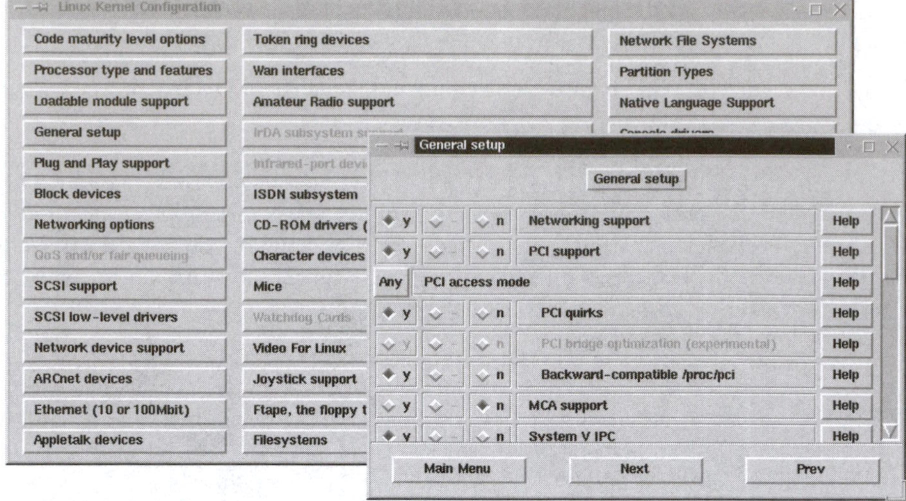

Figure 6.2 Kernel configuration under X.

doubt, please read the very informative help texts available for each option. However, if you have little experience with Linux or any other Unix, even this information will confuse you. Therefore, this section presents further basic information on this subject without, however, dealing in depth with every single option.

Fundamentals

Basically, you have to decide between two types of kernel: monolithic kernels contain all required drivers directly in the kernel and do not support modules. Modularized kernels are capable of including additional modules on top of the integrated kernels during current operation. As a rule, a modularized kernel is the better option.

For many components, you have the choice between three alternatives: YES / MODULE / NO. YES means that this component is directly integrated into the kernel. MODULE means that this component is compiled as a module (only sensible with a modularized kernel). NO means that the component is not compiled at all. With a monolithic kernel, you must specify NO for all components that you do not require (otherwise the kernel becomes unnecessarily large). With a modularized kernel NO will save you some time (because the module does not have to be compiled), but you lose flexibility. Who knows whether you will not need this module at some point in the future?

CAUTION

No matter whether you are building a monolithic or a modularized kernel: you must in any case integrate directly (option YES) all components that you need for booting. If, for example, the root partition is located on a SCSI disk, the corresponding SCSI driver must not be a module, but an integrated part of the kernel. If the root partition is an `ext2` file system (presumably on 99 per cent of all Linux computers), this module too needs to be integrated into the kernel.

Options after options ...

Code maturity level

Here you can specify whether the Alpha driver and other half-finished components should be considered for the configuration. Normally, you will do without them. You need to specify YES only if you want to test brand new kernel components

Processor type

The processor selection (386, 486, Pentium, or Pentium Pro) influences speed and size of the code. Please note that the code is upward compatible, but not downward compatible. 486 code can therefore be executed on any Pentium without problems, whereas Pentium Pro code might cause a crash on a traditional Pentium. *Math emulation* is only needed if you have a very old processor without a coprocessor (such as 386, 486 SX). If you have a motherboard with only one CPU (which is usually the case), you must set the *Symmetric multi-processing* option to NO.

Loadable module support

Specifies whether and how the kernel can handle modules. If you want to build a modularized kernel, you need to set *Enable module support* to YES. *Set version information* refers to whether the kernel should also load modules that were compiled for a different kernel version. Usually, this is not required, therefore NO.

Kernel module loader (in short `kmod`) is a new feature in kernel 2.2, which replaces the `kerneld` program. If you do not want to load kernel modules manually, you better specify YES!

General setup

Network support is needed in any case, even if you do not possess a network. (Many internal commands rely on the network protocol.) *PCI* too must be set to YES for all modern motherboards.

System V IPC is a further form of Linux internal communication used by several programs (especially the DOS emulator) – therefore you should say YES to this option as well.

New distributions exclusively consist of ELF programs. Thus, you definitely need *ELF support*. Often, older programs must be executed in the a.out binary format – therefore you should select YES or MODULE for this option as well.

The *Parallel port support* option refers to the parallel interface to which the printer is usually connected: YES or MODULE.

Plug and play support

Here you can activate the (still rudimentary) support for plug & play cards. Do not expect that thanks to this option the kernel will fully automatically recognize every plug & play hardware device – as a rule, you will still need the `isapnp` utility program.

Block devices

Floppy support is probably a matter of course. Also with *Enhanced IDE support* the correct setting is nearly always YES (not MODULE, because access to EIDE hard disks must already work during booting!). Some additional options concern EIDE special devices and bugfixes. (Some EIDE cards are faulty and the kernel contains special code that circumvents these faults.)

Use DMA by default activates bus master DMA mode, if the motherboard and hard disk are recognized. If this is not the case, the `hdparm` command must be used to activate this performance-increasing mode manually (see page 156). In rare cases, automatic DMA activation leads to problems – in this case you need to specify NO.

Loopback device support is normally only needed if you plan to burn CD-ROMs. This is not the loopback interface known from network configuration, but the possibility of using a file as a file system. When this component is available, you can mount and check an ISO image as a read-only file system (using `mount`).

Multiple devices support allows several hard disk partitions to be combined into one logical partition (RAID, see also page 157).

Some distributions (in particular RedHat) use a RAM disk for loading modules when booting in their default configuration. If you specify YES for the relevant modules (usually a SCSI driver), this detour is omitted. However, in this case you also need to modify `/etc/lilo.conf` accordingly. If, instead, you wish to continue using a RAM disk for booting, you must specify YES with both of the options *RAM disk support* and *Initial RAM disk* (not MODULE!).

Network options

Here, our best advice is that, in case of doubt, you accept all default settings. In any case, you need TCP/IP support. *IP forwarding/gatewaying* is important if your computer is intended to work as a connection between a local network and the Internet or as a PPP or SLIP server. This option is not required for normal use of PPP/SLIP. Some other options in which you will often have to make changes follow below (*Network device support*).

You will find information about many network options in the *Linux Network Administration Guide* of the Linux Documentation Project (see page 79).

SCSI support

If you use a SCSI hard disk, you must answer YES to the first two options; for a streamer or a CD-ROM drive, to the next two options as well. You will also need SCSI support if you want to operate a ZIP drive through the parallel interface.

SCSI Generic Support is only needed for direct addressing of SCSI components. This is mostly the case with CW-Write devices.

SCSI low-level drivers

Here, a number of SCSI cards is listed. Find your card and select the corresponding option (and no other!) with YES, if your root file system is located on a SCSI disk. Also, the driver for ZIP drives on the parallel interface is part of the SCSI low-level components.

Network device support

If you want to communicate with another computer in any form whatsoever, this is the place to select YES. This also applies if your computer is only to be connected to the Internet via PPP/SLIP. *Dummy net support* is often needed for SLIP or PPP configuration. (In kernel 2.2.pre7ac4 this option was to be found in the Arcnet group – but this will hopefully be remedied.)

PLIP allows data exchange via the parallel port (a reasonable choice only in very rare cases); printer access is then no longer possible. *PPP* and *SLIP* are two variations to achieve Internet access via the serial interface. If you do not know which variation your Internet provider prefers (probably PPP), simply select both. (In kernel 2.2.pre7ac4 these options were to be found in the Appletalk group – but this will hopefully be remedied.)

Xy network devices

You need to set the appropriate options to YES or MODULE, if you own a corresponding card. The popular NE-2000-compatible cards belong to the subgroup *Other ISA cards* of the *Ethernet (10 or 100 Mbits)* group. The PCI version of this card can instead be found in the subgroup *EISA, PCI and onboard controllers.* Do not activate a network card that you do not have!

ISDN support

If you want to use ISDN. Information about ISDN can also be found on the following WWW page:

`http://alumni.caltech.edu/~dank/isdn/`
`http://www.suse.com` (support database, keyword ISDN)

CD-ROM drivers

In most cases you will *not* have to select any option, even if you possess a CD-ROM drive. Here, only those CD-ROM drives are listed that have their own interface. Most of the common CD-ROM drives, however, are IDE (see *block devices*) or SCSI drives (see *SCSI support*).

Character devices

The options *Virtual terminal* and *Support for console* must be YES – otherwise you cannot even log in locally.

Standard serial support and *Parallel printer support* are needed to use the serial and parallel interfaces. *Mouse support* refers to mice that are not connected to the serial port – amongst others, the ever more popular PS/2 mice. If you are in doubt, choose YES – then you can activate the appropriate driver in the *Mice* group.

File systems

Quota support allows you to limit the disk space requirements for single users (but requires the installation of additional programs). If you want to access DOS or Windows partitions, you must select *DOS FAT* (base system) and either *MSDOS support* or the extended *VFAT support* (Windows 9x). *Umsdos*, in contrast, is only needed if your Linux is installed in a DOS partition.

ISO9660 is indispensable if you want to use CD-ROM drives. The option JOLIET is of interest if you wish to view the full file name on CD-ROMs for Microsoft Windows as well.

Proc support is needed in any case to allow you to use programs such as `ps` or `top`. *Second extended filesystem* is the most important file system in Linux. Here you *must* specify YES in order to be able to boot.

Network file systems

You will need *NFS support* if you want to use file systems of remote computers via a network. *SMB support* allows use of the Windows file system over the network (similar to NFS for the Unix file system). However, this assumes the installation of additional programs and some configuration work.

Native language support

Some Microsoft file systems (NTFS, Joliet CD-ROMs) support Unicode characters in file names. For these to be recognized, the corresponding language options need to be activated. In any case, you should activate the codepages 437 (US), 850 (Europe) and all other NLS-ISO options. The best way is simply to choose MODULE with all the options!

Console drivers

To enable Linux to display text on VGA cards, the option *VGA text* must be set to YES. *Video mode selection* allows special VGA text modes to be activated via LILO (for example with 80×50 characters).

Sound

If you are not happy with the beep from your built-in speaker, at this point you can select your sound card and set DMA, I/O and interrupt numbers, if needed. As a rule, it is recommended that sound support is activated as a module – otherwise, the sound support will substantially increase the size of the kernel file.

Compiling and installing the kernel

After you have invested some of your time configuring the kernel, it is now the computer's turn to get to work. With the following commands, you will keep your computer busy for a while (about ten minutes on a Pentium 133).

```
root#  cd /usr/src/linux
root#  make dep          # check dependencies
```

```
root#  make clean        # delete old object files
root#  make bzImage      # start compilation
```

TIP Do not forget that Linux is a multitasking system. You can switch to another console and read about some topics in the online documentation, write a letter, and so on. As long as you do not carry out time-consuming operations, you will hardly notice any delay caused by the simultaneous compilation.

The result at the end of this process is the file `bzImage` in the directory `/usr/src/linux/arch/i386/boot`. Depending on the configuration, the compressed kernel should have a size of about 500 Kbytes.

Compiling modules

During kernel configuration, you may choose for a large number of kernel components whether to integrate the component directly into the kernel or to compile it as a module. Then `make zImage` (see above) only creates the generic kernel without the specified modules. The selected modules need to be created separately by means of `make modules`. Scattered all across the kernel code file tree, module files are created that bear the extension `*.o`. In the `modules` directory, links to these files are established.

CAUTION Depending on your computer's configuration, for booting Linux you need at least the drivers for your hard disk (perhaps SCSI), for the file system contained on it (usually `ext2`), plus the modules for elementary network support (without specific hardware drivers).

With `make modules_install` the module files are finally installed where the module management programs (such as `insmod`) expect them to be, namely in the `/lib/modules/`*n* directory (where *n* is the current kernel version).

```
root#  cd /usr/src/linux
root#  make modules
root#  make modules_install
```

Installing the kernel

Obviously, this newly created kernel is not yet active. So far, only a new file has been created, nothing more. The new kernel can only be activated at the next startup of Linux, and even then only if you either create a new boot diskette or call the `lilo` program and activate the new kernel file in the boot program.

Usually, the active kernel file is located in the Linux root directory `/` or in `/boot` and is commonly named `vmlinuz`. Before you move the newly generated kernel into this location, you should rename the old and well-proven kernel file `vmlinuz` into `vmlinuz.bak`:

```
root#  mv /boot/vmlinuz  /boot/vmlinuz.bak
root#  mv /usr/src/linux/arch/i386/boot/bzImage /boot/vmlinuz
```

If Linux is started with LILO, the already existing entries in `/etc/lilo.conf` are extended by a new entry that allows booting of the old kernel (file `/vmlinuz.bak`. Instead of `/dec/hda8`, you must obviously specify the root partition of your own computer. Before you modify this file, please read the section about LILO configuration (page 183)!

```
# LILO configuration file: /etc/lilo.conf
... as before
# boot Linux automatically from /dev/hda8
image = /boot/vmlinuz
  root = /dev/hda8
  label = linux
  read-only
# alternative: 'linuxbak' to boot the old kernel
image= /boot/vmlinuz.bak
  root = /dev/hda8
  label = linuxbak
  read-only
```

The modified LILO configuration file must now be activated by a call to `lilo`. If booting the new kernel leads to a crash, simply try it again, press the Shift key during booting and specify 'linuxbak' as the boot kernel. In this way, you can boot with the old kernel and retry the compilation.

As alternatives to LILO, the new kernel can also be transferred onto a boot diskette, or `loadlin` can be used for booting (see pages 181 or 196).

Update to kernel 2.2

Most up-to-date distributions come with kernel 2.2. If you want to install kernel 2.2 yourself even with an older distribution, here are some tips:

- It is not sufficient simply to exchange the kernel. As a rule, a large number of tools and commands (network commands, process administration, and so on) must be updated as well. Please read `/usr/doc/linux/Documentation/Changes` on this subject. Only relatively recent distributions (RedHat 5.2, SuSE 6.0) are ready for working with kernel 2.2.
- `kerneld` is no longer supported. Usually, this causes no problems. If `kerneld` is started in the Init process, the program simply remains without effect. Nevertheless, you should adapt the Init script accordingly and do without starting `kerneld` if `/proc/sys/kernel/modprobe` exists. Make sure that you deactivate the `kmod` option during kernel configuration.
- Numbering of printer devices has changed. (The first parallel interface is now by default addressed as `/dev/lp0` and not as `/dev/lp1` as before. This behavior can, however, be changed by options passed to the `lp` module – see `parport.txt` in the kernel documentation directory.)

  On my test system (SuSE 6.0, kernel 2.2.pre7ac4), I also had problems with automatic loading of the `lp` module while attempting to prints texts. Printing only works if the modules `parport`, `parport_pc`, and `lp` are loaded in this order. However, only `parport` was automatically activated; access to the printer devices was not possible. This could be remedied either by manually loading the modules or by making the following change in `/etc/conf.modules` (followed by a restart):

```
# Addition to /etc/conf.modules
post-install parport    insmod parport_pc
post-install parport_pc insmod lp
```

This ensures that, after `parport`, `parport_pc` and `lp` are automatically activated one after the other. See also `parport.txt`.

- The devices `/dev/cua`*n* for serial interfaces are no longer supported. You must use `/dev/ttyS`*n* instead.
- The locking behavior of NFS has changed. If you encounter locking problems, you can remedy them by means of the `nolock` option in `mount` or `fstab`.
- The kernel files are larger in size than before. If LILO complains that the kernel file is too large, you need to compile the kernel with `make bzImage` instead of `make zImage`. If this does not help, you need to break up more parts of the kernel treating them as modules.

6.12 Package management (RPM)

Package management helps with the installation of additional packages and with updating or removing of existing ones. This section describes the `rpm` command, which is used for this purpose in nearly all distributions.

Preliminary remarks

RPM is not the only package format. Until recently, most distributions used compressed `tar` archives with the extension `*.tgz` (thus, TGZ format). The Slackware distribution still employs this format. However, it has a number of shortcomings:

- It is extremely difficult to maintain an overview of the currently installed packages (and their versions).
- It is impossible to determine to which package a specific file belongs.
- Package updates are problematic (to put it mildly). For example, an update will also overwrite configuration files, because the TGZ package has no information on which files serve which purpose.
- Dependency information lacks completely. Thus, you can install a package X although the package Y needed for execution is missing.

Part of these limitations can be circumvented by administration of additional information which is managed either inside the package (in a file with a special name) or outside (in a central package description file). Thus, the SuSE distribution recognized package dependencies long before the change to RPM was made.

Nevertheless, during the stormy development of Linux, the need quickly arose for a more modern format. Unfortunately, this immediately resulted in two formats which were more or less developed in parallel and which by now have largely the same features: the RPM (RedHat Package Manager) format and the DEB (Debian) format. Both formats are free (GPL) and can therefore also be used by other distributions.

In this section, we limit ourselves to description of the RPM format which seems to be imposing itself as a *de facto* standard. (Besides RedHat, it is employed, amongst others, in the distributions of Caldera, DLD, and SuSE.)

REFERENCE General information on how to carry out software updates can be found on page 56. Information on handling of TGZ packages is given at the end of this section (see page 220) and in the description of the `tar` command (page 483). If you work with Slackware, you should also read the online documentation on `setup` and `pkgtool`. Tips for handling the Debian tools `dselect` and `dpkg` can be found from page 711 onward.

TIP Some distributions supply the Perl script `alien` which can be used for conversion of packages between the different formats.

RPM basics

Most RPM packages consist of two files: one file is usually located in the `RPMS` directory and contains the binary files needed for the installation of the package (thus, binary package). The second file is located in the `SRPMS` directory and contains the source code employed to assemble the binary package (therefore, source package).

The package name contains a substantial amount of information: `abc-2.0.7-1.i386.rpm`, for example, denotes the package `abc` with version number 2.0.7, `rpm` release 1. (If an error occurred during assembly of a package, or additional online documentation was included, or other changes were made, we find release numbers greater than 1 for a specific version number. Thus the version number refers to the program proper; the release number to the `rpm` assembly.)

The extension `i386` indicates that the package contains binary files for the Intel version of Linux. (Since there are also Linux versions for other processors.) The file containing the source code of the `abc` package has the file name `abc-2.0.7-1.src.rpm`.

As well as the files to be installed, the package file includes a number of management issues: a brief package description, again information on version numbers, positioning inside the group hierarchy (evaluated, for example, by `glint`), dependencies from other packages, and so on. Dependencies exist, for example, when a package assumes a specific programming language such as Perl or a specific library. In this case, these packages need to be installed first.

`rpm` manages a database with information on all installed binary packages. This database is stored in seven `*.rpm` files in the directory `/var/lib/rpm`.

Under no circumstances must the files of the `rpm` database be changed! To keep the files up-to-date, packages must not be removed by deleting their files, but by means of a regular deinstallation (`rpm -u`). The amount of space required for the four files is fairly high (on a system with 600 Mbytes, about 12 Mbytes).

> **NOTE** Despite the `*.rpm` extension, the four database files are not `rpm` packages, but files in an `rpm`-specific binary format. The database only contains information on binary packages; packages installed via source code compilation are not included in the database.

The `rpm` command

For most users, `rpm` only fulfills administrative tasks. Advanced users, however, can employ `rpm` also to assemble their own packages – this aspect of `rpm` usage will, however, not be discussed.

> **TIP** Depending on the distribution, other, more user-friendly programs are available as alternatives to `rpm`: `glint`, `kpackage`, `yast`, and so on. An overview can be found in a separate section from page 732 onward.

The advantage of direct employment of `rpm` is that, on the one hand, you save on the overhead of other programs (use without X); on the other hand, `rpm` provides substantially more possibilities for obtaining information on packages and their files.

```
rpm --install [options] file_name
rpm --install [options] ftp://ftp_server/file_name
```

`-i` or `--install` installs the specified package. If it is a binary package, it is automatically installed at the predefined location in the `root` directory. The second variation automatically establishes an FTP connection.

If the additional option `--test` is used, `rpm` does not perform any changes, but merely displays what would happen during an actual installation.

The installation location can be changed by means of the additional option `--root directory`.

With the `--nodeps` option you can install a package even if `rpm` believes that various dependencies are not met. The `--force` option forces an installation (even if `rpm` believes that the package is already installed).

With the `--noscripts` option, automatic execution of installation programs is disabled. (This may, however, lead to the consequence that the program you just installed does not work as expected.)

> **TIP** In the current version, it is unfortunately impossible to install only a single file or a selection of files. You can only install the entire package (or nothing). One possible remedy is the `mc` file manager, which displays the contents of `*.rpm` files as a virtual directory and is capable of extracting individual files.

If the specified package is a source package, the program code and the configuration files are installed in `/usr/src`. The location of the installation can in this case be set by a change in `/etc/rpmrc`.

```
rpm --upgrade [options] file_name
rpm --upgrade [options] ftp://ftp_server/file_name
```

With `-U` or `--upgrade` you can update an existing binary package. Automatic backups are created of changed configuration files of the current package; all other files of the current package are deleted. With the additional option `--oldpackage` you can replace a newer package with an older one. For upgrades as well, `--nodeps` can be set to have package dependencies ignored.

```
rpm --verify [options] package_name
```

With `-V` or `--verify` you can check whether any files of a package have changed with respect to the original installation. (If no file has changed, `rpm` yields no output.) In contrast to the installation, only the package name, not the entire file name, is specified as a parameter (for example, `abc` for the package file `abc-2.0.7-1.i386.rpm`).

```
rpm --erase [options] package_name
```

The option `-e` or `--erase` removes an existing package. If, in addition, you use the option `--nodeps`, the package is removed even if other packages depend on it.

```
rpm --query -a
rpm --query [options] package_name
rpm --query -f [options] file
rpm --query -p [options] package_file
```

The option `-q` or `--query` offers many different ways of application which make the syntax slightly confusing. The first three syntax variations refer to installed packages; the fourth variation can be used to obtain information on a not yet installed `*.rpm` file.

In the simplest form, with the additional option `-a`, `rpm` supplies an unsorted list of all packages.

If you specify a package name as a parameter (for example `abc`), `rpm` checks whether the package is installed. If this is the case, `rpm` returns the complete name with version and release number (`abc-2.0.7-1`).

With the additional option `-f` you can determine to which package a specific files of your system belongs. This is particularly useful with configuration files. `rpm -qf /etc/fdprm`, for example, returns the package name `util-linux-2.5-7`.

The additional option `-p` allows you to obtain information on a not yet installed package. In this case, the parameter must be the file name of a `*.rpm`file. This option can also be applied to source code packages.

The last three syntax variations can be combined with some further options. Then, `rpm` supplies not only the package name with version and release number, but also some additional information:

`-i` : brief description of the package, compressed size
`-l` : list of all files in the package
`-lv` : as above, but with files size, access rights, and so on
`-c` : list of all configuration files of the package
`-d` : list of all files with online documentation on the package
`--scripts`: list of all installation programs

```
rpm --query [options] --whatprovides name
rpm --query [options] --whatrequires name
rpm --query [options] --provides [-p] package_file
rpm --query [options] --requires [-p] package_file
```

The above query options are used to determine package dependencies. The options `whatprovides` and `whatrequires` can be used to search for all installed packages which provide or require the package or the library `name`. Please make sure that the spelling is correct. These two options are not suitable for searching through not yet installed packages.

The options `provides` and `requires` allow you to generate a list of all packages and libraries provided or required by a specific package. These options can also be used for not yet installed package files (option `-p`). `provides` and `requires` are so-to-speak the reverse procedures of `whatprovides` and `whatrequires`. In the one case, dependencies are sought that result from a package; in the other case, packet names are sought that satisfy these dependencies.

All four options can be combined with `-i`, `-l`, `-lv`, `-c`, and `-d` (see above).

Examples

`root# rpm -i /cdrom/RedHat/RPMS/xv-3.10a-5.i386.rpm`
installs the graphics program `xv`.

`root# rpm -qa`
supplies a list of all installed packages.

`root# rpm -qa | grep XFree86`
supplies a list of all installed packages whose names begin with `XFree86`.

`root# rpm -qi perl`
supplies information on the Perl packages (provided it is installed).

`root# rpm -ql perl`
lists all files in the Perl package.

`root# rpm -qip /cdrom/RedHat/RPMS/perl-5.003-4.i386.rpm`
supplies information on the Perl package on the CD-ROM.

```
root# rpm -qf /usr/lib/libz.so
```
indicates the package of origin of the file `/usr/lib/libz.so`.

```
root# rpm -qp --provides xpm-3.4h-3.i386.rpm
```
indicates which packages/libraries are provided by the `xpm` package.

```
root# rpm -qp --requires pine-3.95-2.i386.rpm
```
indicates which packages/libraries are required for operation of `pine`.

```
root# rpm -q --whatprovides libc.so.5
```
indicates which (already installed) package provides the `libc` library.

```
root# rpm -q --whatrequires libc.so.5
```
supplies a nearly endless list of all installed packages that depend on the `libc` library.

TIP

Finding a file: In spite of all undisputed advantages of `rpm`, a frequent problem arises: in which (not yet installed) package do we find a specific file? (If you work with `glint`, there is an additional problem: where in the RedHat hierarchy do we find a specific package?) The answer to both questions is supplied by the following command. It displays all available information on all packages of a directory on screen via `less`. In `less` you enter a search text with / and thus search for file names.

```
root# rpm -qpli /cdrom/RedHat/RPMS/* | less
```

Package dependencies

Your first-time confrontation with dependencies will probably be when you get the following error message during an installation attempt:

```
root#  cd /cdrom/RedHat/RPMS
root#  rpm -i vga_tetris-0.4-3.i386.rpm
failed dependencies:
        libvga.so.1 is needed by vga_tetris-0.4-3
        libvgagl.so.1 is needed by vga_tetris-0.4-3
```

Thus, `vga_tetris` can only be installed when `libvga` and `libvgagl` are available. If you now search for the `libvga` package on the CD-ROM, you will be astonished to discover that this package does not exist at all. The dependency list may contain library names, package names, and so-called virtual package names. The search for the required package appears like this:

```
root#  rpm -qpi --provides *.rpm | less
```

In `less`, you use / to search for the text `libvga`. In this way, you discover that both `libvga` and `libvgagl` are contained in the package `aout-libs`. (This package includes libraries in the old `a.out` format, which are only required for compatibility reasons with old Linux programs.) After you have installed the `aout-libs` package, the installation of `vga_tetris` will work. (With a bit of bad luck, `aout-libs` is in turn dependent on other packages which you must install beforehand.)

NOTE When you read the `rpm` documentation, you might expect that a package search can be carried out more easily with the option `--whatprovides libvga`. This option is, however, only designed for use with already installed packages, which is of no help with installation problems.

Package dependencies also apply to deinstallation. You cannot, for example, remove a package on which other programs are still dependent. Thus, if you have installed both `svgalib` and `vgq_tetris`, and now try to remove `svgalib`, you get the following error message:

```
root#  rpm -e aout-libs
removing these packages would break dependencies:
        libvgagl.so.1 is needed by vga_tetris-0.4-3
        libvga.so.1 is needed by vga_tetris-0.4-3
```

In some cases – for example if you have installed individual packages not with `rpm` but with `tar` – `rpm` complains about non-satisfied dependencies although the missing files are present. (They are merely missing in the `rpm` database.) In such cases, you can force installation or deinstallation with `--nodeps`. However, please use this option only when you really know what you are doing!

TIP Extensive online documentation on `rpm` can be found in `man rpm`, in the RPM-HOWTO, and in the README files in `/usr/doc/rpm` or `/usr/doc /packages/rpm`.

`rpm` user interfaces

Distribution-specific tools

Although by now most distributions use the same package format, exchange of packages between different distributions continues to be difficult. Reasons for this are not only a different preconfiguration and different installation paths, but also the management of dependency information for which no standard exists.

For this reason, practically every distribution is supplied together with a separate program which builds on `rpm`, but which also provides additional functions. Two of these programs are described in Appendices B and C:

`gnorpm` (RedHat): page 732
`yast` (SuSE): page 741

RPM tools for the X Window System

The unfathomable RedHat package hierarchy of `glint` has driven many users to despair. Alternatives to this program are, amongst others, `xrpm`, `kpackage` (KDE), `kpackviewer` (also KDE), and `mc` (page 496).

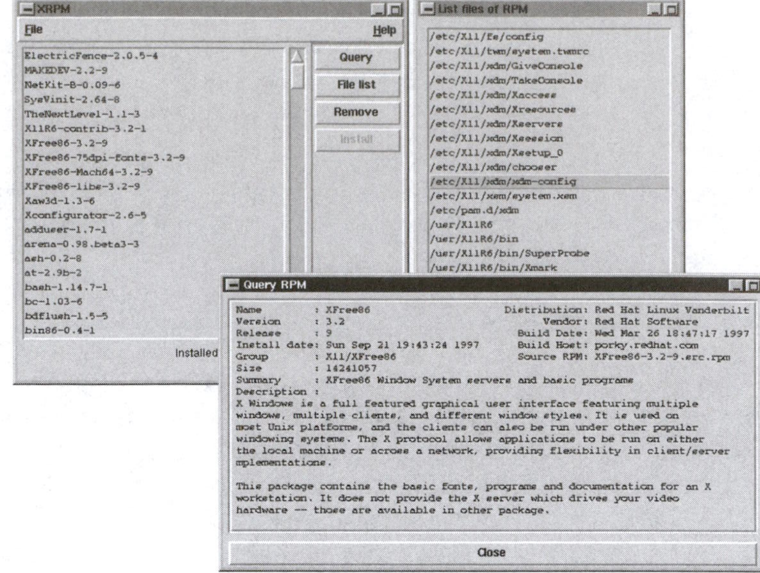

Figure 6.3 Package management with `xrpm`.

Manual installation of additional programs with `tar`

Experienced Linux users in particular often have the problem that Linux software is to be installed which is not organized in the form of a package of a specific distribution. Whole Gbytes of Linux software in `tar` format can be found on various Linux Internet servers or on CDs containing copies of these files (so-called server mirrors).

The compressed archives usually have the extensions `*.tgz` or `*.tar.gz`. These archives must be installed on your computer by means of the `tar` program. (Details of the handling of `tar` can be found on page 483.)

```
root#  tar -tzf archiv.tar.gz                 # display contents of archive
root#  tar -xzf archiv.tar.gz                 # install all files relative
                                              # to current directory
root#  tar -xzf archiv.tar.gz  "*.tex"        # install only *.tex files
root#  tar -xzf archiv.tar.gz -C directory    # install into a directory
```

Often the software is only present as source code and needs to be compiled prior to being used. This presumes that you have already installed the GNU C compiler with its various tools (and sometimes also groff, texinfo, awk, Tcl/Tk, or Perl).

CAUTION

Installation of software packages with `tar` circumvents the package management of your system. Therefore, the RPM databases do not 'know' anything about the programs that you have installed. For this and other reasons, it is always preferable to install packages which have been specially prepared for the current distribution.

XFree86

The X Window System (X for short) is a collection of functions and protocols which display graphic information on screen and administer the mouse and keyboard. The functions are also available for network operations.

XFree86 is a free implementation of the X Window System. Originally, it was only available for operating systems with Intel processors (386, 486, and so on; thus the number 86 in the name), but today it also runs on many other processors.

This chapter describes different aspects of the the configuration of the XFree86 server, providing at the same time some basic knowledge of graphics hardware. Further focal points are the use of keyboard and mouse under X, the handling of X resources, and some internals such as installation of additional character sets.

REFERENCE

X constitutes the basis for a graphical user interface for Linux. However, under Linux/Unix, the term 'user interface' must be taken with a pinch of salt: unlike MS Windows or the Macintosh world, the look and feel of X programs are affected by the library used by the currently running program, the currently active window manager, and so on. X itself does not provide a user interface. More information on this subject and on `fvwm`, KDE, and GNOME follows in the next chapter.

7.1 Configuring the X server

As a rule, you cannot use X directly after installation, but you must first configure the system (while you are still working in text mode). In practice, you must specify which graphics card and which monitor you are using. On this basis, the configuration program determines the possible graphic modes and writes these into a configuration file. Depending on the distribution, different X servers and configuration programs may be available. Here follows a brief overview of the structure of this relatively long section:

This section is based on XFree86, version 3.3.3. This version was being supplied with most distributions at the time of writing this book.

Documentation

There exists a vast amount of online documentation about XFree86. A very useful and up-to-date source of information are the `man` pages for XFree86: there are pages for `XFree86` (overview), `Xserver` (general options for the operation of X) and, depending on the installation, for `XF86_Mono`, `XF86_VGA16`, `XF86_SVGA`, together with texts for specific graphics cards, such as `XF86_Mach64`. The `man` text for `XF86Config` (please be aware of correct upper and lower case spelling) provides a description of all keywords permitted in the configuration file.

A very good overview is given by the HOWTO text for `XFree86`. Finally, the directory `/usr/X11R6/lib/X11/doc` contains many `README` texts. A first introduction is given by `Quickstart.doc`, an overview of the changes against the previous version can be obtained in `RELNOTES`. The `README.`*`Chip`* files contain information on specific graphics chips.

> **NOTE**
>
> Further information on the XFree86 project and on the currently up-to-date version can be found on the Internet:
>
> `http://www.XFree86.org`
>
> In some distributions (such as SuSE) the HTML files available from that address are supplied as a part of the documentation package.

Commercial X servers

Besides the free X server of XFree86, there are commercial servers (MetroX, AcceleratedX). The advantage of these servers is that they support graphics cards which are not (or not yet) supported by XFree86. (The background is often a legal one: some manufacturers of graphics cards – fortunately, increasingly fewer – are not prepared to make their intefaces public. The source code of XFree86, however, is – and will remain – freely available.)

The active X server is determined by the link from `/usr/X11R6/bin/X` to the server program. If you want to change your X server, you must change this link. In some distributions, `/usr/X11R6/bin/X` points to `/etc/X11/X`. In this case, only the latter link points to the server. To obtain further information on commercial servers and their configuration, please consult the relevant product documentation.

A minimalist X Glossary

X Window System

The X Window System (X for short) is basically a collection of functions to draw points, rectangles, and so on, on a screen. X also includes a network protocol that allows you to execute an X program on computer A and display the results (via a network) on computer B. The current version is X11R6.1, but most Linux distributions still use X11R6. The X Window System was developed at MIT (Massachusetts Institute of Technology).

X server

The X server is the interface between the X Window System and the hardware (graphics card, mouse). The most commonly used servers under Linux are the free XFree86 server and the two commercial servers MetroX and AcceleratedX.

XFree86 is part of X11R6 and represents a free port of the X system for computers with Intel 386 and compatibles. XFree86 has been developed by the *XFree86 Procject, Inc.* (*The XFree86 Project, Inc., c/o AIB Software Corporation, 1145 Herndon Parkway, Suite 200, Herndon, VA 22070, USA. Email: XFree86@XFree86.org*). The best feature of XFree86 is the support of countless graphics cards. XFree86 is not only available for Linux, but also for other Unix systems. The current version (January 1999) is 3.3.3.1.

TIP: If you are interested in the history of XFree86, you should read the XFree86 chapter of the Linux User Manual (see References).

Virtual screen

The X server is capable of managing a virtual screen that is larger than the section actually visible on the monitor. Usually, the virtual screen is set to at least 1024×768 points, even if the monitor can only display 800×600 points flicker free. Scrolling of the visible section is immediate, as soon as you move the mouse to the edge of the screen.

Window manager

The window manager is an X program which is responsible for the administration of the windows. Under X, several window managers are available which differ in usage and through variations in the visual layout of the window frames. For a long time, `fvwm` was the most widely used window manager under Linux; however, with the development of KDE and GNOME, things have got moving again in the world of window managers. Information about choice, configuration and handling of window managers can be found from page 262 onward.

Virtual desktop

A virtual desktop is a graphical pane that actually consists of several screens arranged next to and on top of each other. Since you have only one monitor, you cannot view several virtual screens at once. You can, however, easily switch between these screens and, for example, run some shell windows on one screen, the Emacs editor on a second screen, and the page-filling program `ghostview` on a third screen.

Virtual desktops are usually provided directly by the window manager or by an additional module of the window manager. Just to add to the confusion, the `ConfigXF86` configuration program uses the term 'virtual desktop,' although it actually refers to a virtual screen; as you can see, there is no single naming convention.

X resources

Most configuration details (such as the size of the character set, colors, and so on) of the programs running under X are controlled through X resource files. These files constitute central reference points for the configuration of the X programs (but not of the X basic system). More details on this subject follow from page 248 onward.

Motif

Motif is a graphical interface based upon X. In Motif, additional control elements (widgets) are defined which give the interface its typical look and feel. Motif includes its own set of application programs (editor, file manager, and so on). Motif is subject to license, thus it cannot be freely copied like Linux. Single programs with a Motif-like interface have, however, been developed as freeware and are also available under Linux.

OpenLook

OpenLook is a further interface based on X, alongside Motif. OpenLook was released some time ago by Sun (amongst others, in order to increase its diffusion). For this reason, the OpenLook window manager and some OpenLook application programs have been included in several Linux distributions.

CDE

CDE stands for Common Desktop Environment. It is a user interface which again builds on Motif and which contains additional components for facilitating the handling (help system, toolbars, and so on). CDE is an attempt to create a common user interface for different Unix systems. Under Linux, however, CDE is still of very little importance, due to its high price (on top of the price to be paid for Motif).

KDE and GNOME

KDE and GNOME are two free user interfaces and represent modern alternatives to Motif, Openlook, and CDE. KDE consists of its own window manager and a vast number of programs and utilities which together result in a homogeneous, easy-to-use desktop. GNOME provides in principle the same functions, but is based on a different library and therefore looks slightly different. Furthermore, GNOME does not have its own window manager. KDE and GNOME will be extensively described in the next chapter.

Monitor and graphics card fundamentals

It might not be absolutely necessary to understand all the information given in this section in order to carry out a proper X configuration. However, it considerably facilitates the configuration process if you do not have to follow instructions blindly, but rather are fully aware of what you are doing. And as soon as configuration problems occur, there is no way round such background information anyway.

Image construction

The image on the monitor is generated by an electron beam that scans the whole screen surface line by line, causing tiny points to light up (or not, if the point is intended to be black). In order to achieve a flicker-free image, this process is repeated several times per second (between 60 and 100). The information as to which point of the screen surface is to be represented in which color is provided by the graphics card. Inside the monitor, this information controls the intensity of the electron beam.

Horizontal flyback (HSync)

Screen scanning starts in the upper left corner of the screen. From there, the electron beam moves to the right, scanning the first line. Subsequently, the electron beam flies back to the beginning of the line and simultaneously moves one line down. During this horizontal flyback, the electron beam has an intensity of 0, so that the flyback is not visible on the screen. The horizontal flyback is triggered by the HSync impulse, which is transmitted by the graphics card to the monitor. (Physically, the flyback is realized by a change in the magnetic fields that deflect the electron beam in the area of the screen surface. Such changes cannot be made infinitely fast, that is, the flyback takes some time (several microseconds).)

Vertical flyback (VSync)

After all lines have been scanned in this way and the electron beam is now in the lower right corner of the screen, the VSync impulse triggers vertical flyback. During this flyback, the electron beam moves back to the upper left corner of the screen. Obviously, its intensity is again set to 0 – otherwise, it would leave a luminous trace all the way across the screen. For technical reasons, vertical flyback takes magnitudes longer than horizontal flyback. During this lapse of time, several lines could be scanned.

Frequencies

The image construction rating is characterized by three frequencies (see below). The unit for frequencies is Hz (Hertz) – cycles per second. Similarly, kHz and MHz indicate 1000 and 1 000 000 cycles per second.

Vertical frame frequency (vertical refresh)

The vertical frame frequency indicates how many times (per second) the whole screen area is redrawn. The larger this number, the more stable the image appears. From around 70 frames per second (70 Hz) onwards, the image appears to be flicker free.

Horizontal line frequency (HSync)

This frequency indicates how many lines per second are scanned by the electron beam. With an image resolution of 640×480 points (thus, 480 lines) and a frame frequency of 60 Hz, the horizontal line frequency amounts to 31.5 kHz. (If you are checking my calculations, it is true that 60 times 480 only makes 28.8 kHz. The slightly higher frequency is needed to account for the time used by the vertical fly-back.)

Pixel frequency (video bandwidth)

This frequency indicates how many image points (pixels) are transmitted from the graphics card to the monitor in the space of one second. With 640×480 points and 60 Hz, the outcome is a value of 18.4 MHz. Due to the overhead caused by horizontal and vertical flyback, the actual pixel frequency is 25 MHz.

Interlace mode

Interlace mode is a reliable method for developing a headache in a very short time and eye trouble in the long run. Here, for the construction of the image, not every line is considered, but only every second line. Thus, the first frame is composed of lines 1, 3, 5, and so on, the second image of lines 2, 4, 6, and so on. In this way, a higher resolution can be achieved in spite of a low pixel frequency. The result, however, is a slightly flickering image if you do not use a monitor with an extremely persistent phosphor.

The monitor

The image construction is determined by two hardware components, the monitor and the graphics card. The monitor is probably easier to understand from the technical specifications viewpoint. For modern monitors, the relevant data are:

- the vertical synchronization range (frame frequency, for example 50 to 90 Hz),
- the horizontal synchronization range (line frequency, for example 30 to 57 kHz),
- the maximum bandwidth (pixel frequency, for example 75 MHz).

Older monitors cannot be set to any of the frequencies within these ranges, but only support a few fixed frequencies.

Synchronization problems occur when the graphics card sends a stream of data to the monitor, which cannot be correctly interpreted. This may happen when synchronization impulses are transmitted too early, too late, or too weakly, or when the frequency limits of the monitor are exceeded.

CAUTION

Exceeding the frequency limits (in particular, the maximum line frequency) – which happens when the graphics card supplies too much data too fast – may be fairly dangerous. In such a case, the electron beam of the monitor can no longer follow the data, parts of the screen or even the whole screen are irradiated for too long and too intensively, and thus they overheat and in a relatively short time (a matter of a few seconds) they are destroyed.

Exceeding the maximum bandwidth is, however, quite uncritical (as long as the maximum line frequency is kept). The result is usually a smudged image, because the signal amplifier of the monitor is overloaded. For this reason, in more recent XFree86 configuration programs the bandwidth is no longer taken into account.

The graphics card

The main task of the graphics card is to supply pixel data for image construction. (In addition, the card should support drawing operations – but this is not relevant here.) All current graphics cards can generate several graphic modes with different resolution and frequency – maybe even modes which your monitor might not be able to cope with.

Frequencies play an important role for the graphics card as well. While the monitor must understand the data stream supplied at a given pixel frequency, generation of this pixel frequency in the graphics card is a (technical) problem. Older graphics cards can only generate a few predefined frequencies, while modern cards are equipped with a freely programmable frequency generator. The frequencies provided by older graphics cards are an important element in the configuration of the video driver.

Colors

Colors are no problem as far as the monitor is concerned. The monitor simply receives an analog value that reflects the intensity of a color component (red, green, blue). It is irrelevant whether 16 colors, 256 colors, or more are displayed.

For the graphics card, on the other hand, colors do constitute a problem: on the one hand, the greater the number of colors, the more data must be processed. An image with 256 colors takes up twice the memory space of one with 16 colors. This memory has to be read continuously at very high speed. Modern graphics cards reach data streams of up to 200 MBytes per second.

On the other hand, each digital pattern of a pixel must be converted into an analog signal. The digital/analog converters (DAC) required for this purpose, however, work only up to a certain frequency. For many video cards, the DAC frequency is lower than the bandwidth theoretically supported by the card. Also, some graphics card manufacturers seem to have grown into a habit of changing the DAC chips all the time; for this reason, you must enter the precise denomination of the DAC chip into the configuration file for some graphics cards.

Accelerator cards

These are graphics cards where the drawing operations are supported by a dedicated graphics chip. While with older graphics cards the computer itself must change every pixel in a graphical operation, accelerator cards are capable of performing some operations, such as moving an image area, on their own. This takes some load off the computer (the CPU); the whole systems runs faster. The disadvantage: each manufacturer uses different chips to accelerate elementary graphical operations; thus, for each family of cards a specific graphics driver is needed.

The configuration process

The aim of the following explanations is to achieve a flicker-free monitor image of the highest possible resolution. Further details of X configuration (X resources, window manager configuration) are the subject of later sections from page 262 onward.

The central configuration file for XFree86 is `XF86Config`. This file contains all the relevant data relating to your graphics card and monitor in text format. If you want to modify this file, you must log in as `root`.

Unfortunately, depending on the distribution, `XF86Config` is found in different locations. (`/usr/X11R6/lib/X11/XF86Config` is usually only a link somewhere into the `/etc` directory.)

`/etc/X11/XF86Config`	Debian, RedHat
`/etc/XF86Config`	SuSE
`/usr/X11R6/lib/X11/XF86Config`	XFree86 default

Depending on the distribution, a whole palette of configuration programs is there to help you with the creation of `XF86Config`:

`XF86Setup`	page 230
`xf86config`	page 234
`xvidtune`	page 234
`Xconfigurator` (RedHat)	page 725
`sax` (SuSE)	page 740

Independently of which configuration program you use, you will often have to retouch the configuration file manually – more on this from page 235 onwards.

CAUTION

Never use an XFree86 configuration file borrowed from a friend or a colleague, downloaded over the Internet or obtained from somewhere else without adapting the monitor section to the data of your monitor first (see below) – otherwise you risk the premature demise of your monitor!

Video cards supported

The first precondition for a configuration of X is that you must know which video driver you need. Currently, XFree86 comes with 11 video drivers. In most distributions, you are already prompted to selected one of these drivers during the installation of Linux. (If this has not been the case, the relevant driver must be installed now, which is no problem.) The following list includes the most important drivers for Intel PC hardware. For other hardware platforms (such as DEC) different drivers are available.

`XF86_MONO`	monochrome driver (black and white)
`XF86_VGA16`	16 colors, standard VGA (needed for `XF86Setup`)
`XF86_SVGA`	standard driver for Super-VGA (incl. Matrox)
`XF86_8514`	IBM8514 (XVGA)
`XF86_AGX`	AGX graphic processor (IIT)
`XF86_I128`	AGX graphic processor (Number Nine Imagine 128)
`XF86_Mach8`	Mach8 graphic processor (ATI)
`XF86_Mach32`	Mach32 graphic processor (ATI)
`XF86_Mach64`	Mach64 graphic processor (ATI)
`XF86_P9000`	P9000 graphic processor (Diamond Viper etc.)
`XF86_S3`	S3 graphic processor
`XF86_S3V`	S3-ViRGE graphic processor
`XF86_W32`	ET4000/W32/ET6000 graphic processor (Tseng)
`XBF_NeoMagic`	graphics cards with NeoMagic chip set
`XFCom_Cyrix`	Cyrix MediaGX CPU
`XFCom_Rendition`	Rendition Verite V1000, V2100, V2200
`XSuSE_Elsa_GLoria`	GLoria, Winner 2000/Office, Permedia

The first three drivers in the following list run on most VGA cards, but do not always make use of their special features. The VGA-16 driver is needed, in particular, for the configuration process. The SVGA driver is often an emergency solution if it is not possible to get a special driver for your own card to run. However, it also contains highly optimized code for some graphics cards (such as the Matrox card) – see `man XF86_SVGA`. The remaining drivers are specially optimized for specific graphics cards.

All drivers, except for the monochrome and the 16-color driver, support the 256-color mode, with, in most cases, the possibility of setting an arbitrary resolution. Most drivers for special graphics cards also support graphic modes with more colors (15, 16, 24, and 32 bit color coding).

The drivers are installed into the `/usr/X11R6/bin` directory. The required driver is selected by a link from `/usr/X11R6/bin/X` to the driver file. In some distributions, `/usr/X11R6/bin/X` points to `/etc/X11/X` or to `/var/X11R6/bin/X`. In this case, only the latter link points to the server.

```
user#  ls -l /usr/X11R6/bin/X
lrwxrwxrwx 1 root root X -> ../../../etc/X11/X
user#  ls -l /etc/X11/X
lrwxrwxrwx 1 root root /etc/X11/X -> ../../usr/X11R6/bin/XF86_Mach64
```

If you do not know which chip works on your graphics card, you should read your card's documentation. If this does not help (or if you do not find any manuals), you can execute the `SuperProbe` program. In most cases, this program reliably detects your graphics hardware. In the worst case, it can cause a crash, destroy the character set or lead to synchronization problems. Therefore, you should execute this program only if you do not have several hours of work lying around in still unsaved files. Or, to be more accurate: before executing `SuperProbe`, use `umount` to unmount all file systems that you do not need any longer and then execute `sync`.

On the author's computer, the result of `SuperProbe` looks as follows:

```
root#  SuperProbe
First video: Super-VGA
        Chipset: ATI 88800GX-D (Port Probed)
        Memory:  2048 Kbytes
        RAMDAC:  ATI 68860 15/15/24-bit DAC w/pixel-mux
                 (with 6-bit wide lookup tables (or in 6-bit mode))
                 (programmable for 6/8-bit wide lookup tables)
        Attached graphics coprocessor:
                Chipset: ATI Mach64
                Memory:  2048 Kbytes
```

Another alternative for obtaining information on your graphics card is provided by the virtual file `/proc/pci`, which contains information on the cards connected to the PCI bus:

```
root#  cat /proc/pci
PCI devices found: [...]
  Bus  1, device   0, function  0:
    VGA compatible controller: ATI Mach64 GB (rev 92).
      Medium devsel.  Fast back-to-back capable.  IRQ 226.
        Master Capable.  Latency=64.  Min Gnt=8.
      Prefetchable 32 bit memory at 0xe3000000.
      I/O at 0xd800.
      Non-prefetchable 32 bit memory at 0xe2000000.
```

In both cases it is therefore clear that the Mach64 driver is required.

TIP

Before you buy a new graphics card, you should make absolutely sure that the card is already supported by XFree86! XFree86 supports many, but not all, graphics cards (and not all of them with the same reliability). You will find more information about which graphics cards are currently supported in the `README` files of XFree86 or on the XFree86 Web server: `www.xfree86.org`.

The XF86Setup configuration program

Since version 3.2, `XF86Setup` is the default configuration program of XFree86 and is by now supplied with all distributions. To use the program, however, some conditions must be met:

- The program must be installed. Depending on the distribution, the program is contained in a separate package. In addition, the VGA-16 driver is needed for execution (yet another package which is often not installed).
- Your graphics card and your monitor must support the VGS standard mode (640×480 pixels with 16 colors).
- Your computer should be fairly well equipped (memory, CPU) – otherwise, `XF86Setup` is unbearably slow.

Mouse

`XF86Setup` is executed in text mode and first starts the VGA16 X server before it appears as an X program with mouse support, buttons, and so on. Ideally, the program recognizes the connected mouse straight away; otherwise it should be set in the first configuration step. If needed, the program can be entirely controlled with [Tab] and the cursor keys. Also, some of the buttons can be selected by pressing [Alt], followed by the initial letter.

With no-name mice, selecting the mouse type is often a matter of chance. As a first attempt, you should try *Microsoft compatible* (also works with some three-button mice) or *Mouseman*. Manufacturers' names are not always decisive, a Logitech mouse might well observe the Microsoft or the Mouseman protocol. With APPLY you simply adopt the settings and can test them immediately. You should press all three mouse buttons – the corresponding fields in the mouse symbol (on the right-hand side of Figure 7.1) should become black.

If the mouse does not react at all, you may have to select a different device. The most probable ones are `/dev/mouse` (a link to the actual device), `/dev/ttyS0` or `/dev/ttyS1` (the first or second serial port), and `/dev/psaux` (PS/2 mice).

If you work with a two-button mouse, you should also activate the EMULATE3BUTTONS option. Then you can simulate the missing middle mouse button by pressing both buttons simultaneously. (This is only a makeshift solution. Go on, invest some money in a three-button mouse – it's worth it.)

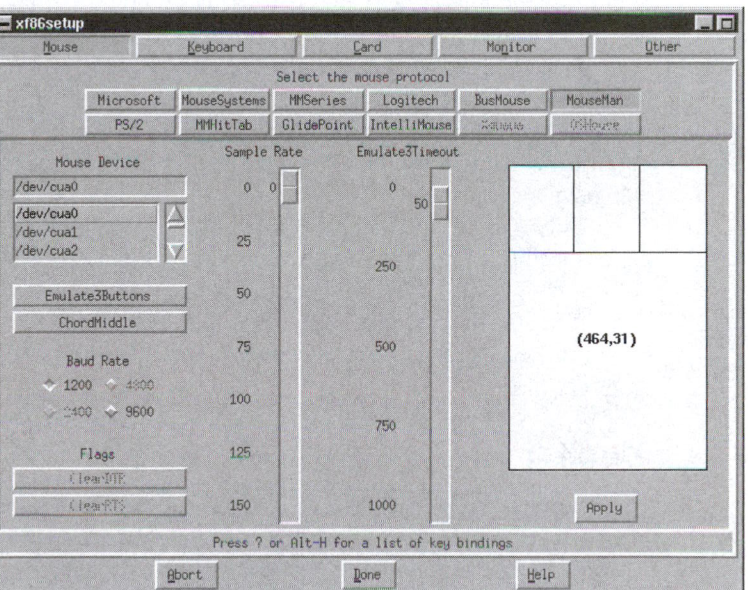

Figure 7.1 Mouse setting with `XF86Setup`.

> **TIP**
>
> If you install X on a notebook with a trackpoint as mouse substitute, you should set PS/2 and the `/dev/psaux` port. It is also highly recommended that you check the Linux notebook page on the Internet:
>
> `http://www.cs.utexas.edu/users/kharker/linux-laptop`

Keyboard

After configuring the mouse (do not forget APPLY), the next step is to set up the keyboard. The settings for a U.S. keyboard are:

MODEL: Generic 101-key PC (or Generic 104-key PC with a Windows keyboard)
LAYOUT: U.S. English
VARIANT: –
GROUP SHIFT/LOCK BEHAVIOR: R-Alt switches group while pressed

In the option field CONTROL KEY POSITION, you can turn the [CapsLock] key into an additional [Control] key and thus deactivate [CapsLock] – but that is a matter of taste.

Graphics card

To select your graphics card, you will be offered a seemingly endless list in which you must look for your graphics card. This sounds easier than it is – or are you sure whether you have an *ATI Graphics Expression with 68875 RAMDAC* or whether *ATI Mach 64* would be the better choice? Before you take your computer to pieces and look at your graphics card to try to determine which chips are actually soldered onto that board, you should opt for the least specific alternative which you think might be correct. If this is sufficient to load the correct X driver, the details are usually recognized automatically.

Only if you have a very precise knowledge of your graphics hardware can you make specific indications on additional options, available graphics memory, and so on, via the DETAILED SETUP button.

If you have no idea at all, you should employ the `SuperProbe` program mentioned earlier, which in many cases recognizes the hardware being used (but in rare cases can also cause a crash).

Monitor

The configuration program wants to know the permissible ranges for the horizontal line frequency (kHz) and for the vertical frame frequency (Hz). You can either select one of the proposed monitor types or enter the values directly.

You will find the necessary data in the manual or data sheet of your monitor (and, with a bit of luck, also on the back of your monitor itself). For a number of monitors, you can also find this data in the file `doc/Monitors` (after the keywords `VertRefresh`, and `HorizSync`). Background information about the meaning of this data is given from page 225 onward.

CAUTION

If you specify excessively high values for VertRefresh or HorizSync, you risk the premature demise of your monitor! XFree86 uses these values to exclude from the very beginning those graphic modes that might not be compatible with your monitor.

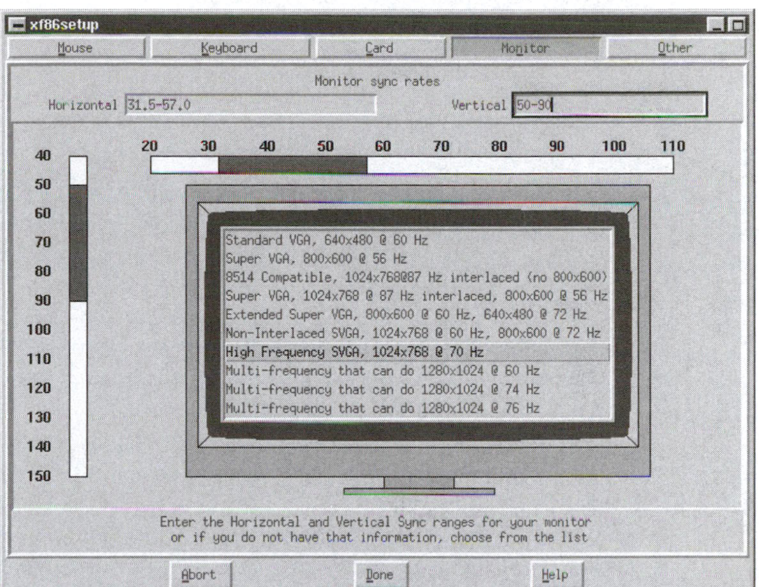

Figure 7.2 Monitor setup with XF86Setup.

Terminating the configuration

In the fifth step of `XF86Setup`, the menu item OTHER, you can without problems adopt the default settings. If you subsequently click on DONE, the X server is started with your settings. If everything goes well, your monitor will display a stable image. You can now decide via a mouse click whether you want to store the settings, further optimize the image position with `xvidtune` (see page 234), or leave the program with QUIT.

If, in contrast, the monitor is not capable to synchronize after the start of X, there are two alternatives: one is the key combination Alt+Ctrl++, where the + key of the numeric keypad is used; this allows you to change to a lower-resolution graphics mode. If that does not help, you need to abort the configuration program with Alt+Ctrl+Backspace, restart it, and repeat the whole configuration step by step.

The configuration program `xf86config`

`xf86config` is the text-based alternative to `XF86Setup`. The program is not excessively user-friendly, but usually leads to the desired goal. The settings are in principle the same as in `XF86Setup` – therefore, only some complementary details are described.

After monitor and graphics card setup, `xf86config` prompts for identification and description strings. Here it is enough to press [↵], thus accepting the default names and strings. The sole purpose of these strings is to make your `XF86Config` somewhat more 'readable.'

After a request for confirmation, `xf86config` carries out a start of the VGA driver with the option `-probeonly`. Here, `X` is not really started – only the pixel frequencies supported by the graphics card are detemined. However, the X trial run does not work with all graphics cards. Therefore it is often sensible to skip this point with [N].

Now the configuration program proposes a list of graphics modes to choose from. The abbreviation bpp indicates the bits per pixel: 8 bits for 256 colors, 16 bits for 32768 or 65536 colors, and 24 bits for true color mode (2^{24} colors). However, only a few Accelerated-VGA drivers support more than 256 colors. (The other drivers simply ignore these settings in the configuration files.)

In most cases, the list can be left as is. Very high-resolution modes (for example 1280×1024 pixels), are automatically removed at the start of X if they are not supported by your graphics card or your monitor.

After a final request for confirmation, the configuration program saves the configuration file just created. Make sure that the file is stored at the correct location (or copy the file to the location required for your distribution).

On the author's computer, `xf86config` was in the main successful. Some additional work was required with the keyboard configuration. Also, the order of graphics modes in the `Modes` line had to be changed – `xf86config` uses the lowest-resolution mode (640×480 points) as a default.

The `xf86config` configuration program has the regrettable peculiarity of filling the configuration file with countless additional sections which, in practice, are not needed at all. This, plus the countless comments make the configuration file longer and harder to read than necessary. Details on manual configuration follow from page 235 onward.

The `xvidtune` program

The `xvidtune` program is not a configuration program, but a tool for optimizing an existing configuration file. (A KDE variation of `xvidtune`, called `kvidtune`, is currently under development.)

With `xvidtune`, you can change size and position of the image for all modes (buttons PREV and NEXT). Changes in image position can be tested with TEST (where the old mode is restored after a few seconds) or permanently set with APPLY. With [R] (restore) you get back to a stable image even if the monitor is no longer synchronized and the mouse can no longer be operated. As soon as you terminate the program, all settings are saved in `XF86Config`.

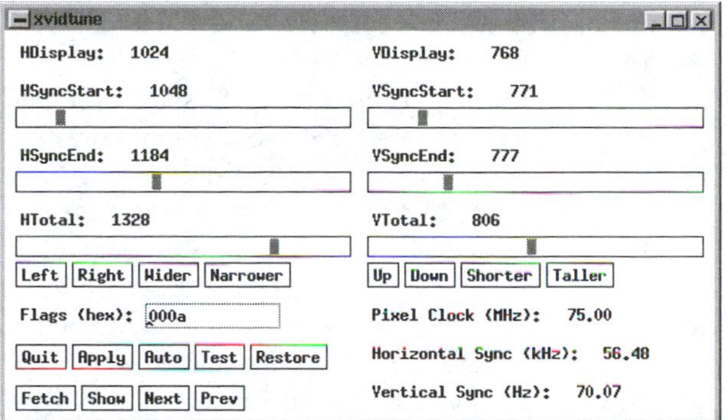

Figure 7.3 `xvidtune` for fine tuning of the image position.

CAUTION

Please take seriously the warnings that are displayed at the start of the program. Incorrect use of the program risks destroying your graphics card and/or your monitor.

The structure of `XF86Config`

This section describes the configuration file `XF86Config`. You will need this information if you wish to optimize the configuration file manually – which, in spite of the greatly improved configuration programs, can often not be avoided. `XF86Config` essentially consists of four parts:

- In the first part, global options are set, mainly for mouse, keyboard and directory locations (sections `Files`, `ServerFlags`, `Keyboard`, and `Pointer`).
- The second part contains one or more `Monitor` sections which specify the monitor ratings and the graphic modes supported by the monitor.
- The third part contains one or more `Device` sections which specify the graphics card's technical data.
- The configuration file ends with one or more `Screen` sections. In these, single `Monitor` and `Device` sections are combined.

NOTE

At this point, only the `Monitor`, `Device`, and `Screen` sections are described. Correct setting of these three sections is sufficient to achieve a stable graphical representation. Information on the other sections is given from page 242 (keyboard and mouse) and from page 250 (character sets) onward.

For a correct configuration, theoretically only *one* `Monitor`, `Device`, and `Screen` section is needed. Unfortunately, some configuration programs (in particular, `xf86config`) have the unpleasant habit of supplying endless configuration files full of redundant information that only causes confusion. So, which sections are actually used?

The easiest way to find out is to start with the last part of the configuration file. Out of all `Screen` sections, the one that corresponds to your video driver will apply. If you work with a Super-VGA driver (and `/usr/X11R6/bin/X` actually points to this driver), then the `Screen` sections for the monochrome driver, the 16-color driver and the group of accelerated VGA drivers are superfluous. You can 'tidy up' the configuration file and simply delete these sections from the file. (But remember to save the original state of the configuration file under a different name first.)

Once you have identified the relevant `Screen` section, you also know the relevant `Monitor` and `Device` sections, since their names are indicated with the keywords `Monitor` and `Device` at the beginning of the `Screen` section. Now you only have to find the `Monitor` and `Device` sections in which the same names are indicated after the keyword `Identifier`.

If you work with the Super-VGA driver, for example, the following three sections contain all relevant data:

```
Section "Device"
    Identifier  "sigma legend II"
    ...
EndSection
Section "Monitor"
    Identifier  "nec 4d"
    ...
EndSection
Section "Screen"
    Driver      "svga"              # for the Super-VGA driver
    Device      "sigma legend II"   # reference to the graphics card
    Monitor     "nec 4d"            # reference to the monitor
    ...
EndSection
```

Device section

The main objective of the device section for the graphics card is to list the pixel frequencies supported by the graphics card and (if necessary) to specify additional information about the RAM DAC used on the card.

First the pixel frequencies: usually, all frequencies supported by the graphics card are simply listed in one or more `Clock` lines, in MHz. The frequencies can be either determined with `X -probeonly` or, if this does not work, extracted from the files `Devices` or `modeDB.txt` (directory `/usr/X11R6/lib/X11/doc`).

Most graphics cards not only support a specific number of fixed frequencies, but are equipped with a freely programmable frequency generator. In this case, no

`Clock` lines are needed. Instead, the type of frequency generator must be specified with the keyword `ClockChip`.

All further settings and options strongly depend on the graphics card used. They are described in the `README` files and (in great detail) in the driver-specific `man` pages (for example, `man XF86_SVGA`).

The following example shows the device section for an old graphics card in the author's computer (an ET4000 Super-VGA card). The two essential entries are the correct `Clocks` line (taken from `modeDB.txt`) and the option `"legend"`, without which the setup would not function (`man XF86_SVGA`).

```
Section "Device"
    Identifier "sigma legend II"
    VendorName "sigma"
    BoardName "legend II"
    Clocks 25 28 0 40 36 40 45 58 32 36 31 35 50 48 33 65
    Option "legend"
EndSection
```

The following lines apply to another graphics card used by the author. This time, the setting of the graphics memory size was decisive for correct functioning.

```
Section "Device"
   Identifier      "Primary Card"
   VendorName      "Unknown"
   BoardName       "ATI Xpert@Work, 3D Rage Pro"
   VideoRam        8192
EndSection
```

Monitor section

The monitor section starts with three frequency specifications: the maximum video bandwidth (pixel frequency in MHz), the permissible range for the horizontal line frequency and the permissible range for the vertical frame frequency. These specifications should not be a problem. (The meaning of these frequencies has been explained in the Fundamentals section at the beginning of this chapter.) Considerably more problems are caused by the graphic modes that have to be entered here as well. Two syntax variations are possible:

```
ModeLine "640x480"  25.175 640  664  760  800   480  491  493  525
# or
Mode "640x480"
  DotClock   25.175
  HTimings   640  664  760  800
  VTimings   480  491  493  525
  Flags
EndMode
```

From a contents point of view, the two specifications through `ModeLine` and `Mode` are equivalent: both describe a graphic mode with 640×480 pixels. The character string `"640x480"` is also the name of this mode. The numeric value 25.175 specifies the pixel frequency (video bandwidth) in MHz. The pixel frequency must match one of the `Clock` values in the `Device` section in order to validate the mode. If several homonymous modes are specified, X uses the first valid one.

Now to the next four values (expressed in pixels) for the horizontal timing: a single screen line with 640 *visible* pixels is actually composed of 800 *virtual* pixels. The first 640 pixels are actually displayed. During the remaining 160 pixels, the electron beam is moved back to the beginning of the next line by the Hsync impulse. During this time, the electron beam has an intensity of 0.

`640`	display 640 screen pixels
`664`	blank 24 further pixels
`760`	generate a 96-pixel-long HSync impulse
`800`	blank another 40 pixels, this amounts to a total of 800 virtual points

The indications for the vertical timing are interpreted in exactly the same way (expressed in screen lines):

`480`	display 480 lines
`491`	blank 11 lines
`493`	generate a 2-line-long VSync impulse
`525`	blank another 32 lines, this amounts to a total of 525 virtual lines

The last values of the quadruples and the pixel frequency allow the horizontal line frequency and the vertical frame frequency to be determined: 25.175 MHz divided by 800 pixels per line results in a line frequency of 31.469 kHz. The line frequency divided by 525 lines per image results in a vertical frame frequency of 60 Hz. The `ModeLine` settings give no information about the number of colors available in this mode – from the monitor's point of view, this does not play a role. (Many graphics cards, however, can display high resolution modes only with a smaller number of colors.)

A whole palette of predefined `ModeLine` lines can be found in the configuration file created by `xf86config`, and in the files `Monitors` and `README.Config`. Depending on the capabilities of your graphics card and your monitor, you can or must adapt these values manually in order to obtain the best possible image.

If, for example, you want to shift the image to the right, you must increase the distance after the HSync impulse. In order to keep the total number of pixels (800) unchanged, you must either shorten the time before the HSync impulse or the length of the HSync impulse itself. You may, for example, want to try out `640 660 752 800`.

If you want to widen or narrow the image, you must change the proportion of the number of visible pixels to the virtual pixels. The following settings widen the image: `640 660 752 790`. However, this leads to a small change in horizontal and vertical frequency and not all monitors can handle this.

In many graphics cards, you can even change the visible resolution. The following settings increase the horizontal resolution from 640 to 656 points: `656 676 772 800`.

Similarly, you can also vary the settings for the vertical timing. Whether this leads to a stable image, however, strongly depends on your monitor and your graphics card technical data.

> **TIP** For fine-tuning, you can also use the `xvidtune` program or its KDE variation `kvidtune`, which allow you to vary part of the timing values interactively during normal operation of X.

Various options can be added to the `ModeLine` lines: `Interlace` for the interlace mode (only possible with an odd number of virtual lines), `+/-Hsync` and `+/-Vsync` to change the polarity of the synchronization impulse, plus `Composite` and `+/-Csync` for a combined synchronization signal (includes both HSync and VSync).

The following example shows the author's `Monitor` section for his nearly stone-age NEC 4D monitor. Three resolutions are defined: 640×480 points at 71 Hz, 816×612 points at 75 Hz, and 1024×768 points at 63 Hz.

```
Section "Monitor"
    Identifier "nec 4d"
    VendorName "nec"
    ModelName "4d"
    BandWidth 75
    HorizSync 30-57
    VertRefresh 50-90
    ModeLine "640x480"  31    640  664  704  832     480 489 492 520
    ModeLine "816x612"  50    816  824  960 1040     612 612 614 635
    ModeLine "1024x768" 65   1024 1065 1065 1260     768 780 785 810
EndSection
```

As a second example, here is the `Monitor` section for a more recent screen.

```
Section "Monitor"
   Identifier      "iiyama 450"
   VendorName      "unknown"
   ModelName       "unknown"
   HorizSync       31.5-102
   VertRefresh     40-100
   Modeline "1280x1024" 157.50 1280 1344 1504 1728
                               1024 1025 1028 1072 +hsync +vsync
   Modeline "1152x864"  137.65 1152 1184 1312 1536
                                864  866  885  902 -hsync -vsync
   Modeline "1024x768"  115.50 1024 1056 1248 1440
                                768  771  781  802 -hsync -vsync
EndSection
```

Screen section

The `Screen` section indicates which `Monitor` section is to be combined with which `Device` section for which VGA driver. The section contains one or more `Display` subsections. Each subsection applies to a specific color depth (8, 16, or 24 bpp, that is, *bits per pixel*).

Each `Display` section contains a list of all graphic modes to be supported. This list begins with the keyword `Modes` and contains the names of the graphic modes defined above in `ModeLine`. The order is significant – the first mode is taken as the default mode. You can switch to the other modes in order with Ctrl+Alt++ or - (numeric keypad).

Graphics cards with sufficient memory allow you to use `Virtual` to define a virtual screen which is larger than the currently visible section. With the mouse you can move around this virtual screen without delays. You should, however, not use the whole available memory for the virtual screen, but should leave some space for a font cache (this leads to a significant speed increase). The keyword `ViewPort` specifies the first visible pixel at the start of X (only of interest if the virtual screen is bigger than the actual resolution).

TIP

Working with a virtual screen requires getting used to. If the virtual screen automatically set up by most configuration programs bothers you, you need to comment out the `Virtual` instruction. (In this case, the size of the virtual screen is oriented towards the highest-resolution graphics mode specified in the `Screen` section.)

```
Section "Screen"        # for an SVGA card
    Driver "vga256"
    Device "sigma legend II"
    Monitor "nec 4d"
    Subsection "Display"
        Depth    8   # 8 bpp, thus 256 colors
        Modes    "1024x768" "640x480" "816x612"
        Virtual  1024 900
        ViewPort 0 0
    EndSubsection
EndSection
```

With some accelerated VGA drivers, several `Display` sections with different color depth (8, 16, 24, or 32 bpp) can be specified simultaneously (see `man XF86_Accel`. At the start of the X server, usually the 8-bpp mode is activated. The `Display` sections with higher resolutions come into play only if in `startx` a higher color depth is explicitly set by means of `-- -bpp 16` or `24`. Alternatively you can change the default mode by specifying `DefaultColorDepth` *n* in the `Screen` section.

```
Section "Screen"
   Driver            "Accel"
   Device            "Primary Card"
   Monitor           "Primary Monitor"
   DefaultColorDepth 24
   SubSection "Display"
      Depth          8
      Modes          "1280x1024" "1152x864" "1024x768"
   EndSubSection
   SubSection "Display"
      Depth          15
      Modes          "1280x1024" "1152x864" "1024x768"
   EndSubSection
   SubSection "Display"
      Depth          24
      Modes          "1280x1024" "1152x864" "1024x768"
   EndSubSection
EndSection
```

Testing X

After setting up `XF86Config`, X is usually started by means of the `/usr/bin/startx` command. After the X server, this script files also starts a window manager (for example `fvwm`, see next chapter). During the startup of X, some messages are displayed (still in the text console). As long as the configuration file does not contain syntactical errors or disagrees with the detected hardware, the graphic mode is activated. Ideally, a stable image should appear straight away – if this happens, the configuration has been successful.

Depending on the configuration, some application programs are automatically launched at the start of X. In addition, you can use the mouse buttons to call up a menu to start further programs. At the beginning, the most important program is certainly `xterm`. Like a text console, it allows you to enter commands and start other programs.

REFERENCE

You will find further information about the different possibilities for starting X and for selecting and configuring the window manager from page 262 onward. Some X programs are described in Chapter 15 from page 491 onward.

Details about how to start X can also be found in the `man` pages for `startx`, `openwin`, `xdm`, `xinit`, and `X`.

If no visible image appears after the execution of `startx` (that is, if the monitor remains black) or if an image appears, but the monitor cannot synchronize this image (the image 'runs'), you can try switching to a different graphic mode. Usually, the configuration file specifies several graphic modes (for example, 640×480 points, 800×600 points, 1024×768 points, and so on), between which you can switch during normal operation of X with Ctrl+Alt+ + or - (on the numeric keypad). Depending on the monitor, a stable image is likely to be displayed in at least some of the modes.

If synchronization of the screen does not succeed, you should exit X as soon as possible to safeguard your monitor. To do this, you press Ctrl+ Alt+Backspace. Under normal circumstances, you should find yourself in text mode again (that is, in the text console in which you started X). If you strike a bad patch, the screen stays dark or it is impossible to display a stable image. The only thing that helps in this, fortunately very improbable, case is a restart (with `shutdown` or Ctrl+Alt+Del). In other words: if bad luck strikes, you must reboot your computer after your X test trial – and you have to do it blind because you can no longer work in text mode either. Therefore: terminate all currently running programs *before* you start experimenting with X.

In order to allow you to read the output generated during the startup of X even when difficulties occur, you can reroute this output to a file by means of xstart `xstart >& log`. Instead of `xstart` you can also execute `X -probeonly`: here, the VGA driver tries to test your graphics card frequencies without actually starting X. Thus, you get back to text mode immediately. This is a relatively problem-free way of checking whether your configuration file is syntactically correct. You will get the same message as with `xstart`.

7.2 Mouse and keyboard under X

This section deals with peculiarities of the mouse and keyboard under X. We deal extensively with the manifold problems that occur when trying keyboard configuration. In addition, important keyboard shortcuts and mouse operations will be described. (Also, please check the Keyboard HOWTO text.)

Keyboard configuration

Under X, the keyboard is a source of permanent frustration. Programs designed for text mode no longer react correctly to most function keys (Home, End, and so on) under X. Even with true X programs, whether or not they will recognize the most important key combinations is something of a gamble. The main cause of this is the different origins of the programs – some come from the world of Motif, others have been developed under OpenLook, and so on.

Surprisingly enough, it is not the foreign language special characters that cause problems, but the function keys (down to the everlasting Unix problem of how to differentiate between Backspace and Del). In this section we will try to provide the most important background information and present the different files that affect the keyboard under X.

Keyboard options in `XF86Config`

If you use an XFree86 X server, the file `XF86Config` is the central point for keyboard configuration. For a U.S. keyboard, the `Keyboard` section should look as follows (`"pc104"` for a Windows keyboard):

```
# Keyboard setting in XF86Config
Section "Keyboard"
   Protocol        "Standard"
   XkbRules        "xfree86"
   XkbModel        "pc101"
   XkbLayout       "us"
   XkbOptions      "grp:switch"
EndSection
```

Numeric keypad

Under X, the numeric keypad is by default set to cursor mode (without NumLock). In previous XFree86 versions it was possible to activate NumLock automatically by entering the instruction `Xleds 1 2 3` in the `Keyboard` section of `XF86Config` and the instruction `xset led 2` or `3` in `xinitrc`. Since XFree version 3.3 this no longer works (probably because of the changed protocol for processing keyboard events). Thus you need to activate NumLock via the keyboard.

CAUTION

Please note that an activated NumLock causes big problems in interaction with various programs and in particular with the `fvwm2` or `fvwm95` window managers: in the same way as Shift or Ctrl, NumLock is regarded as a state which is, however, not taken into account in the common `fvwm` configuration files. The consequence: various window operations, in particular a window change via mouse click or keyboard shortcut no longer work. More about this unpleasant feature can be found in the description of `fvwm` from page 272 onward.

Changing key assignments with xmodmap

`xmodmap` allows you to change the assignment between a key and the character generated by pressing it. With XFree86 X servers, the use of `xmodmap` is required only in exceptional cases – for example to solve the everlasting Backspace/Del problem.

With `xmodmap -pke`, the current keyboard table is displayed in the syntax required for `xmodmap`. `xmodmap file` processes the definitions given in the file, `xmodmap -e definition` allows you to redefine a single key. Application examples can be found in the following subsections.

Backspace and Delete

Once upon a time there was a computer which had a keyboard without a Del key. In those days, computer users had modest expectations: they were glad that they could correct their input at all and were happy to put up with Backspace. This is when the first version of Unix saw the light of day. Since then, eons have gone by. Computers became more powerful and keyboards somewhat more user-friendly. Yet, the distinction between Backspace and Del proved to be such an obstinate problem that even computer geniuses never found a solution. And as long as Unix (and Linux) are alive and well, their users will still have to suffer ... .

After this – obviously imaginary – fairy tale, back to reality: after starting Linux, you can use the `xev` program to check how X reacts internally to various keys being pressed. In many (older) Linux distributions you will find that pressing Del and Backspace lead to the same Keysym text ‘Delete.’ This is the character string that is passed to X programs when a key is pressed. Thus, it is no wonder that X programs are unable to differentiate between Del and Backspace.

In order to make differentiation possible, `xmodmap` must be used. The following instruction ensures that, in future, pressing Backspace results in the Keysym string ‘BackSpace.’

```
# Addition to xinitrc (only required in older XFree86 versions)
xmodmap -e "keycode 22=BackSpace"
```

Depending on the distribution, you will find `xinitrc` in `/etc/X11/xinit` or in `/usr/X11R6/lib/X11/xinit`. If the home directory contains the file `.xinitrc`, this file takes precedence over the global `xinit`.

NOTE The internal key numbers used in text mode (for `loadkeys` and `showkey`) and under X (for `xmodmap` and `xev`) do not correspond! In text mode, the Backspace key is number 14, under X 22.

For more advanced X programs, this instruction is sufficient and Backspace and Del work satisfactorily. Other programs will not know what to do with `BackSpace` and continue interpreting the `Delete` string as `BackSpace`. With such programs, a modification in `~/.Xdefaults` or `~/.Xresources` sometimes works wonders (see also page 248).

Keys in text mode programs

Even under X, you will often find yourself working with programs that were designed to be used in text mode (`jed`, `pine`, and so on). For such programs, the above instruction is of little use. The weirdest reaction comes from the `jed` editor: Backspace now calls the online help, and Del takes on the effect of Backspace.

Under X, text mode programs are executed in a terminal or shell window created by the `xterm` program. This allows you to achieve correct support for nearly all traditional programs with a single change in the `xterm` resources. Simply insert the following lines into the `~/.Xdefaults` or `~/.Xresources` file (depending on the distribution):

```
! in ~/.Xdefaults or ~/.Xresources
*VT100.Translations: #override \
       <KeyPress>BackSpace: string(0x7f)\n\
       <KeyPress>Delete: string(0x04)\n\
       <KeyPress>Home: string(0x01)\n\
       <KeyPress>End: string(0x05)
```

This setting actually refers to the VT100 widget – which is, however, the basis of `xterm`. The Keysym string `BackSpace` is substituted with character code 127 and the Keysym string `Delete` with character code 4 (this corresponds to Ctrl+D). Following the same pattern, Home can be assigned to Ctrl+A and End to Ctrl+E, so that these keys too can be used, as in text mode, to jump to the beginning or the end of a line.

Thus, the four keys are interpreted correctly by a large number of programs. These settings have also been tested with Emacs in text mode (`emacs -nw`), with `jed`, `jove`, `pine`, `bash`, and so on.

In order to force the X version of Emacs to recognize Backspace and Del, you must include the following line in `~/.emacs`:

```
; in ~/.emacs
(global-set-key [delete]  'delete-char)   ;<Del> delete character
```

> **NOTE** However, keyboard simulation for text mode programs is not yet one hundred percent perfect: for example, the Emacs emulators `jed` and `jove` do not recognize the Alt key. If these programs are to be used under X, the Esc key must be used in key combinations instead of Alt. Also, the above `.Xdefaults` setting does not apply to the `cmdtool` and `rxvt` programs which can be used as terminals as well.

Direct keyboard settings via xmodmap

If you *only* work with conventional programs under X, there is yet another solution: you could use `xmodmap` to assign the keys Backspace, Del, Home, and End the codes 0x7f, 4, 1 and 5 (instead of the strings `BackSpace`, `Delete`, `Home`, and `End`).

```
# in xinitrc (this is not recommended at all!)
xmodmap -e "keycode  22=0x7f"  # <Backspace> yields code 127
xmodmap -e "keycode 107=0x04"  # <Del> yields Ctrl+D
xmodmap -e "keycode  97=0x01"  # <home> yields Ctrl+A
xmodmap -e "keycode 103=0x05"  # <End> yields Ctrl+E
```

Text mode programs executed under `xterm` or another terminal program will now receive the same codes they already know from text mode. However, true X programs will also receive the character codes defined above and will not know how to handle them (apart from very few exceptions). Therefore, this solution must be considered a dead end road.

Global key combinations

When working under X, the following key combinations usually apply:

X keyboard shortcuts	
Ctrl+Alt+Backspace	terminate X
Ctrl+Alt+Fn	switch to text console 1 to 6
Alt+F7	switch back from a text console to the X Window System
Ctrl+Alt++ / -	change graphic mode

The key combinations Ctrl+Alt+Backspace, ++ and +- can be deactivated by means of the keywords `DontZap` and `DontZoom` in the `Server` section in `XF86Config`.

Under X, the key combination Ctrl+Alt+Del *cannot* be used to reboot Linux. For a restart, you either have to switch to a text console and press Ctrl+Alt+Del there, or enter the command `shutdown -r now` in a terminal window.

Further keyboard shortcuts are defined by the active window manager – see page 262.

Input focus

In the X Window System, several programs can run simultaneously – but only one program at a time can accept input from the keyboard. Depending on the window manager configuration, either the program that was last clicked is considered to be active, or the one that is currently under the mouse pointer. It is mainly the second variation that causes problems to people used to working with MS Windows. The remedy is a different configuration of the window manager – see page 276.

The way some programs administer the input focus within one window (for example, try the SEARCH command in `xman`) appears even more unusual: input can only be made in the field on which the mouse pointer is situated. Since the input fields are often rather small, a tiny shift of the mouse is often enough to send your input into oblivion. For this reason, many recent programs follow Motif's behavior, where the input focus is fixed in a field by a mouse button click.

Configuring the mouse

If you use an XFree86 X server, the `Pointer` section in `XF86Config` is responsible for mouse configuration. The two most important options, `Device` and `Protocol`, specify the interface to which the mouse is connected (usually `/dev/mouse` or `/dev/ttyS0`) and which protocol from the following list the mouse is using: `BusMouse`, `Logitech`, `Microsoft`, `MMSeries`, `Mouseman`, `MouseSystems`, `PS/2`, `MMHitTab`, `Xqueue`, and `OSMouse`. In case of doubt, you will have to experiment. However, please remember what you learned during your `gpm` configuration (page 141).

If you have a two-button mouse, you can use the `Emulate3Buttons` option to specify that simultaneous pressing of both mouse keys can be used to emulate the missing third button. `Emulate3Timeout` specifies the delay with which the pressing of single keys is processed. Some Logitech three-button mice only work when the `ChordMiddle` option is used.

```
# Mouse setting in XF86Config
Section "Pointer"
    Protocol    "Microsoft"
    Device      "/dev/mouse"
    # Emulate3Buttons     # only for 2-button mice
    # Emulate3Timeout 50  # delay in ms
    # ChordMiddle         # only for some Logitech 3-button mice
EndSection
```

gpm as a mouse server

There are some very exotic three-button mice on which all three buttons work under `gpm`, but only two work under X. In such cases, `gpm` can be used as a server – that is, `gpm` continues to be responsible for mouse control and passes the mouse events on to X. To do this, you must start `gpm` with the additional option `-R`. Then, `gpm` creates the file `/dev/gpmdata`. Communication with X is carried out via this FIFO file, that is, the file must be specified in `XF86Config` as a device, and `MouseSystems` must be specified as the protocol. Do not forget to deactivate `Emulate3Buttons`.

```
# Mouse setting in XF86Config, if rpm -R is used as mouse server
Section "Pointer"
    Protocol    "MouseSystems"
    Device      "/dev/gpmdata"
EndSection
```

CAUTION

While `gpm` can mean the solution to many a mouse dilemma, there are other mice where `gpm` and X do not agree. In this case, `gpm` must be halted with `gpm -k` before X is started. The `gpm -k` instruction can, for example, be included in `xinitrc`.

Using the mouse

Copying and pasting text with the mouse

In practically all X programs, you can use the mouse to copy sections of text and subsequently paste them into another position (or into a different program). The mouse is used as in text mode under `gpm`. Text sections are marked by keeping the left mouse button depressed. The marked text is automatically copied into a buffer. When you press the middle mouse button, the text is pasted at the position of the active insertion point. The right mouse button can be used to change the size of a marked text section.

Using scroll bars

Many X programs are equipped with standardized scroll bars (for example, `xterm`). The size of the gray scroll box indicates the relative size of the visible section. While the look is more or less similar, the handling differs strongly from MS Windows standard practice.

The scroll boxes are moved by pressing and holding the middle mouse button. Clicking the left mouse button moves the scroll box downward, clicking the right mouse button moves it upwards. The current position of the mouse indicates how much the scroll box is to be moved: if the mouse is way up inside the scroll box, the window contents will be scrolled one line, if it is way down the bottom, the window contents will be scrolled a whole page.

Making the mouse pointer invisible

Usually, under X the mouse pointer is always visible. Particularly in programs that are primarily operated via the keyboard, this can be rather annoying – the pointer often covers characters one would like to see. The remedy is the `unclutter` program. It is started as a background process and automatically hides the mouse pointer when it is located on a window and has not been moved for several seconds. The pointer becomes immediately visible again when the mouse is moved or a mouse button is pressed. In the Debian distribution, `unclutter` is included in the standard delivery; with most other distributions, the package must be downloaded from the Internet.

X resources

Resources are a particular feature of the X system. They allow easy setting of the properties of most X programs – from the background color of an `xterm` window to the character fonts in Emacs. For a better understanding of the concept of resource files, we need to undertake a little excursion into the internals of the X system.

> **NOTE**
> Obviously, there are X programs which use their own configuration files (in addition or exclusively). A frequent reason for not using X resources is the attempt to find a uniform configuration process for different computer platforms. During the search for the greatest common denominator, X resources must often fall by the wayside.

Basics

X programs are composed of so-called widgets. Widgets are graphic control elements for specific tasks. Thus, there are widgets for text fields, for buttons, and so on. Widgets have certain features – for example, `font` for the character set, `background` for the background color, and so on. Widgets can be embedded hierarchically – for example, inside a frame widget for a menu there can be several button widgets for the individual menu commands.

The complete denomination of an X program detail – for example, the background color of the VT100 widget of the `xterm` program – is given by the combination of all components. The components are joined by dots. The following line in the resource file sets the background color to white:

```
xterm.vt100.background: white
```

In most X programs, this concept is extended with additional private resources. For this reason, not only can the properties of widgets be changed, but also many global settings. (The difference is interesting insofar as the setting of widget properties works automatically without having to add a single line of code to the X program. For this reason, `man` texts for X programs often only describe the program-specific extensions of this resource concept.) The following line is a typical example for a program-specific resource setting (here, for the `seyon` terminal emulator).

```
Seyon.hangupBeforeDial: off
```

Another detail of resource setting is worth mentioning: in the composition of names, the wildcard `*` can be used. It has the same meaning as in file names, but can also extend over several components of resource names. For example, the first of the following two lines causes all background areas of every program and widget to be colored yellow, with the sole exception of those widgets which have been explicitly set to a different color. The second line makes all `seyon` program widgets turn blue.

```
*background: yellow
seyon*background: blue
```

Resource files

Resource files can be stored in different locations in the directory tree. Depending on the distribution, these files are automatically recognized in the following locations. The files are listed in increasing order of precedence.

Locations of X resource files

default settings exclusively for the `xdm` login:
`/etc/X11/xdm/Xresources` or
`/usr/X11R6/lib/X11/xdm/Xresources`

optional local default settings, in many systems recognized only by `startx` (but not by `xdm`):
`~/.Xresources`

global default settings for a specific program:
`/usr/X11R6/lib/X11/app-defaults/progname`

current user's local settings:
`~/.Xdefaults` (in RedHat)
`~/.Xresources` (in SuSE)

The `Xresources` files are read in only once at the start of X (see page 267). The settings in the `app-defaults` directory and those in `.Xdefaults`, on the other hand, are read at the start of every X program.

Absolute precedence over all resource files mentioned above is given to options which are directly specified at program start. Obviously, this also applies to programs started by `xinitrc` or via `fvwm`.

The syntax used for resource files has probably become clear from the above examples. Upper and lower case spelling usually plays no role (but there are some exceptions!). Comments are marked differently: instead of the `#` known from other programs, they begin with an exclamation mark. Also, comments must be on lines of their own – resource settings are not allowed to have appended comments.

The easiest way to change resource settings is to take existing `.Xdefaults` files as a model and to copy the lines that you can use into your own `.Xdefaults` file (and possibly change some settings). Examples of resource settings can be found in the files of the `app-defaults` directory.

TIP Detailed information about permitted resource settings can also be found in the `man` texts for the program in question. The general concept of resources is described in the `man` texts for `X` and `xrdb`.

7.3 X fonts

Management of character sets under X and the use of these fonts in X programs is a very complex subject which, for reasons of space, cannot be dealt with in all its aspects. The following information should, however, be sufficient to understand the system and to add new fonts.

TIP

If you want to delve deeper into character sets, the following two addresses offer an excellent starting point:

`http://www.gimp.org/fonts.html`
`http://www.nwalsh.com/comp.fonts/FAQ`

Basically, X has non-scalable and scalable fonts. Non-scalable fonts are present as bitmaps in a limited number of sizes (for example, in 8, 10, 11, 12, 14, 17, 18, 20, 24, 25, and 34 points). Such fonts can also be displayed in any other size (X simply reduces or increases the characters of the nearest font); however, characters created in this manner look ugly and are very hard to read.

In scalable fonts, in contrast, only the *shape* of each character is described. When a character is used for the first time, the X server generates a bitmap out of the mathematical description of that character. The quality of the result is good, but the very first display may take some time and (when using many fonts and sizes at the same time) require a lot of memory and disk space.

NOTE

Under Microsoft Windows, fonts generally look smoother than in the X Window System. This is due to the fact that antialiasing is used to draw the characters edges as grayscale pixels. Unfortunately, the X Window System does not support antialiasing (version 11, releases 6.3 and 6.4). Individual programs, such as `gimp`, `ghostview`, `xdvi`, or `acroread` provide an antialiasing option; however, this effect is achieved via a very time-consuming calculation of the page in a higher resolution.

Microsoft Windows is currently still ahead of the X Window System on another aspect too: nearly all fonts can be printed on any printer. Under X, this works only in exceptional cases (with some PostScript fonts that are also available as X fonts).

Font management

Font files are usually located in subdirectories of `/usr/X11R6/lib/X11/fonts`. With non-scalable fonts, there is a separate file for each font size and attribute; with scalable fonts, one file is sufficient for all sizes.

Each font directory also includes the file `fonts.dir`, which is responsible for the coordination between the font files and the internal font names of X.

NOTE The X font naming conventions are described in the context of the Gimp text command on page 678. A list of all available fonts can be generated by means of `xlsfonts`. You can, however, also use the more user-friendly programs `xfontsel` or `kfontmanager` (KDE).

To enable XFree86 to find the font files, the paths leading to the font directories must be listed in the `Files` section of `XF86Config`. (This section also contains the path to a file with the names of the RGB colors which, however, are of no interest here.)

```
# Excerpt from XF86Config
Section "Files"
   RgbPath     "/usr/X11R6/lib/X11/rgb"
   FontPath    "/usr/X11R6/lib/X11/fonts/misc:unscaled"
   FontPath    "/usr/X11R6/lib/X11/fonts/75dpi:unscaled"
   FontPath    "/usr/X11R6/lib/X11/fonts/100dpi:unscaled"
   FontPath    "/usr/X11R6/lib/X11/fonts/URW"
   FontPath    "/usr/X11R6/lib/X11/fonts/freefont"
   FontPath    "/usr/X11R6/lib/X11/fonts/Type1"
   FontPath    "/usr/X11R6/lib/X11/fonts/Speedo"
   FontPath    "/usr/X11R6/lib/X11/fonts/misc"
   FontPath    "/usr/X11R6/lib/X11/fonts/75dpi"
   FontPath    "/usr/X11R6/lib/X11/fonts/100dpi"
   FontPath    "/opt/StarOffice40/fonts/type1"
EndSection
```

The keyword `unscaled` means that, with all fonts of the directory in question, X does not attempt any scaling of its own. This keyword can also be employed with non-scalable fonts. This leads to the effect that unscalable fonts can definitely only be used in the predefined sizes.

In the above font list, some paths are specified twice, the first time with the `unscaled` addition and later once again without it. The consequence: when searching for a font in a specific size, X first tries a matching non-scaled bitmap standard font. If no matching font can be found, scaled fonts are considered as well. If this search also fails, the makeshift solution is adopted to have the X server increase or reduce the size of a non-scalable font – with the unsatisfactory results mentioned earlier.

NOTE The order of paths in `XF86Config` has a decisive influence on the display quality. When an X program requires a font without precise specification of all parameters, the first matching font is returned on the basis of the path order in `XF86Config`. (Only in exceptional cases do X programs really specify all parameters of a fonts – including the name of the manufacturer, and so on.) Therefore, unscaled fonts that can be displayed crisply in all sizes should appear at the beginning of the `Files` section.

XFree86 standard fonts

75-dpi fonts

The XFree86 basic package contains exclusively non-scalable fonts for a screen resolution of 75 dpi. (Information on the dpi value and how to change it follows on page 255.) The standard fonts include, amongst others, Courier, Helvetica, New Century Schoolbook, Times, and Utopia by Adobe, Lucida by B&H, and Charter by Bitstream. These fonts are usually installed in the following directories:

```
/usr/X11R6/lib/X11/fonts/75dpi
/usr/X11R6/lib/X11/fonts/latin2/75dpi
/usr/X11R6/lib/X11/fonts/misc
```

100-dpi fonts

A separate package is avaibale for XFree86 which, with the exception of the `misc` fonts, includes the same fonts for a higher screen resolution of 100 dpi. Please note that this package is not always installed automatically. An installation can even make sense if you want to keep the 75 dpi set as a default, because some programs (such as LyX) take all installed fonts into account to achieve an optimum text display.

```
/usr/X11R6/lib/X11/fonts/100dpi
/usr/X11R6/lib/X11/fonts/latin2/100dpi
```

Speedo and Type-1 fonts (scalable)

Finally, XFree86 comes with several Speedo and Type-1 fonts – in SuSE, for example, in the `xfntscl` package. These fonts are usually not installed automatically.

Speedo is the name of the font format adopted by Bitstream. Type-1 fonts follow the format specifications of Adobe. Their great advantage is that as PostScript fonts they are also suitable for printing without any additional conversion tools. Generally, both font types are scalable.

The package includes the Courier and Utopia fonts by Adobe, together with Charter and Courier by Bitstream. (Courier fonts are thus multiply available under X – scaled and not scaled, by different manufacturers, and so on. You may, for example, use the fonts dialog of Gimp to explore the subtle differences.)

```
/usr/X11R6/lib/X11/fonts/Speedo
/usr/X11R6/lib/X11/fonts/Type1
```

NOTE

Obviously, manufacturers such as Adobe, Bitstream, and others offer many more fonts than the few supplied together with XFree86. The problem: these fonts are usually not freely available, but must be bought (as any other commercial product). Most of the fonts supplied with XFree86 are only available because they were released – almost as a gift – by these companies.

Additional fonts

URW fonts (GhostScript)

For GhostScript, the URW font foundry has donated a package of scalable PostScript standard fonts (AvantGarde, Bookman, Courier, Helvetica, New Century Schoolbook, Palatino, Times, Symbol, ZapfChancery, and ZapfDingbats). The fonts look very similar to the Adobe originals; they can be distributed under the terms of the GPL and can therefore also be used outside GhostScript. They are usually installed in the following directory:

```
/usr/X11R6/lib/X11/fonts/URW
```

If the fonts have not been supplied with your distribution (depending on the GhostScript version), you can also find the files on the Internet:

```
http://www.gimp.org/urw-fonts.tar.gz
```

Gimp fonts

Gimp users have put together a collection of fonts which are either free or available as Shareware. Obviously these fonts too can be used outside Gimp. Since the copyright terms of some of these fonts are somewhat questionable, you will rarely get these fonts on a CD. The usual location is:

```
/usr/X11R6/lib/X11/fonts/freefont
```

On the Internet, you find the fonts under the following address:

```
ftp://ftp.gimp.org/pub/gimp/fonts/
```

NOTE

After installation of new fonts, you need to specify the paths of the relevant directories in `XF86Config` and subsequently restart X. The fonts can only be used correctly if the `fonts.dir` file is included in the directories.

`fonts.dir` can be generated from `fonts.scale` by means of the `mkfontdir` program. (For scalable fonts, `fonts.dir` and `fonts.scale` are identical.) However, you must put together the information for `fonts.scale` yourself or look for it on the Internet. With Type-1 fonts, the Perl script `type1inst` relieves you from this task. This program too can be found on the Internet, for example under:

```
ftp://sunsite.unc.edu/pub/Linux/X11/xutils
```

Font server

Usually, X looks after the task of reading fonts files and converting them into a format that allows a screen representation. However, this task can also be delegated to an external program which runs in the background (even on another computer). This program is called a font server.

There may be two reasons for configuring a font server: on the one hand, X is blocked during scaling of fonts, which is annoying in particular on computers with a very slow CPU (temporary blocking of the mouse). On the other hand, there are font servers which are able to handle fonts that X usually cannot display (for example, TrueType fonts).

To make you understand the principle of a fonts server, first an example to show the configuration of `xfs`. This program is supplied with XFree86, but it is usually not employed because the same functions are handled by the X server anyway.

Before you can start `xfs`, you must create a configuration file. Its name is not predefined; here we use `/etc/xfs-config`. Information on the structure of this file can be found in the `man` text for `xfs`.

```
# /etc/xfs-config
# Paths for fonts
catalogue = /usr/X11R6/lib/X11/fonts/URW,
  /usr/X11R6/lib/X11/fonts/freefont,
  /usr/X11R6/lib/X11/fonts/Type1,
  /usr/X11R6/lib/X11/fonts/Speedo,
  /usr/X11R6/lib/X11/fonts/misc,
  /usr/X11R6/lib/X11/fonts/75dpi,
  /usr/X11R6/lib/X11/fonts/100dpi
# set 12 point as default size (in decapoints)
default-point-size = 120
# 100 or 75 dpi default resolution
default-resolutions = 100,100,75,75
```

Now you can start `xfs` in a text console. (If you want to start it automatically, you should create appropriate Init-V files – see also page 124. In the Debian distribution, such files are part of the delivery.)

```
root#  xfs -config /etc/xfs-config -port 7100 &
```

With this, `xfs` runs as a background process and can be addressed via the TCP-Port 7100. To enable X to find the font server, `XF86Config` needs to be modified.

```
# Addition to XF86Config
Section "Files"
   ...
   FontPath   "tcp/localhost:7100"
EndSection
```

TrueType fonts

Apple Macintosh and Microsoft Windows computers use a different font format than Unix computers, namely TrueType. Owing to the wide distribution of these operating systems, there is a huge range of economical and in many cases even free TrueType fonts. If you want to use these fonts under Linux as well, you need to install a font server that can handle this font format. (RedHat 6.0 comes with a preinstalled TrueType font server.)

The following description focuses on the most popular program for this purpose: `xfsft`. This is an `xfs`-compatible font server which, in addition, can handle TrueType files. The program is available on the Internet both as source code and as a binary file. (The documentation is part of the source package; thus you need it in any case.)

```
http://www.dcs.ed.ac.uk/home/jec/programs/xfsft/
```

To be able to test the program, you obviously need TrueType fonts. The following example is based on the Verdana font which is supplied with Microsoft Windows. (Please note that font files are subject to copyright and cannot be copied freely.)

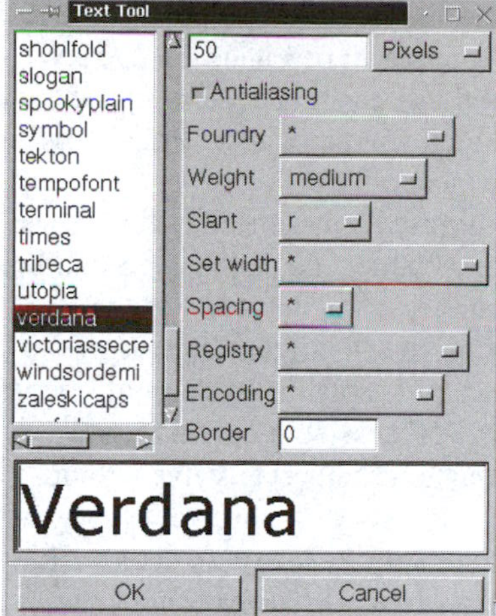

Figure 7.4 The Verdana font in the fonts dialog of Gimp.

First you need to create a new directory (for example `/usr/local/fonts/truetype`). Into this directory, you copy all TrueType files with the extension `*.ttf`. Subsequently, you need to create `fonts.dir`. In the first line, this file contains the number of entries; in the following lines, the X font information. You can either create this file manually (following the example of the `fonts.scale.sample` sample file supplied together with `xfsft`) or employ the `ttmkfdir` program which you can find on the Internet:

```
http://www.darmstadt.gmd.de/~pommnitz/xfsft.html
```

In the simplest case, `fonts.dir` for the file `verdana.ttf` could look as follows. (The second line is only split for reasons of space.)

```
1
verdana.ttf \
  -microsoft-verdana-medium-r-normal--0-0-0-0-p-0-iso8859-1
```

Entry in the configuration file and start of `xfsft`, plus insertion in XF86Config are exactly the same as with `xfs`. Do not forget to include the TrueType directory in the configuration file.

Setting the dpi value

dpi stands for *dots per inch* and specifies the screen resolution. An example: if your screen width is 36 cm (19-inch monitor) and the horizontal resolution 1280 pixels, then about 90 pixels are displayed per inch ($1280 / 36 \times 2.54$).

Which role is played by the dpi value? To make text well readable independently from screen size and graphics resolution, differently sized fonts should be used in function of the dpi value. If, for example, you operate your 17-inch monitor with a resolution of 1280×1024 pixels, the letter 'A' must be composed of more pixels to make it look the same size as an 'A' on an 19-inch monitor with a resolution of 800×600 pixels. In other words: if the X Window System and the programs used under it recognize and evaluate the correct dpi value, characters will not appear either so tiny that they cannot be read or unnecessarily clumsy.

So much for the theory. Practice is again more complex. On the one hand, XFree86 is generally preset to 75 dpi; on the other hand, the X Window System is usually only provided with fonts for 75 and for 100 dpi (which defeats the setting of a different value); finally, a large number of X programs simply ignore the dpi information.

To achieve an optimum font display in spite of all this, all sorts of tricks are employed: manual adaptation of the font size in `.Xdefaults`, modification of the zoom factor in text processing programs, and so on. However, once a system is configured in such a way, one can usually live with it.

Perfectionists will, however, still want to know how to set the dpi factor properly. Unfortunately, `XF86Config` does not allow you to specify the monitor size. (With this information, the X server could calculate the dpi factor itself on the basis of the current resolution.) Instead, you can resort to another two measures (also in combination):

- Start X by means of `startx -- -dpi` *n*, explicitly indicating the dpi factor calculated for your monitor or required for other reasons. (The general rule is: the higher the dpi value, the larger the employed fonts.) If you do not want to specify the dpi factor every time, you can also modify `xserverrc` instead (see page 268).
- Change the order of the `FontPath` lines in `XF86Config` in such a way that the `100dpi` lines are always put before the corresponding `75dpi` lines. (If you do that, in case of doubt, X uses the larger fonts. The default configuration is set exactly to the opposite.)

  Make sure that the 100-dpi fonts are installed. (Check the `/usr/X11R6/lib/X11/fonts/100dpi` directory.)

```
# XF86Config: precedence of 100-dpi over 75-dpi fonts
Section "Files"
  ..
  FontPath    "/usr/X11R6/lib/X11/fonts/75dpi"
  FontPath    "/usr/X11R6/lib/X11/fonts/100dpi"
  ..
EndSection
```

As already stated, not all X programs take these settings into account, and even program that try to do so are limited by the choice of available fonts. (One of the few programs that evaluates the dpi factor at least for text display is LyX. However, the size of the menu texts still does not change.)

> **TIP** If you use a font server (such as `xfs`, see above), remember that its configuration also plays a role.

7.4 X in multiuser operation

In text mode, you can log in on each text console under a different name. Under X, this is not that easy. When you work with `startx`, you need to exit X and re-execute `startx` under a different login. Also, when you use `xdm`, you need to terminate the current session (and thus all running programs) and log in again.

In many cases, it is only necessary to quickly execute a command as `root` – having to leave X for this would not be very user-friendly. Since X is optimized for network operation, it is hardly surprising that there are several alternatives for working under a foreign login under X. However, some rules must be observed which, initially, are often overlooked.

su

The easiest way to quickly change user name is provided by the command `su` *name*. If you do not execute the command as `root`, you are prompted for the password of the relevant user. Inside the terminal window (usually `xterm`) you can now execute commands under the changed name until you change back to normal mode with `exit` or Ctrl+D. Even starting of X programs works, which is not a matter of course, as the following paragraphs will show.

> **TIP** To make `su` a fully-fledged substitute for a `root` login, you need to use the option `-l`. This ensures that all login start-up files (for example, for correct definition of `PATH`) are read in again.

telnet, rlogin

Another two possibilities for working locally under a different login are provided by `telnet localhost` (with subsequent login, including the password) or `rlogin -l` *name* `localhost` (with subsequent password prompt). For reasons of security, neither of the variations can be used to log in as `root`.

Execution of commands or programs that run within `xterm` causes no problems. The attempt to start an X program, however, ends with an error message:

```
user$  xman
Error: Can't open display:
```

The reason: the environment variable `DISPLAY` is not initialized. The following instruction solves this problem:

```
user$  export DISPLAY=localhost:0
```

`telnet` and `rlogin` can also be used to log in on a different computer via network. To ensure that X programs can be started, `DISPLAY` must now be set to the network name of the local computer. (The variable specifies on which computer the X program is to be visible.) Generally, however, this is still not sufficient because, for security reasons, the local computer refuses to execute X programs of a foreign computer. You can deactivate this safety mechanism in an `xterm` window of the local computer for a specific user or computer name by means of `xhost +`*name*. `xhost +` switches the protection off completely. (This is a security risk!)

To illustrate the process with an example: you work on the local computer `jupiter`, but would like to start an X program on the more powerful `saturn` computer (and control it at the local computer). You will need to execute the following commands:

```
user$  xhost +saturn
user$  rlogin saturn
password:  ******
user$  export DISPLAY=jupiter:0
user$  netscape     # Netscape runs on saturn, but is locally
                    # displayed (on jupiter)
```

Although you execute all three commands in the same `xterm` window, from the `rlogin` onward, all commands are no longer executed locally, but on the `saturn` computer. The local computer is exclusively responsible for input and output. (With X programs, all graphics command are now transmitted over the network.)

TIP

In principle, X programs can be executed externally even if you only operate a PPP connection. In practice, however, the insufficient network connection speed prevents reasonable work. In such cases, remedy is brought by the `dxpc` package which compresses the X data stream for transmission. However, this package needs to be installed (and started) on both computers involved.

`http://ccwf.cc.utexas.edu/~zvonler/dxpc`

xterm

Particularly in `fvwm` configuration files it is often desirable to start `xterm` with a command and at the same time provide a login for `root`. The required command looks like this:

```
xterm -title "root" -bg red -e su -l - &
```

The new `xterm` window is visually emphasized by the title 'root' and a red background color.

`xterm` can also be combined with `telnet` or `rlogin`. The following lines present some examples:

```
xterm -e telnet localhost &          # login for local computer
xterm -e telnet -l name jupiter &    # login for 'name' on 'jupiter'
xterm -e rlogin localhost &          # login for local computer
xterm -e telnet -l name jupiter &    # login for 'name' on 'jupiter'
```

7.5 Screen savers

As already mentioned, you can use the command `xset s` *n* in `xinitrc` to obtain that after *n* seconds of inactivity the screen turns black and automatically becomes visible again after a mouse movement. If the only purpose is to protect the monitor, this is sufficient.

However, there is an entire collection of pretty screen savers for Linux, which in most distributions can be activated manually (`xlock` and `xlockmore` packages). The `xlock` program can also be used to lock keyboard and screen when you leave your computer for a short time – thus the name `lock`. It would obviously be a good idea if these screen savers could also be started automatically.

This task is carried out by the `xautolock` program which, however, is not supplied with all distributions. (You can find it on the Internet, for example in the Sunsite archive or on one of the countless mirrors). `xautolock -time` *n* `&` is simply started as a background process in `xinitrc`. *n* specifies the number of minutes of inactivity after which the screen saver is to be started. If you do not want to use `xlock` (default setting) as a screen saver, you can specify a different program by means of the option `-lock`.

An alternative to `xautolock` is `xscreensaver -timeout` *n*. This program is, however, incompatible with `xlock`; thus a different program must be used for displaying the screen saver graphics. Suitable programs, such as `qix`, `helix`, and others, are usually supplied together with `screensaver`. Every program is suitable for displaying a background pattern, as long as it can access the `root` window of X. Selecting this program is, however, somewhat confusing: to ensure that `xscreensaver` uses a specific program (and not some default program which is probably not even installed), the following settings are needed in `~/.Xdefaults` (here with `xdaliclock`, a futuristic clock, as screen saver):

```
! xscreensaver
xscreensaver.monoPrograms:
xscreensaver.colorPrograms:
xscreensaver.programs:      xdaliclock -bg black -fg darkblue -root
```

TIP

If you use KDE or GNOME, you can set the screen saver in a very user-friendly way. KDE and GNOME are described in the next chapter.

If you require a screen saver in text mode, you simply execute `setterm -blank` *n*, where *n* specifies the number of minutes after which the screen saver becomes active.

X user interfaces (fvwm, KDE, and GNOME)

This chapter deals with the handling of the X Window System. This strongly depends on which window manager and (if you use one at all) which desktop system you use. The introduction of the chapter describes the functions of a window manager and in what ways it differs from a whole desktop system. Subsequently, the three currently most important representatives of their kind, namely fvwm, KDE, and GNOME are described in detail.

> **NOTE**
>
> X experts will shudder at the title of this chapter. Is this author again lumping together different things! The reason for this is quite clear: `fvwm` is a window manager, KDE is a package of X programs that includes a window manager, and GNOME is another package of programs, but this time without a window manager. Fear not: these subtleties will be explained in the next pages.
>
> The common denominator of this chapter is the user interface with which you are confronted as a typical Linux user – and the chances are that it is one of the variations mentioned in the title.

8.1 Introduction

Window managers

Primarily, a window manager takes care of how program windows are displayed on the screen. It provides windows with a title bar and buttons, and assists in their management (moving, minimizing, switching programs via mouse click). Furthermore, many window managers offer an option for starting frequently used programs via a menu.

These seemingly elementary functions are *not* provided by the X Window System. This is both an advantage and a disadvantage: the advantage is that the user interface is not restricted by X system functions and can be organized in almost any way by the window manager. The disadvantage is that, as a result of this flexibility, Linux computers cannot be handled in a unique way, since each user has a different opinion as to which is the best window manager.

Visually, the influence of the window manager can be seen in the design of the windows. Of course, window frames look different in each window manager and, obviously, handling of the windows varies too.

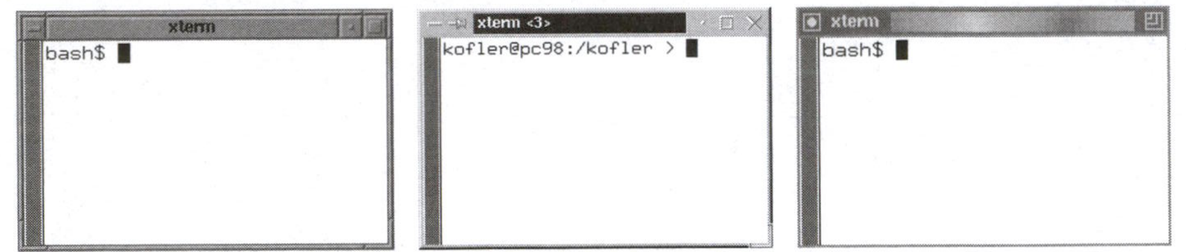

Figure 8.1 The `xterm` terminal window, displayed by the window managers `fvwm 1.2`, `kwm`, and `twm`.

NOTE

As though the window manager and the GUI libraries were not causing enough confusion, modern libraries for X programming additionally support so-called *themes*. This is a further option to vary the look of standard elements (buttons, scroll bars) and thus to design an even more customized, colorful, exotic (and so on) desktop.

Themes are supported by several window managers and enjoy increasing popularity under KDE and GNOME. Since version 1.1, KDE assists configuration with a separate theme manager. There are dozens of pre-configured themes for the Enlightenment window manager.

Depending on the distribution, Linux offers you the choice between a number of different window managers. The following list, which does not set out to be complete, names some of the most popular representatives of their kind:

- `fvwm` has been the most popular manager during recent years. It is available in three versions (1.2, 2.0, and 95). (It is not known what the abbreviation `fvwm` stands for; perhaps Free Virtual Window Manager.)
- If you use KDE, it is very likely that you will also use `kwm`, that is the KDE Window Manager. (KDE is more than just a window manager – more about that later. With KDE you can also use a window manager other than `kwm` – however this rarely makes sense.)

- GNOME does not possess a window manager of its own, but can be used with any window manager of your choice. It works particularly well with window managers that are 'GNOME compliant.'
  Perhaps the most popular window manager for GNOME is Enlightenment, which is the default window manager for future RedHat distributions. Also quite popular are Blackbox, Icewm and WindowMaker, which are not completely GNOME compliant yet. Furthermore, there are plans for the development of a GNOME-friendly configuration for `fvwm2`.
- Finally, `twm` (Tab Window Manager) should be mentioned, because it is the only window manager which is a fixed component of the X system. Although it is notoriously difficult to handle, it is often used as a stopgap when no other window manager is installed, or if there are start-up problems.

Desktop environment

What is a desktop? There is probably no definite answer to this question. The following list outlines some features:

- A desktop environment offers a user interface for elementary operations (handling of files, and so on).
- Handling is as intuitive as possible (drag & drop, icons).
- Menus and dialog texts appear in the predefined language.
- The actual desktop incorporates a package of uniformly operated utilities for frequently used operations (for example, a text editor, a calculator).
- All desktop components can be easily configured (by means of dialogs, not cryptic text files).
- For all components or programs, extensive online documentation is available in an easy-to-read format (HTML).
- Transfer and utilization of data of different desktop programs is not complicated.
- Internet functions (such as access to ftp directories) are transparently supported by all components. Local and external data can be processed in the same way.

In the course of Unix history, there have been several attempts to facilitate handling with the aid of various desktops. The best known of these are two commercial systems: Motif consists of a library for X programming, a collection of utilities, and a window manager. Regarding ease of handling, the Common Desktop Environment (CDE) went a step further than Motif. However, neither of the systems managed to set a true standard. The multitude of functions long enjoyed by Microsoft Windows or Apple Macintosh users was denied to Unix (and thus Linux) users.

KDE (K Desktop Environment) and GNOME (GNU Network Object Model Environment) are supposed to change this. Both are desktop environments which claim to create a modern, easy-to-handle, and most of all free desktop for Linux.

KDE and GNOME are relatively young projects – they started in October 1996 and August 1997, respectively.

From the user's point of view, KDE and GNOME differ mainly in two points: the number of functions and the 'look and feel'. With regard to the number of functions, KDE is still (at least for the moment) far ahead of GNOME. Thus, there are many more KDE programs than GNOME programs. The appeal of KDE and GNOME is due to their modern looks, which even seasoned Windows and Macintosh fans cannot help but admire.

Of course there are also technical differences: the systems are based on different libraries (Qt or Gtk – see the following section). KDE incorporates a window manager, whereas GNOME must be used in combination with a foreign window manager. This results in higher flexibility (nobody will be deprived of their favourite window manager), but is detrimental to the goal of creating uniform handling.

The KDE versus GNOME debate

Disregarding the decade-long discussion as to whether Emacs or vi is the best editor on earth, no other topic has inspired so much discussion in Linux-specific newsgroups as the question which desktop was better for Linux, KDE or GNOME. This book does not want to add to the debate. Nevertheless, a short historical digression might explain why until further notice there will be *two* competing desktops for Linux.

Basically, KDE and GNOME fans agreed that Linux needed a new, modern, easy-to-handle desktop. The core of the conflict was not the question as to whether KDE or GNOME was more beautiful, more functional, and so on. In fact, at the core of the debate were the libraries onto which the two desktops are built. (Both these libraries provide functions for X programming, such as the design of menus, toolbars, and so on.)

KDE is based on Qt, a commercial library of the TrollTech company. This library can be used free for free software projects; however, in comparison to the GPL/LGPL, there were a lot of restrictions (particularly for Qt $1.n$).

GNOME, in contrast, is based on the Gtk (Gimp Tool Kit), a library which was originally developed only for the user interface of Gimp. (Gimp is an image processing program – see Chapter 20.) The Gtk is truly free software and is subject to the LGPL.

KDE supporters argue that the free distribution of Qt is sufficient. However, for the developers of GNOME (and many others), it was not acceptable that the desktop of a free operating system was in the hands of a company which, for example, wanted to retain full control over modifications and corrections to their library.

The debate also split the distributors into two factions. While some distributions simply supplied both desktops (as far as available) and left the choice to the users, RedHat in particular categorically refused to supply KDE because of the above copyright problems. (Of course, KDE packages for RedHat were available on the Internet and many non-original RedHat CDs included KDE.)

Thus there was some danger that the technically excellent KDE could fail because of licensing problems. This danger appears to have been overcome, since TrollTech announced that Qt would get a new licence with version 2.0, namely the QPL (Q Public Licence). Admittedly, in one aspect this licence is still more restrictive than the LGPL (it is only valid for free Qt software, but not for commercial Qt programs). At least, however, it ensures that Qt will remain free in future and can be modified without TrollTech's permission.

Thanks to the new license, it can be expected that in future most distributions will include KDE as well as GNOME. KDE and GNOME developers will try even harder than before to decide this bizarre competition by offering better, easier to handle functions. In this respect, the double-tracked desktop development certainly has its advantages. Furthermore, developers are attempting to implement some of the features, such as drag & drop, to be compatible, so that in future simultaneous utilization of KDE and GNOME programs (which is already possible) will cause even fewer problems.

Finally, you might like to know the author's opinion, although a comparison is very difficult. It is certain that at the moment KDE has a big lead where number and quality of additional programs and documentation are concerned. The fact that almost all KDE programs are equipped with (reasonably translated!) foreign language menu and dialog texts – with a current choice between 25 languages, from Catalan (`ca`) to Chinese (`zh_TW`) – is also very convenient. On the other hand, RedHat wholeheartedly supports GNOME, and therefore GNOME surely has every chance of establishing itself at least in the English-speaking world as a quasi-standard. The dream of the author is of peaceful side by side existence, so that users can have the best of both worlds without having compatibility problems: for example KDE as desktop, `gmc` as file manager, `klyx` as LaTeX interface, `gnumeric` as spreadsheet, and so on.

KDE and GNOME application programs

Lately it has become customary to view every program based on the Qt library as a part of KDE, and similarly every gtk program as a GNOME component. However, this is not quite correct: neither the window manager nor a potentially active desktop system have any influence on the programs you can use under X. The only prerequisite for the execution of programs is that the necessary libraries are installed. In principle, there is no objection to using the GNOME file manager under KDE (and vice versa). However, problems have to be expected with features that go beyond individual programs (drag & drop, data exchange, and so on).

In spite of KDE and GNOME, standardization of the user interfaces of all important Linux programs is not to be expected in the near future. For a large number of programs, special versions for KDE and/or GNOME have been created (for example `kghostview` is a KDE variation of `ghostview`), but these programs only rarely prove to be of the same quality as the originals. Moreover, it is neither sensible nor desirable that all programs are ported: the cost of maintenance as well as the (storage) problems with multiple installations would become huge.

A more positive aspect is that KDE and GNOME have noticeably inspired the development of new application programs. Even if it may appear strange that the double-track desktop situation is to be followed by separate GNOME and KDE office packages – if only some of these components can be developed to a state of general usability, much will be gained.

> **NOTE**
> In this book, X application programs – irrespective of whether they have been specially optimized for a particular desktop system – are described in the appropriate chapters (for example all Internet tools in the Internet Chapters 9 and 10). A description of various X tools and utilities can be found in Chapter 15. This chapter only describes the basic functions of fvwm, KDE and GNOME.

Problems

There only remains to be said that the new desktop systems do have their teething troubles. The first big difficulty occurs when you try to install additional programs that have not been supplied with the respective distribution. This virtually never works! Either the required libraries are missing completely or they are too old. Any attempt to install a new library will fail because of package dependencies or will cause incompatibility problems with programs that have worked so far. For the moment, the average Linux user has virtually no chance of getting a new KDE or GNOME program which has been downloaded from the Internet up and running quickly by him or herself.

A second problem is a lack of stability. KDE and GNOME were developed at incredible speed. The logical consequence is that the many new programs do not yet have the same stability as their predecessors which have stood the test of time.

And that is not all: the beautiful icons and marvellous features obviously cost memory space and CPU performance. Working with KDE and GNOME is only really enjoyable on a powerful computer. If this not available, `fvwm` is certainly the better choice.

So do not be dazzled by the beautiful, new, and colorful desktop world under Linux: however positive the development as a whole, and however great the prospect of Linux distributions offering for the first time more (and not less) ease of operation than Microsoft Windows may be, there is currently chaos with almost daily changing versions, libraries, and so on.

8.2 Selecting your window manager or desktop environment

When you run `startx` after installation of a distribution and configuration of XFree86, the default window manager or desktop provided by the respective distribution will automatically appear on your screen. This section explains what happens at the start-up of X, and which files you need to modify in order to activate a different window manager or desktop environment.

First, a brief overview of the configuration files which strongly depend on the relevant distribution. If you start X with `startx`, one of the following files is usually responsible for starting the window manager (local files – if present – take precedence):

`~/.xinitrc`	(local)
`~/.Xclients`	(local, only RedHat)
`/etc/X11/xinit/xinitrc`	(global, RedHat, Debian)
`/etc/X11/xinit/Xclients`	(global, only RedHat)
`/usr/X11R6/lib/X11/xinit/xinitrc`	(global, default setting, SuSE)

If, on the other hand, X is automatically started by `xdm` at system start-up, the following files are concerned:

`~/.xsession`	(local)
`/etc/X11/xdm/Xsession`	(global, RedHat, Debian)
`/usr/X11R6/lib/X11/xdm/Xsession`	(global, default setting, SuSE)

NOTE

In SuSE, you can easily set the default window manager with Yast when you are logged in as `root`. In addition, users can select their own preferred window manager by modifying the variable `$WINDOWMANAGER`.

In RedHat since version 6.0 you can use the easy-to-handle `switchdesk` tool to choose your default desktop system (GNOME, KDE, or 'Another Level,' an `fvwm` incarnation). `switchdesk` modifies `~/.Xclients`.

The X start-up process

It has already been mentioned that there are several possibilities for starting the X Window System: `startx` or `xdm` for a start as a background process (daemon) with a login window. (If you regularly work with `xdm` you can also modify the default runlevel in `/etc/inittab` and thus enable an automatic start of X on start-up of the computer (see also page 124.) If you use the Open Look window manager, you must use `openwin` instead of `startx`.

The following subsections describe what happens during the execution of the X start-up programs and which configuration files can be modified so that X starts the required window manager (and maybe some other programs) correctly.

startx

The sole task of the `/usr/X11R6/bin/startx` script file is to pass client and server options to `xinit`, which is responsible for the X start-up proper.

```
startx [client_options] [-- [server_options]]
```

`startx` executes the command `xinit client -- server`. `client` and `server` are character strings of arbitrary length – including empty strings – made up as follows:

Client

If client options are passed to `startx`, `startx` passes these (and only these) to `xinit` unchanged.

Otherwise, `startx` looks for the file `~/.xinitrc`. If the file exists, its name is passed.

Otherwise (depending on the distribution) `startx` looks for `/usr/X11R6/lib/X11/xinit/xinitrc` or `/usr/X11R6/lib/X11/xinit/xinitrc`. If the file exists, its name is passed. (In some distributions, this is not a file, but a link to `/etc/X11/xinit/xinitrc` – this is where configuration takes place.)

Otherwise, no parameters are passed to `xinit`.

Server

If server options are passed to `startx` (that is, parameters after `--`), `startx` passes these (and only these) to `xinit` unchanged.

Otherwise, the same procedure is repeated as for the client: look for `~/.xserverrc`, look for `xserverrc`, or do without any options. Finally, an example of how `.xserverrc` might look to start X with a preset dpi of 200 (see also page 255):

```
exec X -dpi 200
```

Normal case

The large number of possible configurations makes the start-up process look a bit confusing. The normal case is very much simpler: `startx` is executed without any parameters at all; `xinit` is passed either the local configuration file `.xinitrc` or the global configuration file `xinitrc`; a configuration file for the server does usually not exist, that is, the choice of server is left to `xinit`.

The command `startx -- exec X -bpp 16` causes the usual `xinitrc` file to be used, but passes the option `-bpp 16` to the server (to make it support 65536 instead of 256 colors). If you want this as default setting, you can use the keyword `DefaultColorDepth` *n* in the `Screen` section of `XF86Config`.

`xinit [client options] [-- [server options]]`

`xinit` first starts the server (specified after `--`) and then the client program. If no server is specified (the normal case), `xinit` automatically starts the server `/usr/X11R6/bin/X`. If no client is specified, `xinit` automatically starts `xterm` as the only client.

Usually, the client is specified through an `xinitrc` file. This is a shell script which first starts various X clients (for example, `xterm`, `arena`, and so on) and then uses `exec` to start the required window manager.

Please note that longer running X programs must be started in the background by means of a postfixed `&` (otherwise, the window manager would only be started after client termination, which makes no sense). Please also note, however, that the window manager must be started in the foreground, since X is terminated as soon as the client script is terminated (and with it, the last program started through it). In the simplest case, `xinitrc` looks like this:

```
#!/bin/sh
# xinitrc minimal version
# (~/.xinitrc or /etc/X11/xinit/xinitrc
#              or /usr/X11R6/lib/X11/xinit/xinitrc)
xterm -ls -geometry 80x30+10+10 &              # shell window
exec fvwm                                      # window manager
```

Normally, `xinitrc` is slightly more complex. On the one hand, it contains code that causes `Xresources` and `Xmodmap` files to be read in automatically. On the other hand, in some distributions, it contains code that starts the file `~/.Xclients` instead of the programs directly specified in `xinitrc`. This allows you to create `~/.Xclients` in the home directory only for a private configuration (and otherwise use the global `xinitrc`). The following listing shows a modified variation of `xinitrc` for RedHat.

```
#!/bin/sh
# xinitrc example (RedHat)
# $XConsortium: xinitrc.cpp,v 1.4 91/08/22 11:41:34 rws Exp $
userresources=$HOME/.Xresources
usermodmap=$HOME/.Xmodmap
sysresources=/usr/X11R6/lib/X11/xinit/.Xresources
sysmodmap=/usr/X11R6/lib/X11/xinit/.Xmodmap
# if local or global Xmodmap files (rarely) and/or
# Xresources files (frequently) exist, they are loaded
if [ -f $sysresources ]; then
    xrdb -merge $sysresources
fi
if [ -f $sysmodmap ]; then
    xmodmap $sysmodmap
fi
if [ -f $userresources ]; then
    xrdb -merge $userresources
fi
if [ -f $usermodmap ]; then
    xmodmap $usermodmap
fi
# if ~/Xclients exists: execute
if [ -f $HOME/.Xclients ]; then
    exec $HOME/.Xclients
elif [ -f /etc/X11/xinit/Xclients ]; then
    exec /etc/X11/xinit/Xclients
else
    xclock -geometry 50x50-1+1 &
    xterm -geometry 80x50+494+51 &
    xterm -geometry 80x20+494-0 &
    if [ -f /usr/X11R6/bin/fvwm ]; then
        exec fvwm
    else
        exec twm
    fi
fi
```

In the case of RedHat, the file `/etc/X11/xinit/Xclients` exists, so that the last `else` block will not be used.

> **TIP** Please note that starting programs automatically can not only be carried out through `xinit` or `xclients` files, but also through the configuration file of the window manager. This applies particularly to `fvwm`! Thus, if you wonder where all these automatically started programs come from, check the `fvwm` configuration files (see page 272).

Modifying `xinitrc`

If you want to select a different window manager without using the distribution-specific control mechanisms, simply copy the global file `xinitrc` into your home directory and name it `~/.xinitrc`. Start-up of the window manager is carried out with `exec`.

```
# in ~/.xinitrc: start fvwm2
exec fvwm2
```

The corresponding line to start KDE is shown below. It starts the KDE window manager as well as a range of KDE core components.

```
# in ~/.xinitrc: start KDE
exec startkde
```

The procedure to start GNOME seems to depend on the distribution. With RedHat 6.0, `exec gnome-session` starts GNOME *and* the window manager set in the GNOME control center (default: Enlightenment). With SuSE, you have to explicitly start a window manager and then use `panel` instead of `gnome-session`.

```
# in ~/.xinitrc: start GNOME 1.0
exec gnome-session                              # RedHat
[your favorite windows manager] & exec panel    # SuSE
```

`xdm`

`xdm` conceptually differs from `startx` and `openwin` insofar as the user must log in under X (as in a text console). As soon as the user exits X with a command to terminate the window manager, `xdm` again shows the login window. Thus, `xdm` is capable of starting X over and over again (and, if required, with different window managers for different users). `xdm` is particularly useful if several people use the same computer to work under X at different times. In most distributions, `xdm` is preconfigured in such a way that it uses the same configuration files as `startx`.

When `xdm` is to be used, the computer is usually configured so that `xdm` is started automatically within the Init process. Therefore, the runlevel must be changed in `/etc/inittab` – see also page 124. As a trial, `xdm` can also be started directly by `root`. A further variation is to change the runlevel as `root` by means of `init` *n* – however, depending on the configuration, this will terminate almost all running programs.

CAUTION When working with `xdm`, X should not be terminated with Ctrl+Alt+Backspace. This key combination not only terminates the window manager, but X as a whole. This may cause problems when `xdm` needs to restart X. If you use XFree86 as your X server, you can deactivate the 'magic' key combination by means of the keyword `DontZap` in the `Server` section of `XF86Config`.

The look of the `xdm` login window can be controlled through the `Xresources` file. The syntax is the same as for the other resource files (see page 248). `Xresources` only applies to `xdm` (not to the programs started by `xdm`!). `Xresources` is located in one of the following directories, depending on the distribution:

`/etc/X11/xdm/Xresources`	(RedHat, Caldera, Debian)
`/usr/X11R6/lib/X11/xdm/Xresources`	(Default setting, SuSE)

When it is executed, `xdm` starts the X system, but no window manager. The X system only provides a window for logging in. Moreover, in some distributions a colorful logo is displayed via `Xsetup_0` and `xbanner`. The shell script `Xsession` is executed only after a successful login. (All files mentioned have the same path as `Xresources`.)

`xdm` checks whether the file `.xsession` is present in the home directory of the currently logged in user. If so, the file is executed. `.xsession` has the same function as `.xinitrc` (see above), that is, it is responsible for additional X resources, for starting programs and for starting the window manager. In many cases, a link to `.xinitrc` is sufficient, if the file exists.

The following lines list the file `/etc/X11/xdm/Xsession` of the RedHat distribution. In other distributions, this file looks completely different in some parts. It serves only as an example to demonstrate the general process.

```
#!/bin/bash -login
# /etc/X11/xdm/Xsession in RedHat
# evaluate parameters passed to Xsession (rare)
case $# in
1)
        case $1 in
        failsafe)
                exec xterm -geometry 80x24-0-0
                ;;
        esac
esac
# save error messages in ~/.xsession-errors
# or in /tmp/xses-<user>
for    errfile    in    "$HOME/.xsession-errors"    "$TMPDIR-/tmp/xses-
$USER"    "/tmp/xses-$USER"
do
        if ( cp /dev/null "$errfile" 2> /dev/null )
        then
                chmod 600 "$errfile"
                exec > "$errfile" 2>&1
                break
```

```
        fi
done
# remove xdm login banner (RedHat-specific)
freetemp
# start X programs
startup=$HOME/.xsession
resources=$HOME/.Xresources
# execute ~/.xsession, if the file exists
if [ -x "$startup" ]; then
        exec "$startup"
# execute ~/.Xclients, if the file exists
elif [ -x "$HOME/.Xclients" ]; then
        exec "$HOME/.Xclients"
# execute /etc/X11/xinit/Xclients, if the file exists
elif [ -x /etc/X11/xinit/Xclients ]; then
        exec /etc/X11/xinit/Xclients
# only if no configuration file can be found:
# start X session manager
else
        if [ -f "$resources" ]; then
                xrdb -load "$resources"
        fi
        exec xsm
fi
```

Further `xdm` options and controls are described in the corresponding, very extensive, `man` text. The documentation for `xbanner` (which, in RedHat, is located in `/usr/doc/xbanner`) is also very informative.

There is a separate X daemon, `kdm`, for the KDE system. This program is described on page 289.

8.3 fvwm (Virtual Window Manager)

There are very good reasons why `fvwm` is the standard window manager for nearly all Linux distributions. The program combines ease of use with low memory consumption. Its configuration possibilities are practically unlimited (keyboard shortcuts, menus, icons, modules such as GoodStuff, and so on). Nobody seems to know any longer what the F in the abbreviation actually stands for – the `man` text suggests the terms 'feeble,' 'famous,' or 'foobar.'

`fvwm` is currently available in several versions. Version 1.2*n* has the lowest memory consumption. Version 2.0 offers far more configuration possibilities, but of course the syntax of the configuration file has changed. `fvwm95` is a variation of `fvwm` 2.0. Its look and feel is surprisingly similar to that of Windows 95. `fvwm95` is described briefly from page 278 onward.

`http://www.hpc.uh.edu/fvwm`

Finally, a word of warning: configuring `fvwm` is more addictive than any video game you can think of and you will end up doing nothing else for days on end! Do not get involved with it in the first place!

NOTE The decision as to which window manager is used is made in `xinitrc`. If you want to change the default window manager, you have to change either the global file `xinitrc` or the local file `~/.xinitrc` (see page 266).

The NumLock problem

A problem of all `fvwm` versions is that, since X11R6, NumLock is a modifier, like Shift or Ctrl. At the moment, this fact is not taken into consideration by `fvwm` or in the commonly supplied `fvwm` configuration files. If, for example, Alt+Tab is defined as the key combination for switching windows, this combination will not work whenever NumLock is active.

There are two ways of solving this problem: adaptation of the `fvwm` configuration file or modification of the keyboard layout by means of `xmodmap`.

fvwm configuration

In the case of key combinations, it is relatively easy to put things right. First you have to determine with `xmodmap` which modify number NumLock has on your system.

```
root#  xmodmap
shift       Shift_L     (0x32),  Shift_R   (0x3e)
lock        Caps_Lock   (0x42)
control     Control_L   (0x25),  Control_R (0x6d)
mod1        Alt_L       (0x40)
mod2        Num_Lock    (0x4d)
mod3        Mode_switch (0x71)
mod4
mod5        Scroll_Lock (0x4e)
```

In the above example, this is number 2. Now have a look at the `fvwm` configuration file (whose name varies depending on the `fvwm` version, see below) and look for lines similar to the following two:

```
#           Context  Modifier  Function
Key Tab     A        M         CirculateUp
Key Tab     A        SM        CirculateDown
```

These lines cause the function `CirculateUp` to be executed by Alt+Tab and the function `CirculateDown` to be executed by Shift+Alt+Tab in all contexts (thus, independently from the position of the mouse). M stands for meta, which corresponds to Alt on PC keyboards. (In `fvwm2` and `fvwm95`, the commands `Next [CurrentScreen *] Focus` and `Prev [CurrentScreen *] Focus`, respectively, have to be used instead of the `circulate` commands.)

Now you can extend the configuration file by two more lines:

```
Key Tab     A        M2        CirculateUp
Key Tab     A        SM2       CirculateDown
```

Forthwith, `fvwm` recognizes the two key combinations even when NumLock is active. Similar modifications are also possible for mouse combinations.

If `fvwm` is configurated in such a way that the input focus of the keyboard can be set to a specific window by a mouse click, a problem remains: this type of window switching only works if NumLock is deactivated. The keyword `ClickToFocus` has no facilities for specifying modifiers.

Modifying key tables

The second solution deactivates the [Num] key and redefines the numeric keypad, so that numbers can be entered even without NumLock.

```
! file to be read by xmodmap
! redefines numeric keypad to be used without NumLock
keycode 79 = 7
keycode 80 = 8
keycode 81 = 9
keycode 83 = 4
keycode 84 = 5
keycode 85 = 6
keycode 86 = plus
keycode 87 = 1
keycode 88 = 2
keycode 89 = 3
keycode 90 = 0
keycode 91 = comma
! deactivates NumLock key
keycode 77 =
```

This file must be read at each start-up of X. To do this, you can either copy the file under the name **`~/.Xmodmap`** into your home directory or install it as a global configuration file under the name `/usr/X11R6/lib/X11/xinit/`**`.Xmodmap`**. The file should be processed automatically during the start-up process in most distributions (see page 267). If this does not work, copy **`Xmodmap-numeric`** to `/etc/X11` and insert the following command in `xinitrc`:

```
# Addition to ~/.xinitrc or /etc/X11/xinit/xinitrc
#                        or /usr/X11R6/lib/X11/xinit/xinitrc
xmodmap /etc/X11/Xmodmap-numeric
```

fvwm 1.2n

A description of `fvwm` is difficult insofar as practically everything can be configured: from the look of the windows to the reaction to the click of a specific mouse button. Each distribution has its own configuration files, which partly define countless keyboard shortcuts, assign the most disparate functions to the mouse, depending on which button was pressed where, and so on.

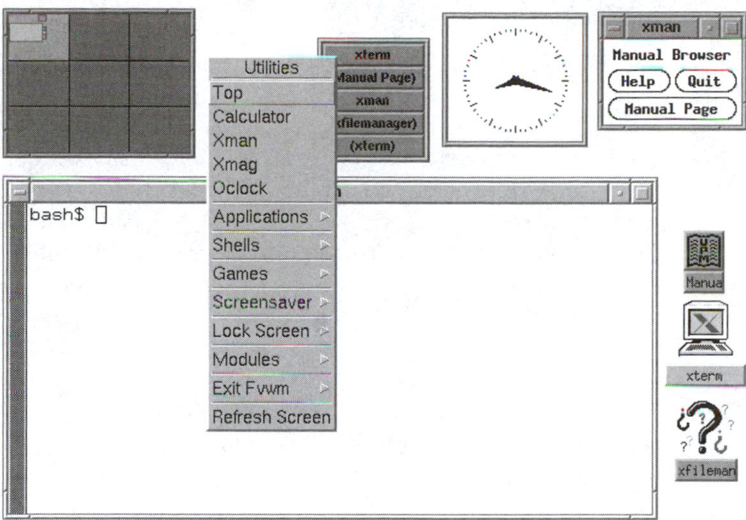

Figure 8.2 The X interface of `fvwm`.

Menus

In `fvwm`, all three mouse buttons are assigned their own menus. If the left mouse button is pressed while the mouse is over the screen background, a menu pops up to start the most important X programs (terminal window, editors, `xman`, `seyon`, and so on). You can also exit or restart `fvwm` through this menu.

> **NOTE**
>
> Not all programs listed in this menu will actually be available. In this case, there is simply no reaction when the corresponding menu item is clicked upon.
>
> In some distributions, the `fvwm` configuration file is recreated at each installation (SuSE) or even at each startup (RedHat). Admittedly, this takes time, but it has the advantage that the menus only list commands that can actually be executed.

The menu activated with the middle mouse button is one that you will probably need much less frequently: it allows you to move and resize windows, and so on. These actions can be performed directly on the window, without the aid of a menu.

Pressing the right mouse button displays a menu that lists all X programs currently running. Selecting one of these entries activates the corresponding program. If the corresponding window has been iconized, it is automatically restored to its previous size. In addition, `fvwm` automatically switches to that part of the virtual desktop in which the program is running.

Virtual desktop, Pager, GoodStuff

The X server can only manage one screen (which can be bigger than the section visible on the monitor, if sufficient video memory is available). `fvwm` goes one step further: windows may be placed in different virtual screens. Several screens can be combined into a 'desk,' several desks into the virtual desktop.

At the beginning, one screen will probably be sufficient. Several screens are useful for network operation (all connections to a particular computer on one screen), for program development (editor and debugger in different screens), and so on.

> **TIP** If you work with a virtual desktop, it is usually useful to activate the X server's virtual screen (keyword `Virtual` in the `Screen` section of `XF86Config`).

The module `FvwmPager` is responsible for managing the virtual desktop. With a click of the left mouse button, you can select the active screen. With the middle mouse button you can move a window arbitrarily across all screens directly in the pager. With the right mouse button, you can place the visible screen section over the actual screen borders (but this very seldom makes sense).

Depending on the configuration, `fvwm` can be set up in such a way that the visible screen automatically scrolls across the whole desktop as soon as the mouse is moved to a screen border. This has not been included in the sample configuration, because this behavior can be rather confusing to begin with.

The module `FvwmGoodStuff` needs addressing at this point: this is a kind of command headquarters in which buttons for starting X programs can be placed. In the sample configuration, only one button for `xterm` has been included.

GoodStuff can also house other modules and display their contents. In the sample configuration, the pager has been integrated into GoodStuff. (Otherwise, the pager would be a window of its own.)

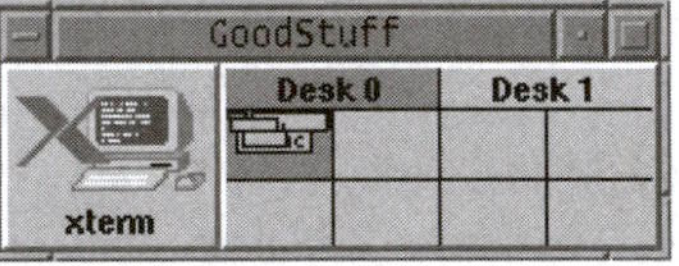

Figure 8.3 GoodStuff

GoodStuff is usually configured in such a way that it always stays in the same position ('sticky'), independently of the currently visible section of the desktop.

Configuration

The `fvwm` configuration is carried out either through `~/.fvwmrc` or, if this file is not present, through the global file `system.fvwmrc`. Depending on the distribution, this file is located in one of the following directories:

`~/.fvwmrc`	(local)
`/etc/X11/fvwm/system.fvwmrc`	(global, RedHat)
`/usr/X11R6/lib/X11/fvwm/system.fvwmrc`	(global, Caldera, SuSE)

TIP

> Online information about the configuration of `fvwm` can be found in the very extensive `man` texts for `fvwm`, `FvwmIconBox`, `FvwmPager`, and `FvwmWinList`.
>
> If you want to try out a new configuration, the fastest and easiest way is to restart `fvwm`, which can usually be done with a menu command. At a restart, all X programs are preserved (including the editor to modify `.fvwmrc`).

The following paragraphs describe some particularly important keywords of the configuration file, without any claim to completeness:

`ClickToFocus`

A window only becomes active (gets the input focus) when it is clicked upon. If the keyword is prefixed with the comment character `#`, a window gets the input focus as soon as the mouse is moved over it. At the beginning, this can be rather confusing, but it certainly saves a whole lot of mouse clicks. As already mentioned, `ClickToFocus` only works if NumLock is not active.

`AutoRaise` *n*

Specifies the time in milliseconds after which a window is shifted to the top when the mouse cursor is placed over it. This setting is useful when `ClickToFocus` is deactivated: in this case, after a short time, the active window also becomes the topmost window.

`IconBox` *x1 y1 x2 y2*

Specifies the area where icons should be placed. Negative values refer to the right and/or bottom screen border.

`DeskTopSize` *n*, `DeskTopScale` *n*, `Pager` *x y*

These three keywords control the size and position of the window for the virtual desktop. If this window irritates you and you only need one screen, you can comment out these three lines.

`OpaqueMove` *n*

Specifies the percentage of screen size up to which windows are visibly moved together with their contents. With $n = 0$, only the frames are moved, independently of the window size; this is the fastest way. If you have a fast computer (and above all a fast graphics card), you should try $n = 100$ – it looks very impressive!

`fvwm` 2.0

Version 2.0 of `fvwm` is brimming with new functions, even more possibilities for configuration and visual layout and a slightly higher memory consumption. The popular GoodStuff module has been rechristened: it is now called `FvwmButtons`. Windows can be ‘pinned’ to the screen via the menu item STICK. Now, the window is highlighted by horizontal lines in the title bar. When you work with a virtual desktop, the window is displayed on each desktop (whereas normal windows are only visible on the desktop where they were started).

The most prominent difference is that the old `.fvwmrc` configuration files can no longer be used. In order to facilitate the conversion, most distributions supply the `fvwm2` or `fvwm95` package together with the script `fvwmrc_convert` which can be used to translate old configuration files into the new syntax.

Probably the most frequent adaptation request concerns the basic functions of the mouse. Many keywords known from `fvwm` 1.24 also exist in `fvwm2`. However, these must now be used with `Style`. The following two lines show how to set the two most important mouse modes:

```
Style "*" ClickToFocus    # window gets focus by clicking on it
Style "*" MouseFocus      # window gets focus when mouse pointer
                          # is over it
```

If you use `MouseFocus`, it is useful that the active window is moved automatically into the foreground after a short period. This function is no longer performed by `fvwm`, but by the module `FvwmAuto`. This module is activated via a line in the `fvwm` configuration file.

```
Module FvwmAuto 200       # move window with focus into
                          # foreground after 200 ms
```

The names of the configuration files have changed as well:

`~/.fvwm2rc`	(local)
`/etc/X11/fvwm2/fvwm2rc`	(global, Debian, RedHat)
`/usr/X11R6/lib/X11/fvwm2/.fvwm2rc`	(global, `fvwm` default, SuSE)

TIP

`fvwm2` is extensively documented: besides the `man` text for `fvwm2`, there is a highly informative FAQ text (in the RedHat distribution, it can be found in the `/usr/doc/fvwm-2*` directory).

fvwm95-2

Although, strictly speaking, `fvwm95-2` is only a variation of `fvwm2` (different default settings in the configuration file, an additional module to simulate the Windows launch bar), the visual difference is surprising. X suddenly looks like Windows 95 and behaves in nearly the same way. (It remains to be seen whether this is an advantage or not.) `fvwm95-2` does not presume `fvwm2`. (`fvwm2`, however, usually comes with more online documentation, which also applies to `fvwm95-2`.)

The 95 version is started in `xinitrc` or in `xsession` by means of the command `fvwm95-2`. The following files are used for the configuration.

`~/.fvwm2rc95`	(local)
`/etc/X11/fvwm95-2/fvwm2rc95`	(global, RedHat)
`/usr/X11R6/lib/X11/fvwm95-2/system.fvwm2rc95`	(global, default)

TIP

In RedHat, `fvwm95-2` is the default window manager. The configuration is carried out through a whole range of files, which are processed by X at each start-up ('Another Level', see page 267).

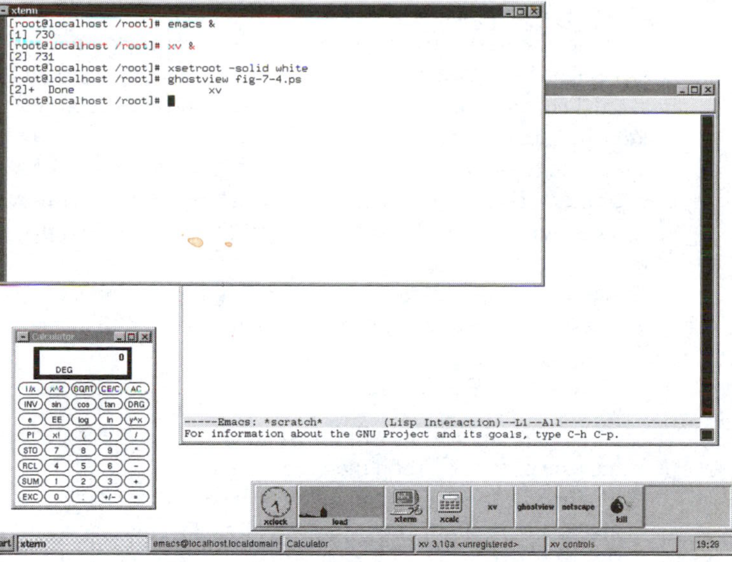

Figure 8.4 `fvwm 95.`

8.4 KDE

This section provides an introduction to the core components of KDE 1.1. Up-to-date information can be found on the KDE website `www.kde.org`.

REFERENCE

This chapter is limited to KDE basics. KDE programs which can be used independently of KDE under Linux are described (ordered by topic) in other chapters of this book, for example the KDE email client in the chapter about email and news. The following list shows the most important programs together with the respective page numbers.

`kdehelp` : help system, page 79
`kppp` : PPP configuration, page 318
`kmail` : email program, page 350
`kfm` : file manager, page 500
`kghostview`: PostScript viewer, page 520
`kdvi` : DVI viewer, page 522
`klyx` : word processing program, page 631

Installation and start

KDE is supplied with most distributions and can be installed without problems. If this is not the case (such as with old RedHat distributions), you need to download the KDE binary packages which are appropriate for your distribution from an FTP server. (The starting point for searching for packages is `www.kde.org`.) Please make sure that the packages of the default library correspond to your distribution (libc5 or glibc alias libc6, see page 120)!

The basic package for KDE 1.1 consists of three packages: `kdesupport`, `kdelibs`, and `kdebase`. As well as these, there is a whole range of optional packages with additional programs (such as `kde-games` or `kde-admin`). Furthermore, for execution of KDE, you will need a package with the Qt library.

After you have installed these packages with the appropriate package manager (for example with `rpm`), you should execute `ldconfig` to ensure that `ld` finds the Qt library. You should also add the path to the KDE binary files `/opt/kde/bin` to `PATH`. To do so, you need to change `/etc/profile`:

```
# Addition to /etc/profile
PATH=$PATH:/opt/kde/bin
```

This modification will only become valid at the next login. (In a text console, you execute Ctrl+D and then log in again.)

Finally you need to modify `xinitrc`, so that KDE is actually used as a window manager and desktop at the start-up of X. The crucial command is:

```
# Change in xinitrc or ~/.xinitrc
exec /opt/kde/bin/startkde
```

`startkde` is a script file which starts the window manager `kwm` as well as a number of KDE components (for example, the desktop panel). Now you only need to execute `startx`, and a few seconds later KDE should appear on the screen.

NOTE

Depending on the distribution, there are different possibilities for setting KDE as the default desktop. Please consult the section about X start-up on page 267.

You should also definitely read the `INSTALL` or `README` files, which provide additional distribution-specific information. In RedHat 5.1 systems, for example, you need to install the `ncurses-3` package for KDE to work.

At the first KDE start-up, the subdirectory `.kde` is created in the home directory, and filled with numerous configuration files. Then you are prompted to change the password in `~/.kde/share/apps/kdm/magic`. You can use any text editor to do this. The meaning of the password is not clear from the documentation. If you do not modify it, everything seems to work correctly anyway.

Survival rules

- Double clicks are frowned upon in KDE and are only used in exceptional cases. A single click is sufficient to start programs, open directories, and so on.
- In many programs and KDE components, a context menu can be called by clicking the right mouse button.
- Almost all KDE programs can handle drag & drop. For example, you can drag a text file out of the file manager and drop it on the editor program (`kedit`). (If the previous text has been changed in the editor, the new text is shown in

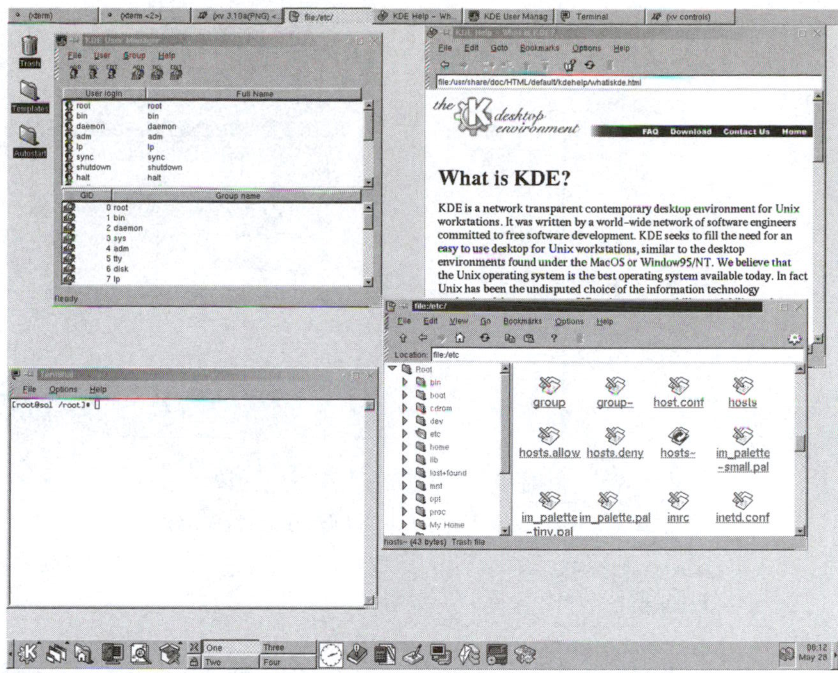

Figure 8.5 The K Desktop Environment.

an additional instance of the editor; in any other case the new text replaces the old one.) When releasing the mouse button, in some cases a context menu is displayed which gives you a choice between COPY, MOVE or LINK. Esc aborts the operation.

- KDE programs are usually configured directly via a menu. (In some central KDE components, configuration is carried out in the KDE control center – see below.) Basically, manual modification of configuration files is possible, but only seldom necessary – for example if no corresponding configuration dialog exists for individual options.
- Never leave KDE with Ctrl+Alt+Backspace! Instead, use the LOGOUT button (the X icon on the panel). KDE then stores information about currently running programs and attempts to restore the current state as exactly as possible at the next start-up. (However, this only works satisfactorily with KDE programs.)

Configuration

Important KDE components are configured via the KDE control center (`kcontrol`). This program is started via the start menu of the KDE panel. However, now and then you need a sixth sense to guess in which part of the hierarchical list field the required option is located.

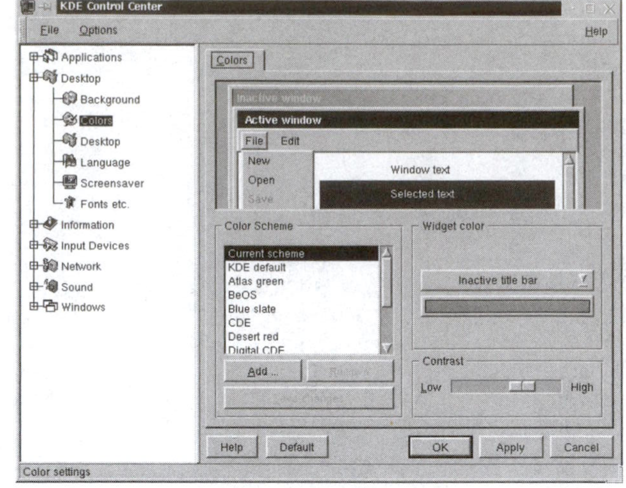

Figure 8.6 The KDE control center.

Language

A typical feature of KDE is that, for most programs, all the menu and dialog texts are available in various languages. The default configuration, however, displays English texts. If you prefer menu texts in another language, choose the requested language in DESKTOP|LANGUAGE. (Programs that are not available in other languages will still display the English texts.)

Font size

You can choose fonts and sizes for menu and dialog texts in DESKTOP|FONTS ETC. However, many KDE programs are not able to adapt their dialogs to the font size. In the case of too large a font size, text is truncated; in the case of a small font, buttons remain disproportionately large.

In the same dialog, you can specify whether control boxes, selection lists, buttons, and so on, should be drawn in the style of Windows 9x or whether the Unix look and feel should be preserved.

Positioning of windows

The place where new windows appear can be specified in the WINDOWS|PROPERTIES dialog. Depending on the setting, the KDE window manager carries out the placing of windows itself or leaves this task to you. (However, the author could not find a thoroughly satisfying setting to work with programs that frequently open small windows (Gimp).)

On the same dialog sheet, you can specify whether only the window frame or its contents too should be moved, and whether the window contents should be redrawn immediately when the size is modified. Both options only make sense on powerful computers.

When you move windows, they 'magically' snap to the borders of the desktop as well as to the borders of other windows. The extent of the snap zones can be modified in the DESKTOP|DESKTOP dialog. (0 switches the snap function off.)

Window title animation

If the window is too narrow to display the whole window title, the window title moves in the title line like in a newsflash. This more irritating than useful animation can be switched off in WINDOWS|TITLEBAR.

Screen saver

KDE contains a whole palette of screen savers. The configuration is carried out in DESKTOP|SCREENSAVER.

Further configuration options will be described in the following sections.

The KDE panel

The KDE panel (KPanel for short) is the central control component of KDE. It assists with starting of programs, switching between running programs, switching between different desktops, and so on. In the default configuration, KPanel is displayed at the bottom of the screen; buttons with a list of all running programs (comparable to the Windows taskbar) are shown at the top of the screen (see Figure 8.5).

The two most important icons of KPanel are the three-dimensional letter K, which leads to the KDE start menu, and the window icon which permits easy switching between currently running programs. (The contents of this menu are also displayed via Ctrl+Esc or after clicking the middle mouse button on the desktop.)

The remaining preconfigured icons are used for starting various KDE programs (file manager, help system, and so on) and save the often laborious navigation through the levels of the start menu. Finally, the letter X icon for shutdown of KDE and the padlock icon for temporary locking of the screen are important. (Work in KDE can only be continued after entering the login password. Until then, a screen saver is activated.)

Panel configuration

Options for the look of the panel can be set via the context menu as well as via APPLICATIONS|PANEL in the KDE control center. There, together with other items, the panel and taskbar positions can be determined (top, bottom, or left). The taskbar can also be made invisible. (To switch between running programs, the WINDOWLIST panel icon or various mouse or keyboard shortcuts can be used.)

Now to the contents of the panel: the displayed icons can be moved with the middle mouse button. With the right mouse button, you can call a context menu. Its commands can also alter the properties of the entry. The icon form can be modified on the dialog sheet EXECUTE by clicking on the square icon buttons. This triggers the display of an almost endless list of premanufactured KDE icons. (As long as no icon is set, the icon button is displayed as an empty, gray surface.)

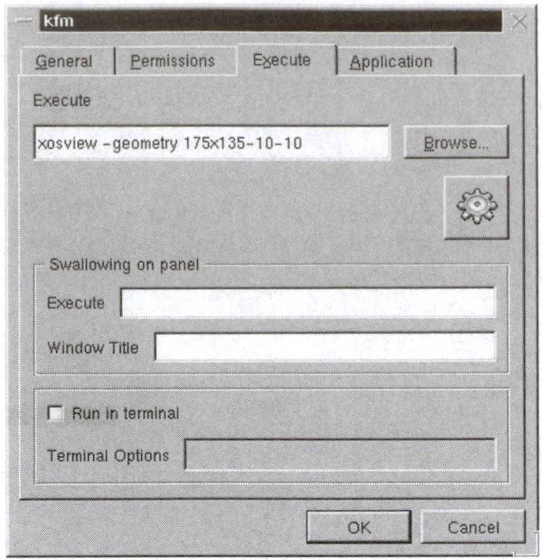

Figure 8.7 Properties of a panel icon.

The icon list displayed on the panel is extended via the KDE start menu, entry PANEL|ADD APPLICATION. The menu contains a list of all programs appearing in the start menu.

This immediately raises the question of how the start menu can be modified: you need to execute PANEL|EDIT MENUS. The menu editor that appears now (`kmenuedit`) shows the current start menu as well as the individual menu (which is simply a submenu of the start menu). Now you can open individual submenus by clicking on them (and by repeated clicking close them again). Via a context menu, you can change existing entries; with drag & drop you can copy individual entries; and with the middle mouse button you can change the order of the entries.

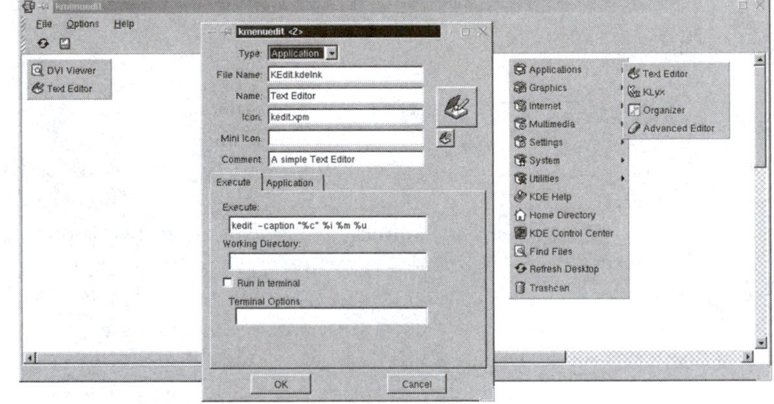

Figure 8.8 The KDE menu editor.

Executing programs in an icon

Usually, programs are displayed in a separate window at start-up. However, in a few cases it makes sense for the output of the program to appear directly in an icon on the panel. To configure an icon in such a way, you have to fill in both panel text fields. The window title is crucial: this is where you specify the text that the program displays in the window title (when it is started normally). KPanel requires the text to catch the window (so to speak). For the settings to become valid, you need to restart the panel via the context menu. The program is started immediately (not only when you click on the icon).

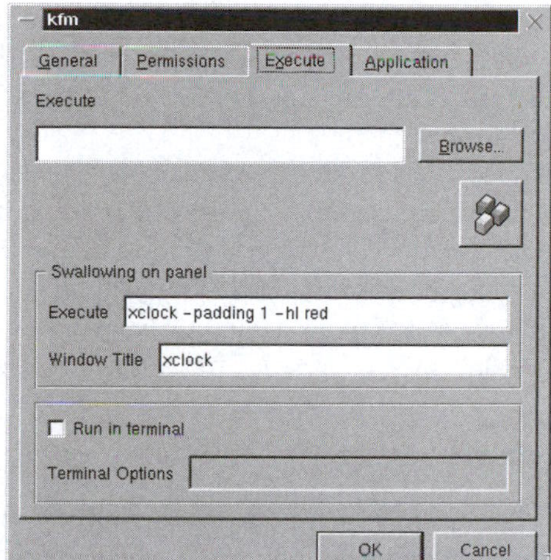

Figure 8.9 `xclock` displays the time of day in an icon.

Panel tools

Panel tools are small programs which display status information at the right or bottom border of the KPanel. Important examples are `kbiff` (displays whether new mail has been received), `kcpumon` (displays CPU load), and `kapm` (displays battery capacity in laptops).

If you want the panel tools to be started automatically, you must create a link to the program concerned in the Autostart directory. To do this, you simply drag the program icon from the file manager (directory `/opt/kde/bin`) onto the Autostart folder on the desktop and then select the option LINK.

Desktop management

Virtual desktops

In the default setting, KDE manages four virtual desktops, between which you can switch with the KPanel buttons ONE to FOUR or with Ctrl+Tab. A further option for switching windows is to move the mouse beyond the bottom or right border of the desktop. However, a switch is only carried out if you specify the appropriate settings in DESKTOP|DESKTOP. This function takes some time to get used to.

The number of desktops (a maximum of eight) can be modified in the control center under APPLICATIONS|PANEL|DESKTOPS. By double clicking on the KPanel buttons you can assign more meaningful names to the desktops.

With DESKTOP|BACKGROUND you can individually set the background of each desktop. (Differing color processes or background bitmaps facilitate orientation in the desktops.)

Windows are usually only visible on the desktop on which they have been started. However, you can 'pin down' a window, so that it remains visible at the same place even if you switch desktops. To pin down a window, just click on the pin symbol at the left border of the window title.

If you want to move a window from one desktop to another, you can also resort to the window menu, entry TO DESKTOP|DESKTOP NAME.

Desktop pager

A so-called desktop pager (`kpager`) can assist with the management of the desktop. This is a program which offers a reduced view of all desktops. Windows can simply be activated with the mouse and moved between different desktops.

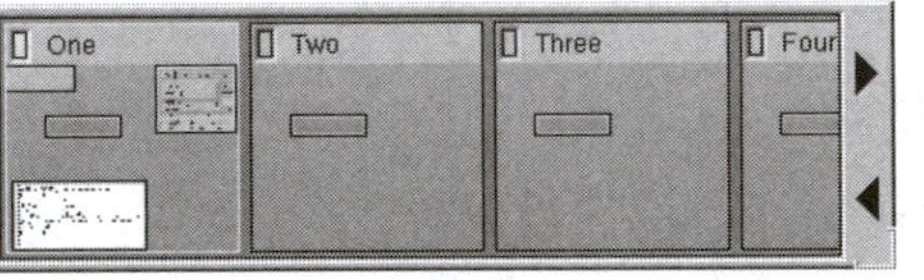

Figure 8.10 The KDE desktop pager.

Icons on the desktop

In the default configuration, KDE displays three icons on the desktops. These are symbols for the directories in `~/Desktop`. With drag & drop or via the context menu NEW, you can put any number of additional icons on the desktop. These can also be, for example, links to files, or other directories, but also symbols for devices or partitions (device icons).

Handling of icons is in itself problem-free, so only the creation of a device icon will be described in more detail. Let us assume that you wish to create an icon for the CD-ROM drive. To do this, you activate the desktop context menu NEW|DEVICE and name the object `cdrom.kdelnk`. Then you click on the icon with the right mouse button and change its properties on the DEVICE dialog sheet. There you need to specify the device name, the mount point, and the file system (see Figure 8.11). In addition you should specify two distinguishable icons which illustrate the status of the device (that is, whether it is currently mounted into the file system).

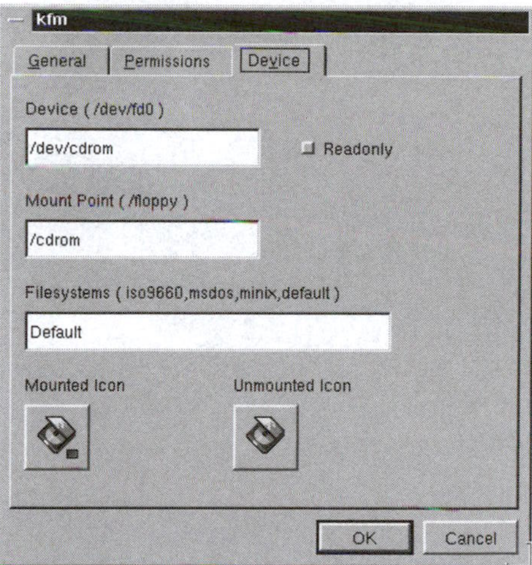

Figure 8.11 CD ROM icon.

If you now click on the icon, the CD-ROM is mounted into the directory tree at the point `/cdrom`. Simultaneously, the KDE manager is started and displays the contents of the CD-ROM. To unmount the CD-ROM from the directory tree (`umount`), simply click on the icon with the right mouse button and execute UNMOUNT.

Disk Navigator

Besides numerous bug fixes and improvements of details, the Disk Navigator is the only true novelty of KDE 1.1 against KDE 1.0. It is a nondescript extension to the KDE start menu, which helps you to quickly open a window for a specific directory with the file manager or a shell terminal. At the same time, you can easily access the most recently used programs and directories without working your way through the meanders of embedded menus or directory hierarchies. Once you have tried out the Disk Navigator even for only a couple of minutes, you will never want to do without its advantages again.

To start the file manager in a specific directory, simply use the menu entries of the Disk Navigator. For each subdirectory, a separate submenu is provided. When you select the OPEN FOLDER entry together with Shift a terminal window is opened in which the selected directory is set as the current directory.

Under the RECENT menu entry, the four most recently selected files, directories, or programs started via the KDE menu are displayed. The number of entries,

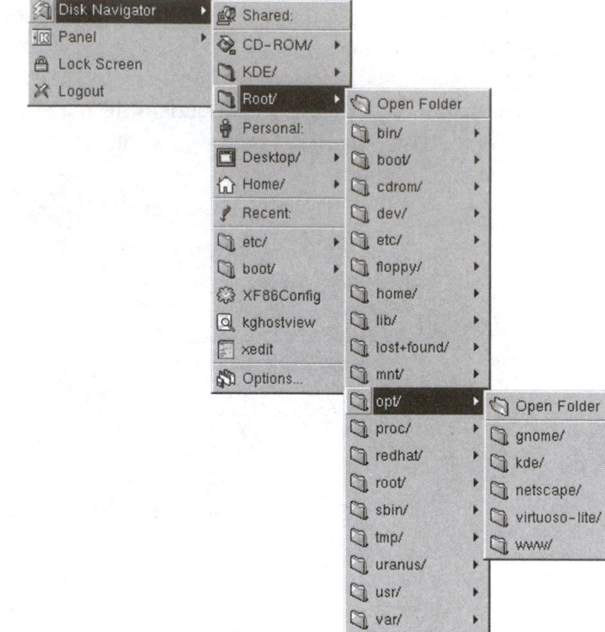

Figure 8.12 The KDE Disk Navigator.

as well as the entries in the PERSONAL and SHARED areas of the menu can be freely configured via the OPTIONS command.

KDE internals

rc files

Most KDE programs store status settings (font size, options, and so on) in the file `~/.kde/share/config/`*name*`rc`. This is a text file which is structured similarly to the `*.ini` files known from Windows 3.1. The program icons displayed on the KPanel, for example, are stored in `~/.kde/share/config/kpanelrc`. (By the way, the names of the files containing the screen saver settings are not *name*`rc`, but *name*`.kssrc`.)

Application-specific directories

Some KDE programs have so much configuration data that a single file would be too unwieldy. Such programs usually create a separate configuration directory in `~/.kde/apps`, for example `~/.kde/apps/klyx`.

kdelnk files

Links to programs or objects represented as icons in KDE (on the desktop, in the start menu, on the panel), are stored in text files with the extension `.kdelnk`. For example, the whole KDE start menu consists of a number of directories that contain `.kdelnk` files (path /opt/kde/share/applnk). In directories, the file .directory takes on the role of the .kdelnk file.

.kdelnk files can contain a lot of information, for example, the object names in several languages, the name of the icon, information regarding the file type, and so on. KDE recognizes several object types for .kdelnk files: programs, directories, devices (links to devices or partitions), FTP and URL links, and MIME data types.

KDE directories

The following list summarizes the locations of the most important KDE directories:

```
~/.kde/share/applnk          Personal menu
~/.kde/share/apps            Program-specific data
~/.kde/share/config          Local configuration settings
~/.kde/share/icons           Local icons
~/.kde/share/mimelnk         Local MIME types
~/Desktop                    Desktop information
~/Desktop/Autostart          Automatic start of programs
~/Desktop/Templates          Template for new kdelink objects
~/Desktop/Trash              Trash bin
/opt/kde/bin                 Programs
/opt/kde/share/applnk        Start menu
/opt/kde/share/apps          Program-specific data
/opt/kde/share/config        Global configuration settings
/opt/kde/share/doc           Online documentation (multilingual)
/opt/kde/share/icons         Icons
/opt/kde/share/locale        Menu and dialog texts (multilingual)
/opt/kde/share/mimelnk       MIME data types
/opt/kde/share/toolbar       Icons for toolbars
/opt/kde/share/wallpapers    Background bitmaps
```

The KDE display manager (kdm)

If you want to be greeted by KDE dialogs immediately after computer start-up, you can use the KDE display manager kdm instead of xdm (page 270). This program allows you a very easy X login. You can even select your favorite window manager. Configuration of kdm is carried out mainly in the KDE control center under APPLICATIONS|DESKTOP MANAGER. (However, individual options described in the online documentation have to be set directly in kdmrc.)

TIP With the kdm LOGOUT button, you can initiate a shutdown after a request for confirmation (that is, you can terminate Linux).

TIP In SuSE, you can use yast to set the environment variable DISPLAYMANAGER to kdm. With this, kdm (instead of xdm) is automatically used in runlevel 3. In other distributions, you need to modify the corresponding Init file yourself (usually /etc/rc.d/init.d/xdm or /etc/init.d/xdm).

Mouse and keyboard shortcuts of the KDE window manager

The following tables give an overview of the default shortcuts of the KDE window manager. (Like so many other things, these shortcuts too can be configured. In KDE 1.0, direct modification of `kwmrc` is required; since KDE 1.1, you can use the control center instead.)

Mouse shortcuts on the desktop	
Middle mouse button	Menu with a list of all running programs
Right mouse button	Menu with a few elementary commands

Mouse shortcuts in the window title	
Middle mouse button	Move window to the very bottom
Right mouse button	Window menu (maximize, minimize, move)
Double click	Maximize window

Mouse shortcuts inside a window	
Left mouse button + Alt	Move window
Middle mouse button + Alt	Move window to the very bottom
Right mouse button + Alt	Change window size

Keyboard shortcuts	
Ctrl+Esc	List of all running programs
Alt+Tab	Switch active program
Ctrl+Tab	Switch virtual desktop
Ctrl+Alt+Esc	Kill window (`xkill`)
Alt+F2	Start program
Alt+F3	Display window menu
Alt+F4	Close window, terminate program
Ctrl+F1 to F8	Activate virtual desktop 1 to 8

8.5 GNOME

This section provides a first introduction to the core components of GNOME. The basis for the present description is the RedHat 6.0 default configuration (that is, GNOME 1.0 in combination with Enlightenment 0.15).

REFERENCE

This section limits itself to GNOME fundamentals. GNOME programs which can be used under Linux independently of GNOME are described in other chapters of this book according to their contents. The following list shows the most important programs together with their page numbers.

`gnome-help-browser`	: help system, page 79
`gmc`	: file manager, page 499
`ee`	: graphics format conversion, page 517
`gftp`	: FTP client, page 338
`gimp`	: image processing, page 659
`gnome-linuxconf`	: system configuration, page 730
`gnorpm`	: package management, page 732

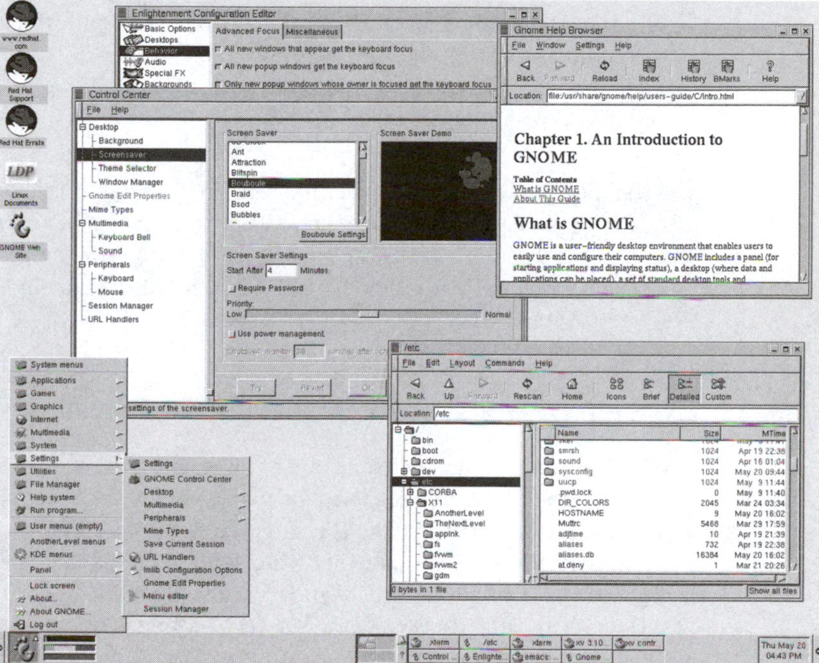

Figure 8.13 The user interface of GNOME.

Survival rules

- In contrast to KDE, icon actions (such as the start of a program) are triggered by a double click.
- In many programs or GNOME components, the right mouse button can be used to call a context menu.

- Nearly all GNOME programs can handle drag & drop. You can, for example, drag a text file out of the file manager and drop it onto the editor program (`gedit`) or move icons from the start menu to the desktop. If, in addition to the left mouse button, you press Ctrl, you copy the object. (The responsibility for management and representation of icons lies with the `gmc` file manager. This program must therefore be started first in order to be able to use icons on the desktop.)
- GNOME programs can usually be configured directly via menus. (Some central GNOME components are configured in the GNOME Control Center – see below.) Usually, it is also possible to change configuration files manually, but this is seldom needed – for example, if no configuration dialog exists as yet for a particular option.
- Do not exit GNOME with Ctrl+Alt+Backspace! Instead, use the LOG OUT command of the Start menu. Then GNOME stores information about currently running programs and tries to restore the current state as precisely as possible at the next GNOME start-up. (However, this only works satisfactorily with GNOME programs.)

NOTE Although GNOME facilitates the handling of programs in many regards, there are obviously some flaws, such as the still unsatisfactory keyboard support. Quite a large number of operations can only be executed with the mouse. In many programs, it is not even possible to call up menus with Alt and the initial letter.

Configuration

GNOME provides an incredible number of possible configurations. Invest some time in experimenting – it will definitely be worth your while! Working is simply much more pleasant when the desktop is configured to the user's personal preferences.

Important GNOME components are configured via the GNOME Control Center (`gnomecc`). This program is started via the Start menu of the GNOME panel: SYSTEM | GNOME CONTROL CENTER. Its handling is so easy that no further explanations are needed at this point.

Language

The GNOME Control Center provides no separate entry for setting the required language for menus, dialogs, and so on. Instead, the system setting of the environment variables `$LANG` and `$LC_ALL` is evaluated. (These variables are best set in `/etc/profile`. The configuration files for RedHat are described on page 736).

Window manager

All settings that do not directly concern GNOME, but the window manager, must be set via the window manager's own configuration program or by direct modification of its configuration file.

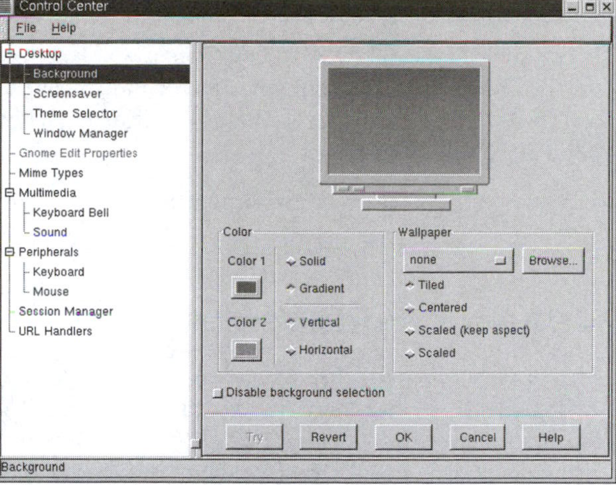

Figure 8.14 The GNOME control center.

A particularly user-friendly configuration is offered by Enlightenment: in DESKTOP | WINDOW MANAGER, the GNOME Control Center provides a button for starting the `e-conf` configuration editor. In this program, you can change every conceivable detail, from the style of the window wallpaper to the behavior of input focus, mouse, and keyboard (with freely definable shortcuts).

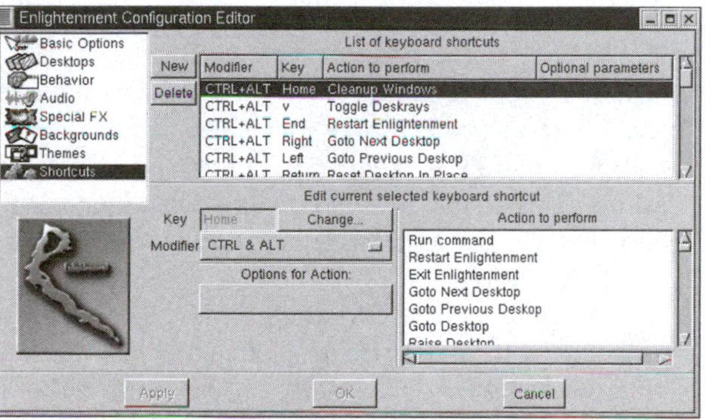

Figure 8.15 The Enlightenment configuration editor.

> **TIP**
>
> When the mouse is positioned for a sufficiently long time at the border of a desktop area, Enlightenment interprets this as the desire to change to the next desktop area. If this behavior irritates you, you can easily switch it off in `e-conf`: simply deactivate the EDGE FLIP RESISTANCE option in the DESKTOP dialog sheet.

Font size in menus, dialogs, and so on

If you consider the GNOME default font as too large or too small, you need to modify the file `~/.gtkrc`. (This configuration file influences the look of the GTK library used by GNOME to display menus, dialogs, and so on.) The following example sets an 18-point Helvetica default font:

```
# ~/.gtkrc
style "user-font"
   font="-adobe-helvetica-medium-r-normal--18-120-*-*-*-*-*-*"
```

Desktop management

The responsibility for display and management of the icons visible on the desktop (which can be placed there, for example, via drag & drop from the file manager or the Start menu) lies with `gmc`. When you quit this program with EXIT, all desktop icons disappear as well. To make them reappear, you need to start `gmc` again.

Drives

`gmc` creates icons for all devices for which all users are allowed to execute `mount` and `umount`, that is, for all devices marked in `/etc/fstab` with the option `user`. Usually, such devices are the CD-ROM and diskette drives.

A double click on the relevant icon causes the device to be mounted into the file system (if this has not yet been done) and a `gmc` window with the contents list to appear. The device can be unmounted via the context menu command UNMOUNT DEVICE.

Virtual desktops

Virtual desktops are managed by the window manager. If you use Enlightenment, please note that this window manager manages not only several virtual desktops positioned on top of each other, but also several so-called 'desktop areas' for each desktop. This double feature provides a maximum of flexibility, but can also be quite confusing. (In the RedHat default setting, however, there is only one desktop with 2×2 desktop areas.)

A visual feedback for this organization of the virtual megascreen is supplied by the GNOME pager, which is integrated into the GNOME panel (see below). This applet is mainly used for quickly changing the active desktop area.

The GNOME panel

The central control unit of GNOME is the `panel`. It includes the Start menu, together with icons for quick starting of programs. In addition, there is a number of so-called GNOME applets which show their output in small areas of the panel (for example the CPU load, or the battery status of laptops).

The panel can be moved on the screen with the right mouse button (left, right, top, bottom). Various details of appearance can be modified via the context menu entries GLOBAL PROPERTIES and THIS PANEL PROPERTIES (color, background bitmap).

Start menu

The GNOME Start menu contains a collection of the most important GNOME programs. It can be easily edited with the GNOME menu editor `gmenu` (SETTING | MENU EDITOR). Internally, the system part of the Start menu is constituted by a collection of links in the `/usr/share/gnome/apps` directory. The user-specific part of the menu is mapped in the `~/.gnome/app` directory.

To place individual start buttons of important programs directly into the panel, you simply move the corresponding icons via drag & drop from the Start menu to the desired location. (Subsequently, you can change the button's properties – such as the program to be called, the icon, and so on – by means of the context menu.) With the panel context menu entry ADD DRAWER, you can even integrate another menu (in addition to the Start menu) into the panel.

> TIP
>
> All elements inside the panel can be easily moved with the right mouse button. If one panel is not sufficient, you may use several panels, which can be created by means of ADD NEW PANEL and then configured in the same way as the main panel.

Panel applets

Besides the Start menu, some embedded programs, so-called applets, are usually executed in the panel as well. In the default configuration, these are the pager, which allows easy switching between desktops and windows, and the clock. A number of additional applets can be integrated into the panel via the Start menu, by means of the PANEL | ADD APPLET command.

Pager

The pager consists of two parts: the left-hand part shows a reduced image of all desktops. With the left mouse button, you can select the active desktop area.

The right-hand part of the pager shows buttons for all programs running in the active desktop area. The color of the icons indicates whether the program window is currently open (black-and-white icon) or the program is minimized (colored icon).

You activate the required program with the left mouse button. Although this causes the program to receive the input focus, its window is not automatically brought into the foreground, which can sometimes be irritating. You have two possibilities for making a hidden window visible: either you press Ctrl+Alt+↑ after activating the program, or you double-click the button in the pager with the middle mouse button. This first iconizes the program window, and then restores it to its previous size and position, placing it at the same time in front of all other windows. Neither of these solutions is really elegant – but this will certainly be improved in the further development of GNOME.

QuickLaunch

This applet allows easy starting up of some frequently used programs, thus saving the way through the hierarchies of the Start menu. The required programs are simply

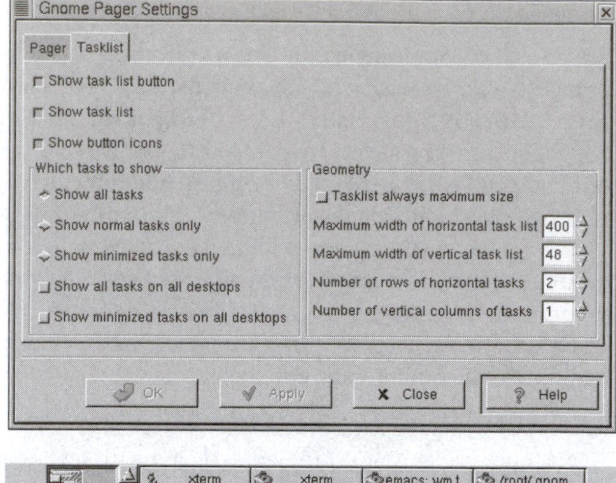

Figure 8.16 The GNOME pager (bottom) and its configuration dialog (top).

moved by drag & drop from the Start menu into the applet, where they are shown as small icons. A click of the mouse starts the program.

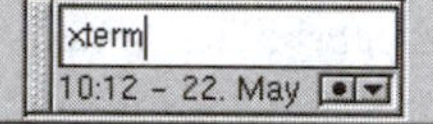

Figure 8.17 QuickLauncher applet.

Mini Commander

This applet is one of the author's favorites! It provides a small input line in which commands can be executed. (Finally you need no longer change to a terminal window for this purpose.) In the applet, Tab can be used for expansion of (unique) command names. With the History button, you can easily recall the most recently used commands. And thanks to the configuration dialog, it is even possible to define arbitrary abbreviations (macros).

Figure 8.18 Mini Commander.

> **TIP**
> The Mini Commander applet can be dragged out of the panel with the mouse and is then displayed in a separate window of its own.

Monitors

Another useful feature is finally represented by various monitor applets, which indicate CPU load, swap file size, battery status (of laptops), mailbox contents, and so on. Take a look into the ADD APPLETS submenus and just try the programs out!

Internals

`.desktop` files

Similarly to KDE, GNOME too has files in which information on programs, directories, and so on, is stored. The files have the extension `.desktop`; directory information is stored in `.directory` files. Information on the required sort order of entries inside a directory is managed in `.order` files.

The following lines show the file `~/.gnome/apps/emacs.desktop`, thanks to which an icon for Emacs is shown in the personal part of the Start menu.

```
[Desktop Entry]
Name[en_US]=GNU Emacs
Exec=emacs
Icon=/usr/share/pixmaps/emacs.png
Terminal=false
MultipleArgs=false
Type=Application
```

Desktop icons

Information on which objects (files, WWW addresses) the icons refer to is stored in the `~/.gnome-desktop` directory. All further information (icon name, position on the desktop, labeling, and so on) is instead stored in `~/.gnome/metadata.db`.

GNOME directories

The following list summarizes the locations of the most important GNOME directories:

```
~/.gnome                      local configuration files
~/.gnome/apps                 personal menu
~/.gnome-desktop              icons on the desktop
/usr/share/applets            menu for Panel applets
/usr/share/control-center     links to the Control Center components
/usr/share/gnome/apps         GNOME Start menu
/usr/share/gnome/help         online documentation (multilingual)
/usr/share/locale             menu and dialog texts (multilingual)
/usr/share/pixmaps            icons
```

Mouse and keyboard shortcuts of Enlightenment

The following tables summarize the default shortcuts of the Enlightenment window manager valid for RedHat 6.0. Please note that these shortcuts are configurable (dialog sheet SHORTCUTS in `e-conf`).

Mouse shortcuts on the desktop	
Middle mouse button	Start menu for some important programs
Right mouse button	desktop and `gmc` commands

Mouse shortcuts in the window title	
Right mouse button	window menu (maximize, minimize, move)
Double click	minimize window (reduce to title bar)

Mouse shortcuts inside the window	
Left mouse button + Alt	move window
Middle mouse button + Alt	change window size
Right mouse button + Alt	window menu (caution, default entry CLOSE!)

Keyboard shortcuts	
Alt+Tab	switch active program
Alt+F1, F2 ...	switch to desktop area *n*
Alt+Shift+cursor keys	switch desktop area
Ctrl+Alt+←	previous desktop
Ctrl+Alt+→	next desktop
Ctrl+Alt+↑	window to the very top
Ctrl+Alt+↓	window to the very bottom
Ctrl+Alt+I	reduce window to icon
Ctrl+Alt+R	reduce window to title bar
Ctrl+Alt+S	pin window down (stick/unstick)
Ctrl+Alt+X	close window (caution)

Part III
Internet

Going Internet with Linux

The Internet is such a multifaceted subject that clear limits had to be set for this and the following chapters (otherwise, they would have stretched to a whole book). The three chapters describe how you can use Internet services with a PC, a modem, and a phone line. They are explicitly addressed to private Linux users who cannot access a university for hardware and support or do not enjoy the benefit of a company network.

This chapter discusses the PPP and SLIP protocols and the Internet services telnet/rlogin, FTP and WWW (World Wide Web). The two following chapters discuss the creation of an email and a news system. Particular attention will be given to the offline mode which helps to keep telephone costs down.

Just to contain your expectations for this chapter, a list of what will *not* be dealt with in this book: the UUCP protocol, ISDN as an alternative to a normal phone connection, setting up an Internet server, its connection to a local network, setting up safety mechanisms (firewalls), setting up a PPP/SLIP server (so that your computer can be phoned up), and so forth. If you want to use Linux as a network server, you should get yourself a book especially dedicated to this subject.

NOTE: Prerequisites for this chapter are the correct configuration of the modem (page 166) and a basic network configuration (page 171). For initial experiments, the terminal emulators `minicom` or `seyon` are often useful too (page 525).

9.1 Internet basics

There have been few subjects more written about in the past few years than the Internet. This section provides a brief overview of the most important concepts.

Internet Services

Email

The most well-known and probably still most important use of the Internet is the sending of electronic mail. More recent email protocols (MIME) also allow transmission of binary data.

Discussion forums

Discussion forums are an extension of the email concept. After you have registered with a discussion forum, you receive a copy of each (email) message sent to this discussion forum. Many of these forums exist for very specialized subjects – for example, knowledge exchange about a specific aspect of quantum physics or the development of SMP (Symmetric Multi Processing) for Linux. Discussion forums have the advantage that they always keep you up to date. On the other hand, you will continually receive lots of mail which you will have to digest first.

News

Newsgroups are a public variation of the above-mentioned discussion forums. The main difference is that contributions are not automatically forwarded to you. Instead, you must use a news reader to search the existing texts for news that is of interest to you. News is more difficult to configure, but easier to use.

FTP

FTP stands for *File Transfer Protocol* and allows transmission of any (binary) files. A particular variation is *anonymous FTP*: on many big Internet servers (especially in universities) huge hard disks exist whose files you can access without a password. In this way you can, for example, fetch the most up-to-date Linux patches.

`telnet`, `rlogin`

`telnet` allows you to work on a remote computer as if it were your own (provided you have the password). All input you enter on your keyboard is executed by the remote computer connected via the Internet, but all results are displayed on your computer. Very similar functions are offered by `rlogin`, but with more safety features.

World Wide Web

WWW documents contain formatted text, graphics and cross-references (links). For reading WWW documents you need a so-called WWW browser, such as Netscape Navigator or Communicator.

Internet via telephone

A fully fledged Internet connection is implemented through a leased line with high transmission capacity. This form of Internet connection can only be afforded by universities (and connected students' residences) and major enterprises. There, a server connects the local network with the Internet and thus provides Internet access to all computers connected to the university or enterprise network.

For private users, so-called Internet providers offer a less expensive connection via a phone or an ISDN line. The basic principle is simple: the provider company has a full Internet connection. For a fee, the company creates a working directory for you on its server and gets you an internationally valid email address. You can now communicate with this computer via modem and phone.

PPP, SLIP

As a rule, the PPP protocol (less frequently the SLIP protocol) is used for connection with the provider. These protocols permit establishment of a TCP/IP link via a telephone line or via ISDN. As long as this link between your computer and the server of the provider is upheld, your computer is a true member of the Internet. However, configuration and putting into operation are often a time consuming affair (for details, see page 304 onward).

UUCP

A less and less frequently used alternative to PPP/SLIP is UUCP. The abbreviation stands for Unix to Unix Copy. Originally, this program package was developed to allow data exchange between Unix computers via phone lines (meanwhile, however, UUCP also works via TCP/IP). UUCP originated as a separate network, independent of the Internet, but is today – at least partly – interlinked with the Internet. The biggest disadvantage of UUCP is that only two Internet services (email and news) are available.

TCP/IP

The Internet is an international network of local networks. The term Internet refers not only to the physical cabling, but also to the data transmission protocol TCP/IP, the world-wide unique identification of all Internet members through numbers, and the various services (applications) of the Internet. TCP stands for *Transmission Control Protocol*, and IP for *Internet Protocol.*

TCP/IP fulfills two essential tasks, amongst others. It identifies each computer by a unique IP number (for example, 135.212.37.12) and it ensures that data sent to a given address does indeed reach the addressee. In order to achieve this, the data is subdivided into smaller packets and sent to the nearest Internet node. The computer running there (the server) looks at the address of the data and, depending on free line capacity, forwards the packets to the next computer. In this process different packets may well take different routes and arrive at the destination at different times. Here, the packets are reassembled into the original data.

As a rule, the user is not confronted with the Internet address numbers but uses names instead, such as `name@department.company.uk`. This specifies user `name` in the department network of a larger company network in the United Kingdom.

Thanks to so-called *domain name servers* (DNS), the TCP/IP software is able to determine the corresponding IP number from this address. A DNS is a program that runs on the computers of all Internet nodes. It manages a database containing the assignment of IP numbers and names. If the DNS comes across an unknown name or an unknown IP number, it contacts other DNSs via the Internet to gather the missing information.

In the Unix world, and increasingly also under other platforms (Windows), TCP/IP is also used as the protocol for *local* networking. This has the advantage that whether a message is sent to the computer in the next room or to a university in Japan makes no difference, neither from the user's nor from the software point of view.

Finally, we wish to clarify the terms file server, gateway and router: a file server is a computer which centrally manages the data for a group of other computers (and thus facilitates central administration and backup). A gateway also takes care of the communication between the local area network and the Internet. Routers are computers at Internet nodes (that is, where long-distance transmission cables meet) and play a particularly important role in the forwarding of TCP/IP packets.

In part, server, gateway and router functions are carried out by a single computer. Many file servers (especially in the university domain) provide huge amounts of information and data (archives) which Internet users can access worldwide via anonymous FTP.

9.2 PPP basics

PPP stands for *point to point protocol* and allows an Internet connection between two computers via a serial connection (modem plus phone line). Besides PPP, there is the now rarely used protocol SLIP (*serial line IP*).

In its basic format, an Internet connection via PPP or SLIP is easy. The TCP/IP Internet transmission protocol is simply transmitted via a phone line. Transmission speed is lower than in a local Ethernet network or a dedicated Internet connection via a leased line, but apart from that, there are no restrictions.

But there is a snag: your computer becomes a true Internet computer (even though you are effectively connected to the Internet only for half an hour now and then) and must therefore be configured as such. And it is this configuration which represents the major obstacle. (In a university or company network, such configuration tasks are usually carried out by specialists. Thus, many Internet users, who often have much better technical means than yourself at their disposal, have never been faced with such configuration problems and are in most cases unable to be of any help.)

Overview

In this section, we will discuss the following aspects of a PPP or SLIP connection:

- Glossary (page 305): the data sheet supplied by your Internet provider, which contains the technical specifications for establishing the connection, is usually strewn with unknown technical terms.
- System requirements (page 307): in order to make PPP work, the kernel must be compiled correctly. Furthermore, the loopback interface (the local variation of the TCP/IP network) must be configured properly.

- Manual PPP configuration (page 309): first trials with PPP are usually conducted by manually executing the commands `minicom`, `pppd`, and so on.
- Testing and error detection (page 312): this subsection describes how to find out whether a connection has actually been established and what to do in order to identify possible sources of errors.
- Starting and stopping PPP by means of scripts (page 313): once the manual PPP start-up has worked, you will probably want to start PPP with less effort in future. The scripts `ppp-on` and `ppp-off` will help with this.
- Menu-driven PPP configuration (page 317): there are numerous programs which try to relieve you from the labor of PPP configuration. However, the prerequisite for a successful application is a basic understanding of PPP.
- SLIP configuration (page 323): if your Internet provider still offers SLIP, you will find some information on this subject.

TIP This chapter contains quite a lot of basic information about PPP. If you simply want to get it working without any delay, and you already have some PPP experience (for example from a corresponding configuration for Microsoft Windows), you can skip the part on basics and try the tools described from page 317 onward. If you are lucky, PPP will be up and running within two minutes. If you are unlucky, you can always go back to reading about its basics.

NOTE The most important prerequisite for PPP is the correct configuration of your modem and serial interface. See page 166.

Additional documentation about PPP/SLIP can be found in the HOWTOs, in the Network Administrator's Guide by Olaf Kirch, in the SuSE installation manual (very practice-oriented!), in the `man` pages for `chat`, `dip`, `pppd`, and `slattach`, and in the README files for PPP and SLIP.

Glossary

The most important condition for a correct Internet configuration is that your Internet provider has supplied you with all necessary data. Usually, this is a list full of strange-looking words and numbers which will look more or less like the table below. (All passwords and IP numbers are obviously imaginary. It will therefore be useless trying to establish a connection using these data.)

```
Phone number:                123456
Email address:               hofer@provider.de
User name (Login):           hofer
Your PPP/SLIP password:      abc5EfG
Domain name server (DNS):    199.85.37.2
SMTP mail server:            mail.provider.de
Pop mail server:             pop.provider.de
News server (NNTP):          news.provider.de
WWW proxy:                   www-proxy.provider.de (Port: 8080)
```

Let us now explain the terms occurring in the above list: the table starts with the phone number. This is the number you must dial with your modem in order to contact the Internet provider.

Email address

The email address specifies where other Internet users can send email for you to read either interactively or via PPP/SLIP. Usually, the mail address consists of your name or an abbreviation or a composite word, the character `@` and the domain name of the Internet provider (in the above example, `provider.de`).

User name and password

User name and password are required to establish a PPP or SLIP connection with the provider. As a rule, the user name is the same as the name in the email address, but this need not necessarily be the case.

Depending on the provider, PPP utilization is recognized automatically, or you have to start PPP after login via an explicit command, such as `ppp`. Some providers differentiate between PPP and interactive utilization via different user names and passwords. If you have established the connection by means of a terminal emulator, only strange characters are displayed forthwith. In order to make your computer react properly to this data, you must now quit the terminal emulator and take over the connection with either `slattach` (SLIP) or `pppd` (PPP). Details follow further below.

IP number

As soon as the PPP/SLIP connection is established, you are a member of the Internet! However, in the above list you will look in vain for the IP number under which you can be reached on the Internet. The reason: Most providers manage a pool of IP addresses and dynamically assign these at each login. In other words: at each login, you receive a different IP address, namely the first of your provider's numbers that happens to be free.

> CAUTION
>
> This connection is bidirectional – that is, you have access to external computers, but other Internet users theoretically have access to your computer too. Now is the time for you to protect all user names on your computer with passwords, if you have not already done so in the first place!

Further data may be specified for mutual identification only for PPP (and not for SLIP). Besides the password, this mutual identification is an additional safety mechanism which works in both directions (not only you, but also the provider must transmit an identification number before a TCP/IP connection is established).

Name server

The above list also contains an IP number which refers to a server of your Internet provider. This server determines the IP numbers corresponding to Internet addresses used by you (such as `www.addison-wesley.de` in the Web browser). Thus, the domain name server (DNS) is of great importance for the proper functioning of your Internet connection.

Mail server

You need the two mail server addresses to be able to hand your own emails to your provider for posting and to collect temporarily stored mail from there. (These addresses are already quoted in Internet-typical notation without IP numbers – thus their use requires successful access to the DNS.)

News server

If you want to read newsgroup articles or write them yourself, you also need the address of the news server.

Proxy

A proxy server manages a cache for the most recently used WWW documents. Usually, each Internet provider runs a proxy server to minimize the amount of data to be transmitted. This is briefly how it works: one after the other, in quick succession, two persons want to read the same document which is potentially located in Australia. The first time, the file has to be transmitted from Australia to the readers' country. The second time, it is already present in the proxy cache of the provider and is therefore available much faster. You can enter the proxy address when you are configuring your Web client (for example Netscape Communicator) in order to speed up WWW access.

Kernel and network requirements

Kernel configuration

The Internet software can only be used when the corresponding code parts are contained in the kernel or at least can be loaded as modules. The following list contains the most important code parts:

- General networking: networking support
- Networking: TCP/IP networking
- Network device support: network device support
- Network device support: dummy network driver support
- Network device support: PPP and/or SLIP support
- Character devices: standard/generic serial support

The kernels supplied with the various distributions all comply with these prerequisites. (Information about kernel recompilation can be found on page 199.)

Network configuration

An appropriate configuration of Linux network functions is required in order to be able to use PPP or SLIP. The starting point for this section is the configuration of the loopback interface described on page 171. This can be easily checked with `ping localhost` – no error message must be received.

```
root#  ping localhost
PING localhost (127.0.0.1): 56 data bytes
64 bytes from 127.0.0.1: icmp_seq=0 ttl=64 time=0.0 ms
64 bytes from 127.0.0.1: icmp_seq=1 ttl=64 time=0.0 ms
   <Ctrl>+<C>
--- localhost ping statistics ---
2 packets transmitted, 2 packets received, 0% packet loss
round-trip min/avg/max = 0.0/0.0/0.0 ms
```

In addition, a maximum of two files must be extended or newly created, `/etc/hosts` and `/etc/resolve.conf`. Depending on the distribution, you can use the relevant configuration program to modify these files (such as `yast` with SuSE, `linuxconf` with RedHat)

`/etc/resolv.conf`: This file must be extended by the IP address of the Internet provider's name server. The name server (also DNS for domain name server) is responsible for the translation of unknown Internet addresses into the corresponding IP numbers. This task is carried out by the Internet provider's program and is of no further interest here.

```
# /etc/resolv.conf
domain galactic.network
nameserver 199.85.37.2
```

NOTE

In SuSE Linux, you should not modify `resolv.conf` but, instead, configure the name server with Yast (SYSTEM ADMINISTRATION|NETWORK CONFIGURATION|CONFIGURATION NAMESERVER) or enter it directly into `/etc/config.rc`.

`/etc/hosts`: The file contains a list of known IP numbers: 127.0.0.1 is the standard IP number for the loopback device. Additional lines can be used to assign the computer its IP number within the local area network. Only if your provider has assigned you a static IP address (which is unlikely) should you enter this address in `hosts`. (If you are not part of a local network and your Internet provider assigns IP addresses dynamically, `/etc/hosts` only contains 127.0.0.1 for the loopback interface.)

```
# /etc/hosts
# for the loopback interface (always required)
127.0.0.1        localhost
# for the local network (only if one exists, obviously!)
192.168.1.5      jupiter.galactic.network  jupiter
# for PPP/SLIP (only if a static IP address is known)
199.85.96.166    jupiter.galactic.network  jupiter
```

NOTE

As a rule, it is not possible to choose domain and login names corresponding to the email address supplied by the provider (and it makes no sense either).

The fact that the same computer has several IP addresses is not a problem. As a rule, even PPP with a static address works without an entry in `/etc/hosts` – the local PPP daemon and the PPP program of your provider negotiate automatically which IP address is going to be used. Thus, for your first attempt, you might as well leave `/etc/hosts` as it currently is.

9.3 PPP configuration

To be able to use PPP, the kernel must support PPP. In addition, you need the programs `pppd` and `chat`. Usually, both programs are part of a separate PPP package.

Manual configuration

The first step to a PPP connection consists in using a terminal emulator (such as `minicom` or `seyon`) to dial your Internet provider's phone number and log in with your PPP login name and the corresponding password. For the sample data in this section, this login process looks more or less like the following listing. With ATDT the modem is requested to dial the specified number. After some time, the modem answers with the success message CONNECT. Now the Internet provider comes up with the login prompt.

```
ATDT123456
CONNECT 57600/REL
Internet Provider login: hofer
Password: qwe44trE
PPP session beginning.... ~/}#.!}!}!}}8}!}$~
```

If everything has gone right so far, the terminal emulator starts to display strange characters. These result from the fact that, after your successful login, the Internet provider has started its PPP program and wants to establish a PPP connection with your computer. With some providers, PPP startup is not carried out automatically; instead, you have to enter an additional command (such as `ppp`). If necessary, you need to ask your provider for the name of the command.

In order to make this PPP connection actually usable, you must quit the terminal emulator and subsequently start `pppd`. It is essential that, while doing this, you do not interrupt the established phone connection. If you work with `minicom`, quit the program with Ctrl+A, Q. With `seyon`, use the CANCEL button and, in the confirmation request that now appears, tell the program not to hang up.

When calling `pppd`, you must specify your modem device and the keywords `crtscts` and `defaultroute`. With this, `pppd` takes control of the serial interface and establishes a PPP connection. `defaultroute` causes `pppd` to exchange IP addresses with the partner program of the Internet provider.

```
root# /usr/lib/ppp/pppd /dev/ttyS1 crtscts defaultroute &
```

All examples of this chapter assume that your modem is connected to the second serial port (that is, to `/dev/ttyS1`).

Instead of `defaultroute`, you can also use the syntax `ownIP:foreignIP`, if fixed IP addresses are to be employed. If the IP address of your Internet provider's PPP server is not known, it is sufficient to specify your own IP address.

```
root# /usr/lib/ppp/pppd /dev/ttyS1 crtscts 199.85.96.166: &
```

If the Internet provider assigns IP addresses dynamically (that is, if you are assigned a different IP address with each login), you must use the keyword `noipdefault`.

```
root# /usr/lib/ppp/pppd /dev/ttyS1 crtscts noipdefault &
```

NOTE

`pppd` can only be executed by `root`. (More precisely, problems do not occur when starting `pppd`, but only when this program attempts to link the new Internet connection into the TCP/IP system with programs such as `ifconfig` and `route`.) However, the PPP connection established by `root` can subsequently be used by all logged-in users.

Establishment of the connection can be controlled through additional options. These options can be stored either in `/etc/ppp/options` or in the current working directory in `.ppprc`.

CAUTION

`pppd` requires that the file `/etc/ppp/options` exists. If this is not the case, simply execute `touch /etc/ppp/options`.

Most distributions supply a preconfigured version of the `options` file. If `pppd` does not work, the problem is often caused by the option settings in this file! Try to comment out all the options set there.

Instead of the normal PPP, many Internet providers use Van Jakobsen Compressed PPP. This PPP variation provides additional data reduction (corresponds to CSLIP). Linux recognizes this PPP variation automatically; no special options or settings are required.

PPP authentication

There are different options for carrying out the PPP login:

- In the above example, the user name and password had to be entered manually in a terminal program, which is, however, only suitable for initial testing. On page 313 you will be introduced to the program `chat` which, besides the dialing process, also automates this simple form of identification. (In many PPP configuration programs, this variation is called script-based, because `chat` utilizes a script-like configuration file.)
- A more elegant form of PPP identification is PAP (Password Authentication Protocol). In the easiest case, this means that login name and password are stored in the file `/etc/ppp/pap-secrets`, in the following form (for the example of this chapter):

  ```
  #in /etc/ppp/pap-secrets
  "hofer"        *        "qwe44trE"
  ```

  Now, `name hofer` (or whatever the login name may be) must be submitted to `pppd` as an additional parameter. `pppd` automatically reads the corresponding password from `pap-secrets`. (This file can contain any number of name/password pairs.) The login process can be made more secure by means of further PAP options, that is the password is encoded before transmission, and so on.

- Rather less frequently, CHAP (Challenge/Handshake Authentication Protocol) is used for identification – for example, when Windows NT is used as a PPP server. In this case, the `pppd` configuration file is `etc/ppp/chap-secrets`.

> **TIP** Extensive information about PAP and CHAP can be obtained through `man pppd` or by looking at the PPP-HOWTO.

Testing the connection

In order to test whether the PPP connection has been successfully established, your next step is to execute `ifconfig`. The result should look more or less like the following listing: besides the loopback device, there is now a PPP connection (device name ppp0) from your own IP address 199.85.96.166 to the IP address of the Internet provider 199.85.37.3. Up to now, no data has been transmitted and therefore all packet indications are 0.

```
root#  ifconfig
lo     Link encap:Local Loopback
       inet addr:127.0.0.1  Bcast:127.255.255.255  Mask:255.0.0.0
       UP BROADCAST LOOPBACK RUNNING  MTU:3584  Metric:1
       RX packets:14 errors:0 dropped:0 overruns:0 frame:0
       TX packets:14 errors:0 dropped:0 overruns:0 carrier:0
       collisions:0

ppp0   Link encap:Point-to-Point Protocol
       inet addr:199.85.96.166  P-t-P:199.85.37.3  Mask:255.255.255.0
       UP POINTOPOINT RUNNING  MTU:1006  Metric:1
       RX packets:7 errors:0 dropped:0 overruns:0 frame:0
       TX packets:7 errors:0 dropped:0 overruns:0 carrier:0
       collisions:0
```

Next, you can check whether data transmission works. For this purpose, you use the `ping` program which sends small test data packets to a specified IP address, which in this case should be the address of the Internet provider known from `ifconfig` (in the above example, 199.85.37.3).

```
root#  ping 199.85.37.3
PING 199.85.37.3 (199.85.37.3): 56 data bytes
64 bytes from 199.85.37.3: icmp_seq=0 ttl=255 time=252.2 ms
64 bytes from 199.85.37.3: icmp_seq=1 ttl=255 time=210.3 ms
64 bytes from 199.85.37.3: icmp_seq=2 ttl=255 time=210.3 ms
    <Ctrl>+<C>
--- 199.85.37.3 ping statistics ---
3 packets transmitted, 3 packets received, 0% packet loss
round-trip min/avg/max = 210.3/224.3/252.2 ms
```

Even a name server test is now possible. Call `ping` once again, but specify the domain name of the provider instead of the IP address. This name is not known on your computer – thus, the name server specified in `/etc/resolv.conv` is contacted. The result should not differ from the above example (the only difference will be the IP address).

```
root#  ping provider.de
PING 199.85.37.3 (199.85.37.3): 56 data bytes
64 bytes from 199.85.37.3: icmp_seq=0 ttl=255 time=252.2 ms
64 bytes from 199.85.37.3: icmp_seq=1 ttl=255 time=210.3 ms
64 bytes from 199.85.37.3: icmp_seq=2 ttl=255 time=210.3 ms
    <Ctrl>+<C>
--- 199.85.37.3 ping statistics ---
3 packets transmitted, 3 packets received, 0% packet loss
round-trip min/avg/max = 210.3/224.3/252.2 ms
```

If everything functions as it should, you are ready to try out a proper Internet application. Particularly suited for testing is `ftp`, because larger amounts of data are transmitted, and this allows you to check the stability of the connection. Furthermore, handling `ftp` is quite straightforward (see also page 335) and, as a rule, it does not assume any further configuration work.

If it does not work

If problems arise at the very first step – that is, during connection setup with the terminal emulator – you should contact your Internet provider. After the login, the terminal emulator should display strange characters which result from the PPP communication. The online LED of your modem must still be on after quitting the terminal emulator – otherwise, the connection has been interrupted.

`pppd` uses `syslog` to log its error messages, warnings, and so on, in a file in the `/var/adm/` or `/var/log/` directory (depending on the setting in `/etc/syslog.conf`). When problems occur, you should look at the end of these files. If you specify the optional keyword `debug` when calling `pppd`, logging is even more extensive.

Some Internet providers automatically terminate the connection when no more data is transmitted for a given time (usually, between 1 and 5 minutes). In principle, this is very useful, because a forgotten PPP connection will not lead to an astronomical phone bill. On the other hand, it can be very irritating when you are under continuous pressure while reading WWW documents.

If you frequently experience problems with such unwanted interruptions, you can eliminate them by means of the mentioned program `ping` command. The following command transmits a small data packet to the provider every 30 seconds, ensuring some Internet traffic in periods of inactivity.

```
root#  ping -i 30 provider.de
```

TIP If you are completely lost, look at the excellent PPP-HOWTO document!

Terminating the connection

To terminate the connection you must terminate the background program `pppd`. To do this, determine the process number of `pppd` by means of `ps -x` and then terminate the program with `kill`.

```
root#  ps -x | grep pppd
  195 v02 S      0:00 pppd /dev/ttyS1 crtscts defaultroute
root#  kill 195
```

CAUTION The PPP connection remains active until it is terminated by one side (either you or your Internet provider). During all of this time, you obviously incur phone charges! Since PPP runs invisibly and unnoticed, even when you are not using any Internet services, you must remember to terminate the connection yourself.

Establishing the connection automatically (ppp-on, ppp-off)

In the above example, we have used a terminal emulator for dialing and logging in before executing `pppd`. For some first attempts, this method is certainly to be recommended, in order to familiarize yourself with the mechanism. In the long run, it is too long-winded. In this section we therefore introduce the two scripts `ppp-on` and `ppp-off` which allow you to establish or terminate a PPP connection by means of a single command.

NOTE There is an even easier possibility: with the aid of the `diald` program, your computer can be configured in such a way that a PPP connection is automatically established as soon as you access the Internet. If you do not request any data for some time, the connection is terminated.

`diald` is not described in detail in this chapter. Further information can be found in the `man` texts for `diald` and `diald-examples`. In addition, there is an extensive `diald-faq` document. `diald` can also be configured with `yast` (SuSE).

chat

A fundamental prerequisite for easy establishment of a connection is the `chat` program: it allows you to automate dialing and logging in. `chat` is passed several character strings. It waits until the first string arrives from the modem, then sends the second string (ATZ for a modem reset), waits for the third string (OK), sends the fourth one (dial the phone number with ATDT), waits for the fifth string (a Login/login prompt with an upper or lower case initial), and so on. `chat` expects input from the standard input and writes character strings to the standard output. In order to make `chat` communicate with the modem, you must redirect both input and output to `/dev/ttyS1`.

The following command shows how `chat` is employed as a `connect` parameter of `pppd`. The `chat` parameter consist of character strings which are alternately sent to and expected from the modem.

```
root# pppd lock connect \
  'chat -v "" ATZ OK ATDT123456 ogin: hofer word: qwe44trE' \
  /dev/ttyS1 115200 modem crtscts defaultroute debug
```

It is much clearer to control `chat` not by means of options but by means of a file. This file is usually stored in the directory `/etc/ppp`, for example under the name `ppp.chat`. Now `chat` is simply executed with the option `-f file_name`. A viable `/etc/ppp/ppp.chat` file for the above connection might look like this:

```
TIMEOUT 20
ABORT "NO CARRIER"
ABORT BUSY
ABORT "NO DIALTONE"
ABORT ERROR
"" +++ATZ
OK ATDT123456
CONNECT ""
ogin: hofer
word: qwe44trE
```

This file has the additional advantage that a failure to establish a connection due to various reasons (line busy, and so on) is immediately recognized.

Please note that this file is only an example. The details depend on your Internet provider's protocol. Thus some providers do not ask for login with 'login' but with 'user name.' Other providers do not automatically start PPP after a connection has been established, but an additional command is required after the password. For example, the provider responds to the login with 'welcome' and expects the command 'ppp.' In this case, you simply extend the `chat` command with these two keywords.

To explore this mechanism, it makes sense on the first attempts to use `minicom` or `seyon` (see above). Many providers offer ready-made login scripts – but of course only for Windows! Nevertheless, have a look at one of these files – often the communication mechanism is easily recognizable.

TIP

When `pppd` and `chat` are used as in the above listing, both programs log details of the connection process in `/var/log/messages` (or in `/var/adm/messages` or in a different log file, depending on the configuration of `/etc/syslog.conf`). This is very useful for detection of errors. However, as soon as establishing a connection works reliably, you should delete the option `-v` and the keyword `debug`.

TIP

Most Internet providers offer the possibility of carrying out the PPP login with PAP, too. For this, you delete the final two lines of `ppp.chat` and enter the login and password data into `/etc/ppp/pap-secrets` instead (see page 310). Also, you pass `pppd` the additional parameter `name` *username*.

Establishing a connection with `ppp-on`

Practice proves that `chat` alone is not yet the optimum. It often happens that no connection is established at all (because the phone number is busy) or that the PPP communication fails (for example, because the Internet provider's server is temporarily overloaded). This has led to the development of the `ppp-on` program, which automatically carries out several attempts and is easier to configure. Some special features of this shell program are worth mentioning:

- The program assumes that the `chat` parameters are stored in `/etc/ppp/ppp.chat` (see above).
- First, it checks whether the serial interface is blocked by another program (minicom, seyon). The `LOCKDIR` and `DEVICE` variables may have to be adapted.
- After the start of `pppd`, it checks whether the program is actually running (or whether no connection has been established). For this, `ifconfig` checks whether the PPP network interface is active. Usually it takes some time before both sides agree upon modem speed and PPP modalities (typically between 20 and 30 seconds).
- If problems occur, the line is interrupted with `ppp-off`, and a new attempt is started after 30 seconds.

```
#!/bin/sh
# ppp-on: establish PPP connection
LOCKDIR=/var/lock       # lock directory
DEVICE=ttyS1            # serial port
INTERFACE=ppp0          # PPP interface
DIALLIMIT=15            # number of dial-in attempts
CONNECTLIMIT=15         # number of tests whether ppp is running

# Locking control
if [ -f $LOCKDIR/LCK..$DEVICE ]
then
    echo "PPP device is locked"
    exit 1
fi

# if possible, increase serial interface speed
# stty ispeed 115200 < /dev/$DEVICE

# several dial-in attempts (variable i)
i=0
while [ 1 ]; do
  echo -n "dialing ... "
  pppd lock connect \
    'chat -v -f /etc/ppp/ppp.chat' \
    /dev/$DEVICE 115200 modem crtscts defaultroute debug &
  sleep 10
```

```
    # did we get a connect?
    echo -n "trying to establish ppp ."
    j=0
    while [ $j -lt $CONNECTLIMIT ]; do
      # test with ifconfig whether ppp connection is running
      echo -n "."
      x=$(/sbin/ifconfig | grep $INTERFACE | wc -l)
      if [ $x -ne 0 ]; then
        break 2   # exit from both loops
      fi
      sleep 2
      j=$[j+1]
    done

    # It did not work
    echo
    echo -n "no connect (busy?) or no ppp"

    # New dialing attempt?
    i=$[i+1]
    if [ $i -ge $DIALLIMIT ]; then
      echo "after $DIALLIMIT tries, "
      echo "try running this script again later :-("
      ./ppp-off  # just to make sure
      exit 1
    fi
    echo ", I'll try again soon ..."
    ./ppp-off    # just to make sure
    sleep 30
  done

  # Display success message
  echo " ppp is up!"
  /sbin/ifconfig
```

Switching off the modem loudspeaker

In many modems, the loudspeaker is only switched off after a connection has been established. Although the little noises in the background are quite useful during the first attempts (for example, you can hear the busy signal), they become irritating in the long run. In most modems, it is possible to switch the loudspeaker off. You need to look up the required command in your modem manual. For US Robotics modems, for example, it is ATM0. The command is confirmed by OK. You must also insert an additional line in `/etc/ppp/ppp.chat` (ideally immediately after the `ATZ` line):

```
ATM0 OK
```

Optimizing the connection for `telnet`

If you frequently work with `telnet` via a slow PPP connection, you may be able to achieve better response times by minimizing the blocksize to be transmitted. (Data transfer via TCP/IP connections is carried out in blocks. The smaller these blocks are, the more communication overhead is produced. At the same time, however, the number and frequency of the transmitted blocks increase, which is sensible if small amounts of data (such as individual keyboard entries) are to be usually sent.)

Setting of the block size is carried out via the two `pppd` options `mru` and `mtu` (maximum receive unit and maximum transmit unit). The default setting for both is 1500, and the smallest reasonable setting is 296 (256 bytes of data plus 40 bytes for the TCP/IP header).

The resulting additional `pppd` parameters look as follows:

```
pppd mru 296 mtu 296 ...
```

You can check the current setting of `mtu` with `ifconfig`, as soon as a PPP connection has been established.

Terminating the connection with `ppp-off`

For an easy termination of a PPP connection, you can use the shell program `ppp-off`. This program terminates `pppd` through a `kill` command.

```
#!/bin/sh
# ppp-off: terminate ppp
INTERFACE=ppp0
MODEM=/dev/ttyS1

# look for ppp0 PID file
if [ -r /var/run/$INTERFACE.pid ]; then
  # terminate process with kill
  kill -INT `cat /var/run/$INTERFACE.pid`
  # delete lock files
  if [ ! "$?" = "0" ]; then
    echo "removing stale $INTERFACE pid file."
    rm -f /var/run/$INTERFACE.pid
    exit 1
  else
    echo "$INTERFACE link terminated"
    exit 0
  fi
else
  # ppp was not active at all
  exit 0
fi
```

Menu-driven PPP configuration

Tools for easy PPP configuration are common as grains of sand! The following section briefly describes the three variations `kppp`, `linuxconf`, and `yast`. An alternative for friends of Tcl/Tk is `tkppp`. A PPP tool for GNOME, namely `gnome-ppp`, is also being developed.

The prerequisite is in any case that you already have some PPP experience. The pretty menus and dialogs certainly save a lot of typing, but if you do not understand which input the program expects, you will fail after all. (To tell you the truth: even the author – usually quite happy with text-based tools – soon got used to the easy handling of `kppp`. This tool is really great!)

kppp (KDE)

After the first start-up of `kppp`, a new account needs to be created. First you click on SETUP, then on ACCOUNTS, and finally on NEW.

On the DIAL dialog sheet, you specify the name and phone number for this account. Usually, the simplest authentication procedure is PAP. For this, you must enter your user name and password in the main window. If, instead, you opt for SCRIPT-BASED, you need to enter the `chat` character string pairs on the LOGIN SCRIPT dialog sheet (as in a manual configuration). You only need to specify a DNS address if you have not configured `/etc/resolv.conf` properly. For the remaining settings, you can mostly use the default settings.

After entering the access information, you need to configure the device (that is, the serial interface), the modem, and `pppd`. Usually it is sufficient to select the correct device for the serial interface.

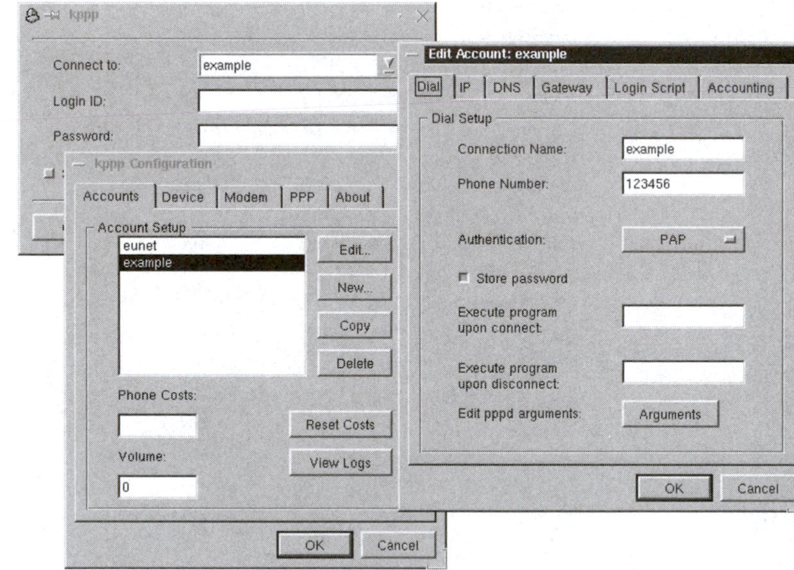

Figure 9.1 PPP configuration with `kppp`.

Now you are ready to proceed. With CONNECT, `kppp` attempts to set up PPP. During this process, the modem communication is displayed in a terminal window, which is helpful for error detection. Once the connection has been established, DETAILS displays the volume of data so far transmitted.

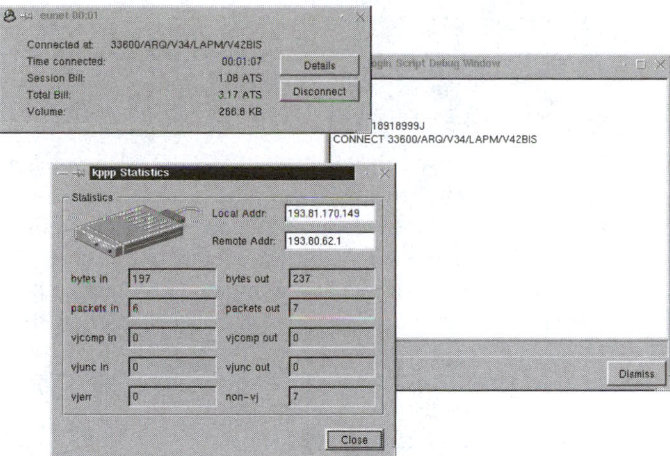

Figure 9.2 Information about the PPP connection.

One of the most attractive features is the telephone charges counter of `kppp`. To use it, accounting must be enabled for the relevant account on the ACCOUNTING dialog sheet, and a phone company must be selected. (The program contains charges regulations for surprisingly many tariffs worldwide.) The logging files with a summary of data and charges incurred can then be displayed via VIEW LOGS on the ACCOUNTS sheet of the SETUP dialog.

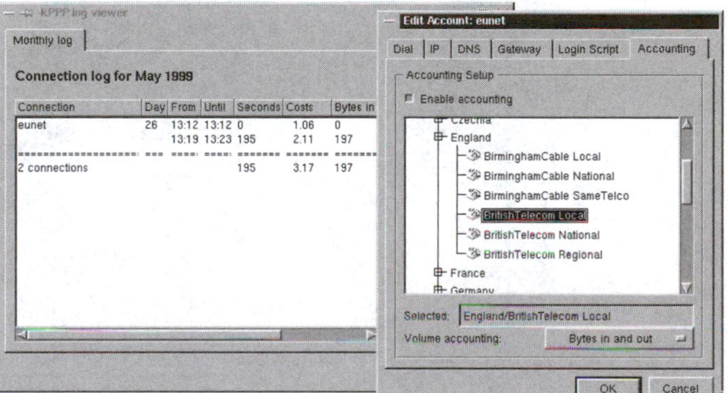

Figure 9.3 Counting phone charges with `kppp`.

CAUTION

When kppp displays the message 'pppd died unexpectedly,' there are two highly probable reasons for this: either `/etc/ppp/options` is missing completely, or `/etc/ppp/options` or `~/.ppprc` contain the keyword `lock`. (This means that pppd is responsible for locking. Most of the time, this makes sense, but not in connection with kppp, which takes on this task by itself. Delete `lock`!) In case of doubt, simply have a go with a completely empty `/etc/ppp/options` file. Please also read the excellent online documentation!

kppp is usually installed as a SETUID program. This means that the program has `root` privileges irrespective of who is executing it. Although this is a gap in security (the online documentation explains how it can be filled), it has one great advantage: in contrast to other scripts introduced in this chapter, it can be used by all users (not only by `root`) without any significant problems. The only prerequisite is that all users are allowed to execute pppd. This is achieved by the following command:

```
root#  chmod a+x /usr/sbin/pppd
```

`linuxconf` (RedHat)

In the hierarchic main menu of `linuxconf`, the PPP configuration is hidden under SETTINGS|NETWORK|CLIENT|PPP. With the NEW button, you create the new PPP device ppp0. In the INTERFACE dialog, you must enter the phone number, serial interface, login name, and password. If you want to carry out identification with PAP (usually the simplest alternative), you must activate the appropriate option – it is not enabled in the default setting.

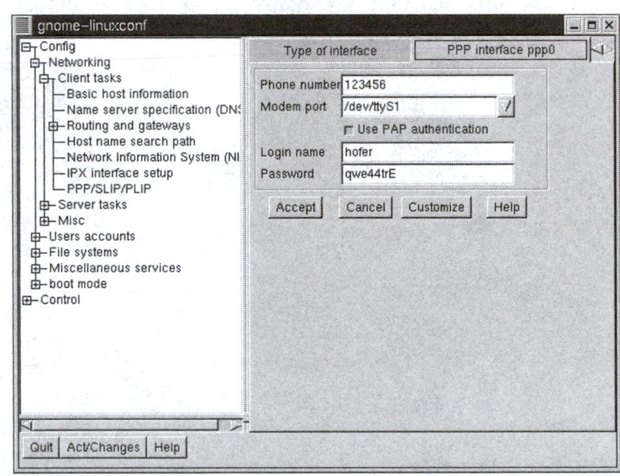

Figure 9.4 PPP configuration with `linuxconf`.

CONFIRM takes you back to the main dialog. By clicking on the interface name `ppp0`, you get into a new dialog with further configuration options. There you can set the speed of the serial interface and various pppd parameters. An interesting option

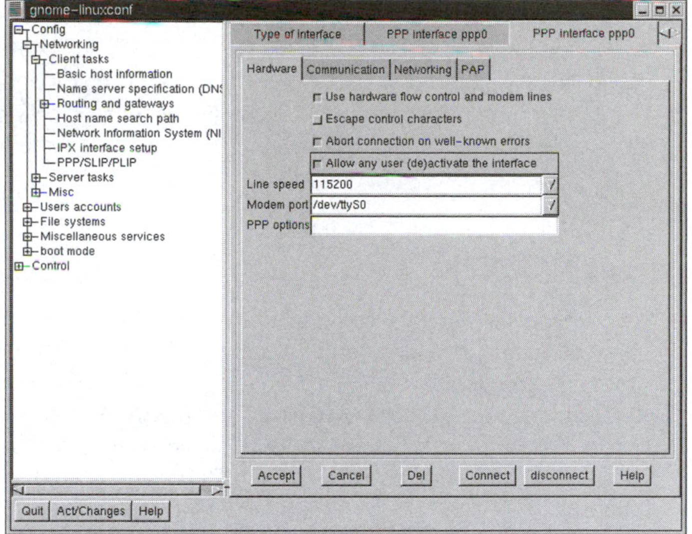

Figure 9.5 Further PPP options in `linuxconf`.

is ALLOW ANY USER TO (DE)ACTIVATE PPP, which ensures that subsequently not only `root` can resort to PPP.

With CONNECT and DISCONNECT it should now be possible to try out PPP. In the tested version of `linuxconf` (1.12 in RedHat 5.2), however, this did not work. Instead, the `usernet` program must be started (Figure 9.6). With this, you can easily activate and deactivate PPP as well as all other network interfaces with a click of the mouse. The current state is displayed by a red or green button.

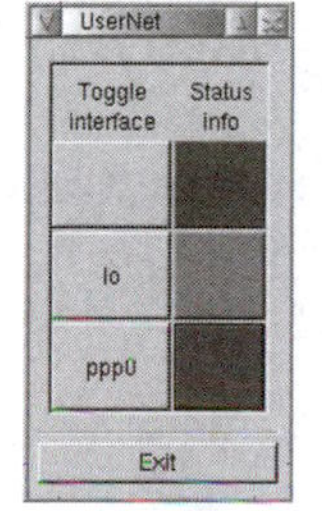

Figure 9.6 (De)activating PPP.

If you want to switch PPP on or off by means of a command (that is without X), you can use the `usernetctl` command instead of `usernet`. The following two commands illustrate the syntax:

```
root#  usernetctl ppp0 up
root#  usernetctl ppp0 down
```

> **CAUTION**
>
> While PPP configuration with `linuxconf` worked straight away, `usernet` and `usernetctl` have proved to be unreliable in RedHat 5.2. In particular, it was in some cases impossible to deactivate PPP. (This can lead to an unpleasant surprise on your next phone bill!) The only remedy was an explicit `kill` for `pppd`. (The process ID can easily be determined with `cat /var/lock/LCK....ttySn`.)

`yast` (SuSE)

A prerequisite for PPP configuration with `yast` is the installation of the `suseppp` package which contains various configuration data for a range of (mostly German) Internet providers.

In `yast`, SYSTEM ADMINISTRATION|NETWORK CONFIGURATION| NETWORK BASE CONFIGURATION leads to the start dialog for network configuration. There you select the device MODEM PPP with [F5]. [↵] or [F6] now lead to the PPP dialog.

The PROVIDER input field allows you to select one from a list of predefined providers. If your provider is missing, you must select GENERIC.

Subsequently, you need to enter login name, password, phone number, and IP number of the name server. The options DEFAULTROUTE and (for the moment) DEBUG should remain activated. The AUTOMATIC DIAL option should, however, remain deactivated until you have manually tested the scripts.

In AUTHENTICATION you can choose between PAP, CHAP, and TERMINAL. In most cases, the preset PAP is correct. (Information on other procedures can be obtained by pressing [F1] or by reading the `man` page for `pppd`.)

The remaining fields can be left blank for the moment – they only become relevant if you want to configure Internet services such as email and news with `yast`, too. You can now set additional modem parameters with [F4] (in particular, the speed of the serial interface).

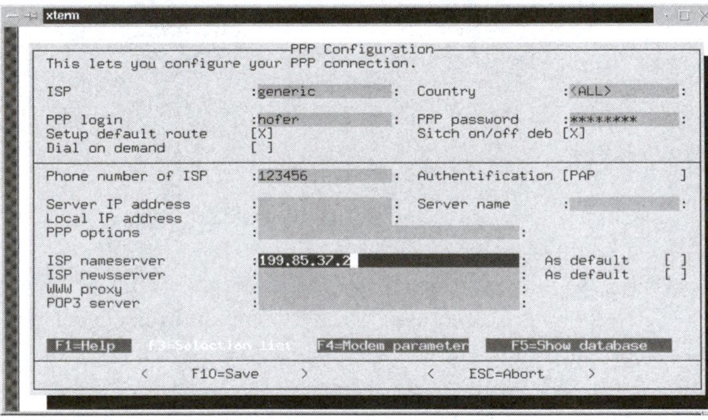

Figure 9.7 PPP configuration with `yast`.

F10 takes you back to the main dialog, where you must activate the new network device with F4. Subsequently you leave this dialog too with F10. The result is two new files in `/etc/suseppp`, usually `generic.chat` and `generic.options`. (If your provider was on the list provided by SuSE, the name of the provider is specified instead of `generic`.)

Now you can start and stop PPP with the following two commands:

```
root#  /etc/suseppp/scripts/ppp-up generic debug
root#  /etc/suseppp/scripts/ppp-down
```

If one exists, you must specify the provider's name instead of `generic`. Once this works, you can of course also do without the debug option. It causes additional logging information in `/var/log/messages`.

If everything is working, and you want PPP to be started automatically and without prompts for confirmation at each Internet access (for example, if you want to read an Internet page with Netscape), you activate the AUTOMATIC DIAL option in the PPP dialog. Subsequently, you first have to execute `init 1` and then `init 2` in a text console for the setting to become valid. (Restarting the computer is, of course, another possibility.)

From now on, `diald` monitors the network, starts PPP for each inquiry, and stops it when there has not been any Internet traffic for some time. You can set the timeout intervals in `/etc/suseppp/diald/generic.diald`.

9.4 SLIP configuration

SLIP (Serial Line IP) allows TCP/IP communication via a serial interface, as does PPP. CSLIP is a variation of SLIP in which the protocol information is compressed (but not the data). SLIP/CSLIP is, so-to-speak, the predecessor of PPP. However, because of its limited security mechanisms it is increasingly losing significance.

To automate establishing of connections, you need the `dip` program, which is usually located in the `/usr/sbin` directory. You might have to install the appropriate package.

Unfortunately, I did not have a chance to actually try out SLIP, so the information given here must be taken with some reservation. It is mainly based on available documentation: the HOWTO text on `NET-2`, the files in `/usr/doc/dip`, the `man` texts for `slattach` and `dip`, and finally on the Linux Network Administration Guide.

Establishing the connection

As with PPP, a connection is established manually by using a terminal emulator to make a connection with your Internet provider and to log in. Subsequently, you quit the emulator without interrupting the line. Now you can take over the serial interface with `slattach` for exclusive use with SLIP. If you want to work with SLIP (and not with CSLIP), you must specify the option `-p slip`.

```
root#  /usr/sbin/slattach /dev/ttyS1 &
```

After SLIP has taken over the serial interface, this new Internet connection must be registered. This is done with the commands `ifconfig` and `route`:

```
root#  ifconfig sl0 199.85.96.166 pointtopoint 199.85.37.3 up
root#  route add default dev sl0 &
```

With this, the connection with your Internet provider is established. It can now be checked with the same methods as PPP (`ifconfig`, `ping`).

Terminating the connection

To terminate a SLIP connection, you must deactivate the above commands in reverse order:

```
root#  route del default
root#  ifconfig sl0 down
root#  kill n   # n must be substituted with the PID of slattach
```

Subsequently, the still active phone connection must be terminated using a terminal emulator (hangup).

Automation

Establishing a SLIP connection manually is only acceptable for first experiments. For establishing SLIP connections automatically, the `dip` program is provided. It combines the functions of the PPP programs `chat` and `pppd`; that is, it looks after both the login on the phone line and the registration of the new Internet connection. When `dip` is called up, a script file containing `dip` commands is passed to it. Some distributions supply the file `sample.dip` as an easily adaptable example.

```
root#  /sbin/dip /usr/doc/dip/sample.dip  # establish connection
root#  /sbin/dip -k                       # terminate connection
```

NOTE

For trial purposes, `dip` can also be executed interactively, by starting the program with the `-t` option. Subsequently, the program accepts commands such as `dial`, `send`, `mode` until it is terminated with `exit`.

9.5 World Wide Web (WWW)

Introduction

For reading WWW documents you need a separate program, a so-called browser. Well-known browsers are the Netscape Communicator and (under Windows) the Internet Explorer. Besides the standard WWW functions, they also integrate other Internet services (FTP, news, email, and so on). Apart from these, numerous small web browsers exist, such as Arena, Lynx, and `kfm` (the KDE file manager).

Before these programs are described, we must explain some terms which are used in connection with the WWW:

HTML

HTML stands for *hypertext markup language* and denotes the document format for use with the WWW (World Wide Web). HTML instructions are enclosed within angle brackets, for example, `<H1>` for a first-order heading. HTML documents are coded in ASCII format and can, in principle, be created with any editor. An easier way to create your own HTML documents, however, is to use a dedicated HTML editor or a text processing program equipped with an HTML export filter.

http

http (usually written in lower case) stands for *hypertext transfer protocol* and defines how HTML documents are transmitted over the network. As a rule, you as a user will not be concerned with this – you may, however, have noticed that all WWW addresses begin with `http://`. If you want to provide WWW documents over the Internet yourself (and do not wish to use the services of an Internet provider for this purpose) you must configure your own http server. Under Linux, for example, this can be done with Apache. Configuration of your computer as an Internet server is, however, not dealt with in this book.

URL

URL stands for *universal resource locator* and means a WWW address in the format `type://....` Possible type names are, for example, `ftp`, `http`, `https` (same as `http`, but with encryption) and `file`.

Bookmarks

Bookmarks are used to store the current WWW address in a list. This page can then be quickly retrieved at a later stage.

Cache

Some WWW browsers manage a separate *cache* in which the WWW documents that have been accessed most recently are stored locally on the hard disk. At a repeated access, it only checks whether the document has changed. If this is not the case, no new transmission takes place and the local file is used instead.

Proxy

In addition to this, most WWW servers (universities, Internet providers) manage a *proxy cache* which, in principle, fulfills the same tasks as a local cache, but for several users at a time. When a second user accesses the same WWW document as the first, the proxy copy is used. Thus, the proxy cache does not reduce the amount of data transmitted to your computer; instead, it reduces the data flow between your Internet server and the rest of the world, thus avoiding long waiting times for frequently used documents.

A special variation of a proxy is provided by the program `wwwoffle`: if it is installed locally on the computer, web sites that have been visited once can be read again at a later point without an Internet connection. The program can also transmit previously selected Web documents or directories in one go and thus minimize the time of the telephone connection with the Internet. More information on this cost-saving utility can be found on page 332.

> **TIP** Many Linux-specific links to the Internet can be found on the author's homepage:
>
> `http://www.addison-wesley.de/Service/Kofler/ehome.html`

Netscape

The programs Netscape Navigator (up to version 3) and Communicator (as from version 4) are more than mere WWW browsers: the built-in functions include email and news management, a Java interpreter, and so on. Since the licence of the Communicator was changed in the fall of 1997, and both program and source code are freely available, the program is part of each Linux distribution (and is also supplied with this book).

After installation, depending on the configuration (and distribution), the browser can be started by means of one of the following commands: `netscape`, `communicator`, or `netscape-communicator`. At the first start-up, after various copyright messages and warnings have been displayed, the directory `~/.netscape` is created, in which local configuration data, bookmarks, and temporarily stored files (cache) are stored.

Usage

As with other WWW browsers, use of Netscape is not complicated at all. The document to be displayed can be selected via FILE|OPEN PAGE or FILE|OPEN PAGE|CHOOSE FILE or via direct input of the address in the LOCATION field. If the name of a local directory is specified, Netscape automatically displays all files and subdirectories; you can move to the file you are interested in with a click of the mouse.

With BOOKMARKS|ADD BOOKMARK you can store the address of the current document in the bookmark list. (This also works for local files; thus, for example, you can create a bookmark that points to the HOWTO index.) The bookmark list will quickly become too long to handle. With COMMUNICATOR|BOOKMARKS|EDIT BOOKMARKS you open a separate window in which you can reorganize your bookmarks into directories, sort them and relabel them.

Another nice feature is the command FILE|NEW|NAVIGATOR WINDOW(short, Alt+N): it can be used to open an additional WWW window. This allows you to download and read several WWW documents in parallel which in turn leads to a better usage of waiting time – very relevant with lower transmission speeds.

If you do not want to display a file pointed to by a link, but instead transfer it to your computer, you can simply click on the link with the right mouse button. The command SAVE LINK AS opens a file selection dialog box where you can specify in which directory and under which name the file is to be stored.

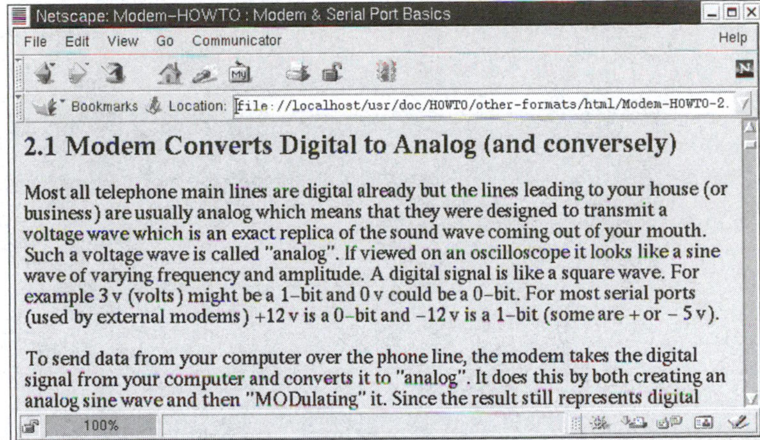

Figure 9.8 A WWW page in Netscape Communicator.

TIP

The FTP, email and news functions of Netscape (together with their configuration options) are described in the following sections (see pages 338, 348, and 372).

Configuration

Configuration of Netscape is carried out with EDIT|PREFERENCES. Several subgroups provide countless configuration options of which only the most important ones are described.

Fonts

Under the category APPEARANCE|FONTS you can set the desired font and size, as well as other options.

Small icons in the toolbar

In the category APPEARANCE you can define a space-saving display of the toolbar with the option PICTURES ONLY.

Start page

After startup, Netscape automatically attempts to establish a connection to `home.netscape.com`. If you want to prevent this, you can select the option BLANK PAGE in the category NAVIGATOR or specify a different Internet address.

File types / programs:

When you click on a link that does not point to an HTML file or to an image, Netscape usually does not know how to deal with the file. For example, it could display the file as a text file, load the file and display it with a different program (PostScript files, for example, by means of `ghostview`) or store the file on the hard disk (for example with (compressed) archive files). Some default settings can be found under the category

NAVIGATOR|APPLICATIONS. Figure 9.9 illustrates the configuration for display of PostScript files.

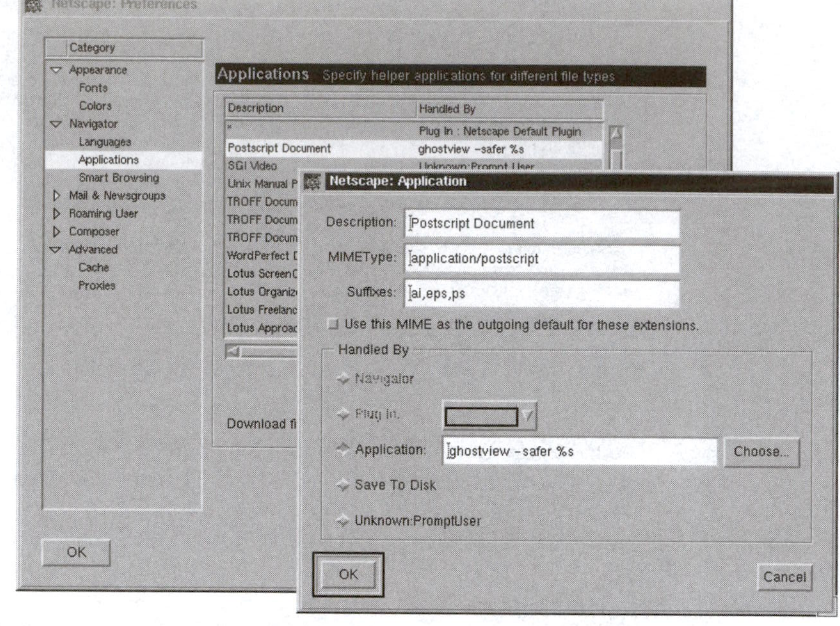

Figure 9.9 Netscape Communicator configuration.

Images

If you do not want images to be transferred automatically, deactivate AUTOMATICALLY LOAD IMAGES in the ADVANCED category. Now that much less data needs to be transmitted, documents are displayed faster. If you want to view an image, simply click on the icon displayed as a placeholder. By clicking the IMAGES button, all the images of the document are downloaded.

Java, JavaScript

Java and JavaScript are two programming languages for executing programs that can be integrated into WWW documents. If you wish to deactivate Java and/or JavaScript for security reasons, you can do this via options of the ADVANCED category.

Cache/Proxy

The Communicator manages a local cache for the most recently downloaded documents. Cache parameters can be set in the ADVANCED|CACHE category. If you have enough space on your hard disk, increase the disk cache! If your Internet provider manages a proxy cache, you should enter its address in the ADVANCED|PROXIES category under MANUAL PROXY CONFIGURATION.

Smart Browsing

Since version 4.5, the Communicator has a new feature: when you click on the WHAT'S RELATED button, the program offers you a selection of comparable Web pages. However, this function is not uncontroversial. To make it work, Netscape stores a list of all Web pages you visit (and this is not done not locally, but on a server of the Netscape Corporation). From a data protection point of view, this is at least a dubious procedure. If you have reservations about it, you can easily deactivate this function in the category NAVIGATOR|SMART BROWSING.

Problems

Lock file

Netscape should only be started once. (If you start it more than once, there will be problems with management of bookmarks, caches, and so on.) Consequently, any attempt to start the program a second time triggers a warning. Netscape recognizes that it is already running with the aid of the file `~/.netscape/lock`.

You may however receive this warning even if Netscape is currently not running at all. In this case, you did not exit Netscape properly when you last used it (crash), that is `~/.netscape/lock` has not been deleted. In this case, you will have to delete the file manually:

```
user$  rm ~/.netscape/lock
```

TIP
There is only rarely any reason to start Netscape more than once. First, you can open any number of windows with Alt+N. Second, you can display a new document in a running Netscape instance with the command `netscape -remote "openUrl address"`.

`talkback`

Since version 4.5, the program `talkback` is supplied together with Netscape. This program occasionally establishes a connection to Netscape's company server, and thus supplies the company with feedback about utilization and potential difficulties of Netscape. In particular, the program is started automatically when there is a problem with the execution of Netscape.

CAUTION
Whether this uninvited and mostly even unnoticed behavior is desirable from a data protection point of view will be left open. The real problem is of a different kind: `talkback` may in the worst case lead to a complete loss of keyboard and mouse control – and then only the reset button remains (which will result in the loss of all unsaved data and, if you are unlucky, in a faulty file system).

Therefore, you should deactivate `talkback` for your own good. To do this, you need to start the program. It is located in a subdirectory of the Netscape directory, in SuSE in `/opt/netscape`.

```
user$  /opt/netscape/talkback/talkback
```

Now you execute SETTINGS|TURN TALKBACK OFF and terminate the program. This puts an end to all the Talkback hubbub.

Arena

Arena was the first freely available and reasonably user-friendly Web browser for X. In comparison with other WWW browsers, `arena` is limited to the absolute minimum: the program is capable of displaying WWW documents at various levels of scaling (Zoom) and of following cross-references contained in them. More cannot be said: further functions are not provided (not even the management of a bookmark list). Arena is controlled through an easily understandable button bar and, apart from the cursor keys, no keyboard shortcuts exist.

For reading online documentation and for first experiments with the WWW, Arena is certainly sufficient. The program has the additional advantage that screens are built up quite quickly and memory consumption is limited. However, it cannot offer the comfort and stability of Netscape.

`kfm` (KDE file manager)

The program `kfm` is not only a file manager but also a quite adequate Web browser. Its operation is problem-free. Configuration is carried out with OPTIONS|CONFIGURE BROWSER.... (see also page 500).

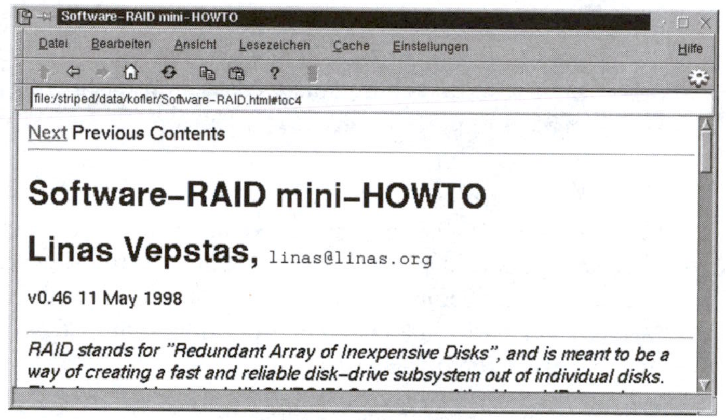

Figure 9.10 Reading HTML files with `kfm`.

> **TIP** Please note that in `kfm`, WWW addresses have to be entered in full, that is with the preceding characters `http://`. Netscape fills in this information automatically, whereas `kfm` interprets addresses without `http://` as file names.

Lynx

Lynx has one big advantage over other WWW browsers: the program runs in text mode. This advantage is seen by many users as a disadvantage, because many features of the WWW obviously get lost (text attributes, pictures). On the other hand, Lynx is very easy on memory consumption and computing capacity, and it does not assume an X installation.

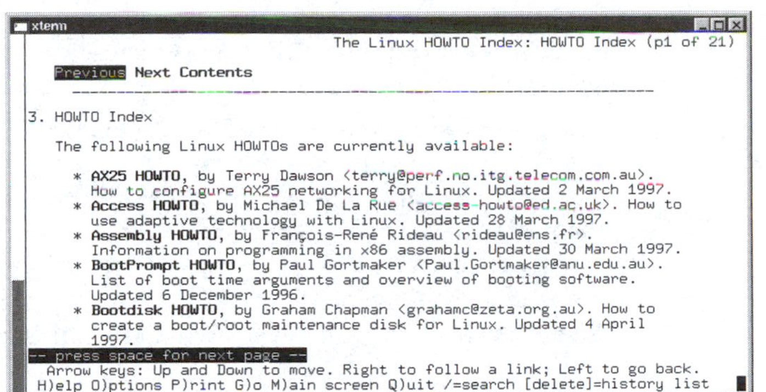

Figure 9.11 Lynx – reading HTML files in text mode.

Handling Lynx is simple: usually, the program is started by passing it a WWW address or the name of an HTML file. Lynx loads the document and displays the first page. Subsequently, the following keyboard shortcuts apply:

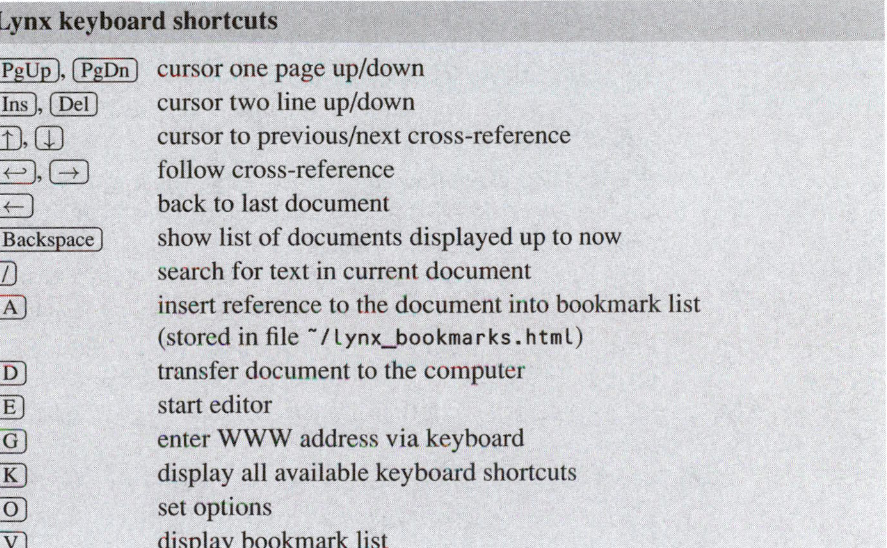

Lynx keyboard shortcuts	
PgUp, PgDn	cursor one page up/down
Ins, Del	cursor two line up/down
↑, ↓	cursor to previous/next cross-reference
↵, →	follow cross-reference
←	back to last document
Backspace	show list of documents displayed up to now
/	search for text in current document
A	insert reference to the document into bookmark list (stored in file `~/lynx_bookmarks.html`)
D	transfer document to the computer
E	start editor
G	enter WWW address via keyboard
K	display all available keyboard shortcuts
O	set options
V	display bookmark list

Lynx can also be started by passing it a directory: the program displays a list of all the directory's files and subdirectories which can be selected in the same way as cross-references. Text files in ASCII format can be displayed directly in Lynx.

More recent versions of Lynx display headings and links in different colors and can be controlled with the mouse. (With the left button, you follow a link; the right button takes you back to the previous page.) These features can be activated with the options `-color` and `-use_mouse`.

Lynx has yet another function: the program can be used as an HTML → ASCII converter, and thus converts HTML documents into a readable text file. The following command illustrates this application:

```
user$ lynx -dump source.html > target.txt
```

TIP

Lynx has an extensive `man` text. `lynx -help` gives an overview of all command options available. During operation, [K] can be used to display a list of all keyboard commands. Help is called with [H] or [?] – however, the help texts are read over the Internet. If you use Lynx for reading local files only and you have no network connection, you cannot use this help function.

Surfing offline (WWWoffle)

Usually, Web documents can only be read 'online,' that is, while your computer is connected (via PPP) to the Internet. The WWWoffle program seems to promise the opposite but cannot, of course, work miracles either. Nevertheless, the program is extremely useful:

- It manages a cache which stores all WWW documents that have been read. You can read all these documents without problems at a later date, even if you are not connected to the Internet at the time. (In principle, this corresponds to the 'offline' mode of Internet Explorer.)
- When you click offline on links of documents that are not locally available at the moment, WWWoffle earmarks the document. Whenever a new Internet connection is established, all earmarked documents are transmitted at once. Afterwards, the connection can be terminated. Now you can read the required documents in peace and without incurring further phone charges.
- Reading single documents is often unsatisfying. With WWWoffle, you can therefore mark whole groups of documents (which are connected from a starting page via links) for transmission. Any link depth can be specified.

TIP

WWWoffle can do much more than is explained here. You should read the extensive online documentation, and check the WWWoffle-Homepage:

`http://www.gedanken.demon.co.uk/wwwoffle/`

Installation and configuration

For most distributions, WWWoffle is available as a preconfigured package. After installation, you only need to adapt the configuration file `wwwoffle.conf` (usually in `/etc/wwwoffle`) to your requirements. Usually it is sufficient to specify the proxy server of your Internet provider:

```
# Change to /etc/wwwoffle/wwwoffle.conf
...
Proxy
{
 http://* = www-proxy.provider.de:8080
}
```

Subsequently, you start the WWWoffle daemon with the following command.

```
root#  wwwoffled -c /etc/wwwoffle/wwwoffle.con
```

As a next step, you must configure your Web browser to take WWWoffle into account. For this, you need to deactivate the cache (its task is now taken on by WWWoffle) and specify `localhost:8080` as WWW and FTP proxy server.

If you use Netscape Commnicator, you need to execute EDIT|PREFERENCES. Reduce the size of the disk cache to 0 on the ADVANCED|CACHE dialog sheet. On the ADVANCED|PROXIES dialog sheet, you manually set the WWW and FTP proxies to `localhost` and port 8080.

> **NOTE** Now you have two proxy servers which you should not mix up: on your computer, WWWoffle functions as local proxy server. This is the proxy server with which your Web browser communicates. WWWoffle, in turn, reads WWW documents from the proxy server of your Internet provider.

Now it is time for a first test to see whether WWWoffle is running properly: enter the address `http://localhost:8080` into your Web browser. With this, the Web browser reads a start page created by WWWoffle, where you can find additional information and control features for WWWoffle.

Handling

WWWoffle will now run almost fully automatically. You merely need to tell the program whether an Internet connection is currently established or not. Each time you start PPP, you need to carry out the following command:

```
user$  wwwoffle -online
```

When you terminate PPP, the corresponding command is:

```
user$  wwwoffle -offline
```

If, in offline mode, you click on a locally unavailable link, a message is displayed in the Web browser that the page is earmarked for later transmission (Figure 9.12).

To ensure that the transmission is effectively carried out, you need to execute a further `wwwoffle` command the next time you are connected to the Internet:

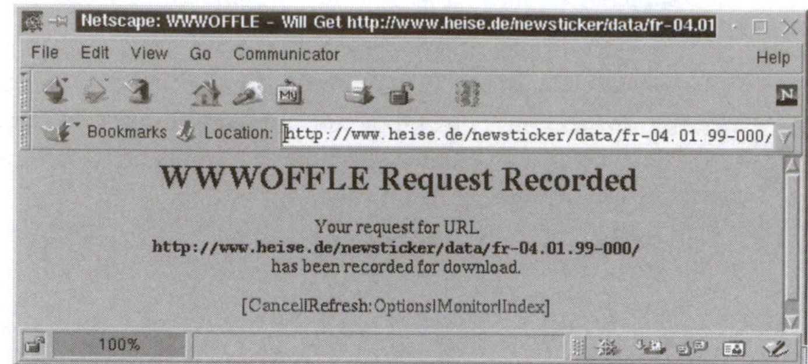

Figure 9.12 The WWW document will be transmitted later.

```
user$ wwwoffle -fetch
```

If you want to transmit a whole WWW directory with the next `fetch` command, you need to specify the directory in WWWoffle beforehand, by entering the address `http://localhost:8080/refresh-options/` in your Web browser.

Automating WWWoffle

In the long run, manual execution of `wwwoffled` at each computer start-up and `wwwoffle` at each PPP status change is unsatisfactory. However, the program is not difficult to automate. You just need to ensure that `wwwoffled` is started within the Init-V process. For this purpose, most distributions provide a `rc.local` file. (Information on the Init-V process can be found on page 124.)

The process is particularly easy for SuSE users. Here, the `wwwoffle` package is completely preconfigured. For an automatic start, you only need to modify one line in `/etc/rc.config`(using `yast` or a text editor):

```
# Change to /etc/rc.config
START_WWWOFFLE="yes"
```

Integration of the `wwwoffle` commands into the `ppp-on` and `ppp-off` scripts introduced from page 313 onward is also without problems:

```
# at the end of ppp-on
wwwoffle -online
wwwoffle -fetch

# at the beginning of ppp-off
wwwoffle -offline
```

> **NOTE**
>
> `wwwoffle` stores the transmitted WWW documents in the directory `/var/spool/wwwoffle`. (It is of course possible to specify a different directory in `wwwoffle.conf`.) When the files have reached a certain age, they are automatically deleted. Nevertheless, the directory may grow faster than you would like. A more sophisticated control over the time files are to be deleted and the maximum size the directory may reach is provided in the `purge` section of `wwwoffle.conf`.

Problems

During operation of `wwwoffle`, occasionally the program refused to reload certain pages that were already in the cache from the Internet. Instead, the Web browser reported after a while that the file was empty. Direct access to the page (after the `localhost` proxy setting had been deactivated), in contrast, did not pose any problems.

The cause of the problem is still obscure; the solutions mentioned in the FAQs were not successful. Deleting the cache for the web address concerned, however, seemed to help. To do this, point your web browser to the address `http://localhost:8080/index/http/?none`. Now you can see a list of all Web sites contained in the `wwwoffle` cache. Click on the link `[Del All]` at the Web site which is causing difficulties. The next attempt to access a page of this Web site should work again.

9.6 File transfer protocol (FTP)

FTP allows transmission of binary files between computers linked to each other via the Internet. It is immediately obvious that FTP is a practical way of exchanging data with far away colleagues. The great popularity of FTP, however, is due to anonymous FTP: many big Internet servers belonging to universities and Internet providers offer all users access to so-called FTP archives. This access (unlike normal FTP) is not blocked by a password. In order to use anonymous FTP, you simply specify `anonymous` as the user name and your email address as the password.

The number of programs you can use for FTP is incalculable: besides the classic `ftp` command, you can use the following programs:

- Netscape, Lynx, Emacs, and XEmacs
- `mc`, `gmc`, `kfm` (file managers)
- `mirror`, `wget` (scripts for recursive transmission of whole FTP directories)
- `ncftp` (FTP client with an easy-to-handle, text-based user interface; a special feature is that an interrupted transmission can be continued.)
- `xftp` (FTP client with an X user interface)

Some of these programs, however, only support downloading of files via anonymous FTP (but not uploading of files or FTP with an individual login).

This section is primarily limited to a description of `ftp`, which you should use for your first attempts. Once you have gathered some experience with `ftp`, you will not have any problems handling the other programs – all the programs mentioned above are decidedly easier to handle than `ftp`!

Many data archives are mirrored, that is, they are periodically transferred from one Internet server to another (daily or weekly, mostly at night). The reason for this mirroring is that users can always access the geographically closest server without fear of finding out-of-date data. You should always try to access an FTP server located as near to you as possible.

When you need a file, but you do not know on which FTP server it is stored, you can search for it at the following Web address:

`http://ftpsearch.com/`

The `ftp` command

An FTP session is initiated with the `ftp` command. Since files are to be transferred from/to the current directory, you should first use `cd` to change into the required working directory. At the call of `ftp`, the required Internet address of the FTP server is specified.

After the connection has been established and you have entered your user name and password, you are ready to go: you can use the `cd`, `pwd`, and `ls` commands, which have the same meanings as under Linux, to find your way through the directories of the FTP archive. In order to transfer a file from the FTP archive into the current directory of your computer, you execute `get file`. The file name remains unchanged. Conversely, you can use `put` to transfer a file from your current directory into a directory of the FTP archive. (Obviously, this works only if you have write access rights for that directory. With anonymous FTP, this is mostly restricted to a single directory with a name such as `/pub/incoming`.)

NOTE

Before you transfer a file, you must first switch into binary mode with `binary`. In text mode, FTP interprets the files as texts and tries to convert them into the format of the current computer. Binary files become unusable through such a conversion. (Luckily enough, most FTP servers are configured in such a way that binary is the default setting.)

An FTP session is terminated with the command `quit` or `bye`. The following table summarizes the most important commands which can be executed during an FTP session:

ftp commands	
`?`	displays a list of all FTP commands
`!`	allows execution of shell commands
`ascii`	switches into text mode
`binary`	switches into binary mode
`bye`	terminates FTP
`cd dir`	changes into the specified directory
`close`	terminates the connection with the FTP server
`get file`	transfers the file from the FTP archive into the current directory
`help command`	displays brief info about the specified command
`ls`	displays the list of files
`mget *.pattern`	transfers all matching files from the FTP archive into the current directory (see also `prompt`)

`open`	establishes a connection with the host computer (if the first attempt has failed)
`prompt`	activates/deactivates the automatic request for confirmation prior to transmitting each file with `mget`
`put file`	transfers the file from the current archive into the FTP archive
`quit`	terminates FTP
`user`	allows a new login (if the first attempt has failed)

Example

The following example shows how the PPP package 2.2 is copied from the FTP server `ftp.redhat.com`. For reasons of space, some of the texts and directories displayed on screen have been shortened. In order to improve readability, all received texts have been indented by a few characters with respect to user input.

TIP

In spite of the shortened texts, the example shows that during an FTP session vast amounts of text are displayed. Therefore, try to work in an X shell window or in the shell mode of Emacs, where you can scroll through already displayed text without problems. `less` cannot be used in FTP sessions.

```
user$  ftp ftp.redhat.com
    Connected to speedy.redhat.com.
    Please use a mirror if possible

    FTP Site                 Directory
    ========                 =========
    ftp.gwdg.de              /pub/linux/install/redhat
    ...

    speedy.redhat.com FTP server (Version wu-2.4.2-academ[BETA-9](1)
    Thu Feb 29 15:50:44 EST 1996) ready.
Name (ftp.redhat.com:kofler): >  anonymous
    331 Guest login ok, send your complete e-mail address as password.
Password: >  kofler@ping.at
    Welcome to the Red Hat Software Linux archive.
    There are currently 72 users using this ftp archive.
    Guest login ok, access restrictions apply.
    Remote system type is Unix.
    Using binary mode to transfer files.
ftp>  ls
    ...
    drwxrwxr-x    3 root      root           1024 May 24 20:26 mirrors
    drwxr-xr-x    5 506       506            1024 May 21 14:23 pnp
    drwx--x--x    3 root      root           1024 May 27 17:10 private
    drwxr-xr-x   15 root      root           1024 Jun  5 16:16 pub
    dr-xr-xr-x    3 root      root           1024 Sep  9  1994 usr
```

```
...
ftp>  cd pub
    Please read the file README
      it was last modified on Fri Mar 15 17:30:04 1996 - 83 days ago
ftp>  ls
    ...
    drwxr-xr-x  10 504     504          1024 Jun  5 21:08 contrib
    drwxrwxr-x   2 root    root         1024 May 31 21:07 current
    drwxr-xr-x   7 root    root         1024 May  9 18:38 devel
    ...
ftp>  cd contrib/RPMS
ftp>  ls p*
    ...
    -rw-rw-r--   1 504   504     19428 Mar  1 01:17 portmap-3.0-1.i386.rpm
    -rw-rw-r--   1 504   504    707936 Feb  8 22:06 postgres95-1.0-2.i386.rpm
    -rw-r--r--   1 504   504     81095 Apr 28 00:02 ppp-2.2.0f-1.i386.rpm
    -rw-r--r--   1 504   504     82548 May 17 22:52 privtool-0.96-1.i386.rpm
    -rw-r--r--   1 504   504     11003 Apr  3 22:24 procmeter-1.1-1.i386.rpm
    ...
ftp>  get ppp-2.2.0f-1.i386.rpm
    PORT command successful.
    Opening BINARY mode data connection for
    ppp-2.2.0f-1.i386.rpm (81095 bytes).
    Transfer complete.
    81095 bytes received in 28.3 secs (2.8 kBytes/sec)
ftp>  bye
```

In order to keep the amount of data to be transferred as small as possible, files on FTP servers are usually compressed with `compress` or `gzip`. The only exceptions are smaller text files. After the data transfer, you must use `gunzip`, `compress` or, with archive files, `tar` to decompress the files.

Modern FTP clients

Access to an anonymous FTP server with programs such as Netscape Communicator, `gftp` (the GNOME FTP client), `gmc`, or `kfm` is much easier than with the `ftp` command: you simply specify the address of an FTP server instead of the WWW address. Please take care to use the correct syntax (here, an example for the RedHat FTP server):

```
ftp://ftp.redhat.com
```

The FTP client executes the login procedure as `anonymous`and displays a list of all files and directories in which you only have to click on the requested file.

TIP

If you do not want to use an FTP server as `anonymous`, many FTP clients recognize the following syntax:

```
ftp://server@username
```

Subsequently, you are automatically prompted to enter your password.

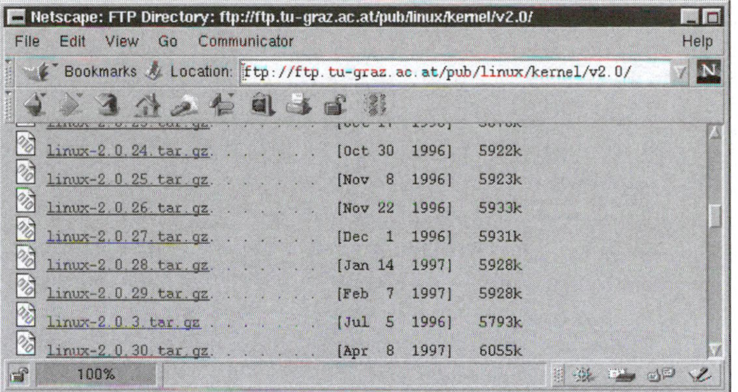

Figure 9.13 FTP with Netscape.

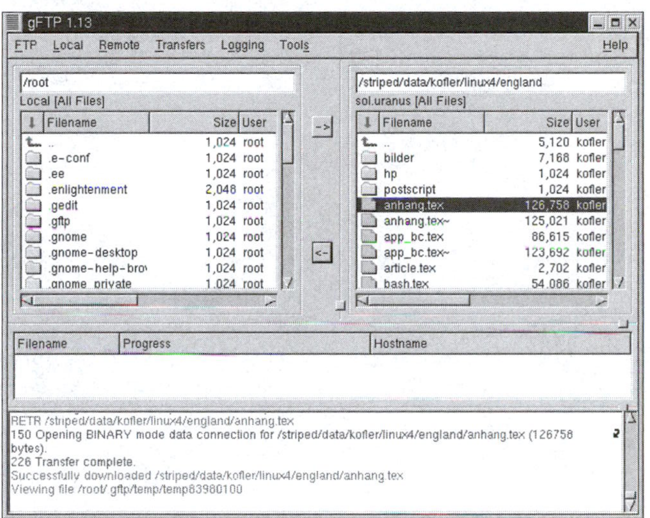

Figure 9.14 FTP with the GNOME FTP client.

9.7 `telnet` and `rlogin`

`telnet` and `rlogin` are amongst the most impressive Internet tools. They allow you to work on a remote computer as if it were standing in front of you. This obviously assumes that both computers are networked and support `telnet` and/or `rlogin`. If you have a computer with an Internet connection in your university or company, you can log into it from your Linux computer at home and start `pine` on it to read your email, to check whether a longer job is still running or if it needs to be restarted with a different set of parameters, and so on. Since both `telnet` and `rlogin` are usually used in text mode, even a slow modem connection is sufficient to allow you to work in a reasonable way.

For the user, `telnet` and `rlogin` look pretty much the same. The programs differ internally through the protocols they use (`rlogin` is safer). Both programs (`telnet`, `rlogin`) are passed the complete name of the computer on which you want to work. When the computer has been found in the network, you log in with user name and password. (When `rlogin` is configured accordingly and the second computer knows you, no password is needed.) For logging out, you use `exit`.

```
kofler@saturn$  telnet jupiter.galactic.network
Trying 192.168.1.2...
Connected to jupiter.galactic.network.
Escape character is '^]'.

Red Hat Linux release 4.2 (Biltmore)
Kernel 2.0.29 on an i586

jupiter.galactic.network login:  kofler
Password:  *******
Last login: Fri Jun  7 07:17:23 from saturn
...
kofler@jupiter$  exit
logout
Connection closed by foreign host.
```

Reference

In principle, you can also start X programs during a `telnet`/`rlogin` session. The X programs are executed on the remote computer (fully exploiting, for example, the existing hardware), but they are displayed on the local X server and also receive keyboard and mouse input from there. Since now the whole X protocol must be transmitted through the network, working in this way with a modem connection requires more patience than you are likely to be willing to invest. Further details regarding the security mechanisms of X (`xhost`, `DISPLAY` variables) can be found on page 257.

Email

This chapter deals with the basics, configuration, and operation of an email system. While the usage of email is extremely easy, its optimum configuration may be difficult. The main emphasis is on offline use, which helps minimize telephone costs.

10.1 Basics

Email stands for *electronic mail* and denotes the sending of messages (letters) over the Internet. It is one of the oldest and still one of the most important applications of the Internet. Originally, email was only designed for sending 7-bit ASCII texts. Today, email also copes with foreign language special characters and HTML texts. Furthermore, any type of file (images, and so on) can be sent via email.

If you use email in conjunction with PPP/SLIP, you can configure your email system as a so-called offline system. The name refers to the fact that email is read or written while there is no connection to the network. Only for transmitting messages to or from the provider must a brief Internet connection be established. This method has the advantage of saving you a lot of telephone costs. You only need to establish a connection to the provider for a short period required for collecting new mail or for sending the mail messages you have written.

Some email programs can also be configured in such a way that a continuous network connection must be open for their operation. This variation can certainly be viable in local networks; this book, however, limits itself to offline configuration.

In the context of this chapter, we will deal with the following aspects of email:

- Internals of mail programs under Linux (page 342): even if you already have some experience with email, you will still find a lot of valuable information here.

- Working techniques for handling mail programs (page 345): this section is mainly addressed to email novices. It describes some basic terms and working techniques, such as utilization of folders and address books, sending of binary files via email, and so on.
- Configuration and operation of stand-alone systems (page 348): these are programs which execute all email functions themselves (receiving, reading, writing, and sending). This category of email programs includes Netscape and KDE Mail. These programs are very easy to configure and to use.
- Setup of a classical Unix email system (page 359): instead of carrying out all functions with a single program, you can distribute these tasks between several programs. Configuration requires a little more effort, but it provides better possibilities for automation and a wider choice of other email clients (such as `pine`).

NOTE At first sight, email looks easier than it actually is. Once a system is configured, its use is certainly problem-free, but the path to a proper configuration is varied. For reasons of space, some advanced aspects are not dealt with in this chapter, such as signature and encryption of email messages (`pgp`) and automatic processing and answering of email (`procmail`).

Internals of mail management

The typical email configuration on a Microsoft Windows PC uses *one* program (for example Netscape or Outlook) for all email tasks, that is, for both reading and writing, as well as receiving and sending of messages. In practice, the email system works as a stand-alone system.

The typical email configuration on a Unix server is the exact opposite – here, different programs are used for the individual tasks:

- First, there is a so-called *mail transport agent*, which deals with sending and forwarding of email. Usually, the `sendmail` program is used for this purpose; occasionally, also `smail`. The program runs in the background and is constantly on stand-by.
- Second, there is a vast choice of *mail user agents* (which are also often called *mail clients*). These programs represent the user interface for the end user, allowing email to be read and written. Each user can make use of an email client of his or her choice, for example `pine`, `elm`, Emacs, or Netscape. All email clients assume that incoming email is available in the `/var/spool/mail/`*`name`* directory, and that email messages to be sent can simply be passed on to the local *mail transport agent*.

After this introduction, back to Linux: there is no such thing as a 'typical' configuration, as Linux is employed both in the private sector (one or few users, Internet access via PPP) and as a server (many users, Internet access often via a leased line). This book deals primarily with the first species, that is, Linux as a private workstation.

If you do not want to spend much time on configuration, you should opt for an all-rounder among the email programs, and thus for a program that unifies the tasks of *mail transport agent* and *mail user agent*. Besides Netscape, the KDEmail program `kmail` also offers this kind of service.

The alternative is to configure a more or less 'classical' email system (from the Unix point of view) and optimize it for offline operation. In this case, you will have to familiarize yourself with the programs `sendmail` and `fetchmail`. These two programs transmit your email messages to the provider and collect the messages sent to you.

Although the `sendmail/fetchmail` variation involves significantly more configuration effort, it definitely has its advantages: first, you now have an unlimited choice of email clients. For example, you can now use the extremely efficient email program `pine` (the author's favorite). A later switch to another email program is also easily possible. Second, the system can be better automated, that is, sending and receiving of email can be carried out by means of scripts.

This book – as if it could be any other way – deals with both variations.

- Netscape:
  - Configuration for stand-alone operation: page 348
  - Configuration as a client for `sendmail/fetchmail`: page 349
- KDEmail:
  - Configuration for stand-alone operation: page 350
  - Configuration as a client for `sendmail/fetchmail`: page 351
- `pine`:
  - Configuration as a client for `sendmail/fetchmail`: page 351
- `sendmail` and `fetchmail`:
  - Configuration for offline operation: page 359

Tip A separate mail client for GNOME, named Balsa, is currently being developed. Unfortunately, the program could not be taken into account in this edition.

Where is mail stored?

Caution – this question sounds simpler than it is! The answer is twofold: first, we will discuss email reading, then email sending.

Reading messages with POP

Let us assume that you have a POP account with an Internet provider. (POP stands for *Post Office Protocol* and is currently the most common protocol to collect messages from Internet providers.) If a friend sends you an email, the message first arrives on the server of your Internet provider.

The next time you connect to your provider, you can fetch the message (making use of POP). As mentioned above, you can use different programs for this purpose – which will determine the next location of the message.

If you use a stand-alone program, it immediately stores the message in a local `inbox`file. Messages remain in this file until they are moved to a different folder or are deleted. (Many email programs keep the messages in the file even when they are already marked as deleted or moved and are no longer displayed in the program. Only the explicit command to compress the folder (FILE|COMPACT in Netscape) finally removes the messages.)

Now for the second variation: if you fetch your messages from the Internet provider with `fetchmail`, they are temporarily stored in the file `/var/spool/mail/`*name*. Every email program that is configured as a client can access this file. The remaining procedure, however, depends on the program:

- `pine`, `mutt`, and `elm` only modify this mail file after confirmation. Both programs display the messages in an `Inbox` folder, although the messages are still in `/var/spool/mail`. (Generally it is not desirable to leave too many messages in `Inbox`. Move the messages into local folders!)
- The programs `Mail`, GNU Emacs, XEmacs, Netscape, and `kmail` remove all messages from `/var/spool/mail` and transfer them into a local file.

The following table shows the `Inbox` location for various email programs (in their default configuration):

```
elm          /var/spool/mail/username
GNU Emacs    ~/RMAIL
kmail        ~/Mail/inbox
Mail         ~/mbox
Netscape     ~/nsmail/Inbox
mutt         /var/spool/mail/username
pine         /var/spool/mail/username
XEmacs       ~/#*VM-MAIL*#
```

The behavioral details of the different mail programs are described here to save you the search for 'lost mail'. Mail is never deleted without asking first. It is just transferred to a different location where it can only be processed by a specific program (not by all programs).

No matter how the message has made its way from the Internet provider to the local email program, its last location is usually a folder, that is, a local text file.

NOTE

The most important alternative to POP is IMAP. This abbreviation stands for *Internet Message Access Protocol*. The essential difference to POP is that messages remain on the Internet provider's server. Thus, IMAP is not designed for offline operation. However, the protocol has its advantages for people who access their email from various locations/computers/operating systems, because all messages are centrally managed (and do not end up on various computers, partitions, and so on). In this book, IMAP is not considered any further.

Sending messages

To conclude, some words about messages that you send yourself. Their location after sending also depends on the configuration. In stand-alone systems, messages are usually stored in a folder named `outbox` until they are forwarded to the Internet provider. Subsequently, they end up in the `sent-mail` (or a similar) folder so that you always know what you have sent to whom.

Things look slightly different when the email program works as a client. In that case, the program forwards the message immediately after writing to `sendmail`. If `sendmail` cannot straight away pass the message on to the Internet provider (for example because there is no Internet connection at the moment) it is temporarily stored in the directory `/var/spool/mqueue`. In this directory, each message is stored in a separate file under a rather cryptic file name. Normally, you should not modify anything in this directory – `sendmail` itself will deal with the files temporarily stored here. A list of the queued mail can be displayed with `mailq` .

Glossary, working techniques

For a better understanding of the email program descriptions in the next section, the following paragraphs explain a few terms and working techniques, which are similar in all email programs. If you already have some email experience, you can skip this section.

The email header

Email header	
`From: address`	email address of the sender
`To: address`	email address of the addressee
`Subject: contents`	brief description of the contents (one line)
`Reply-To: address`	do not reply to `From:`, but to this reply address
`Cc: address`	a copy of the message is sent to the Cc address
`Bcc: address`	same as Cc:, with the exception that the main addressee is not informed that the message has also been sent to another person (blind carbon copy)

Folders

If you receive several email messages per day for several weeks and simply store them, you will quickly discover that this is not sufficient. Before long you will lose orientation in the long list of messages stored in `inbox` and `sent-mail`. For this reason, email messages can be stored in different folders. You can create folders with arbitrary names (for example, `private` for private messages, `linux` for Linux-specific email, and so on). You can also delete messages from a folder or transfer them into other folders.

Many users employ the email program as a mini-database for archiving various pieces of text, news and even WWW pages. This is possible because many WWW and news browsers are capable of sending the current document as email. Although the email program has not been designed as a database (and therefore becomes rather slow when too many messages are stored in a folder), handling is in most cases so easy that these disadvantages are gladly accepted.

In principle, the email program decides how the individual email messages are combined and stored in a folder. Under Linux/Unix, almost all programs comply with the unwritten rule that all email messages in a folder are simply stored as a very long text file. This has not the considerable advantage that it is possible to continue using the existing email archive when changing email program. (At most, it needs to be moved to a different directory.)

NOTE

Almost as expected, the Outlook email program, which is quite popular under Microsoft Windows, does not keep to this standard. Thus, it is not easily possible to use Outlook folders in a different email program.

Searching for text in the email archive

The internal organization of email folders is fairly easy, but to find a message in them is somewhat more difficult. (An exception to this rule is Netscape, which provides a workable search function.) In such cases, the remedy is simply to apply the `grep` command to the email file.

The following command searches all 1998 sent-mail files for the text enclosed in double quotes. For each entry found, the file name and the relevant line of text are displayed.

```
user$ grep "search text" ~/mail/send-mail-*98
```

The `grep` options `-3` (three lines before and after the detected line) and `-n` (display line number) allow the search result to be displayed in more detail.

TIP

You can also load a whole email folder into a text editor and search it there. However, make sure that you do not modify the text – otherwise the email program might get confused about the organization of the messages.

Address books

The most laborious and error-prone step when writing an email message is inputting the address. The abbreviations are often hard to remember and typing errors have fatal consequences. However, the problem is not too dramatic, as when you are writing a reply to an email message (using REPLY), the address is inserted automatically.

Nevertheless, you may wish to write a new message, in which case it is nice to be able to take the address from an address list. All email programs support the management of address books. Addresses can be extracted from existing email messages to minimize typing effort (and the probability of errors).

Signature

It is a matter of politeness in the Internet community to finish off email messages and news articles with a few lines of text which, apart from data such as company name, address, and so on, may also contain personal statements ('I love Linux'). To relieve you from having to enter the text repeatedly, most email programs automatically insert the contents of the file `~/.signature` at the end of the message.

Binary files

Email messages usually consist only of ASCII text, which does not cause problems to any of the email programs. In addition, all modern email programs support the mail standard MIME. This abbreviation stands for *Multipurpose Internet Mail Extensions*. MIME can be used for easy transfer of binary files. In some email programs, you can even view images and HTML files directly in the email program.

Problems arise when your addressee does not have a program that supports MIME. In this case, the coded file is displayed directly as text. This will look more or less like the following listing.

```
--1371616636-894403337-790290599:#100
Content-Type: TEXT/PLAIN; CHARSET=US-ASCII; NAME="picture.ps"
Content-Transfer-Encoding: BASE64
Content-ID: <Pine.3.89.9501170859.B100@hofer.muenchen>
Content-Description: Image
IOZJRyAyLjENCjgwIDINCjEgNCAwIDEgLTEgMCAwIDAgMC4wMDAwMCAxIDAu
MDAwIDE4NiAyMTQgMTY4IDE2OCA2OSA5NCAzMDQgMzMODQoxIDQgMCAxICOx
...
MCAwLjAwMDAwIDAgMTIgMTA1IDM3NCAxMjkga2psa2psamxramxqbGtqbGtq
--1371616636-894403337-790290599:#100--
[EOB]
```

uuencode and uudecode

The commands `uuencode` and `uudecode` are a relic from the past, when MIME had not yet been established as a standard. They are used to convert a binary file into ASCII format or to recreate the original binary file from an ASCII file. In this way, it is possible to send binary files even with stone-age email programs. In the unlikely event that you receive such an email or send one yourself, here is the syntax of the two commands:

```
user$  uuencode file name > uufile
user$  uudecode uufile
```

`uuencode` encodes `file` and stores the result in `uufile`. `name` specifies which file name should be stored within the encoded file. Generally, the same name is specified for `file` and `name`. `uudecode` can thus restore the file name without further information.

10.2 Netscape Messenger

The Messenger component of Netscape allows you to read and write email and news. From the Netscape main window, you start Messenger with COMMUNICATOR|MESSENGER or with Alt+2.

Before you can use Messenger you need to enter your full name and your email address on the EDIT|PREFERENCES|MAIL|IDENTITY dialog sheet. Some further specifications are optional, such as the file name of the signature, or the reply address. (This is only required when the addressee should not send a reply to your sender address but to a different one.)

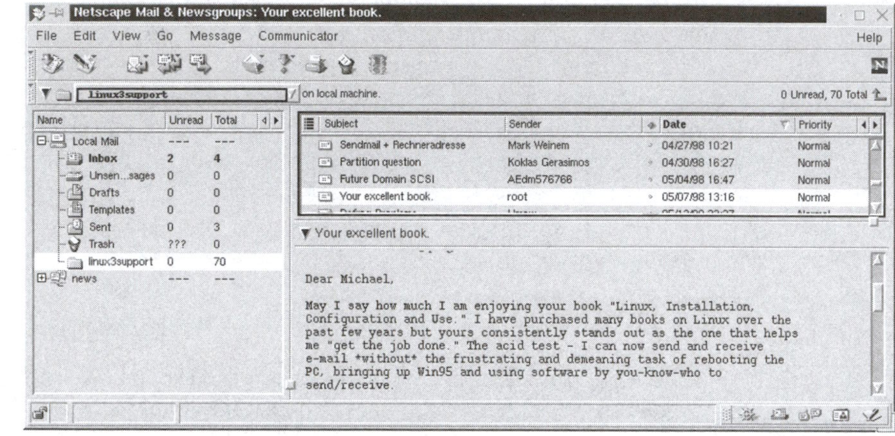

Figure 10.1 Reading email with Netscape.

Configuration as a stand-alone system

If you want to use the mail functions *without* additional programs such as `sendmail` or `fetchmail`, the following settings are required on the MAIL SERVERS sheet in the PREFERENCES dialog:

INCOMING MAIL SERVERS: here you specify the Internet address of your Internet provider's POP server (`pop.provider.de` for the sample user from page 305). As USER NAME, you must indicate the login name for the POP account. This may or may not be the same name as in your email address (that is `hofer`). When you establish a connection for the first time, you are prompted for a password. If you want Netscape to remember this password forthwith, you must activate the appropriate option. (The encrypted password is then stored in `~/.netscape/preferences.js`.)

The option CHECK FOR MAIL EVERY ... MINUTES should be deactivated – it does not make sense in offline operation. Finally, you can also specify whether read email should remain on your Internet provider's server. This setting is extremely useful for first experiments (otherwise, an email might occasionally get lost in the configuration muddle), but it absolutely needs to be deactivated later on, or your email list at the provider's will grow until all your available storage space is filled.

Under OUTGOING MAIL SERVER you enter the name of your provider's server to which all your email to be sent is forwarded for delivery (`mail.provider.de` for the sample user `hofer`).

If you do not specify a different directory, all email folders (including `Inbox`) are usually stored in the directory `~/nsmail`.

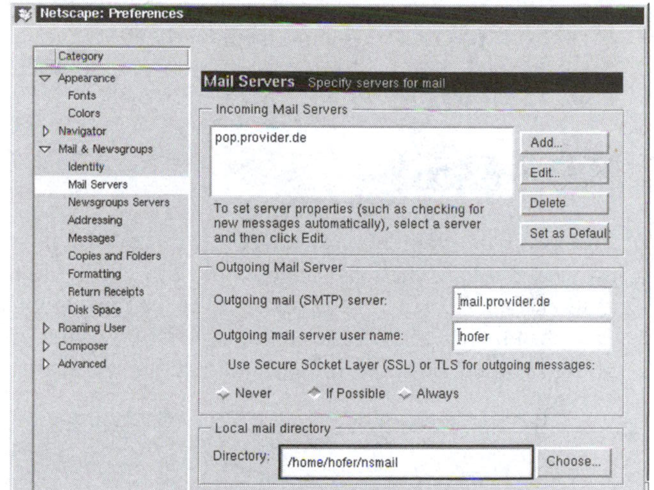

Figure 10.2 Configuration as a stand-alone system.

Configuration as a client for `sendmail/fetchmail`

If Netscape is only to be used for reading local email (and `sendmail` and `fetchmail` deal with forwarding of messages, see page 359), some configuration details look slightly different:

As INCOMING MAIL SERVER you now use the `movemail` program, which is supplied together with Netscape. As USER NAME you need to specify the name under which your email is stored in `/var/spool/mail` (as a general rule, your local login name). You should activate the option CHECK FOR MAIL EVERY ... MINUTES and specify a short period (one minute) – it certainly does not involve a lot of effort to check the contents of a local file once a minute.

While reading email messages, Netscape creates a lock file in `/var/spool/mail`. However, this only works, if the program is allowed to write data in this directory. Therefore, the access rights for `/var/spool/mail` may have to be extended:

```
root#  chmod a+w /var/spool/mail
```

This has the disadvantage, that any user can now arbitrarily store files in this directory. The only alternative would be to use an external `movemail` program with SETUID privileges which reads the mail messages from the directory.

As OUTGOING MAIL SERVER you specify `localhost`. You can do without entering the OUTGOING MAIL USER NAME.

Usage

Usage of Messenger should not pose any problems. Two further points regarding utilization as a stand-alone system: to read mail, you establish an Internet connection and execute the command FILE|GET NEW MESSAGES. Subsequently you can terminate the PPP connection.

Now you can read your emails in peace. When you write replies, you use FILE|SEND LATER for sending them. Only after you have finished writing all your email messages you establish a connection to your provider and execute FILE|SEND UNSENT MESSAGES.

10.3 KDE Mail

The `kmail` program belongs to KDE, but can of course be used independently. It provides similar functions as Netscape with the additional advantage of KDE integration (drag & drop). A further bonus is the fairly good keyboard handling. On the other hand, `kmail` is not as mature as Messenger and provides fewer configuration options (which, however, makes configuration easier).

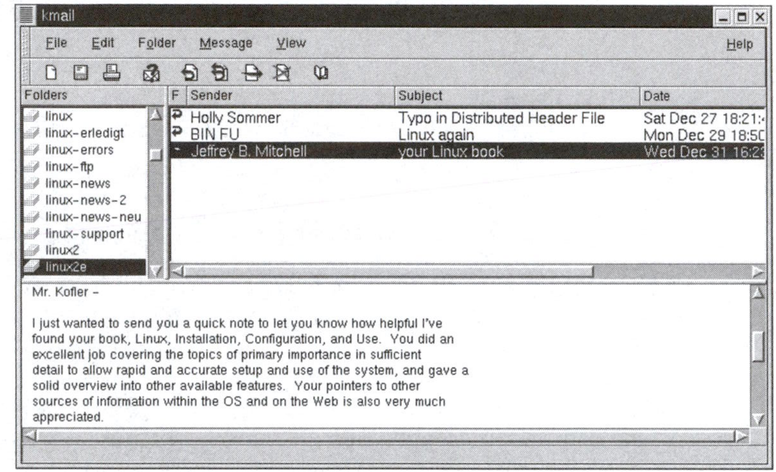

Figure 10.3 Reading email with `kmail`.

Some email folders (`inbox`, `outbox`, `sent-mail`, and `trash`) are automatically created in the directory `~/.Mail` at the first startup. The configuration of the program is carried out with FILE|SETTINGS. On the IDENTITY dialog sheet, you specify your full name and your email address.

Configuration as a stand-alone system

SENDING MAIL: on the NETWORK dialog sheet, you specify the address of your provider's server as SMTP server (`mail.provider.de` for the sample user `hofer`). Usually, the correct port number is 25.

INCOMING MAIL: here you must create a new POP account, which you can name as you wish. The entries for user, password, and POP server should not pose a problem. As a rule, the port number is 110.

NEW COMPOSER: activate the option SEND LATER, so that completed email messages are only sent when you execute the command FILE|SEND QUEUED.

Configuration as a client for `sendmail/fetchmail`

SENDING MAIL: here you only need to activate the SENDMAIL option.

INCOMING MAIL: here, too, you cannot cause much damage – create a local mailbox and specify the path to the local email directory (usually `/var/spool/mail/`*user*).

Usage

As in Messenger, usage should be obvious. To check for new messages, you execute FILE|CHECK MAIL. (In stand-alone operation, you must activate PPP first). To send replies, the already mentioned command FILE|SEND QUEUED is used.

10.4 pine

`pine` is one of the classic email clients under Linux and Unix. The program runs in text mode which, in the age of graphical user interfaces, is seen as a disadvantage by some users. However, do not disregard the advantages:

- `pine` is a relatively 'old' program, that means it is mature and stable.
- `pine` can be operated very efficiently via the keyboard. You will appreciate this advantage when you process huge quantities of email.
- `pine` also runs in a text console or via `telnet` or `rlogin`. (If your computer has a permanent connection to the Internet, this is a crucial aspect: you can login world-wide with `telnet` to process your email.)

Unfortunately, the handling of `pine` is not quite as intuitive as that of the preceding programs, so this section is rather long. Do not be deterred by it!

> TIP
>
> Further information on `pine` (including an excellent collection of FAQs) can be found on the Internet:
>
> `http://www.washington.edu/pine`

Configuration

In contrast to the programs (Netscape and `kmail`) described above, `pine` cannot be used as a stand-alone program for offline operation. The use of `pine` requires either a permanent connection to the Internet or the configuration of `sendmail` (page 359) and `fetchmail` for offline operation (see page 363).

`pine` can either be configured by means of the [S] (setup) command or by direct modification of the file `~/.pinerc`. (The first variation provides handy online help with [?], while the second variation is significantly more efficient for `pine` experts.)

If the configuration file does not exist, it can be created with `pine -conf > .pinerc`. The configuration file is extensively documented, so modifying the settings should not pose any problems. In the following sections, only a few important setting options are discussed.

Account data

In its default configuration, `pine` uses `sendmail` for sending own email messages and reads incoming mail from `/var/spool/mail/`*user*.

`personal-name``=Manfred Hofer`

This setting specifies your full name which is to be used as the sender. If `personal-name` is not set, `pine` uses the name contained in the `passwd file`.

`user-domain``=provider.de`

This setting uses the specified domain name in the sender's address. This is practical when the domain name of your computer (for example, `galactic.network`) does not match your email address with your Internet provider (`provider.de`). Thus, when you use the above setting and log in as `hofer`, `pine` uses `hofer@provider.de` as the sender's address.

`feature-list``=allow-changing-from`

In some cases, the modification of the domain name is not enough – namely when your email name differs from the login name. Unfortunately, in `pine` it is rather laborious to enter a different sender in the `From:` field. In order to make it work at all, you have to activate the function `allow-changing-from` in `From:`. (You need to use an editor to modify the configuration file.)

`customized-hdrs``=From:hofer@provider.de`

As a second step, you can now set the requested `From:` text in the `customized-hdrs` field.

Optimizing control

`enable-aggregate-command-set`

Allows simultaneous processing of several emails (see page 357).

`enable-bounce-cmd`

Activates the BOUNCE command (see page 356).

`enable-tab-completion`

Allows completion of folder names with Tab (as in the shell).

`use-current-dir`

File operations are carried out relative to the directory from which `pine` was started. (Without this setting, the home directory is used.) The setting is useful if you frequently send attachments, store emails in files (EXPORT), and so on.

`signature-file=file_name`

Specifies a file which `pine` automatically integrates into each message you write. It may be a logo, your address, phone or fax numbers, and so on – that is, all of those things you do not want to keep typing in all the time.

`editor=/usr/bin/emacs`

Specifies the editor you can start with Ctrl+_ (that is, Shift+Ctrl+-), if the standard editor of `pine` is not sufficient for you.

`character-set=ISO-8859-1`

Specifies the character set used on your computer. If this entry is missing, `pine` assumes that your computer only recognizes the US-ASCII character set which may cause problems with foreign language special characters.

> **TIP** Extensive online information on `pine` is available via the help functions of the program (RELEASE NOTES and HELP in the main menu, Ctrl+G in the editor). Furthermore, there is a fairly short `man` text.

Usage

There are at least three folders in `pine`: `inbox` for newly received mail, `sent-mail` for messages written by yourself and sent with `pine`, plus `saved-messages` for messages transferred there from `Inbox` by means of the SAVE command. If you specify a different folder name in SAVE, `pine` automatically creates a new folder with that name.

With the exception of `inbox`, `pine` stores its folders in the directory `~/Mail`. For the `inbox` folder, `pine` does not create a separate file, but accesses the mail file in `/var/spool/mail`.

At the beginning of each month, old emails are transferred (after a request for confirmation) from `sent-mail` to `sent-mail-mmm-yy`, where `mmm` is an abbreviation for the month and `yy` the last two digits of the year. This prevents the `sent-mail` folder from growing forever. In addition, you can use this opportunity to delete old `sent-mail` folders. All other folders are not affected by this tidying-up process.

After start-up, `pine` comes up with the following menu:

```
PINE 4.05   MAIN MENU                         Folder: INBOX  4 Messages

          ?     HELP               -  Get help using Pine
          C     COMPOSE MESSAGE    -  Compose and send a message
          I     FOLDER INDEX       -  View messages in current folder
          L     FOLDER LIST        -  Select a folder to view
          A     ADDRESS BOOK       -  Update address book
          S     SETUP              -  Configure or update Pine
          Q     QUIT               -  Exit the Pine program

 Copyright 1989-1998.  PINE is a trademark of the University of Washington.
                   [Folder "INBOX" opened with 0 messages]
? Help                     P PrevCmd                R RelNotes
O OTHER CMDS L [ListFldrs] N NextCmd                K KBLock
```

Thus, when you want to read your current mail, you use FOLDER LIST to select the `inbox` folder. Then `pine` displays a list of all messages (each with date, sender, size in bytes and subject line):

```
    1  Dec 13 Susanne Spitzer  (4,411) Re: CDs and Books
    2  Dec 16 Susanne Spitzer  (2,310) Re: Delivery date for Linux CD
    3  Dec 18 christian mock   (2,493) Re: Query about mail under PPP (fwd)
  N 4  Dec 21 Michael Kofler     (401) test mail to myself
```

New, not yet read mail is marked with a preceding letter N. Now you can use the cursor keys to select a mail message and read it with [↵].

Inside an email list, the cursor keys will work, provided the keyboard has been configured correctly. In addition, the following keyboard commands are available:

`pine` keyboard shortcuts	
[N]	Next email
[P]	Previous email
[+]	One page down
[-]	One page up
[W]	Search for text within email list (search is limited to headings)

While you are reading an email message, you have some additional commands at your disposal. Available commands are displayed in two command lines at the bottom of the screen. Commands are selected by entering their initial letter.

```
? Help       M Main Menu  P PrevMsg   - PrevPage  D Delete    R Reply
O OTHER CMDS V ViewAttch  N NextMsg  Spc NextPage U Undelete  F Forward
```

OTHERS displays the names of further rarely required commands:

```
? Help       Q Quit       L ListFldrs  I Index    Y Print     S Save
O OTHER CMDS C Compose    G GotoFldr   W WhereIs  T TakeAddr  E Export
```

The meaning of most commands is evident, anyway. Some explanation is needed for DELETE, UNDELETE, and SAVE. With DELETE you mark a message as deleted. For the time being, however, the message still remains in the list: it is only deleted when exiting `pine` (and even then only after a request for confirmation). With UNDELETE, a delete marker can be removed.

SAVE also marks a message as deleted, but at the same time the message is copied into another folder. The proposed folder is `saved-messages`, but you can specify the name of a different folder which will be created with this command, if it does not yet exist.

EXPORT transfers the current message into a text file. This is especially useful if you wish to process the message later on with a text editor or another program (for example, for decoding a uuencoded message).

The commands COMPOSE, REPLY, and FORWARD all lead to the `pine` editor. COMPOSE is used to write a completely new email message. With REPLY you answer the current message. `pine` automatically fills in the `To:` and `Subject:` fields and can insert the original message into the reply, indented with > characters. With FORWARD, you send the unaltered message to a second addressee (but you are also allowed to add extra information to the message).

Handling the `pico` editor poses no great problem. The cursor keys work, but Home and End often create problems. In any case, however, the following `Ctrl` keyboard shortcuts do work:

`pico` keyboard shortcuts

Ctrl+^	sets a marking point
Ctrl+K	deletes the current line or the marked text
Ctrl+U	inserts the deleted text n
Ctrl+R	inserts a text file into the message
Ctrl+X	sends the message t
Ctrl+C	aborts writing of the message
Ctrl+_	starts the editor specified in `~/.pinerc`
Ctrl+A	jumps to the beginning of the line (equivalent to Home)
Ctrl+D	deletes characters (equivalent to Del)
Ctrl+E	jumps to the end of the line (equivalent to End)
Ctrl+H	deletes characters backwards (equivalent to Backspace)

TIP If, while writing a message, you wish to access an old email message or read new email, you can interrupt the process with Ctrl+O. The partially ready message is then stored in the `postponed-messages` folder and can be completed later on (as soon as you select COMPOSE). You can even store several partially ready messages.

With `pine`, you can manage not only your email, but also your email address book. In the main menu, ADDRESS BOOK leads you to a list which contains all stored addresses. If you select the COMPOSE command from there, `pine` automatically inserts the current address into the address field of the message to be written. Vice versa, while reading a message, you can use the TAKEADR command to insert the sender's address into the address book. The address book is stored in the text file `~/.addressbook`.

> **TIP** The address book is very useful for managing small mailing lists. For example, you can define an entry 'sales' and enter all addresses of employees of the sales department. If you want to send an email to this group you only need to enter 'sales' as the address.

Sorting messages, searching for texts

Messages are usually stored in a folder in the order in which they are received. With the SORTINDEX command (shortcut `$`) you can change the order. However, the new sorting order is not stored. A permanent sorting order – which is then, however, applied to all folders – can be selected in the configuration menu (see above).

Unfortunately there is no real search function in `pine`. WHEREIS only ever refers to visible text, that is to say, either to the list of email headings or to a specific email.

Sending and receiving binary files with `pine`

If you want to send a file together with the email message you are currently writing, you must place the input cursor into the `Attchmnt:` field and execute the command Ctrl+J. Now, `pine` asks you for the name of the file you want to transmit, then for a comment about this file (a brief explanation of the file contents and/or data format). You can also attach more than one file to an email message.

The opposite occurs when you receive an email message with an attached file. In this case, `pine` only displays the normal message. Some info lines tell you that further files are attached to the message. You can now view these files with VIEWATTCH and/or store them as separate files on your computer. For processing the first attachment, you must specify attachment number 2 (because `pine` assigns the number 1 to the normal message). Viewing an attached file obviously only makes sense when the binary file is in text format (which tends to be the exception).

Attached files are coded by `pine` in a special text format. In order to prevent transmission problems, only ASCII characters are used, which increases the amount of transmitted data by about 25% compared with the actual file size.

Old email programs simply send binary files as encoded ASCII text. Such emails can be recognized by the fact that, in front of an endless list of ASCII characters, a line of the form `begin 664 file_name` can be found. `pine` cannot automatically extract binary files encoded in this way. You need to move the message with EXPORT to another file and subsequently (after you have left `pine`) execute `uudecode file` (see also page 347).

Forwarding emails (forward/bounce)

If you have several email accounts – for example one at your university or in your company and a second private one – you may often wish to forward individual emails from one account to the other. As a rule, this is done by means of the FORWARD command. This command, however, has the disadvantage that the sender changes. An email message originally sent by XY now looks as though it had been sent by you. (This is certainly correct: with FORWARD, you send an existing email message as if it was a new one – maybe even with additions.) If you use the BOUNCE command instead of FORWARD, the sender remains unchanged. To make BOUNCE available, you need to activate the command in the `pine` configuration (see above, option `enable bounce`).

If you do not want to forward individual emails, but all emails from one address to the other, you can usually employ the file `~/.forward` for this purpose. (The prerequisite is that the email system of the respective computer interprets this file correctly. This is the case in most Unix systems.) The content of `.forward` typically looks like this:

```
hofer@provider.de
\hofer
```

Here, all incoming mail for the user 'hofer' (login name for the account in which `.forward` is located) are forwarded to the address `hofer@provider.de`. At the same time, a copy of the emails is stored locally (second line; otherwise you could read your emails only on your private account and not on your local computer).

Processing groups of emails

If you receive a lot of email, processing each individual message soon becomes tiresome. Often one wishes to delete all emails that satisfy a certain criterion together, or move them to a specific folder, and so on. `pine` provides the appropriate commands. However, these must first be activated in the configuration (`enable-aggregate-command-set`, see above).

You can now select a group of emails with SELECT (keyboard shortcut [;]). Several options are available: selection of a group of emails based on their number (use this variation in combination with the sort command), selection of all emails containing a certain text as sender, subject, and so on, selection of all emails of a specific range of dates, and so on. To select individual emails you can also use [:] instead of [;] – this command refers to the email which currently contains the cursor. Selected messages are marked by an X in the left-hand column.

As a second step, you can now process all selected emails with APPLY – for example delete, store, or forward them, extract addresses, and so on.

Alternatives to `pine` (`elm`, `mail`, Emacs)

`pine` has been extensively described as an important representative of text-oriented email clients. To conclude, we will give some brief information on alternatives to `pine`. The common denominator of these programs is that, like `pine`, they can be used in text mode and that they require configuration of `sendmail` and `fetchmail` (or equivalent programs).

elm

elm is not quite as user-friendly as pine, but still easy enough to operate. After the first start-up elm creates the directory ~/.elm in which all elm-specific files are stored.

In order to prevent elm from using vi as its editor, you must either set the environment variables EDITOR and VISUAL in the profile file correctly (see page 139) or specify the file name of your favorite editor in the editor= option of the configuration file ~/.elm/elmrc:

```
# in ~/.elm/elmrc
editor=/usr/bin/emacs
```

elm is menu driven, with the most important available commands being displayed at the bottom of the screen. A complete list of commands can be obtained with ? (help function). As standard, elm transfers read messages into the file ~/Mail/received. (You can prevent this when exiting elm by answering N to the corresponding request for confirmation.)

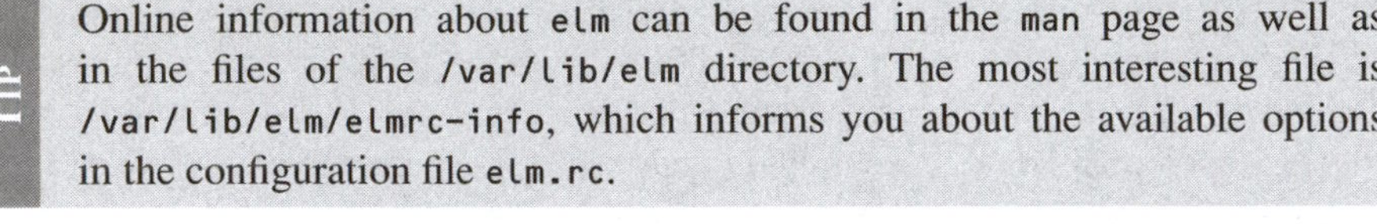

TIP Online information about elm can be found in the man page as well as in the files of the /var/lib/elm directory. The most interesting file is /var/lib/elm/elmrc-info, which informs you about the available options in the configuration file elm.rc.

mutt

mutt is seen as the successor of elm. The most important differences are the extensive configuration possibilities (color, keyboard shortcuts, and so on). Further information about this program is available on the Internet:

```
http://www.cs.hmc.edu/~me/mutt/index.html
```

Mail

The minimum specification a mail program can be limited to is evident in the Mail program, which can also be called as mail or mailx. When it is started without parameters, it displays a numbered list of all unread mail messages. When you enter a number, the corresponding email message is displayed on screen once.

When Mail is started with a mail address as a parameter, the program waits for the input of a mail text. As soon as you terminate a line that consists only of one dot with ↵, Mail considers this to be the end of the mail message and sends it to the specified address.

Thus, Mail offers no comfort at all. However, this program has one advantage over the other mail programs: it is extremely well suited to shell programming and thus for all applications for mail management automation. Online information about Mail can be obtained with man Mail.

CAUTION

If you do not quit `Mail` with [X], all read email messages are removed from the local mail file and transferred into the file `~/mbox`. You can read these messages again only if you view `mbox` with an editor. (This behavior can be changed through configuration of the file `/etc/mail.rc` or `~/.mailrc` – see `man Mail`.)

Using Emacs as a mail program

Properly speaking, GNU-Emacs und XEmacs are text editors and not mail programs (see Chapter 16 from page 537 onward). However, by means of the commands TOOLS|READ MAIL or APPS|READ MAIL, both programs can be put into a very sophisticated mail mode (the user surface of XEmacs being far more attractive).

The mail mode of both Emacs versions has one particular feature which at first may be a little irritating: the programs read the entire mail file `/var/spool/`*name* and transfer all messages into their own mail file `~/RMAIL` (GNU-Emacs) or `~/#*VM-MAIL*#` (XEmacs). Mail read in this way can now only be processed with the corresponding program (but not with any other mail program).

10.5 `sendmail` and `fetchmail` offline configuration

Sending mail (`sendmail`)

The `sendmail` program is used to send email from one computer to the other. The application described here – sending of a couple of emails from one person to the Internet provider – means letting `sendmail` run idle. The program is really designed for sending large amounts of email, with numerous options allowing very complex operations to be controlled (automatic modification of sender and addressee, rejecting incorrect addresses, automatic warnings if mail cannot be delivered, and so on). In fact, the program is employed world-wide by innumerable universities and Internet providers to deliver millions of emails each day.

These possibilities of application explain why configuration of `sendmail` is a fairly complex affair (which this chapter cannot even outline, let alone explain). An alternative to `sendmail` is represented by `smail`. Although this program is notoriously easy to configure, it is employed much less frequently.

Most Linux distributions are configured in such a way that `sendmail` is started as a background process (daemon) during the Init process (page 124).

Email that cannot be delivered immediately, because no Internet connection is active, is temporarily stored in the `/var/spool/mqueue` directory. `sendmail` periodically undertakes further delivery attempts. When email cannot be delivered for a longer period of time, `sendmail` sends a warning to the sender.

Even if your computer is only infrequently connected to the Internet via PPP, `sendmail` should run as a background process, since the program also deals with the computer-internal mail delivery. (For example, in case of faults or problems, various programs automatically send mail to `root`.)

Online information can be obtained with `man sendmail`. Depending on the distribution, additional information can be found in `/usr/doc/packages/sendmail`. Further sources of help are the Mail-HOWTO) and Chapter 15 of the Linux Network Administration Guide.

Configuration

`sendmail` is controlled via the configuration file `/etc/sendmail.cf`. All distributions include at least one ready-to-use configuration file. Some distributions, for example Slackware and SuSE, offer a choice of several configuration variations depending on the intended use: for local networks without Internet connection, for UUCP, and so on. The most suitable variation for offline operation is the one with Internet connection and name server support (DNS).

Even if the preset configuration files already function fairly well, they will frequently need some minor changes to adapt `sendmail` optimally to the peculiarities of PPP/SLIP operation. Fortunately, `sendmail.cf` is well provided with comments, so that the meaning of many settings quickly becomes evident.

Before modifying `sendmail.cf`, you should first stop and subsequently restart `sendmail`. In RedHat Linux, you need to execute the following commands:

```
root#  /etc/rc.d/init.d/sendmail stop
root#  /etc/rc.d/init.d/sendmail start
```

In SuSE the paths are slightly different:

```
root#   /sbin/init.d/sendmail stop
root#   /sbin/init.d/sendmail start
```

Host name problems

`sendmail` logs status and error messages in the `/var/log/mail*` file (the exact file name depends on the distribution, see `/etc/sylog.conf`). If you experience problems with `sendmail`, you should check this file.

A particularly frequent problem is the message 'unqualified host name (localhost) unknown.' Subsequently `sendmail` goes to sleep for one minute before it resumes work. The cause of this problem is usually that `localhost` is used as the computer name. In this case, `/etc/hosts` looks like this in some of the distributions (for example in SuSE):

```
# /etc/hosts: sendmail conplains about unqualified host name
127.0.0.1       localhost
127.0.0.2       localhost.localdomain         localhost
```

Although most programs can actually cope with this, `sendmail` cannot. The Unix-conformant solution is to choose a different computer name (`myhost`, if you cannot think of anything better). From this, `yast` generates the following file `/etc/hosts` which `sendmail` can agree with too. (Of course, `/etc/HOSTNAME` too must now contain the name `myhost`.)

```
# /etc/hosts: this will work (SuSE)
127.0.0.1       localhost
127.0.0.2       myhost.localdomain        myhost
```

The other alternative is to continue using `localhost` as the computer name and in exchange specify the full computer name for `localhost` in `/etc/hosts`. (However, this is in breach of the golden rule according to which `localhost` is considered to be *fully qualified* even without extension.) RedHat Linux is usually configured in this way if the network has only been set up as loop-back.

```
# /etc/hosts: and this works too (RedHat)
127.0.0.1       localhost.localdomain      localhost
```

Setting the sender's address

When you send mail via PPP/SLIP with `elm`, `Mail`, or Emacs, `sendmail` automatically inserts `loginname@hostname.domainname` as the sender's address. This is undesirable – the addressee cannot reply to this address, but must use your mail address at your Internet provider (in this chapter's example: `hofer@provider.de`).

A small change in `/etc/sendmail.cf` ensures that, instead of the host and domain names, `sendmail` uses a different sender. In the masquerade line, which begins with the letters `DM`, you specify the required sender's domain name. This causes `sendmail` to assemble the sender out of the login name, the `@` character and the masquerade text.

```
# alternative modification in /etc/sendmail.cf
# specify fixed computer name
DMprovider.de
```

CAUTION

Neither setting affects `pine`! `pine` builds the sender field for itself. How `pine` can be told to indicate the specified sender has been described on page 351. In Netscape and `kmail` too the sender is directly inserted by the program.

In general `sendmail` only sends emails and not news articles. The sender of news articles must also be set separately – see pages 376 and 380 for the programs `slrn` and `tin`.

Calling Internet providers as relays

In its standard setting, `sendmail` *itself* looks after forwarding your messages. Normally, however, you can leave this task to your Internet provider. For this, you tell `sendmail` that it is to deliver your mail only to the mail system of the Internet provider (and not any further).

This has an essential advantage: even if you send a message to another continent and the Internet connections are jammed, you can deliver your mail to your Internet provider without delay and thus save telephone costs. On your provider's system, we once again find `sendmail` (or another mail transport agent) which automatically forwards your mail as soon as it becomes possible.

The necessary change in `sendmail.cf` is again limited to one line: you must specify the address of your Internet provider's mail server in the line that begins with `DS` and is normally empty:

```
# modification in /etc/sendmail.cf
# "Smart" relay host (may be null)
DSprovider.de
```

Changing timeout settings

`sendmail.cf` contains a separate section in which various timeout settings can be specified. These settings control the behavior of `sendmail` if an email message cannot be delivered for a given period of time.

Often, these times have to be increased, since otherwise you will receive irritating email messages from `sendmail` which inform you about undeliverable email. If you write a message in the morning, but decide to send it only in the evening via PPP (because during the day you have no access to your provider or simply to save telephone costs) you are well aware that this message is undeliverable and do not require any warning.

```
# modification in /etc/sendmail.cf
# after one day, the sender of an undeliverable
# email message receives a warning; but sendmail
# still attempts to deliver
O Timeout.queuewarn=1d
# after five days, an undeliverable email message
# is returned to the sender
O Timeout.queuereturn=5d
```

The frequency with which `sendmail` attempts delivery of email is controlled at the start of `sendmail` with the option `-q`*time* (for example, `-q1h` for hourly delivery attempts). In RedHat, starting is carried out via `/etc/rc.d/init.d/sendmail`; in SuSe via `/sbin/init.d/sendmail`.

Creating your own `sendmail.cf`

`sendmail.cf` is built in such a complex way that the file is normally not edited directly, but generated by recompiling `m4` macro files. The advantage of this procedure is that the source files for `sendmail.cf` are more easily understandable and therefore easier to adapt than `sendmail.cf` itself.

A precondition for the creation of completely new configuration files is the installation of the `sendmail` configuration files (which are not included in all distributions) and the macro processor `m4`, whose function is best compared to that of the preprocessor of a C compiler. Furthermore, you need a lot of fundamental `sendmail` knowledge. (The 'official' documentation is the 800-page book *sendmail* published by O'Reilly.)

The source files for `sendmail.cf` are usually located in the `/usr/share/sendmail` or `/usr/src/sendmail` directory. The subdirectory `cf` contains several ready-made configuration files from which you can generate a new sendmail.cf file with a call to m4. In the following instructions, instead of linux.smtp.mc, you can obviously specify any of the many other sample files contained in the cf directory.

```
root#   cd /usr/src/sendmail/cf
root#   m4 linux.smtp.mc > sendmail.cf
root#   mv /etc/sendmail.cf /etc/sendmail.cf.backup
root#   cp sendmail.cf /etc
```

During execution of m4, various configuration files from the directories domain, mailer, ostype, and so on, are read in and processed. A detailed description of this process and the meaning of the various settings can be found in the file /usr/src/sendmail/README.

mailq

mailq or the equivalent command sendmail -bp displays a list of all mail messages which have been sent by a mail program, but which could not yet be forwarded (for example, because no Internet connection was available). Thus, mailq is a simple method for determinining whether there are any unsent emails lying around.

Sending local mail

You can also try out email on your computer if you have no Internet connection. As the address, you simply enter the login name of the addressee (for example hofer or root). In some programs (pine, Netscape) you must append @localhost to the addressee's name, for example root@localhost. The reason: some email programs automatically supplement the abbreviation root with @hostname.domainname, which is in itself correct but may cause problems to the local delivery via sendmail.

Fetching mail via POP (fetchmail)

While sendmail forwards the mail you have written to your Internet provider, the fetchmail program has exactly the opposite task: it fetches mail addressed to you from your Internet provider and appends the messages to the local mail file in /var/spool/mail. (Automatic delivery of your email to your computer is not possible, because the PPP/SLIP connection cannot be kept open continuously.)

Communication between the Internet provider and fetchmail is based on the *Post Office Protocol* (in short POP). There are two variations of POP, namely POP2 and POP3. Most Internet providers currently use POP3.

Some email programs (Netscape, kmail) can also be configured in such a way that they fetch your mail from the provider via POP. The use of fetchmail, however, allows better automation of the process.

NOTE Instead of fetchmail it is also possible to use the older program popclient. This program works in a similar way, but is less easy to configure and also no longer maintained. fetchmail is the successor of popclient.

`fetchmail` configuration

`fetchmail` is usually called without parameters. The program reads all information needed for communication with the POP server from `~/.fetchmailrc`. For the configuration file to be accepted by `fetchmail`, very restrictive access rights need to be set (`chmod 600 ~/.fetchmailrc`). The following line illustrates the structure of this configuration file using the configuration example of this chapter:

```
poll pop.provider.de protocol pop3 username hofer password qwe44trE
```

After `~/.fetchmailrc` has been set up, a `fetchmail` call with the additional option `-v` (verbose status messages) looks like this:

```
root#  fetchmail -v
```

Now `fetchmail` checks whether any email for the user `hofer` has arrived at the POP server `pop.provider.de`. The transmission protocol used is the currently prevailing protocol POP3. If there is any email, it is transmitted and forwarded to the local `sendmail`. This program deals with the actual delivery to the local user `hofer`. (The local address is derived from the original address. Email originally addressed to `hofer@provider.de` is thus sent to `hofer@localhost`.

Keywords in `~/.fetchmailrc`	
`poll` *`popserver`*	specifies the POP server
`protocol` *`protocol`*	the required protocol (`POP2`, `POP3`, `APOP`, `KPOP`, `IMAP`)
`username` *`name`*	mail name
`password` *`password`*	password
`is` *`localname`*	optional, delivery name
`mda "`*`program`*`"`	optional, program for message delivery
`keep`	optional, do not delete messages at the server (for testing!)
`silent`	optional, prevent status messages

With one exception, all commands can also be issued in form of options when calling `fetchmail`. This exception concerns the password. Without `~/.fetchmailrc`, you always need to enter the password interactively.

The keyword `is` allows email names defined by the provider to be redirected to other local user names. If, for example, your email address on a university account is `s123456@uni-xy.de`, but the emails are to be read under the login `hofer`, the `~/.fetchmail` line reads as follows:

```
poll pop.uni-xy.de protocol pop3 username s123456 is hofer ...
```

The keyword `keep` is especially useful during the test phase. It prevents emails from being deleted at the provider after having been read by fetchmail. You will not therefore lose emails because, for example, the local delivery is faulty. (With `keep`, you read the same email over and over again – which is, of course, absolutely unsuitable for continuous operation.)

Normally, `fetchmail` uses port 25 to address the locally running email server (usually `sendmail`) for local email delivery. Alternatively, you can specify a different program to deal with the task via `mda`. (The abbreviation mda stands for *mail delivery agent.*) A suitable program is the very versatile `procmail` which can also be used to answer emails automatically ('gone on holiday'), to sort emails into different files, and so on. More information can be found in the extensive `man` text and in the `Offlinemailing` Mini-HOWTO.

A less powerful alternative to `procmail` is `deliver`. `deliver` expects the messages to be delivered in the standard input channel. To make these messages arrive in the mailbox of the addressee, the name must be specified as a parameter (`deliver` *name*).

Script for automatic mail delivery via PPP

The next step is now to coordinate PPP connection establishment and sending and receiving of email by means of a central script. This allows you to use your local email program on your computer (be it `pine` or Netscape) whenever you want. If you want to send your own email messages or check whether new mail has arrived, you execute the `offlinemail` program introduced below as `root`. (The script cannot be executed by normal users, since the commands for establishing a PPP connection require `root` privileges.)

The program code for `offlinemail` is surprisingly short. As soon as the script is running satisfactorily, you should delete the `-v` options, which provide useful additional information during the test phase. The call to `sendmail` is needed, in spite of the active `sendmail`, to use the short period in which the Internet connection is open for immediate transmission of temporarily stored emails. (Depending on the configuration, `sendmail` checks only once every 15 minutes whether temporarily stored emails can be send.)

```
#! /bin/sh
# offlinemail
if ./ppp-on; then
  echo "send mail"
  /usr/sbin/sendmail -q -v
  echo "read mail"
  fetchmail -v
else
  echo "error"
fi
./ppp-off
```

The script can only be executed by `root`. Thus, `.fetchmailrc` must be located in the home directory of `root`. To ensure that email is nevertheless delivered to `hofer` and not to `root`, you must insert the keywords `is hofer` in `.fetchmailrc`.

The following lines show how `offlinemail` works in practice:

```
root#  offlinemail
dialing ... trying to establish ppp ........... ppp is up!
send mail
Running JAA00712 (sequence 1 of 1)
hofer@jupiter.galactic.network ... Connecting to provider.de via relay...
220 provider.de SMTP/smap Ready.
>>> HELO jupiter.galactic.network
```

```
250 (jupiter.galactic.network) pleased to meet you.
>>> MAIL From:<hofer@jupiter.galactic.network>
250 <hofer@jupiter.galactic.network>... Sender Ok
>>> RCPT To:<hofer@provider.de>
250 <hofer@provider.de> OK
>>> DATA
354 Enter mail, end with "." on a line by itself
>>> .
250 Mail accepted
hofer@jupiter.galactic.network... Sent (Mail accepted)
Closing connection to provider.de.
>>> QUIT
221 Closing connection

read mail
fetchmail: 1 message for hofer at pop.provider.de
reading message 1 of 1 (1699 bytes) . flushed
ppp0 link terminated
```

In principle, you can further automate your mail system. For example, you can configure `/etc/crontab` in such a way that `offlinemail` is called periodically (say, once an hour).

News

One of the most important sources of information on Linux are the topical discussions in countless newsgroups. There you find tips for solving every-day and exotic problems, opinions about trends in the development of Linux, experiences with the most recent programs, as well as endless debates about topics such as KDE versus Gnome, Emacs versus vi, GNU Emacs versus XEmacs, RedHat versus SuSE versus other distributions, and so on.

This chapter describes the most important programs for reading and writing news articles (Netscape, `tin` and `slrn`). As in the previous chapter, special emphasis will be put on offline configuration, to keep the phone bill low in spite of studying the news. An optimal solution for this is provided by the `leafnode` program.

11.1 Basics

Introduction

News groups are forums for discussion. They can be local (for example, limited to a university or a country) or international. News articles are stored on so-called news servers. Practically all universities and Internet providers operate their own news servers. In the context of this chapter, you will even learn how to establish your own (small) news server on your local computer.

News articles can be read with a news client. If you know answers to questions that have been put or want to ask questions yourself, you can write your own article.

Storage of all news articles in newsgroups (there are thousands of them!) would require incredible amounts of data. For this reason, news servers are set up in such a way that all articles are automatically deleted after a certain time (usually several days). In spite of this restriction, the news articles on big news servers often fill up several gigabytes of a hard disk.

In brief some information about the structure of the chapter:

- Fundamentals: this section explains some general features of news programs (threading, subscription to groups, and so on) and gives an overview of Linux-specific newsgroups.
- News clients (page 371): programs for reading news articles are as common as grains of sand. This chapter contains information on Netscape, `slrn`, and `tin`. These programs can be used online as well as offline.
- Configuration of an offline system (page 380): if you want to read news offline, you will need to install a local news server on your computer. In this chapter, the `leafnode` program is introduced, which is particularly suited for small news servers.

Glossary, working techniques

News clients and servers

As was the case with 'mail program' in the previous chapter about email, the term 'news program' is also ambiguous. News clients provide the user interface for the news system, allowing reading and writing of news. Common clients are Netscape, `tin` und `slrn`.

News servers deal with management and transmission of news. World-wide, thousands of news servers are in operation which are connected to each other via the Internet. Most frequently, the `inn` program is used, which allows huge news archives to be managed. For smaller news servers, the `leafnode` server introduced in this chapter is more suitable, because the program is easier to configure.

When anywhere on the planet a news article is written, copies of this article are made available world-wide on all servers which have the appropriate newsgroup in their archive. (For reasons of space, not all servers can store all groups.) Since news travels through many servers, this can take quite long – even one or two days.

Space requirements for millions of articles written world-wide every day are of course very high. In large servers, the archives comprise scores of Gbytes! For this reason, news has to be deleted after a certain period (depending on the configuration, after a few days or weeks). News is thus a short-lived medium!

TIP

Automatic deletion of articles has an essential influence on the reading of newsgroups: If you come across an interesting article, you should immediately store it locally. Otherwise you may want to access it again the next day and the article is gone (in Internet jargon: The article has 'expired'). The easiest way to store an article is to send it as an email to yourself (`name@localhost`). Then you can store the article in a folder in the email program, which gives you a chance to find it again. (Simply create appropriate folders, for example `linux-news`.)

There are two possibilities for communication between the news client, which is executed locally on your computer, and the news server of your Internet provider:

- In an online configuration (which is very simple), a direct connection between client and server is established. You select the news you are interested in from a list of all new ones. These are transmitted to the client and displayed in the same way as Web pages. Therefore, while you are reading news, there has to be a continuous connection to the Internet.
- For an offline configuration, you need to create a separate (small) news server on your local computer. At regular intervals (for example, daily), you call your provider, and the local news server contacts the provider's server: then all new articles are transmitted to the local computer; at the same time, all articles you have written yourself in the meantime are sent on to their journey through the Internet. Depending on how many newsgroups you regularly read, this takes a few minutes.

  Subsequently you can close the Internet connection. Now the news clients can access the local server to read and write news articles. (Of course, not all newsgroups are available there, only a limited selection.)

The configuration type which is actually cheaper (that is, which involves the lowest phone bills) depends very much on your reading habits. If you only occasionally look at a few newsgroups, an offline configuration does not make sense. Too many news articles you would never read would be transmitted to your computer. Offline configuration, in contrast, is ideal for intensive and most of all stress-free news reading

Subscribing

The news server whose articles you read usually hosts a lot more newsgroups than are of interest to you. It can become rather irritating when, amongst a thousand newsgroups, you have to select the one you are interested in over and over again. For this reason, all news programs allow you to mark newsgroups that interest you. Depending on the program, these newsgroups are called 'subscribed' or something similar. In all programs it is possible to choose between displaying only the subscribed newsgroups or all groups (for example, in order to subscribe to a new group).

This setting has no influence on which articles are actually available on the computer or can be transmitted. The subscription setting is simply a filter to select certain groups from all available newsgroups in order to facilitate your work.

The newsgroups that are subscribed are usually (depending on the news client) stored in the file `~/.newsrc`. Miraculously, the same format applies to most news programs, so that the file does not have to be re-created for each program.

Threading

Sometimes, real discussions take place in newsgroups. A asks a question, B answers, C corrects the answer, B defends his/her point of view, D supplies yet another answer to A's question, and so on. Hierarchically, it looks like this:

```
A: How can I do this?
  B: Re: How can I do this?
    C: Re: How can I do this?
      B: Re: How can I do this?
  D: Re: How can I do this?
```

The problem is that the articles do not arrive at the news server in this order. Between A's question and B's answer, several other articles may be sent. When reading articles, however, it would be useful if one could read articles connected in such a way in one block.

Therefore, most of the better news programs try to use the subject lines of the articles and some internal information which is not displayed to order the articles by subject, thus creating a thread. Netscape boasts a particularly elegant way of representing threads.

Writing news articles

Before you send off ('post') your first questions or answers, follow some basic rules:

- Address articles with which you only intend to check the correct functioning of your system to test groups set up for this purpose (for example `de.test`).
- Use such test news to check whether you have set up your sender properly. It should contain your name and your email address. (To prevent spam, that is unwanted automatic emails, news articles often show an intentionally incorrect email address, for example `kofler@nospam.ping.at`.)
- Read the articles of the newsgroups for a couple of days first. Maybe the question answers itself or you realize that you are in the wrong newsgroup.
- Do not ask any questions that have already been answered in FAQs.
- Stay calm and polite. (Language in the newsgroups is often unnecessarily aggressive or emotional.)
- Avoid cross-posting (that is, simultaneously addressing several newsgroups).
- News articles often end with a signature, which can contain your name (as if you were signing it), address (for businesses or universities), an aphorism or whatever you choose. This signature is read from a file created for this purpose (mostly `~/.signature`). Limit yourself to the essential and do not blow up your articles with huge signatures!
- When you react to other articles, never quote more than absolutely necessary. But quote enough to make sure that the context is still clear when the original article is no longer available. (A quotation usually consists of pieces of the original text indented with `>`.)

Each article, including the one you have just finished writing yourself, is displayed in the news program. However, it can take some time before this happens. This should not lead you to assume that something has gone wrong and you need to send the same article again. Be patient, and you will see the fruits of your labor: during this time, the article is processed by the news server and finally inserted into the news database. If your news program does not automatically look for new articles, you must ask it to do so (in Netscape, for example, with FILE|GET MORE MESSAGES).

If you have a local news system, expect a reaction time of about one minute. If you work online, it can take much longer; maybe your provider's news server is currently doing something else. (It is a typical beginner's error to send news articles repeatedly in the belief that it did not work the first time.)

Linux-specific newsgroups

Newgroups exist for all possible subjects: politics, sports, culture, science, computers, and so on. Newsgroups can be moderated or unmoderated. Moderated groups are the exception. In such groups, only articles accepted by the moderator are inserted. This leads to the quality of the articles being significantly higher, but the speed is slower (because the moderator cannot just sit there day and night reading news articles). The following list presents some newsgroups that are of interest for Linux:

International (English) newsgroups	
`comp.lang.*`	discussion groups about various programming languages
`comp.os.linux.announce`	official announcements (moderated)
`comp.os.linux.*`	a number of further Linux-specific groups
`comp.sys.*`	manufacturer-specific discussion groups (hardware/software)
`comp.sys.ibm.pc.hardware.*`	PC hardware
`comp.os.unix.*`	Unix questions
`comp.windows.x.*`	discussion groups about the X Window System
`gnu.*`	various newsgroups about GNU software

TIP

Often it is difficult to find the right newsgroup for a specific question. In such cases, invaluable help is provided by news search engines, in which you can search a huge archive of old and new news articles for keywords in their contents. The most well-known search engine of this kind has the following address:

```
http://www.deja.com
```

You can use this search engine with every Web browser; that is, you do not need a news configuration.

11.2 News clients

Linux offers a wide choice of programs for reading and writing news. This chapter limits itself to three variations, namely Netscape and the two text-oriented programs `slrn` and `tin`. If you are not happy with any of these programs, there follows an incomplete selection of programs you might wish to try out as well:

- `pine`: configuration via SETUP|CONFIG. For online reading, the news server of the Internet provider must be specified as NNTP server. For offline reading, no specification of the news server is needed; however, the text `News *[]` must be entered in the `news-collection` field. Unfortunately, `pine` is not capable of threading. The handling is similar to reading email.
- `nn`, `trn`: these are another two news clients for the text console.
- GNU Emacs/XEmacs: as everybody knows, there is nothing that cannot be done with these programs!
- `krn`: this is the news client of the KDE system. The program looks promising, although the version supplied with KDE 1.0 was too unstable for practical use.
- `knews`, `xvnews`: another two news clients with X interface. In spite of its initial letter, `knews` is *not* part of the KDE project.

Netscape Messenger

You start Messenger with COMMUNICATOR|MESSENGER or with Alt+2 from the Netscape main window. Before you can use the program, you have to enter your full name and your email address on the EDIT|PREFERENCES|MAIL|IDENTITY dialog sheet.

Access to the external server

You create a new news server with ADD on the NEWSGROUPS SERVERS configuration sheet. As the server name, you enter the Internet address of your provider (`news.provider.de` for the sample user `hofer` from page 305). As a rule, the correct PORT is 119. Subsequently, you make this server your default server with SET AS DEFAULT and delete the sample server `news` defined by Netscape.

The meaning of the NEWSGROUP DIRECTORY has remained a mystery. It is better to leave this directory as it is.

Access to the local server

When you have installed a local news server (see page 380), the only difference to the above explanations is that you enter `localhost` as the server name.

Usage

The required newsgroup can be selected from the same list field that contains the mail folders. At the first start-up, however, only the name of the news server, but not one single newsgroup is displayed.

Click on the server entry with the right mouse button and execute SUBSCRIBE TO NEWSGROUPS. Now Netscape transmits a list of all available newsgroups. In online operation via a modem, this will take a few minutes. This waiting time occurs only the first time. Netscape stores the list in `~/.netscape/xover-cache/host-server/hostinfo.dat`.

Subsequently, a hierarchical list of all available newsgroups is displayed in a dialog box. This list is often extremely large (20,000 newsgroups and more). Searching for required newsgroups is aided by the SEARCH dialog sheet in which, for example, you can filter out all newsgroups which contain 'linux' in their name. (It is, however, not permitted to use search patterns containing *.) When you have found the required group, simply click on the SUBSCRIBE button or activate the selection tick mark.

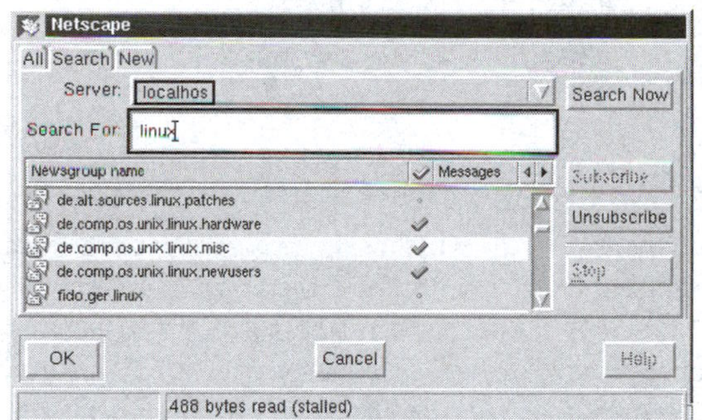

Figure 11.1 Subscribing to newsgroups with Netscape.

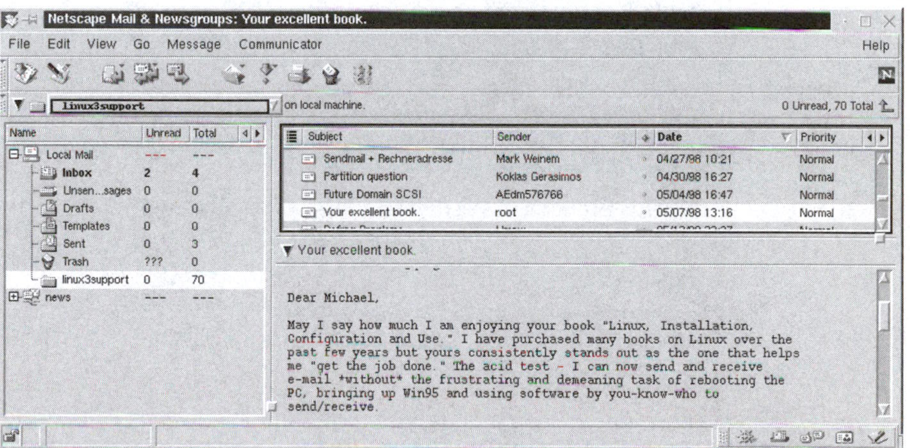

Figure 11.2 Reading news with Netscape.

> **NOTE** To be able to use the FILE|GET NEW MESSAGES command to update the list of news articles, you need to configure Netscape also as a mail client. This is rather annoying because it makes it impossible to use Netscape only as a news client without using it as an email client.

`slrn`

According to the RedHat package description, `slrn` is the best news reader on earth! Before you can share this opinion, you have to take a little time to get used to `slrn`. The great features are hidden behind an unyielding interface, which even in the age of KDE and Gnome copes without icons. (This section of course does not do justice to `slrn` at all. However, it should suffice for a first approach.)

> **TIP** Up-to-date information on `slrn`, including a very helpful collection of FAQs, can be found on the Internet:
>
> `http://space.mit.edu/~davis/slrn`

Start

Independently of whether the program is used for accessing a local server or an external server via the Internet, the server name must be set in the environment variable `NNTPSERVER`. Alternatively, the name can also be specified with the option `-h`. (The server name for the sample user from page 305 is `news.provider.de`. If you install `leafnode` (as described on page 380) as your local news server, the server name is simply `localhost`.)

In order to be able to start `slrn`, either `.jnewsrc` or `.newsrc` must be located in the home directory. If neither is the case (because so far no other news client has been used), `slrn` issues an error message.

```
hofer$ slrn
slrn 0.9.5.2 (Dec 11 1998 21:07:03)
Reading startup file /var/lib/slrn/slrn.rc.
Unable to open /home/hofer/.jnewsrc.  I will try .newsrc.
slrn fatal error: Unable to open /home/hofer/.newsrc.
```

This problem is easily remedied. Try again, and this time use the following options:

```
hofer$ slrn -f ~/.newsrc -create
slrn 0.9.5.2 (Dec 11 1998 21:07:03)
Reading startup file /var/lib/slrn/slrn.rc.
Connecting to host localhost ...
Connected to host.  Posting Ok.
--The next step may take a while if the NNTP connection is slow.--
Creating /home/hofer/.newsrc...........
```

Reading the list of all stored newsgroups may take some time – but luckily this is only needed at the first start-up.

`srln` now shows a (still empty) list of all subscribed newsgroups. To display all groups – including the ones you have not yet subscribed to – enter Shift+L * ↵. Instead of *, you can enter any pattern, such as `*.os.*` for all newsgroups involving operating systems.

> **NOTE**
> Depending on which server you or your Internet provider are using, Shift+L may not work: no groups are displayed. This is particularly likely if you use `leafnode` as a news server. Quit `slrn` with `Q`, and use an editor to insert the following line into the configuration file `~/.slrnrc`:
>
> ```
> set read_active 1
> ```

As soon as you see the list of groups, you can subscribe to the required newsgroups with S. U cancels the subscription. If you now execute Shift+L a second time, only the subscribed groups are displayed.

Usage

To read the news of a group, you select the group with the cursor keys and press ↵. Now `slrn` displays a list of all articles out of which you can select the required article, again using the cursor keys and ↵.

In the text window now appearing on screen, you can scroll with Spacebar and Backspace. With H and Z you view/hide the news text or the news list. Further commands can be found in the following table:

`slrn` keyboard shortcuts	
Q	quit current view or `slrn`
?	online help
List of articles	
C	mark all articles as 'read' (catchup)
Esc, U	mark all articles as 'unread' (uncatchup)
Spacebar	scroll news forward
Backspace	scroll news backward
H	view/hide news text
Z	view/hide news list
F	send reply (follow up) to an article as a news article to the newsgroup
R	send reply (reply) to an article as email directly to the author
Shift+P	write new article (post)
Group list	
S	subscribe to groups
U	cancel subscription to a group (unsubscribe)
Shift+L	display all groups or only subscribed groups

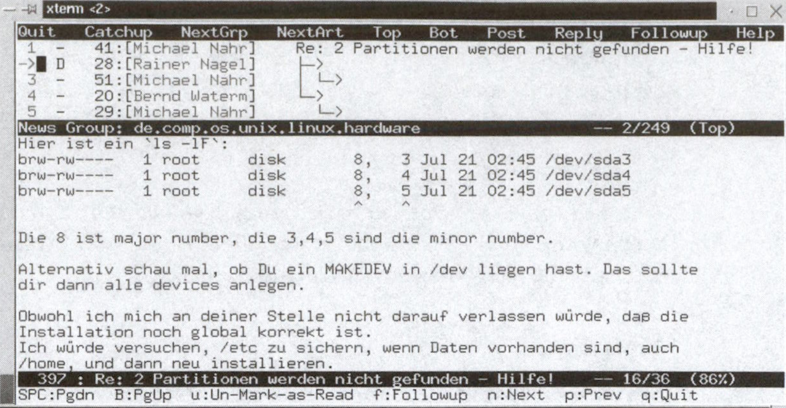

Figure 11.3 Reading news with `slrn`.

Configuration

Appearance, operation, and functional extent of `slrn` can be extensively modified by means of the configuration file `~/.slrnrc`. Setting options and syntax are documented in the accompanying example file `slrn.rc` (usually in the directory `/var/lib/slrn`).

Sender's address

`slrn` normally employs the user name, host name, and domain name to build the sender's address. In an offline configuration, this is only rarely a good solution; rather, the email address of the Internet account should be used. The following lines in `.slrnrc` set up the following sender's address: `hofer@provider.de (for the sample user Hofer)`.

```
username "hofer"
hostname "provider.de"
realname "sample user Hofer"
```

> **CAUTION**
> The address of the sender will be entered correctly in all news articles, but it is not valid for the REPLY command with which you send an email directly to the author of a news article. In the current version of `slrn`, it seems to be impossible to influence the sender's address of emails. As is customary under Unix, the email address is made up out of login name, host name, and domain name. Only the `sendmail` configuration may potentially be able to solve the problem.

Editor

`slrn` has no editor of its own and starts `vi` as a default editor. You can prevent this by setting the `EDITOR` or `VISUAL` environment variables appropriately.

Colors

The preset colors of `slrn` occasionally make it impossible to read the text. A slight modification works wonders: the following line causes headings (in the help text too) to be displayed in blue on a white background.

```
color headers blue white
```

Mouse control

With the following line, many functions of `slrn` can also be controlled via the mouse:

```
set mouse 1
```

Besides menu control and selection of groups or individual news articles, there are a number of not so obvious mouse shortcuts.

`slrn` mouse shortcuts	
In the 'News Group' status line:	
Left button	scroll list forward
Right button	scroll list backward
Middle button	close list view
In the article status line:	
Left button	jump to the next unread news article
Right button	jump to the previous unread news article
Middle button	view/hide quoted text (`> text`)
In the article text:	
Left button	scroll text forward
Right button	scroll text backward
Middle button	close text view

tin

`tin` is a handy program which may leave you with a rather meager first impression, but which is actually much more efficient in its handling than some other programs (such as Netscape). As with `slrn`: do not be deterred by the very simple interface!

Start

Just like `slrn`, `tin` too evaluates the contents of the environment variable `NNTPSERVER` or the file `/etc/nntpserver`, where the name of the news server must be specified (for example `localhost` or `news.provider.de`). Alternatively, the server name can be specified with the option `-g`.

> **NOTE**
>
> The first `tin` obstacle might already be the start. Depending on how the program is compiled, it will display a few error messages after start-up (which might not even be visible in `xterm`) and then quit immediately. In this case, `tin` expects a news archive in `/var/spool/news`, as it would be created by the server `inn`.
>
> `tin` can read such an archive without contacting the news server. However, this rather exotic feature fails if no local server at all or a different local server (for example `leafnode`) is used. Try to start `tin` with the option `-r`:
>
> ```
> user$ tin -r
> ```

Usage

At the first start-up, `tin` transfers a list of all known newsgroups from the server into the local `.newsrc` file. If the Internet connection to the server runs only via a modem, this will take several minutes. (The waiting time occurs only at the first start-up.) Subsequently, `tin` displays the still empty list of subscribed groups.

Press [Y] to display the long list of all unsubscribed newsgroups. Now, you can use the cursor to move to the required newsgroups and subscribe to a single group with [S]; or you can use [Shift]+[S] to subscribe to all groups that match a given pattern. For example, you could enter `comp.os.linux.*` to select all Linux groups. Press [Y] once more – then the screen should look more or less as follows:

```
                Group Selection (localhost  3)               h=help

   1    32  comp.os.linux.hardware
   2    92  comp.os.linux.misc
   3     3  comp.os.linux.networking
   4     2  comp.os.linux.x

  <n>=set current to n, TAB=next unread, /=search pattern, c)atchup,
g)oto, j=line down, k=line up, h)elp, m)ove, q)uit, r=toggle all/unread,
  s)ubscribe, S)ub pattern, u)nsubscribe, U)nsub pattern, y)ank in/out
```

The numbers in the second column indicate how many articles you have not yet read. In order to read the articles in a newsgroup, simply move the cursor into that line and press [↵] or [→]. Now, the structure of the screen will look something like this:

```
   1        e2fsck signals error. Disk defective?     Joerg Mertin
   2   + 2  MC in color?                              Kai Straube
   4   + 3  lpd - no daemon present                   Joachim Zobel
   6   + 2  Problems with kernel compilation          Stefan Janke
```

The second column needs some explanation. If it contains a number, we have a thread containing n unread articles. With the cursor keys, you can select an article or a thread. With [→] you can read the article. [↓] takes you to the next article, [←] back to the list. Once an article has been read, the plus sign or the threading number is removed. When you quit the list and later visit it again, read articles are no longer displayed at all.

TIP: If you want to have a second look at an article you have already read, you must use [Z] to mark the whole group as 'unread.'

The following list summarizes `tin`'s most important keyboard shortcuts. Please note that some shortcuts only apply in some `tin` windows (for example, only when an article is currently displayed).

`tin` keyboard shortcuts	
[↑], [↓]	previous/next article or group
[→]	read newsgroup or article
[←]	back one hierarchy level
[Tab]	jump to the next unread article
[/]	search for text
Processing news	
[F]	send the newsgroup a reply (follow up) to the article as a news article
[R]	send a reply to an article as email directly to the author (in the article window)
[W]	write new article
[T]	mark an article
[M]	send (marked) articles or threads as email
[S]	store (marked) articles or entire thread in a file
[C]	mark all articles in this group as 'read'
[Z]	mark all articles in a group as 'unread'
Processing groups	
[S]	subscribe to the group
[Shift]+[S]	subscribe to several groups (with pattern) (the group must be visible, press [Y] beforehand)
[U]	cancel subscription to a groupn
[Shift]+[U]	cancel subscription to several groups (with pattern)
[Y]	show all newsgroups or only subscribed newsgroup

Many additional commands are described in the very informative `man` text. Online help can be called with [H], but only displays a list of keyboard shortcuts. Depending on the distribution, further information can be found in `/usr/doc/tin*`.

TIP: You can speed up the start-up of `tin` by using the option `-nq`. In that case, `tin` only considers the already subscribed groups. It is not possible to subscribe to additional groups, nor does `tin` check whether new newsgroups have become available on the server.

Configuration

`tin` can be extensively configured. You can either modify the file `~/.tin/tinrc` directly or call the configuration dialog from inside the program with Shift+M. Besides other things, this allows you to activate colors and mouse support.

Editor

`tin` has no editor of its own and starts `vi` as its default editor. You can prevent this by setting the `EDITOR` or `VISUAL` environment variables appropriately.

Sender's address

`tin` normally employs the user name, host name, and domain name to build the sender's address. In an offline configuration, this is only rarely a good solution; rather, the email address of the Internet account should be used. For this purpose, a modified sender's address can be set with Shift+M (option `mail_address` in `tinrc`).

CAUTION

As with `slrn`, in `tin` too the modified sender's address is only valid for news articles, not for email sent with `tin` via REPLY. You should use your email program to reply directly to news articles.

11.3 Offline news configuration (leafnode)

`leafnode` is a news server specially optimized for small news archives (a few dozen groups maximum). Thus, `leafnode` is particularly suitable for managing a news archive on private computers without permanent Internet access.

TIP

You can find the most up-to-date version of `leafnode` together with further information on the Internet:

`http://wpxx02.toxi.uni-wuerzburg.de/~krasel/leafnode.html`

REFERENCE

The most popular alternative to `leafnode` is `inn`. This program is generally used for very large news archives, but can also be employed for private use. The only basic disadvantage is the rather difficult configuration.

In the first edition of this book, this chapter included instructions for installing an offline news server with `inn`. This text had been made available by Markus Dickebohm, which is most gratefully acknowledged. If you would rather use `inn` than `leafnode`, the (German) text is still available on the Internet:

`http://www.uni-koeln.de/~acp66/linux`

Installation and configuration

By now, many distributions supply `leafnode` as a preconfigured package. (In RedHat, you can find the program in the `contrib` directory which is often supplied on an additional CD-ROM. If not, you will need to download the fairly small package from a RedHat FTP server to your computer.)

The information in this chapter refers to version 1.8.1, but should also be valid for version 1.6 and all versions after 1.8. (`leafnode` 1.7 is defective and should not be used!) Please note that, depending on the distribution, the paths of the `leafnode` binary files may vary (`/usr/sbin` or `/usr/local/sbin` or `/usr/local/bin`). Please check where the binaries are located on your computer and use the correct path.

config

The configuration of `leafnode` is carried out in the file `config`, which is normally located in `/usr/lib/leafnode/config` (in SuSE in `/etc/leafnode`).

The most important setting in this file concerns the news server or news servers from which `leafnode` is supposed to read news articles. For the sample user from page 305, this is `news.provider.de`. The keyword `expire` specifies for how many days unread news threads should be kept on the server. The default setting is 20.

`initialfetch` specifies how many news articles are to be read the first time after subscribing to a newsgroup. If you do not set a limit, `leafnode` will transfer all available news articles – and that may take ages!

The `maxfetch` limit is valid for current operation. Each time `leafnode` searches for new articles, a maximum of this many articles is transferred. If you only very rarely (say, once a week) transfer the news articles of a popular newsgroup (for example `comp.os.unix.linux.misc`), you should select a higher value – otherwise your local news archive will be incomplete. Too high a value is also not a good idea – transfer of many news articles takes quite a long time. (As a rule of thumb: transfer of two to three news articles per second is a realistic value.)

```
# /usr/lib/leafnode/config
server = news.provider.de
expire = 20
initialfetch = 500
maxfetch = 1000
```

These settings should be sufficient for your first experiments. The `config` file supplied together with `leafnode` is well commented, so that the setting of further options should not be a problem.

/etc/nntpserver

This file specifies which server should be contacted by local clients. Since `leafnode` is now running on your computer, you will need to enter `localhost`.

$NNTPSERVER

This environment variable too is evaluated by some news clients and must therefore also be set to `localhost`. (In SuSE, you set `$NNTPSERVER` in the file `/etc/rc.config`)

`/etc/inetd.conf`

This file specifies which programs are responsible for which Internet services. For the `nntp` news protocol, you must enter the exact path to the program `leafnode`. Please make sure that the file has no other `nntp` entries!

```
# in /etc/inetd.conf
nntp stream tcp nowait news /usr/sbin/tcpd /usr/local/sbin/leafnode
```

To make the `inetd` daemon take the modification of `/etc/inetd.conf` into account (without restarting the computer), you must execute the following command. It does, in fact, not terminate `inetd` at all. The signal `-HUP` means that the configuration file is to be read in again.

```
root#  kill -HUP `cat /var/run/inetd.pid`
```

Now you can execute a test as to whether `leafnode` actually starts. First, you establish a `telnet` connection to the NNTP server for `localhost`. If everything is working correctly, `leafnode` responds. After this, you can exit `telnet` with Ctrl+], Ctrl+D.

```
user$  telnet localhost nntp
Trying 127.0.0.1...
Connected to localhost.localdomain.
Escape character is '^]'.
200 Leafnode NNTP Daemon, version 1.8.1 running at localhost.localdomain
<Ctrl>+<]> <Ctrl>+<D>
```

Operation

Fetching the list of newsgroups

With this, the configuration is concluded for the moment. Establish a connection to the Internet, and execute the `fetch` command that belongs to `leafnode`:

```
root#  /usr/local/sbin/fetch -vvv
Read active groups every 90 days
Unsubscribe unread groups after 7 days
Unsubscribe groups that have been read once after 2 days
Trying to connect to news.provider.de ... connected.
LIST ACTIVE done 915854522 seconds ago, getting all groups
...
Disconnected from news.provider.de
```

`fetch` transfers the list all newsgroups stored on the Internet provider's news server. This may take a few minutes. (A simple way of finding out whether data is being transmitted via PPP is the `ifconfig` command. It displays the number of data packets transmitted so far. When you execute `ifconfig` twice in in a row, the number of packets should change.)

Reading news articles

Now, `leafnode` is ready for operation. At this point, you can use any news client you like (Netscape, however, only from version 4.5 onward) and subscribe to newsgroups. As only the list of newsgroups has so far been loaded, but no articles, you will enjoy only somewhat limited reading. In fact, `leafnode` displays one dummy article per newsgroup, which you need to display in your news client to tell `leafnode` that you are interested in the corresponding newsgroup.

After you have done this for a few (but, for the moment, not too many!) newsgroups, check the directory `/var/spool/news/interesting.groups`:

```
user$  ls -l /var/spool/news/interesting.groups/
-rw-rw-r--  news  news   0 Jan  9 comp.os.unix.linux.hardware
-rw-rw-r--  news  news   0 Jan  9 comp.os.unix.linux.misc
-rw-rw-r--  news  news   0 Jan  9 comp.os.unix.linux.newusers
```

For each newsgroup whose articles are to be read, `leafnode` has created an empty file with the name of the newsgroup. Now, establish another Internet connection and execute `fetch`. This time, articles are actually transferred from your Internet provider's news server to the local news server. (The option `-v` can be used to control how extensively the program reports about its actions. The more 'v's you specify, the more verbose the reports will be.)

```
root#  /usr/local/sbin/fetch -vv
Trying to connect to news.provider.de ... connected.
LIST ACTIVE done 120239 seconds ago, issuing NEWGROUPS
Read server info from /var/spool/news/leaf.node/news.provider.de
comp.os.unix.linux.newusers: considering articles 24077-24305
comp.os.unix.linux.newusers: 202 articles fetched, 0 killed
comp.os.unix.linux.misc: considering articles 30645-30874
comp.os.unix.linux.misc: 212 articles fetched, 0 killed
comp.os.unix.linux.hardware: considering articles 12376-12471
comp.os.unix.linux.hardware: 84 articles fetched, 0 killed
Disconnected from news.provider.de
```

When you start your news client again, you should be able to read the transferred articles. From now on, `leafnode` works practically on its own: the program logs the newsgroups you are interested in. As soon as you have not read a group for a few days, transfer of its articles is stopped. You might even want to integrate the `fetch` program into the `ppp-on` script file, so that you automatically read news each time you establish an Internet connection via PPP.

NOTE

You can also manually delete the files in `/var/spool/news/interesting.groups/` if you have activated a group by mistake. Conversely, you can also activate new groups by simply creating the corresponding file with `touch`. However, please note that all files in `/var/spool/news` must belong to the user `news`. Therefore, you need to execute `chown news.news *` for all manually created files.

Sending your own articles

When you write an article with a news client, `leafnode` first stores it temporarily in the directory `/var/spool/news/out.going`. Only when you execute `fetch` the next time are the articles transmitted to the Internet provider's news server. When fetching new articles, your own article too will be fetched from the external news server.

This means that articles you have written are only visible in the article list after the next `fetch`. (If you are unlucky – if the Internet provider's news server is momentarily very busy – two `fetch` commands may be needed.) Therefore, do not worry that the command has not worked if your articles are not displayed at once!

Deleting old news articles

Little by little, the transferred news articles fill up the numerous subdirectories of `/var/spool/news`. Even with only a few newsgroups, the archive soon grows to 10 to 20 Mbytes. To prevent unlimited growth, you need to delete old articles. This is the task of the `texpire` program, which is also supplied with the `leafnode` package. The program must be executed by the user `news`.

```
root#  su news
news#  /usr/local/sbin/texpire -v
texpire 1.8.1: check mtime and atime
comp.os.unix.linux.hardware: 97 articles deleted, 833 kept
comp.os.unix.linux.misc: 217 articles deleted, 2213 kept
comp.os.unix.linux.newusers: 178 articles deleted, 2229 kept
total: 436 articles deleted, 5042 kept
news#  <Ctrl>+<D>
root#
```

This program should be executed periodically (for example once a day or once a week). The process can be easily automated by registering the program with the `crontab` command. `crontab` starts an editor and, after its termination, carries out all necessary modifications in the `/var/cron` files. (Caution: `crontab` automatically starts `vi` if you do not set a different editor in `$EDITOR`.)

```
root#  crontab -u news -e
```

If you want `texexpire` to be executed every night at 20:00 hrs, you must enter the following line in the editor:

```
0 20 * * * /usr/local/sbin/texpire
```

The first number specifies the minutes, the second one the hours. Choose a time at which your computer is usually running.

Part IV
Application

12 The `bash` – a modern command interpreter

The main topic of this chapter is the ‘bourne again shell’ (in short, `bash`). This program is automatically started after logging in and subsequently allows input and execution of Linux commands – thus the term command interpreter. At the same time, the `bash` provides its own programming language which can be used to write shell programs (shell scripts).

The description of the `bash` is spread across two chapters. The present chapter deals with the use of the `bash` as a command interpreter, where the major subjects are an introduction to `bash` usage, input and output redirection, communication between processes (pipes, command substitution) and the management of shell variables.

Chapter 13 from page 405 onward explains the programming possibilities offered by the `bash`, describes the most important language elements and provides examples of their use. The chapter concludes with a reference section listing the most important commands for programming the `bash` and a table of all its special characters.

12.1 What is a shell?

`bash` stands for ‘bourne again shell’ and is a typical example of Unix word-play. It is a successor to the Bourne shell, which together with the Korn shell and the C shell is one of the three classic Unix shells. Under Linux, all three shells are available, but as a standard usually only the `bash` is set up.

Now, what is a shell? A shell is a kind of interface between the Linux system and the user. In the first place, the shell is used for calling Linux commands and programs and thus represents a kind of command interpreter (comparable, for example, to `COMMAND.COM` in the MS-DOS world).

At the same time, the shell provides a powerful programming language which can be used to automate repetitive tasks. Some special shell commands allow the use of variables inside these programs, construction of branching expressions and loops, and so on. Depending on the personal preferences of their authors, the resulting programs are called batch files, shell scripts, shell procedures, or similar names. However, in all cases they are simple text files which are executed (interpreted) by the shell. More details can be found in Chapter 13 from page 405 onward.

TIP

There is a substantial `man` text (5000 lines) to document the `bash`, and an equally voluminous `info` file which can be read with the command `info -f/usr/info/bash`. In addition, some distributions supply the HTML file `bashref.html`, which presents the same contents in a properly formatted way.

NOTE

This chapter describes `bash` version 2.0. Older distributions still use version 1.14. In normal application, there is hardly any visible difference. More has changed for the programmer (see also page 405) – but here too, except for very few details, the two `bash` versions are compatible. If you do not know the shell version you are working with, simply execute the following command:

```
user$ echo $BASH_VERSION
2.02.1(1)-release
```

Changing to a different shell

Under GNU/Linux, the `bash` is considered the standard shell. However, other shells are available, depending on how you installed Linux. These shells are characterized by a slightly different command input syntax and different commands for programming. The decision for or against one or the other shell is mainly a question of personal preferences, habits, and so on. The fact that this book only describes the `bash` is mainly down to space restrictions.

If you have installed more than one shell, you can switch between shells at any time during normal operations: with `bash` or `sh` you get into the `bash`, with `ash` into the shell of the BSD system (ideal for computers with little RAM), with `ksh` or `pdksh` into the Korn shell, and with `csh` or `tcsh` into the C shell or its variation tcsh. `exit` brings you back into the last active shell.

Please note that all shells distributed with Linux are GNU or public domain versions. For this reason, there can be some differences – usually very small – from the original shells.

If you do not know in which shell you are currently working, the easiest way to find out is to enter the command `echo $0`. This command is available in all three shells with the same meaning and displays the file name of the current shell.

```
user$  echo $0
-bash
```

TIP If you have now become curious to find out more about different shell versions: there are very extensive `man` texts available for `ash`, `ksh`, and `tcsh`.

Changing the default shell

Each user registered under Linux may have his or her own default shell. This shell is automatically started after logging in. If you want to change your default shell, you have to edit the file `/etc/passwd`. The shell is the last entry in the line for each user.

Instead of directly modifying the `passwd` file, which only `root` is authorized to do, you can also call the command `chsh` (change shell). The shell programs are stored in the `/bin` directory. Thus, you must specify `/bin/csh` if you want to work with the C shell. A list of usable shells can be found in `/etc/shells`.

12.2 Command input

Your first contact with the `bash` occurs during normal command input. The `bash` supports you with a number of useful keyboard shortcuts and special keys. In particular, you can use the ↑ and ↓ cursor keys to reprocess the most recently input commands, which saves a lot of typing. When you log out from a shell, the most recently entered commands are stored in a file and are thus available when you next log in. (If you work under the same user name on several terminals, only the commands of one of these terminals will be stored.)

Command lines can be edited in the same way as in a text editor, that is, you can insert and delete characters in any position. The keyboard mapping of the `bash` is almost entirely configurable. In particular, you can assign your own commands to special keys (such as function and cursor keys). In addition, you can switch between `emacs` and `vi` mode. Thus, for all basic editing commands, the same keyboard shortcuts apply as in the selected editor. Usually, the default setting is `emacs`. All keyboard shortcuts in this chapter are specified for the `emacs` mode.

TIP Information about configuration of the `bash` can be found on page 137, which also contains a description of the correct setup of the `.inputrc` configuration file.

Expansion of command and file names

Possibly the biggest difference in command input between the `bash` and other shells (especially the usual MS-DOS command interpreter) is the automatic expansion of file names by means of Tab. As soon as you have entered the first letter of a command or file name, you can press the Tab key. If the name can already be uniquely identified, it is expanded to its full length. If there are several names that start with the same letters, the expansion is only performed up to the point where these start to differ. In addition, a beep is sounded to indicate that the name is probably not yet complete.

An example will make the concept of expansion easier to understand. On my computer, for example, the input

```
user$ em [Tab] com [Tab]
```

is automatically expanded to

```
user$ emacs command.tex
```

where `emacs` is the name of a command (to call an editor). In order to complete `em`, the `bash` searches all directories specified in the `PATH` variable for executable programs. `command.tex` is a text file located in the current directory and is uniquely identifiable through the specification of the first three letters. The expansion also works for file names preceded by several directories. If you input

```
user$ ls /usr/doc/ger [Tab]
```

the `bash` expands this input to

```
user$ ls /usr/doc/german/
```

taking into account all file and directory names in the `/usr/doc` directory. If a unique expansion is not possible (beep), you can simply press [Tab] again. Then the `bash` displays all possible expansions underneath the current input line. The input

```
user$ e [Tab] [Tab]
```

leads to the output

```
user$  e
echo       elif       emacs-nox    eqn    exec        expand
ed         elm        emacsclient  esac   exit        export
editres    elmalias   enable       etags  exmh        expr
egrep      else       encaps       eval   exmh-async
eject      emacs      env          ex     exmh-bg
```

Now the input can be continued. The file list that will actually appear on your computer obviously depends on which files are contained in your current directory, which programs are installed in your Linux system, and so on.

TIP

Programs and commands in the current directory are only considered for command expansion if the current directory is contained in the `PATH` variable. (`echo $PATH` displays `PATH`. The current directory is abbreviated with '`.`'.) For reasons of safety, some Linux distributions lack the current directory in `PATH`. In order to execute programs from the current directory, `./name` must be entered. The `PATH` setting can be changed in `/etc/profile`.

NOTE

The automatic command expansion hides the location of a program file. With `whereis name`, all standard directories for program files are searched, which in most cases leads to success. `which` searches `PATH` and determines the program that was executed when the command name was input without a path specification. `which` is of interest where several versions of a program exist, located in different directories.

Similar expansion mechanisms work for the names of home directories (`~ro` [Tab] yields `~root/`) and variables (`$PA` [Tab] yields `$PATH`).

Important keyboard shortcuts

The following table presumes that the `bash` is configured for `emacs` mode. If on your computer some keys produce a different reaction, please read the configuration hints on page 137. If you work under X, the keyboard management of X may well get in your way, even with a correct `bash` configuration – see from page 242 onward.

`bash` keyboard shortcuts	
↑, ↓	scroll through the most recently entered commands
←, →	move cursor backward / forward
Home, End	move cursor to beginning / end of line
Ctrl+A, Ctrl+E	as above, if Home or End do not work
Alt+B, Alt+F	move cursor one word backward / forward
⟵, Del	delete character backward / forward
Alt+D	delete word
Ctrl+K	delete to end of line
Ctrl+T	swap the two preceding characters
Alt+T	swap the two preceding words
Tab	expand command or file name
Ctrl+L	clear screen
Ctrl+R	search for previously entered commands

The Ctrl+R keyboard shortcut needs some words of explanation. This shortcut allows you to search for already entered commands: press Ctrl+R at the beginning of the line and enter the first character of the required command line. The `bash` then displays the first matching line. Pressing Ctrl+R several times toggles between different matching lines. Tab stops the search and allows you to edit the selected line.

Alias abbreviations

One further way to make typing easier when inputting commands into the shell can be obtained through the `alias` command. `alias` is used to define abbreviations. When a command line is evaluated, the first word is checked to see whether it contains an abbreviation. If so, the abbreviation is substituted with the complete name.

Abbreviations for specific combinations of options or for file names are not possible, as the `bash` does not search the remaining parameters of a command for abbreviations. However, the `bash` recognizes special cases in which several programs are named in one command line (pipes, command substitution, sequential execution of commands with ';') and searches all command names for abbreviations.

```
user$  alias cdb='cd /home/mk/book'
```

The above command defines the abbreviation `cdb`, which allows a quick change to the frequently used directory `/home/mk/book`.

`alias` calls can also be embedded. Please note that `alias` abbreviations take precedence over commands bearing the same name. This can be used to prevent unwanted calls of commands:

```
user$  alias more=less
```

From now on, each attempt to call the `more` command leads to the start of the more powerful, but otherwise equivalent, program `less`. If you really need `more`, you must specify the complete path (`/bin/more`).

`alias` abbreviations can be deleted with `unalias`. Otherwise, they remain valid until you exit the shell (that is, at most until you log out). If you need specific abbreviations more frequently, you may incorporate their `alias` instructions into the `.profile` file in your home directory.

NOTE A similar effect can be achieved with shell programs stored under a concise file name. Shell scripts have the additional advantages that they can cope with parameters (`$1`, `$2`, and so on) and that they can be employed in a much more flexible way (see page 405).

12.3 Input and output redirection

Three so-called standard files are involved in every command execution in the `bash`. The term 'file' might be slightly misleading; precisely speaking, these 'standard files' are not true files, but file descriptors that can be treated as files at operating system level.

- Standard input: this is where currently executing programs read their input (for example, when text is entered into an editor). In general, the standard input is the keyboard.
- Standard output: this is where all program output is directed (for example, the listing of all files through `ls`). In general, the standard output is the screen (the current terminal or, under X, the current terminal window).
- Standard error: error messages too are generally displayed on the current terminal.

It is often desirable that the three standard files are changed when certain commands are executed. For example, the contents list of the current directory may have to be written to a file instead of being displayed on screen. Thus, the standard output must be redirected into a true file. In the `bash`, this is achieved through the `>` character:

```
user$  ls *.tex > contents
```

Now, the text file `contents` contains a list of all `*.tex` files in the current directory. This form of output redirection is certainly the most frequent application. There are a number of further variations: `2> file` directs all error messages into the specified file. `>& file` directs both the standard output and the error messages into the specified file. If the double `>>` is used, instead of `>`, the output is appended to the end of an already existing file.

Input redirection is obtained with `< file`: commands expecting input from the keyboard now read from the specified file.

> CAUTION
>
> It is not possible to process a file and simultaneously write the result back to the same file.
>
> `sort fl1 > fl1` or `sort < fl1 > fl1` lead to `fl1` being deleted!

Pipes

Pipes are constructed with the `|` character. This means that the output of the first command is used as the input for the second command. In practice, you will probably use pipes most frequently in connection with the commands `more` or `less`, when you want to view longer output page by page.

```
user$  ls -l | less
```

With the above command, the contents list of the current directory is defined and written into a pipe. The `less` command, which is executed in parallel, reads its input from the pipe and displays the result on screen.

Instead of pipes, you can also use so-called FIFO files for input and output redirection. FIFO stands for 'first in first out' and realizes the idea of a pipe in file form. FIFOs are much more laborious to type in, but they clearly show what the `|` character actually does. In practice, they are used to make two completely independent programs communicate with each other (for example, `gpm` and the X server – see page 246).

```
user$  mkfifo fifo
user$  ls -l > fifo &
user$  less < fifo
```

The three commands shown above do the following: first a FIFO file is created, then `ls` is started as a background process which writes its output to a file. `less` reads the data from the file and displays it on screen.

Output multiplication using tee

Sometimes the output of a program has to be stored in a file, but you want to watch the progress of the program on screen as well. In this case, the output must be doubled, with one copy being displayed on screen and the second copy stored in a file. This task is carried out by the `tee` command:

```
user$  ls | tee contents
```

The contents list of the current directory is displayed on screen and at the same time stored in the file `contents`. This is done by first redirecting the standard output to the `tee` command. This command displays the standard output on screen and stores a copy of the output in the specified file. You can tell that this is really a duplication of the output if you redirect the standard output of `tee` into a file as well:

```
user$  ls | tee contents1 > contents2
```

The result is two identical files `contents1` and `contents2`. The above command is simply an example. The next (and last) example is somewhat more difficult to understand, but it makes more sense:

```
user$  ls -l | tee contents1 | sort +4 > contents2
```

Again, in `contents1`, we find the 'normal' contents list which `ls` has automatically sorted by filename. The copy has been passed to `sort`, then it is sorted by file size (fifth column, thus option +4) and stored in `contents2`.

Syntax summary

Input and output redirection	
`command > file`	directs standard output to the specified file
`command < file`	reads input from the specified file
`command 2> file`	directs error messages to the specified file
`command >& file`	redirects output *and* error messages
`command >> file`	appends standard output to the specified file
`command1 | command2`	passes output of `command1` to `command2`
`command | tee file`	displays the output and simultaneously stores a copy in the specified file

12.4 Command execution

Normally, you start commands by simply entering the command name. Inside the command line, you can specify a number of special characters which are evaluated by the `bash` before the command is actually executed. In this way, you can start commands in the background, specify several similar file names using wildcards (for example, `*.tex`), substitute the results of one command in the parameter list of another command, and so on.

Background processes

The most important and most frequently used special character is `&`. If it is appended to the end of a command line, the `bash` starts the corresponding program in the background. This is mostly useful for time-consuming programs, since work with other commands can continue immediately.

```
user$  find / -name '*sh' > result &
[1] 334
```

The above command searches the whole file system for files that end in the letters 'sh'. The list of files is written to the file `result`. Since the command is executed in the background, work can continue immediately. The output `[1] 334` means that the background process has the PID number 334. PID stands for process identification. The PID number is of interest if the process is to be prematurely terminated with `kill`. The number in square brackets indicates the number of background processes started by the `bash` and is generally of no interest.

> **TIP** If you forget the `&` character when starting a command, you do not need to wait until it terminates nor stop it brutally with Ctrl+C. Instead, you should interrupt the program with Ctrl+Z and continue it with `bg` as a background process.

Execution of several commands

After the `&` character you can also specify an additional command. In this case, the first command is executed in the background, while the second one is executed in the foreground. In the following example, the above `find` command is again started in the background, and at the same time `ls` displays the current directory list:

```
user$  find / -name '*sh' > result & ls
```

If a semicolon is entered instead of the `&` character, the `bash` executes the commands one after the other and in the foreground:

```
user$  ls; date
```

The above command first displays the current directory list and then the current date. If these two pieces of information are to be redirected to a single file with `>`, both commands must be enclosed in parentheses. This causes the two programs to be executed by the same shell (normally, a new shell is started for each command).

```
user$  (ls; date) > contents
```

Now the file `contents` contains the file list produced by `ls` and the current date determined by `date`. The parentheses cause the two programs to be executed by the same shell and therefore yield a common result. (Normally, a new shell is started for the execution of each command.)

The character pairs `&&` and `||` can be used to execute commands conditionally, that is, depending on the result of another command:

```
user$  command1 && command2
```

executes `command1`. Only if this command is executed successfully (no error, return value =0) is `command2` executed.

```
user$  command1 || command2
```

executes `command1`. Only if an error occurred during execution of this command (return value $\neq 0$) is `command2` executed.

Additional possibilities for the construction of conditions and branches are offered by the shell command `if`; however, this is of interest only for shell programming (see page 415).

Syntax summary

command execution	
`command1; command2`	executes the commands one after the other
`command1 && command2`	executes `command2` if `command1` was successful
`command1 || command2`	executes `commmand2` if `command1` yields errors
`command &`	starts the command in the background
`command1 & command2`	starts `commmand1` in the background, `command2` in the foreground
`(command1 ; command2)`	executes both commands in the same shell

12.5 Substitution mechanisms

The term *substitution mechanism* sounds very abstract and complicated. The basic idea is that commands containing special characters are substituted by their results. In the simplest case, this means that during evaluation of the command `ls *.tex` the character combination `*.tex` is substituted by the list of matching files – for example, `book.tex command.tex`. Thus, the `ls` command does not get to see `*.tex`, but a list of actual file names.

The aim of this section is to give a brief summary of the most important mechanisms used in interpreting the command line: wildcard characters for the generation of file names, braces for the construction of character strings, square brackets for the calculation of arithmetic expressions, quotes for command substitution, and so on.

REFERENCE

One substitution mechanism is excluded from this section: the so-called parameter substitution, which allows character strings stored in variables to be analyzed and modified. The general syntax is `${var__text}`, where `var` is the name of a variable, __ stands for one or two special characters, and `text` contains the search pattern or a default setting. This substitution mechanism will be described in detail in Chapter 13, from page 412 onward.

File name generation using wildcards

If you enter `rm *~` and the `rm` command actually deletes all files whose names end with the character ~, then this is the responsibility of the `bash`. The shell searches the current directory for matching files and substitutes `*~` with the corresponding file names.

Permitted wildcards are (exactly one arbitrary character) and `*` (any number (including zero) of arbitrary characters). The character string `[a,b,e-h]*` stands for file names that start with one of the characters `a`, `b`, `e`, `f`, `g`, or `h`. If the first character inside the square brackets is `^` or `!`, all characters are allowed except the ones specified. `~` can be used as an abbreviation for the home directory (see also page 87).

The best way to test the function of special characters is to use the `echo` command. The first command below supplies all files and directories in the root directory. The second command is a variation in which only names that contain one of the letters from `a` to `c` are allowed. The third command proves that the generation of file names also works across several directory levels. (For reasons of space, the output has been greatly reduced. On my computer, for example, `/*/*` results in a list of about 700 files and directories.)

```
user$  echo /*
/CD /bin /boot /cdrom /dev /dist /dosa /dosc /dosemu /dosi /etc
/home /install /lib /local /lost+found /mnt /proc /root /sbin
/test /tmp /usr /var /vmlinuz /zImage

user$  echo /*[a-c]*
/bin /boot /cdrom /dosa /dosc /etc /install /lib /local /proc
/sbin /var /zImage

user$  echo /*/*
/bin/Mail /bin/arch /bin/bash ....
/boot/any_b.b /boot/any_d.b ...
/dev/MAKEDEV /dev/arp /dev/bmouseatixl ...
...
```

TIP

Since generation of file names is not carried out by the program in question, but by the `bash`, the results sometimes look different from what you would probably expect. Thus, `ls *` can lead to a seemingly endless list of files, even though there are only a few files in the current directory. After the expansion of `*`, `ls` is passed a list of all files and directories. `ls`, however, displays not only the names of directories, but also their whole contents. If you just want to have a simple list of all files and directories, you must use the option `-d` which prevents the contents of the directories specified in the parameter list from being displayed.

TIP

If you would like to have feedback on how the `bash` works internally, you can execute `set -x`. In this case, the `bash` shows the internal command line (with all options, including those set elsewhere and the expanded file names) before a command is executed.

Character string generation using braces

The `bash` combines character strings specified in braces into all possible character string combinations. The official term for this substitution mechanism is *brace expansion*. `part{1,2,3}` becomes `part1 part2 part3`. Brace expansion can reduce the amount of typing required for accessing several similar file or directory names. Unlike wildcards, such as `*` and `?`, the advantage is that even non-existent file names can be generated (for example, for use with `mkdir`).

```
user$  echo {a,b}{1,2,3}
a1 a2 a3 b1 b2 b3

user$  echo {a,b,c}{e,f,g}.{1,2,3}
ae.1 ae.2 ae.3 af.1 af.2 af.3 ag.1 ag.2 ag.3 be.1 be.2 be.3
bf.1 bf.2 bf.3 bg.1 bg.2 bg.3 ce.1 ce.2 ce.3 cf.1 cf.2 cf.3
cg.1 cg.2 cg.3
```

Calculation of arithmetic expressions in square brackets

Normally, the `bash` is not capable of executing calculations. If you enter `2+3`, the shell does not know what to do with this expression. If you want to carry out a calculation within the shell, you must enclose the expression in square brackets and precede it with a `$` sign.

```
user$  echo $[2+3]
5
```

Inside the square brackets, most operators of the C programming language are allowed: `+ - * /` for the four fundamental operations, `%` for modulo calculations, `== != < <= >` and `>=` for comparisons, `<<` and `>>` for bit shift operations, `! &&` and `||` for logical NOT, AND, and OR, and so on. All calculations are executed as 32-bit integer numbers (value range between ±2 147 483 648). If values have to be extracted from variables, they must be preceded by a `$` sign (see page 400 about variable management).

> **TIP** An alternative way to execute calculations is provided by the `expr` command. This is an autonomous Linux command which works independently of the `bash` (see page 453).

Command substitution

Command substitution allows you to substitute a command in the command line with its result. For this purpose, the command must be enclosed in two ` characters, or written as `$(command)`. This latter notation is preferable: firstly, it reduces the confusion caused by three different kinds of quote (", ', and `) and secondly, it can be embedded.

However it is written, the command is substituted with its result. This substitution allows embedded calls to several commands, where one command passes its result to the next command. The following example illustrates this very powerful mechanism:

```
user$  ls -l `find /usr/doc -name '*README*'`
user$  ls -l $(find /usr/doc -name '*README*') # equivalent
```

With the above command, first `find /usr/doc -name '*README*'` is executed. The result of this command is a list of all files in the `/usr/doc` directory in which the character string 'README' occurs. This list is now inserted into the command line in place of the `find` command. Now, the command line might look like this:

```
user$  ls -l /usr/doc/xpm33/README /usr/doc/term/README.gz \
    >  /usr/doc/mt-st/README /usr/doc/README.gz
```

This (only internally combined) command supplies the following result:

```
-rw-r--r--   1 root   root   1854 Apr 24 22:49 /usr/doc/README.gz
-rw-r--r--   1 root   root    847 Sep 21  1993 /usr/doc/mt-st/README
-rw-r--r--   1 root   root   5796 Apr 20  1994 /usr/doc/term/README.gz
-rw-rw-r--   1 root   root   5550 Jan 30  1994 /usr/doc/xpm33/README
```

Please note that the same result could not have been obtained by a simple pipe using the | character. `ls` does not expect input from the standard input and therefore ignores the information supplied by `find` through the pipe. Consequently, the following command just displays the contents of the current directory. The results of `find` are not displayed!

```
user$  find /usr/doc -name '*README*' | ls -l  # this does not work
```

There is, however, another solution that does not require command substitution: by means of the command `xargs` data is redirected from the standard input to the command specified after `xargs`:

```
user$  find /usr/doc -name 'README' | xargs ls -l
```

Special characters in character strings

Since in the `bash` practically every character, with the exception of letters and numbers, appears to have some special meaning, it seems to be quite impossible to use these characters in character strings or file names. This problem can be solved in two ways. Either the special character is preceded by a backslash \, or the whole character string is enclosed in single or double quotes. With the use of quotes, you can, for example, delete a file with the name `ab* $cd`:

```
user$  rm 'ab* $cd'
```

Please note the difference between ' (for character string identification) and ` (for command substitution, see above).

Double quotes have a similar effect to single quotes, but they are less restrictive and allow the interpretation of a few special characters ($, \, and `). Thus, in character strings placed within double quotes, shell variables with a prefixed `$` sign will be evaluated.

```
user$  echo "This is the access path: $PATH"
```

As a result, the command supplies the character string 'This is the access path:', followed by the contents of the shell variable `PATH`. If single quotes are used instead of double ones, `echo` outputs the whole character string unchanged. More information about shell variables is given in the next section.

TIP A summary of all `bash` special characters can be found at the end of Chapter 13, on page 435.

Syntax summary

Substitution mechanisms	
Wildcards for file names	
?	exactly one arbitrary character
*	any number (including zero) arbitrary characters (but no .* files!)
[abc]	one of the specified characters
[a-f]	one character out of the specified range
[!abc]	none of the specified characters
[^abc]	same as above
~	abbreviation for the home directory
.	current directory
..	next higher directory
Character string combinations	
ab{1,2,3}	yields ab1 ab2 ab3
Arithmetics	
$[3*4]	arithmetic calculations
Command substitution	
`command`	substitutes the command with its result
$(command)	same as above, alternative notation
Evaluation of character strings	
command "character"	prevents evaluation of special characters
command 'character'	same as above, but more restrictive

12.6 Shell variables

The functionality of the bash and many other Linux programs is controlled by the state of so-called shell variables. Shell variables are comparable to programming language variables, with the difference that they can only store character strings (no numbers). The assignment of shell variables is carried out by means of the assignment operator =. The easiest way to display the contents of a shell variable is to use echo, with the variable name preceded by a $ sign.

```
user$  var=abc
user$  echo $var
abc
```

If the contents of a shell variable are to contain spaces or other special characters, then the whole character string must be enclosed in single or double quotes in the assignment operation:

```
user$  var='abc efg'
```

In the assignment operation, several character strings can be joined together. In the following example, the variable `a` is assigned a new character string which consists of its original contents, the string '`xxx`' and once again its original contents.

```
user$  a=3
user$  a=$a'xxx'$a
user$  echo $a
3xxx3
```

In the following example, the existing variable `PATH` (which contains the list of all directories to be searched for executable programs) is complemented by the `bin` directory in the home directory (abbreviated ~). Now, all commands contained in this directory can be executed without having to specify the complete path.

```
user$  echo $PATH
/usr/bin:/bin:/usr/local/sbin:/usr/sbin:/sbin:/usr/bin/X11:
/usr/bin/TeX:/usr/openwin/bin:/usr/games:.
user$  PATH=$PATH':~/bin'
user$  echo $PATH
/usr/bin:/bin:/usr/local/sbin:/usr/sbin:/sbin:/usr/bin/X11:
/usr/bin/TeX:/usr/openwin/bin:/usr/games:.:~/bin
```

Calculations with variables can be carried out using the square bracket notation discussed above:

```
user$  a=3
user$  a=$[$a*4]
user$  echo $a
12
```

If the result of a command is to be stored in a variable, a command substitution with `$(command)` must be carried out, as described above. In the following example, the current directory is stored in `a`:

```
user$  a=$(pwd)
user$  echo $a
/home/mk
```

The contents of variables are only stored inside the shell. They are lost when the shell is exited (or, at the latest, when the computer is switched off). If specific variables are going to be needed over and over again, their assignments should be carried out in the files `/etc/profile` or `.profile` in the home directory. These two files are automatically executed (if present) when the `bash` is started.

If you want to store the contents of a variable in a file, you can simply execute `echo` with an output redirection:

```
user$  echo $var > file
```

Local and global variables (environment variables)

The terms local and global for the description of variables are taken from the world of programming languages. With regard to shell variables, a variable is considered global if it is passed on at the start of a command or a shell program. Global variables are also often called environment variables.

Please note that all variables created by simple assignment are considered as local. If you want to define a global variable, you must either call `export` or `declare -x`.

There are quite a number of commands for the management of variables within the shell and some of these overlap in their function. Thus, to define a global variable, you can use both `export` and `declare -x`, and so on. With the following table, we will try to reduce the confusion caused by similar commands:

`a=3`	short notation for `let`, `a` is local
`declare a=3`	assigns the local variable `a` a value (as `let`)
`declare -x a=3`	assigns the global variable `a` a value (as `export`)
`export`	displays all global variables
`export a`	turns `a` into a global variable
`export a=3`	assigns the global variable `a` a value
`let a=3`	assigns the local variable `a` a value
`local a=3`	defines `a` as local (only in shell functions)
`printenv`	as `export`, displays all global variables
`set`	displays *all* (local and global) variables
`unset a`	deletes the variable `a`

CAUTION If you create variables for controlling the behavior of other Linux commands, then these variables must always be global. If you want to make use of the shell substitution mechanisms on the one hand and define global variables on the other, simply assign the variables first with `x=...` and then define them as global with `export x`.

CAUTION Variable assignments always apply to only one shell. If you work in several terminals or terminal windows, autonomous and independent shells run in each one. Changing one variable in one shell has no influence on the other shells. You can, however, carry out frequently needed variable assignments in the `.profile` file in your home directory, which is automatically executed at the start of each shell (see page 425).

Important shell variables

In principle, you can create any number of new variables and name and use them as you wish. You should, however, try to avoid existing variables, since these are generally evaluated by the `bash` and frequently also by other Linux commands. An uncontrolled change in these variables may lead to the processing of commands no longer working as expected, Linux suddenly stopping finding files, and so on. This section describes the most important variables in alphabetical order:

BASH
contains the file name of the `bash`.

glob_dot_filenames
controls the expansion of file name wildcards: if the variable is set (to an arbitrary value), `*` will also include file names that begin with a dot. `unset glob_dot_filenames` ends this state.

HOME
contains the home directory path, for example, `/home/mk`.

LOGNAME
contains the login name (user name).

HOSTNAME
contains the host name (computer name).

MAIL
contains the path of the directory in which incoming mail is stored.

MANPATH
contains the paths to all directories that contain `man` pages.

OLDPWD
contains the path of the last active directory.

PATH
contains a list of directories. When the `bash` has to execute a command, it searches all directories listed in `PATH` for the command. The directories are separated from each other by colons.

`PATH` is set in `/etc/profile`. If you want to add a directory to `PATH`, you need to complement `/etc/profile` following the pattern shown below:

```
# Addition to /etc/profile
PATH=$PATH:/opt/kde/bin
```

For reasons of safety (and in order to prevent the involuntary execution of programs in the current directory) most distributions exclude the local directory from `PATH`. If you want to execute programs in the current directory without prefixing them with `./`, you must extend PATH with `.`. An alternative solution is to store your own programs in the `~/bin` directory and to append this directory to `PATH`.

PS1 contains a character string which is displayed at the beginning of each input line (prompt). Amongst others, the following character combinations can be used within this character string: `\t` for the current time, `\d` for the date, `\w` for the current directory, `\W` for the last part of the current directory (thus, X11 for `/usr/bin/X11`), `\u` for the user name, `\h` for the host name (computer name), and `\$` for the prompt character (`$` for normal users, `#` for `root`). `PS1` is set in `/etc/profile`. A typical setting is `"\w\$ "`.

`PS2` as PS1, but the character string is displayed only when several lines of input are entered (that is, the first line was terminated with `\`). A typical setting is `">"`.

`PWD` contains the current directory path.

NOTE

Besides the variables described above, the shell recognizes a number of further variables about which you will find detailed information in the `man` pages for `bash`. In addition, there are many Linux commands whose function can equally be controlled through (global) shell variables. A typical example is `less`, which displays foreign language special characters when the variable `LESSCHARSET` is assigned the character string `latin1`. The meaning of such command-dependent variables is documented in the `man` pages for the command in question.

bash programming

Shell programs are simple text files containing some Linux and/or `bash` commands. After the start of a shell program, these commands are executed one after the other. The shell program can be passed parameters, as with any normal command. These parameters can be evaluated inside the program.

Since the simple sequential execution of a few commands does not leave much room for complex tasks, the `bash` supports shell programming with commands for the construction of loops and branches. With this, you have a true programming language at your disposal for which you need neither a compiler nor knowledge of C. (Admittedly, this comparison is a bit lame: C programs execute much faster, support several types of variables, offer a large number of special functions, and so on. Nevertheless, the possibilities of the `bash` are more than sufficient to cope with a surprisingly high number of problems.)

Typical applications of shell programs are the automation of frequently needed command sequences for installation of programs, system administration, creation of backups, configuration and execution of single programs, and so forth.

NOTE: This chapter builds on the `bash` fundamentals laid out in Chapter 12. In particular, you should be familiar with input and output redirection, command substitution and the handling of variables.

13.1 Introduction

Let us assume that you frequently enter the command `ls -ltr` in order to create a list of files in the current directory ordered by date (the most recent file last). Each time, you try again to remember which combination of options will get you there. Thus, it would be a good idea to define a new command, `lt` (list time), which fulfills exactly this task.

To do this, you start your favorite editor and write the text file `lt`. For the time being, this file consists of only one line, namely `ls -ltr`. Enter these characters, save the file and quit the editor.

> **TIP** If you do not wish to call the editor, you can create the file with `cat`: enter the command `cat > lt`. Now, the command expects to receive data from the standard input (keyboard) and writes it into the file `lt`. Thus, enter `ls -ltr` and ↵. Then terminate `cat` with Ctrl+D (this corresponds to EOF, end of file). You can view the resulting file with `cat lt`.

The attempt to execute the newly created file `lt` results in the error message 'permission denied'. The reason is that the access bits (x) for file execution are generally deactivated for newly created files. However, you can change this immediately with `chmod`. Now, `lt` supplies the required list of files ordered by last modification date. (The following lines show only a small part of this list.)

```
user$  lt
bash: ./lt: Permission denied
user$  ls -l lt
-rw-r--r--    1 user    mk            8 Oct 20 10:47 lt
user$  chmod a+x lt
user$  lt
...
-rw-r--r--    1 user    mk       112088 Oct 20 09:28 bash.tex
-rw-r--r--    1 user    mk        74126 Oct 20 09:28 grundl.tex
-rwxr-xr-x    1 user    mk            8 Oct 20 10:47 lt
```

> **TIP** When the variable `PATH` does not contain the current directory '`.`', you can execute `lt` only by means of the command `./lt`. Generally, only those programs can be executed that are contained in a directory specified in `PATH` or whose path is specified completely and uniquely.

However, the new command has not turned out particularly well: it still ignores all further parameters specified in the call. Thus, `lt *.tex` does not display a sorted list of all `*.tex` files, but yet again a list of *all* files.

This limitation can be easily remedied. The variable `$*` predefined inside the `bash` contains all parameters specified in the call of a shell program. If the program code in `lt` is changed into `ls -ltr $*`, the `bash` passes all parameters specified with the call of `lt` on to `ls`. (An overview of predefined `bash` variables can be found on page 411.)

In order to make the example more interesting, the new command will now be extended to display an info line at the end of the file list which indicates how many files have been displayed and what their total use of disk space is. Furthermore, `tee` is used to redirect the contents list into a temporary file in addition to its being displayed on screen.

Now, `cut` extracts from the file those columns that contain the file size. Via command substitution, this list of byte sizes is passed to a `for` loop and summed. The result is finally formatted in groups of thousands and displayed.

```
#!/bin/sh
# shell file lt: second variation with additional info line
tempfile=/tmp/lt.$$
ls -ltr $* | tee $tempfile
sum=0
num=0
for i in $(cut $tempfile -b 33-41); do # command substitution
  i=$i##*[^0-9,' ']*                    # eliminate text characters
  if [ i ]; then                         # only if i contains characters
    sum=$[$sum+$i]
    num=$[$num+1]
  fi
done
echo -n "$num files, "
# format byte indication in groups of thousands
if [ $sum -ge 1000000 ]; then
  echo -n $[$sum/1000000]","
  printf '%.3d,' $[($sum % 1000000)/1000]
  printf '%.3d'  $[$sum % 1000]
elif [ $sum -ge 1000 ]; then
  echo -n $[$sum/1000]","
  printf '%.3d' $[$sum % 1000]
else
  echo -n $sum
fi
echo " bytes"
rm $tempfile                             # delete temporary file
```

A test run shows the behavior of the extended command:

```
user$  lt *.sty
-rw-r--r--   1 root     root         1760 Aug  2 10:22 nfpalatt.sty
-rw-r--r--   1 root     root          349 Aug  4 23:29 makeidx.sty
2 Files,  2,109 Bytes
```

Some points of this sample program need clarifying: the first interesting detail is the temporary file `/tmp/lt.`*nnn*. The name of this file is constructed with **`tmp.$$`**, where **`$$`** is a `bash` variable which contains the process number of the currently running shell. At the end of the program, the temporary file is deleted with `rm`.

The `for` loop processes the result of the `cut` command, that is, a list of numbers, which is inserted by means of the command substitution mechanism described on page 398.

Once again, this loop checks each element of the list to see whether it is a number or not. With **`${i##*[^0-9,' ']*}`** the whole character string is eliminated if it does not consist of digits and spaces exclusively. This test is necessary because `ls` sometimes produces lines that exclusively contain text (for example, a directory name). If `I` is not empty, that is, if it contains a number, then the value is added to the variable `sum`. At the same time, the variable `num` is incremented by 1.

Finally, for output of the info line, the resulting sum is subdivided by commas into groups of thousands. The number in each group is determined by division and modulo calculations. The distinction between numbers greater or equal 1 000 000, greater or equal 1 000 and smaller numbers is necessary to prevent small values from being output in the form 0,0,123. The `printf` command is required to achieve a three-digit display of numbers (such as '027' when a file has a size of 12,027 bytes).

bash version 2

`bash` version 2 has been available for some time, although some distributions still supply version 1.14, which is considered to be very stable. (Execute `echo $BASH_VERSION`.)

Programmers may have some problems with the new `bash` version: the `bash` was practically fully adapted to the POSIX standard. Some syntax variations which were still tolerated by `bash` 1.14, are now considered as syntax violations and lead to error messages. In particular, this concerns missing semicolons in command chains which up to now used to be accepted:

bash 1.14: `{ command1; command2; command3 }`
bash 2.0: `{ command1; command2; command3; }`

A similar problem can occur with `case-esac` blocks: the last command of such a construction was up to now also executed when the two closing semicolons `;;` were missing. Since version 2, these semicolons are mandatory.

Many more details about new features and potential incompatibilities (which have nearly exclusively been caused by errors in the previous `bash` implementation can be found in the files containes in the `/usr/doc/bash/` or `man bash` directories.

Formal aspects of shell programs

All shell files should begin with a line composed of the characters `#!` and the required shell name, so that the required shell is started automatically to execute the file. `bash` shell files should begin with `#!/bin/sh`. This makes the program portable and executable on other computers where the Bourne shell is installed instead of the `bash`. (Under Linux, `/bin/sh` is a link to `/bin/bash`.)

As long as you write shell programs only for your own use and a change of shell or the use of your program by other users is improbable, you can do without the shell identification. The same applies when you are sure that other shells will have no difficulties in executing your file, that is, if you have not used any shell-specific special features. Most problems derive from the syntax differences between the C shell and most other shells.

CAUTION

Shell scripts can only be executed if the access bits for read access (r) and execution (x) are set (`chmod a+rx file`). The first line of a shell script must not contain any foreign language special characters, not even in comments. Otherwise, the `bash` refuses to execute the file and comes up with the message 'cannot execute binary file.'

When you write a collection of your own shell scripts for day-to-day use, it is a good idea to store them in some central place, for example in the `~/bin` directory. If subsequently you make the following change in `.profile`, these scripts can be executed without having to specify the complete path.

```
# Addition to ~/.profile
PATH=$PATH':~/bin'
```

TIP Online texts about shell programming can be obtained with `man bash` and with `info -f /usr/info/bash`. `help` displays an overview of `bash`-internal commands. `help command` gives further information about the specified command.

Other script languages

'Script language' is the technical term that denotes programming languages which process commands contained in a text file. Script languages stand in contrast to 'true' programming languages, such as C, in which the program must previously be compiled. Script languages have the advantage that they are usually much easier to learn.

If you find the possibilities of the `bash` no longer sufficient, you should consider the additional script languages available to you under Linux: thus, for example, the `ksh` can manage arrays, whereas the `tcsh` uses a syntax similar to that of C (and often very different from that of the `bash`).

Two languages which are completely independent of the peculiarities of a shell language are `perl` and `awk`. `perl` stands for 'Practical Extraction and Report Language' and is especially suited to processing text files. You can use `perl` to analyze, modify, and do other things to texts. `perl` combines the capabilities of the `sed` (stream editor) with those of a programming language. A similar aim but a different syntax is presented by the `awk` programming language. The name `awk` is combined out of the initials of the original authors, Alfred Aho, Peter Weinberger, and Brian Kernighan.

Another easy-to-learn script language is Tcl/Tk. Many commands are similar to those of the `bash` – but the extent of the Tcl/Tk language goes far beyond that of the `bash`. Tcl/Tk has two special features: the language can be extended with C functions and thus adapted to the requirements of the programmer and it is suitable for easy interface programming under X. A few program lines are sufficient to realize dialogs with buttons, list arrays, and so on in Tcl/Tk.

The last language worth mentioning is Python, which is very popular in the Linux scene (but not only there). In contrast to other script languages, Python is object oriented. Furthermore, in the design of the language great emphasis has been put on the fact that the structure of the code remains as clearly visible as possible. (Thus, lines in loops, conditions, and so on, *must* be indented.) There is yet another argument in favor of Python: the language is extremely well-documented. (In some distributions, the documentation needs to be installed separately because of its size; in SuSE, for example, the documentation can be found in the `pyth_doc` package.)

13.2 Variable management in shell programs

Introductory information on handling variables has already been given in Chapter 12 from page 400 onward. We have already mentioned the difference between normal shell variables and environment variables. In addition, we have described the most important variables of the `bash`, such as `PATH` and `PWD`.

This section deals with further aspects of variable management which are especially relevant for shell programming. In particular, we will discuss the scope of variables, some variables predefined in the `bash` (such as `$*` and `$?`), the parameter substitution mechanism for analyzing and processing character strings in variables, and finally the input of variables in shell programs.

Scope of variables

In order to understand the subtleties of variable management during the execution of shell programs, you need some basic knowledge about how commands and shell programs are started.

To execute a command or a program, the `bash` creates a new process with its own PID number (a Linux-internal number for identification and management of a process). Only shell variables declared as environment variables (`export` or `declare -x`, see page 400) are passed to the new process. When a command is started in the foreground, the `bash` retreats into the background and waits for the end of the command. Otherwise, both programs (that is, the `bash` and the program started in the background) run in parallel.

The start of a shell program is a special case. This is because the processing of a shell program is not carried out in the currently running shell, but in a subshell specially started for this purpose. Thus, two instances of the `bash` are running, one as its command interpreter, the other for the execution of the shell program. When yet another shell program is started inside this program, a third instance of the `bash` is started, and so on. Execution of separate subshells for shell programs is needed in order to be able to execute several shell programs in parallel and without mutual interference (and, if required, in the background).

The concept of subshells affects variable management insofar as each (sub)shell has its own set of variables. As with the start of any other program, the interactive shell passes only those variables to the subshell that have been declared as environment variables. Subsequently, the variables in the two shells are completely independent of each other, that is, a change to a variable in one shell has no influence whatsoever on variables in the other shell.

Sometimes it would be desirable to declare some new variables with a shell command or to modify existing variables of the interactive shell permanently. In order to achieve this, you can also execute shell programs inside the current `bash`, thus without the automatic start of a subshell. You do this by preceding the file name of the shell program with a dot and a space (this is the short notation for the shell command `source`).

An example: you want to write a shell program which adds the path of the current directory to the environment variable `PATH`. The necessary program `addpwd` is very simple:

```
#! /bin/sh
# shell program addpwd adds the current directory to the path
#
PATH=$PATH":"$(pwd)
```

Thus, the variable `PATH` is assigned its previous contents, a colon, and finally, via command substitution, the result of the `pwd` command. The following test run shows that the contents of the `PATH` variable in the current shell are only changed when `addpwd` is started with a preceding dot. (Inside the subshell that was started at the first call of `addpwd`, `PATH` is obviously changed – this change, however, is valid only as long as `addpwd` is running.)

```
user$  echo $PATH
/usr/local/bin:/usr/bin:/bin:/usr/local/sbin:/usr/sbin:/sbin:
/usr/bin/X11:/usr/bin/TeX:/usr/openwin/bin:/usr/games:.
user$  addpwd
user$  echo $PATH
/usr/local/bin:/usr/bin:/bin:/usr/local/sbin:/usr/sbin:/sbin:
/usr/bin/X11:/usr/bin/TeX:/usr/openwin/bin:/usr/games:.
user$  . addpwd
user$  echo $PATH
/usr/local/bin:/usr/bin:/bin:/usr/local/sbin:/usr/sbin:/sbin:
/usr/bin/X11:/usr/bin/TeX:/usr/openwin/bin:/usr/games:.:/home/mk/book
```

Variables predefined by the shell

Inside shell programs, several variables predefined by the `bash` can be accessed. These variables cannot be changed through assignments; they can only be read. The names of these variables are constructed from various special characters. In the following table, the variables are indicated with their preceding `$` symbol.

$ variables	
`$?`	return value of the last command
`$!`	PID of the most recently started background process
`$$`	PID of the current shell
`$0`	file name of the currently executed shell script (or of the symbolic link that points to the file)
`$#`	number of parameters passed to the shell program
`$1` to `$9`	parameters 1 to 9
`$*` or `$@`	total of all parameters passed

Some additional remarks about the application of these variables: `$0` to `$9`, `$#` and `$*` are used for the evaluation of the parameters passed to the batch program. Nearly every sample script in this chapter shows their use.

Another interesting command in connection with parameter evaluation is the `bash` command `shift`. This command shifts the passed parameters through the nine variables `$1` to `$9`. When you execute `shift 9`, the first nine parameters passed to the program are lost; in exchange, the next nine parameters can now be easily accessed. `shift` without further specification shifts the parameter list by one parameter.

`$?` can be used to construct conditions in order to make the further course of the program depend on the result of the last command processed. In principle, it is also possible to specify a command directly as a condition in `if`. The variable `$?` has the advantage that it prevents instructions from becoming too long and unclear (see page 416).

The variable `$$` contains the PID (process identification number). This numerical value is used internally by Linux for process management. The PID is unique, that is, in the whole system, there exists no other process with the same number. For this reason, the PID value is particularly useful for the creation of a temporary file. For example, you could use `ls > tmp.$$` to store a list of all files in the file `tmp.`*nnn*. Even if the same batch file runs simultaneously in another terminal, there will never be a name conflict between the temporary files because the two shells have different PIDs.

Parameter substitution

Under the heading parameter substitution, the `bash` provides several commands for processing character strings stored in variables. The syntax of this substitution mechanism is `${var__pattern}`, where __ stands for one or two special characters which specify the type of substitution command. Please note that the variable name is specified *without* a preceding `$` character. However, if the pattern is to be read from a variable, the `$` character must precede that variable.

`${var:-default}`
: if the variable is empty, the construction yields the default setting as a result, otherwise it yields the contents of the variable. The variable is not changed.

`${var:=default}`
: as above, but at the same time the contents of the variable are changed if it has been empty up to now.

`${var:+new}`
: if the variable is empty, it is not changed. If it is already occupied, the current contents are replaced with a new setting. The construction returns the new contents of the variable.

`${var:?error_message}`
: if the variable is empty, the variable name and the error message are displayed, then the shell program is terminated. Otherwise, the construction returns the contents of the variable.

`${#var}`
: returns the number of characters stored in the variable (0, if the variable is empty). The variable is not changed.

`${var#pattern}`

compares the beginning of the variable contents with the specified pattern. If the pattern is recognized, the construction returns the contents of the variable minus the shortest possible text that matches the search pattern. If the pattern is not found, the entire contents of the variable are returned. In the search pattern, the same wildcards can be used as for the construction of file names (`* ? [abc]`). In no case is the variable changed:

```
user$  dat=/home/mk/book/book.tar.gz
user$  echo ${dat#*/}
home/mk/book/book.tar.gz
user$  echo ${dat#*.}
tar.gz
```

`${var##pattern}`

as above, except that now the longest possible character string that matches the pattern is eliminated:

```
user$  dat=/home/mk/book/book.tar.gz
user$  echo ${dat##*/}
book.tar.gz
user$  echo ${dat##*.}
gz
```

`${var%pattern}`

as `${var#pattern}`, except that the pattern matching now takes place at the end of the variable contents. The shortest possible character string is eliminated from the end of the variable. The variable itself remains unchanged.

```
user$  dat=/home/mk/book/book.tar.gz
user$  echo ${dat%/*}
/home/mk/book
user$  echo ${dat%.*}
/home/mk/book/book.tar
```

`${var%%pattern}`

as above, except that the longest possible character string is eliminated.

```
user$  dat=/home/mk/book/book.tar.gz
user$  echo ${dat%%/*}

    -- no output --
user$  echo ${dat%%.*}
/home/mk/book/book
```

> **TIP** On page 421 you will find an example which makes extensive use of the substitution commands introduced above for the purpose of copying or renaming groups of files (`regmv *.ps *.eps`).

`${!var}`
yields the contents of the variable whose name is contained as a character string in `var`.

```
user$  abc="123"
user$  efg=abc
user$  echo ${!efg}
123
```

> **NOTE**
>
> The syntax `${!var1}` is only allowed from `bash` version 2 onward. If, in an older version of the `bash` you want to determine the contents of a variable whose name is specified in another variable, you must use the following syntax (which is also allowed in version 2):
>
> ```
> user$ eval var2=\$${var1}
> ```

Reading in variables with `read`

You can use the `bash` command read to accept input during execution of a shell program. Usually, you first call `echo` to display a short text which tells the user which input you expect (for example, y/n, a numerical value, and so on). When you use the option `-n`, input starts directly after the `echo` text and not in the following line. During execution of the subsequent `read` command, the `bash` waits until the user enters a line and terminates it with ⟨↵⟩.

In the following sample program, the `while` loop is executed until the character string in the variable `a` is no longer empty. A test run shows the function of the tiny program:

```
user$  readvar
Enter a number:  a
Invalid input, please try again
Enter a number:  12
12
$ readvar
: a
12
12
```

After the input via `read`, the entire contents of the variable are deleted via parameter substitution if a character occurs which is not a digit, a minus sign, or a space. This check is obviously not perfect (the strings `"12-34-5"` and `"12 34"` are both legal), but is fairly efficient. Information about `while` can be found on page 419.

```
#! /bin/sh
# readvar: read numerical value
a=                          # delete a
while [ -z "$a" ]; do
  echo -n "Enter a number: "
  read a
```

```
  a=$a##*[^0-9,' ',-]*  # eliminate character strings that contain
                         # characters other than 0-9, the minus sign
                         # or spaces
  if [ -z "$a" ]; then
    echo "Invalid input, please try again"
  fi
done
echo $a
```

13.3 Branches

Branches in shell programs can be constructed with the commands `if` and `case`. While `if` is better suited for simple case decisions, `case` is better suited to the analysis of character strings (pattern matching).

`if` branches

In the shell file `iftst`, an `if` condition is used to test whether two parameters were passed. If not, an error message is displayed. The program is terminated by `exit` with a return value not equal to 0 (to indicate an error). Otherwise, the contents of the two parameters are displayed on screen.

```
#! /bin/sh
# shell file iftst
#
if test $# -ne 2; then
  echo "This command must be passed exactly two parameters!"
  exit 1
else
  echo "Parameter 1: $1, Parameter 2: $2"
fi
```

A short test run shows the behavior of the program:

```
user$  iftst a
This command must be passed exactly two parameters!
user$  iftst a b
Parameter 1: a, Parameter 2: b
```

The branching criterion is the return value of the last command preceding `then`. The condition is satisfied when this command yields a return value of 0. If `then` is written in the same line (and not in the following one), the command must be terminated with a semicolon.

CAUTION

Please note that in the `bash` the truth values for True (0) and False (not equal to 0) are defined exactly the other way round compared to most other programming languages! Commands which are terminated correctly yield the return value 0. Any value other than 0 indicates an error. Some commands return different error values depending on the type of error.

In the above example, the condition is constructed with the aid of the `bash` command `test`. The operator `-ne` stands for not equal. `test` is generally used when two character strings or numbers are to be compared, when a check is to be made whether a file exists, and so on. The command is described in the next section.

The above program can also be formulated in a different way: instead of the `test` command, a short notation with square brackets can be used. One space must be inserted both after `[` and before `]`!

Furthermore, the second `echo` command can be removed from inside the `if` structure because, due to the `exit` instruction, all lines after `fi` are only executed if the condition has been satisfied.

```
#! /bin/sh
# shell file iftst, second, equivalent variation
#
if [ $# -ne 2 ]; then
  echo "This command must be passed exactly two parameters!"
  exit 1
fi
echo "Parameter 1: $1, Parameter 2: $2"
```

We conclude with a more practical example: the shell file `savequit` saves all `*.tex` files in the compressed archive file `backup.tgz`. If no errors have occurred during creation of the archive file (operator `&&`), the resulting file is copied onto a diskette in drive A:. The criterion for the `if` condition is the return value of `mcopy`. When everything goes well (and drive A: does not contain a full diskette or contains no diskette at all), the computer is subsequently switched off with `shutdown`.

```
#! /bin/sh
# shell file savequit: save *.tex-files, switch off system
#
if tar -czf backup.tgz *.tex && mcopy -n backup.tgz a:; then
  shutdown -t 5 -h -q now
fi
```

The same program can also be arranged more clearly by specifying the `tar` and `mcopy` commands in a separate line. In `if`, the result of the two commands is then checked with the aid of the variable `$?`:

```
#! /bin/sh
# shell file savequit: save *.tex-files, switch off system
#
tar -czf backup.tgz *.tex && mcopy -n backup.tgz a:
if [ $? = 0 ]; then
  shutdown -t 5 -h -q now
fi
```

Formulation of conditions with `test`

In the `bash`, it is not possible to specify conditions directly – such as a comparison between a variable and a value. Firstly, the whole idea of the `bash` is based on the fact that all actions are carried out via a unique command concept, and secondly, special characters such as `>` and `<` are already used for other purposes. For this reason, you must use the `bash` command `test` to formulate conditions in loops and branches. (By the way, `test` also exists as a proper Linux command outside the `bash`. It has primarily been integrated into the `bash` in order to achieve a higher processing speed.)

`test` yields the return value 0 (true), if the condition is satisfied, or 1 (false), if the condition is not satisfied. In order to reduce typing effort, a short notation in square brackets can be used. The command is described in more detail in the reference section at the end of this chapter (see page 433).

`test` is used in three areas of application: for the comparison of two numbers, for the comparison of character strings and for testing whether a file exists and has given properties. The following examples show some possible applications:

`test "$x"`
: checks whether `x` is occupied (that is, the result is false when the character string contains 0 characters, otherwise it is true).

`test $x -gt 5`
: checks whether the variable `x` contains a numeric value greater than 5. If `x` does not contain a number, an error message is displayed. Besides `-gt` (greater than), the following comparison operators can be used: `-eq` (equal), `-ne` (not equal), `-lt` (less than), `-le` (less equal) and `-ge` (greater equal).

`test -f $x`
: checks whether a file with the name specified in `x` exists.

When `test` is to be executed interactively in the shell, the variable `$?` (return value of the last command) must be read with `echo` after the `test` command:

```
user$  a=20
user$  test $a -eq 20; echo $?
0
user$  test $a -gt 20; echo $?
1
```

case branches

`case` constructions are started with the keyword `case`, followed by the parameter to be analyzed (usually a variable). After the keyword `in`, several character string patterns can be specified against which the parameter is compared. The same wildcard characters are allowed as for file names. The pattern is closed with a round parenthesis), thus for example `--*)` for the recognition of character strings that start with two minus signs. Several patterns can be separated from each other with `|` – in this case, all patterns are checked (for example, `*.c|*.h)` for the recognition of `*.c` and `*.h` files in the same branch).

The commands following the parenthesis must be terminated with double semicolons. If an `else` branch is needed, the last pattern to be specified must be `*` – all character strings match this pattern. During processing of a `case` construction only the first branch in which the parameter matches the specified pattern is taken.

The following `casetst` example shows the application of `case` for classifying the passed parameters into file names and options. The loop for the variable `i` is executed for all parameters passed to the shell. Inside this loop, each parameter is analyzed with `case`. If the parameter starts with a '`-`', it is appended to the end of the variable `opt`, otherwise to the end of `dat`.

```
#! /bin/sh
# shell file casetst
opt=         # delete opt and dat
dat=
for i do     # loop for all passed parameters
  case "$i" in
    -* ) opt="$opt $i";;
    *  ) dat="$dat $i";;
  esac
done         # end of loop
echo "Options: $opt"
echo "Files:  $dat"
```

A sample run of the shell file proves the functionality of this simple case differentiation. Parameters passed in arbitrary order are classified into options and file names:

```
user$  casetst -x -y dat1 dat2 -z dat3
Options:  -x -y -z
Files:   dat1 dat2 dat3
```

Following the same scheme, `case` branching can also be used for classifying given file extensions (by specifying `*.abc` in the search pattern). If you want to get more deeply involved in `case` analyses, you should have a look at the shell file `/usr/bin/gnroff`. This file processes the parameters passed in the syntax of `nroff` in such a way that the related command `groff` can handle them.

13.4 Loops

The `bash` has three commands for the construction of loops: `for` executes a loop for all elements of a given list. `while` executes a loop until the specified condition is no longer satisfied, whereas `until` executes a loop until the condition is satisfied for the first time. All three loops can be prematurely exited with `break`. `continue` skips the remaining body of the loop and continues the loop with the next cycle.

for loops

In the first example, the variable `i` is assigned the character strings '`a`', '`b`', and '`c`' one after the other. In the body of the loop, that is, between `do` and `done`, the contents of the variable are displayed. Please note that a semicolon is required both at the end of the list and at the end of the `echo` command. You can only omit these semicolons when you spread the input over several lines (which, in script files, is quite often the case).

```
user$  for i in a b c; do echo $i; done
a
b
c
```

The list for `for` can also be built with the same wildcard characters as for file names or with `{...}` constructions for the generation of character strings (page 397). In the following example, all `*.tex` files are copied into `*.tex~` files. (In Unix/Linux, the `~` character at the end of a file name usually identifies a backup file.)

```
user$  for i in *.tex; do cp $i $i~; done
```

If `for` loops are constructed without `in ...`, the loop variable is passed all parameters passed at the call one after the other (in practice, this corresponds to `in $*`). An example of such a loop can be found in the description of `case`.

`while` loops

In the following example, the variable `i` is assigned the value 1. Then, in the body of the loop between `do` and `done`, the variable is incremented by 1 until the value 5 is exceeded. Please note that the conditions must be specified with the command `test` or its short notation with square brackets, just as with `if` branches.

```
user$  i=1; while [ i -le 5 ]; do echo $i; i=$[$i+1]; done
1
2
3
4
5
```

`until` loops

The only difference between `until` loops and `while` loops is that the logical negation of the condition is formulated. Therefore, the following example is equivalent to the `while` loop above. For formulating the condition `i>5` (greater than), the `-gt` comparison operator is used.

```
user$  i=1; until [ $i -gt 5 ]; do echo $i; i=$[$i+1]; done
1
2
3
4
5
```

13.5 Shell program samples

The Linux system is strewn with examples of `bash` programming, even though this may have escaped you. Many of the commands you executed during installation, configuration and administration of Linux were actually `bash` programs.

Starting with the current directory, the following `find/grep` command searches the whole directory tree for shell programs, recognizing all files that are marked as executable and contain the character string `\#! ... sh`. The list of all files is stored in `list` in the home directory. Execution of this command takes some time because the entire file system is searched.

```
user$  cd /
user$  find -type f -perm +111 -exec \
   >     grep -q '#!.*sh' {} \; -print > ~/list
```

Text conversion filters

On page 503, you find a description of the commands `fromdos`, `todos` and `recode` which convert text files between DOS and Linux. If the only task is to eliminate a carriage return character at the end of each line (DOS → Linux) or to insert it (Linux → DOS), you can obtain the same result by means of two small shell files.

First, we will look at the conversion from DOS to Linux, in which all CR characters must simply be eliminated. This can be done by employing the `tr` command. This command reads data from the standard input, replaces or deletes single characters and writes the result to the standard output. `tr -d '\r'` removes superfluous spaces. In order to make the call of `dos2linux` as easy as possible, the following program provides three application variations:

```
user$  dos2linux file
user$  dos2linux source_file target_file
user$  dos2linux < source_file > target_file
```

In the first variation, `dos2linux` reads the specified file and writes the result back to the same file. In the second variation, the source file is read and the result is written to the target file. In the third variation, `dos2linux` is used as a filter. This would also allow you to use the program in the following form:

```
user$  cat text.dos | dos2linux > /dev/lp1
```

The specified text file is directed with `cat` to the standard output, filtered by `dos2linux` and finally directed to the first parallel interface (printer).

The program code for `dos2linux` contains few surprises. The three syntax variations are distinguished by the number of parameters. If more than three parameters are passed, the command displays a help text. Text output is carried out by `cat`, using the << operator to interpret the text of the current file as standard input until the pattern 'EOF' occurs.

```
#! /bin/sh
# dos2linux: eliminates CR characters
if [ $# -eq 0 ]; then    # use as filter
  tr -d ''
elif [ $# -eq 1 ]; then  # process one file
  mv $1 $1.$$
  tr -d '' < $1.$$ > $1
  rm $1.$$
elif [ $# -eq 2 ]; then  # process two files
```

```
  tr -d '' < $1 > $2
else
  cat << EOF
dos2linux: eliminates CR characters in text files
Usage: dos2linux file
       dos2linux source_file target_file
       dos2linux < source_file > target_file
EOF
fi
```

Now we will look at the conversion from Linux to DOS. In order to append a CR character to the end of each line, the `sed` program must be used. The stream editor is characterized by great flexibility in the processing of text files and, unfortunately, equally great non-transparency of its syntax.

```
#! /bin/sh
# linux2dos: inserts a CR character at each end of line
if [ $# -eq 0 ]; then    # use as filter
  sed -e s/$/^M/
elif [ $# -eq 1 ]; then  # process one file
  mv $1 $1.$$
  sed -e s/$/^M/ < $1.$$ > $1
  rm $1.$$
elif [ $# -eq 2 ]; then  # process two files
  sed -e s/$/^M/ < $1 > $2
else
  cat << EOF
linux2dos: inserts a CR character at each end of line
Usage: linux2dos file
       linux2dos source_file target_file
       linux2dos < source_file > target_file
EOF
fi
```

In the present example, a global replace command is executed in which each end-of-line is substituted by CR. Please note that `^M` is not composed of the two characters `^` and `M`, but represents one character with the (decimal) code 13. How such characters are input varies from editor to editor. In Emacs, you must enter Ctrl+Q, Ctrl+M. The usage of `linux2dos` is the same as `dos2linux`.

Both programs can also be used as filters for printing text files when the printer produces an endless string of characters because of missing CR characters or produces lots of empty lines because of superfluous line feeds.

`mv` and `cp` for regular expressions

Because of the automatic substitution of special characters such as `*` and `?`, commands such as `mv *.bak *.old` are not possible in Linux. In such cases, advanced `bash` users enter a tiny for loop in order to include all required files, and use substitution commands to change the file names (see page 412). The following instruction, for example, substitutes all `*.eps` files with `*.ps` files:

```
user$  for i in *.eps; do mv $i ${i%.*}.ps; done
```

Such solutions may well prove the power of the `bash`, but in the end, they are far too long-winded for the day-to-day management of files. It is therefore obvious that such operations need to be simplified. The two commands presented here, `regmv` and `regcp`, represent variations of `mv` and `cp`. A character string enclosed in single quotes must be passed as a parameter. Both the source file pattern and the target file pattern must contain exactly one asterisk. The following examples show the application of the two commands:

```
user$  regmv '*.eps *.ps'      # renames all *.eps files as *.ps files
user$  regmv 'pic*.eps b*.ps' # renames pic*.eps files as p*.ps files
user$  regmv '*~ *.old'        # renames all *~ files as *.old files
user$  regcp '* *.dup'         # makes a duplicate copy *.dup of all files
user$  regcp '#*# *.bak'       # copies #*# files, new name *.bak
```

The program code of these two commands is admittedly not too easy to understand. In principle, it is nothing but a repeated application of the command substitution already used in the previous example.

For the following description of the command, we assume that the command was passed the character string `pic*.eps p*.ps`. This parameter is split into two parts at the position of the space and stored in two variables (`pic*.eps` in `source` and `p*.ps` in `target`). Subsequently, `source` and `target` are in their turn split into two parts at the position of the `*` (`pic` in `source1`, `.eps` in `source2`, and so on).

If `source` and `target` contain character strings at all, a check is made as to whether the number of characters in `source` is exactly one higher than that in `source1` and `source2`. If this is not the case, either too many wildcards have been passed or none at all. An analogous check is also made for `target`.

The instruction `files=$(echo $source)` does not simply cause a duplication of `source`. On the contrary, for execution of `echo`, the usual expansion of wildcards is carried out. Therefore, `files` subsequently contains the list of all files that match the source pattern. The following test checks whether any expansion has taken place at all. If not, there are no files that match the source pattern and the command is aborted with an error message.

If everything has gone well, the copy command for each file found is executed in the `for` loop. Piece by piece, the new file name is assembled in the variable `tmp`. In the first step, the first part of the source pattern (`pic`) is eliminated from the file name, in the second step the second part (`.eps`) is removed. In the third step, the file name is expanded with the two parts of the target pattern (`p` and `.ps`).

Each command is also displayed on screen in order to provide the user with feedback on what is actually happening. The `-i` option in `cp` causes `cp` automatically to display a request for confirmation before an already existing file is overwritten.

The program code of `regmv` looks exactly the same as that of `regcp`, with the sole exception that the command `mv -i` is executed instead of `cp -ip`.

```
#! /bin/sh
#  regcp: copies files using patterns
#  Example: regcp *~ *.old
if [ $# -eq 1 ]; then
```

```
  source=$1%% *          # fist part of parameter (before space)
  target=$1##*           # second part (after the space)
  source1=$source%*    # first part of source pattern
  source2=$source#*    # second part (following *)
  target1=$target%*    # first part of target pattern
  target2=$target#*    # second part (following *)
  # Check whether source or target are empty
  if [ -z "$source" ]; then
    echo regcp: Source pattern is missing
    exit
  fi
  if [ "$source" = "$target" ]; then
    echo regcp: Target pattern is missing or same as source pattern
    exit
  fi
  # Check whether source and target contain exactly one * each
  if [ $[ $#source1 + $#source2 +1 ] -ne $#source ]; then
    echo regcp: Source pattern must contain exactly one *
    exit
  fi
  if [ $[ $#target1 + $#target2 +1 ] -ne $#target ]; then
    echo regcp: Target pattern must contain exactly one *
    exit
  fi
  # Check whether any source files are found at all
   files=$(echo $source)  # source files to be processed
  if [ "$ files" = "$source" ]; then
    echo "regcp: cannot find any $source files"
    exit
  fi
  # copy
  for i in $files; do
    tmp=$i#$source1         # eliminate character preceeding *
    tmp=$tmp%$source2       # eliminate character following *
    tmp=$target1$tmp$target2   # assemble target file name
    echo "cp -ip $i $tmp"
    cp -ip $i $tmp
  done
else
  echo "regcp: copies files using patterns"
  echo "The whole parameter must be enclosed in '"
  echo "Source and target pattern must contain exactly one *"
  echo
  echo "Example: regcp '*.bak *.old'"
fi
```

Endless loop for starting LaTeX automatically

The following example not only demonstrates the possibilities of shell programming, but also the multitasking capabilities under Linux. When you work with LaTeX or any compiler, your modus operandi will probably look like this: you edit the text or the program, start LaTeX or the compiler, analyze the error messages, make some changes, start the compiler, and so forth. Under Linux, you will probably use two terminals or shell windows, so that you never have to leave the editor. For compiling, you simply switch to the corresponding window/terminal and restart the compiler from there.

However, there is an even easier way: when you start the `latexauto file` shell program listed below, an endless loop checks every three seconds whether your LaTeX file has changed or not. If so, LaTeX is executed automatically. If LaTeX is successful, `dvips` immediately transforms the resulting `*.dvi` file into a PostScript file which can then be viewed with the `ghostview` program running in the background.

In practice, this means that your text file is *automatically* translated after each save operation – you do not even have to quit the editor. The end of the translation is signalled with a beep, so that you can then switch to the window/terminal in which `latexauto` is running.

```
#!/bin/bash
# latexauto: automatic translation of LaTeX files
#
tmp2=$(ls -l --full-time $1.tex)
while true                                # endless loop
do
  if [ "$tmp1" != "$tmp2" ]; then         # check for changes
    tmp2=$(ls -l --full-time $1.tex) # update tmp2
    echo "new attempt"
    latex $1 && dvips $1 -o test.ps
    echo -e "                          # beep
  fi
  sleep 3                                 # 'sleep' for three seconds
  tmp1=$(ls -l --full-time $1.tex)        # periodically update tmp1
done
```

The above program has several special features: thanks to the loop condition `while true` it just runs on until it is manually stopped with Ctrl+C. The check as to whether the file specified as the parameter has changed is carried out by comparing the two variables `tmp1` and `tmp2`. In these variables, the size and date of last modification of the specified file are stored by means of `ls`. Saving the file in the text editor leads to a change in `tmp1`. In order to prevent the program from using too much CPU time through continuous comparisons, `sleep 3` is executed after each check. This puts the program into a state of rest for three seconds. During this time, it uses practically no CPU time.

Following the same principle, you can also create a backup program that runs in the background. This program could check every five minutes whether a given file (or several files) have been modified. If so, the files are copied into their own separate backup directory.

The `profile` file

Two particular shell files are `/etc/profile` and `~/.profile`. The first file is automatically executed at every start of the `bash`, that is, independently of who uses the shell. In this way, `profile` allows presetting of important variables (such as `PATH` or `MANPATH`) and the definition of abbreviations.

In order to allow local adaptation of the shell as well, the `.profile` file from the home directory of the current user is executed after `/etc/profile`. A number of examples of applications of the `profile` file can be found in Chapter 6 about Linux configuration.

13.6 Shell programming command reference

The following reference provides a brief description of the most important commands for shell programming, in alphabetical order (without any claim to completeness!). Many of the commands described here are built-in `bash` commands, but a number of regular Linux commands particularly suited to shell programming have also been included.

REFERENCE

A reference list of the most important Linux commands can be found in Chapter 14 from page 437 onward. All commands described there can obviously also be used in shell programs. The current reference only contains commands that are *typical* of shell programming and normally not used in direct command input in the shell. A reference list of all special characters that can be used in command input – and obviously in shell programming too – can be found at the end of this chapter.

Variable management and parameter evaluation

`alias`	defines an abbreviation
`declare`	defines an (environment) variable
`export`	defines an environment variable
`local`	defines local variables in a function
`read`	reads a variable
`readonly`	displays all write-protected variables
`shift`	shifts the parameter list
`unalias`	deletes an abbreviation
`unset`	deletes a variable

Handling of character strings

`basename`	determines the file name of a path
`dirname`	determines the directory of a path
`expr`	performs pattern matching

Branches, loops

`break`	terminates a loop prematurely
`case`	starts a case distinction
`continue`	skips the body of the loop
`exit`	terminates the shell program
`for`	starts a loop
`function`	defines a new function
`if`	starts a branch
`local`	defines local variables in a function
`return`	terminates a function
`source`	executes the specified shell file
`test`	evaluates a condition
`until`	starts a loop
`while`	starts a loop

Output

`cat`	displays a file on screen
`echo`	displays a line of text
`printf`	allows formatted output as under C
`setterm`	changes letter types, clears the screen

Miscellaneous

`dialog`	displays a dialog box
`dirs`	displays a list of stored directories
`eval`	evaluates the specified command
`file`	tries to determine the type of a file
`popd`	changes to the directory last stored
`pushd`	stores the current directory and changes to a new one
`sleep`	waits for a given period of time
`trap`	executes a command when a signal occurs
`ulimit`	controls the resources taken up by the shell
`wait`	waits for the end of a background process

`alias` `abbreviation='command'`

`alias` defines an abbreviation (see page 391).

`basename` `character_string [extension]`

`basename` supplies the file name of the specified path. Thus, `basename /usr/man/man1/gnroff.1` leads to the result `gnroff.1`. If an extension is specified as the optional parameter, this extension is removed from the file name (if it exists).

```
break [n]
```

`break` prematurely terminates a `for`, `while` or `until` loop. The shell program is continued with the command following the end of the loop. With the specification of an optional numerical value, *n* loop levels can be terminated.

```
case expression in
  pattern1 ) commands;;
  pattern2 ) commands;;
  ...
esac
```

`case` is used for the construction of multiple branches. The branching criterion is a character string (usually a variable or a parameter passed to the shell program). This character string is compared with the patterns one by one; the patterns can also contain the wildcards for file names (`*?[]`). In a `case` branch, you can also specify several patterns separated by `|`.

As soon as a pattern matches, the commands between the closing parenthesis `)` and the two semicolons are executed. Subsequently, the program is continued with the command following `esac`.

```
cat << end
```

In this syntax variation, `cat` reads text from the current shell file and displays it on screen until the character string '`end`' occurs. In this way, `cat` can be used for easy output of larger amounts of text without having to execute an `echo` command for each line. Obviously, the syntax `<< end` can also be used for all other commands to read text from the current file until the character string 'end' is encountered.

```
continue [n]
```

`continue` skips the body of a `for`, `while` or `until` loop and continues the loop with the next cycle. This process can also be executed for outer loop levels by means of the optional numerical value.

```
declare [options] var[=value]
```

`declare` assigns shell variables a (new) value and/or various properties. When the command is called without parameters, all known variables are listed together with their contents. There must be no spaces before or after the equal sign.

`-r` the variable can be read, but no longer modified.

`-x` the variable is defined as an environment variable and is therefore available to other commands and in subshells.

`dialog [--clear] [--title text] [dialog options]`

`dialog` can be used for the display of dialogs. Properly speaking, the command has nothing to do with the `bash`, but is an autonomous program for text-oriented input and output of data. This brief description is based on version 0.6 which has for some time now been supplied together with many Linux distributions.

The options `--clear` and `--title` can be combined with any of the other specified dialog options. `--clear` causes the dialog to be removed from the screen once it is terminated. (Afterwards, the whole screen will be blue! Execute `setterm -clear` to get it back to normal.) `--title` allows you to set a dialog title. `dialog` offers the following types of dialog:

`--msgbox text height width`
: displays a message text which must be confirmed with ↵.

`--infobox text height width`
: as above, but without confirmation. The program is immediately continued. The dialog box stays on screen until the screen is cleared.

`--yesno text height width`
: displays a dialog box for a yes/no decision.

`--inputbox text height width`
: allows the user to enter a line of text.

`--textbox file height width`
: displays the text file (cannot be edited, but can be scrolled).

`--menu text h b men_height men_item1 men_text1 men_item2 men_text2 ...`
: allows selection of an option (a menu item).

`--checklist text height width list_height option1 text1 status1 option2 text2 status2 ...`
: allows simultaneous selection of several options.

`dialog` yields a return value of 0 if the dialog was terminated with OK or YES, 1 if it was terminated with CANCEL or NO, or 255 if it was terminated with Esc. In dialog types that supply a text, a menu title or a list of options, the results are written into the standard error file. Therefore, results normally need redirection into a temporary file by means of `2> tmp`. Once the input is terminated, this file can be evaluated.

Dialog boxes can be controlled both with the keyboard and with the mouse (since version 4.0). Unfortunately, display or input of foreign language special characters is not (yet) possible.

Example

```
user$  dialog --clear --inputbox \
       'Enter a file name' 10 60 2> tmp
```

The above command prompts the user to enter a file name. This name can be subsequently read from the file `tmp`. You can check whether the dialog has aborted by evaluating `$?`.

`dirname character_string`

`dirname` supplies the path of a complete file name. Thus, `dirname /usr/bin/groff` yields `/usr/bin`.

`dirs`

`dirs` shows the list of directories stored with `pushd` – see page 432.

`echo [options] character_string`

`echo` displays the specified character string on screen. The character string should be enclosed in single or double quotes.

- `-e` recognizes the special characters `\a` (beep), `\n` (end of line) and `\t` (tab) in the character string, amongst others. Thus, `echo -e "\a"` can be used to output a warning beep.
- `-n` does not change to a new line when output is terminated. Output can be continued with a further `echo` instruction.

`eval $var`

`eval` interprets the contents of the variable as a command line, evaluates this line (with all known substitution mechanisms) and finally executes the command. `eval` is needed whenever a command stored in a variable is to be executed and the command contains various special shell characters.

Example

```
user$  com="ls | more"
user$  $com
ls: |: No such file or directory
ls: more: No such file or directory
user$  eval $com
```

The command stored in the variable `com` can only be executed through the use of `eval`. The first attempt to execute the command fails because the `bash` no longer evaluates the pipe character `|` after having substituted `$com` with its contents.

`exec command`

`exec` starts the specified command as a substitution for the current `bash`. The command can, for example, be used to start a different shell. In any case, the running shell is terminated. (With a normal command start, the `bash` remains active in the background until the command is terminated.)

`exit [return_value]`

`exit` terminates a shell program. When no return value is specified, the program returns 0 (OK).

`export [options] variable [=value]`

`export` declares the specified shell variable as an environment variable. This makes the variable available to all called commands and subshells. Optionally, a variable assignment can be made. When the command is called without parameters, all environment variables are displayed.

`-n` converts an environment variable back into a normal shell variable. With this option, the program has exactly the opposite effect to when it is used without options.

`expr character_string : pattern`

`expr` can be used to evaluate arithmetic expressions, compare two character strings, and so on. `expr` differs from `test` and the substitution mechanism `$[...]` insofar as it can execute pattern comparisons of character strings in the syntax variation specified above (regular expressions). All wildcards described with `grep` can be used in the pattern (see page 459). The pattern must normally be enclosed in quotes in order to prevent evaluation of special characters by the shell.

As a result, `expr` returns the number of characters that match the pattern. When the pattern or parts of the pattern are enclosed between `\(` and `\)`, `expr` supplies the matching character string.

Examples

```
user$  expr abcdefghi : a.*g
7
user$  expr abc_efg_hij : '.*_\(.*\)_.*'
efg
```

`file [options] file`

`file` tries to determine the type of the file specified as the parameter. As a result, `file` supplies a character string with the file name and the file type (for example, 'test.ps: PostScript text conforming'). *Warning:* Text files containing foreign language special characters are not classified as text files, but as 'data'. There are also other cases where classification does not work reliably for all file types.

`-z` tries to determine the data type of a compressed file, by evaluating the file `/etc/magic`.

```
for var [in list;] do
  commands
done
```

`for` builds a loop. All list elements are assigned to the specified variable, one after the other. The list can also be constructed with the wildcards used for file names or with `{...}` elements for assembling file names. When no list is specified, the variable cycles through all parameters passed to the shell (thus, `in $*`).

```
[ function ] name()
  { commands }
```

`function` defines a subfunction which can be called inside the shell in the same way as a new command. Inside the function, `local` can be used to define local variables. Functions can be called recursively. The functions can be passed parameters in the same way as these are passed to commands. Inside the function, these parameters can be read from the variables `$1`, `$2`, and so on.

```
if condition; then
  commands
[elif condition; then
  commands]
[else
  commands]
fi
```

The `if` command starts a branching construction. The block following `then` is only executed when the condition is satisfied. Otherwise, an arbitrary number (optional) of `elif` conditions are evaluated and, if needed, the equally optional `else` block is executed.

Several commands can be specified in the conditions, the last of which must be followed by a semicolon. The criterion is the return value of the last command. Comparisons and other tests can be carried out with the `test` command (see page 433). Instead of `test`, a short notation in square brackets is allowed. Please note that a space must be inserted both after `[` and before `]`.

```
local var[=value]
```

`local` defines a local variable. The command can only be used in a user-defined function (see `function`). There must be no spaces before or after the equal sign.

```
popd
```

`popd` changes back to a directory previously stored with `pushd`. The directory is removed from the directory list.

`printf format para1 para2 para3 ...`

`printf` allows you to generate formatted output using the syntax of the C command `printf`. Detailed information on available formatting options can be obtained with `man 3 printf`.

`pushd directory`

`pushd` stores the current directory and subsequently changes to the specified directory. With `popd`, you can switch back to the original directory. `dirs` displays a list of all directories stored.

`read [var1 var2 var3 ...]`

`read` reads a line of text into the specified variables. `read` expects its data from the standard input. When no variable is specified, `read` writes the input into the variable `REPLY`. When exactly one variable is specified, `read` writes the entire input into this variable. When several variables are specified, `read` writes the first word into the first variable, the second word into the second variable ... and the remainder of the input into the last variable. Words are considered to be character strings separated by spaces or tabs.

The `read` command does not provide the possibility of outputting an info text as the input prompt. It might therefore be a good idea to inform the user of the purpose of the input by means of `echo -n`, prior to execution of `read` commands.

`readonly`

`readonly` displays the write-protected variables of the shell. Variables can be protected against modification with `declare -r`.

`setterm [option]`

`setterm` modifies various settings of the terminal. When the command is executed without specifying an option, it displays a list of all available options. Some options have already been described on page 479. Useful options for shell programming are:

`-bold on | off`
: activates/deactivates bold face. In text consoles, the text does not appear in bold face, but in a different color from other text.

`-clear`
: clears the screen.

`-default`
: restores colors and text attributes to their default settings.

`-half-bright on | off`
: highlighted type on/off.

`-reverse on | off`
reverse type on/off.

`-underline on | off`
underlined type on/off.

`shift [n]`

`shift` shifts the parameter list passed to the shell program through the predefined variables `$1` to `$9`. When `shift` is used without parameters, the parameters are shifted by one position, otherwise by *n* positions. `shift` is of particular help when more than nine parameters are to be accessed. *Warning:* Parameters shifted out of the variables with `shift` can no longer be accessed. They are also removed from the variable `$*`.

`sleep time`

`sleep` puts the running program into a state of rest for the specified time. During this time, the program uses practically no CPU time. Time is normally specified in seconds. Optionally, the letters 'm', 'h' or 'd' can be appended to specify the time in minutes, hours or days.

`source file`

`source` executes the specified shell file as though all commands contained in it were entered instead of the source command. After execution of the file, the running shell program is continued with the next line. No new shell is started to execute the specified file. Therefore, all variables (including the parameter list) are also valid for the specified file. Execution of `exit` in this file does not lead to a return to the program containing the source command, but to an immediate termination of program execution. The short notation for source is `.␣file` (␣ stands for a space).

`test expression`

`test` is used for the formulation of conditions and is mostly applied in `if` branches and loops. Depending on whether the condition is satisfied, it returns the truth values 0 (true) or 1 (false). Instead of `test`, you can also use the short notation `[ expression ]`, with a space inserted after `[` and before `]`.

Character strings

`[ cs ]`	true if the character string is not empty
`[ -z cs ]`	true if the character string is empty (0 characters)
`[ cs1 = cs2 ]`	true if the character strings match
`[ cs1 != cs2 ]`	true if the character strings differ from each other

When character strings from variables are to be compared, the variables should be enclosed in quotes (for example, `[ "$a" = "$b" ]`). Otherwise, errors can occur when a variable contains several words separated by spaces.

Numbers

`[ n1 -eq n2 ]`	true if the numbers are equal
`[ n1 -ne n2 ]`	true if the numbers are not equal
`[ n1 -gt n2 ]`	true if *n1* is greater than *n2*
`[ n1 -ge n2 ]`	true if *n1* is greater or equal *n2*
`[ n1 -lt n2 ]`	true if *n1* is less than *n2*
`[ n1 -le n2 ]`	true if *n1* is less or equal *n2*

Files (in extracts)

`[ -d file ]`	true if file is a directory
`[ -e file ]`	true if the file exists
`[ -f file ]`	true if file is a simple file (and not a device, a directory ...)
`[ -L file ]`	true if file is a symbolic link
`[ -r file ]`	true if the file can be read
`[ -s file ]`	true if the file has a size of at least 1 byte
`[ -w file ]`	true if the file can be written to
`[ -x file ]`	true if the file can be executed
`[ file1 -ef file2 ]`	true if both files share the same I-node (equal file) (equal file)
`[ file1 -nt file2 ]`	true if file1 is newer than file2

Joint conditions

`[ ! cond ]`	true if the condition is not satisfied
`[ cond1 -a cond2 ]`	true if both conditions are satisfied (and)
`[ cond1 -o cond2 ]`	true if at least one of the conditions is satisfied (or)

`trap [command] n`

`trap` executes the specified command when the specified signal occurs in the `bash`. When no command is specified, the program or the `bash` ignores the signal. A list of all available signals and their associated numbers can be obtained with `trap -l`.

`ulimit option limit`

`ulimit` limits the maximum system resources taken up by the shell and processes started from inside this shell. Sizes are generally expressed in Kbytes.

`-d memory`
: limits the memory dedicated to the data segment of processes.

`-f file_size`
: prevents creation of files larger than the specified limit. Only functions in the `ext2` file system.

`-s memory`
: limits stack space.

```
unalias abbreviation
```

`unalias` deletes an existing abbreviation. When the command is called with the option `-a`, it deletes all known abbreviations.

```
unset variable
```

`unset` deletes the specified variable.

```
until condition; do
  commands
done
```

`until` is used for the construction of loops. The loop is executed until the specified condition is satisfied. The criterion is the return value of the command specified as the condition. Comparisons and tests are carried out with the command `test` or its short notation in square brackets (see page 433).

```
wait [process_number]
```

`wait` waits for termination of the specified background process. When no process number is specified, the command waits for termination of all running processes started by the shell.

```
while condition; do
  commands
done
```

`while` is used for the construction of loops. The loop is executed until the specified condition is not satisfied for the first time. The criterion is the return value of the command specified as the condition. Comparisons and tests are carried out with the command `test` or its short notation in square brackets (see page 433).

13.7 Special characters reference

A large number of special characters can be used for various actions, both when entering commands and when writing shell programs. The following table summarizes all special characters dealt with in Chapter IV (bash – a modern command interpreter) and in this chapter.

<table>
<tr><th colspan="2">bash special characters</th></tr>
<tr><td>;</td><td>separates several commands</td></tr>
<tr><td>:</td><td>a shell command that does nothing</td></tr>
<tr><td>.</td><td>starts a shell program without its own subshell (. file)
(corresponds to source file)</td></tr>
<tr><td>#</td><td>starts a comment</td></tr>
<tr><td>#!/bin/sh</td><td>identifies the shell required for the shell program</td></tr>
<tr><td>&</td><td>executes the command in the background (com &)</td></tr>
<tr><td>&&</td><td>conditional command execution (com1 && com2)</td></tr>
<tr><td>&></td><td>redirection of standard output and standard error</td></tr>
<tr><td>|</td><td>constructs pipes (com1 | com2)</td></tr>
<tr><td>||</td><td>conditional command execution (com1 $||$ com2)</td></tr>
<tr><td>*</td><td>wildcard for file names (any number of characters)</td></tr>
<tr><td>?</td><td>wildcard for file names (one arbitrary character)</td></tr>
<tr><td>[abc]</td><td>wildcard for file names (one character out of ‘abc’)</td></tr>
<tr><td>[expression]</td><td>short notation for test</td></tr>
<tr><td>~</td><td>abbreviation for the home directory</td></tr>
<tr><td>></td><td>output redirection into a file (com > file)</td></tr>
<tr><td>>></td><td>output redirection; append to existing file</td></tr>
<tr><td>>&</td><td>redirection of standard output and standard error</td></tr>
<tr><td><</td><td>input redirection from a file (com < file)</td></tr>
<tr><td><< end</td><td>input redirection from the current file until ‘end’</td></tr>
<tr><td>(...)</td><td>execute commands in the same shell ((com1; com2))</td></tr>
<tr><td>{...}</td><td>groups commands</td></tr>
<tr><td>{ , , }</td><td>assembles character strings (a{1,2,3} → a1 a2 a3)</td></tr>
<tr><td>[...]</td><td>short notation for test ...</td></tr>
<tr><td>$</td><td>identification of variables (echo $var)</td></tr>
<tr><td>$!</td><td>PID of the most recently started background process</td></tr>
<tr><td>$$</td><td>PID of the current shell</td></tr>
<tr><td>$0</td><td>file name of the shell script being executed</td></tr>
<tr><td>$1 bis $9</td><td>the first nine parameters passed to the command</td></tr>
<tr><td>$#</td><td>number of parameters passed to the shell program r</td></tr>
<tr><td>$* or $@</td><td>all passed parameters</td></tr>
<tr><td>$(...)</td><td>command substitution (echo $(ls))</td></tr>
<tr><td>${...}</td><td>various special functions for processing character strings</td></tr>
<tr><td>$[...]</td><td>arithmetic evaluation (echo $[2+3])</td></tr>
<tr><td>"..."</td><td>prevents evaluation of most special characters</td></tr>
<tr><td>'...'</td><td>prevents evaluation of all special characters</td></tr>
<tr><td>`...`</td><td>command substitution (echo `ls`)</td></tr>
<tr><td>\character</td><td>undo the effect of the special character</td></tr>
</table>

Command reference

This chapter contains a reference list of the most important Linux commands, in alphabetical order. In this context, use of the term command is slightly problematic. To be accurate, Linux makes no distinction between commands such as those described in this chapter and much more complex programs (for example, editors or programming languages) which are described in separate dedicated chapters. In addition, this chapter describes several commands which are not true Linux programs, but commands of the currently active shell (mostly the `bash`; see Chapter 12). A typical example is the frequently used `cd` command for changing the current directory.

The aim of this chapter is to provide a uniform overview of all commands needed for the standard use of Linux for file system administration, starting and stopping processes, processing text files and carrying out other management tasks. This aim has been the final criterion for the selection of commands in this chapter. Some rarely needed commands have been left out altogether, and others will be described in chapters where they fit in better from a contents point of view (such as the commands for shell programming, which you will find in Chapter 13).

NOTE Depending on the extent of the Linux distribution installed on your computer, some of the commands described here may be missing or may have to be installed separately. This applies particularly all to the `mtools` commands for processing DOS diskettes, which are often supplied as a separate package.

14.1 Command overview by subject

File management

`cat`	concatenates several files into one file
`cd`	changes the current directory
`cp`	copies files
`ln`	establishes hard and symbolic links to files
`ls`	displays the contents list
`mkdir`	creates a new directory
`mv`	moves files and changes file names
`rm`	deletes files
`rmdir`	deletes directories
`split`	splits a file into files of specified size
`tee`	duplicates the standard output

Finding files

`find`	finds files by name, date, size, and so on
`locate`	finds files in a previously prepared database
`whereis`	finds files in typical `bin` directories
`which`	searches the `PATH` directories for commands

Accessing MS-DOS diskettes

`fdformat`	formats a diskette (low level)
`mattrib`	changes the attributes of a file
`mcd`	changes the current directory
`mcopy`	copies files to/from Linux
`mdel`	deletes files
`mdir`	displays the directory list
`mformat`	creates a DOS file system
`mlabel`	changes the name of a diskette
`mmd`	creates a new directory
`mrd`	deletes directories
`mread`	copies files from DOS to Linux
`mren`	renames files
`mtype`	displays the contents of text files
`mwrite`	copies files from Linux to DOS

Processing text

`cat`	displays a file or concatenates several text files into one file
`csplit`	splits a text at specified points into several single files
`cut`	extracts columns from each row of text

`expand`	expands tabs into spaces
`fold`	splits long lines of text into shorter ones
`fromdos`	converts DOS end-of-line characters into Linux format
`grep`	searches for text within a file
`head`	displays the first lines of a file
`less`	displays files page by page (also backwards)
`more`	displays files page by page
`paste`	concatenates several texts line by line
`recode`	converts between different character sets
`sed`	stream editor (programmable editor)
`sort`	sorts files
`tac`	displays files ‘the other way round’ (last line first)
`tail`	displays the end of a file
`todos`	converts Linux end-of-line characters into DOS format
`tr`	substitutes given characters with other ones
`uniq`	eliminates lines that occur more than once in a text file
`zcat`	displays a compressed text file
`zless`	displays a compressed text file (also backwards)
`zmore`	displays a compressed text file page by page

Compressing and archiving files

`bunzip2`	decompresses files compressed with `bzip2`
`bzip2`	compresses files; more powerful than `gzip`
`compress`	compresses files
`cpio`	transfers archive files between different file systems
`gunzip`	decompresses files compressed with `gzip`
`gzip`	compresses files; more powerful than `compress`
`mt`	controls the streamer (forward/backward winding, and so on)
`tar`	joins several files (and directories) into one file
`uncompress`	decompresses files compressed with `compress`

Process administration

`bg`	continues a process in the background
`fg`	continues a process in the foreground
`halt`	terminates Linux and halts the computer
`kill`	sends signals (mostly for premature termination of a process)
`nice`	starts a process with decreased priority
`ps`	displays a list of currently running processes
`pstree`	as `ps`, but shows dependences in a better way
`reboot`	terminates Linux and restarts the computer
`shutdown`	terminates Linux
`top`	displays a list of all processes every five seconds

User and group administration

`adduser`	registers a new user (interactive)
`chsh`	changes the default shell after logging in
`groups`	displays the groups of the current user
`passwd`	changes the password of a user

File system administration

`badblocks`	checks whether data media (diskettes) contain bad sectors
`dd`	copies blocks of data between devices (low level)
`dumpe2fs`	displays internal information about an ext2 file system
`e2fsck`	repairs an ext2 file system
`fdformat`	formats a diskette
`fdisk`	partitions the hard disk
`fsck`	repairs a file system (front end)
`mkfifo`	creates a FIFO file (a named pipe)
`mkfs`	creates a file system
`mknod`	creates device files
`mkswap`	creates a swap file or partition
`mount`	mounts a device (for example, a hard disk) into the file system
`swapoff`	deactivates a swap file or partition
`swapon`	activates a swap file or partition
`tune2fs`	modifies system parameters of an ext2 file system

Screens and terminals

`reset`	restores the character set assignment
`restorefont`	restores the VGA character set
`restore-palette`	restores the VGA color palette
`setfont`	changes the VGA character set
`setterm`	changes various terminal settings

Online help

`apropos`	finds `man` pages concerning a specified subject
`info`	starts the `info` system
`man`	displays the description of a command
`whatis`	displays a short description (one line) of a command

Miscellaneous

`alias`	defines an abbreviation
`cksum`	calculates the CRC checksum for a file

`date`	displays date and time
`dmesg`	displays the kernel messages of the boot process
`expr`	executes simple integer calculations
`free`	displays the free memory (RAM and swap storage)
`hash`	displays the hash table
`ldd`	displays the libraries needed to run a program
`lpr`	prints a file
`printenv`	only displays the environment variables
`rdev`	changes some bytes in the kernel file
`set`	displays all variables known to the shell
`sum`	calculates the checksum for a file
`tty`	displays the device name of the current terminal
`type`	displays the type of a command (for example, shell command)
`unalias`	deletes an abbreviation
`uname`	displays name and version number of the operating system

REFERENCE

The `bash` is described in Chapter 12. This Linux standard shell is not simply your interpreter when you enter commands. The shell also allows you to write simple shell scripts (that is, batch files). This least complicated form of Linux programming is very often used to make simple tasks automatic (such as the execution of a backup). In their application, shell scripts often look like true programs. Chapter 13 gives an introduction to the basics of shell programming, together with some examples which will also make use of the commands described in this chapter.

14.2 Alphabetical command reference

Most of the commands described in this chapter can be controlled by a number of options. Options must be specified before all other parameters. Options begin either with one hyphen `-` followed by one or more letters, or with two hyphens `--` for the specification of longer option names (which are equivalent to the option letters, but are more expressive).

The following two `ls` commands are equivalent and both display all files and directories in the `/root` directory, taking into account all files (with the exception of `.` and `..`) whose names start with the `.` character. (A detailed description of the command and its options can be found on page 464.)

```
user$  ls -l -A /root
user$  ls --format=long --almost-all /root
```

With many commands, several options can be specified as a group (that is, `-ab` instead of `-a -b`). Some commands can also cope with options specified after the parameter(s) proper. This should, however, not lead you to believe that this applies to all commands!

```
user$  ls -lA /root
user$  ls /root -lA
```

With a very small number of commands, the order of the parameters impacts on the way the command is executed. If mutually exclusive options are specified, the option specified last is generally the one that applies.

In order to keep this chapter down to a reasonable size, only the most important options are described for most commands. A complete overview of all command options can usually be obtained by typing `command_name --help` ↵. More detailed information is usually contained in the manual pages which can be displayed by means of `man` *name* or `man 1` *name*. For some commands, the `man` pages only contain a reference to the `info` texts which, correspondingly, are displayed by means of `info` *name*.

adduser name

`adduser` registers a new user. Depending on the distribution, the command works interactively (asking for confirmation of all input) or alternatively fully automatically. `adduser` can only be executed by `root`.

alias [abbreviation [=command]]

`alias` defines a new abbreviation or displays an existing abbreviation. When you use `alias` without any parameters, it displays all defined abbreviations. `alias` is a `bash` command and is described in detail on page 391.

Example

```
user$ alias ll="ls -l"
```

defines the abbreviation `ll` for the command `ls -l`.

apropos subject

`apropos` provides a list of all `man` texts which contain information about the specified subject. If `apropos` does not work, there is a high probability that the underlying databases are missing. They can be generated with `makewhatis` (see page 71).

badblocks device blocks

`badblocks` checks the number of blocks of the data medium specified by `block`. The command is mostly employed for checking diskettes:

```
user$ badblocks /dev/fd0 1440
```

bg [process]

`bg` continues an interrupted process in the background. If no process number is specified, `bg` applies to the last interrupted process (interruptions are mostly carried out with Ctrl+Z). Otherwise, the process must be specified either by its name or by its `bash`-internal job number (not the PID). `bg` is a `bash` command.

`bunzip2 file.bz2`

`bunzip2` decompresses a file previously compressed with `bzip2`, automatically removing the extension `.bz2` from the file name. `bunzip` is a link to `bzip2`, with the `-d` option activated.

`bzip2 file`

`bzip2` is a relatively new command for compression of files. Generally, this command yields files that are about 20 to 30 per cent smaller than those generated by `gzip` (page 460). However, the CPU time needed for compression is significantly longer.

`-c` or `--stdout` or `--to-stdout`
: leaves the file to be (de)compressed unchanged and redirects the result to the standard output (generally, to the screen). From there, it can be redirected into an arbitrary file by means of `>`.

`-d` or `--decompress` or `--uncompress`
: decompresses the specified files instead of compressing it (equivalent to `bunzip2`).

`-1` to `-9`
: specifies the amount of memory required for the compression algorithm (`-1` needs only 1.1 Mbytes, while `-9` requires a hefty 6.7 Mbytes). The default setting is `-9` and yields the best results.

`cat files`

`cat` displays the contents of the specified text file on screen. For longer texts, however, you should use the `more` or `less` commands which stop the display after each page and (`less` only) also allow you to move backwards through the text (see also `tac` on page 482 for a reverse text display, with the last line being displayed first).

`cat` is often used to concatenate several files into one larger file. To do this, the standard output must be redirected into a file by means of `>` (see example).

If by mistake `cat` is applied to binary files (instead of text files), the character set of the text terminal may be destroyed – that is, instead of letters and numbers, strange-looking characters are displayed. Remedy: execute the `reset` command

Example

```
user$  cat part*.tex > total.tex
```

concatenates the files `part1.tex`, `part2.tex`, and so on, into a single file `total.tex`.

`cd [directory]`

`cd` changes into the specified (sub)directory. If no directory is specified, `cd` changes to the home directory. If the directory is specified as `-`, `cd` changes to the most recently used directory. The current directory can be displayed with `pwd`. (`cd` is not a Linux command, but a shell command.)

`chattr [options] [+/-csSu] files`

`chattr` changes the version of the file plus an additional six file attributes which are supported only in `ext2fs` file systems (Linux standard). The file version indicates how many times the file has already been modified. The attributes are set with `+` and deactivated with `-` (thus, for example, `+S` to activate the sync attribute). The `c` and `u` attributes are not yet supported by the Linux kernel.

`+/-a` (append)
: The file cannot be deleted or overwritten, but extended by appending new data at the end.

`+/-c` (compressed)
: The file is automatically compressed/decompressed.

`+/-s` (secure deletion)
: During deletion, the file is overwritten with random data so that it cannot be reconstructed.

`+/-S` (synchronous update)
: Each modification of the file is immediately executed physically and not stored in an intermediate buffer.

`+/-u` (undelete)
: During deletion, the file is not deleted physically and can be 'salvaged.'

`-R` The command is recursively executed for all subdirectories as well. This only makes sense for file specifications using wildcards.

`-v version`
: This changes the stored version number of the file.

`chgrp [options] group files`

`chgrp` changes the group membership of files. The owner of a file can assign it only to his/her own group(s). For most users, this command is only meaningful if they belong to more than one group. `root` can carry out arbitrary assignments.

`-R` or `--recursive`
: Recursively changes the group membership of files in all subdirectories as well. This option only makes sense if files are described using wildcards (such as `*.tex`).

`chmod [options] changes files`

`chmod` changes the nine access bits of files. Together with each file, information is stored about whether the owner, the group members or other users can read, write or execute the file. Changes to the access bits are carried out by means of the character combination group `+/-` *`access type`*, for example `g+w` to give all users in the group write access privilege. The group can be specified through the characters `u` (user), `g` (group), `o` (others) or `a` (all). The access type is described by `r` (read), `w` (write) or `x` (execute).

If the access type `s` (setuid) is used instead of `x`, the executed program behaves as though it were executed by the owner of the file (see example). When the setuid bit is set for files belonging to privileged users (for example, `root`), this can constitute a considerable safety risk. Ordinary users can execute the program as if they were `root`. Please make sure that ordinary users can only perform those tasks for which the program is actually designed.

Alternatively, the access type can be specified with an octal number, where `u`, `g` and `o` are assigned one digit each. Each digit is a combination of the values `4`, `2` and `1` for `r`, `w` and `x`. Thus, `660` means `rw-rw----`, and `777` means `rwxrwxrwx`.

`-R` or `--recursive`
: also changes the access rights of files in all subdirectories. This option only makes sense if files are described using wildcards (such as `*.tex`).

Examples

```
user$  chmod a+rx savefile
```

allows all users to execute the file `savefile`. This file could, for example, be a shell script (a batch file) for the creation of a backup.

```
user$  chmod -R o-rw *.doc
```

denies all users outside the owner's group read and write access privileges for all `*.doc` files in the current directory and in all subdirectories.

```
root#  chmod a+xr /usr/bin/local/newsflash
root#  chmod a+w /usr/bin/local/newsflash
root#  chmod u+rws /usr/bin/local/newsflash
root#  chown news.news /usr/bin/local/newsflash
```

allows all users to execute `newsflash`. Because of the setuid bit, however, `newsflash` behaves as if it had been started by the user `news`.

chown [options] user[.group] files

`chown` changes the owner and (optionally) the group membership of a file. The owner of a file can only be changed by `root`, whereas the group can also be changed by other users (see `chgrp`).

`-R` or `--recursive`
: also changes the group membership of files in all subdirectories.

chsh [user]

`chsh` changes the default shell which is automatically called after logging in. The choice is between all shells registered in `/etc/shells`, usually `/bin/bash`, `/bin/csh` and `/bin/ksh`. `chsh` modifies the file `/etc/passwd` by entering the new shell. The shell of another user can only be changed by `root` (whereas each user can arbitrarily change his/her own shell).

`cksum file`

`cksum` determines the checksum and the length of the file in bytes. The checksum can be used to find out quickly and reliably whether two files are identical (for example, after a data transmission via a modem or when a virus infection is suspected). `cksum` supplies more reliable results than the related `sum` command.

`clear`

`clear` empties the screen (the text console). The command corresponds to the DOS command `cls`.

`cmp [options] file1 file2`

`cmp` compares two files byte by byte and supplies the position of the first discrepancy. When the files are identical, the command does not display any message at all (see also `diff` on page 451).

`-c` or `--show-chars`
: displays the first text character in each file where the files differ from one another.

`-l` or `--verbose`
: supplies a list of all discrepancies.

`compress [options] file`

`compress` compresses or decompresses the specified file. Compressed files are indicated by `.Z` appended to the file name. A more powerful command than `compress` is `gzip` (see page 460).

`-d` decompresses the specified file instead of compressing it (corresponds to `uncompress`).

`cp [-options] source target`
`cp [-options] files target_directory`

`cp` is used to copy files. Single files can be renamed. When several files are to be processed (for example, through the specification of wildcards), these can only be copied to a different directory, but not renamed. Instructions of the type `cp *.tex *.bak` are not allowed. Commands comparable to `cp` are `mv` for moving and renaming files, and `ln` for the creation of links. Amongst others, `cp` supports the following options:

`-a` or `--archive`
: preserves all attributes of the file. `-a` is an abbreviation for `-dpR`.

`-b` or `--backup`
: already existing files are not overwritten, but renamed as backup files (file name plus `~`.

`-d` or `--dereference`
: only copies a link reference, but not the file pointed to by the link.

`-i` or `--interactive`
: asks for confirmation before overwriting existing files.

`-l` or `--link`
: creates hard links instead of copying the files. When `cp` is used with this option, it has the same functionality as `ln` (see page 463).

`-p` or `--preserve`
: leaves information about owner, group membership, access rights and the date and time of last modification unchanged. Without this option, the copy belongs to the user who executes `cp` (user and group), and the date and time are set to the current date and time.

`-R` or `--recursive`
: also copies subdirectories and the files they contain.

`-s` or `--symbolic-link`
: creates symbolic links instead of copying the files or directories. With this option, `cp` has the same functionality as `ln -s` (see page 463).

`-u` or `--update`
: copies files only if this does not cause a homonymous file with a more recent date to be overwritten.

Another command well suited to copying whole directory trees (especially between different hard disk partitions) is `tar` (see page 483).

Example

```
user$  cp book/*.tex .
```

copies all `*.tex` files from the subdirectory `book` into the current directory, which in the above command is denoted by a single dot.

`cpio command [options] [pattern]`

`cpio` combines several files into an archive and copies them to another storage medium (for example, to a streamer) or to another directory. Similarly, the command can also be used to read such data. Under Linux, `cpio` is not very widely used; `tar` is more popular. The greatest advantage of `cpio` is that voluminous archives can be automatically distributed onto (and read back from) several data supports (similar to the DOS programs `BACKUP` and `RESTORE`).

`cpio` is, for example, needed for the installation of programs which have been recorded by their manufacturers on diskettes or tapes using `cpio`. The three central `cpio` commands are:

`-o` (output) for storing data. The files are combined into one archive and written to the standard output.

`-i` (input) for reading archived data.

`-p` (pass through) for the transfer of archives between different directories.

These three main commands can be controlled through various options. Details can be found in the `man` pages.

`csplit [options] file split_position`

`csplit` splits a text file at predetermined positions into several single files. The split position can be specified either directly by a number of lines or by a search pattern. As a result, the command produces the files `xx00`, `xx01`, and so on, and displays their lengths on screen. Through the specification of appropriate options, 'prettier' file names can be generated. The `cat` command can be used to combine these single files back into the original file. (See also `split` on page 481 for splitting files of any type – even binary – into smaller files of *n* bytes each.)

Specification of the split positions

The split positions are specified either as a number of lines or as a search pattern. In the first case, the file is split after *n* lines, in the second case before or after the occurrence of the search pattern. When `csplit` is used to split the file several times (which is normally the case), the number of times the operation is to be repeated must be specified after the number of lines or the split pattern.

n splits the file after *n* lines.

`/pattern/`
: splits the file after the line preceding the occurrence of the pattern. (The line which contains the pattern becomes the first line of the next file.)

`/pattern/+n`

`/pattern/-n`
: splits the file *n* lines after (+) or before (-) the occurrence of the pattern.

`{n}` splits the file into *n*+1 files (not just into two files).

Options

`-f file` or `--prefix=file`
: uses the specified file name to name the output files.

`-k` or `--keep-files`
: already created files are not deleted when an error occurs. This option must always be used with pattern specifications of the form `n {*}`. Patterns are specified as in `grep`.

`-z` or `--elide-empty-files`
: prevents the creation of empty files. Without this option, empty files can occur, especially when the first line of the source file matches the search pattern.

Examples

```
user$  csplit -k -f part. total.txt 100 {*}
```

splits `total.txt` into the files `part.00`, `part.01`, and so on. Each file is 100 lines long.

```
user$  csplit -k -f part. total.txt '/^% ---/' {*}
```

as above, except that the file is split every time a line begins with the text `% ---`.

`cut [options] file`

`cut` extracts the columns specified by the options from each line of a text.

`-b` *`list`* or `--bytes` *`list`*
: extracts the characters specified in a list. Single characters may be separated by commas (but not by spaces). Alternatively, entire ranges can be specified, such as `-b 3-6,9,11-15`.

`-f` *`list`* or `--fields` *`list`*
: as above, but applying to fields (data records) which must be separated by tab characters.

`-d` *`character`* or `--delimiter` *`character`*
: specifies the separation character for `-f`; this character is to be used instead of the tab character.

`-s` or `--only-delimited`
: eliminates all lines that do not contain data that corresponds to the `-f option`. Cannot be used together with `-b`.

Example

```
user$  ls -l | cut -b 1-11,56-
```

uses `cut` to filter the file list obtained with `ls`. As a result, only the access rights and the file names (characters 1 to 11 and all characters from the 56th character onward) are displayed.

`date [options] [time]`

`date` displays the current date and time or changes them. (Changes can only be carried out by `root`.) `date` can display the time in various formats (see the `man` texts).

`-s` sets the date and/or time (instead of just displaying them).

`dd [options]`

`dd` transfers data between different storage media (hard disk, diskette, and so on) and, if required, carries out a data conversion. The command can be used to exchange data between different computer architectures.

`dd` can not only copy single files, but also accesses devices directly. This can be used to copy entire hard disks (or partitions), modify the boot sector of a hard disk, and so on. There is no need to create a file system on the hard disk or diskette first.

When `dd` is used without options, it reads the data from the standard input (keyboard, terminated by Ctrl+Z) and writes to the standard output (the screen). Please note that the options of `dd` must be specified without preceding minus signs!

`conv=`*`mode`*
: converts the data during the copying process. There exist various settings for *mode*, such as `lcase` (upper case into lower case letters), `ucase` (lower case into upper case letters), `swab` (swaps 2 bytes at a time), and so on.

`bs=`*`n`*
: specifies the block size for input and output files. (The block size determines how many bytes are read or written at once.)

`count=`*`n`*
: copies only *n* blocks (and not all data).

`ibs=`*`n`*
: specifies the block size of the source file.

`if=`*`source_file`*
: specifies the source file (instead of the standard input).

`obs=`*`n`*
: specifies the block size of the target file.

`of=`*`target_file`*
: specifies the target file (instead of the standard output).

Examples

```
user$  dd if=/dev/hda of=/boot/bootsector.bak bs=512 count=1
```

transfers the boot sector of the first IDE hard disk into the backup file `bootsector.bak`.

```
user$  dd if=/vmlinuz of=/dev/fd0
```

copies the kernel directly into the first sectors of the diskette, which can then be used as a boot diskette.

`df [options]`

`df` provides information about the points in the directory tree where hard disks (or partitions) or other drives are mounted and how much free storage is available on each.

`-i` or `--inodes`
: instead of the free storage in Kbytes, information is displayed about the available I-nodes.

`diff [options] file1 file2`

`diff` compares two text files. The result is a list of all lines that differ from one another. The command is relatively 'intelligent,' that is, when lines have been added in one file, only this fact is signalled as a change. Subsequent lines are again recognized as identical, although their line numbers are now different. Thus, this program can be effectively used to quickly document the differences between two versions of a program listing.

`-b` regards multiple spaces and empty lines as single spaces/lines.

`-w` completely ignores spaces and empty lines.

`dmesg`

Messages displayed by the kernel during the boot process can be viewed at a later stage by means of `dmesg`. Such kernel messages can, for example, help determine which hardware has been recognized. Depending on the setting in `/etc/syslog.conf`, kernel messages are also stored in `/var/log/messages`.

The texts of the Init-V process (page 124) displayed after the boot process are not stored and can therefore not be viewed with `dmesg`. Some programs or so-called daemons, however, write their logs or error messages into various `/var/log/xxx` files.

`du [options] [directory]`

`du` provides information about the storage used by files or directories. When a file specification is given in the directory parameter (for example, `*` or `*.tex`), `du` provides a list giving the sizes of all files. When only a directory is specified, `du` calculates the storage used by all subdirectories. The sizes always include the storage used by all subdirectories. The last figure indicates the total storage used by all files and subdirectories below the specified directory. All sizes are given in Kbytes.

`-b` or `--bytes`
: indicates the sizes in bytes (instead of Kbytes).

`-c` or `--total`
: displays the total space as the last value. This option is only needed when `du` is applied to files (and not to directories). With this option, it is easy to determine how much space is occupied by all files with a given extension (for example, `*.tex`).

`-s` or `--summarize`
: displays *only* the total space. This option only makes sense when the storage of directories is shown.

`-S` or `--dereference`
: only displays the storage used by the specified directory itself. The storage used by subdirectories is not taken into account.

Examples

```
user$  du -bsS
129377
```

The files of the current directory use 129 377 bytes.

```
user$  du
101     ./a/a1
4       ./a/a2
114     ./a
5       ./b
251
```

The storage used by the files in `a1` is 101 Kbytes, in `a2` 4 Kbytes, in `a` (including `a1` and `a2`) 114 Kbytes, in `b` 5 Kbytes and in the current directory (including data and `b`) 251 Kbytes.

```
user$  du -S
101     ./a/a1
4       ./a/a2
9       ./a
5       ./b
132     .
```

With the `-S` option, `du` displays the storage used in the directories themselves. (The sum of these values is again 251 Kbytes.)

```
user$  du -c *.tex
100     emacs.tex
26      grundl.tex
126     total
```

The `*.tex` files in the current directory occupy a total of about 126 Kbytes.

`dumpe2fs device`

`dumpe2fs` provides a large amount of information about the state of the file system (see also page 107).

`e2fsck [options] device`

`e2fsck` checks the integrity of an ext2 file system and, if needed, carries out repairs. The command can be started via `fsck`. Its most important options are described on page 458.

`echo character string`

`echo` displays the specified character string on screen. For faster execution, `echo` is implemented as a shell command in most shells. `echo` is mainly useful for shell programming, and is used to output information for the user during execution of a shell script. When the character string contains spaces or special characters, it must be enclosed in single or double quotes (see also page 399).

`expand [options] file`

`expand` substitutes all tab characters with a corresponding number of spaces. When no options are specified, `expand` assumes a tabulator distance of eight characters. The result is displayed on screen and can be redirected into a file by means of `>`.

-n changes the tabulator distance to *n* characters.

`expr expression`

`expr` evaluates the specified expression arithmetically or performs a pattern match for character strings. The specified variables, numbers and operators must be separated by spaces. A short description of all permitted operators can be found in the `man` pages for `expr`.

When you use the `bash` as a shell, you can also calculate without using `expr` by simply entering arithmetic expressions in the form `$[expression]`.

Example

```
user$  expr 2 + 3
```

yields the result 5.

`fdformat [-n] drive`

`fdformat` carries out a low-level formatting of a diskette. A diskette prepared in this way can subsequently be used to install a file system with `mformat` or `mkfs`, to write a backup copy with `tar` or to write a boot kernel with `dd` (see pages 468, 468, 450 and 483).

The option `-n` prevents a subsequent verification of the diskette. The diskette drive is specified by means of a device file, for example `/dev/fd0H1440` for formatting a 3.5-inch HD diskette in drive A. The following device files are commonly used:

`/dev/fd0`	3.5-inch diskette HD in A: (default 1.4 Mbytes)
`/dev/fd0d360`	5.25-inch diskette in A:
`/dev/fd0D720`	3.5-inch diskette DD in A:
`/dev/fd0H1440`	3.5-inch diskette HD in A:
`/dev/fd0H2880`	3.5-inch diskette with 2.88 Mbytes in A:
`/dev/fd1d360`	5.25-inch diskette in B:
`/dev/fd1D720`	3.5-inch diskette DD in B:
`/dev/fd1h1200`	5.25-inch diskette HD in B:

If you use `fdformat` without having previously accessed the diskette, the command comes up with the error message ‘no such device.’ This can be remedied with `mdir`, which accesses the diskette and reads its parameters. In future Linux versions, `fdformat` will probably be replaced by `superformat`.

Example

```
user$  fdformat /dev/fd0 > /dev/null &
```

formats an HD diskette in drive A. Through the specification of `&`, the process is carried out in the background, so that you can continue working immediately. Furthermore, the specification of `> /dev/null` redirects the output of `fdformat` into oblivion, so that you are not continuously disturbed by the message 'Formatting *n*'.

`fdisk [options] [device]`

`fdisk` is used to partition a hard disk. The command can only be executed by `root`. When no device file is specified, `fdisk` automatically refers to the first IDE hard disk (`/dev/had`). `fdisk -l` displays a list of all partitions on all IDE and SCSI disks. The usage of the command is extensively described in the context of Linux installation (see page 33).

The command should never be used on a hard disk where one of the partitions is currently mounted into the Linux file system. If this cannot be avoided, you must restart your computer after changing the partition table to make the changes take effect. (`fdisk` issues a warning on this matter which you should definitely take seriously!)

After you have configured your system, you should produce a printout of the result of `fdisk -l` and keep it in a place where you will be able to find it again. This information is often sufficient to be able to restore a destroyed partition tabel of a hard disk.

`fg [process]`

`fg` continues a process in the foreground. When no process is specified, `fg` applies to the last process interrupted or the last process started in the background. Otherwise, the process must be specified through its name or its `bash`-internal job number (not PID). `fg` is a `bash` command. It can also be written using the short notation `%process`. Many programs (processes) can be interrupted by means of Ctrl+Z.

`file file`

`file` tries to determine the type of the data in a file. To do this, the command evaluates the file `/etc/magic`. The result is displayed on screen (for example, `data`, `text`, `executable`, and so on). Warning: text files containing foreign language special characters are interpreted as `data` (not as `text`).

`find [path_specification] [search_options]`

`find` helps to find files in the many branches of the directory tree. Several search criteria (such as file name patterns, file size, date and time of last modification, and so on) can be specified. In addition, it is possible to take all files which satisfy those conditions and apply further selection criteria with a different program (for example, `grep`). Thus it is possible, for example, to find all `*.tex` files which have been modified in the past three days and which contain the text 'graphics programming.'

Unfortunately, the vast number of possible search criteria also means that the description of all `find` options takes ten `man` pages, which is likely to put you off. Thus, before you read all those details, it would be a good idea to look at the examples below to see how the command can be used.

The GNU `find` syntax differs slightly from the `find` variations of various Unix systems. There, a path must be specified, whereas the GNU `find` uses the current directory as a default directory. In most cases, you *must* use the `-print` option, because otherwise files are sought, but the results are not displayed!

General options

Unlike practically all other Linux commands, `find` automatically searches all subdirectories. If this is not desired, the number of subdirectories must be restricted with `-maxdepth`.

`-depth`
: processes the current directory first, and then the subdirectories. (Depending on where you think the file to be sought might be, this can be significantly faster.)

`-follow`
: also processes directories included through symbolic links.

`-maxdepth` *n*
: restricts the search to *n* directory levels. With `-maxdepth 1`, no subdirectories are searched at all.

Search criteria

Several search criteria can be specified simultaneously. These criteria are logically joined with AND. The search is aborted as soon as the first criterion is not satisfied – thus, the order of criteria can impact on the speed of the command. Criteria can also be grouped with `\(` and `\)`, negated with `!` and, by means of `-o`, joined with the logical OR.

`-ctime` *n*
: finds files that were last modified exactly *n* days ago. When a `+` precedes the number, all files older than *n* days are found. A preceding `-` finds files younger than *n* days.

`-group` *group_name* or `-nogroup` *group_name*
: finds files that belong (or do not belong) to the specified group.

`-name` *search_pattern*
: finds files whose names match the specified search pattern. When the search pattern contains wildcards, it must be enclosed in quotes.

`-path` *search_pattern*
: finds files whose names match the specified search pattern. This option goes further than `-name`, because the search pattern is applied not only to the file

name, but also to the path that leads to it. This option is more flexible than the direct path specification in the first argument of `find`, because here the wildcards include the `/` character (see example below).

`-perm` *`access_bits`*
: finds files whose access bits exactly match the specified octal value (see `chmod`). When the octal value is preceded by a `-`, it is sufficient that the file contains at least one of these access bits, whereas a preceding `+` means that the file may have more extensive access rights.

`-size` *`file_size`*
: specifies the required file size. Usually, this is indicated in multiples of 512. Thus, `3` denotes files between 1024 and 1536 bytes. With the additional characters `c` or `k`, the size can be specified in bytes or Kbytes. A preceding `+` finds all larger files, a `-` all smaller files. Thus, `-size +10k` finds all files that are larger than 10 Kbytes.

`-type` *`character`*
: restricts the search to given file types. The most important characters are `f` for regular files, `d` for directories and `l` for symbolic links.

`-user` *`user_name`* or `-nouser` *`user_name`*
: finds files that belong (or do not belong) to the specified user.

Actions when finding a file

`-exec` *`command [options]`* `{} \;`
: calls the specified command and passes it the name of the file that has satisfied all criteria processed up to this point. The command can now check whether the file satisfies additional criteria. A typical program called through `-exec` is `grep` (see example below). `{}` acts as a placeholder for the file name. `;` terminates the command call, that is, further `find` options can be specified after it. `\` is necessary within the shell to prevent `;` from being interpreted as a special character.

`-print`
: displays the names of the files found on screen. This option is the default setting as long as you do not use `-exec`.

`-printf` *`format`*
: displays the names of the files found and other information on screen. The format character string can be used to specify how the output is to be displayed and which additional information is to be output (for example, file size, date and time of last modification, and so on). The syntax of the format character string is described in the `man` pages.

`find` is a relatively slow command, especially when the whole directory tree is to be searched. The commands `locate`, `whereis` or `which` often provide the same result in a much shorter time (see pages 463 and 489). If you have installed KDE, `kfind` provides a more user-friendly interface to `find` and `grep`.

Examples

```
user$  find
```

supplies a list of all files in the current directory and in all subdirectories.

```
user$  find -name '.e*'
```

finds all files in the current directory and in all subdirectories whose names begin with `.e`.

```
user$  find / -path '*latex/*.tex'
```

finds all `*.tex` files in a directory that ends in `latex`. (This search pattern is sufficient to find the files contained in `/usr/lib/texmf/tex/latex` in a relatively short time!)

```
root#  find /home -group users -ctime -5
```

finds all files in the (sub)directories of `/home` that belong to users of the `users` group and that have been modified in some way (contents, access rights, and so on) during the past five days. `-ctime +5` finds files modified more than five days ago, `-ctime 5` those modified exactly five days ago.

```
user$  head `find -name '.e*'`
```

displays the first ten lines of all `.e*` files on screen. Please note that the search pattern is enclosed in left quotes, whereas the whole `find` command as an argument of `head` is enclosed in right quotes. If you use another command instead of `head`, you can copy, delete, compress and do other things with the files found.

```
user$  find -name '*.tex' -type f -exec grep -q emacs {}  \; -print
```

searches all `*.tex` files for the character string 'emacs.' If the string is found, the file name is displayed on screen. Please note that the `-print` option must not be specified before `-exec` – otherwise, all `*.tex` file names are output, independently of whether 'emacs' was found or not (see also `grep` on page 459).

```
user$  find -name '*' -maxdepth 1 -size -10k -exec grep -q \
   >  case.*in {} \; -print > result
```

searches all files in the current directory which are smaller than 10 Kbytes for the regular expression `case.*in`. The list of files found is stored in the file `result`. The restriction of the files size to 10 Kbytes is used to exclude the (mostly much larger) binary files from the search.

`fold [options] file`

`fold` breaks text lines at a length of 80 characters and displays the result on screen.

`-w n` or `--width n`
: sets a maximum text width of *n* characters.

`-s` or `--spaces`
: tries to break the lines at a space (that is, between two words). Thus, the line length will become less than or equal to *n* characters.

`free`

`free` displays how the available memory space (RAM and swap area) is used.

`fromdos file`
`fromdos < source > target`

`fromdos` replaces all carriage return/line feed combinations in the specified file with simple line feeds. This is used to display DOS text files under Linux without the irritating `^M` characters at the end of each line (see also `recode` on page 476 and `todos` on page 486).

`fsck [options] device`

`fsck` checks the integrity of the file system and, if needed, carries out repairs. Instead of the device file, the directory (mount point) where the data resource is mounted in the file system can be specified.

Depending on the type of the file system, `fsck` calls the programs `e2fsck`, `fsck.xias` or `fsck.minix`. Thus, `fsck` is only an interface to further programs. Other file systems currently cannot be checked. Therefore, you cannot check the integrity of a mounted DOS partition.

`fsck` can best be compared to the DOS command `chkdsk`. It can only be executed by `root`. After a given number of boot processes, the command is executed automatically (that is, during Linux startup). In addition, the command is executed automatically after the computer has been switched off in an uncontrolled manner (power failure, total system crash).

A file system check can also be carried out on a currently active file system. When errors are found, changes should only be made when the device is not mounted into the file system (that is, you have to execute `umount` first). However, you cannot unmount the root device (that is, the hard disk (partition) containing the root directory `/`). Nevertheless, `fsck` can be executed if the system was booted read-only (and this is the case when problems occur during a routine file system check directly after starting the system).

When `fsck` finds errors in the file system and repairs them (which normally leads to a loss of data), the system must be subsequently restarted with `reboot`! Erroneous files (or what remains of them) are stored in the `lost+found` directory.

`-A` checks all file systems named in `/etc/fstab`.

`-t` *`type`*
specifies the file system type (for example, `ext2`).

The following options only apply to `e2fsck`, which is called by `fsck` in a standard Linux file system. (Obviously, `e2fsck` can also be called directly, without going through `fsck`).

`-n` answers all confirmation requests with `n` (no), and does not carry out any changes.

`-p` carries out repairs (changes) in the file system without asking for confirmation.

`-y` answers all confirmation requests with `y` (yes), and carries out changes.

Before you execute `fsck` and `e2fsck`, please read the manual pages of these commands. They also contain a description of all additional options. It might well be the case that the online documentation is more up to date than this book. During the development of Linux, the organization and administration of the file system have already changed (and improved) several times, which has also had its effects on `fsck`. Further changes cannot be ruled out.

`grep [options] search_pattern file`

`grep` searches the specified text files for a search pattern. Depending on the options used, the command subsequently displays the text passages found or simply indicates in how many lines the search pattern was found. `grep` can be combined with `find` to search all files that satisfy certain conditions.

`-n` displays not only the line containing the text, but also the *n* lines directly preceding and following the line.

`-c` shows the number of lines in which the search pattern has been found, but not the lines themselves.

`-f` *`file_name`*
reads the options from the specified file (for complex or frequently used search patterns).

`-i` does not differentiate between upper and lower case spelling.

`-l` only displays the file names in which the search pattern has been found.

`-n` displays the line number together with each displayed line.

`-q` does not supply any on-screen display and merely returns the value 0 (search text found) or 1 (not found). This option is useful when `grep` is called by other programs (see the `find` example on page 454).

`-w` only finds whole words. With this option, the search pattern 'grey', for example, would no longer be recognized in 'greyhound'.

Structure of the search pattern

The search pattern generally consists of two components: the characters to be searched for and the number of times these characters may occur:

`abc`	the character string 'abc'
`[abc]`	one of the characters a, b or c
`[~abc]`	none of the characters a, b or c (thus, an arbitrary different character)
`[a-z]`	one of the characters between a and z

`.`	an arbitrary character
`?`	the preceding character may occur zero or one times
`*`	the character may occur an arbitrary number of times (including zero times)
`+`	the character may occur an arbitrary number of times, but must occur at least once
`{n}`	the character must occur exactly *n* times
`{,n}`	the character may occur at most *n* times
`{n,}`	the character must occur at least *n* times
`{n,m}`	the character must occur at least *n* and at most *m* times

When special characters such as `? * + [ ] ( )` or `!` are to be used in the search pattern, they must be preceded by a `\`. Some groups of characters have predefined patterns, such as `[:digit:]` for digits (see `man` page).

Finally, some examples: `'abc'` searches for exactly this character string. `'[a-z][0-9]+'` searches for character strings that begin with a lower case letter, followed by one or more digits. `'\(.*\)'` searches for arbitrary strings containing at least one character enclosed by round parentheses.

`grep` applies the search pattern line by line. Text passages interrupted by a line break cannot be recognized. Obviously, `grep` is not capable of finding character strings in compressed files – for this purpose, you will have to resort to the `zgrep` command (see the corresponding `man` page).

Examples

```
user$  grep emacs *.tex
```

searches all `*.tex` files in the current directory for the character string 'emacs'. Displays a list of all lines found (each one preceded by the file name) on screen.

```
user$  grep -c arctan\(.*\) *.c
```

determines how many times the function `arctan` is used in the specified `*.c` files.

`groups`

`groups` displays a list of all groups to which the current user belongs. This list includes the main group specified in `/etc/passwd` plus the groups optionally specified in `/etc/group`.

`gunzip file`

Uncompresses the specified file, independently of whether it was compressed with `gzip` or `compress`. The `.gz` or `.Z` label in the file name is automatically removed. `gunzip` is a link to `gzip`, with the `-d` option automatically activated.

`gzip [options] file`

`gzip` compresses or uncompresses the specified file. Compressed files have the label `.gz` automatically appended. `gzip` is only suitable for the compression of single files.

If you want to store several files (or whole directories) in one compressed file, you must additionally use the `tar` command (see page 483).

`-c` or `--stdout` or `--to-stdout`
: leaves the file to be (un)compressed unchanged and redirects the output to the standard output (usually, to the screen). From there, it can be redirected to a file by means of `>` (see the example below).

`-d` or `--decompress` or `--uncompress`
: uncompresses the specified file instead of compressing it (corresponds to `gunzip`).

`-r` or `--recursive`
: also (un)compresses files in all subdirectories.

`-n, --fast, --best`
: controls compression speed and quality. `-1` corresponds to `--fast` and causes fast compression, but slightly larger files. `-9` corresponds to `--best` and leads to higher computing times, but smaller files. Default setting is `-6`.

Examples

```
user$  gzip *.tex
```

compresses all `*.tex` files in the current directory. The results are the corresponding `*.tex.gz` files.

```
user$  gzip -c file > backup.gz
```

compresses `file`, but leaves the file unchanged and writes the result to `backup.gz`.

halt [options]

`halt` terminates all running processes. Subsequently, Linux stops and no longer reacts to any input.

hash [option]

`hash` displays the contents of the hash table, that is, the table in which the shell memorizes the path names of all previously executed commands. This accelerates repeated execution of an already known command, since it is no longer necessary to search for the program in all `PATH` directories. `hash` is a built-in `bash` command.

`-r`
: deletes the hash table of the `bash`. This becomes necessary when the directory of a program contained in the hash table changes. Otherwise, the `bash` will no longer find the command. In the `tcsh`, the `rehash` command must be used instead of `hash -r`.

head [options] file

`head` displays the first ten lines of a text file on screen.

`-n` *`lines`*
displays the specified number of lines.

`hostname [name]`

`hostname` displays or changes the current network name of the system. When used with the option `-a`, the complete host name is displayed (including the domain name).

`id`

`id` displays the name and ID number of the user, his/her primary group and any other groups he/she belongs to.

`info [command_name]`

`info` starts the homonymous online help system, which documents various GNU tools and the Emacs editor. You will find the texts easier to read if, to read them, you use the Emacs editor. The info system is extensively described on page 74.

`kill [-s signal] process_number`

`kill` sends signals to a running process. When `kill` is used without the `-s` option, the SIGTERM signal (15) is sent to terminate the process forcibly (hence the name of the command). In particularly obstinate cases, `-9` or `-s SIGKILL` or the shorter `-KILL` will help. In such cases, however, the process has no chance of doing any clearing up before it is terminated.

`kill` can also be used to send 'harmless' signals. Frequently, `-1` or `-s SIGHUP` or `-HUP` is used to ask a daemon to reread its configuration files. This allows configuration data to be modified without having to stop the daemon completely and then restart it again.

The necessary process number (PID) is best determined by means of the `ps` command (see page 475).

`ldd program_file`

`ldd` displays all files needed to execute the program (together with their paths). This command can be used to determine very quickly if libraries are missing, and if so, which ones. More information about libraries can be found on page 120.

`less [options] file`

`less` displays the specified text file page by page. The command is a (more powerful) variation of `more`. It is often used as a filter (for example, `ls -l | less` for a pagewise display of a very long directory list).

The most important commands during the use of `less` are: [h] to display a short help text, the cursor keys to move around in the text, [↵] to scroll one line down,

[Spacebar] to scroll one page down, [b] to scroll one page back, [/] to input a search text and [q] to terminate `less`. (There are a large number of additional commands which are described in the `man` page.)

Various options can also be specified when calling the command – the most important are:

`-p search_text`
: displays the first line in which the search text was found.

`-s` several empty lines are reduced to one empty line.

`less` has difficulties with foreign language special characters. This problem can be easily solved by assigning the variable `LESSCHARSET` the character string `latin1` – this is best done directly in `/etc/profile`. These and other `less` configuration options are described on page 139.

Example

```
user$  less command.tex
```

displays the file `command.tex` on screen.

`ln [options] source [target]`
`ln [options] files target_directory`

`ln` establishes hard or symbolic links to files and directories. (You will find some information about what links are and how they are used in Chapter 5 from page 98 onward.) The same functionality as offered by `ln` can also be obtained with the `cp` command, by specifying the options `-l` or `-s`.

`-b` or `--backup`
: renames already existing homonymous files as backup files (name plus ~) instead of overwriting them.

`-d` or `--directory`
: creates a hard link to a directory. Only `root` is allowed to execute this operation. All other users can create symbolic links to directories.

`-s` or `--symbolic`
: creates symbolic links. (Without this option, `ln` creates hard links.)

Example

```
user$  ln -s abc xyz
```

creates the symbolic link `xyz` to the already existing file `abc`.

`locate pattern`

`locate` is the most important and most frequently used command for a quick search for files. It searches the database `locatedb` for files where the specified pattern occurs in the complete file name (including the path). Since `locate` makes use of a database, it is extremely fast when compared to `find`. However, files created or moved after establishing the database obviously cannot be found.

`locate` assumes that the `locatedb` database has been previously established with `updatedb`. The database is usually stored in `/var/lib`. Depending on the system, `updatedb` can be automatically started at regular intervals by means of `crond` or executed manually after major system changes. (If you are the only person using your computer, the second alternative is more reasonable.)

Examples

```
root#  updatedb
```

updates the `locate` database. This command must be executed by `root` prior to the first use of `locate` or after changes to the file system.

```
user$  locate XF86config
```

determines the location of `XF86config`. (This varies depending on the distribution.)

```
user$  locate dvips
```

finds all files whose names contain 'dvips' (this is usually quite a lot).

```
user$  locate '*dvips'
```

finds files whose names end in 'dvips'. This can be used to track down the binary file, possible links to it and homonymous directories.

```
user$  locate '*X*doc*' | less
```

finds the online documentation for X and displays the files with `less`.

logname

`logname` displays the login name (user name).

logout

With `logout`, a user terminates his/her work on a text console or with an X shell. Often it is also possible to use the short form Ctrl+D instead of `logout`.

lpr file

`lpr` prints the specified file. A precondition is that the printer daemon `lpd` has been correctly configured by means of the file `/etc/printcap`. If this is not the case, you can start a printout with the command `cp file /dev/lp0`, where `/dev/lp0` is the device name for the first parallel interface. Information about configuration of `lpd` can be found on page 163.

ls [-options] [path]

`ls` displays a list of all files and directories and essentially corresponds to the DOS command `DIR`. When `ls` is used without any further parameters or options, the command supplies a multi-column table, sorted by files name, in which all files, links and directories contained in the current directory are shown.

Now to the most important options of `ls` (a complete list can be obtained with `ls --help`, a description with `man ls`):

`-a` or `-all`
: also displays files whose names begin with a dot. A very similar effect can be achieved with the option `-A`, with the sole difference that the files `.` and `..` (references to the current and the parent directory) are not shown.

`--color`
: uses different colors for different file types (links, directories, and so on). Many systems use an `alias` definition of the type `alias ls='ls --color'` (for example in `/etc/profile`, which causes `ls` automatically to use colors). The configuration of color effects can be carried out either through the system variable `$LS_COLORS` or the file `/etc/DIR_COLORS` (details can be found in the `man` text).

`-d` or `--directory`
: only displays the name of the directory, but not its contents. This option is useful, for example, when a directory name is given as a path and the access rights of this directory are to be checked (but not its contents).

`-i` or `--inode`
: displays the I-node of the file in addition to all other details. (The I-node is an internal file identification number which is needed for Linux-internal file management.) This option can be used to recognize links (since files joined by links share the same I-node).

`-I` *`file`* or `--ignore` *`file`*

`-I`*`pattern`*
: excludes the specified files from being displayed. For example, `-I*ps` prevents files whose names end with `ps` being displayed. When `-I` is not followed by a single file, but by a file pattern, there must be no space between `-I` and the pattern!

`-l` or `--format=long` or `--format=verbose`
: displays further information in addition to the file name: file size in bytes, access rights, and so on. For each file, an entire line is used (instead of the space-saving multi-column display).

`-L` or `--dereference`
: displays the contents of the original directory (and not the path of the link) for symbolic links to directories. An example of the use of this option can be found on page 99.

`-o` or `--no-color`
: does without different colors or letter types. The `$LS_COLORS` system variable is ignored.

`-p` or `-F`
: appends a special character to the file name that denotes the type of the file. In some Linux distributions, this option is activated as a standard by means of an

alias abbreviation in `/etc/profile`. The most important special characters are: / for directories, @ for symbolic links, * for executable files and | for FIFOs (see page 393).

`-r` or `--reverse`
reverses the sorting order. This option is frequently used in combination with `-t` or `-S`.

`-R` or `--recursive`
also displays files in subdirectories (like `/S` with the DOS command `DIR`).

`-S` or `--sort=size`
sorts the files by size (the largest file first).

`-t` or `--sort=time`
sorts the files by time and date of last modification (the most recent file first).

`-u` or `--sort=access`
sorts the files by time and date of the last read access. This option must be specified together with `-t` (otherwise, `ls` does not sort at all).

`-X` or `--sort=extension`
sorts the files by their extension (the character combination after the last `.` in the file name).

The output of `ls` with the `-l` option needs some explanation. A typical line looks something like this:

```
-rw-r--r--   1 michael  users        3529 Oct  4 15:43 header.tex
```

Thus, we are talking about the file `header.tex`, which was last modified at 15:43 on 4 October of the current year. The file is 3529 bytes long and belongs to somebody from the `users` group whose user name is `michael`. The ten characters at the beginning of the line specify file type and access rights. File type indicators can be the hyphen `-` for a normal file, `d` for a directory, `b` or `c` for a device file (block or char) and `l` for a symbolic link. The next three characters (`rwx`) specify whether the user is allowed to read, write or execute the file. Analogous information follows for the members of the group and for all other system users.

In contrast to the DOS command `DIR`, `ls` does not show the entire space taken up by all listed files together. This is the task of `du` (see page 451).

In one respect, `ls` differs substantially from the DOS command `DIR`: while `DIR /S *.abc` lists all `*.abc` files in all subdirectories, the seemingly analogous command `ls -R *.abc` fails. The reason is that the file name expansions for `*.abc` are not executed by the command itself, but by the command interpreter (`bash`, see Chapter 12), and only apply to the the current directory. If you want to find files in arbitrary subdirectories, you must use `find` (see page 454).

Examples

```
user$  ls -ltr /root
```

displays all files in the `/root` directory and sorts them by date (the most recent file last).

```
user$  ls -ld */.
```

displays all directories (no files) of the current working directory.

`lsattr [options] files`

`lsattr` shows the state of the four additional attributes managed by the `ext2fs` file system: `c` (compressed), `s` (secure deletion), `S` (sync) and `u` (undelete), together with the version of the file (see also `chattr` on page 444).

`-a, -R`
as with `ls`, see above.

`-v` displays the version of the file.

`man [group] [options] name`

`man` displays online information about the specified command or file. The search can be restricted by specifying a group. The most important groups are 1 (user commands), 5 (configuration files) and 8 (system administration commands). The option `-a` displays all `man` texts found (otherwise, only the first one is displayed). `man` is extensively described on page 69.

`mattrib [+/-ahrs] files`

`mattrib` reads or changes the attributes of files on MS-DOS format diskettes. `mattrib` is the (alphabetically) first command of a whole series of commands collected under the generic term `mtools` (see page 473).

`mcd directory`

`mcd` makes the specified directory on an MS-DOS format diskette the current working directory of all `mtools` commands. This can also be used to set the default drive (`A:` or `B:`).

`mcopy [options] source target`
`mcopy [options] files target directory`

`mcopy` copies files from or to MS-DOS format diskettes. Generally, the command functions in the same way as `cp`, but the meaning of the options is different. The two main options are:

`-n` does not issue a warning before overwriting a file.

`-t` replaces the DOS carriage return/line feed combination with a simple line feed character. This eliminates the irritating `^M` characters at the end of each line of a text file imported from DOS (see also page 503). This option must only be used for text files!

`mdel files`

`mdel` deletes the specified files on an MS-DOS format diskette.

`mdir [path]`

`mdir` displays the contents of an MS-DOS format diskette.

`-w` lists only the file names in a multi-column table. By default, the file names are displayed line by line with some additional information.

`mformat drive`

`mformat` creates an MS-DOS file system on a diskette already preformatted with `fdformat` (see also page 453).

`mkdir directory`

`mkdir` creates a new directory. The two most important options are:

`-m mode` or `--mode=mode`
: sets the access rights of the new directory as specified in *mode* (see `chmod` on page 444).

`-p` or `--parents`
: also creates intermediate directories. When you execute `mkdir a/b/c` and the directories data and `a/b` do not yet exist, they are created as well.

`mkfifo file`

`mkfifo` creates a FIFO file (first in first out). In principle, FIFO files function the same way as pipes and allow data exchange between two programs.

Example

```
user$  mkfifo fifo
user$  ls -l > fifo &
user$  more < fifo
```

creates a new FIFO file, redirects the contents list into this file and reads it from there with `more`. `ls` must be started as a background process by specifying the option `&`, because the `ls` process terminates only after `more` has read all data from `fifo`. The display of a contents list via `more` could be obtained much more easily without a FIFO file, namely with `ls -l | more`.

`mkfs [options] device [blocks]`

`mkfs` creates a file system on a diskette previously formatted with `fdformat` or on a hard disk partitioned with `fdisk`. `mkfs` can only be executed by `root`. Depending on the file system specified, the program calls up one of the programs `mkfs.minix` or `mke2fs`, `mkxfs`. When an MS-DOS file system is to be created on a diskette, the `mformat` command must be used instead of `mkfs`.

`-t` *`file_system`*

specifies the type of file system. Currently supported file systems are `minix` (default setting), `ext2` (standard Linux file system) and `xias` (as an alternative to `ext2`). When the `-t` option is not specified, `mkfs` tries to determine the file system by looking through `/etc/fstab`. The `-t` option must be specified as the first option!

Options for `mke2fs`

Further options are passed to the program that actually creates the file system. Therefore, they depend on the type of file system. Here, we only present options for `mke2fs`, which is used most frequently. The internals of this file system are described on page 107. The options of the other `mkfs` programs are described on the corresponding `man` pages.

`-b` *n*

specifies the block size (default: 1024 bytes). *n* must be a power of 2 greater than or equal to 1024 (that is, 1024, 2048, 4096, and so on).

`-c` executes a check for bad blocks on the data support prior to creating the file system.

`-i` *n*

specifies after how many bytes an I-node is created. The default setting is 4096, which means that 256 I-nodes are created for a total capacity of 1 Mbyte. (Thus, a maximum of 256 files plus directories can be stored, independently of how small the files are.) The minimum value for *n* is 1024. The choice of a value greater than 4096 carries the implication that more space is available for actual data. However, when a large number of very small files is to be stored, the available I-nodes may well be too few.

`-m` *n*

specifies what percentage of the data support is to be reserved for `root` data (default: 5 per cent).

Example

```
root#  mkfs -t ext2 /dev/fd0
mke2fs 0.5a, 5-Apr-94 for EXT2 FS 0.5, 94/03/10
360 inodes, 1440 blocks
72 blocks (5.00%) reserved for the super user
First data block=1
Block size=1024 (log=0)
Fragment size=1024 (log=0)
1 block group
8192 blocks per group, 8192 fragments per group
360 inodes per group
```

```
Writing inode tables: done
Writing superblocks and filesystem accounting information: done
```

The above command creates an `ext2` file system on a diskette previously formatted with `fdformat`.

`mknod device_file {bc} major_number minor_number`

`mknod` creates a new device file. Usually, device files are located in the `/dev` directory and are used to manage the hardware accessed under Linux (hard disks, interfaces, RAM, and so on). Device files are characterized by three items of information: the `major` and `minor` device numbers specify the driver with which the device can be accessed. The characters `b` or `c` specify whether the device works buffered or unbuffered. Creation of new device files can only be carried out by `root` and assumes a basic knowledge of Linux internals.

A detailed description of all devices and the required device numbers can be found in the file `/usr/src/linux/Documentation/devices.txt`.

Example

```
root#  mknod /dev/sbpcd b 25 0
```

creates a device file for a CD-ROM drive of the types Matsushita, Panasonic and CreativLabs. (These rather obsolete first-generation CD-ROM drives are not addressed via the standardized EIDE interface, but via a proprietary interface.)

`mkswap device/file`

`mkswap` sets up a device (a hard disk partition) or a file as a swap area. `mkswap` can only be executed by `root`. In order to allow the newly created swap area to be used, it must subsequently be activated with `swapon`. Now, in case of insufficient RAM, Linux can swap memory into this area.

`mlabel drive`

`mlabel` displays the name (volume label) of the MS-DOS diskette in the specified drive. Subsequently, you are asked to enter a new name and confirm it with [↵].

`mmd directory`

`mmd` creates a new directory on an MS-DOS diskette.

`more file`

`more` displays the contents of a text file page by page. After each page, the display is interrupted, and `more` waits for keyboard input. The most important key commands are [↵] (one line down), [Spacebar] (one page down), [B] (one page up) and [Q] (quit).

Further keyboard commands are described on the `man` page for `more`. The most important options when calling `more` are:

`-s` displays only one empty line even when several consecutive empty lines occur in the text.

`+`*`line_number`*
starts the display with the specified line number.

`+\`*`text`*
starts the display with the first occurrence of the specified search text.

A related command is `less` (see page 462), a more powerful command than `more`. For example, `less` allows backward scrolling even when it is used as a filter.

Example

```
user$  ls -l | more
```

displays the contents of the current directory page by page. The example shows the use of `more` as a filter program.

```
mount
mount [options] device directory
```

`mount` mounts a data resource (hard disk, diskette, CD ...) into the Linux file system. As parameters, the device name of the data resource (for example, `/dev/cdrom`, see pages 37 or 102) must be specified together with the directory (mount point) in which the file system of the data resource is to be linked into the current file system. Calling the command without parameters displays a list of all currently available data resources.

The structure of the file system at the start of Linux is controlled through the file `/etc/fstab`. The data in this file essentially corresponds to the parameters of `mount` (see also page 147).

For all drives registered in `/etc/fstab`, `mount` can be used in an abbreviated form in which only the device or the mount directory is specified. `mount` then reads the missing data and options directly from `fstab`.

`umount` is used to remove data resources from the file system (see page 488). Both `mount` and `umount` can usually only be executed by `root`, but drives registered in `fstab` with the option `user` are an exception. (This is commonly the case with CD-ROM drives.)

`-r` prevents writing operations on the data resource (read only).

`-t` *`file_system`*
specifies the file system. Some of the possible options are `ext2` (for Linux hard disks (or partitions)), `msdos` for MS-DOS data resources, `vfat` for the Windows 95 file system with long file names, `hpfs` for data resources in the OS/2 file system (read only) and `iso9660` for CDs.

A more extensive discussion of `mount` options can be found in the context of the description of `/etc/fstab` on page 147.

Examples

```
root# mount -r -t msdos /dev/hda3 /dos
```

allows files to be read from a DOS partition. The partition is accessed via the `/dos` directory.

```
root# mount /cdrom
```

mounts the CD-ROM drive into the file system. The command presumes that the remaining parameters for the CD-ROM drive are present in `/etc/fstab`.

```
root# mount -t iso9660 -r /dev/mcd /cdrom
```

as above, but this time with all parameters for an old Mitsumi CD-ROM drive (in case the `fstab` entry is missing).

`mrd directory`

`mrd` deletes the specified directory from the MS-DOS diskette (only if it is empty).

`mread dos_file linux_file`

`mread` copies the specified file from the MS-DOS diskette into the Linux file system. The command is a restricted variation of `mcopy` which allows copying in both directions.

`mren old_name new_name`

`mren` renames a file on an MS-DOS diskette.

`mt [-f device] command`

`mt` is used for the control of streamers. The default device is `/dev/tape`. If your streamer cannot be accessed under this name, you must specify the device file exactly (for example, `-f /dev/nst0` for a SCSI streamer). The most frequent applications of `mt` are the rewinding of tapes with the command `rewind` and the ejection of tapes with `offline`. `setblk` can be used to modify the block size, and `stat` displays status information about the streamer settings.

An overview of further commands can be found in the `man` pages for `mt` or `mt-st` (Slackware). Background information is contained in `st_info.txt` or `mt-st`; one of these files is normally installed together with `mt`.

There are two `mt` variations: one GNU and one BSD. Most distributions automatically supply the BSD variation. The GNU variation lacks many commands of its BSD counterpart.

`mtools`

`mtools` is a program which allows easy and problem-free access to MS-DOS format diskettes. The `mtools` commands (such as `mattrib`, `mdir`, and so on) are realized through links to the central program `mtools`. `mtools` itself cannot be executed directly, but only through these links. (This chapter describes neither all of the `mtools` commands nor all of the options. Please consult the extensive online documentation.)

In principle, MS-DOS diskettes can be mounted into the file system in the same way as all other drives, using `mount`, but this is more laborious than using the the `mtools` commands (see also page 104).

The `mtools` commands have some features in common: drive specifications are the same as under DOS, that is, `A:` or `B:`. When no drive is specified, the commands automatically access `A:` or the working directory specified through `mcd`. In path specifications, directories can be separated with both `/` and `\`. The wildcard `*` functions as under Unix, which means that `*` (and not `*.*`) must be specified in order to process all files. File names are restricted to the DOS conventions (eight plus three characters).

The configuration file for `mtools` is `/etc/mtools`. If you have problems using the `mtools` commands, you can set the correct drive type there. As a rule, however, no modifications to the configuration file will be necessary.

`mtype file`

`mtype` displays a text file from an MS-DOS diskette on screen. The command essentially corresponds to the Unix command `cat`.

`mv source target`
`mv files target_directory`

`mv` renames a file or moves (one or more) files to a different directory. The effect of `mv` is essentially the same as that of the `cp` command, when after copying the source files are deleted. The most important options are:

`-b` or `--backup`
: renames already existing homonymous files as backup files (name plus ~), instead of overwriting them.

`-i` or `--interactive`
: asks for confirmation before overwriting existing files.

Example

```
user$  mv *~ backup
```

moves all backup files in the current directory (that is, all files whose names end with ~) into the `backup` subdirectory.

`mwrite linux_file dos_file`

`mwrite` copies the specified file from the Linux file system onto an MS-DOS diskette. The command is a restricted variation of `mcopy`, which allows copying in both directions.

`nice [options] program`

`nice` starts the specified program with reduced or increased priority. The command is normally used to start programs that are not too time-critical (background programs) with a low priority in order not to affect the rest of the system too adversely.

`+/- n`

sets the `nice` value. As standard (that is, without `nice`) programs are started with a `nice` value of 0. A value of –20 means highest priority, a value of +19 lowest priority. Values less than 0 can only be specified by `root`, that is, most users can only use `nice` to start programs with reduced priority. Without this option, `nice` starts the program with a nice value of +10.

`nl [options] file`

`nl` numbers all non-empty lines of the specified text file. By setting the various options, numbering can be obtained page by page, for headers and footers, and so forth.

`passwd [user_name]`

`passwd` without parameters allows the password of the current user to be changed. First the old password must be entered, then the new password twice in succession. The new password is registered in encrypted form in the `/etc/passwd` file. Each user has the right to modify his/her own password. However, the password must be at least six characters long and it must contain either digits or both upper and lower case letters.

When `passwd` is called with a user name, that user's password can be altered. This `passwd` variation can only be called by `root`. The old password does not have to be specified, that is, `root` can change the password even if the user has forgotten his/her password. The above restrictions do not apply to `root`, that is, `root` can define a password consisting of a single character. However, not even `root` is allowed to specify no password at all (that is, to enter nothing but ↵).

If you want the password to be skipped altogether for specific users (for example, `guest`), you can (as `root`) delete the password data from the text file `/etc/passwd`. The data is located between the first and second colons, that is, immediately after the user name.

`paste file1 file2 ...`

`paste` combines the lines of the specified files into new (longer) lines and displays the result on screen. Thus, the first line of the resulting text is composed of the first line of the first file plus the first line of the second file, and so on. The components of the new lines are separated by tab characters. With `> target_file`, the result can be stored in a file.

`printenv`

`printenv` displays all environment variables. Environment variables depend on the current shell. The shell variables of the `bash` can be displayed with `set`.

`ps [options]`

`ps` displays a list of running processes (programs). This command is particularly useful in connection with `kill`, in order to terminate hanging programs by force (see page 462). `ps` is equipped with countless options which are extensively described in the online manual (`man ps`). There, you can also find explanations of the meaning of the vast amount of information output by `ps`.

In contrast to other commands, `ps` options can also be used without the prefixed hyphen (for example `ps ax`, to display all currently running processes). The most important options are:

- `-a` also displays processes of other users.
- `-l` displays various additional information (memory usage, priority, and so on).
- `-m` displays detailed additional information, especially about memory usage.
- `-u` displays a vast amount of additional information, in addition to the process number, such as the names of the users of all processes. This option automatically includes `-a`.
- `-x` also displays processes not associated with any terminal, such as Linux-internal processes for the administration of the system (so-called daemons).

`pstree [options] [pid]`

`pstree` displays on screen a tree of all processes. Such a tree clarifies which process was started by which other process. When a process number is specified, the tree begins at that point (otherwise, it begins with `init`, that is, with the first process executed at system start-up).

`pwd`

`pwd` displays the current directory. `pwd` is not a proper Linux command, but a shell command of the `bash`.

`rdev`

`rdev` allows you to change some bytes in the Linux kernel file (usually `/vmlinuz` or `/zImage`) which control the VGA text mode, the size of the RAM disk and some other settings. When `rdev` is called without parameters, it simply displays the current boot device (that is, the name of the hard disk partition on which the directory tree starts with the root directory `/`).

Many of the kernel settings can also be controlled via LILO (VGA mode, root device, and so on). This is more transparent and thus to be preferred. Therefore, the use of `rdev` only makes sense when the kernel is to be transferred directly (without LILO) onto a boot diskette.

`kernel_file device`
: changes the root device of the kernel file.

`-R` *`kernel_file`* `1`
: mounts the file system as read-only at first, so that during booting a file system check can be carried out.

`-v` *`kernel_file`* *n*
: sets the VGA mode. The following values are permitted for n: `-1` for standard VGA mode (80×25 characters), `-2` for extended VGA mode (80×50 characters), `-3` for a request for the desired mode during the boot process, or a value greater than 0 to set that particular mode of the VGA card.

Example

```
user#  cp /vmlinuz /dev/fd0
user#  rdev /dev/fd0 /dev/hda3
user#  rdev -R /dev/fd0 1
```

The above commands create a boot diskette: the kernel file `/vmlinuz` is copied onto an empty diskette. `/dev/hda3` is set as the partition for the root directory. Starting the Linux system from this boot diskette will only succeed when the root directory is in fact contained in this partition (see also page 30).

`reboot [options]`

`reboot` terminates all running processes and subsequently restarts the computer. When the computer is in runlevels 1 to 5, `shutdown` is called for this purpose.

`recode charset1:charset2 file`
`recode charset1:charset2 < source > target`

`recode` carries out a character set conversion from character set 1 to character set 2. `recode` knows an extensive list of character sets which can be viewed with `recode -l`. `recode` does not belong to the standard system in all Linux distributions.

Example

```
user$  recode ibmpc:latin1 < dosfile > linuxfile
```

converts all end-of-line and foreign language characters in the file `dosfile` into the character set ISO Latin 1 used under Linux. The result is stored in `linuxfile`.

`reset`

`reset` restores the character set mapping which was destroyed by the output of special characters on the screen. `reset` also resets the terminal settings to the default setting previously stored with `setterm -store`. `reset` should be executed every time strange symbols suddenly appear on screen instead of letters and digits. If `reset` does not help, `setfont` or `restorefont` must be executed.

`restorefont -w file`
`restorefont -r file`

`restorefont -w` stores the currently valid VGA character set in a file. When the command is used with the `-r` option, this file can be read in again in order to restore a destroyed character set (normally caused by the X system). `restorefont` can only be executed in a text console and not under X.

Remember in which file you have stored the character set. If one day X really destroys your character set, you must be able to enter the command blindly. An even better idea is to write a small shell script (for example, `newfont`) which carries out this call. Copy this file into `/usr/bin` and set the x bit for all users. As an alternative to `restorefont` you can call `setfont` in order to load one of the predefined character sets.

`restorepalette`

`restorepalette` restores the VGA color palette for the text mode. With some VGA cards, this can become necessary after switching between X and a text console. `restorepalette` can only be executed in a text console and not under X.

`rm [options] file`

`rm` deletes the specified files. Provided that the `-r` option is not used, directories are not deleted. If you want to delete single directories, you must use the `rmdir` command (see below). When files whose names contain special characters are to be deleted, the file names must be enclosed in single quotes. The most important options of `rm` are:

`-f` deletes without asking for confirmation (including directories). Caution!

`-i` or `--interactive` or `-v` or `--verbose`
displays a request for confirmation prior to the deletion of each single file.

`-r` or `-R` or `--recursive`
: also deletes files in all subdirectories (warning!). When the entire contents of a subdirectory are deleted, the subdirectory itself is deleted as well.

Examples

```
user$  rm *~
```

deletes all backup files (files whose names end with ~) in the current directory.

```
user$  rm -r backup
```

deletes the file or the directory `backup`. When `backup` is a directory, all subdirectories and files contained in it are deleted too!

```
user$  rm '#'*
```

deletes all files whose names begin with the symbol `#`. The quotes are necessary to prevent the shell from interpreting the `#` character as a comment.

`rmdir [options] directory`

`rmdir` deletes the specified directory. `rmdir` can only be executed when the directory is empty. Any existing files must previously be deleted with `rm` (if necessary, using the `-r` option). The most important option is:

`-p` or `--parents`
: also deletes subdirectories in the specified directory (provided that the directories do not contain any files).

`sed [options] command [< source > target]`

`sed` is a so-called stream editor. The command is normally used as a text filter to find and process (delete, substitute with other characters, and so on) given characters or character combinations in the source text. `sed` is controlled by commands which are applied either to all lines of the text or only to lines that satisfy given conditions. Unfortunately, handling `sed` is rather complicated and, because of the many special characters, completely unsystematic. For these reasons, we will do without a detailed description and simply give two examples:

```
user$  sed 1,3d < test
```

deletes the first to third lines of the file `test` and displays the rest of the file on screen (standard output). Here, `d` stands for the `sed` command *delete*. `1,3` specifies the address range to which this command is applied.

```
user$  sed s/a/A/ < test
```

replaces every 'a' with 'A'. Here, `s` stands for the command *regular find and replace*. The texts enclosed in `/` are the search pattern and the replacement text. Since no address range is specified, the command is applied to all lines.

`set`

`set` displays all variables known to the shell (including the environment variables which can also be displayed with `printenv`). `set -x` causes the `bash` to display, prior to the execution of each command, the internal command line after resolution of `alias` abbreviations and file name expansion. `set` is not a Linux command, but a command of the `bash` shell.

`setfont charset`

`setfont` reads a character set file from the `/usr/lib/kbd/consolefonts` directory and activates this character set in the VGA text mode. `setfont` cannot be used under X. Usable character sets are `default8x16` (for 25-line text mode) and `default8x9` (for 50-line text mode).

`setterm [option]`

`setterm` allows you to modify various terminal settings. When the command is executed without specifying an option, it displays a list of all possible options. Important options are:

`-blank n`
: activates the screen saver after *n* minutes without input activity.

`-clear`
: clears the screen.

`-inversescreen on` or `off`
: inverts the screen display (black text on a white background) or reverts to the normal setting.

Some additional options which are of interest in shell programming (changes to letter types, and so on) are described on page 432.

`shutdown [options] time [message]`

`shutdown` is the safest way to terminate Linux. You must specify either a time of day (hh:mm), the number of minutes from the current time of day onward (`+m`) or the keyword `now` (that is, immediately). `shutdown` can only be executed by `root`. Often Linux is configured in such a way that users without `root` privileges can restart the computer with Alt+Ctrl+Del.

`shutdown` informs all other users that the system is going to be shut down shortly and will no longer allow new logins. Subsequently, all processes are warned that they will be stopped shortly. Some programs (such as `emacs`, `vi` ...) react to this warning by saving all open files in backup copies.

`-c` aborts an already started `shutdown` process (provided this is still possible).

`-f` same as `-r`, but faster.

`-h` after closing down the system, it is halted, that is, it no longer reacts to any input. The screen displays the message 'system halted'. Subsequently, the computer can be switched off.

`-n` carries out the shutdown particularly quickly (bypassing the Init-V processes).

`-r` after closing down the system, a restart is carried out.

`-t` *`seconds`*
specifies the time between the warning message and the kill signal for the processes (default: 20 seconds).

Example

```
root#  shutdown -h -t 3 now
```

closes down the system with lightning speed. When you choose this `shutdown` variation, no text editors or other programs with unsaved files should be running, as a time of three seconds is often not sufficient to make safety backups.

`sort [options] file`

`sort` sorts the specified file and displays the result on screen. Foreign language special characters are not sorted lexically correctly (but by their character codes, that is, they appear after all other letters). `sort` can be controlled with a large number of options, of which only the most important are described here.

`-c` checks whether the file is sorted or not.

`-f` treats upper and lower case letters as equivalent.

`-m` merges two or more presorted files into one large sorted file. This is faster than joining the files first and sorting them afterwards.

`-o` *`result_file`*
writes the result into the specified file. This file may be the file to be sorted.

`-r` sorts in reverse order.

`-ts` specifies the separator character between two columns (the default is 'white space', that is, an arbitrary mixture of space and tab characters).

`+n1 [-n2]`
only considers the characters between the *n1*th (inclusive) and the *n2*th (exclusive) column. Column numbering starts with 0! Columns are normally separated by space or tab characters, but see `-t`. When *n2* is not specified, all characters from *n1* up to the end of line are considered.

The command `sort file > file` does not have the desired effect, but leads to `file` being deleted. When you want to redirect the result of the `sort` command into a file, you must either specify a different file name than the name of the file to be sorted or use the option `-o`. `sort` does not deal accurately with foreign language special characters.

Example

```
user$  ls -l | sort +2
```

sorts the contents list passed by `ls` by user and group names. Files with identical user and group names are sorted by size.

`split [options] file [target_file]`

`split` divides the specified file into several single files. Depending on the selected option, the source file is split every *n* bytes, Kbytes or lines. When no target file is specified, the command produces the files `xaa`, `xab`, and so on. When a target file is specified, this file name followed by the character combinations `aa`, `ab`, and so on is used for the resulting file names.

`-n` or `-l n` or `--lines=n`
: splits the source file into single files of *n* lines each.

`-b n` or `--bytes=n`
: splits the source file every *n* bytes. The letters `k` or `m`, when specified after *n*, stand for Kbytes or Mbytes.

`-C n` or `--line-bytes=n`
: same as `-b`, but the files are split at the end of lines and are therefore in most cases a few bytes smaller than *n*.

Examples

```
user$  split -c 1430k backup.tar disk.
```

splits the archive file `backup.tar` into single files of 1430 Kbytes each and names them `disk.aa`, `disk.ab`, and so on. These files can subsequently be stored on diskettes.

```
user$  cat disk.* > total.tar
```

combines the single files back into one complete file.

`su [options] [user]`

`su` (substitute user) without options changes into `root` mode without the laborious logoff and login (but obviously with password input). Thus, `root` becomes the active user until the next `exit` command.

Optionally, a different user than the default user `root` can be specified with `su`. When `su` is executed by `root`, it is not even necessary to enter a password when changing users.

`-l` or `--login`
: at the change of users, all login files are read. This is required for a proper configuration of `PATH`.

`sum file`

`sum` calculates a 16-bit checksum and determines the number of blocks the file occupies on the hard disk (see also `cksum` on page 446).

`swapoff device`

`swapoff` deactivates the specified swap file or hard disk partition (see `swapon`).

`swapon device`

`swapon` activates the specified device (usually a hard disk partition), or the file specified instead of it, as a swap area. The partition or file must previously have been formatted with `mkswap` as a swap area. `swapon` is automatically executed at Linux startup for all swap areas listed in `/etc/fstab`. The command can only be executed by `root`. The correct setting of `fstab` in the context of system configuration is described on page 147.

`sync`

Executes all buffered write operations on all hard disks. When an orderly termination of Linux is not possible, that is, when the commands `shutdown`, `reboot` and `halt` can no longer be executed and the computer does not react to Ctrl+Alt+Del, `sync` should be executed immediately before switching off. This is, however, only an emergency solution!

`tac file`

`tac` displays the specified text file on screen in reverse order, that is, last line first (see also `cat` on page 443).

`tail [options] file`

`tail` displays the last ten lines of a text file on screen.

`-n` *`lines`*
: displays the specified number of lines.

`-f`
: reads the file at regular intervals and displays all new lines. In this form, `tail` is particularly useful for viewing log files.

Example

```
root#  tail -f /var/log/messages
```

displays the last ten lines of `messages`. When new lines are added, these are displayed as well (so that after a short time the whole screen is used – not just ten lines).

```
tar action [options] files
tar action [options] directories
```

`tar` combines several files or whole directories into a so-called archive and extracts their components out of the archive again. Originally, `tar` was designed as a tool for reading and writing data on a streamer. Therefore, as standard, `tar` accesses the installed streamer (usually `/dev/tape` or `/dev/rmt0`). When you want to create an archive in a file (for example, in order to save this file subsequently on a diskette) you must specify the option `-f` *`file`*.

Since `tar` also compresses the files to be archived with `compress` or `gzip`, depending on the options, its functionality can be compared with typical compression programs under DOS (for example, LHA). Its main application – apart from saving data onto streamers – is to pack several files or directories into a handy file which is as small as possible. Practically all Linux CDs contain archive files created in this way.

The typical extension for archive files is `.tar`. When the archive file is compressed, extensions are usually named `.tgz`, `.tpz` or `.tar.gz`.

`tar` is controlled in two steps: first, an action must be specified for `tar` to carry out, and second, this action can in turn be controlled by one or more options. Even though actions and options look the same, there is an essential difference: exactly one (no more and no less) action must be specified before all other options. All actions are briefly described in the next few lines, but only the most important options are listed (see `man` pages). If you do not want to be bothered with the countless `tar` options, the program `xtar` provides a user-friendly interface for the most important commands.

On many Unix systems the control of `tar` is (mostly) carried out with the same commands and options, but their syntax is different: all commands and options are specified in one block, without the usual option hyphens, for example `tar cvf name.tar path`. GNU `tar` also understands this syntax.

Actions

`-A` or `--catenate` or `--concatenate`
: appends a further archive to an existing archive. Only suited for streamers (not for archive files).

`-c` or `--create`
: creates a new archive, that is, any existing archive is overwritten.

`-d` or `--diff` or `--compare`
: compares the files of the archive with the files of the current directory and detects possible discrepancies.

`-r` or `--append`
: extends the archive with additional files.

`--delete`
: deletes files from the archive. Only suited for archive files (not for streamers).

`-t` or `--list`
: displays the contents list of the archive.

`-u` or `--update`
extends the archive with new or modified files. This option cannot be used for compressed archives. Caution: the archive will get larger and larger, because already existing files are not overwritten! The new files are simply appended to the end of the archive.

`-x` or `--extract`
extracts the specified files from the archive and copies them into the current directory. The files are not deleted from the archive.

Options

`-C` *`directory`*
extracts the files into the specified (instead of the current) directory.

`-f` *`file`*
uses the specified file as the archive (instead of accessing the streamer).

`-I` compresses or uncompresses the whole archive with `bzip2`. See also `-z`.

`-L` *`n`* or `--tape-length` *`n`*
specifies the capacity of the streamer in Kbytes. When the size of the archive exceeds the capacity, `tar` requests the magnetic tape to be changed.

`-N` *`date`* or `--after-date` *`date`* or `--newer` *`date`*
only archives files which are more recent than the specified date.

`-T` *`file`* or `--files-from` *`file`*
archives or extracts the file names specified in the file.

`-v` or `--verbose`
displays all file names on screen during processing. When `-v` is used in combination with the `t` command, additional information about the files is displayed (file size, and so on).When the option is specified twice, the information becomes even more extensive.

`-W` or `--verify`
checks the correctness of the archived files immediately after writing. Cannot be used for compressed archives.

`-z` or `--gzip`
compresses or uncompresses the whole archive with `gzip`. This option is very useful for creating `*.tgz` files, but if data is actually to be stored on a streamer, this option may be dangerous:

One single error on the tape can invalidate the whole archive. (Files are destroyed even without compression, but usually the damage is much more limited.) DAT streamers are themselves capable of compressing the data to be processed (this is faster, but not as efficient as `gzip`). The `-z` option is incompatible with the `tar` versions of most other Unix dialects.

Examples

```
user$  tar -cv text/book
```

stores all files in the current directory and its subdirectories on the default streamer and displays the stored files on screen.

```
user$  tar -cvf /dev/nst0 text/book
```

as above, but for the streamer connected to `/dev/nst0` (in case the default streamer of `tar` does not correspond to your streamer).

Generally, you should always specify a path when creating archives. This makes unpacking easier later on (because the files are automatically extracted into subdirectories, which avoids possible disorder in the current directory).

```
user$  tar -czf book.tgz text/book
```

archives all files of the directory `text/book` and all subdirectories in the compressed file `book.tgz`.

```
user$  find . -mtime 7 -print > /tmp/lastweek
user$  tar -cT /tmp/lastweek
```

stores on tape all files that have been modified during the past week.

```
user$  tar -tzf backup.tgz
```

displays all files in the archive.

```
user$  tar tIf linux-2.2.0-pre7.tar.bz2
```

displays all files of a Linux archive compressed with `bzip2`.

```
user$  tar -xzf backup.tgz
```

extracts the archive into the current directory.

Always look into your archives with `tar -t` before unpacking them. By doing so, you will establish whether path information is stored in the archive and where the files are going to be installed. Thus, you can create a new directory and change to this directory before you run `tar -x`, or you can use the `-C` option to prevent the uncontrolled writing of files in your local directory.

```
user$  tar -xzf backup.tgz -C /tst
```

extracts the archive into the directory `tst`.

```
user$  tar xzfC backup.tgz /tst
```

as above, in an alternative notation.

```
user$  tar -xzf backup.tgz '*.tex'
```

only extracts `*.tex` files from the archive. Please note the quotes for the search pattern which prevent immediate evaluation by the shell!

```
root#  (cd /dir1 ; tar cf - .) | (cd /dir2 ; tar xvf -)
```

copies all files from `/dir1` to `/dir2`. The advantage as opposed to a normal `cp` command is that symbolic links are copied as such (and not the data pointed to by the links). The above command is particularly useful for transferring whole directory trees from one partition to another.

DAT data exchange between different Unix systems

The exchange of DAT streamer tapes read and written on different Unix systems often causes problems (there is no sign of a standard!). The following paragraphs give some hints which are in part the result of the author's own experience, and in part based on relevant articles found in Linux newsgroups.

The most probable cause of errors is the number of blocks (option `-b`) which must match when reading and writing. It would appear that the `tar` commands in every Unix variation use a different number of blocks as their default setting. In GNU `tar`, the default setting is `-b 20`. You may also have to change the default setting of the streamer with `mt setblk n`. On some Unix systems, besides the manufacturer's original `tar`, you will also find an installation of GNU-`tar`, which in this case often must be addressed as `gtar`.

If nothing helps, there are still other ways of exchanging data via a DAT tape. One variation consists in using the `cpio` command. Still one level below, we find the `dd` command, that is, for writing you use `dd if=`*`file`*` of=/dev/`*`streamer`*, for reading `dd if=`*`streamer`*` of=/dev/`*`file`*. With the `dd` option `conv=swap`, you can even invert the byte order, if necessary.

If you do not want to do without `tar`, you can also use pipes. Then, the command for writing data to a DAT tape looks like this:

```
root#  tar -cvf - data | dd obs=10240 of=/dev/tapedevice
```

For reading you use:

```
root#  dd ibs=10240 if=/dev/tapedevice | tar -xvf -
```

SGI

For writing of data on an SGI system, it has proven useful to address the device `tps0d3ns` directly; `tar cvBf /dev/rmt/tps0d3ns files`. To be able to subsequently read the data under Linux, you must first set the block size to 512: `mt setblk 512`. Now `tar` should function without further problems.

```
tee file
```

`tee` duplicates the standard input, displaying one copy and saving the other copy in a file. In practice, this is useful when the output of a command is to be viewed on screen but simultaneously also saved in a file. A simple redirection into a file with `>` would result in nothing being seen on screen.

Example

```
user$  ls -l | tee contents
```

displays the contents list of the current directory and simultaneously stores it in the file `contents`.

```
todos file
todos < source > target
```

`todos` appends a carriage return character to each of the lines of the specified text file. Thus, the text file can be processed under DOS as usual (see also `fromdos` on page 458 and `recode` on page 476).

`top [q]`

Every five seconds, `top` displays a list of all running processes, with the processes listed in the order of their share of CPU time. When the optional parameter `q` is specified, `top` continuously updates the list and takes up the whole of the remaining CPU time. Pressing [Q] terminates the program. If at all possible, the program should be executed in its own terminal (window).

`touch [options] files`

`touch` changes the time and date of the last modification stored with the file. When the command is used without options, the current time is stored. If the file does not yet exist, a new file of 0 bytes is created.

`-d` *`time`*
: stores the specified time (date and time of day).

`-r` *`file`*
: uses the stored modification time and date of the specified file.

`tr [options] cs1 [cs2] [ < source > target]`

`tr` substitutes all characters of character string 1 in the specified source file with the corresponding characters of character string 2. The character strings should be of equal length. Characters that do not occur in the first character string remain unchanged. It is not possible to replace a single character with several characters (for example, ö with `"o`) – for this purpose, commands such as `recode` or `sed` must be used.

`-d` the characters specified in character string 1 are deleted. Character string 2 does not have to be specified.

Example

```
user$  tr a-z A-Z < text.lin
```

replaces all lower case letters in `text.lin` with upper case letters.

`tty`

`tty` displays the device name of the terminal (`/dev/tty1` to `tty6` for the text consoles, `/dev/ttyp`*`n`* for X shell windows).

`tune2fs [options] device`

With `tune2fs`, various system parameters of an ext2 file system can be modified at later times.

`-c` *n*

specifies after how many `mount` operations the partition is to be checked for errors during booting (`mke2fs` default: 20 `mount` operations). If you start and stop Linux once (or several times) per day, it is sensible to specify a slightly higher value. Thus you avoid that every couple of days a time-consuming integrity check of your data is carried out.

`-i` *n*

specifies how often (in days) the partition is to be checked for errors during booting (`mke2fs` default: 180 days).

`-m` *n*

specifies how many per cent of the data resource are to be reserved for `root` data (`mke2fs` default: 5 per cent).

The command must only be applied to partitions which are currently not mounted into the file system! Do not forget to execute `umount` beforehand! (For changing the root partition, you will need to boot the computer with an emergency or installation diskette.)

`type` `command`

`type` determines whether the specified command is a shell command (for example, `cd`) or an `alias` abbreviation. The message 'command is hashed' means that the command is a Linux command already executed during the current session and that the `bash` has stored its path name in a hash table (see also `hash` on page 461). `type` is a `bash` command, so that `type type` leads to the message 'type is shell builtin'.

`umount` `device`
`umount` `directory`

`umount` removes a data resource from the Linux file system. The data resource is specified either by its device name or by the directory in which it is mounted into the file system. The command can only be executed by `root`. An error message is displayed if there are still open files on the specified data resource (see also `mount` on page 471).

`unalias` `abbreviation`

`unalias` deletes the specified abbreviation. `unalias` is a `bash` command. The usage of abbreviations is described in more detail on page 391.

`uname` `[options]`

`uname` displays the name of the operating system (that is, Linux). Through the specification of options, other information can be displayed as well.

`-a` displays all available information, namely operating system, version number, date and time, plus the processor (for example, i486).

`uncompress file`

`uncompress` uncompresses a file previously compressed with `compress`. The extension `.Z` is automatically removed. `uncompress` is a link to `compress`, with the `-d` option activated automatically.

`uniq file`

`uniq` displays the lines of a text file on the standard output, eliminating consecutive identical lines. In presorted files, `uniq` eliminates all lines occurring more than once.

Example

```
user$  sort test | uniq > test1
```

sorts the file `test`, eliminates duplicate lines and stores the result in `test1`.

`wc files`

`wc` counts the number of lines, words and characters in the specified files. When several files are specified using wildcards, `wc` also calculates the total number of lines, words and characters. `wc` is well suited for combining with other programs.

Example

```
user$  find / -type f -print | wc
```

displays the total number of all files. (`find` supplies one line for each regular file, then `wc` counts the lines.)

`whatis file`

`whatis` gives a brief description (usually one line) of the specified command or keyword. `whatis` descriptions only exist for subjects for which `man` texts are installed. When `whatis` does not work, this is probably due to missing databases, which can be generated with `makewhatis` (see page 71).

`whereis file`

`whereis` searches all 'usual' paths for binary files, `man` files and source code for the specified file name. `whereis` is less thorough than `find`, but significantly faster. The `man` page for `whereis` lists the directories that are searched.

`which command`

`which` searches all paths specified in `PATH` for the command. As an answer, `which` supplies the complete name of the command that would be executed at a command input. This can be of great help when several versions of a command exist in different directories.

```
who [options]
```

`who` displays a list of all currently logged in system users. (Even when you work alone on your computer, you can still log on under different names on different text consoles.)

`-m` displays the user name of the currently active console. The command `who am i` has the same meaning.

```
write username
```

`write` allows you to send a message to another user. After the execution of the command, all characters entered up to Ctrl+D are sent to the terminal of the other user.

```
zcat file.gz
zless file.gz
zmore file.gz
```

These three commands function in the same way as `cat`, `less` and `more`. The only difference is that files compressed with `gzip` can be read directly (without prior decompression with `gunzip`). This is particularly useful when the files are located on a CD-ROM.

`less` can be configured in such a way that it can be used for both compressed and non-compressed files (see page 139).

Tools and utilities

This chapter describes a number of small programs without which day-to-day work with Linux would be practically unthinkable. The main difference with the commands introduced in Chapter 14 lies in their handling: most of the programs introduced here are provided with a user interface; thus, control is carried out interactively and not by means of countless options.

The spectrum covered by this chapter is fairly wide:

- X utilities (`xterm`, `xclock`, `xcalc`, and so on)
- file managers
- programs for conversion of documents and graphics between various formats (DVI, PS, HTML, data exchange between DOS and Linux)
- programs for display of documents and graphics
- program for generating screenshots
- terminal emulators (`minicom`, `seyon`)
- programs for writing CD-ROMs

Reference

Commands such as `ls` or `cp` are not described in this chapter – see Chapter 14. Furthermore, all Internet tools have been left out – see Chapters 9 and 10. Finally, sufficient space for a detailed description has been dedicated to the programs (X)Emacs, LaTeX, LyX and Gimp – see Chapters 16, 18, 19 and 20.

15.1 X utilities

This section lists a few simple X programs. The intention is not so much to give instructions for using such programs, but rather to draw attention to their existence.

`xterm` and other terminal programs

The X program with which you will probably be working most of the time is `xterm`. This is a terminal window in which Linux commands can be executed. You can work with an arbitrary number of terminal windows under X, just as you can work with several text consoles in text mode. If you have executed a command in one window which takes longer than you thought, you can simply use the window manager menu to open a new window.

As opposed to text consoles, `xterm` has the advantage that all input and output is stored over a longer period of time. Thus, you can use the scroll bar to view less recent output again. The scroll bar can be set by means of the following lines in a resource file:

```
xterm*scrollBar:        true
xterm*saveLines:        1000
```

TIP With the Ctrl key kept depressed, the three mouse buttons can be used to call up various menus that allow you to set different properties of `xterm`. For example, you can change the letter size during normal operation.

Obviously, you can also set the required letter size in a resource file. (Other resource settings for support of the Del, Home and End keys have already been described on page 244.)

```
xterm*VT100*font:       9x15
```

`xterm [options]`

When `xterm` is called through script files (for example, `.Xsession` or `xinitrc`) or through `fvwm`, the various command options come into play:

`+cm` activates the ANSI color codes. This is needed to make programs with color display function properly (for example `ls`).

`-e command options`
: executes the specified program in `xterm`. `-e` must be used as the last option.

`-fn charset -fg color -bg color`
: specifies the required letter type together with background and foreground colors.

`-geometry 80x35+100+200`
: starts `xterm` in a size of 35 lines times 80 columns at the pixel coordinates (100/200).

`-ls` when the shell is started in `xterm`, `.profile` is evaluated. This is important to ensure that various `alias` abbreviations, environment variable definitions, and so on are read in.

`-sl` *n*
specifies the number of lines to be stored (same as `saveLines`).

`-title name`
specifies the window title.

TIP If you would like to use all the features of `xterm`, you should read through the `man` pages: the extent of more than 30 pages gives an idea of how far `xterm` is configurable!

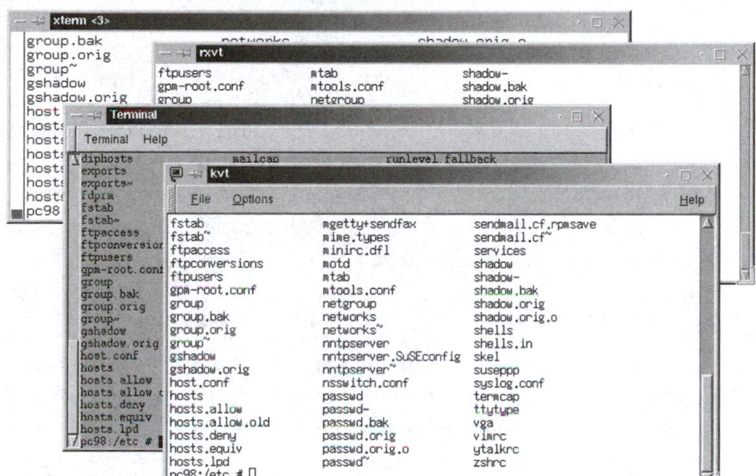

Figure 15.1 At first sight, the terminal variations only differ by different scroll bars.

Apart from `xterm`, several other terminal programs are available under X. In principle, usage is always the same; differences occur in configuration, representation of colored text (`ls`), keyboard shortcuts, memory consumption, and so on.

- `gnome-terminal`: the name says it all; user-friendly configuration
- `kvt`: the KDE variation, equally user-friendly configuration
- `nxterm`: similar to `xterm`, supplied with RedHat
- `rxvt`: optimized with regard to minimum memory consumption

X standard tools (`xclock, xcalc`)

As well as `xterm`, several other programs are traditionally supplied together with the X Windows System. Thus, these programs are available on practically every

Unix/Linux computer, independently from X version, distribution, and so on. Here is a list of the most important tools, in alphabetical order:

xbiff

The program indicates with a letter box symbol whether new mail has arrived.

xcalc

The program simulates a simple scientific pocket calculator. (The KDE variation can be started with `kcalc`; in GNOME, the commands are `gcalc` and `genius`.)

xclock

The program displays the current time of day. As well as the classic `xclock`, there are numerous variations which are mostly known for their extravagant design (such as `xdaliclock`).

xev

The `xev` program is of great help in exploring keyboard management. It opens a new window and subsequently shows all X events (mouse, keyboard, and so on) in the terminal window in which the program was started. This program can also be used to determine which code is assigned to a given key and which corresponding `KeySym` character string is generated by the X system.

xlsfonts

`xlsfonts` displays a list of all available character sets. Similarly to `ls`, the list can be restricted through a search pattern. This pattern must be enclosed in quotes to prevent it from being evaluated by the `bash`:

```
user$  xlsfonts '*24*'
```

xmodmap

The `xmodmap` program can be used to change keyboard assignments for X. This program is useful for getting rid of problems such as differentiation between [Backspace] and [Del] (see page 243).

In this context, the `xkeycaps` program is worth mentioning. Although it is not part of the usual X Window Tools and is therefore lacking in many distributions, it is an incredibly useful program for creating and modifying `xmodmap` configuration files.

xrdb

`xrdb` is used to read in additional resource files. The command is mostly used in the `xinitrc` files for starting the X system. It can also be used to try out changes to an `xresources` file immediately. (Modified resources which are not located in

`~/.Xdefaults` must be reread with `xrdb` – otherwise they only take effect after a restart of X.) `xrdb -query` displays the currently stored resource information.

xset

`xset` is used to change the X server settings. The program can also be used to set the reaction time of the screen saver and the state of NumLock. The following instructions can be entered into the `xinitrc` files used for starting X:

```
user$  xset s 60     # blacken screen after 60 seconds
user$  xset led 3    # switch NumLock on
```

xsetroot

`xsetroot` changes the pattern and/or the color of the X background. As a rule, the program is used with the `-solid` option to define a plain background:

```
user$  xsetroot -solid blue
```

Text display, text editors

Obviously, all editors designed for text mode can also be used under X. In addition, there is a large number of pure X editors:

- `xedit` is characterized by a very austere user interface.
- `xjed` is an X variation of `jed`; however, the advantages against the pure text version are not too great.
- The `asedit` and `axe` editors are less frequently supplied with distributions, but are much more attractive in their handling. `asedit` impresses more with its pretty layout than with its functionality. `axe` excels in outstanding online documentation and good configurability.
- `kedit` and `gedit` are the editors belonging to KDE and GNOME. Their handling (cursor control, selecting, copying and pasting text, and so on) is largely oriented towards the Microsoft Windows standard.

`xless` and `kless` (the KDE variation) are variations of the highly popular `less` command. Their basic advantage is the scroll bar.

System and process control, CPU monitoring

`xosview` displays the most important system load parameters in the form of colored bar graphs: CPU load, memory consumption, swap partition usage, network activity, serial interface status, and interrupt activity. More detailed information on the parameters displayed can be found in the `man` page for `xosview`.

`xsysinfo` is a slimmed-down version of `xosview`. Only CPU load and memory consumption are shown. Only `xcpustate` is even more austere. `xload` finally uses a small diagram to show the number of actively running processes (thus, the CPU load).

GNOME

`logview` helps to keep a clear view of endless log files. `gtop` combines the functions of `ps` and `top`; the program displays information on running processes, their memory and CPU usage, and so on. It also allows you to terminate processes that got out of control.

The mini-programs `cpuload_applet`, `cpumemusage_applet`, `diskusage_applet` and `drivemount_applet` display status information on various system parameters in the GNOME panel.

KDE

`ktop` and `kpm` are KDE variations of `gtop`. `kcpumon` shows the CPU load as an icon in the KDE panel.

15.2 File managers

There is certainly no shortage of file and program managers for X. This section, however, lists only those that have stood the test of daily practice:

- `mc`: Midnight Commander, a professional program with color and mouse support; its handling is similar to Norton Commander. The program is particularly suitable for use in a text console.
- `tkdesk`: file manager written in the Tcl/Tk programming language; very powerful and flexible; however, not part of all distributions.
- `kfm`, `gmc`: these two file managers are part of the KDE and GNOME projects, but can also be employed independently.

Midnight Commander (`mc`)

The Midnight Commander is an easy-to-handle file management tool which strongly resembles the Norton Commander commonly used under DOS, but it is extended with a number of Unix-specific details (handling of links, modification of access rights, processing of `ftp` directories, and so on).

`mc` is menu driven. The program supports the mouse both in text mode (`gpm` must be installed) and under X.

Two half-screen windows each display the files of one directory. You can use either the mouse or Tab to switch between the two windows. The right mouse button is used to highlight files, which can subsequently be deleted, or moved or copied into the opposite window. Many commands can be executed both with the mouse (menu) and with function keys (see status line).

Obviously, you can also use the keyboard to select files: Ins selects/deselects the file under the cursor. + and - (on the numeric keypad) select/deselect a group of files. In order to do this, you must specify a file name pattern (for example, `*.bak`).

Ctrl+S (search) moves the cursor to the first file that matches the specified initial characters.

You can also enter commands via your keyboard in a command line at the bottom of the screen. In this line, you can use Alt+Tab as a keyboard shortcut for the expansion of incomplete file names (the same as Tab in the `bash`). In order to ensure that the results of a command do not stay hidden behind the `mc` user interface, you can temporarily switch this interface off and back on again with Ctrl+O.

Two of the most outstanding features of this program are the display of the directory tree (LEFT | TREE) and the ability to show the size of directories during the standard file view (COMMAND | SHOW DIRECTORY SIZE). Unfortunately, the two views cannot be combined.

Another feature worth mentioning is the possibility of changing file names within COPY or MOVE commands. Unlike standard Unix practice, wildcards are also allowed in the target names, which allows you, for example, to rename all your `*.bak` files as `*.old` files.

In view of the comprehensive online help which you can call up with F1, this short description should be sufficient to whet your appetite. Once you have got used to `mc` (this should take no more than about half an hour), you will never want to do without this program again.

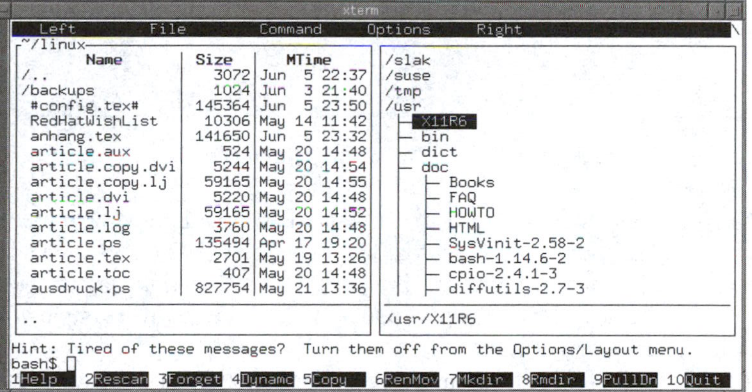

Figure 15.2 The Midnight Commander.

> **TIP** `mc` is particularly suited to view the contents of `*.rpm` packages and of `*.tar` or `*.tgz` archives and to extract individual files. The contents of the archives are represented in the same way as a subdirectory.

Tcl/Tk file manager (`tkdesk`)

`tkdesk` is based on the Tcl/Tk programming language, which means that the correct versions of its libraries must be installed. At program start, a three-level browser window and an icon bar are opened. In the browser window, three directory levels can be represented. The number of directory levels is variable. In addition, an arbitrary number of browser windows can be opened. Inside the directory windows, several colors are used to identify the different file types.

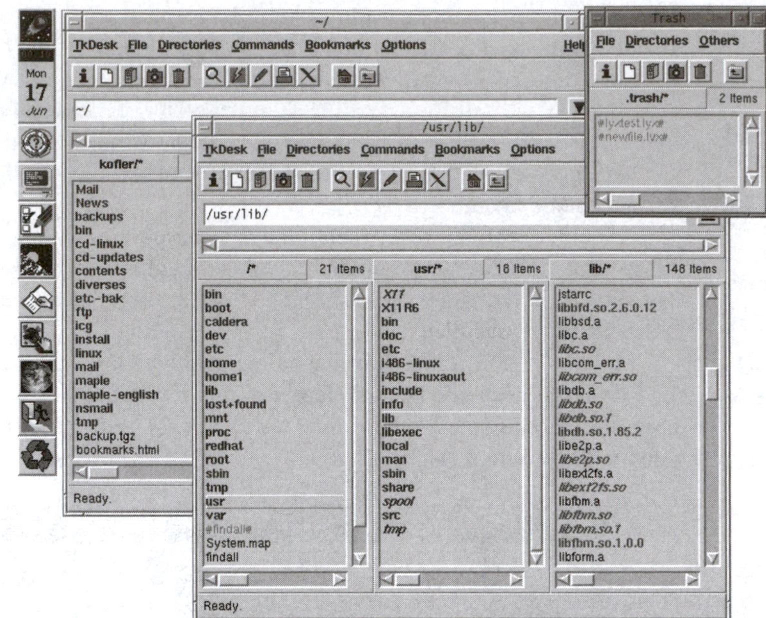

Figure 15.3 The `tkdesk` file manager.

In each directory list, files can be highlighted with the left mouse button. With the middle mouse button, the highlighted files can be moved into another directory, even across browsers (drag and drop). The right mouse button leads to a context menu with various commands. `tkdesk` has its own simple editor which is also used to display text files.

Apart from easy and intuitive handling, `tkdesk` differs from other file managers because of a number of rather special features:

- When files are deleted, they are copied into a trash can which can be emptied separately (via its own window). (Backup copies of homonymous files can, however, be only simply stored.)
- Important directories can be stored as bookmarks as in a WWW browser.
- The DISK USAGE command provides a very clear display of the disk space usage of individual directories.
- `tkdesk` is in practice arbitrarily configurable.
- The file manager is equipped with excellent online help.

The GNOME file manager (`gmc`)

As the name suggests, the GNOME file manager `gmc` is derived from the `mc` program described above. Visually, however, this is no longer apparent – the program has received a very modern user interface which, in many regards, is oriented toward Windows Explorer (for example, in the excellent representation of the directory tree, in the list view of files with various sorting possibilities, and so on.)

However, the version shipped together with GNOME 1.0 is not yet fully mature. One irritating factor is that many operations can only be performed with the mouse (but not via the keyboard). By the time you read this book, a new version will certainly have been released. An update is definitely worthwhile!

Just like `mc`, `gmc` has no problems handling `ftp` directories and displays the contents of `*.rpm` packages, `*.tar` and `*.tgz` archives, and virtual directories.

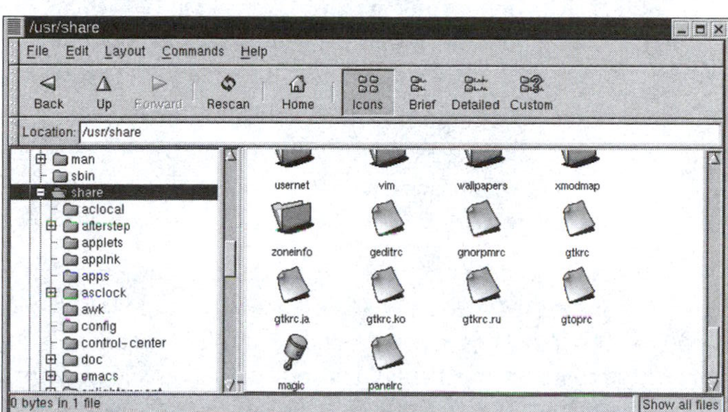

Figure 15.4 The GNOME file manager.

Obviously, `gmc` is interlinked with the other GNOME programs – a double click on a `*.gif` file starts the graphics program `ee`, and so on. (The fact that `ee` is started rather than, for example, `netscape` or `xv`, is due to the MIME settings which specify the connection between file types and programs. You can change these settings in the GNOME control center.)

NOTE `gmc` also takes care of the management of icons on the GNOME desktop (see also the GNOME section from page 290 onward). For this reason, it is usually not very sensible to leave the program with EXIT. If, nevertheless, you do this (instead of just closing the window), you can always restart the file manager with `gmc`.

TIP If you click on a file with the right mouse button, you can display the file (VIEW), modify it (EDIT), and so on. The editor to be used for this purpose can be set in the GNOME control center (Dialog sheet GNOME EDIT PROPERTIES).

The KDE file manager (`kfm`)

`kfm` is the KDE file manager. Files can be represented either as icons or in text format. Handling is practically without problems, although some smaller details are still annoying (such as the lack of sorting possibilities for file lists). If you want to select a file with the mouse without immediately opening it, you need to press Ctrl together with the mouse button. This is easier via the keyboard – simply press Spacebar. Special features of `kfm` are:

- The contents of `tar` archives can be viewed and processed in the same way as a directory.
- With image files, the image contents can be displayed as an icon (VIEW | SHOW THUMBNAILS).
- HTML documents are displayed directly – thus, `kfm` is also a Web browser. Important directories, no matter whether locally on the hard disk or on the Internet, can be marked with bookmarks. (These are stored as `*.kdelink` files in the directory `.kde/share/apps/kfm/bookmarks`.
- When clicking on documents with known file name extensions, the corresponding programs for viewing the contents are automatically started (such as `kview` for images, `kdvi` for `*.dvi` files, and so on.

  New document types can be defined with EDIT | MIME TYPES and FILE | NEW | MIME TYPE. Subsequently, the features need to be specified via the PROPERTIES context menu. A similar procedure is followed for setting up new programs for display and processing of such documents: first EDIT | APPLICATIONS, then FILE | NEW | APPLICATION.

`kfm` keyboard shortcuts

Alt+←	back to previous directory/WWW file
Alt+→	Undo for Alt+←
Alt+↑	one directory level up (`cd ..`)
Ctrl+F	find files
Ctrl+S	select files following a pattern
Ctrl+T	open terminal window for the current directory

TIP

`kfm` should, if possible, be started from within a KDE menu. For a start from outside, you need to use the option `-ws`, thus `kfm -ws`.

TIP

If, as a normal user, you want to execute `kfm` with `root` privileges, you simply execute `kfmsu`. (You need neither exit X nor execute `su`. You are automatically prompted for the `root` password.) `kfm` now shows a red bar next to the menu bar and provides some additional commands (EDIT | GLOBAL MIME TYPES and EDIT | GLOBAL APPLICATIONS).

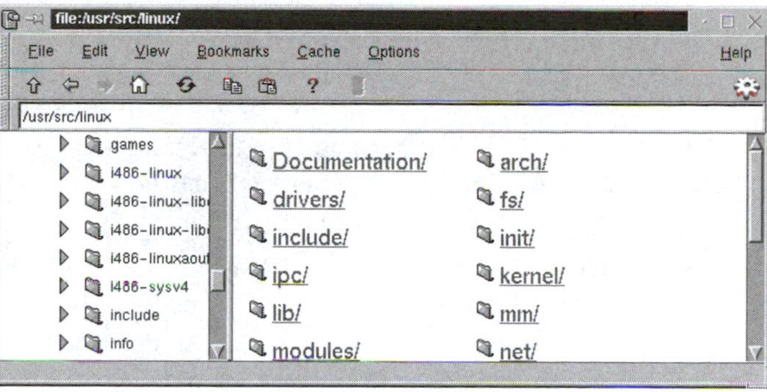

Figure 15.5 The KDE file manager.

`kzip`

`kfm` is very good at handling `tar` archives, but not `zip` archives commonly used under Windows (WinZip, and so on). In such cases, `kzip` comes to the rescue. As with all KDE programs, files can be exchanged between different KDE applications via drag and drop.

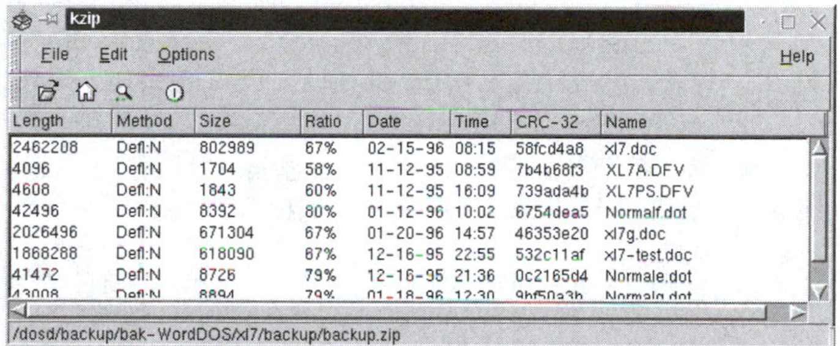

Figure 15.6 Processing Windows ZIP archives.

15.3 Document and graphics conversion

Linux documents and graphics are present in the most disparate formats. The following list is intended to provide an overview:

- ASCII: Linux uses an 8-bit character set which largely corresponds to the ANSI set used by Microsoft Windows
- DVI (Device Independent Format): DVI files are the result of the LaTeX typesetting program. DVI files stand in the middle of the road leading from a LaTeX source text (TEX file) to a printer file (mostly PS).

- Graphics formats: for historical reasons, there are an endless number of graphics formats (GIF, TIF, JPEG, and so on). Conversion and processing of such files can be carried out by means of a whole range of programs.
- HTML (Hypertext Markup Language): although the HTML format was originally developed for the Internet, it has now established itself as an important format for online documentation.
- `man` files: the source texts for the `man` texts are present in the format of the `groff` text formatting system.
- PCD (Photo CD): you will encounter PCD files if you want to process the pictures of a Photo CD under Linux.
- PS, EPS (PostScript): PostScript is a page description language for specific printers. Under Linux, this format plays a much bigger role than under Windows. Practically all Linux programs can generate printing files only in this format. Thus, PostScript represents the printer standard in the Linux world (and, more generally, in the whole Unix world). But even if you do not own a PostScript laser printer, you need not despair. With `gs` (GhostScript) you can convert PostScript files into the format of many other printers.
- SGML (Standard Generalized Markup Language): this is a variation of HTML. The source texts of most Linux HOWTOs are present in SGML format.
- TEX (LaTeX): TEX files contain the source code for a LaTeX or TeX translation. (For reasons of space, only the TEX files are supplied as documentation of some programs; conversion into other formats is left to the user.)
- TEXI (TeXInfo): this is a variation of TEX files used specially for creation of online documentation in the `info` format.

This section presents a number of tools which allow you to convert documents from one format into another. If, for example, you first want to read a `*.tex` file containing the documentation of a program on screen and then print it on an Epson inkjet printer, the following conversion steps are required:

TEX → DVI using `latex`; display for example with `xdvi`
DVI → PS using `dvips`; display for example with `ghostview`
PS → printer file using `gs`

REFERENCE

With an appropriate printer configuration, this conversion can be carried out automatically – see also page 162 and the Printing-HOWTO.

Programs for display of different documents are discussed in the next section from page 518 onward.

Depending on the printer, there may be several ways of obtaining a printout. You can, for example, first convert an ASCII file into a PostScript file with `a2ps` and subsequently print this file via `gs` on an HP Laserjet. The detour via the PostScript format often looks longwinded, but may lead to higher-quality results.

The following table (sorted by source formats) provides an overview of the most important conversion programs available under Linux and shows the pages where these programs are explained:

Conversion programs		
`to/fromdos`	ASCII → ASCII (DOS/Linux conversion)	page 503
`a2ps`	ASCII → PS	page 505
`mpage`	ASCII → PS	page 506
`dvips`	DVI → PS	page 507
`dvilj`	DVI → HP Laserjet format	page 508
`xv`	graphics conversion	page 515
`ee`	graphics conversion	page 517
`gimp`	graphics conversion	page 659
`lynx`	HTML → ASCII	page 331
`html2ps`	HTML → PS	page 514
`groff`	`man` page → ASCII, DVI or PS	page 511
`rman`	`man` page → HTML	page 513
`xpcd`, `hpcdtoppm`	PCD → graphics format XY	page 517
`pdf2ps`	PDF → PS	page 515
`gs`	PS → various printer formats	page 509
`mpage`	PS → PS (several pages on one sheet)	page 506
`psutils`	PS → PS (tools for processing PS files)	page 510
`ps2pdf`	PS → PDF	page 515
`sgml2xy`	SGML → ASCII, `info`, HTML, TEX	page 513
`latex`, `tex`	TEX → DVI	page 587
`latex2html`	TEX → HTML	page 513
`pdflatex`	TEX → PDF	page 515
`makeinfo`	TEXI → `info` file	page 512
`texi2html`	TEXI → HTML	page 513

Text conversion DOS ↔ Linux (`fromdos`, `todos`)

When you try to exchange texts between DOS/Windows and Linux, you will encounter two problems: line ends are marked differently (this applies to DOS and Windows), and different characters sets are used, which affects foreign language special characters (only applies to DOS).

Some details in brief: under both DOS and Windows, the end of a line is marked by a character combination of carriage return and line feed. Unix and Linux do not require the carriage return character and are happy enough with the line feed. This means that a DOS file, when viewed with a Linux editor, shows a `^M` character pair at each end of line. Conversely, a Linux file viewed in a DOS editor turns into an endless snake of characters, because DOS and some Windows programs (such as the `NOTEPAD` editor) do not recognize the ends of lines.

Now a few words about foreign language special characters: DOS, Windows and Linux use three different character sets. DOS generally uses a variation of the ASCII character set, Windows uses the ANSI character set and Linux uses the ISO 8859/1 character set. In all three character sets, the characters with codes from 0 to 127 are identical. Differences appear in the remaining 128 characters, which contain the foreign language special characters (accents, umlauts, and so on). The Windows and Linux character sets are more similar to each other – for example, umlauts are coded in the same way (unfortunately, other characters are not).

Manual conversion of text files

There are two variations for the solution of these problems: when only the ends of lines are to be changed, the commands `fromdos` and `todos` can be used:

```
user$  fromdos file                  # DOS -> Linux
user$  todos file                    # Linux -> DOS
```

When conversion of special characters between DOS and Linux is also required, the GNU tool `recode` is better suited.

```
user$  recode ibmpc:latin1 file  # DOS -> Linux
user$  recode latin1:ibmpc file  # Linux -> DOS
```

Care must be taken when calling these four commands – the original file is replaced with the new one. The following variations, in which `dos` and `linux` are used as names for text files, are much safer.

```
user$  fromdos < dos > linux       # DOS -> Linux, only ends of lines
user$  todos < linux > dos         # Linux -> DOS, only ends of lines
user$  recode ibmpc:latin1 < dos > linux    # D -> L, incl. spec. chars
user$  recode latin1:ibmpc < linux > dos    # L -> D, incl. spec. chars
```

`recode` can cope with more than 100 different character sets. Details of other character sets and further application possibilities can be obtained by executing `info recode`.

`recode` must not be used with `ibmpc` to convert Windows texts. This is because the ANSI character set used in Windows employs different codes for foreign language special characters.

> **NOTE** On page 420, you will find an example of `bash` programming which shows how you can program your own simple conversion tools with the aid of the commands `tr` and `sed`.

Automatic conversion

If you have a DOS/Windows partition mounted in your Linux file system, you can carry out the end-of-line conversion automatically, either by specifying the option `-o conv=auto` in the `mount` command or by entering the option `conv=auto` into `/etc/fstab`. When you read a text file from Linux, all ends of lines appear correctly.

Conversely, when you write DOS files, their carriage return characters are inserted – it feels like heaven!

Automatic conversion only affects ends of lines. The character set (foreign language special characters in DOS text files) remains unchanged. A list of all file extensions excluded from automatic conversion can be found in the file `/usr/src/linux/fs/fat/misc.c`.

> **CAUTION** The snake in the grass is the recognition of text files. Any file that does not have a well-defined extension (such as `*.exe`, `*.dll`, `*.gif`, and so on) is interpreted as a text file. If the file is a binary file, it is incorrectly interpreted during access. If, for example, you use `tar` to carry out a backup of a DOS partition, the chances are that part of the backup file is unusable! Thus, although the option `conv=auto` is very convenient, it is a serious source of danger! Please activate this option only if you are completely aware of the damage you may cause.

ASCII → PostScript conversion (`a2ps`, `mpage`)

Since PostScript printers expect each output in the form of commands, it is not possible to send an ASCII file straight to the printer without prior processing. For ASCII to PostScript format conversion, you can use the `a2ps` and `mpage` commands.

```
a2ps [options] ascii_file > ps_file
```

In the default setting (that is, without options) `a2ps` formats the text in a two-column page in landscape format. Both columns are automatically supplied with frames and headers. In the following list, only those options are indicated that do not apply as default settings anyway.

- `-1` prints one column (instead of two columns in landscape format).
- `-8` uses the ISO Latin character set. Allows printing of foreign language special characters, but only on Level 2 PostScript printers.
- `-Fn` sets the letter size to *n* points. This automatically affects line spacing and the number of lines per page. *n* is specified using a floating point number.
- `-p` portrait format instead of landscape.
- `-nd, -nL, -nH, -nu`
  prints no date, no login info, no header, no file name.
- `-ns` prints no frame around the text.

There is a detailed `man` page for `a2ps`. An overview of all options can be obtained with `a2ps -h`. In this help text, the default settings are marked through the use of upper case letters.

NOTE

On my PostScript printer, some problems have occurred with files produced by `a2ps`: files with special characters (option `-8`) and `man` files using the backspace character (code 8) could not be printed. The reason: `a2ps` partly uses PostScript commands which are only officially defined with PostScript Level 2. On older Level 1 printers (depending on the implementation), these commands may or may not be present, and they are obviously missing on my printer. `ghostview`, by the way, has no problems with either of the special cases. Also, a conversion into HP Laserjet format with `gs` and a printout in this mode (which is possible with most PostScript printers) works fine.

If you want to output ASCII texts on a printer which is not PostScript compatible, you can usually do without the detour via `a2ps` and `gs` (GhostScript). Simply try to copy the file to your printer interface with `cp file /dev/...`. After this command, you will often have to send a form feed character with `echo -e "\f" > /dev/...` in order to start the printout (of the last page).

Many printers can cope with pure ASCII text and automatically start a new page when the current page is full. You will, however, have to do without orderly line and page breaks, headers, page numbers and similar pleasantries.

```
mpage [options] source_files > target_file
```

`mpage` processes the specified source files (ASCII or PostScript format) and writes the new PostScript file to the standard output (which is redirected into the target file). The following list gives only the most important options (there are many more!).

`-1   -2   -4   -8`
: arranges one, two, four or eight pages on one sheet. With two and eight, landscape format is used. Default is four pages.

`-A` output is done in DIN A4 format (default: US Letter).

`-C ISO-8859.1`
: uses the ISO-8859/1 coding for the character set. This option is necessary to print texts containing foreign language special characters. Other code tables can be found in `/usr/lib/mpage`.

`-c` when printing several files, a new sheet is not started for each file.

`-f` long lines are run over several lines (default: they are truncated).

`-j` *n–m*
: only prints sheets *n* to *m* (default: all).

`-l` prints in landscape format with 55 lines and 132 columns and a proportionally smaller letter size (default: portrait, 66 lines, 80 columns).

`-L` *n*
: prints *n* lines per page and adjusts the letter size accordingly (default: 66 lines).

`-o` does not print frames around the pages.

`-v` prints the sheet number too (default: only the page number).

`-W` *n*

prints *n* columns per page and adjusts the letter size accordingly (default: 80 columns).

Like `a2ps`, `mpage` can generate a PostScript file from an ASCII file. Compared with `a2ps`, it has two additional features: firstly, `mpage` can print up to eight pages on one sheet (but you will need a magnifying glass to read them), and secondly, `mpage` accepts both ASCII files and PostScript files as input. Thus, you can reformat an existing PostScript file in a space-saving manner and then print it with two pages per sheet. (This does not work with all PostScript files. `mpage` is compatible with `dvips`, the most important PostScript generator in the Linux world.)

Default settings can be changed with the environment variable `MPAGE`. The variable can be preset in `/etc/profile`. A reasonable setting (for international business) is:

```
# Addition to /etc/profile
export MPAGE='-A -C ISO-8859.1'
```

DVI → PostScript conversion (`dvips`)

`dvips [options] file`

The `dvips` program converts `*.dvi` files into PostScript format. The program automatically appends the extension `.dvi` to the file name. `*.dvi` files are the result of the programs TeX and LaTeX (see Chapter 18 from page 587 onward). `*.dvi` files are frequently supplied as online documentation for various programs.

`-A` converts only odd pages.

`-B` converts only even pages.

`-i -S` *n*

splits the output into files of *n* pages each. The files are automatically numbered in sequence. This option is important when a longer document is to be output to an imagesetter. Most imagesetters can only expose a relatively small number of pages (typical values are between 20 and 50) at a time.

`-l` *last_page*

terminates the conversion with the specified page.

`-o` *target_file*

writes the result to the specified file (instead of passing it on to the `lpr` program).

`-p` *first_page*

starts the conversion with the specified page.

`-pp n1,n2-n3,n4,n5,n6-n7`
: prints the specified pages. Please note that there must be no spaces in the page list.

LaTeX documents generally do not use the original PostScript character sets, but character sets specially created for LaTeX. This has the advantage that a subsequent conversion of the PostScript file into the format of a different printer is possible with almost no loss of quality. If the LaTeX character sets have not been calculated during a previous printout (as compressed bitmap files), then for each missing character set, `dvips` automatically starts the LaTeX font program Metafont. For this reason, a first-time conversion of a LaTeX document into a PostScript file can take a relatively long time.

REFERENCE `dvips` is normally installed in such a way that it generates LaTeX character sets at a resolution of 300 dpi (dots per inch). If you want to print the LaTeX document to a printer with a different resolution, you must modify the file `/usr/TeX/lib/texmf/dvips/config.ps`. All further information on this subject, which is LaTeX-specific, can be found on page 623.

```
dvilj   [options] dvi_file
dvilj2p [options] dvi_file
dvilj4  [options] dvi_file
dvilj4l [options] dvi_file
```

`dvilj` is a variation of `dvips` used for a direct conversion of `*.dvi` files into the format of HP Laserjet compatible printers. If you do not possess `dvilj`, you must first use `dvips` to generate a PostScript file and subsequently convert it into HP format with `gs`. This is more long-winded, but entails no loss of quality.

`-gfile`
: writes the result to the specified file.

`-gpage_number`
: starts the printout with the specified page number.

`-l` prints in landscape format.

`-sn` sets the paper format. The following are some of the values that are permitted for *n*: 26 for DIN A4, 90 for DL size envelopes (11×22 cm^2) and 91 for C5 size envelopes (16.2×22.9 cm^2).

`-tpage_number`
: terminates the printout with the specified page number.

Calling `dvilj` without any options causes the specified DVI file to be processed. As a result, the program supplies a homonymous file with the extension `.lj` for printing on a 300 dpi HP Laserjet printer. The commands `dvilj2p`, `dvilj4` and `dvilj4l` work in a similar way, but specifically support the specified models (including 600 dpi resolution and built-in TrueType and Intellifont character sets).

The detour via `dvips` is also recommended when a single page contains more than 16 different typefaces (this causes `dvilj` to fail) or when the LaTeX text uses PostScript typefaces. `gs` cannot exactly represent PostScript typefaces either, but it still supplies much better results than `dvilj`.

TIP If you want to print out `*.dvi` files containing PostScript character sets, you should take the detour via `dvips` and `gs` – the result will definitely be better. `dvilj` relentlessly replaces all PostScript character sets with a 10-point LaTeX standard typeface.

NOTE `dvilj` possesses a very detailed `man` page. There you will find information about the remaining options and about how to obtain a double-sided printout (by first printing the odd pages, and then the even pages on the reverse side of the sheets you have just printed).

PostScript → printer format conversion (`gs`)

GhostScript (that is, the `gs` program) can convert PostScript documents into a large number of printer formats (including a fax format). When LaTeX character sets are used in the PostScript document, there is no loss of quality, but if original PostScript character sets are used, `gs` must employ the character set files of `/usr/lib/ghostscript/fonts` instead, not all of which can match the quality of the original fonts.

```
gs [options] postscript_file [quit.ps]
```

In order to make `gs` function correctly, at least two options must be specified: `-sDEVICE=` to set the output format and `-sOutputFile=` to specify the file into which the result is to be written. As a rule, it is also reasonable to use the options `-sPAPERSIZE=a4` and `-dNOPAUSE`.

`-dNODISPLAY`
: suppresses the display of various messages on screen. Also, it is no longer necessary to confirm the completion of each page with ↵.

`-dSAFER`
: all files are exclusively opened as read-only. This option must be used when `gs` is used as a filter (for example, for a print spooler).

`-q`
: suppresses various status messages (*quiet*).

`-r`*`resolution`*
: sets the graphics resolution. This option is necessary for conversions into the format of various dot matrix printers.

`-sDEVICE=`*`printer_format`*
: specifies the format into which `gs` is to convert the PostScript file. A list of all possible formats can be obtained with `gs -h`. Amongst the most important for-

mats are `deskjet`, `djet500`, `laserjet`, `ljet3`, `ljet4`, `necp6`, `bj10e` and `bj200` and `ibmpro`. PostScript files which contain only one page (one image)can also be converted into various graphics formats, such as `tiffg3` or `png256`. A conversion into ASCII text is not possible.

`-sOutputFile=`*`file_name`*
: writes the result of the conversion to the specified file.

`-sPAPERSIZE=`*`paper_size`*
: specifies the paper size of the output. In most cases, `a4` must be used, since otherwise `gs` defaults to the American letter size format which is slightly smaller.

`gs` works interactively and comes up with an input prompt after having processed the last page. In order to make it clear to `gs` that the conversion is over, you must enter Ctrl+D. If you want to avoid this input, you can specify a second file called `quit.ps` which is loaded from `/usr/lib/ghostscript/` and only contains the text 'quit'.

The following instruction converts `test.ps` into the HP Laserjet 3 format. The result is written to `test.hp`. `quit.ps` causes `gs` to be terminated immediately afterwards.

```
user$  gs -sDEVICE=ljet3 -sOutputFile=test.hp \
   >     -sPAPERSIZE=a4 -dNOPAUSE test.ps quit.ps
```

`gs` exists in various versions which are subject to different copyrights: the most recent version is always 'Aladdin Ghostscript *n*'. Although this version is freely available on the Internet, a commercial distribution (such as in Linux distributions) is only possible with a license agreement. Older versions, after a while, get the name 'GNU Ghostscript *n*'. They are subject to the GPL, that is, distribution is (almost) unrestricted. Depending on the agreement with Aladdin Enterprises, Linux distributions are therefore partly shipped with Aladdin and partly with GNU Ghostscript. For the end user, GNU Ghostscript has the disadvantage that the latest drivers are not yet implemented. Up-to-date information on the different Ghostscript versions can be found on the Internet:

`http://www.cs.wisc.edu/~ghost/`

The `man` text for `gs` is fairly comprehensive. In addition, the directory `/usr/share/ghostscript/`*n.n*`/doc` contains further information about the internals of GhostScript.

PostScript tools (`psutils`)

With `ghostview`, you can also select individual pages from a file and store them as separate PostScript files. If you wish to automate this and other similar tasks, the commands of the `psutils` package will be very useful. Some commands are self-contained programs, others `bash` or Perl scripts.

For reasons of space, this section cannot contain a detailed description of the large number of commands – but just looking at the listing should give you a good idea. More details can always be found in the corresponding `man` pages.

`epsffit`	adapts the size of an EPS file
`extractres`	analyzes the file and supplies `%%IncludeResource` comments for all necessary fonts, files, and so on
`fixfmps`	adapts FrameMaker files to the `psutils` conventions
`fixmacps`	adapts Macintosh files to the `psutils` conventions
`fixscribeps`	adapts Scribe files to the `psutils` conventions
`fixtpps`	adapts Troff/Tpscript files to the `psutils` conventions
`fixwfwps`	adapts WinWord files to the `psutils` conventions
`fixwpps`	adapts WordPerfect files to the `psutils` conventions
`fixwwps`	adapts MS Write files to the `psutils` conventions
`getafm`	generates AFM files for the description of fonts
`includeres`	includes the comments generated with `extractres` into a PostScript file
`psbook`	arranges the pages of a text in such a way that whole sheets (for example, with 16 pages each) can be printed
`psmerge`	merges several PostScript files into a single file
`psnup`	arranges several scaled-down pages on one sheet
`psresize`	changes the required paper size of a document. This command solves the common problem of printing out PostScript documents generated for the US Letter format
`psselect`	extracts single pages from a PostScript file
`pstops`	arranges the pages of a document in a new order

The above commands can only work when the PostScript files contain comments complying with the DSC standards. (DSC stands for Document Structuring Conventions. The comments are not printed, but contain important information about the size of a page, beginning and end of pages, and so on.) EPS files are single-page PostScript files which contain special commands for embedding into other documents (in particular, bounding box specifications regarding the size of the image).

Processing PostScript files generated under MS Windows is usually rather laborious; even the above commands do not always lead to the desired results. In any case, if you want to have a (remote) chance of success, you must not forget to activate the option for generation of DSC-compliant PostScript files in your Windows PostScript printer driver.

If the task is only to format a PostScript file in such a way that several reduced pages are printed per sheet, the `mpage` program described on page 506 is usually easier to handle than the above commands.

Formatting man texts (`groff`)

`groff` is a higher-level command used to control a whole family of text formatting programs, amongst others `gtroff` for the text itself, `geqn` for mathematical formulae, `gpic` for illustrations, `gtbl` for tables, `grefer` for cross-references, and so on. The `groff` programs taken together thus constitute a typesetting system, in its concept comparable to LaTeX, but less sophisticated in its formatting capabilities and therefore easier to handle.

In practice, the `groff` programs play a fairly secondary role – with one exception: `groff` is used to format the `man` texts. Thus, `man` texts are formulated in a `groff`-compatible syntax. They become easily readable ASCII texts only after `groff` formatting.

The following description of `groff` explains only those options that are needed to convert `man` sources into `*.dvi` or PostScript files.

```
groff [options] file [> target_file]
```

`-m`*`name`*
: uses the macro file `tmac.name` in the `/usr/lib/groff/tmac` directory. For conversion of `man` texts, the name used must be `andoc`.

`-T`*`format`*
: determines the output format. Default setting is `ps` for PostScript. Other possible settings are `dvi` (for `dvi` files), `ascii` for ASCII texts (yields the results known from `man`), and `latin1` (as `ascii`, but with foreign language special characters).

If a `man` text is present not only in its formatted version, but also as source text, `groff` can be used to convert this file into a high-quality PostScript file. `man` sources can be found in the `manx` directories (x stands for 1 to 9, n, g), for example in `/usr/man/manx`. The following command converts the `man` source file `groff.1` into PostScript format and writes the result into the file `test.ps` in the home directory:

```
user$  groff /usr/man/man1/groff.1 -mandoc > ~/book/test.ps
```

The same result – although with less extensive control possibilities – is achieved with the following command:

```
user$  man -t groff  > ~/book/test.ps
```

NOTE

In some Linux distributions, the `man` texts are only available preformatted, so that `groff` cannot be applied. In such cases, however, the `rman` command allows the formatted `man` page to be converted into another format (PostScript, HTML, and so on) (see page 514).

Formatting of info texts (Texinfo)

`info` texts are created by means of Texinfo. The great advantage of the Texinfo system is that the same source files (extension `*.texi`) can be used to create both an `info` and a DVI file. The resulting `*.dvi` files can be converted into PostScript files by means of `dvips` and subsequently printed. Thus, `*.texi` files are suited both for creation of online documentation and generation of typographically excellent manuals. (LaTeX and `dvips` are described in a separate chapter from page 587 onward.)

Conversion of a `*.texi` file into an `*.info` file is carried out by means of the command `makeinfo name.texi`. With complex documents combined out of several files (for example, the Emacs manual) you will often find the file `Makefile` which controls the translation process. In this case, you only need to execute `make` in the relevant directory.

```
user$  makeinfo name.texi
```

Translation into a DVI file is done with a sequence of three commands. (Actually, one `tex` run would be sufficient – however, in this case the index and the cross-references would be missing.) `dvips` is then used to generate a PostScript file. The translation can only be carried out when TeX is installed.

```
user$  tex name.texi
user$  texindex name.??
user$  tex name.texi
user$  dvips name.dvi -o name.ps
```

Thus, you can use the above command sequence to generate your own manuals for GNU C, Emacs, and so on. The only precondition (besides an installation of TeX) is that the `*.texi` files must be available.

TIP

Texinfo has an extensive online documentation – hardly surprisingly in the `info` system.

NOTE

For reasons of space, many Linux distributions only supply the ready-made `*.info` files. The `*.texi` files can, however, always be found in the original GNU packages:

```
http://www.gnu.org
```

HTML conversion

Texinfo → HTML

`texi2html` is a Perl script which generates one or more HTML files from one `*.texi` file. The `-split_chapter` and `-split_node` options allow you to combine long texts into shorter sections. This leads to a large number of single files, but improves reading speed enormously. (Have you ever tried to read a `*.html` file of 2 Mbytes?)

Info → HTML

`info2html` follows a completely different approach: the Perl program is installed into the cgi directory of an http server. If a reference to an info text occurs on a WWW page, the program generates an 'on-the-fly' conversion of the existing `*.info` file into the `*.html` format. The advantage of this procedure is that no `*.texi` files are needed and that the disk space requirement is practically nil. All existing `*.info` files can be accessed transparently. The disadvantage: without a running http server, nothing happens.

LaTeX → HTML

In principle, `latex2html` works the same way as `texi2html`: the Perl script generates one or more `*.html` files from one LaTeX file. Formulae and LaTeX special characters are translated into `*.gif` images – this, however, assumes the presence of the large graphics package `netpbm`.

Usually, the application of `latex2html` is not as easy as `texi2html`: on the one hand, the computing power requirements (CPU, RAM) are huge, and on the other, the conversion achieves the desired outcome if and only if nothing but LaTeX standard commands have been used (not various self-defined macros, additional packages, and so on). For this reason, the attempt to convert this book into an `*.html` book failed miserably. For simpler texts, however, the conversion works perfectly. The program is mainly used to convert scientific publications written in LaTeX into a WWW-usable form.

Man → HTML

`rman` (short for RosettaMan) converts formatted man pages into other formats (ASCII, HTML, SGML, LaTeX and so on). The special feature of `rman` is that it does not have to start from the `groff` source texts for `man` pages, but can cope with the already formatted `man` pages themselves. `rman` can, like `info2www`, also be employed in cgi scripts. The help system of the SuSE distribution uses `rman` to convert `man` texts into HTML texts on demand.

The following example shows the use of `rman`: the `man` page for `ls` is converted into HTML format and written to the file `ls.html`.

```
user$  rman -f html /var/catman/cat1/ls.1 > ls.html
```

Linuxdoc-SGML

While the programs described above are tools to convert 'old' online documentation into a new format, the Linuxdoc-SGML software package has been created from the start with the purpose of generating files in different formats (ASCII, HTML, PostScript) from one and the same source text. Texts are entered as SGML documents. (SGML stands for Standard Generalized Markup Language and has a similar syntax to the WWW language HTML.) SGML texts can then be converted into different formats by means of `sgml2txt`, `sglm2html`, and so on. Nearly all HOWTO texts and many other Linux documents have been written using Linuxdoc-SGML.

HTML → PS

If you want to print an HTML file, you can use a Web Browser (for example Netscape). However, for automatic conversion from HTML into PostScript format, the Perl script `html2ps` is far better. Its handling is very easy: `html2ps -D name.html > name.ps`. The option `-D` causes `html2ps` to insert DSC-conformant comments into the PostScript file, which greatly facilitates its further processing. If `html2ps` is not part of your distribution, you can find the converter on the Internet:

```
http://www.tdb.uu.se/~jan/html2ps.html
```

PDF conversion

LaTeX → PDF

With the LaTeX command `latexpdf` you create a `*.pdf` file from a `*.tex` file (instead of a `*.dvi` file). While the application of the command is extremely simple, the results for complex documents using various fonts and macro packages (such as the `*.tex` files of this book) are usable only to a very limited extent. In some cases, the resulting PDF files could not even be properly displayed by `acroread`. `latexpdf` is part of the supply only since teTeX 0.9 and is therefore missing in many older distributions.

PS → PDF

`ps2pdf source.ps target.pdf` creates a PDF file from an arbitrary PostScript file. The command is based on GhostScript. The results are only usable if the PostScript file exclusively contains texts in the Courier, Times and Helvetica fonts. Otherwise, bitmaps are used for character representation, which both reduces the quality and makes file size grow hugely. Furthermore, the resulting PDF file is not even compressed.

PDF → PS

The opposite way is taken by `pdf2ps source.pdf target.ps`. This command too resorts to GhostScript.

Graphics conversion

xv

The most popular tool in the Unix world for conversion of graphics files between different formats is without any doubt `xv`. You can use it to read graphics files in the most varied formats and store them in a different format. At the same time, it offers various operations for image processing (rotate, mirror, and so on) and color manipulation (brightness, contrast). Furthermore, `xv` can be used to do screen shots, that is, to store a window or the whole screen in a graphics file of arbitrary format. Last, but not least, you can use `xv` as a file manager (button VISUAL SCHNAUZER).

> **NOTE** Unlike most other Linux components, `xv` is shareware. Commercial use is only permitted after licensing. The license agreement is displayed by clicking on the LICENSE button.

A few quick words about handling `xv`: when it starts up, a colorful logo is displayed. The actual control window only appears after clicking on the logo with the right mouse button. Through the control window, you can load a file. When `xv` recognizes the graphics format, it displays the file in a graphics window.

Now, you can carry out some elementary processing steps directly via buttons in the control window. Should you want to change brightness, contrast or other color settings, clicking on WINDOWS | COLOR EDITOR provides you with a separate window with countless setting possibilities.

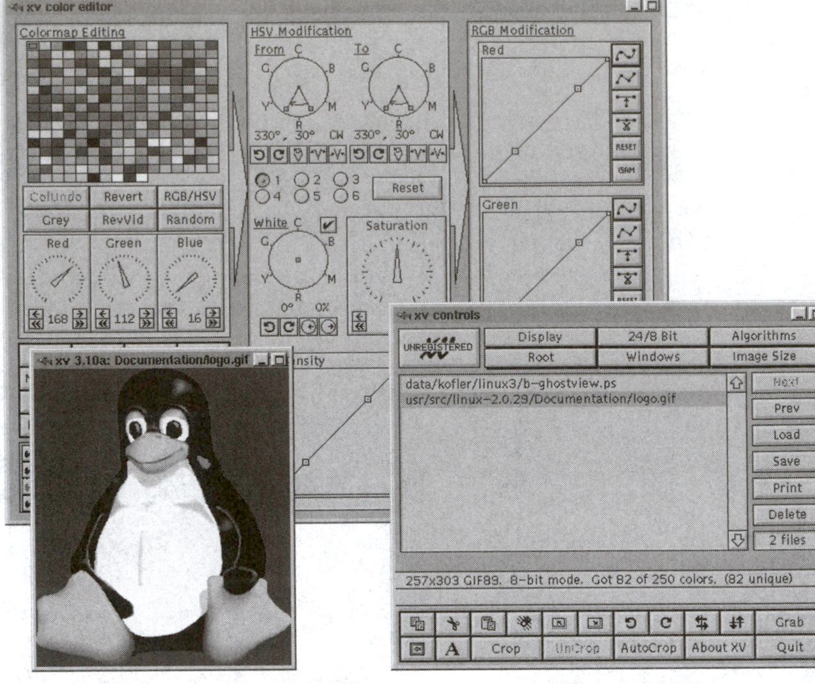

Figure 15.7 The Linux logo, shown with xv.

If you work in 256-color mode, you can modify each color separately. The required color can be selected directly in the image with the middle mouse button.

> **NOTE**
> For images in true color, this possibility does not exist; you can, however, reduce the image to 256 colors by means of 24/8 BIT | 8 BIT MODE. You should, however, ascertain that an optimum image quality can be maintained by executing 24/8 BIT | BEST 24->8 first.

Independently of 24- or 8-bit color mode, you can change the brightness distribution both for the entire color spectrum and for single color components (red, green, blue). To do this, you just move the brightness distribution control points.

The ALGORITHMS menu provides various algorithms for image processing. For example, you could blow up a low-resolution bitmap image to double the size with IMAGE SIZE | DOUBLE SIZE and subsequently blur the pixels by means of ALGORITHMS | BLUR.

With the left mouse button, you can mark an arbitrary section of the image and subsequently crop the image down to that area with CROP. This allows you to store only part of an image. (However, all image processing steps are carried out for the entire image. When you execute UNCROP, the complete image is displayed again.)

After processing your image, you can use SAVE to store it in one of the following formats (to mention just a few): BMP, GIF, IRIS, JPEG, PBM, PostScript, TIFF.

At this point, a variety of additional options can be set (color/black&white, compression factors, and so on). Thus, xv represents an incredibly powerful tool for image processing and converting.

TIP xv boasts a 100-page manual which is supplied as a PostScript file (xvdocs.ps) in most distributions.

Electric Eyes

The GNOME program Electric Eyes is started by means of the command ee. Control is carried out either via context menus (right mouse button) or a dialog which is displayed with EDIT | SHOW EDIT WINDOW. In its current version, the program is easy to use (see also the help text available in HTML format), but it is still far from being a replacement for xv (as extolled in the RedHat manual).

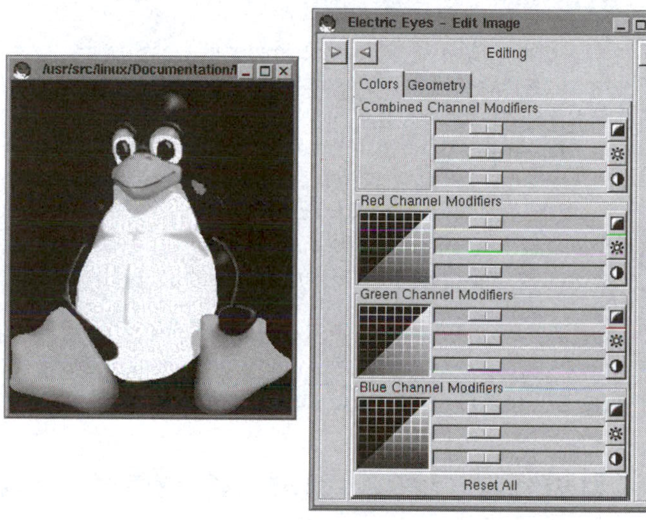

Figure 15.8 The Linux logo, displayed with Electric Eyes.

xpcd, hpcdtoppm (Photo CD)

The easiest way to read pictures on a Photo CD is the xpcd program. Previously, the CD must, as usual, be mounted into the file system with mount. Then, xpcd /cdrom shows a contents list of the CD. Subsequently, you can view the individual pictures in different resolutions and save them in JPEG, PPM or TIFF format. For automatic conversion of several files into PPM format you can also use the command hpcdtoppm instead.

Figure 15.9 The contents of a Photo CD.

Other programs for image processing and graphics conversion

If you think that the `xv` and `ee` image processing functions are not flexible enough, you should take a look at the `gimp` program. The program is extensively described in Chapter 20 from page 659 onward.

If, on the other hand, you are confronted with exotic graphics formats or if you want to convert a whole collection of files into another format by means of a script (thus without user interaction), there are other alternatives: the program package Image Magick provides both single commands and an interactive interface. For conversion, a proprietary intermediate format (MIFF) is used.

A similar approach is also followed by the NetPBM package (formerly Portable Bitmap Utilities). Here, the PBM format is used as an intermediate format. If, for example, you have to convert hundreds of MS Windows bitmaps into PostScript format, these utilities are the right choice.

15.4 Displaying documents and graphics

Displaying PostScript files (`ghostview`, `kghostview`, `gv`)

In principle, `ghostview` is nothing but a graphical user interface for the already introduced `gs` (GhostScript) program. `ghostview` allows you to view/read PostScript files on screen. `ghostview` can cope with both single PostScript graphics and documents running to hundreds of pages. If the document corresponds to the PostScript standards, you can freely jump between page numbers. Otherwise, the file can only be read sequentially (that is, page after page without the possibility of skipping pages or leafing back).

Depending on the distribution, `ghostview` is compiled with different widget libraries. This has the consequence that `ghostview` buttons and scroll bars look different than shown in Figure 15.10. However, this difference only concerns the visual outcome; the function of the program remains the same.

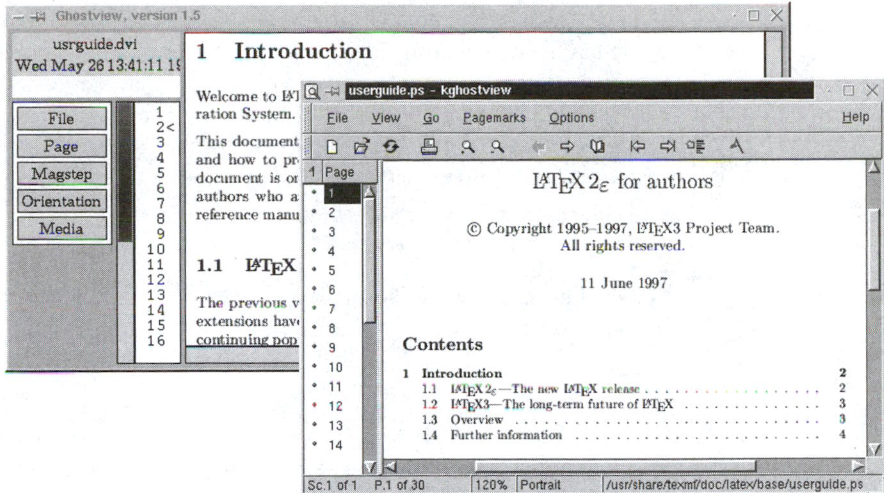

Figure 15.10 A page from the LaTeX 2_ε user guide, shown with `ghostview` and `kghostview`.

Usually, `ghostview` is called either without any parameters or with the file name of the file to be viewed. The program is completely menu-driven. In order to open new files, a window is displayed that allows easy file selection with the mouse. A mouse click on any point of the image section opens a small window which contains a magnification of the area around the mouse pointer. You can change to another page to be displayed by clicking on a page number with the middle mouse button.

As a quick alternative to mouse control, a number of keyboard shortcuts are provided, the most important of which are summarized in the following table.

`ghostview` keyboard shortcuts	
PgUp, PgDn	previous/next page
Spacebar, ↩	next page
↑, ↓	rotate view by 90 degrees
Backspace, Del	previous page
+, -	change zoom factor
O	open new file
Q	quit the program
R	reopen modified file
H, L	move image section left/right
U, D	move image section up/down

`ghostview` allows you to extract single pages or page sections from the document and store them in separate files. In order to do this, mark the required area by moving the mouse while keeping the mouse button depressed and subsequently execute the SAVE | MARKED PAGES command.

If you attach great importance to high-quality representation (and are prepared to put up with longer computing time and higher memory consumption in return), you should activate the antialiasing function. This means that the PostScript representation is first generated in a higher resolution and then reduced to a grayscale image. To do this, you either select the option `-sDEVICE=x11alpha` when starting `ghostview` or you extend `~/.Xdefaults` with the following line:

```
! activate Ghostview antialiasing in ~/.Xdefaults
Ghostview*arguments: -sDEVICE=x11alpha
```

> **TIP** Detailed information on the handling of `ghostview`, together with a summary of all command options and keyboard shortcuts, can be found in the `man` text.

`kghostview`

The KDE variation of `ghostview` is `kghostview` and impresses with its substantially easier handling. (Hard-boiled `ghostview` users will, however, miss their usual keyboard shortcuts.)

`gv, ggv`

The `gv` program is yet another `ghostview` variation. The program looks more modern than `ghostview`, but does not offer any essential additional functions. RedHat Linux is currently only shipped with `gv`. `ghostview` is merely a link to `gv`. `ggv`, finally, is the GNOME variation of `gv`.

Viewing DVI files (`xdvi, kdvi`)

In principle, `xdvi` does the same for `*.dvi` files as `ghostview` does for PostScript files. The program allows you to view `*.dvi` files on screen and to leaf through their pages forward and backward.

`xdvi` is started with the file name of the `*.dvi` file as the only parameter. Subsequently, the buttons NEXT, PREVIOUS, and so on can be used to leaf through the document. When you move the mouse over the image section while keeping the mouse button depressed, a magnified section of the rectangle under the mouse pointer is displayed (without visible delay). The following table gives an overview of the most important keyboard shortcuts for the control of `xdvi`.

`xdvi` keyboard shortcuts	
PgUp, PgDn	previous/next page
Spacebar, ↩	next page
Backspace, Del	previous page
↑, ↓, ←, →	move image section
G	go to the previously entered page number
V	(de)activate the display of PostScript graphics

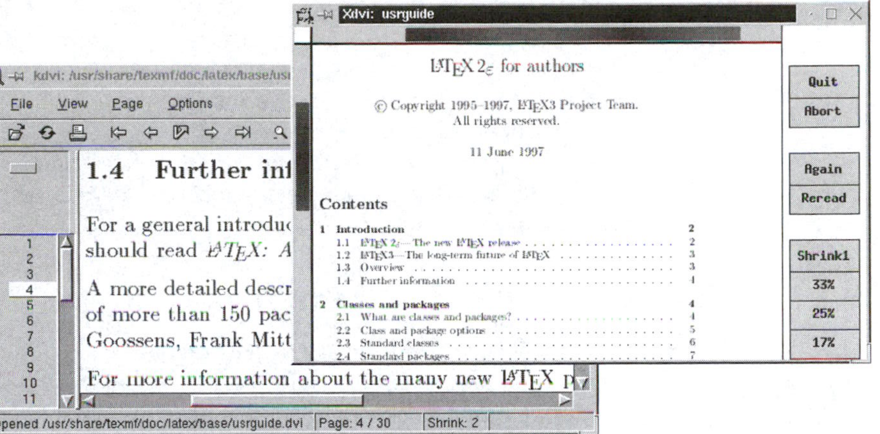

Figure 15.11 A page of the LaTeX 2_ε user guide shown with `xdvi` and `kdvi`.

You can freely choose between `xdvi` and `ghostview` for processing LaTeX texts. Both programs have advantages: `xdvi` usually displays the pages somewhat faster. When LaTeX original fonts are used, `xdvi` provides the better image quality, whereas when PostScript fonts are used, `ghostview` comes off better.

In the teTeX distribution, `xdvi` can be configured through the file `XDvi` (directory `/usr/lib/texmf/texmf/xdvi`). The file has four entries: `mfmode` specifies the printer types, `pixelsPerInch` the resolution in dpi, `shrinkFactor` the scaling-down factor inside `xdvi` and `paper` the paper size. The first two settings should match the parameters used with `dvips` for the generation of PostScript files. In this way, you will avoid unnecessary creation of bitmap font files, which is wasteful in terms of both time and disk space.

Resolution and printer type must match (see file `MakeTeXPK` or page 623). The higher the dpi number chosen, the greater the scaling-down factor (otherwise, `xdvi` displays the text pages far too large). If you print your `*.dvi` files on a 300 dpi laser printer, the following settings are reasonable:

```
XDvi*mfmode: cx
XDvi*pixelsPerInch: 300
XDvi*shrinkFactor: 4
XDvi*paper: a4
```

If you want to check what the result of imagesetting with 1270 dpi would look like pixel by pixel, you can use the following settings:

```
Dvi*mfmode: linoone
XDvi*pixelsPerInch: 1270
XDvi*shrinkFactor: 16
XDvi*paper: a4
```

`kdvi`

The KDE variation of `xdvi` is `kdvi`. In contrast to `kghostview`, `kdvi` provides substantial improvements with respect to the original – in particular the display of page numbers, which allows much easier navigation through large documents. The printing function too is worth noting – you can use `kdvi`, for example, for easy creation of a PostScript file that contains four pages per sheet. (`kdvi` resorts to the mentioned programs `dvips`, `dvilj`, `mpage` and `psnup`.)

Viewing PDF files (`acroread`)

PDF files can be displayed with the mentioned programs `ghostview` and `kghostview`, and with the special programs `xpdf` and `acroread`. Of all these programs, `acroread` provides by far the best results (extremely sharp text representation). Furthermore, it is the easiest one to handle.

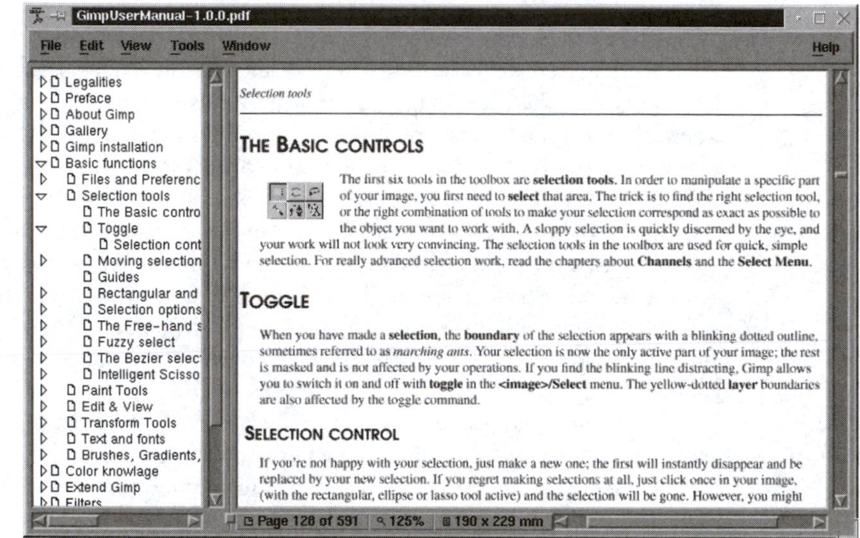

Figure 15.12 A page of the Gimp User Manual, displayed with `acroread`.

`acroread` is a commercial program of Adobe Systems Inc. (who also invented the PDF format) which can, however, be freely distributed. Nevertheless, `acroread` is unfortunately still missing in many distributions. If needed, you can always find the program on the Internet:

```
http://www.adobe.com
```

Handling of the program does not pose problems. The only peculiarity which is often overlooked is the possible division of the window for showing a hierarchic contents list (see Figure 15.12). However, this works only with documents which are provided with such a contents list in the first place.

Viewing graphics files

The KDE program `kview` allows easy display of graphics files of the formats BMP, EPS, GIF, ILBM, JPEG, PCX, PNM, TGA, XBM and XPM. The `kfax` program which also belongs to KDE fulfills the same task for fax files.

REFERENCE

Most of the other Linux programs for viewing graphics files can also be used for image processing or conversion. They are therefore described elsewhere in this book:

`xv`: page 515
`ee`: page 517
`gimp`: page 659

15.5 Creating screenshots

A screenshot is a copy of the current screen or window contents in a graphics file. Besides the programs described in this section, Gimp too has an elementary screenshot function (command XTNS | SCREENSHOT).

TIP

If you want to represent several windows in one screenshot, you should previously set the screen background to white to prevent it from disturbing the image:

```
user$ xsetroot -solid white
```

If the screenshot program is not capable of selecting the desired area, simply create a screenshot of the entire screen. Subsequently, you can use an image processing program – for example `xv` – to extract the required section.

xv

The `xv` program already mentioned on page 515 can also be used to create screenshots. To do this, you first click on the GRAB button and subsequently on a window or on the background of the X system. This causes `xv` to read the contents of the window or the whole screen. Subsequently, this image can be processed and saved as described above.

NOTE

Depending on the X server and the video card, the screenshot function of `xv` can cause problems whose origin I have not been able to identify. In particular, `xv` seems to have problems with the desktop change of the KDE window manager. Try to use `ksnapshot` instead.

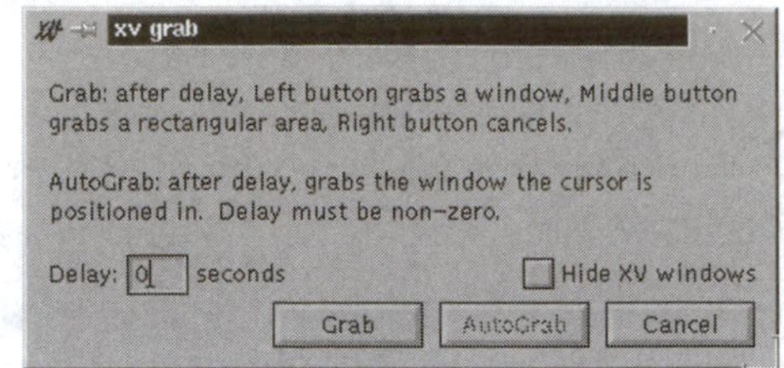

Figure 15.13 The screenshot control window of `xv`.

xgrab

The handling of `xgrab` is completely different from `xv` – you must set all options in advance: the required screen area (a window, the whole screen or a rectangle previously marked with the mouse), the graphics format (PostScript or various bitmap formats), possibly some PostScript options (for illustrations, PS-FIGURE must usually be selected), and the file name.

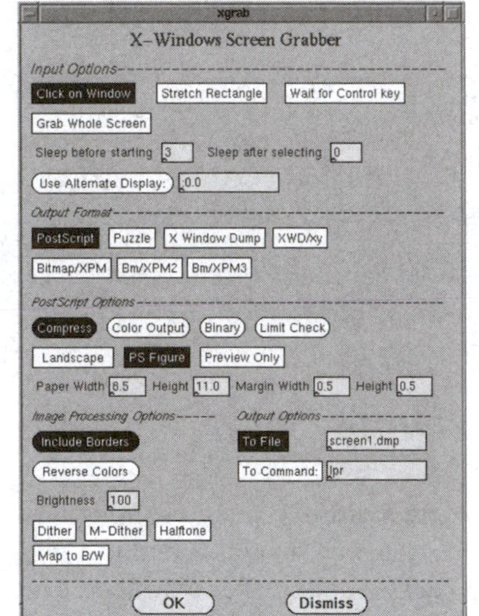

Figure 15.14 The control window of `xgrab`.

When you click on OK, the control window disappears from the screen. After a preset time, during which you can, for example, select a menu, the current screen contents at that particular instant are stored in the file. A few moments later, the control window appears again. `xgrab` does not provide for viewing the generated images – either `xv` or `ghostview` will have to be used.

ksnapshot

The `ksnapshot` program is part of KDE. Its main advantage is that it fully agrees with KDE and (as opposed to, for example, `xv`) does not get disconcerted by its desktop management. Handling is easy: first you specify the file name, the graphics format for the snapshot file, and the delay time for launching the snapshot function. The snapshot function is then triggered by means of GRAB. The resulting image is not automatically stored – you need to click on SAVE.

TIP The default setting of GIF as graphics format has not proven successful because color halftones are often marred by dithering (that is, alternating use of two similar colors). Try to use a different format – BMP or XPM, for example – and sunsequently convert the file into another format with `xv`. (In `xv`, you should use the option 24/8-BIT | BEST 24 → 8 BIT.) With this, you will achieve a significantly higher image quality.

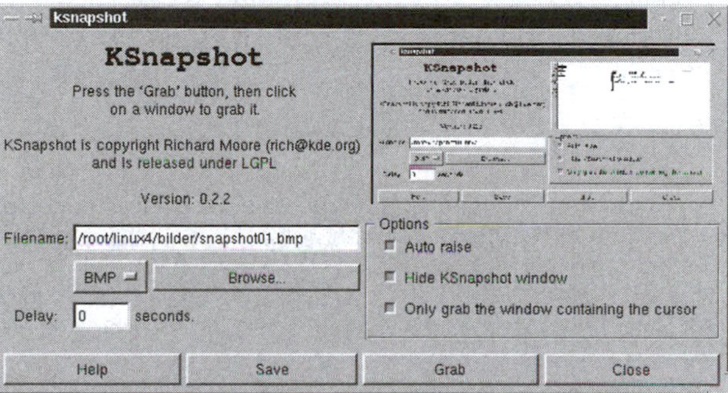

Figure 15.15 The control window of `ksnapshot`.

15.6 Terminal emulators

You will need a terminal emulator whenever you want to use your modem to communicate in text mode. The terminal program reads your keyboard input and transmits it to the modem. At the same time, it reads the data arriving from the modem and displays it on screen. Thus, you use a terminal emulator when you work with an interactive Internet online connection or when you use a mailbox.

The rather quaint name 'terminal emulator' has its origin in the fact that in the old days, terminals used to be self-contained devices consisting of a screen and a keyboard, attached to a central Unix computer via a serial interface.

A terminal emulator is an ideal program for getting to know your modem better. You can communicate with your modem by simply inputting commands (directly as ASCII characters). If, for example, you enter `ATZ` ↵, you are requesting your modem to reset. After several seconds, the modem answers with the character string `OK`, which is displayed on screen by the terminal emulator.

With `ATDT45678` you dial the number 45678 and establish a connection. When the connection is successfully established, the modem answers with `CONNECT`; when the line is engaged, with `BUSY`. At this point, the modem switches from command mode to normal working mode in which text input is not interpreted as commands but transmitted via the phone line. By entering `+++` (these characters have a kind of Escape function), you switch back into command mode. Now the connection can be terminated with the `ATH` (hangup) command.

TIP If you are still connected to an old-fashioned telephone exchange with pulse dialling, the character string for dialling is `ATDP45678`.

Linux offers you a choice of two very powerful programs, namely `minicom` (for text mode) and `seyon` (for X), which will be described in the next two subsections.

NOTE Under Linux you are faced with a different kind of terminal emulator every time you log in to a text console. In order to make this possible, the `getty` program or its `mingetty` variation runs on every non-active text console. These programs access Linux-internal devices for communication with text consoles.

minicom

`minicom` is a terminal program for text mode. Its handling resembles the DOS program TELIX. `minicom` accesses the modem via the device file `/dev/modem`. In order to configure `minicom`, you should start the program as `root` with the option `-s`. Now, instead of `/dev/modem`, you can specify the serial interface directly (for example, `/dev/ttyS1`). This is necessary when several programs access the serial interface and your system also answers incoming calls (for example, to receive faxes). Together with the serial interface, you can also set the requested transmission speed. The configuration is stored in `/etc/minirc.dfl`.

Usually, `minicom` is configured in such a way that it can only be used by `root`. To allow the program to be used by other users as well, `root` must enter their names into the configuration file `/etc/minicom.users`. This is normally the second step after setting up the serial interface.

`minicom` is menu-driven. The main menu (a kind of help text) is called with Ctrl+A, Z. By entering an additional letter, you are led into submenus, for example for modification of various configuration data. Once you know the corresponding letters, you can circumvent the main menu and call a command directly with Ctrl+A and a letter (for example, Ctrl+A, D for dialling).

Apart from the extension of `minicom.users`, usually no further configuration of `minicom` is needed; that is, the default settings can stay unchanged. You can enter the configuration menu with Ctrl+A, O if you are using a modem that does not use the AT command set, if you want to transmit additional initialization commands to the modem, and so on. The configuration should be carried out by `root`, which will make it valid for all `minicom` users.

Independently of the remaining configuration data, `minicom` manages a phone list which can be accessed with Ctrl+A, D. Additions to the list are again made via menus. For each number, you can specify the required type of terminal emulation (VT 102 or ANSI) and a script file to be automatically executed after the connection has been established (see below). Which terminal emulation you must use depends on the computer you are contacting via the modem.

The phone list is stored in each user's current home directory under the name `.dialdir`; that is, you can only access numbers which you have defined yourself.

`minicom` keyboard shortcuts	
Ctrl+A, D	dial, establish connection
Ctrl+A, G	execute script file (go)
Ctrl+A, H	terminate connection (hangup)
Ctrl+A, L	protocol screen output in a file
Ctrl+A, Q	terminate program without modem reset (quit)
Ctrl+A, R	receive files
Ctrl+A, S	send files
Ctrl+A, X	terminate program with reset (exit)

File transmission

Most mailboxes and Internet providers offer the possibility of transmitting single files (in both directions) in binary format, using a special command. For this purpose, `minicom` supports the data transmission protocols `x/y/zmodem`. A data transmission from the local computer is started with Ctrl+A, S (send), and the opposite direction is selected with Ctrl+A, R (receive). Subsequently, the required protocol is selected.

The data transmission itself is carried out by calling the utility programs `sz`, `sb`, `sx`, `rz`, `rb` or `rx`. For these programs, the device name of the modem must be specified in the environment variable `RZSZLINE`.

```
# Addition to /etc/profile
# substitute ttyS1 with the name of your interface
export RZSZLINE="/dev/ ttyS1"
```

Online information about `sz`, `sb`, `sx`, `rz`, `rb` and `rx` can be obtained with the commands `man rz` and `man sz`.

Script programming

Now you will probably ask yourself what else can be programmed in a terminal emulator. But after having logged in to an Internet system or a mailbox for the tenth time and having finally worked your way through to the mail system via five menu levels, you will definitely feel the desire to automate such repetitive tasks.

For such purposes, `minicom` provides a simple script language. This language is used to recognize certain keywords (such as 'login', 'password') and to react to them with the transmission of character strings (the user name, the password, and so on). Script files are not directly executed by `minicom`, but by the `runscript` interpreter.

The following list summarizes the most important commands of this interpreter. A complete overview of all commands is given by `man runscript`.

`minicom` script commands	
`# comment`	comment
`exit`	terminates the script program
`expect { "pattern" command "pattern" command ... }`	executes one of the commands as soon as the corresponding pattern has been recognized
`goto label`	jumps to the line labeled with `label:`
`print "character string"`	displays the character string on screen
`send "character string"`	transmits the character string to the modem
`sleep n`	waits *n* seconds
`timeout n`	limits the waiting time of `expect` to *n* seconds

The syntax of `runscript` is not always very intuitive. A particularly irritating command is `expect`: it only works if both curly brackets are placed in separate lines of their own and the { bracket is followed by a space (although no further commands are allowed in this line anyway). Thus, writing `runscript` programs is mainly a matter of patience (using the tried and tested trial and error method).

To test script programs, you can execute them directly with `runscript` without starting `minicom` first. The patterns which the program expects from the modem must now be entered via the keyboard.

The following example shows a script for a typical login on a Unix system. The program waits for the character string 'ogin' (in order for both 'Login' and 'login' to be recognized), then sends the user name, waits for 'word:', then sends the password, and so on.

```
print "Login trial"
expect
  "ogin:"
  timeout 20 goto error

# here the user name must be entered
send "moser"
expect
  "word:"
  timeout 5 goto error

# here the password must be entered
send "sfd4kDs"
exit
error:
print "Something must have gone wrong!"
```

You should create a separate directory for the storage of script files. To ensure that `minicom` finds the files, you must set the directory with Ctrl+A, O, FILENAMES AND PATHS, C.

Please check the access rights of this directory and the files contained in it to make sure that nobody but yourself can read these files. After all, the above file contains your password for your Internet account! If you integrate the script file into your phone list (it provides a separate entry for script files), `minicom` executes the file automatically as soon as a connection has been established. Much more complex tasks can also be automated following the pattern of the above file.

seyon

`seyon` essentially carries out the same functions as `minicom`, but runs under X and is slightly easier to handle. The program is controlled through buttons which are for the most part labeled very clearly. (Some additional functions can be executed via the MISC button. There, for example, you will find the CAPTURE button. After clicking it, all input and output is written to the file `~/.seyon/capture` – unfortunately strewn with countless special characters.)

Because of its easy handling, this section mainly concentrates on the correct configuration of `seyon`. Very extensive online information about `seyon` can be obtained with `man seyon` or by clicking on the HELP button.

In general, `seyon` will run immediately, without long-winded configuration settings. You may have to specify the `-modems /dev/ttySn` option in the calling command to tell `seyon` which interface it should use for accessing the modem.

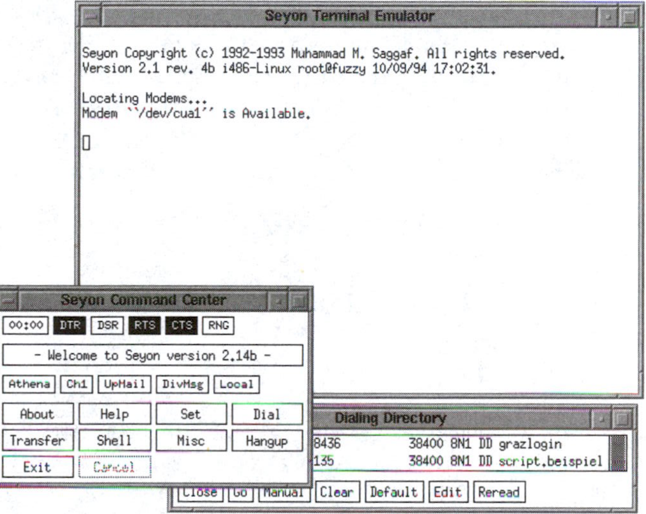

Figure 15.16 The `seyon` terminal emulator.

Configuration

`seyon` is controlled through several configuration files. Most files are located in the `~/.seyon` directory, such as the initialization file `startup`, the phone list `phonelist` and the definition of various transmission protocols in `protocols`. Sample configuration files for copying into your own home directory can be found in `/root/.seyon`.

Various additional settings can be carried out in `~/.Xdefaults`. Probably the most important setting in `.Xdefaults` is that of the serial interface:

```
! in ~/.Xdefaults
! Setting of the serial interface for seyon
Seyon.modems:   /dev/ttyS1
```

In `phonelist`, only two specifications per line are compulsory: the phone number and a text to identify this number. All further indications are entered in the form `OPTION=...`. The two most important options to be set are `SCRIPT` (automatic execution of a script file after the connection has been established) and `BPS` (required transmission speed). The phone list can also be extended during normal operation of `seyon`.

```
# ~/.seyon/phonelist
123456 tugraz     SCRIPT=grazlogin BPS=38400
234567 mailboxxy  SCRIPT=xylogin   BPS=38400
```

`startup` contains some general configuration settings, such as the required transmission speed, the number of bits to be transmitted, and so on.

Script programming

Similarly to `minicom`, `seyon` too is equipped with a script language. However, this language has a much more powerful syntax which resembles that of the `bash`. In comparison to the experiences encountered with `minicom`, script programming for `seyon` is sheer pleasure. Usually, script files are stored in the `~/.seyon` directory.

A precise definition of all script commands is given in the `man` text. The following table summarizes the most important commands.

`seyon` script commands	
`# comment`	comments
`echo "character string"`	displays the character string on screen
`exit`	terminates the script program
`goto label`	jumps to the line labeled with `label:`
`pause n`	waits for n seconds
`transmit "character string"`	transmits the character string to the modem
`waitfor "character string" [n]`	waits for a maximum of n seconds before the modem receives the specified character string; if n is not specified, the timeout is 30 seconds

Please note that transmit does not transmit carriage return characters! An end of line must be explicitly specified with the two characters `^M`. `^` can also precede various other control characters. The following minimal sample can be used to automate a login into a Unix system (specification of user name and password).

```
# ~/.seyon/script.sample
echo "Login Script"
waitfor "ogin:" 10
transmit "moser^M"
waitfor "word:" 3
transmit "asd4jKl^M"
```

15.7 Writing CD-ROMs

This section provides an introduction to ISO image creation and CD-ROMs writing under Linux. The main focus will be on single-session data CDs in ISO 9660 format, whereas various other variations (audio CDs, multi-session CDs) will not be considered.

To begin with, an overview of the most important steps:

- Before you can write a CD-ROM, you need to prepare the data, that is, create an ISO image of the data processed for the CD-ROM file system. Usually, the `mkisofs` command is employed for this purpose.
- For writing the CD-ROM, you can choose between the programs `cdwrite` (old, not being developed any further) and `cdrecord`. If none of these programs supports your CD-R drive, you can also create the CD under Windows or another operating system; most CD-R programs are able to write the ISO image created with `mkisofs`.
- Depending on kernel version and SCSI hardware, it may be necessary, before writing a CD-ROM, to patch and recompile the kernel.
- Finally, you should check the CD-ROM. Various programs are available which can either be used to read all data blocks or all files or to compare the contents of the CD-ROM with an existing file system.
- Instead of the command-oriented programs `mkisofs` and `cdrecord`, you can also use the X program `xcdroast`, which allows you to carry out both steps with the aid of a user-friendly interface.

TIP

Up-to-date versions of the programs discussed in this section can be found on the Internet:

```
ftp://ftp.ge.ucl.ac.uk/pub/mkhfs
ftp://ftp.fokus.gmd.de/pub/unix/cdrecord/
http://www.fh-muenchen.de/home/ze/rz/services/projects/xcdroast
```

Creating and testing an ISO image

The easiest way to create an ISO image is when you want to copy a data CD (not an audio CD!) unchanged:

```
root#  dd if=/dev/cdrom of=/usr/local/iso.img bs=2048
```

```
mkisofs [options] -o iso_file directory
```

The normal case is, however, that you first put together the data for a new CD-ROM in a directory and subsequently generate an ISO image. This is exactly what `mkisofs` does: the command creates a file which contains all files of a directory and which is formatted according to the ISO-9660 conventions (optionally with Rockridge extension).

`-a` Files beginning with `#` or ending with `~` are considered as well. Usually, this is not the case, because such files are mostly backup files.

`-b` *`file`*
The specified file is stored as a boot image. At computer start-up, this file is automatically executed (provided the BIOS is configured accordingly). The size of the file must correspond exactly to what will fit on a 3.5 or 5.25 inch diskette (1.2, 1.44 or 2.88 Mbytes).

`-c` *`name`*
This option specifies the file name under which the so-called boot catalog should be stored on the CD. The catalog is created by `mkisofs`. When specifying the name, you merely need to ensure that there is no conflict with an existing file. (The `man` text for `mkisofs` recommends using a name such as `boot.catalog`.)

`-D` The ISO standard allows for a maximum of eight directory levels. `mkisofs` usually sticks to this standard and, if needed, modifies the directory hierarchy (and the names of the affected files). The `-D` option prevents this; however, on some systems which require strict adherence to the ISO standard this may lead to problems.

`-f` Symbolic links are followed, that is, the contents of files or subdirectories specified in this manner are included into the ISO image. (Without this option, only the link is stored in the ISO image. However, symbolic links can only be mapped to CDs with Rockridge extension.)

`-o` *`file`*
The ISO image is stored in *file*.

`-R` The ISO image uses the Rockridge extension to store information on long file names.

`-r` As `-R`, but UID and GID are set to 0 for all files (corresponds to `root`). At the same time, all R access bits are set; in addition, all X access bits if at least one X bit was set in the original file (see also `chmod` on page 444).

`-T` The file `TRANS.TBL` is written into each directory; this specifies the short ISO-9660 name under which files with long Unix names can be found. (This is necessary to allow association to long file names under DOS/Windows as well.)

`-V` *name*

This option specifies the volume ID, that is the name of the CD-ROM (max. 32 characters) as shown, for example, under Windows.

Example

```
root#  mkisofs -o /mnt/dos/iso.img -r -T -V Linux_3_98 /master
```

The above command writes all files contained in the `/master` directory into the file `linimg.raw`. For reasons of space, this file is stored on a DOS partition which is mounted into the file system at the mounting point `mnt/dos`. `master` itself is *not* a directory in the ISO image.

```
root#  mkisofs -o /mnt/dos/iso.img -r -T /master \
   >   -b /images/boot.img -c boot.catalog
```

As above, but this time a bootable CD is created.

TIP

If you do not use the option `-r`, here are some tips: make sure that all files in the `master` directory are owned by `root` and are readable by all!

```
root# chown -R root.root /master
root# chmod -R a+r /master
```

Testing the ISO image

Provided that you have compiled your kernel with the *Loopback device support* option (category *Block devices*) or the corresponding module `loop.o` is available and can be activated on demand by means of `insmod`, you can mount the newly created file `linimg.raw` in read-only mode into the file system:

```
root#  mkdir /iso-test
root#  mount -t iso9660 -o loop,ro /mnt/dos/linimg.raw /iso-test/
```

You can now test the contents of the future CD-ROM (access rights, `TRANS.TBL`, and so on) via the `iso-test` directory. You need to use a kernel version of 2.0.31 or later – otherwise Linux signals an I/O error for the last file of the image although the ISO image is all right!

Hybrid CDs

Hybrid CDs contain the data itself only once; however, they allow access to this data via different file systems, depending on the operating system. On a Macintosh, the CD-ROM is recognized with the HFS file system; under Windows 9x/NT, as an ISO-9660 CD with Joliet extension; under Unix, equally as an ISO-9660 CD, but with Rockridge extension. Thus, hybrid CDs allow CD-ROMs with long file names which are correctly recognized on (almost) all operating systems. Sounds like magic, doesn't it?

ISO images for hybrid CDs can be created with the `mkhybrid` command, which is a variation of `mkisofs`. `mkhybrid` works in the same ways as `mkisofs`, but supports some additional options:

`-h` Creates a hybrid CD with HFS information (Macintosh).

`-j` Employs the Joliet extension (Microsoft Windows).

Writing CDs with cdrecord

`cdrecord` transfers an appropriately formatted file (ISO image for data CDs) to the CD-R drive. In principle, `cdrecord` is multi-session capable, that is, the CD can be extended in several sessions. This description is, however, limited to single-session CDs where all data is transferred in one go.)

```
cdrecord [options] dev=channel,id,lun isoimage
```

`driver=`*`name`*
: Specifies the type of CD-R drive. Supported types are displayed with `cdrecord driver=help`. `cdrecord -checkdrive dev=`n, n, n can be used to determine the type of the existing CD-R drive.

`-dummy`
: The write process is only simulated. Ideal for testing!

`-eject`
: Ejects the CD after the write process. Some CD-R drives require ejection before the next CD can be written, even if the last one was only simulated with `-dummy`.

`fs=`*`n`*
: This option specifies the size of the FIFO buffer used for buffering the data transfer between hard disk and CD. Reasonable values lie between 2 and 8 Mbytes (thus `fs=2m` or `fs=8m`).

`speed=`*`n`*
: This option *without* a prefixed hyphen specifies the writing speed (usually 1, 2 or 4).

`-v` `cdrecord` displays verbose messages on what is currently happening.

Some brief information on specifying the CD-R drive: `cdrecord` expects this information not as a device name, but in the form of three numbers: the SCSI bus number (usually 0), the SCSI ID of the device, and finally the Logical Unit Number (LUN, usually also 0). The easiest way to determine the numbers is to execute `cat /proc/scsi/scsi`:

```
root#  cat /proc/scsi/scsi
Attached devices:
Host: scsi0 Channel: 00 Id: 04 Lun: 00
  Vendor: TOSHIBA  Model: CD-ROM XM-3601TA Rev: 0725
  Type:    CD-ROM                          ANSI SCSI revision: 02
```

```
Host: scsi0 Channel: 00 Id: 05 Lun: 00
  Vendor: TEAC     Model: CD-R50S-000      Rev: 1.0E
  Type:   CD-ROM                           ANSI SCSI revision: 02
Host: scsi0 Channel: 00 Id: 06 Lun: 00
  Vendor: HP       Model: HP35480A         Rev: T503
  Type:   Sequential-Access                ANSI SCSI revision: 02
```

In the above example, the correct identification of the Teac-CD-R drive would be `dev=0,5,0`.

Examples

```
root#  cdrecord -dummy -v speed=2 fs=4m dev=0,5,0 /mnt/dos/iso.img
root#  cdrecord -v speed=2 fs=4m dev=0,5,0 /mnt/dos/iso.img
```

Theoretically, it is possible to join `mkisofs` and `cdrecord` with a pipe. The advantage: you save the space of the ISO image. The disadvantage: this method requires extremely fast and reliable hardware.

```
root#  mkisofs -r -T -V Linux_3_97 /master | \
    >  cdrecord -v fs=8m speed=4 dev=0,5,0 -
```

Testing CDs

In particular with your first CD-ROMs created under Linux, you should check whether the CD-ROMs contain the required data and whether this data can also be read. (Ideally, you should not perform this test with the CD-R drive, but with a different CD-ROM drive.)

The following command compares the contents of the CD-ROM with that of the `master` directory file by file and byte by byte. All differences are written into the file `diff.log` in the home directory.

```
root#  diff -qrd /data /cdrom/  >& ~/diff.log
```

In a second window or a second console, you can follow the creation of `diff.log`:

```
root#  tail -f ~/diff.log
```

If you have used the `-T` option with `mkisofs`, the CD-ROM and the original data will differ in each directory by the file `TRANS.TBL`. You can use `grep` to filter these warnings out of `diff.log`:

```
root#  grep  -v TRANS.TBL ~/diff.log | less
```

xcdroast

If you want to carry out assembly, burning and testing of CD-ROMs by means of a user-friendly X program, your choice should be `xcdroast`, which is an X user interface for the `mkisofs` and `cdrecord` programs.

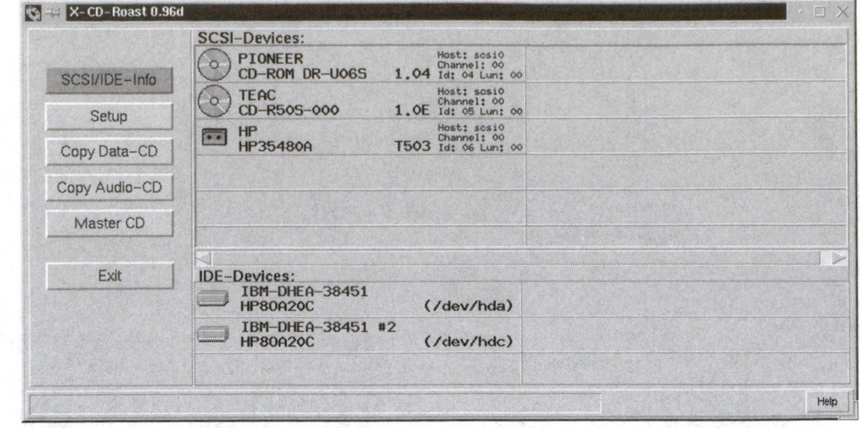

Figure 15.17 `xcdroast` – creating CDs with the ease of windows.

Emacs – king of all editors

Under Linux, you can choose between a large number of editors. Some of them have been briefly described from page 64 onward, and they are well suited for simple tasks. Emacs, however, is without any doubt *the* editor under Linux. If you plan more demanding projects and have to process large amounts of text (even program code) efficiently, there is practically no way around using Emacs.

The most important advantage of Emacs over other editors is that Emacs is extendible and programmable almost without limit. Whether you want to record a simple macro or program a whole online help system such as `info` – Emacs makes it possible! There is another argument in favor of Emacs: it is available on practically every Unix system; in addition, there are versions for most other operating systems (including DOS). Once you know how to handle your Emacs, you will hardly ever need another editor.

Where there is much light, there is much shadow. At first sight, the handling of Emacs may look daunting. The interface is simply strewn with Ctrl and Alt sequences for calling countless commands. It is nevertheless worthwhile memorizing the most important keyboard shortcuts, since many of them can also be used for command input in terminal consoles and/or terminal windows.

TIP In this and the following chapter, Emacs commands that can be executed with Alt+X are set in a slightly smaller typeface, for example, byte-compile-file.

16.1 Quick start

Currently, there are *two* versions of Emacs, GNU Emacs and X Emacs (formerly Lucid Emacs, often in short XEmacs). Both versions show great similarities with regard to keyboard shortcuts and functionality, but have been for years developed in parallel.

Information contained in this and the next chapter applies to both variations, on the basis of versions 20.2 (GNU Emacs) and 20.4 (XEmacs). Issues where the versions differ significantly are explicitly pointed out. By the time you read this book, new versions will have certainly emerged. It is, however, unlikely that there will be changes to the basic functions (which is what this chapter deals with, in any case).

Whether you prefer to work with GNU Emacs or XEmacs is a matter of taste. The programs are started with the commands `emacs` and `xemacs`, respectively. The author wrote the first three (German) editions of this book with GNU Emacs and changed to XEmacs for the fourth edition (and with a faster computer).

Both programs are very stable and are supplied with a wealth of extensions and extensive documentation. XEmacs excels through a visually more appealing menu and a tool bar, and is generally slightly easier to handle. However, it requires significantly more space both on hard disk and in memory. Both GNU Emacs and XEmacs can be used in a text console as well as under X – in this sense, the name XEmacs is misleading.

Some distributions relieve you from the burden of having to make a choice and, for reasons of space, supply only one version; others allow you to choose during installation. (If your distribution provides for a parallel installation in different directories, you can also install both versions simultaneously. Please note, however, that Emacs Lisp files are incompatible with each other.)

> **NOTE**
> When you install Emacs – no matter which version – at a later stage, do not forget that you will usually need several packages: the basic package and the Emacs Lisp package containing the code for many extensions and processing modes. The Emacs Lisp package has in turn two versions, one that is compiled and one that contains the source texts. For execution, the compiled version is sufficient (faster, less space required). In SuSE, by the way, the packages are not named `emacs*` and `xemacs*`, but `ge_*` and `xe_*`.

Besides the two big Emacs versions, there are several smaller variations: `jove` and `jed`, for example, are quite useful mini-versions. (The advantage: much less space requirement both on the hard disk and in RAM.) `jed` in particular, thanks to its built-in help system and its configurability is a good replacement for GNU Emacs in cases of insufficient space and computing power.

> **TIP**
> Even if you work under Windows 9x or Windows NT, an excellent version of GNU Emacs is available. The corresponding XEmacs version was still under development when this book was being written.

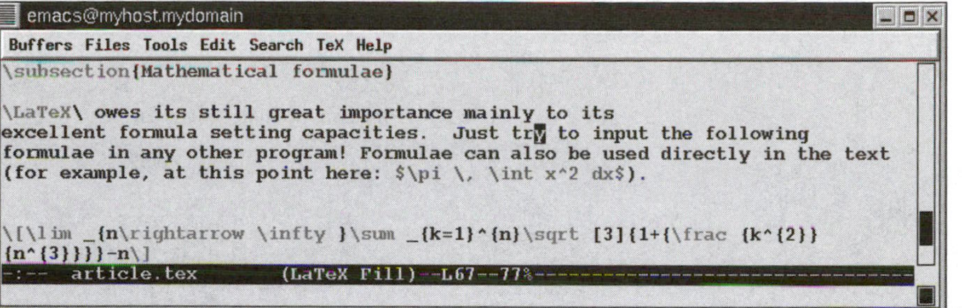

Figure 16.1 GNU Emacs.

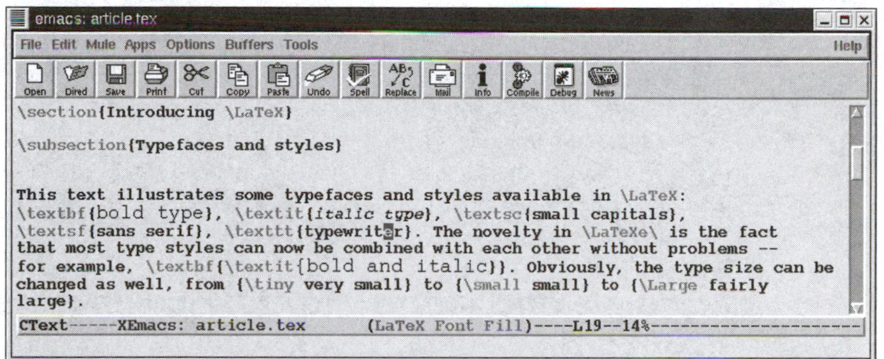

Figure 16.2 XEmacs.

Minimal configuration

In its basic configuration, Emacs can only handle plain ASCII (that is, no characters above decimal code 127 – and therefore no foreign language special characters), both in output and in input. Also, there are problems with certain special keys (for example, Home and Del). The main reason for this is that Emacs not only runs under Linux, but under countless other Unix platforms which are characterized by different keyboard and character set conventions. The basic configuration ensures that Emacs actually does run on each and every platform. All further configuration is left to the user.

Some distributions (for example SuSE) avoid these problems by supplying appropriate configuration files for compiling the program with different default settings for various options. If this is not the case, you can insert individual lines from the following listing into the file `~/.emacs` , if needed. (This file is equally evaluated by Emacs and XEmacs.)

```
; file ~/.emacs
(standard-display-european 1)       ;display foreign language characters
(set-language-environment 'Latin-1) ;correct word boundaries with
                                    ;umlauts and accents
(set-input-mode                     ;enter foreign language characters
```

```
   (car (current-input-mode))
   (nth 1 (current-input-mode)) 0)
(global-set-key [delete] 'delete-char)       ;Del: delete character
(global-set-key [home]   'beginning-of-line) ;Home: beginning of line
(global-set-key [end]    'end-of-line)       ;End: end of line
```

NOTE Information on the everlasting problem of Backspace and Del under X can be found on page 243. If you are interested in more advanced Emacs configuration, you need read about Emacs Lisp programming. This is described in a separate chapter from page 569 onward.

NOTE Current versions of GNU Emacs and XEmacs support input and processing of Asian and other foreign language special characters through the new *MULtilingual Enhancement* (in short, MULE). However, this extension is not yet as mature as other Emacs functions. In the long run, the whole Emacs will be adapted to Unicode. As long as you are happy with common 8-bit character sets (ISO Latin character sets), you do not need MULE. In this chapter, MULE is not described any further.

Loading and saving texts, quitting the program

Emacs is started by entering `emacs` or `xemacs`. When you are working under X and Emacs is installed properly, it will automatically appear in its own window with menus and scroll bars.

When you specify one or more file names when starting the program, these files are automatically loaded. Search patterns are allowed: `emacs Makefile *.[ch]` loads the file `Makefile` together with all `*.c` and `*.h` files in the current directory. Independently of this, you can always use Ctrl+X, Ctrl+F *file_name* Return to load files at a later stage.

To save a modified file, you use the keyboard command Ctrl+ X, Ctrl+S. Subsequently, you can quit Emacs with Ctrl+X, Ctrl+C. If at that point Emacs detects any file which has not yet been saved, a safety confirmation request appears to ask you whether you really want to quit Emacs without saving. If you do want to discard your changes, answer this request with *yes* ↵. You can also save the file under a different name by means of Ctrl+X, Ctrl+W *file_name* ↵.

If you use Emacs on a text console, you can temporarily leave the program with Ctrl+Z. With `fg` you can resume your work. (Under X, Ctrl+Z merely reduces the window to an icon.)

Loading and saving files, terminating Emacs	
Ctrl+X, Ctrl+F *file* ↵	load file (find)
Ctrl+X, I	insert file into existing text

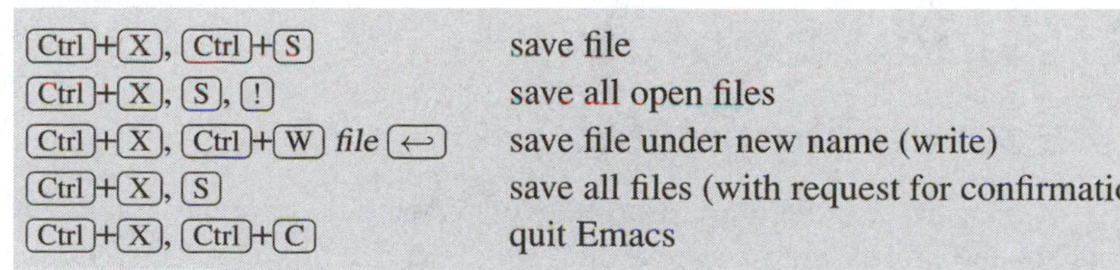

Ctrl+X, Ctrl+S	save file
Ctrl+X, S, !	save all open files
Ctrl+X, Ctrl+W *file* ↵	save file under new name (write)
Ctrl+X, S	save all files (with request for confirmation)
Ctrl+X, Ctrl+C	quit Emacs

When saving, Emacs automatically creates a backup copy `name~` which contains the original text. In addition, Emacs saves the current contents of the file at regular intervals into the file `#name#`. You can go back to this file if you had a power failure or were unable to quit Emacs in an orderly way. At the next attempt to process the file, Emacs automatically comes up with a warning that a backup file exists. With Alt+X recover-file, the old file can be restored.

NOTE

When Emacs is used under X, XEmacs provides an extensive menu and GNU Emacs a rather limited menu allowing you to execute a large number of commands without having to know hundreds of keyboard shortcuts by heart. This chapter does not discuss the menu any further – its use poses no problems anyway.

Elementary commands

Now to the elementary commands for processing a text: when the keyboard is installed correctly, you should be able to move the cursor with the cursor keys and PgUp and PgDn. If this does not work, it will definitely function with the following commands:

Keyboard shortcuts if the cursor keys don't work	
Ctrl+F	cursor one character to the right (forwards)
Ctrl+B	cursor one character to the left (backwards)
Ctrl+P	cursor one line up (previous)
Ctrl+N	cursor one line down (next)
Ctrl+V	text one page up
Alt+V	text one page down

You can enter new text at any position. When you want to delete characters, you can use ← and, in a correct installation, Del as well. Alternatively, you can use the keyboard command Ctrl+D to delete the character at the cursor position.

TIP

With Ctrl+X, U or Ctrl+/ you can undo the last changes. This undo function works for arbitrarily complex commands and is practically unlimited!

When you make a mistake while entering a command, you can abort the command input with Ctrl+G. This is particularly useful if you press the Esc key by mistake.

16.2 Fundamentals

Processing modes

Emacs has various processing modes in which additional commands are available for the processing of special files. A difference is made between major and minor modes: only one major mode can be active at a time, but this can be complemented with several minor modes.

Amongst the most important major modes are C mode (for editing C programs) and LaTeX mode (for editing LaTeX files). When loading a file, Emacs automatically activates the mode it considers suitable (for example, the C mode when the file name ends with `.c`). When Emacs cannot identify a suitable mode, it activates the fundamental mode as a default.

Two of the most important minor modes are fill mode (for processing flow text with paragraphs going over several lines) and abbrev mode (for automatic expansion of abbreviations).

The elementary Emacs commands function in the same way in all modes; thus you do not have to worry about processing modes at this point. Whenever you want to deactivate Emacs' high-handed actions resulting from a special mode (for example, automatic indenting of program lines in C mode), simply switch back into fundamental mode with [Alt]+[X] fundamental-mode [↵]. More detailed information about processing modes can be found from page 558 onward.

Keyboard conventions

Generally, there are three ways of selecting Emacs commands: the menu; using keyboard shortcuts (mostly, a combination involving [Ctrl] or [Alt]); or inputting the whole command name. This third variation begins with [Alt]+[X], thus, for example, [Alt]+[X] delete-char [↵].

Input of commands and other parameters is facilitated by several mechanisms:

- During input, you can expand the command name with [Tab] in the same way as during command input in a shell terminal. Emacs differentiates between upper and lower case spelling. File names can also be expanded. When several possibilities exist, Emacs displays them on screen.
- You can refer back to commands entered previously with [Alt]+[X] by first opening a new command with [Alt]+[X] and then entering [Alt]+[P] (previous) or [Alt]+[N] (next).

In this book, keyboard sequences are specified in such a way that they can be entered on a correctly installed US/UK international keyboard. A plus sign means that several keys must be pressed at the same time, whereas a comma indicates that they must be pressed one after the other. Letters are always indicated in upper case inside their key frames (as they are on a real-life keyboard). Thus, the [Shift] key must only be pressed where explicitly indicated! [Alt]+[X], for example, means that you should press the [Alt] and [X] keys simultaneously, but not [Shift]!

NOTE

In the Emacs documentation, keyboard shortcuts are represented slightly differently: `DEL` does not mean Del, but ←! `C` stands for Control (meaning Ctrl) and `M` for Meta.

On most standard keyboards there is no direct correspondence for the Meta key. Instead of Meta+X, you must press Esc and X (one after the other). Alternatively, in most cases, you can use Alt+X (simultaneously) as well. In this book, we generally indicate the easier Alt key combination.

In some Emacs-compatible programs or when using Emacs in a text console, problems arise with the Alt key. Here, instead of Alt+X, you must employ Esc. Information about correct keyboard installation and Emacs configuration via the `.emacs` file can be found in Chapter 17 from page 569 onward.

TIP

Please note that Emacs differentiates between Ctrl+X, Ctrl+B and the apparently very similar combination Ctrl+X, B. Thus, it really does matter how long you keep the Ctrl key depressed.

Mouse support

You will not be particularly surprised to know that you can use the mouse to change the cursor position, and select and copy text. (The usual X conventions apply, that is, previously selected text is inserted with the middle mouse button.) If you are displaying several texts at a time, you can also move the separation bar between the text areas by means of the left mouse button.

Somewhat more confusing is the handling of the scroll bar: in GNU Emacs it can, as in `xterm`, only be moved with the middle mouse button, whereas in XEmacs, the left mouse button can be used as well.

Further mouse functions depend on the Emacs version. In XEmacs, a position-dependent context menu appears when the right mouse button is pressed. (Try out the right mouse button in different areas of the status line!) In GNU Emacs, in contrast, you can use Shift and Ctrl in combination with the mouse buttons to execute various commands.

X-specific options and resources

When starting Emacs under X, you can perform numerous setting for colors, character set, and so on, by means of command line options. The following table lists the most important options. A complete description can be found in the manual page for Emacs.

Command line options	
`-nw`	start standard Emacs in the shell window (not the X variation in a separate window)
`-fg color`	foreground color (text color; default: black)

`-bg color`	background color (default: white)
`-cr color`	color of the text cursor (default: black)
`-geometry bxh+x+y`	preset size (width times height) and position of the Emacs window; all specifications in text characters
`-fn charset`	starts Emacs with the specified character set

All of the above options can also be set in the `.Xdefaults` configuration file in your home directory. The syntax of possible settings is also described in the manual pages. The following example shows some possible setting for GNU Emacs and XEmacs.

```
! ~/.Xdefaults
emacs.cursorColor: black
emacs.pointerColor: blue
emacs*menubar.background: bisque1
emacs*background: white
xemacs.geometry:81x45
xemacs.font:-adobe-courier-bold-r-normal--18-180-75-75-m-110-iso8859-1
```

Emacs in the text console

This chapter assumes that you are using Emacs under X. However, both Emacs versions can also be started in a text console, although certain restrictions apply: no menu, no tool bar, no scroll bar, no character attributes (bold, italic) in syntax highlighting, and so on.

Some key combinations may well fail (for example Alt+>). If problems occur, you need to work with Esc (see the above hint), modify the keyboard table (see page 135) or change `.emacs` accordingly (page 578).

Problems usually arise with the mouse: it can normally be used only under X. If you have the `gpm` program installed, you can at least use the mouse in text mode for copying and inserting selected text (see page 141). XEmacs recognizes `gpm` automatically, so the mouse can also be used for cursor positioning. In GNU Emacs, the following lines provide more mouse handling facilities:

```
; Addition to .emacs
(or window-system                        ;only in text mode
  (progn (load "t-mouse" 1)))            ;gpm mouse routines as under X
```

NOTE

Even under X you can do without the user interface of Emacs and execute the program directly in a shell window. (This may be sensible when the program runs on a remote computer and only a slow network connection is available.) If you execute Emacs in `xterm`, you can go on using the mouse: simply execute Esc, X xterm-mouse-mode.

16.3 Online help

Emacs provides a number of commands to call online help. The most important one (for getting started) is F1, T (tutorial). Ctrl+X, B, ↵ takes you back to the original text.

If, after the execution of a help command, several text passages (windows) remain on screen, you can use Ctrl+X, O ('oh') to place the text cursor inside the next window. Ctrl+X, 0 ('zero') removes the current window, Ctrl+X, 1 deletes all windows but the current one. Thus, you can use these three commands to toggle between help and text windows and finally remove the help window altogether.

If the help text is displayed in such a way as to take up the whole page, you can use Ctrl+X, B, ↵ to switch back to your original text. (Internally, the management of several texts – such as, for example, your text and the help text – is realized by means of so-called buffers. You can find out more about buffers and windows on page 557.)

Using online documentation

F1, F1	overview of available help commands
F1, A *text* ↵	overview of all commands containing *text* (apropos)
F1, B	overview of all keyboard shortcuts (bindings)
F1, C *shortcut*	brief description of the associated command
F1, F *command* ↵	brief description of the command (function)
F1, Shift+F	Emacs FAQ (Frequently Asked Questions)
F1, I	starts the info system for the display of hierarchical help texts (for usage see page 74)
F1, N	summary of new features in the current version in contrast to previous versions
F1, T	introduction to using Emacs (help tutorial)
F1, Ctrl+F *name*	starts the `info` system and displays information on the specified command
F1, Ctrl+P	information on the concept of free software

The most important source of information about Emacs is the internal `info` system which is officially looked upon as the Emacs manual. In some distributions, this manual is also supplied in HTML format which allows even easier reading.

TIP

In GNU Emacs versions prior to 19.29 you must press the Ctrl+H key combination instead of F1. Further information on GNU and XEmacs can also be found on the Internet:

`http://www.gnu.org/software/emacs/emacs.html`
`http://www.xemacs.org`

Keyboard shortcut reference

The TeX file `refcard.tex` contains a table with the keyboard shortcuts of the most important Emacs commands. It is located in the Emacs `etc` directory (for example, `/usr/share/emacs/20.2/etc/`). If you have an installation of TeX and a PostScript printer, you should carry out the following instructions:

- Load the file `refcard.tex` into Emacs and change the line `\columnsperpage=1` to `..=3`. Save the file.
- Use the file to generate a DVI file:
  `tex refcard`
- Convert the DVI file into a PostScript file:
  `dvips refcard -o test.ps -t landscape`
- Print the file with `lpr test.ps`. (Information on correct printer configuration can be found on page 163.)

The result is a two-page printout whose pages contain three columns each listing nearly all relevant Emacs commands (in landscape format). The commands are ordered by subject (for example, Files, Getting Help, Error Recovery, and so on). Those two pages are constantly somewhere on my desk and are my most important reference source for Emacs!

A further source of information is the Emacs `man` page. However, it only contains details of command options and the setting of X default values for colors, character sets, and so on.

The Info mode

The built-in Emacs online help is stored in the GNU Info format (see also page 74). For reading Info texts, Emacs activates a special Info mode. In this mode, some special keyboard shortcuts apply which are described on page 75. You can follow cross-references and menu entries by simply clicking the middle mouse button. [L] takes you back to the last page viewed.

16.4 Cursor movement

The most important key combinations for cursor movement have already been introduced in the previous section: the four cursor keys plus [PgUp] and [PgDn]. Apart from these, there is a choice of various other commands:

Cursor movement	
[Alt]+[F] / [Alt]+[B]	cursor one word forward / backward
[Ctrl]+[A] / [Ctrl]+[E]	cursor to beginning / end of line
[Alt]+[A] / [Alt]+[E]	cursor to beginning / end of paragraph
[Alt]+[V] / [Ctrl]+[V]	text one page up / down

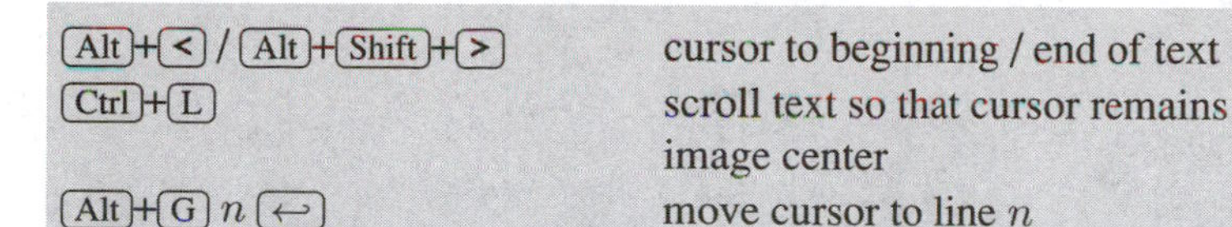

Alt+< / Alt+Shift+>	cursor to beginning / end of text
Ctrl+L	scroll text so that cursor remains in image center
Alt+G n ↵	move cursor to line n

If you want to know which line you are currently working on, you can enter Alt+X what-line ↵; Emacs displays the current line number in the bottom line of the screen. It might be even easier to activate a permanent line number display with Alt+X line-number-mode ↵. Unfortunately, this display stops functioning with very long texts (of more than about one Mbyte). Obviously, the column number can be displayed as well – just activate the column-number-mode!

Emacs is capable of executing any of its commands several times in succession. First, you enter Alt+n, where n is an arbitrary number (it may run to several digits). The digits must be keyed in on the alphanumeric part of the keyboard (not on the numeric keypad on the right-hand side). During the input of the numbers you must keep the Alt key depressed. Subsequently, you enter a command – for example, PgDn. This causes Emacs to scroll the text down by n pages. This process can be used for all Emacs commands (including the input of text characters).

Saving cursor positions in registers

In a longer text it is often desirable to jump quickly back and forth between different places in the text. For this purpose, the current cursor position can be stored in a so-called register. A register is a memory location which is identified by a text character (letter or digit). At a later point in time, this register can be used to jump back to the originally saved position. Note: Registers are not saved when quitting Emacs.

Cursor position registers	
Ctrl+X, r, Spacebar *char* ↵	store current cursor position in *char* register
Ctrl+X, R, J *char* ↵	jump to cursor position stored in *char* register

16.5 Marking, deleting and inserting text

You have already met Del or Ctrl+D and ← for the deletion of single characters. Emacs can also delete larger amounts of text:

Deleting and inserting text	
Alt+D	deletes the following word or the rest of the word after the cursor position
Alt+←	deletes the previous word or the beginning of the word up to the cursor position

Ctrl+K	deletes the rest of the line after the cursor position
Alt+0, Ctrl+K	deletes the beginning of the line up to the cursor position
Alt+M	deletes the following paragraph
Alt+Z, c	deletes all characters up to the next occurrence of c (including the c character)
Ctrl+Y	inserts the most recently deleted text at the current cursor position

If you execute one of these delete commands several times in succession, Ctrl+Y inserts the entire deleted text. Ctrl+Y can be executed more than once and at any point in the text. Thus, this command allows you to move or copy the deleted text to a different place.

The above commands are relatively inflexible because the amount of text to be deleted is preset. However, Emacs can obviously also delete (and subsequently insert) arbitrary sections of text. The method of selecting an area of text is somewhat unusual: you must use Ctrl+ Spacebar to mark the beginning or the end of the area (this mark remains invisible, but Emacs displays the message 'Mark set'). The selected area is defined as the text between the marked point and the current position of the text cursor.

Marking text	
Ctrl+Spacebar	sets an (invisible) marking point
Ctrl+W	deletes the text between the marking point and the current cursor position
Ctrl+Y	inserts the deleted text
Ctrl+X, Ctrl+X	exchanges cursor position and marking point

The double command Ctrl+X, Ctrl+X is mainly used to check which point is currently marked. The second execution puts the cursor back into its original position.

When deleting with Ctrl+W, the first character between the marking point and the cursor position is considered to belong to the marked area, whereas the last character is considered to be outside the area and is not deleted.

After inserting previously deleted text with Ctrl+Y (no matter whether this text was deleted with Ctrl+W or with another command) the first character of the inserted text is considered as the new marking point. For this reason, text inserted with Ctrl+Y can be immediately deleted with Ctrl+W (for example, after an erroneous insertion).

NOTE

If you cannot get used to area selection with Ctrl+X, GNU Emacs also allows you to use the usual Windows form of selection with Shift. To activate this feature, simply execute Alt+X pc-selection-mode. If you want to use this form of selection as a default setting, you will need to insert the following lines into `.emacs`:

```
(custom-set-variables
    '(pc-selection-mode t nil (pc-select)))
```

Unfortunately, there is no corresponding mode for XEmacs.

Intermediate storage of texts in registers

As can be seen from the above paragraphs, Emacs has a standard buffer in which the most recently deleted text is stored so that it can subsequently be inserted with Ctrl+Y. Furthermore, Ctrl+X, U can be used to carry out a multi-level undo.

In addition, Emacs offers the possibility of intermediate text storage in registers. These registers, which are identified by a letter or a digit, can be inserted into a text any number of times. Registers are particularly useful when you frequently need similar formulations or keywords within a text. Registers (and the deletion buffer) are not saved when Emacs is terminated! If you often define the same registers, you should think about defining macros or abbreviations instead which can also be saved (see page 565 and following).

Text registers	
Ctrl+Spacebar	sets an (invisible) marking point
Ctrl+X, R, S *char* ↵	stores the text between the current cursor position and the marking point in the *char* register (register save)
Ctrl+X, R, I *char* ↵	inserts the contents of the *char* register (register insert)

16.6 Elementary editing commands

Inserting and overwriting of text

Usually, Emacs is in insert mode, that is, the newly entered text is inserted into the existing text at the current cursor position. If you want to overwrite the existing text instead, you must use Alt+X overwrite-mode ↵ to switch to overwrite mode. A repeated execution of the command switches back to insert mode. With a correct keyboard configuration, you can also simply use Ins to toggle between modes.

TIP

You do not have to spell out the command overwrite-mode in its entirety. Entering Alt+X ov ↵ is sufficient. Emacs can expand the complete command name on the basis of the two letters. You can also carry out this expansion yourself by using Tab.

Changing upper and lower case spelling

Emacs provides various commands for changing upper and lower case spelling in already typed-in words:

Upper and lower case spelling	
Alt+C	letter at cursor position upper case, all subsequent letters of current word lower case (capitalize)
Alt+L	all letters of word from cursor position onward lower case
Alt+U	all letters of word from cursor position onward upper case
Esc, -, Alt+C	first letter upper case, rest lower case; when cursor stands at beginning of word, previous word is changed
Esc, -, Alt+L	all letters of word up to cursor position lower case; when cursor stands at beginning of word, previous word lower case
Esc, -, Alt+U	all letters of word up to cursor position upper case; when cursor stands at beginning of word, previous word upper case
Ctrl+Spacebar	set marking point
Ctrl+X, Ctrl+L	text between marking point and cursor position lower case
Ctrl+X, Ctrl+U	text between marking point and cursor position upper case

In the current XEmacs version, foreign language special characters are not affected by the above commands. This problem does not arise with GNU Emacs, but instead it interprets these special characters as word boundaries. This can be remedied with the command Alt+X set-language-environment ↵ Latin-1 ↵.

Esc, - can also be put before a number of other commands and modifies their effect. In most commands, Esc, - inverts the direction of action (backward instead of forward).

Exchanging letters, words and lines

A frequent typing error is the exchange of two letters. With Ctrl+T you can easily correct such exchanges. The cursor must be positioned on the second of the two affected letters, thus, in the word 'exhcange', on the 'c'.

Similarly, two words can be exchanged with Alt+T. If the cursor stands at the beginning of a word, this word is exchanged with the preceding one, and if the cursor stands somewhere else in the word, the word is exchanged with the following one. Repeated execution of Alt+T leads to the first of the two words being continually shifted further forward.

Finally, you can use Ctrl+X, Ctrl+T to exchange the current line and the preceding line. Repeated execution of the command leads to the line above the cursor being continually shifted further down.

Tabulators

In some processing modes, Emacs substitutes long sequences of spaces with tabs. The Alt+X tabify command replaces all spaces in a previously marked area with tabs, whereas Alt+X untabify works the other way round and replaces all tabs with spaces.

Tabs are not visible. Whether an empty place in a line contains one tab or several spaces only becomes clear when you move the cursor across it. With tabs, the cursor movement is jerky.

The standard tabulator width is eight characters. With Alt+X set-variable tab-width you can set a different tabulator width. (If you generally want to work with four instead of eight characters per tabulator, you can carry out this setting in the configuration file `.emacs`.)

Manual indenting and outdenting of text

Indenting and outdenting of text is of particular importance for structuring code in program listings. The most important command is called with Ctrl+X, Tab and indents the text between the marking point (Ctrl+Spacebar) and the current cursor position by one space. Prior specification of Alt+*n* indents the marked text area by *n* spaces. With a preceding Esc, - the text is outdented instead of indented.

Indenting and outdenting of text	
Ctrl+Spacebar	set marking point
Ctrl+X, Tab	indent text between marking point and cursor position by one character
Esc, -, Ctrl+X, Tab	outdent text by one character
Alt+*n*, Ctrl+X, Tab	indent text by *n* characters
Esc, -, Alt+*n*, Ctrl+X, Tab	outdent text by *n* characters

With the above commands, spaces can only be inserted and deleted at the beginning of lines. If you want to insert or delete spaces within the lines (for example, for processing tables or for indenting/outdenting comments at the end of program code lines), you must work with so-called rectangle commands. A rectangle is defined by all characters in the area between the marking point and the cursor position.

Rectangle commands	
Ctrl+Spacebar	set marking point
Ctrl+X, R, O	open rectangular area (rectangle open), that is, fill the rectangular area with spaces
Ctrl+X, R, K	delete rectangular area (rectangle kill)
Ctrl+X, R, Y	insert the deleted rectangular area at the current cursor position (rectangle yank)
Alt+X string-rectangle	insert text before each line of the marked area

Besides this, Emacs has some further processing modes in which automatic indenting is carried out. In C mode, for example, program lines are indented or outdented by spaces at each curly bracket (brace, { or }) (see page 558).

16.7 Flow text

Up to now we have assumed that you use Emacs to process texts in which each line constitutes a unit (for example, program listings, configuration files, and so on). Things look slightly different when you want to use Emacs to process flow text. Here, the unit is a paragraph (of one or more lines). When inputting long lines, the text will automatically 'flow' into a new line.

Normally, Emacs does not carry out automatic line breaking. When lines are longer than the screen or window width, a \ character is inserted at the left end and the text is continued in the next line.

If you want to break a single long line, you can execute the Alt+Q command (in all processing modes): this replaces spaces with line breaks at the appropriate points. Thus, a long line is turned into several short lines. Please note, however, that Emacs considers all lines which are not separated from other lines by a completely empty line as a single paragraph. Emacs reformats the whole paragraph (that is, all lines which belong together). In a program listing, the consequences of this command are obviously fatal! Use Ctrl+X, U to undo the command.

NOTE When you process TEX or LATEX files, Alt+Q shows a special feature: lines that begin with a \ character are considered as a paragraph boundary and are not reformatted. In order to carry out line breaking, you must first join the line manually with the previous line and re-execute Alt+Q.

When entering new text, the repeated execution of Alt+Q becomes somewhat irritating. Therefore, a special flow text mode is provided which is activated with Alt+X auto-fill-mode ↵. When Emacs is in this mode, all newly entered text is automatically broken up. Already existing text is not changed by this mode. Also, deleting text does not lead to automatic reformatting, which is why line breaking must often be forced manually with Alt+Q after changes in already existing flow text.

Lines are normally broken after a maximum of 70 characters. You can, however, modify the column where you want lines to be broken with the following command: Alt+X set-variable ↵ fill-column ↵ *n* ↵. Obviously, you can also specify a corresponding setting in `.emacs` (see page 584).

Line breaking in flow text	
Alt+Q	carries out manual line breaking
Alt+X auto-fill-mode ↵	activates flow text mode (automatic line breaking)

Indenting flow text

When you want to enter several paragraphs of indented text, you can preset the first valid column. To do this, you must enter as many spaces or tabs in an otherwise empty line as your text is to be indented. Subsequently, you execute Ctrl+X, . (that is, Ctrl+X, full stop). Now, Emacs indents all lines from the second line of a paragraph onward to the specified indenting column.

The indenting column only applies to newly entered text. Indenting of already existing text must be carried out with the method described above, with no (!) indenting column defined. Therefore, you must deactivate your indenting column by placing the cursor at the beginning of a line and re-executing Ctrl+X, ..

CAUTION

The Ctrl+X, . command actually stores the characters between the current cursor position and the beginning of the line and automatically inserts them at the beginning of a new line created by a line break. If you execute Ctrl+X, . while the characters left of the cursor position contain text, this text is inserted at the beginning of each new line. This can be used to write several lines that start with a given character string (for example, >).

For reformatting larger amounts of text which are indented in various ways, Emacs provides the command Alt+x fill-individual-paragraphs ↵. This command formats the entire area between the marking point (Ctrl+ Spacebar) and the current cursor position. All current indents are maintained.

Indenting flow text	
Ctrl+X, .	defines the indent column by means of the current cursor position; for this, the cursor must be in an empty (!) line
Alt+M	moves the cursor to the beginning of an indented line (similar to Ctrl+A)
Ctrl+Spacebar	sets the marking point
Alt+x fill-individ ↵	reformats the area between the marking point and the cursor position, maintaining the current indents

Text mode

If you often work with indents, the indented text mode might be more convenient than the above procedures: this mode is activated with Alt+X text-mode ↵. When you want to process flow text in this mode (which will normally be the case), you must also activate the appropriate minor mode with Alt+X auto-fill-mode ↵. (Minor modes define some additional commands which can be used in parallel with an arbitrary major mode – see also page 558.)

The only essential new feature of the indented text mode is that, when breaking lines, Emacs automatically and without complicated preparations indents each new line by the same amount as the preceding one. Also, Alt+Q for manual line breaking now follows the first line indent without 'ifs' or 'buts'.

In addition, the indented text mode has two new commands: Alt+S centers the current line, Alt+Shift+S the whole paragraph.

Text mode	
Alt+X text-mode	activates text mode
Alt+X auto-fill-mode	activates the minor mode for flow text
Alt+Q	carries out manual line breaking, on the basis of the current line indent
Alt+S	centers the current line
Alt+Shift+S	centers the current paragraph

If you want to center lines or paragraphs without switching to text mode, you can call the corresponding commands in all other modes with Alt+X center-line ↵ and Alt+X center-paragraph ↵, respectively.

16.8 Searching and replacing

Incremental search

The quickest way to search for text is to use Ctrl+S *search_text*. Compared with the search commands in other editors, this command has a special feature: it starts searching as soon as the first character of the search text has been entered. If, for example, you search for 'second mode' and enter Ctrl+S *sec*, the cursor jumps to the first word that begins with 'sec'. Instead of entering further characters, you can press Ctrl+S again to jump to the next word that starts with 'sec'. (If you only enter lower case letters, Emacs does not differentiate between upper and lower case spelling.)

If at this point you decide that you were actually looking for 'sending mode', you delete the 'c' with ←. Emacs jumps back to the first word (starting with the position where the search began) that begins with 'se'. If you now enter the 'n', Emacs advances to the first word that starts with 'sen'. Just try it out – you will immediately love the concept!

As soon as you press ↵ or a cursor key, Emacs assumes that the search is finished and places the cursor at the found position. The beginning of the search is stored as a marking point. Therefore you can easily move the cursor back to where it was before the search was started – by simply entering Ctrl+X, Ctrl+X. A repeated execution of Ctrl+X, Ctrl+X gets you back to the position of the search text.

By pressing Ctrl+S twice, you can resume the search and jump to the next occurrence of the search text. If you want to search backwards, just press Ctrl+R instead of Ctrl+S.

Incremental search	
Ctrl+S	incremental search forward
Ctrl+R	incremental search backward
Alt+P	selects a previously used search text (previous)
Alt+N	selects a previously used search text (next)
Ctrl+G	aborts the search
Ctrl+X, Ctrl+X	exchanges marking point (start of search) and current cursor position

If at a later time you want to search for text which you have already searched for earlier, you can select a text from the stored list of search texts with Ctrl+S followed by Alt+P (previous) and Alt+N (next).

Pattern search (with regular expressions)

Incremental search finds text which exactly corresponds to the search text. Often, however, it is desirable to search for texts that match a given pattern.

Search for regular expressions	
Ctrl+Alt+S	incremental pattern search forward
Ctrl+Alt+R	incremental pattern search backward
Structure of the search pattern	
`\<`	beginning of a word
`\>`	end of a word
`^`	beginning of a line
`$`	end of a line
`.`	an arbitrary character with the exception of the line feed character
`.*`	an arbitrary number (including 0) of arbitrary characters (like * in file names)
`.+`	an arbitrary number of arbitrary characters (but at least one)

`.?`	zero or one arbitrary character
`[abc..]`	one of the specified characters
`[^abc..]`	none of the specified characters
`\(`	start of a group (see searching and replacing)
`\)`	end of a group
`\x`	special character x, for example, `\\` to search for a `\` character or `\.` to search for a dot (full stop)

The search text differentiates between upper and lower case spelling. Some examples follow which explain the syntax of the search pattern: `\<[Tt]he\>` searches for the article 'the', no matter whether it is spelt with an upper or lower case initial. Occurrences within words (such as in 'Theme' or 'other') are ignored.

`[Tt]he[a-z]+` searches for words that start with 'The' or 'the' followed by at least one letter. The cursor stops at the end of the word (that is, at the first character which is not a (lower case) letter between 'a' and 'z').

The character pairs `\(` and `\)` have no influence on the search itself. However, the characters in the searched text that match the characters in the group can then be used again to build the replacement text (see below).

Searching and replacing

In searching and replacing, Emacs differentiates between the normal command and the extended version with pattern matching. In the normal variation, upper and lower case spelling is ignored in the search. During replacing, the initial letters of words are maintained in the original upper or lower case when the replacement text is completely spelt in lower case. The search and replace command will not be able to find any search text separated by a line feed, because the wildcards * and + have no effect across lines.

Searching and replacing	
Alt+%	command for searching and replacing without patterns
Alt+X query-replace-r ↵	searching and replacing with patterns
Placeholder in the search text: see page 555	
Placeholder in the replacement text (for the variation with pattern matching)	
`\&`	placeholder for the entire text found
`\1`	placeholder for the first `\(...\)` group in the search text

As can be seen from the above syntax summary, when searching and replacing with pattern matching, placeholders for the pattern can also be specified in the replacement string. This allows you to carry out large and complex operations very efficiently. One example will illustrate this feature:

Replace `function(\([^,]*\),\([^,]*\))` with `function(\2,\1)`: at each occurrence of `function`, the two parameters are exchanged. Thus, `function(a+b,2*e)` becomes `function(2*e,a+b)`. The only condition is that there must be no commas in the parameters of the function. When trying to exchange the parameters in `function(f(a,b),g(x,y))`, the command fails.

Please be careful when you use the pattern search and replace command and save your text first. Especially during the first attempts, it often happens that the search pattern finds rather different (and often much larger) texts than you had planned. (With Ctrl+_ (that is, Ctrl+Shift+-) you can undo an erroneous replace command step by step.)

Keyboard shortcuts for processing the found text	
Spacebar or Y	replace, continue search
,	replace, but leave cursor where it is (in order to be able to check the result; when ok, the command can be continued with Spacebar)
← or N	do not replace, continue search
Esc	do not replace, abort command
!	carry out all further replacements without requests for confirmation (caution!)
Ctrl+R	interrupt the command in order to carry out a manual correction at the current cursor position (recursive edit)
Ctrl+Alt+R	resume the command

16.9 Buffers and windows

You can use Emacs to edit several texts at a time. Each text is managed in a so-called buffer. Even when you work on a single text, several buffers exist: one for the text (the buffer name corresponds to the file name (without path)), one for an Info or help window opened at some time during work (buffer names `*info*` or `*help*`), one for the most recently displayed list of possible commands expanded with Tab (`*completions*`), one for the abbreviations list (`*abbrevs*`, if at some time Alt+X edit-abbrevs has been executed; see below), and so on.

Besides the concept of buffers, Emacs also has windows: a window is an area on screen in which a buffer is displayed.

Normally, a single window is used which takes up all available space. For the execution of some commands (for example, the display of help or other Emacs-internal information) the screen is horizontally split into two windows. The screen can also be divided into several horizontal or vertical strips. In each of these areas (windows) a different buffer can be displayed. You can also display the same buffer in two different windows. (This is mainly useful for very long texts: you can work on two different parts of the text without continually having to jump back and forth with long-winded cursor movements.)

> **NOTE** The window concept of Emacs has nothing to do with a window under X, but only means a partial area within a window. If you really need an additional X window of Emacs (for example, to work on two program listings in parallel), you can easily achieve this with FILE|NEW FRAME.

The following commands refer to the currently active window (that is, the window in which the cursor is shown). The commands change the buffer displayed in this window.

Buffer commands	
Ctrl+X, B, ↵	activates the previously used buffer
Ctrl+X, B, *name* ↵	activates the specified buffer
Ctrl+X, Ctrl+B	displays the list of all available buffers in a window; the window can be deleted with Ctrl+X, 1
Ctrl+X, K *name* ↵	deletes the specified buffer; if the buffer contains a not yet saved file, a request for confirmation appears

The following commands only affect the display of buffers in various screen areas (windows). The separation bar between the windows can be moved with the mouse.

Window commands	
Ctrl+X, O	switches to the next window ('oh')
Ctrl+X, 0	deletes the current window ('zero')
Ctrl+X, 1	deletes all windows except the one the cursor is in
Ctrl+X, 2	splits the current window into two horizontal areas
Ctrl+X, 3	splits the current window into two vertical areas
Ctrl+X, <	moves the window contents to the left
Ctrl+X, >	moves the window contents to the right

The buffers themselves are not affected by the deletion of a window (they become invisible, but remain in memory and can be displayed again at any time).

16.10 LaTeX and C modes

A particular feature of Emacs is the existence of various processing modes which modify the functionality of the editor and in addition provide several special commands. This optimizes Emacs for the editing of different text types. When Emacs is used under X, some modes allow color coding of the text (highlighting of keywords and comments – see page 562).

Emacs differentiates between major and minor modes. Only one major mode can be active at any one time. This mode is automatically selected according to the file name extension and keywords in the text. The major mode can be complemented by one or more minor modes. Each file processed in Emacs (that is, each buffer) has its own mode setting. Thus, a manual mode change only affects the currently active buffer. A switch to a different major mode deactivates the previous mode. Activating and deactivating minor modes does not affect the major mode.

Important Emacs major modes

Alt+X fundamental-mode ↵	standard mode (default setting)
Alt+X text-mode ↵	mode for easy text indenting (see page 554)
Alt+X tex-mode ↵	TeX mode (page 559)
Alt+X latex-mode ↵	LaTeX mode (page 559)
Alt+X c-mode ↵	C mode (page 561)

Important Emacs minor modes

Alt+X auto-fill-mode ↵	flow text mode (automatic line breaking; page 552)
Alt+X font-lock-mode ↵	colored syntax marking (page 562)
Alt+X abbrev-mode ↵	abbreviation mode (automatic expansion of abbreviations; page 564)
Alt+X iso-accents-mode ↵	input of foreign language special characters (page 566)

Besides the modes listed above, there are countless additional major and minor modes, including modes for most programming languages available under Linux. An overview can be obtained with F1, A mode ↵. Information about the currently active major mode can be displayed with F1, M.

Tip

When loading a file, Emacs tries to recognize the type of file from the file name extension and the contents of the first few lines and automatically activates the corresponding mode. If this does not work for a particular file, you can insert a comment in the first line of that file which contains the characters `*-* name *-*`. Instead of `name` you must specify the required mode name (for example, `tex`).

TeX and LaTeX modes

These two modes are practically identical, which is why they are described together. They are activated either automatically when loading a file or manually with the commands Alt+X tex-mode or Alt+X latex-mode, respectively.

Two changes in the behavior of Emacs concern special characters: now, instead of the " character, Emacs inserts `` or '', that is, a pair of single quotes. A " character can only be entered directly after a backslash (\). (Page 584 describes how this rather irritating feature can be switched off.)

At the input of every second \$ sign, the cursor briefly jumps back to the preceding \$ sign to show where the mathematical formula started. (Under TEX and LATEX, \$...\$ has the function of a pair of brackets which encloses commands for the definition of a mathematical formula.) Furthermore, Emacs now provides some additional input aids:

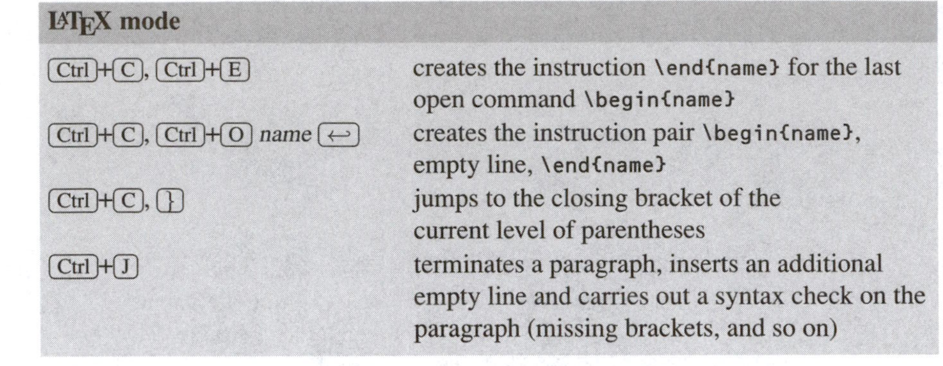

LATEX mode	
Ctrl+C, Ctrl+E	creates the instruction `\end{name}` for the last open command `\begin{name}`
Ctrl+C, Ctrl+O *name* ↵	creates the instruction pair `\begin{name}`, empty line, `\end{name}`
Ctrl+C, }	jumps to the closing bracket of the current level of parentheses
Ctrl+J	terminates a paragraph, inserts an additional empty line and carries out a syntax check on the paragraph (missing brackets, and so on)

Both modes have defined commands for calling TEX or LATEX. These commands, however, only make sense when the whole document is contained in a single file. Under Linux, it is usually more practical to start TEX or LATEX from a separate console or from a shell window.

The Alt+X validate-tex-buffer command is much more attractive: this searches the current text for TEX or LATEX syntax errors. Even though the command sometimes signals errors which are not there (especially when the LATEX command `\verb` or the LATEX environment `verbatim` is used), it has certainly helped me to find many a missing `{` or `}` brace.

NOTE

For professional LATEX/Emacs users, the AUC TEX package provides a considerable enhancement of the LATEX mode: the AUC TEX package defines many additional Emacs macros. One of the most attractive features is that after a LATEX translation you can advance to the next error with a simple click of the mouse. AUC TEX is integrated into more recent XEmacs versions; with GNU Emacs or older XEmacs versions, it must be installed separately. Subsequently, you must insert the line `(require 'tex-site)` into `.emacs`. With this, a range of additional AUC TEX commands is automatically available in LATEX mode. Documentation on AUC TEX can be found in the framework of the Emacs Info documentation and in the file `auc-tex.dvi`.

C mode

The most striking feature of the C mode is that Emacs indents all curly brackets when new text is entered. This visualizes the structure of the program code – almost totally automatically. Nevertheless, it can often be rather irritating when Emacs places your brackets where you least expect them.

How far the brackets are indented for different C structures can be controlled through various Emacs variables. These variables are described in the online help for the current mode (F1, M). In order to change a variable, you enter Alt+X set-variable ↵ *varname* ↵ *value* ↵.

NOTE If you are interested in Linus Torvalds' opinion on reasonable indenting of C program code, you should read the file `/usr/src/linux/Documentation/CodingStyle`. There you will also find some Emacs Lisp commands for use in the configuration file `.emacs`.

In addition to automatic indenting of text when brackets are entered, two separate commands are defined in the C mode for moving the cursor with respect to levels of parentheses:

C mode	
Alt+A	jumps to the beginning of the current parenthesis level
Alt+E	jumps to the end of the current parenthesis level

Much more practical than the input aids are two other features of the C mode: the Etags function and the compilation of C programs from within Emacs.

First the Etags function: `etags` is a Linux command which generates a cross-reference of all C functions that are defined in several files. The program must be activated prior to using the Etags function in Emacs. If Emacs is already running, you can start the command `etags *.[ch]` directly from Emacs with Esc, !. The result of the call is a `TAGS` file which is read into Emacs with Alt+x visit-tags-table.

From now on you can use Alt+. to jump to the definition of any function located in any of the files covered by `etags`. This is enormously helpful, especially in major projects, where functions are often scattered across countless files.

Etags function	
Esc, ! etags *.[ch] ↵	generates the `TAGS` file with cross-references to all function definitions in the `*.c` and `*.h` files covered
Alt+X visit-tag-table ↵	reads the `TAGS` file
Alt+. *function_name* ↵	changes to the file in which the function is defined
Ctrl+U, Alt+.	search for the next occurrence of the function
Alt+X tags-search ↵ *fname* ↵	pattern search for a regular expression

Now to the compilation of the C program: with Alt+x compile you start the compilation from within Emacs. The command used is `make -k` – thus, you must have a `Makefile` in your C program directory. Before the start of `make`, Emacs automatically asks whether you now want to save files which have not yet been saved. Subsequently, Emacs displays the result of the compilation (usually a list of error messages) in a separate window.

Now you can use Ctrl+X, ` to move the cursor to the position of the first error. You can use this command as soon as the first error is displayed (even if the compilation is not yet completed). A repeated execution of Ctrl+X, ` moves the cursor to the following error. Esc, -, Ctrl+X, ` moves the cursor back to the previous error, Ctrl+U, Ctrl+X, ` to the first faulty line.

Ccompiling and correcting code	
Alt+X compile ↵	starts the compilation
Ctrl+X, `	moves the cursor to the next error
Esc, - Ctrl+X, `	moves the cursor to the previous error
Ctrl+U, Ctrl+X, `	moves the cursor to the first error

In general, you can start any program from within Emacs (not only `etags` or `make`). The call is carried out with Esc ! *name* ↵. When a closing & is specified, Emacs starts the program in the background. This has the advantage that you can continue to work with Emacs while the program is still running. The program output is stored in a separate buffer and displayed in a window.

However, it is not possible to interact with the program. If the program detects an error and then waits for input (which, for example, often happens with a call to `latex`), it will wait forever. At this point, the program can only be terminated with Ctrl+C, Ctrl+K (kill). In order to avoid this, you should call only programs that can run independently (even in the case of errors).

Shell script mode

With Alt+X shell-script-mode you can activate the shell script mode. This mode is particularly suited for editing shell scripts (for example, for the `bash`) and configuration files which show a shell-like syntax (which is the vast majority of all configuration files used under Linux).

Syntax highlighting

In combination with many major modes, Emacs can carry out so-called syntax highlighting, where commands, comments, and so on are marked by colors or font attributes. In this way, program code, LaTeX documents, and so on become much clearer.

To activate this feature, you must first activate the corresponding major mode and then execute Alt+x font-lock-mode: now Emacs analyses the entire text and marks the identified elements with colors or font attributes.

TIP

Emacs can only display different font attributes when the active font is available with these attributes. For example, fonts whose names contain something like 8x13 are not suitable (because the italic attribute is not available). You can easily try out different fonts with [Shift] and the left mouse button. The following fonts have given good results:

```
-adobe-courier-medium-r-normal--14-100-100-100-m-90-iso8859-1
-adobe-courier-medium-r-normal--14-140-75-75-m-90-iso8859-1
```

With large texts, syntax analysis takes a very long time; when the text exceeds a certain size, the analysis is no longer carried out at all.

In order to obtain quick syntax highlighting with long texts, you can use the Emacs extension `lazy-lock`. This extension causes syntax highlighting to be executed only for the currently displayed page and not for the entire text. The extension is activated by the following three lines in `.emacs`:

```
(autoload 'turn-on-lazy-lock "lazy-lock"
  "Unconditionally turn on Lazy Lock mode.")
(add-hook 'font-lock-mode-hook 'turn-on-lazy-lock)
```

With really long texts (such as the text of this book, which takes up more than 2 Mbytes), even `lazy-lock` becomes unbearably slow. At that point, it is more reasonable to execute `font-lock-fontify-buffer` manually and wait those 10 or 20 seconds until the process has terminated. (Subsequently, Emacs works at its usual speed.)

LaTeX fontlock problem

When the fontlock mode (no matter whether 'lazy' or not) is used together with the LaTeX mode, Emacs might get confused in its syntax analysis and therefore may mark large areas of text incorrectly. The most frequent cause is a single `$` sign used in a `verbatim` environment or in a single `\verb` command.

The problem can be solved by changing a line in the file `font-lock.el` (the `\"` character is replaced with a space) which will cause no more highlighting of formulae in LaTeX texts. In order for this change to take effect, you must rename `font-lock.elc` or recompile the modified file `font-lock.el`. If only `*.elc` files are installed in your `lisp` directory, you must first install the Emacs Lisp source files. (In many distributions, they constitute a separate package.)

```
; Change in /usr/X11R6/lib/xemacs-20.4/lisp/packages/font-lock.el
; original:
; (put 'tex-mode 'font-lock-defaults
;       '(tex-font-lock-keywords nil nil ((?$ . "\""))))
; new:
(put    'tex-mode 'font-lock-defaults
        '(tex-font-lock-keywords nil nil ((?$ . "  "))))
```

16.11 Advanced functions

Abbreviations

A special feature of Emacs is the ability to use abbreviations without having to carry out any prior preparations. You simply enter the first letters of a word and press Alt+/. This causes Emacs to search for words beginning with these characters, first in the preceding text, then in the following text and finally in all open files. If, for example, you enter env Alt+/ at this point in the text, Emacs replaces 'env' with 'environment'. By pressing Alt+/ again (and again), Emacs offers further options for expansion, for example, 'envelop' and 'envisage'.

> **NOTE** If you want to use the feature of dynamic word expansion in an even easier way, you should assign the `dabbrev-completion` command an easier-to-reach keyboard shortcut (for example, a function key – see page 581).

Dynamic expansion only works if a word is already present in the text and the initial letters match. In some cases, this is not sufficient. For writing email and letters, it would be very handy, for example, if Emacs were able to substitute 'br' with 'Best regards'.

Emacs also supports this kind of predefined abbreviation. Unfortunately, their definition is rather long-winded: first you must enter the abbreviation into your text (for example, 'wheeg'), then call the command Ctrl+X, A, I, G, then type the complete text (for example, 'with the humble expression of my eternal gratitude') and finally press ↵. With this, the abbreviation is stored, and the originally entered characters 'wheeg' are immediately substituted with the new text.

Any time you enter 'wheeg' again in your text, immediately followed by the command Ctrl+X, A, E (abbreviation expand), Emacs replaces the five letters with the above text.

There is an even easier way: with the command Alt+X abbrev-mode ↵ you can activate the abbreviation mode. From now on, Emacs replaces all abbreviations with the complete text if you enter a space or a punctuation mark directly after your abbreviation. (You need no longer ask Emacs explicitly to expand an abbreviation into the full text.) Due to this automatic expansion, you must define your abbreviations in such a way that they do not constitute an existing word (since otherwise, this word would always be replaced with the abbreviation text).

You can view the list of all defined abbreviations with Alt+X edit-abbrevs ↵. The first column in this list contains the abbreviations (enclosed in double quotes), the second column a number which specifies how many times this abbreviation has already been used, and the third column the full text (again in double quotes). The abbreviation list is subdivided into several sections for different Emacs processing modes. With the above command, abbreviations are always defined globally, that is, they work independently of the processing mode and are stored in the section `global-abbrev-table`.

```
(c-mode-abbrev-table)
(text-mode-abbrev-table)
```

```
(lisp-mode-abbrev-table)
(fundamental-mode-abbrev-table)
(global-abbrev-table)
"rt"           6    "\\keys{$\\hookleftarrow$}"
"trl"         19    "\\keys{Ctrl}+\\keys{}"
"lt"          25    "\\keys{Alt}+\\keys{}"
"ky"          22    "\\keys{}"
```

In principle, you can not only view this abbreviation list, but also edit it. The deletion of abbreviations works without problems; you simply remove the corresponding line with Ctrl+K. Usually, you can also enter new abbreviations or alter existing ones, provided you stick to the syntax of Emacs. (Please note in particular that the \ character must be entered twice in order to be inserted into the text once!) Subsequently, you must save the modified abbreviation list inside Emacs with Ctrl+X, Ctrl+S. Ctrl+X, B takes you back to the text you are editing.

Abbreviations	
Alt+/	dynamic expansion of a word
Ctrl+X, A, I, G *text* ↵	defines a global abbreviation text for the previously entered shortcut
Ctrl+X, A, E	manual expansion of an abbreviation
Alt+X edit-abbrevs ↵	activates abbreviation mode (automatic expansion)
Alt+X edit-abbrevs ↵	edit the abbreviation table
Ctrl+X, Ctrl+S, Ctrl+X, B, ↵	saves the abbreviation table inside Emacs, then returns to the text

Abbreviations are usually only valid until Emacs is terminated. The abbreviation list is stored in a buffer in RAM, not in a file. As a rule, it would be desirable if abbreviations that have once been defined could be reused at a later stage. For this purpose, Emacs provides the commands Alt+X write-abbrev-file and Alt+X read-abbrev-file for saving and loading files containing abbreviation definitions.

REFERENCE

With these two commands you can now save and load abbreviations, but the usage of the commands is rather long-winded. In particular, before you quit Emacs, you must remember to save new or modified abbreviations. From page 581 onward, we describe how you can automate the loading and saving of abbreviation files by using a couple of lines in the `.emacs` configuration file.

Macros

Apart from abbreviations, which are merely a typing aid, Emacs also understands true macros in which more complex command sequences can be recorded and later executed again. The recording of a macro starts with Ctrl+X, (and ends with

Ctrl+X,). All keyboard input between these two commands is recorded. With Ctrl+X, E, this macro can be executed.

Emacs always stores only one macro. As soon as you record a new macro, the old one is deleted. You can, however, give the current macro a name before you start to record a new one. This is done with Alt+X name-last-kbd-macro ↵ *name* ↵. Now the macro is stored under the specified name and can be executed at any time with Alt+X name ↵.

However, even named macros are only stored until you quit Emacs. It is not possible to assign a user-defined macro a keyboard shortcut which allows it to be called up more easily. The desire to have both macros and shortcuts available can only be fulfilled by storing the definition of your macro and, subsequently, a keyboard shortcut to be assigned to it in the `.emacs` configuration file. Alternatively you can create a separate macro file; however, you will have to execute it manually with Alt+X *eval-current-buffer* ↵ (whereas `.emacs` is automatically executed at the start of Emacs).

For storing a previously recorded and named keyboard macro in a file, Emacs provides the command Alt+X insert-kbd-macro ↵ *name* ↵. This command inserts the Lisp code corresponding to the macro name into the current file. The command can also be used to insert the Lisp code for all other commands defined in Emacs. However, this code does not look particularly clear since it is strewn with incomprehensible key codes. Thus, editing existing macros is practically impossible.

To summarize, the way to create a permanently available macro is:

- record the macro with Ctrl+X, (and Ctrl+X,);
- test the macro with Ctrl+X, E and, if it does not work as expected, try to record it again;
- name the macro with Alt+X name-last-kbd-macro ↵ *name* ↵;
- load the configuration file `.emacs` from your home directory;
- insert the macro with Alt+X insert-kbd-macro ↵ *name* ↵, then save `.emacs`.

> **NOTE** Macros can be assigned their own keyboard shortcuts. In addition to the macro recording facility described above, Emacs also allows you to program macros in its own Lisp programming language. More on this subject can be found in a separate chapter from page 569 onward.

Entering foreign language special characters

On page 539 we described how Emacs must be configured to allow input of foreign language special characters by loading the 'iso-syntax' library. This allows Emacs to handle special characters which are actually present on the corresponding national keyboards. But what if you have a standard US keyboard or any national keyboard which does not contain the characters you want to enter when writing texts in a different language? For example, if you want to enter characters such as á, à, â, ã or ç on a US/UK or a German keyboard?

For such cases, Emacs obviously has its own special input mode, which you can activate with Alt+X iso-accents-mode. Now, the ", ^, ' and ` keys have a new meaning: if you enter a suitable letter directly afterwards, Emacs combines the two characters into one new letter. Thus, the input " O yields the letter 'ö', " S the letter 'ß'. If you have to input ", you simply enter " followed by an additional space.

New Emacs versions with MULE (*MULti-lingual Enhancement*) have a number of additional alternatives for entering foreign language characters. Execute the command Alt+X select-input-method and then press Tab. Emacs displays a list of over 50 possibilities! The latin-1-prefix variation basically corresponds to the above-mentioned iso-accents-mode.

Using Emacs as a shell

The Alt+X shell command activates the shell mode. Emacs opens a new window and allows you to execute commands in it. The result of these commands is stored in a buffer and can be further processed with all the editor commands. Thus, you can copy the results of a command into another text, or look through the entries of a ten-page file listing, searching for particular texts with Ctrl+S, and so on.

Thus, the shell mode combines the text processing possibilities of Emacs with the command variety of the shell. When you modify a line and terminate it with ↵, this line is interpreted as a new command. In this way, you can correct wrongly spelt commands or modify and re-execute already executed commands in a different variation.

Unfortunately, there are communication problems between Emacs and some shell commands – namely each time the commands want to use specific terminal commands which are not available in Emacs. A typical example is `less` (which you do not need in Emacs anyway; and if you do, simply use `more`).

Client/server operation

Anybody who uses Emacs intensively will inexorably end up carrying out the major part of his/her work under Linux with Emacs – regardless of whether he/she wants to have a quick look at a text file, needs to write an email message or has to manage a complex programming project. However, it makes no sense to start Emacs anew every time you want it – it costs time (and a lot of memory, if there are several instances of Emacs loaded).

In order to avoid these disadvantages, Emacs can be put into a special server mode with Alt+X server-start. (The command can also be executed in the `.emacs` configuration file or with the command line option `-f server-start`. A comparable command for XEmacs, unfortunately, does not exist.)

The handling of Emacs does not change. The only new feature is that you can now start a new Emacs client with `emacsclient file`. The specified file is simply displayed in the currently running Emacs. (When you work in text mode, you must change console; under X, you must change into the Emacs window.)

A new command is provided for terminating an Emacs client: Ctrl+X, #. (Ctrl+C must not be used since it would also terminate the Emacs server.)

In order to have the Emacs client automatically called by various programs, you must preset the `EDITOR` and `VISUAL` environment variables in `/etc/profile` or `~/.profile` to `emacsclient`.

Some programs have to be configured individually in order to call the Emacs client for editing files. In the email program `pine`, for example, the following line must be changed in `~/.pinerc`. Emacs can now be called with Ctrl+_ for writing email messages. Analogous configuration steps are possible for many other programs.

```
# in ~/.pinerc
editor=emacsclient
```

Emacs configuration and programming

The default settings of Emacs – from color layout to keyboard shortcuts – can be arbitrarily modified. Two methods are available: use of the menus and configuration masks designed for this purpose (that is, configuration with the mouse) or direct modification of the configuration file `.emacs` by means of an editor.

To enable you to exploit all the possibilities of `.emacs`, this chapter would need to describe the Emacs-internal Lisp programming language together with all available extension functions and variables. This subject would provide enough material to fill a whole book of its own! This chapter is only a very modest attempt to give a first, practice-oriented introduction.

Things are made even more difficult by the fact that the Lisp dialects of GNU Emacs and XEmacs are not fully compatible with each other and that both versions often provide different extension functions. However – if not explicitly stated otherwise – the basic information contained in this chapter applies to both Emacs versions (GNU version 20.2, X version 20.4).

TIP

Information on some very elementary instructions in `.emacs` for prevention of problems with the keyboard and/or foreign language special characters can be found on page 539.

17.1 Fundamentals

Configuration files

When GNU Emacs starts up, three files – if present – are read in sequence:

```
/usr/share/emacs/site-lisp/site-start.el
~/.emacs
/usr/share/emacs/20.2/lisp/default.el
```

With XEmacs, four files are read:

```
/usr/X11R6/lib/xemacs-20.4/lisp/site-start.el
~/.emacs
~/.xemacs-options
/usr/X11R6/lib/xemacs-20.4/lisp/default.el
```

If, depending on the distribution, the programs are installed in a different directory (`/usr/lib` and `/usr/local` are quite common), the path specifications must obviously be changed. If needed, make use of `locate` to search for the files.

`site-start.el` is the place for global settings which should be carried out in any case, while `.emacs` is for personal configuration settings. `default.el` again applies to all users, but can be individually deactivated with the instruction `(setq inhibit-default-init 1)` in `.emacs`.

The file `.xemacs-options` is automatically created by XEmacs the first time you make changes in the OPTIONS menu and save them. Furthermore, XEmacs appends some additional lines to the file `.emacs` to ensure that `.xemacs-options` is automatically loaded by XEmacs (but not by GNU Emacs).

NOTE

SuSE Linux includes its own `.emacs` file (see the `/etc/skel` directory) which, depending on the Emacs version, automatically loads `.gnu-emacs`or `.xemacs-custom`. Furthermore, changes made through Alt+X customize-browse (see page 572) are automatically stored in `.xemacs-custom` instead of `.emacs`. This mechanism is, however, not standardized.

Directories of Lisp files

Most Emacs functions and, in particular, all Emacs extensions and processing modes are implemented in the Emacs-internal programming language (a dialect of Lisp). In this respect, `.emacs` is nothing special; it just joins the existing basic inventory of Lisp files.

Lisp files are usually located in two directories: the Emacs Lisp directory contains all the Lisp files that belong to standard Emacs. The site Lisp directory is the right place to put additional files that expand the functionality of Emacs. (In principle, these files could also be installed in the Emacs Lisp directory, but they would get lost at the next Emacs update.)

The exact path of these two directories depends on the Emacs installation – if needed, you may use `locate` for searching. The following paths apply to GNU Emacs version 20.2, as supplied with SuSE Linux.

```
/usr/share/emacs/20.2/lisp
/usr/share/emacs/site-lisp
```

Inside Emacs, the `load-path` variable is evaluated when searching for Lisp files. You can view the contents of this variable with Ctrl+H, V load-path.

In order to accelerate the reading of Lisp files, they can be compiled. Compilation is carried out directly in Emacs with the Alt+X byte-compile-file command, which causes Emacs to generate an `*.elc` file from the specified `*.el` file. When Emacs looks for a given Lisp file and both the `*.el` and the `*.elc` versions are available, it uses the `*.elc` version.

For space reasons, most Linux distributions only install the compiled Lisp files. If you are interested in the source code, you must install the `*.el` files separately. The source code offers good examples of professional Lisp programming.

TIP

Beside the Lisp files included in the distributions, the Emacs Lisp archive contains hundreds of additional files which provide Emacs with additional functionality. Thus, before you plunge into the abyss of Lisp programming, you should have a look at this archive. Perhaps the functions you require already exist.

```
http://www.gnu.org/software/emacs/emacs.html
http://www.xemacs.org/elisp-archive.html
http://www.xemacs.org/elisp.html
```

Command line options

When starting the editor, the option `--no-init-file` or short `-q` causes the configuration file `.emacs` *not* to be loaded. This is sensible when an error has occurred during creation of the configuration file and Emacs can no longer be properly controlled. Similarly, `--no-site-file` can be used to prevent `site-start.el` from being executed.

The option `-u file_name` specifies a different configuration file to be loaded instead `.emacs`; `-l file_name` specifies an additional Lisp code file. `-f function` executes the specified function immediately after program start.

Command line options	
`-f function`	executes the specified function after program start
`-l file`	executes another file in addition to `.emacs`
`--no-init-file` or `-q`	starts Emacs without executing `.emacs` and `default.el`
`--no-site-file`	starts Emacs without executing `site-start.el`
`-u file`	executes another file instead of `.emacs`

17.2 Configuration via mouse click

One of the most attractive Emacs innovations in recent years is the new, user-friendly possibility of modifying countless default settings via mouse click. To do this, you simply execute Alt+X customize-browse. Subsequently, Emacs displays a hierarchical menu which can be controlled with the middle mouse button. When you navigate through this menu, you will quickly get an idea of the huge number of configuration possibilities.

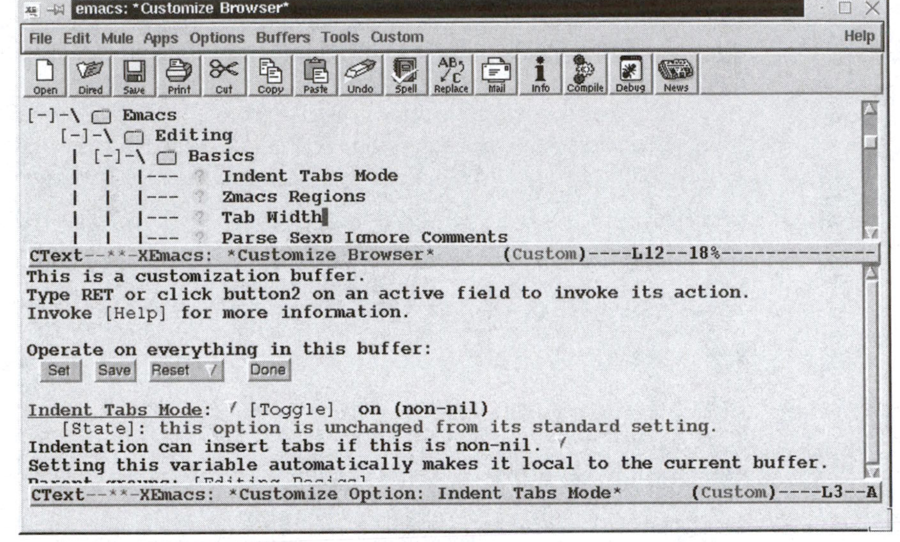

Figure 17.1 User-friendly Emacs configuration.

When you click on one of the icons, the corresponding option, together with a brief help text, is displayed in a second window where it can be changed. In GNU Emacs, mouse operations must always be carried out with the middle mouse button; whereas in XEmacs you may in some cases use the left mouse button as well.

CAUTION

Changes only take effect when you click on the SET button. However, the changes now apply only to the currently running program. If you want to store the changes permanently, you must click on SAVE – and this for each and every change you made. The settings are stored in the file `.emacs`.

customize-browse is available both in GNU Emacs and in XEmacs. In XEmacs, however, menus and configuration options are presented in a visually more appealing and clearer way. In its current version, GNU Emacs still does without icons and represents the same information as ASCII text. The settings stored in `.emacs` automatically apply to both Emacs versions (GNU and XEmacs).

customize-browse has some more variations:

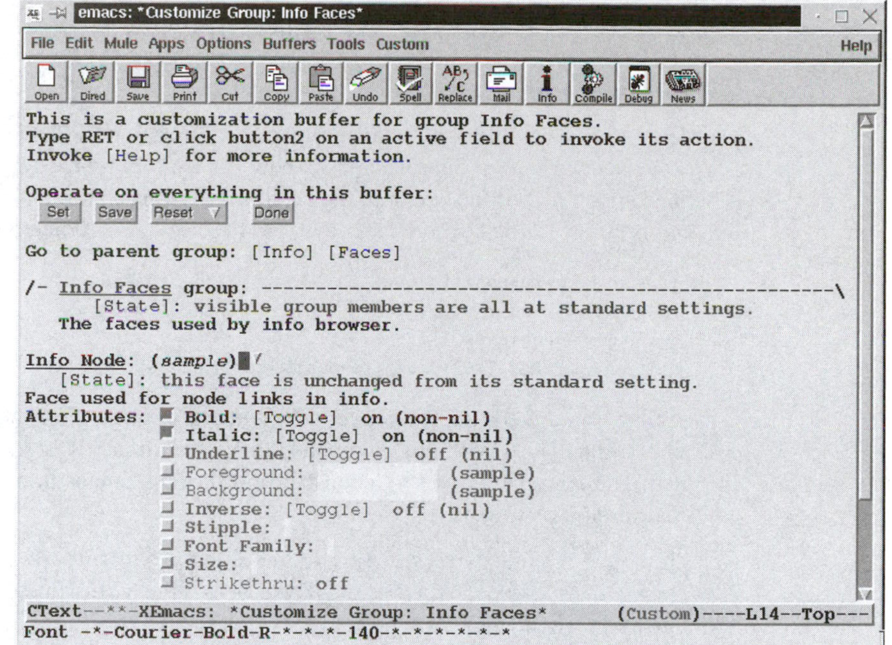

Figure 17.2 Changing the font attributes for headings in info mode.

- Alt+X customize allows the same settings to be made, but navigation is carried out via longwinded dialogs. (customize is the predecessor of customize-browse.)
- In XEmacs, you may also specify your customize settings in an incredibly deeply embedded menu which begins with OPTIONS | CUSTOMIZE | EMACS.
- Alternatively, in XEmacs you can perform many settings with the remaining entries of the OPTIONS menu. Do not forget to store these settings with OPTIONS | SAVE OPTIONS!

  The OPTIONS menu is not an additional variation of the OPTIONS | CUSTOMIZE | EMACS submenu, but an alternative emerged in the course of XEmacs development. The settings are stored in `.xemacs-options` (not in `.emacs`) and apply exclusively to XEmacs (not for the GNU version). Depending on whether the lines for loading `.xemacs-options` are located before or after the other options in `.emacs`, either the menu settings or the customize settings take precedence. To prevent conflicts and confusion, you should not use OPTIONS and CUSTOMIZE settings in parallel. Make up your mind in favor of one or the other of the two variations!

17.3 Programming techniques

Introduction

In order to give you an idea of what an Emacs configuration file looks like, we show a typical code section: in the four lines, a new Emacs function, `jump-to-position`, is defined which moves the cursor to the position previously stored in register 1. This function is assigned the keyboard shortcut [F6] for easy and efficient use.

```
(defun jump-to-position()                   ;definition of a
  (interactive)                             ;new function
  (jump-to-register 1))
(global-set-key [f6] 'jump-to-position)   ;new shortcut F6
```

While you are editing the `.emacs` file, you can execute the command [Alt]+[X] eval-current-buffer [↵]. With this command, all Lisp commands in the active file are executed. The command saves you constantly restarting Emacs in order to try out a modified version of `.emacs`.

CAUTION

If there is a syntax error in `.emacs`, Emacs ignores the file from the faulty line onward. An error message is displayed below the status line, but it becomes invisible when you load a file at Emacs start-up. (In this case, the line is used to display a message about the most recent action – for example about successful syntax highlighting.)

In other words: a syntax error in `.emacs` easily goes unnoticed, and you wonder why subsequent changes in `.emacs` remain without effect. The best way to track the error down is to load `.emacs` into the editor and to explicitly execute the commands contained in it by means of [Alt]+[X] eval-buffer. The incorrect instruction will be identified instantly.

Another very useful command for testing single Lisp instructions is [Alt]+[X] eval-region [↵]. This command only executes the instructions between the marking point ([Ctrl]+[Spacebar]) and the current cursor position.

Executing Lisp code	
[Alt]+[X] eval-current-buffer	execute Lisp instructions in the active buffer
[Alt]+[X] eval-region	execute instructions between marking point and cursor position

Online help about Lisp programming

The Emacs online documentation contains a lot of useful information about Emacs programming: [F1], [F] function_name [↵] gives a short description of the specified Lisp function. [F1], [F], [Tab] supplies a list of *all* available Lisp functions. In order for this list to be viewed, the command must be aborted with [Ctrl]+[G]. Then, you can switch to the buffer containing the list of functions with [Ctrl]+[X], [B] *Com [↵].

If you need the list more often, you should save the buffer to a file (Ctrl+X, W). Similarly, you can obtain information about all variables known to Emacs via the keyboard shortcut F1, V.

You will often want to know the name of a Lisp function which is started via a given keyboard shortcut (for example, if you want to use this function in a function of your own): in this case, you enter F1, C *shortcut*. Emacs then displays the name of the function in the bottom line of the screen.

Help about functions and variables	
F1, F *function_name*	information about the specified Lisp function
F1, F Tab	list of all known functions
F1, V *vname*	information about the specified Lisp variable
F1, V Tab	list of all known variables
F1, C *shortcut*	name of the associated Lisp function

Furthermore, there are two excellent programming handbooks for GNU Emacs: `elisp-manual` describes the GNU Emacs Lisp dialect in about 700 pages. `emacs-lisp-intro` gives a more compact introduction to programming.

Unfortunately, these two documentation packages are supplied only with very few distributions (and then mostly in an obsolete version). However, up-to-date versions in different formats (PostScript, HTML) can obviously be found on the Internet:

```
http://www.gnu.org/manual/manual.html
```

When you work with XEmacs, an extensive Lisp language reference is integrated into the info system. Look for `lispref` in the Info start menu.

Calling Lisp functions

Lisp functions must generally be enclosed in parentheses. The function name and parameters are simply separated by spaces. The accumulation of levels of parentheses typical of Lisp occurs when functions are passed as parameters to other functions.

```
(set-input-mode (car (current-input-mode))
                (nth 1 (current-input-mode)) 0)
```

This instruction allows you to enter foreign language special characters via the keyboard. Three parameters are passed to the function `set-input-mode`, with the first two being determined through other functions: `current-input-mode` supplies a list of four elements, from which `car` extracts the first and `nth` the second element (counting begins with 0; `(car x)` is a short form of `(nth 0 x)`). In a C-type programming language, the above command would look something like this:

```
set-input-mode(car(current-input-mode()),
  nth(1, current-input-mode()), 0);
```

All operations are generally indicated in the notation `(command parameter1 parameter2 ...)`, even simple arithmetic operations, number comparisons, and so on. Comments are initiated with a semicolon.

```
(+ 2 3)            ; corresponds to 2+3
(/ (+ a b) c)      ; corresponds to (a+b)/c
(= c d)            ; corresponds to c=d  (equal)
(<= e f)           ; corresponds to e<=f (less equal)
(/= h i)           ; corresponds to h!=i (not equal)
```

Normally, several instructions are simply written one after the other (each enclosed in round parentheses). For some language elements, however (in particular for the construction of branches with `if`), it is necessary to combine the instructions into a block. This is done using the `progn` function:

```
(progn
  (function1 parameter1 parameter2 ...)
  (function2 parameter1 parameter2 ...)
  (function3 parameter1 parameter2 ...))
```

`save-excursion` works in a similar way to `progn`, with the difference that after the last instruction in the block, the cursor is reset to its original position.

Variables

Local variables are introduced with the function `let`. The scope of these variables is limited to the level of the parentheses enclosing `let`. The two syntax variations differ in that in the first variation the variables are not initialized.

```
(let (var1 var2 var3 ...)                 ; do not initialize variables
  (function1 parameter1 parameter2 ...)
  (function2 parameter1 parameter2 ...)
  (function3 parameter1 parameter2 ...))

(let ((var1 value1) (var2 value2) ...)      ; initialize variables
  (function1 parameter1 parameter2 ...)
  (function2 parameter1 parameter2 ...)
  (function3 parameter1 parameter2 ...))
```

Unlike other programming languages, there are no variable types. Without restriction, variables can store integer numbers, single characters, character strings, lists, and so on. Once a variable is defined, it can be used in instructions without any special marking. Variable assignments are carried out with the function `setq`. You can also use `set`, but in that case the variable name must be preceded by a single quote.

```
(setq var value)             ;corresponds to var=value
(set 'var value)             ;as above
(setq var (+ var1 var2))     ;corresponds to var=var1+var2
```

When `setq` is used to assign a value to a variable that has not been introduced by `let`, the variable is considered to be global. However, care must be taken when naming global variables in order to prevent them from colliding with already existing Emacs variables.

Defining your own functions

User-defined functions are defined with `defun`. Parameters are specified in parentheses after the function name. The keyword `interactive` makes the function generally usable, so that a function call via Alt+X function_name is possible.

```
(defun func1()                        ;function without parameters
  (interactive)
  (function1 parameter1 parameter2 ...)
  (function2 parameter1 parameter2 ...)
  (function3 parameter1 parameter2 ...))
```

When a function requests the user to enter values for the parameters, the `interactive` instruction must contain a character string which describes the parameters:

```
(defun func1(p1 p2 p3)                ;function with parameters
  (interactive "nLine number: \nsText: \nfFile:")
  (function1 parameter1 parameter2 ...)
  (function2 parameter1 parameter2 ...)
  (function3 parameter1 parameter2 ...))
```

The `interactive` character string is split into three parts using `\n`, each consisting of one character for the input type and a short explanatory text. In the above example, after the start of the function, Emacs prompts the user to enter a line number, some text and a file name. Amongst others, the following characters can be used to specify input types in `interactive`: `n` (number), `s` (character string), `b` (existing text buffer), `B` (new text buffer), `f` (existing file), `F` (new file).

The return value of a function is the return value of the last instruction executed within the function.

Branches

Most frequently, branches are constructed with `if`. The syntax is as follows:

```
(if (condition)
  (progn                  ;then block
  (function1 ...)
  (function2 ...) ...)
  (progn                  ;optional else block
  (function1 ...)
  (function2 ...) ...)
)
```

If the `then` block consists only of a single function, `progn` can be omitted. Conditions are mostly constructed with comparisons, such as `(< a 5)` for `a < 5`. Conditions can be logically joined with `(or cond1 cond2 cond3 ...)`, `(and ...)` and `(not cond)`.

Loops

The simplest form of a loop begins with `while`. Unlike `if`, the body of the loop does not have to be indicated with `progn`. The syntax is as follows:

```
(while (condition)
  (function1 ...)
  (function2 ...) ...)
```

Differentiating between GNU Emacs and XEmacs

Both Emacs versions evaluate the file `~/.emacs`. Some Lisp functions are, however, version-dependent, that is, parallel use of both versions may lead to conflicts and syntax errors. To prevent this from happening, you can split the code in `~/.emacs` into three parts: one common section and one section each for each editor. The required code fragment roughly looks like this:

```
; file ~/.emacs
;  common part
... code ...
(defvar running-xemacs (string-match "XEmacs
|Lucid" emacs-version))
; only GNU Emacs
(cond ((not running-xemacs)
... code ...
))
; only XEmacs
(cond (running-xemacs
... code ...
))
```

17.4 User-defined keyboard shortcuts

Basically, it is not very difficult to assign a new keyboard shortcut to a user-defined or a predefined command. Thus, if you often need an Emacs command and have always been irritated by the long-winded call using Alt+X command, you need not despair any longer.

The `global-set-key` command is passed two parameters: the keyboard shortcut enclosed in square brackets and the function name preceded by a single quote.

```
(global-set-key [f1] 'goto-line)
```

In practice, unfortunately, the assignment of user-defined keyboard shortcuts is not as easy as it might look:

- GNU Emacs and XEmacs have a different syntax for composite keyboard shortcuts. In GNU Emacs, Ctrl+X is represented as `[?\C-x]`; in XEmacs, in contrast, as `[control x]`.
- The default meaning of some keyboard shortcuts changes with nearly every Emacs version. (Particularly prone to changes are Del and Backspace. As soon as you thought you had found a reasonable configuration, the next version comes and voids all your efforts ...)
- The code the X server actually supplies to Emacs when you press a key combination highly depends on the X configuration (in particular on `xmodmap`). For this reason Del may behave differently in two Linux distributions, even with an identical Emacs configuration!
- Some key combinations are claimed by Linux, the X server or the X window manager and are therefore no longer available for use in Emacs (for example, Ctrl+Alt+*Fn* to switch between consoles).
- When Emacs is used in a text console, many keyboard shortcuts cannot be processed at all. Furthermore, the meaning of the keyboard shortcuts now also depends on the `loadkeys` program. (Keyboard shortcuts in text consoles will not be treated any further in this context. This chapter assumes that you are using Emacs under X.)
- Finally, several Emacs restrictions must be observed: many keyboard shortcuts are preassigned, and it does not always make sense simply to substitute these shortcuts with one's own shortcuts. Some keys activate a separate level of shortcuts and can only be used in combination with additional keys (for example, Ctrl+X, Ctrl+C, Ctrl+H).

For all these reasons it is completely impossible to write a `.emacs` file that really works in the same way on every computer.

TIP

In order to find out how Emacs reacts internally to a key press, you can use the key combination Ctrl+H C *key*. Emacs displays the internal character string of the pressed key plus the current meaning of this keyboard shortcut. For example, Ctrl+H, C, F5 leads to the message 'f5 is undefined'.

Ctrl+H, C is also a good way to determine the Emacs-internal symbol for special keys. Ctrl+H, C, Home, for example, yields 'home runs ...'. Thus you know that Home is represented by `[home]`.

GNU Emacs syntax for keyboard shortcuts

The entire shortcut is placed in square brackets. Inside the brackets, either single characters (preceded by `?`) or keywords for function keys (without `?`) can be specified.

Combinations with Ctrl are indicated with `\C-z`, where *z* can be any letter (but not a digit or special character). Similarly, the letter S is used for Shift, M for Meta (Esc) and A for Alt. For f unction keys, the backslash character (\) preceding the letters C, S, M and A can be omitted (thus, `[S-f1]`). Some further examples will clarify the syntax:

GNU Emacs keyboard shortcuts			
`[?a]`	A	`[?\C-x ?y ?z]`	Ctrl+X, Y, Z
`[f1]`	F1	`[?\C-x ?Y ?\M-z]`	Ctrl+X, Shift+Y, Alt+Z
`[?\C-x]`	Ctrl+X	`[?\C-x f1]`	Ctrl+X, F1
`[?\M-w]`	Alt+W	`[S-right]`	Shift+→
`[?\e]`	Esc		

XEmacs syntax for keyboard shortcuts

In XEmacs, keyboard shortcuts must in addition be enclosed in parentheses. Keys corresponding to letters are simply coded by the letter itself, with upper and lower case spelling being significant. Status keys are expressed by the keywords `shift`, `control` and `meta` (for Alt). Because of the parentheses, no hyphens are required between the keywords. Generally, these rules lead to more readable code. Some examples:

XEmacs keyboard shortcuts	
`[a]`	A
`[A]`	Shift+A
`[(meta a)]`	Alt+A
`[(control x) (meta a)]`	Ctrl+X, Alt+A
`[(shift end)]`	Shift+End

Key codes of important special keys

In order to save you too much work when experimenting with key combinations, the following list shows the most important special keys under X. The list equally applies to GNU Emacs and to XEmacs. Please note that depending on your Linux distribution and the `xmodmap` setting and versions used, the results may well be different.

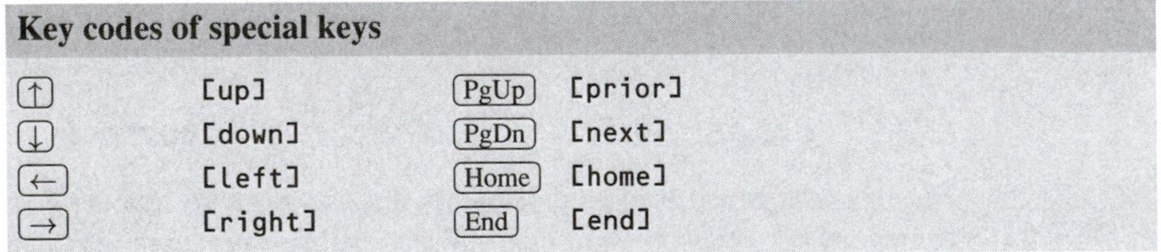

Key codes of special keys			
↑	`[up]`	PgUp	`[prior]`
↓	`[down]`	PgDn	`[next]`
←	`[left]`	Home	`[home]`
→	`[right]`	End	`[end]`

Del	[delete] or [deletechar] or [DEL]
Backspace	[backspace] or [DEL]
Ins	[insert] or [insertchar]
F1 to F12	[f1] to [f12]

17.5 Emacs programming samples

Exchanging two letters

With the key combination Ctrl+T you can exchange the letter at the cursor position with the preceding letter. In principle, this is OK – apart from the fact that, during many years of working with a different text editor, I had been used to exchanging the letter at the cursor position with the next letter – and not with Ctrl+T, but with F11. To make Emacs behave in the same way, the following easily understandable macro has been introduced:

```
(defun swap-char()              ;exchange two letters at cursor position
  (interactive)
  (save-excursion
    (forward-char)
    (transpose-chars 1)))
(global-set-key [f11]           'swap-char) ;F11 under X
```

The function `save-excursion` saves the current cursor position. The cursor is moved one character forward with `forward-char` and the built-in function `transpose-chars` is called to exchange the last two letters. With `global-set-key`, the new function is assigned to the F11 key.

Automatic loading and saving of abbreviations

On page 564, we have described how you can define abbreviations. Such definitions are, however, not loaded or saved automatically when you start or exit Emacs. And this is exactly what the following three lines in `.emacs` provide:

```
(setq-default abbrev-mode t)              ;automatically activate abbrev-mode
(read-abbrev-file "~/.emacs-abbrev")      ;load abbrev. file ~/.emacs-abbrev
(setq save-abbrevs t)                     ;automatically save when changed
```

`setq-default` assigns a variable a default value, where the assignment of `t` corresponds to the truth value `true` of other programming languages.

Opinions about automatic expansion of abbreviations differ. It can be rather irritating when Emacs suddenly recognizes some unwanted character combinations as abbreviations. If you prefer to expand your abbreviations manually, you can remove the first instruction from the above listing and instead define an easily reachable keyboard shortcut for the existing `expand-abbrev` function. With this, abbreviations are only expanded manually by pressing F3.

```
(global-set-key [f3] 'expand-abbrev)      ;expand abbreviations manually
```

Handling of abbreviations becomes even more interesting with the following macro: `expand-abbrev-or-dabbrev` first tries to use an abbreviation contained in the abbreviation table. If no suitable abbreviation is found, the macro calls `dabbrev-expand` in order to expand dynamically. Thus, F3 can be used both for predefined abbreviations and for dynamic expansion at the same time.

```
(defun expand-abbrev-or-dabbrev()     ;expansion of abbreviations with F3
  (interactive)
  (if (not (expand-abbrev))           ;if no abbreviation exists
    (progn
    (dabbrev-expand nil))))           ;dynamic expansion
(global-set-key [f3]  'expand-abbrev-or-dabbrev)
```

The above example also shows the definition of a new Lisp function: the function initiates with the keyword `defun`. Through the `interactive` command, the function is registered as an Emacs command and can thus be called with Alt+X in the same way as all other commands.

Changing upper and lower case spelling

Although Emacs has countless commands to change a letter, a word, or any other area into upper or lower case, it still lacks a command that simply inverts existing spelling: every upper case letter is to be substituted with its lower case equivalent and vice versa.

The resulting function `change-case` is more complex. `let` is used to define the variable `char` in which the character at the current cursor position is stored by means of `char-after(point)`. In the subsequent `if` condition, it checks whether the ASCII code of this character is greater than 64. This is the case for all letters (and several special characters). If so, the `progn` block is executed.

At this point, the sixth bit of the character code is changed (XOR 32). This changes A (code 65) into a (code 97) and vice versa. Subsequently, `insert-char` is used to insert the resulting character at the cursor position, and the original character is deleted.

The `else` part of the `if` condition is only executed if the code for the character under the cursor was less equal 64 (digits, space, new line, point, comma, and so on). If so, the cursor is moved one character forward. Since the `else` block consists of one single function, no `progn` block is required.

Subsequently, the new function is assigned to the function key F12. If F12 is pressed several times in sequence, the cursor moves forward through the text and changes all letters. To undo such a change, F12 must simply be pressed again over the letter in question. The program also works for German umlauts.

```
(defun change-case()                    ;change upper and lower case
  (interactive)                         ;spelling of a character
  (let ((char (char-after (point))))    ;char at cursor position
    (if ( > char 64)                    ;code > 64, thus from 'A'
      (progn                            ;start of then block
      (setq char (logxor char 32))      ;XOR 32 matches upper/lower
      (insert-char char 1)              ;insert changed character
      (delete-char 1)                   ;delete original character
      )                                 ;end of then block
      (forward-char 1)                  ;else block (only 1 command)
    )                                   ;end if
  )                                     ;end let
)                                       ;end defun
(global-set-key [f12]          'change-case)
```

The following function shows that user-defined functions can also be called in other functions. The command stores the current cursor position with `point-to-register` in register number 2, jumps to the beginning of a word, inverts upper/lower case spelling of the first letter and subsequently jumps back to the stored position with `jump-to-position`. Instead of the two functions `point-to-register` and `jump-to-position`, we obviously could have used a `save-excursion` block as in one of the previous examples.

```
(defun change-word-case()               ;change upper/lower case spelling
  (interactive)                         ;of the 1st letter of a word
  (point-to-register 2)                 ;store current position
  (backward-word 1)                     ;jump to beginning of word
  (change-case)                         ;call above function
  (jump-to-register 2))                 ;back to stored position
(global-set-key [f9] 'change-word-case)
```

Color representation

In fontlock mode, Emacs assigns different text attributes, such as 'bold', 'font-lock-keyword-face', 'font-lock-comment-face' to text sections as a function of their syntax. With various `set-face-xxx` commands you can change the appearance of these attributes: you can, for example, specify that Emacs displays text with the 'bold' attribute in green italics. In this way, you can substitute the pale-looking Emacs default settings with some brighter colors.

The condition `(and window-system` ensures that the subsequent commands are only executed when Emacs is running under X (not in a text console). This safety measure is meant for GNU Emacs, which cannot represent colors in text consoles.

```
(and window-system                              ;only under X
  (progn
  (set-face-foreground  'bold "red")            ;bold red
  (set-face-underline-p 'underline nil)         ;no underlining
  (set-face-foreground  'underline "blue")))    ;blue instead
```

A different syntax applies for setting colors in info mode. The following lines have been created with the aid of Alt+X customize-browse.

```
(custom-set-faces
 '(info-xref ((t (:bold t :foreground "blue"))))
 '(info-node ((t (:bold t :italic t :foreground "red")))))
```

Modifying a processing mode

If you want to change Emacs' behavior, not globally, but only for a given processing mode, you must work with `mode-hook` variables. The code stored in these variables is automatically executed as soon as the processing mode is activated. `add-hook` appends a new function to the existing contents of a hook variable.

The following lines modify the $\TeX$ mode of Emacs: every time the $\TeX$ mode is activated, `auto-fill-mode` activates flow text mode as well. To prevent line-breaking in this mode in the 70th text column (the default setting), the `fill-column` variable is set to 79. The final modification regards inputting the " character: in $\TeX$ mode, Emacs has the unpleasant habit of changing this character alternately to '' and ``. In order to prevent this, the variables `tex-open-quote` and `tex-close-quote` are both assigned the character " (code 34).

Finally, we need to explain the keyword `lambda`: similarly to `defun`, this instruction defines a function. The difference lies in the fact that the function does not have to be named. In addition, the preceding quote ' causes the following lines not to be evaluated but to be stored as code.

```
(add-hook 'tex-mode-hook          ;settings for TeX mode
  (function (lambda ()
  (auto-fill-mode)                ;flow text mode
  (setq fill-column 79)           ;full width
  (setq tex-open-quote 34)        ;no fuss with "
  (setq tex-close-quote 34)
  (and window-system
    (progn
    (font-lock-mode 1)            ;color representation
    (set-face-foreground  'font-lock-comment-face  "blue")
    (set-face-foreground  'font-lock-string-face   "red")
    (set-face-foreground  'font-lock-keyword-face  "magenta"))
  )
)))
```

Percentage cursor movement in large texts

Emacs shows in the status line at which percentage range of the text you currently are (thus, about 50 per cent for the middle position). Unfortunately, the text mode lacks a command which allows you to move the cursor quickly to a position that is expressed as a percentage value. (When using Emacs under X, you will not miss this command as much as you would in the text version, since cursor movement is also possible via the vertical scroll bar.)

When executing the `goto-percent` command, the user is first prompted to enter a percentage value (1 to 100). This value is stored in the variable `p` (the function parameter). Subsequently, `goto-char` moves the cursor to the required position which is determined by calculating `(point-max)*p/100`, where the `point-max` function supplies the last character of the text.

```
(defun goto-percent (p)                    ;goto percent value (0-100)
  (interactive "nPercent (0 to 100): ") ;[Idea: Cameron, Rosenblatt:
  (goto-char (/ (* p (point-max)) 100))  ; Learning GNU Emacs]
  (beginning-of-line))                     ;cursor to beginning of line
(global-set-key [f8]  'goto-percent)
```

The above function has the disadvantage that it does not work reliably for texts in excess of 80 Kbytes. Since under Emacs Lisp numbers are only represented with 24 bit precision, calculating the new position causes an overflow. Therefore, the order of calculation must be inverted: `(point-max)/100*p`. This new formula, however, has the disadvantage that in small texts large rounding errors occur. For this reason, the new function uses different formulae depending on the text size:

```
(defun goto-percent (p)                    ;goto percent value (0-100)
 (interactive "nPercent: ")
 (if (> (point-max) 80000)
  (goto-char (* (/ (point-max) 100) p))  ;no overflow: (max/100)*p
  (goto-char (/ (* p (point-max)) 100))) ;no error:  (max*p)/100
 (beginning-of-line))                      ;cursor to beginning of line
(global-set-key [f8]  'goto-percent)
```

LaTeX

TeX is a widely used typesetting program, especially in the Unix world. It has been designed for the production of scientific texts and can be freely copied. TeX has the disadvantage that its handling is relatively complicated. This led to the development of the macro package LaTeX, which makes the formatting of text slightly easier. With LaTeX you can write almost every conceivable document, from a simple letter to a whole book.

The centerpiece of this chapter is the current LaTeX version, namely LaTeX 2_{ε}. On a PC, Linux represents the ideal working environment for LaTeX: in the first instance, LaTeX is a fixed part of all Linux distributions, together with important utility programs (such as `dvips` and `ghostview`) – thus, the otherwise considerable difficulties of getting hold of and installing a LaTeX version for DOS or even for Windows do not even arise. And secondly, the multitasking environment of Linux allows efficient work.

This chapter gives a quick introduction to getting started with LaTeX and summarizes the most important LaTeX instructions. Emphasis is also put on formal and partly Linux-specific aspects of LaTeX usage, such as printing LaTeX files, problems with character sets, and so on.

REFERENCE

If you would like to enjoy the many advantages of LaTeX without having to get into the details of its rather complex handling, LyX represents an interesting complement. LyX is a kind of user interface for LaTeX, which nearly implements WYSIWYG (what you see is what you get). More about this in the next chapter from page 631 onward.

18.1 Introduction

The specific advantages of LaTeX as opposed to other programs lie in its excellent typesetting quality (for example, automatic kerning, that is, in 'Vector' the 'e' is moved nearer to the 'V') and its overwhelming formula setting capacities ($\pi \sum_{i=1}^{n} \frac{a_i x^i}{i!}$). However, LaTeX also has its disadvantages: the handling of the program is simply Stone Age. Seemingly trivial things such as hyphenation or page breaks must often be changed manually in a long-winded process in cases when LaTeX does not produce the required results as standard.

A few words about the origin of TeX and LaTeX: in its original form, TeX was programmed by Donald Knuth, and the associated macro package LaTeX by Leslie Lamport. Since Leslie Lamport has given up further LaTeX development with version 2.09, it is now mainly thanks to Frank Mittelbach and Rainer Schöpf that the current version LaTeX 2_ε has come into being and that development plans for LaTeX 3 are being carried out.

LaTeX and the most important utility programs

LaTeX is a typesetting program and not a word processor. The difference is that LaTeX is not equipped with its own editor, so that the text to be typeset must be written as a completely normal text file with any editor of your choice. This also means that LaTeX is not a WYSIWYG program (what you see is what you get) – on the contrary: all setting instructions must be specified in the text in a rather complex syntax. If, for example, you want to write a word smaller than the surrounding text, the LaTeX syntax for this is `{\small smaller}`.

The next step after text input using an editor is to translate the text file (extension `*.tex`) into a DVI file (extension `*.dvi`). This is a file in which all page layout instructions are specified in a printer-independent, or rather a device-independent, language.

The DVI file is generated by the LaTeX program. Thus, the command `latex file` only reads the specified text file and generates a homonymous file with the extension `.dvi`. This frequently leads to the generation of error messages which are mostly due to syntax errors in the LaTeX file. More detailed information on the handling of error messages and error detection can be found on page 590.

Once the DVI file has been generated, it can be viewed on screen by means of the X program `xdvi`. If you want to print the file, a further step is needed – the conversion of the DVI file into the format of the current printer. While the DOS versions of LaTeX (in particular emTeX) are supplied with large numbers of programs with which DVI files can be converted into specific printer formats, there is really only one program for converting DVI files into PostScript files under Linux: `dvips`.

PostScript files can be viewed on screen with `ghostview`. Thus, the program accomplishes a similar function to `xdvi`. If you own a PostScript printer, you can now print the PostScript file directly by using `cp` to send the file to the parallel or the serial interface (depending on your printer's connection). For all other printers, you must first use the `gs` command to carry out a conversion between PostScript format and the current printer format.

In more detail, the path from a text file `test.tex` in LaTeX format to a printout on an HP Deskjet looks as follows:

```
user$  latex test                                   #yields test.dvi
user$  dvips -o test.ps test                        #yields test.ps
user$  ghostview test.ps &                          #check the result
user$  gs -sDEVICE=deskjet -sOutputFile=test.hp
          -sPAPERSIZE=a4 -dNOPAUSE test.ps          #yields test.hp
user$  cp test.hp /dev/lp0 &                        #printout on LPT1:
```

During execution of `dvips` or `xdvi`, new character sets may have to be generated. In such a case, both commands start the `mf` program (metafont) automatically. Background information on Metafont and PostScript character sets can be found from page 622 onward.

If you own an HP Laserjet compatible printer, you can use the program `dvilj` to generate files directly in Laserjet format, thus saving the detour via a PostScript file.

NOTE

The LaTeX program itself will be the main item in the rest of this chapter. The `dvips`, `dvilj`, `xdvi`, `ghostview` and `gs` programs programs are described together with some other tools and utilities in Chapter 15 from page 501 onward. Another separate chapter, starting on page 631 is dedicated to LyX.

LaTeX online documentation

The available online documentation about LaTeX is rather unsystematic, strongly dependent on the selected distribution (see below) and mostly addressed to expert LaTeX users. The `man` pages very briefly describe the program calls of TeX, LaTeX, and so on, but give no information on the syntax of LaTeX documents. A good introduction is provided in `lshort2e.dvi`. Another very useful text is `essential.dvi`. The files `usrguide.tex`, `fntguide.tex` and `clsguide.tex` summarize the changes in LaTeX 2_ε compared with LaTeX 2.09, in about 80 pages. However, these guides assume that you already have a good knowledge of LaTeX 2.09.

LaTeX on the Internet

Even though the LaTeX distributions supplied with Linux are already huge, there are countless additional LaTeX utilities, extensions and special layouts (for example, for documenting chess game positions, setting sheet music, and so on). Three Internet servers have teamed up under the name CTAN (Comprehensive TeX Archive Network) to collect these LaTeX extensions. Besides these three, there are a large number of additional Internet servers which mirror the entire archive or at least parts of it.

```
http://www.dante.de
ftp://ftp.dante.de/tex-archive
```

```
ftp://ftp.shsu.edu/tex-archive
ftp://ftp.tex.ac.uk/tex-archive
```

Error detection in LaTeX texts

First contact with the LaTeX program is usually frustrating. The program works interactively, reacts to the first error that occurs with a nearly always incomprehensible error message and on top of it all expects you to enter a letter to indicate how it should continue. A typical error message looks something like this:

```
LaTeX error.  See LaTeX manual for explanation.
              Type  H <return>  for immediate help.
! text for \verb command ended by end of line.
\@latexerr ...rcontextlines \m@ne \errmessage #1
                                                  \endgroup
l.46 ...TeX syntax for {\sm\verb?{\small
?
```

In this case, the cause of the error is a `\verb` command in line 46 whose effect goes beyond the end of the line (and this is not allowed). Now you have the following possibilities:

- [↵] continues processing the LaTeX file regardless of the error. This does work occasionally, but more often than not it leads to a number of consequential errors (to which you can also react with [↵]).
- [H] [↵] displays additional information about the error message. However, the info text is of real help only in very rare cases.
- [R] [↵] continues processing, displays further error messages, but no longer expects any input.
- [Q] [↵] as above, but without display of error messages.
- [X] [↵] terminates LaTeX.

Usually you either terminate LaTeX straightaway with [X] when you have recognized the cause of the error, or you continue processing in quiet mode with [Q]. In the second alternative, you can expect that in spite of all the consequential errors that are probably occurring, LaTeX is capable of finishing translating at least the faulty page. In this case, you can view the result (the typeset page) with `xdvi` and from there possibly guess the cause of the error.

In any case, you will have to change to your editor and search for the error in your LaTeX file. In this process, the file `name.log` is of the essence. In this file, all LaTeX error messages are stored (no matter whether they were displayed on screen or not). The name of this log file is a combination of the name of the translated LaTeX file and the extension `.log`. The most important information in this file is usually the line number in which the error occurred.

If you have problems in locating an error, you should try to isolate the critical text passage and copy it into a separate small file. In general, it is recommended that you split large texts across several files (see page 627). When you work with Emacs, you can use the command Alt+X validate-tex-buffer to carry out a syntax check. Although Emacs sometimes signals errors when there are none, it will find most of the missing brackets.

While processing text, LaTeX issues not only error messages, but also warnings. Warnings do not interrupt the translation process. Many warnings begin with a message such as 'overfull hbox' and suggest that LaTeX has problems with line or page breaking. In most of these cases, manual intervention is required (suggested hyphenations, forced page breaks, and so on). These problems are discussed from page 618 onward.

TIP

The interactive behavior of LaTeX – that is, an interruption for each and every error – can be very irritating, especially if the translation is to be automated. If you insert the instruction `\batchmode` at the beginning of the LaTeX file, LaTeX no longer stops at errors (as though you had entered Q at the occurrence of the first error). After the translation has finished, you can take your time to read through the `*.log` file.

CAUTION

While LaTeX is waiting for keyboard input, it does not react to Ctrl+C! If you want to terminate the program during an input, you must press Ctrl+D (for end of file)! This emergency exit is particularly useful when LaTeX has encountered a wrong file name and expects you to specify a different file. An alternative solution is to enter `null`. Then, LaTeX loads the empty file `null.tex` or `null.sty` which has been inserted into the LaTeX directory structure specifically for this purpose.

TIP

In your Linux distribution you will keep finding `*.tex` files which contain online documentation for various programs. If large numbers of mysterious error messages occur when translating such files with LaTeX, the cause is usually that the file is not a LaTeX file but a TeX file. TeX files too have the extension `*.tex`, but they must be translated with `tex file`.

Introductory example

Before the next section provides a systematic description of the most important LaTeX commands, the following example is intended to illustrate the general usage of LaTeX. After their translation, the LaTeX instructions listed below result in the page shown in Figure 18.1. For a longer article, it would obviously make more sense to print the contents list on a separate page and to precede the whole article with a title page – we had to do without this for reasons of space.

```
\documentclass[twocolumn,11pt]{article} % type: two-column article
\usepackage{isolatin1}                  % ISO Latin character set

\parindent0pt          % no first line indent
\parskip1ex            % space between paragraphs
\columnsep1cm          % 1 cm gutter between columns
```

Contents

1 Introducing LaTeX

1.1 Typefaces and styles

This text illustrates some typefaces and styles available in LaTeX: **bold type**, *italic type*, SMALL CAPITALS, sans serif, `typewriter`. The novelty in LaTeX 2_ε is the fact that most type styles can now be combined with each other without problems – for example, ***bold and italic***. Obviously, the type size can be changed as well, from very small to small to fairly large.

1.2 Text blocks and frames

The `minipage` environment is used to place text blocks side by side next to each other.

This is the second, slightly narrower mini-page.

Here, a 5 cm wide minipage was centered by means of one preceding and one following `\hfill` command and framed by means of `\fbox`.

1.3 Bulleted lists

LaTeX has many advantages as opposed to other programs:

- The quality of the results speaks for itself.
- After getting used to the syntax, processing speed is very high.
- LaTeX texts are portable and, in the Unix world, they are frequently used for on-line documentation.

1.4 Footnotes

This paragraph provides two examples for footnotes.[1] Obviously, LaTeX numbers the footnotes[2] automatically.

1.5 Mathematical formulae

LaTeX owes its still great importance above all to its excellent formula setting capacities. Just try to input the following formulae in any other program! Formulae can also be used directly in the text (for example, at this point here: $\pi \int x^2 dx$).

$$\lim_{n\to\infty} \sum_{k=1}^{n} \sqrt[3]{1 + \frac{k^2}{n^3}} - n$$

$$\begin{bmatrix} \frac{\partial}{\partial x} f & \frac{\partial}{\partial y} f \\ \frac{\partial}{\partial x} g & \frac{\partial}{\partial y} g \end{bmatrix}$$

[1] This is the first footnote.
[2] The second footnote.

1

Figure 18.1 The text `article.tex` processed with LaTeX.

```
\begin{document}

\tableofcontents        % contents

\section{Introducing \LaTeX}

\subsection{Typefaces and styles}

This text illustrates some typefaces and styles available in \LaTeX:
\textbf{bold type}, \textit{italic type}, \textsc{small capitals},
\textsf{sans serif}, \texttt{typewriter}. The novelty in \LaTeXe\ is
the fact that most type styles can now be combined with each other
without problems -- for example, \textbf{\textit{bold and italic}}.
Obviously, the type size can be changed as well, from {\tiny very
small} to {\small small} to {\Large fairly large}.

\subsection{Text blocks and frames}

{\small
\begin{minipage}[t]{4cm}
The {\small\verb?minipage?{ en\-vi\-ron\-ment is used to place text
blocks side by side next to each other.
\end{minipage}
\hfill
\begin{minipage}[t]{3cm}
This is the second, slightly narrower mini-page.
\end{minipage}
}

\hbox{}\hfill\fbox{
\begin{minipage}{5cm}
Here, a 5 cm wide minipage was centered by means of one preceding
and one following {\small\tt \char92hfill} command and framed by
means of {\small\tt \char92fbox}.
\end{minipage}
}\hfill\hbox{}

\subsection{Bulleted lists}

\LaTeX\ has many advantages as opposed to other programs:

\begin{itemize}
\item The quality of the results speaks for itself.
\item After getting used to the syntax, processing speed is very high.
\item \LaTeX\ texts are portable and they are frequently used for
on-line documentation in the {\sc Unix} world.
\end{itemize}

\subsection{Footnotes}

This paragraph provides two examples for footnotes.\footnote{This
is the first footnote.} Obviously, \LaTeX\ numbers the
footnotes\footnote{The second footnote.} automatically.
```

```
\subsection{Mathematical formulae}

\LaTeX\ owes its still great importance above all to its excellent
formula setting capacities.  Just try to input the following formulae
in any other program! Formulae can also be used directly in the text
(for example, at this point here: $\pi \, \int x^2 dx$).

\[\lim _{n\rightarrow \infty }\sum _{k=1}^{n}\sqrt [3]1+{\frac
{k^{2}}
{n^{3}}}}-n\]

\[\left [\begin {array}{cc}
{\frac {\partial }{\partial x}}f&{\frac {\partial }{\partial y}}f\\
\noalign{\medskip}
{\frac {\partial }{\partial x}}g&{\frac {\partial }{\partial y}}g
\end {array}\right ]\]

\end{document}
```

If, after reading this section, you are left with the impression that working with LaTeX is a laborious task, you are quite right. You should only go deeper into LaTeX when you are ready to invest a relatively long time in experimenting with it. The path to a truly excellent result is often thorny. In part, manual intervention is required to make LaTeX hyphenate foreign language words correctly and break pages where it makes sense for visual reasons (and not after the first line of a new paragraph).

However, you should also see the advantages: the quality of LaTeX texts speaks for itself. LaTeX is available on practically any computer – LaTeX texts can therefore be exchanged effortlessly between different computer platforms. Furthermore, there is an excellent HTML converter (`latex2html`) which can be used to convert LaTeX texts into HTML format.

In the mathematical/scientific sector, there is no real alternative to LaTeX anyway. Text processing programs such as Word are much too inefficient and, above all, too unstable for extensive scientific texts with formulae and illustrations. What is the use of an all singing, all dancing user interface if a text processing program suddenly crashes with longer texts, no longer finds cross-references, displays a red 'X' instead of illustrations, and so on? Maybe getting familiar with LaTeX takes a couple of days more than with other programs – but this time is quickly recovered when the program continues to work without problems even with documents of 100 or 1000 pages. (Obviously, this book too has been typeset with LaTeX.)

TIP

If you just want to write an occasional letter, you should take a look at the next chapter. It describes the LyX program which provides an easy-to-handle interface to the most important functions of LaTeX.

Problems with different LaTeX distributions

The LaTeX program cannot be taken in isolation, but must be considered in its entirety together with various style files, the Metafont utility program, its character sets, and so on. The whole thing is known as a LaTeX distribution. While LaTeX itself is largely standardized, defined standards are still missing with regard to supplying the remaining components.

During the past years I have worked with four different LaTeX packages and/or distributions. Over and over again there have been changes to the directory tree; single style files which are present in one distribution are missing or have a different name in the next one; in some cases different character sets are installed as default character sets.

These factors mean that LaTeX documents are still not as portable as they should be. When translating a LaTeX text on a different computer, the translation may not succeed at all (missing style file), line and page breaks may be altered (different default character set), hyphenation may not work (incorrect hyphenation table), and so on.

Meanwhile, two LaTeX distributions are dominant under Linux: NTeX (put together by Frank Langbein) and teTeX (by Thomas Esser). Both distributions are huge. teTeX is slightly better structured, has more online documentation and uses a faster system for finding files. For these reasons, most current Linux distributions now supply teTeX. Personally, I have had excellent experiences with both distributions.

TIP All path specifications in this chapter are based on the teTeX distribution 0.9 and the assumption that the installation directory is `/usr/share/texmf`. If you are unable to find a file, try using `which` (for programs) or `locate`.

NOTE One big advantage of teTeX is the structuring of available online documentation in the `/usr/share/texmf/doc` directory. When you execute `make` in this directory, various `*.dvi` and `*.ps` files are automatically created together with the HTML file `helpindex.html` as a central index. Provided your WWW browser is configured correctly (see page 338), clicking on cross-references in the index directly starts `ghostview` or `xdvi`. (A vast part of the teTeX online documentation is also available under NTeX, only it is much more difficult to find the files.)

TIP Problems arising from upgrading from LaTeX 2.09 to the new version LaTeX 2_ε are described on page 629.

The LaTeX directory three

Few program packages under Linux present a more garbled directory structure than LaTeX (on my computer: about 7000 files in 370 directories!). The following table gives a first overview. It mainly follows the teTeX distribution 0.9. All path specifications are relative to `/usr/share/texmf/`.

teTeX directories	
./bibtex	style files for bibtex
./doc	online documentation
./dvips	files for dvips
./fontname	TeX-internal name scheme for character sets
./fonts/source	font definition (Metafont files *.mf)
./fonts/tfm	font size (base for TeX/LaTeX, *.tfm)
./fonts/vf	virtual fonts (for PostScript fonts, *.vf)
./lists	file directory for teTeX packages
./metafont	style files for Metafont (*.mf)
./teTex	teTeX-specific extensions
./teTex/bin	all programs (tex, latex, xdvi, and so on) (/usr/bin contains links to this directory)
./teTex/info	online documentation in info format
./teTex/man	online documentation in man format
./tex	the TeX/LaTeX directory proper
./tex/amstex	amsTeX (macro package for TeX)
./tex/generic	hyphenation tables, foreign languages
./tex/plain	TeXbase
./tex/texinfo	texinfo (macro package for TeX)
./tex/latex	LaTeX (macro package for TeX)
./tex/latex/base	LaTeX base files
./tex/latex/*/	various LaTeX extensions (graphics, different layouts, style files)
./texmf/xdvi	xdvi configuration

Some variable files are located in /var/lib/texmf. Depending on the distribution, various configuration files are located in /etc/texmf. The /usr/share/texmf/ directory tree contains links to these configuration files.

During the conversion of *.dvi files into PostScript format (dvips) or when files are displayed on screen (xdvi), bitmap files of the required fonts are generated. These files have the extension *.pk and are stored in the following directory:

/var/cache/fonts/pk/	font bitmaps (*.pk)

If you suffer from space problems, you can delete the *.pl files without hesitation. However, at the next call of dvips or xdvi, these files have to be generated again, which takes some time.

NOTE

In view of the immense number of files, the search for a given font or style file can take relatively long. The teTeX distribution therefore manages an additional database which contains a list of all TeX files. Essentially, this database consists of the result of ls -R and is therefore called ls-R. When you extend teTeX with additional files, you must always execute the command texhash in order to extend the database as well. Also, you should always try this command first whenever you encounter problems in finding TeX files.

NOTE: Internally, the Kpathsea library is responsible for searching for TEX files. If you are interested in the details, please read `kpathsea.dvi` or the equivalent `info` texts together with the very short `man` pages for `texhash` and `ls-R`.

18.2 Elementary LATEX commands

This section summarizes the most important LATEX commands. The commands introduced here should be sufficient to produce simple LATEX documents. If you want to work with LATEX more extensively, there is no other way but to approach some more detailed literature. Highly recommended are the books by Helmut Kopka (see References on page 757) and the *LATEX Companion* by Michael Goosens, Frank Mittelbach and Alexander Samarin.

Formal details

The text to be processed with LATEX is generated with a text editor. A group of consecutive lines is viewed as a paragraph. Words are separated from each other by spaces or line breaks, paragraphs by at least one empty line. Proper line breaking within a paragraph is carried out by LATEX. Therefore the position where a new line is started in the original text is irrelevant.

LATEX commands always begin with a backslash `\`. When commands need parameters, these must be specified enclosed in curly brackets, for example, `\chapter{Chapter title}`. Some commands also have optional parameters which must be specified enclosed in square brackets, for example `$\sqrt[3]{x}$` for $\sqrt[3]{x}$. Without `[3]`, `\sqrt` yields a common square root, that is, $\sqrt{x}$.

Curly brackets can also be used to restrict the effect of commands. Thus, `{\bf word}` only prints one word in bold, whereas the unbracketed command `\bf` sets the 'bold' attribute until reset by another command.

Environments represent a special type of command. They are opened with `\begin{environment}` and closed with `\end{environment}`. The special formatting features of the environment apply throughout the whole text enclosed between these two commands. Typical environment names are `tabbing` (for tables) or `verbatim` for listings containing special characters.

Within a LATEX text, comments can be started with `%`. This causes LATEX to ignore the remainder of the line from this character onward.

Structuring of texts

LATEX texts begin with the command `\documentclass[options]{type}`. This command determines the text type. In its standard configuration, LATEX has four important text types: `book`, `report`, `article` and `letter`. The first three text types are rather similar to each other and differ mainly in the planned text length. As opposed to `book` and `report`, `article` does not have chapters; its smallest structuring element is the section. In `book`, all pages are automatically equipped with running heads in which, in addition to the page number, the name of the current chapter (even pages) and the name of the current section (odd pages) are indicated. The easiest way to find out about the differences between the three text types `book`, `report` and `article` is to change the first line of the sample file of the previous section by substituting the three text types one by one.

The text type `letter` can be used for letter writing. For reasons of space, however, this text type will not be dealt with in this book. Inside LaTeX, text types are realized through macro files with the extension `*.cls`. These files are stored in the `./tex/latex/base` directory. Some publishing houses, universities, and so on provide their own macro files which are particularly suited for formatting scientific articles, theses, and so on.

Options can be specified in square brackets in front of the text type. Important options are `11pt` and `12pt` (to change the default type size) and `twocolumn` (for two-column texts).

LaTeX document classes	
`\documentclass[options]{type}`	
Text types	
`book`	for long texts (such as books), structuring into parts, chapters, sections
`report`	as above, but for shorter texts; different title page, and so on
`article`	for articles, structuring into sections, subsections as opposed to `book` and `report`, no differentiation between even and odd page numbers
`letter`	for letters (not described in this book)
Options	
`11pt`	standard type size 11 (instead of 10) points
`12pt`	standard type size 12 (instead of 10) points
`twoside`	differentiation between even/odd pages (standard with `book`)
`twocolumn`	two-column text

The text layout can be further controlled with some additional packages. Packages are LaTeX files with the extension `*.sty` which modify various system settings. These packages are loaded with `\usepackage{file}`. The `\usepackage` command(s) must be specified immediately after `\documentclass`.

Additional packages	
`\usepackage{isolatin1}`	for input of foreign language special characters
`\usepackage{epsf}`	for embedding of PostScript graphics

The text itself begins with the command `\begin{document}` and ends with `\end{document}`. The text enclosed by these two commands is processed and typeset by LaTeX. Several commands are available to structure the text:

Document structuring	
`\part{Title}`	part (only for `book` and `report`)
`\chapter{Title}`	chapter (only for `book` and `report`)
`\section{Title}`	section
`\subsection{Title}`	subsection
`\subsubsection{Title}`	subsubsection

LaTeX deals with chapter and section numbering itself. At the same time, LaTeX automatically selects suitable typefaces and vertical text spacing for the titles. In the `book` text type, the text in the `\chapter` and `\section` commands is also taken into account for generating running heads. When the commands are used in the form `\section[short version]{complete version}`, the short version is used for running heads and table of contents, whereas the complete version is used for body text.

If the text is to be equipped with an appendix, this is started with the `\{begin\{appendix}` command and ended with `\end{appendix}`. Inside the appendix, `\chapter`, `\section` can be used, with the chapters now being numbered A, B, C ... .

Thus, the general structure of a typical LaTeX text looks approximately like this:

```
\documentclass[11pt]{article}  % document type: article,
                               % type size 11 points
\usepackage{isolatin1}         % ISO Latin character set
                               % (foreign language characters)

% space for macro definitions, variable assignments, and so on
% possibly table of contents with \tableofcontents

\begin{document}
% the text itself, structured by means of
% \section{...}, \subsection{\hdrsecb ...}, and so on

\begin{appendix}
% the appendix text, again structured by means of
% \section{...}, \subsection{\hdrsecb ...}, and so on
\end{appendix}
\end{document}
```

Fonts and attributes

Other text processing programs have probably got you used to a practically unlimited choice of fonts and sizes. For historical reasons, this is not the case in LaTeX. As a rule, LaTeX restricts your choice to three font families: one standard font used for flow text, headlines, and so on, the `Typewriter` font for program listings and the Sans Serif font for highlighting and other tasks.

These three fonts (or better 'font families') can be formatted with different attributes. The highest number of attributes exists for the standard font, which can be represented as bold, italic, slanted and small caps.

You may not be aware of the difference between italic and slanted: for slanted text, LaTeX uses the normal character set and inclines the letters slightly to the right. For italic text, a separate character set is used in which the characters are somewhat more inclined and also slightly differently shaped. This subtle difference, however, applies only when LaTeX's own fonts are used. This book, in contrast, uses PostScript fonts in which usually no difference can be noted between italic and slanted text.

Standard font	normal	*italic*	SMALL CAPS
	bold	***bold italic***	**BOLD SMALL CAPS**
Sans Serif	normal	*italic*	SMALL CAPS
	bold	***bold italic***	**BOLD SMALL CAPS**
`Typewriter`	`normal`	*`italic`*	`SMALL CAPS`
	`bold`	***`bold italic`***	**`BOLD SMALL CAPS`**

REFERENCE

LaTeX is usually not capable of representing the `Typewriter` font in bold. In the above list, this has been made possible because for setting this book, PostScript fonts have been used instead of LaTeX's own character sets. More information on the subject of LaTeX and PostScript fonts can be found from page 622 onward, where the LaTeX utility program Metafont and the handling of PostScript fonts are discussed.

Now for the commands used to change font families and their attributes. For historical reasons and for reasons of compatibility with previous versions, we are faced with a Babylonian confusion of commands. The following table lists what are currently the 'official' commands of LaTeX 2_ε in the first two columns, the still permitted old syntax in the third column and the outcome in the fourth column. The result of the different commands only appears to be the same (see below):

Font attributes

LaTeX 2_ε		**LaTeX2.09**	**Result**
`\textrm{text}`	`{\rmfamily text}`	`{\rm text}`	Standard (Roman)
`\textsf{text}`	`{\sffamily text}`	`{\sf text}`	Sans Serif
`\texttt{text}`	`{\ttfamily text}`	`{\tt text}`	`Typewriter`
`\textbf{text}`	`{\bfseries text}`	`{\bf text}`	**bold**
`\textmd{text}`	`{\mdseries text}`	`{\rm text}`	normal
`\textit{text}`	`{\itshape text}`	`{\it text}`	*italic*
`\textsl{text}`	`{\slshape text}`	`{\sl text}`	*slanted*
`\textsc{text}`	`{\scshape text}`	`{\sc text}`	SMALL CAPS
`\textup{text}`	`{\ipshape text}`	`{\rm text}`	normal
`\emph{text}`		`{\em text}`	*emphasized*

Some remarks: `\emph` does not simply change to italic type, but toggles the attribute between normal and italic. Thus, inside italic text, `\emph` produces normal type.

The short commands such as `\sl`, `\bf`, and so on seem very attractive because of the minimum typing effort required, but for reasons of compatibility they have a rather idiosyncratic way of functioning: thus, `\bf`, `\it`, `\sl` and `\sc` switch to the standard typeface and deactivate all other attributes! Thus, these attributes cannot be used to combine different attributes. Try to get used to using the more recent `\textxy` commands, such as `\textbf{\textit{text}}`!

Now for the type size: here again LaTeX differs from what you are used to in other text processing programs. There is a standard type size which applies to the entire document. This size can only vary between 10 and 12 points. 10 points is the default setting, but you can alter it to 11 or 12 points with the `\documentstyle` options `11pt` or `12pt`.

Starting from this standard type size, LaTeX automatically calculates suitable sizes for headlines with `\chapter` or `\section`, for footnotes, mathematical formulae, and so on. This size is also used as a reference for the size changing commands:

Font size			
`\tiny`	only readable with a magnifying glass	`\Large`	larger
`\scriptsize`	tiny	`\LARGE`	still larger
`\footnotesize`	very small		
`\small`	small	`\huge`	huge
`\normalsize`	standard size		
`\large`	large	`\Huge`	kingsize

Special characters and accents

A large number of special characters, such as `%` or `$`, are interpreted by LaTeX as commands. Some further special characters only have specific meanings in mathematical mode (for example, `^` and `_`), but they cannot be used in text mode. The following table summarizes the most important special characters:

Meaning of special characters	
`%`	starts comments
`~`	fixed space (for example in `5~cm`)
`{..}`	encloses text areas (for example, for special formatting)
`$formula$`	encloses formulae in flow text
`_`	subscript (only in mathematical mode)
`^`	superscript (only in mathematical mode)

The attempt to represent special characters unchanged in flowing text is a source of permanent frustration: firstly, even after months of working with LaTeX you may well still not remember that a character has a special meaning. Secondly, there is still no single method of representing special characters in normal text. In many cases it is sufficient to prefix the special character with a backslash (for example, `\%` to generate a % sign). If this does not help, the character code can be specified directly with `\char`*n*. The standard ASCII code applies for most text characters.

<table>
<tr><th colspan="6">Representation of special characters</th></tr>
<tr><td>--</td><td>– (n-dash)</td><td>\ae</td><td>æ</td><td>\char34</td><td>”</td></tr>
<tr><td>_</td><td>_ (underscore)</td><td>\AE</td><td>Æ</td><td>\char92</td><td>“</td></tr>
<tr><td>\#</td><td>#</td><td>\aa</td><td>å</td><td>{\tt\char92}</td><td>\</td></tr>
<tr><td>\$</td><td>$</td><td>\AA</td><td>Å</td><td>\char94</td><td>^</td></tr>
<tr><td>\&</td><td>&</td><td>\oe</td><td>œ</td><td>{\tt<}</td><td><</td></tr>
<tr><td>\%</td><td>%</td><td>\OE</td><td>Œ</td><td>{\tt>}</td><td>></td></tr>
<tr><td>\{</td><td>{</td><td>\o</td><td>ø</td><td>\pounds</td><td>£</td></tr>
<tr><td>\}</td><td>}</td><td>\O</td><td>Ø</td><td>\copyright</td><td>©</td></tr>
<tr><td>$|$</td><td>|</td><td></td><td></td><td>$\sim$</td><td>~</td></tr>
</table>

The following table summarizes the LaTeX commands for generation of accented letters:

Accents							
\'a	á	\`a	à	\^a	â	\~a	ã
\.a	ȧ	\=a	ā	\b{a}	a̲	\d{a}	ạ
\u{a}	ă	\v{a}	ǎ	\c{a}	a̧		

A large number of additional special characters is possible in mathematical mode – for example, π with `$\pi$` or $\leftarrow$ with `$\leftarrow$`. A summary of the most important mathematical symbols is given in Section 18.4.

An alternative way of representing texts containing special characters is provided by the command `\verb_text_`. `\verb_ls | more_` yields `ls | more`. In this example, the underscore character was used to enclose the text itself, but you can use any other character provided that it does not occur in the text to be represented. The text inside of `\verb` is set in `typewriter` font. `\verb` cannot be used in a number of environments and certainly not for the definition of macros. `\verb` texts are limited to a maximum of one line. There is no way of representing `\verb` texts in bold face.

When you do not wish to represent just a few characters or words with special characters, but want instead to represent several lines, you can use the `verbatim` environment. This environment is started with `\begin{verbatim}` and terminated with `\end{verbatim}`. All lines specified in between are set unchanged in the `typewriter` font. The `verbatim` environment is particularly suited for program listings, which are usually strewn with special characters.

verbatim environment	
`\verb_text_`	sets the text including all special characters
`\begin{verbatim}`	starts text which is to be output unchanged
`multi-line text with`	
`special characters $ % ^ ~`	
`\end{verbatim}`	end of the `verbatim` environment

Problems occur not only with special characters but sometimes also with spaces. For example, LaTeX eliminates the space required after some commands.

Thus, `\copyright Michael Kofler` becomes '©Michael Kofler'. In order to display a space between © and the following text, the command must be closed with a backslash, thus, `\copyright\ Michael Kofler`.

Foreign language special characters no longer constitute a problem in current LaTeX versions. You must simply specify the instruction `\usepackage{isolatin1}` at the beginning of the text. From then on accented letters, umlauts, and so on, can be used in the text directly. Previous versions needed a rather long-winded notation of the form `"a` for an 'ä'. This notation is still recommended if you plan to use your texts on other UNIX computers (possibly running older LaTeX versions).

NOTE

There are several possibilities for representing the Euro symbol under LaTeX. The easiest one is to use the `textcomp` package and the `\texteuro` command defined there. The result, however, bears little resemblance to the official symbol and is furthermore incompatible with the PostScript fonts used for this book (Times and Futura) – therefore we have to do without an example.

DANTE's German-language LaTeX FAQ quotes some further variations which, however, presume installation of additional packages and/or fonts:

```
http://www.dante.de/faq/
ftp://ftp.dante.de/tex-archive/fonts/euro*
```

Tables

LaTeX has several possibilities for defining tables. At this point, we only describe the simplest variation, namely the `tabbing` environment. The syntax of this environment looks as follows:

Tables

```
\begin{tabbing}
sample \= sample \= \kill        Sample line: \= defines tab stops
term1 \> term2 \> term3\\        Table: \> for tab, \\ for end of line
term4 \> term5                   last line without\\
\end{tabbing}
```

Tables are initiated with a sample line. This line defines the positions of the left-ranged tab stops with `\=`. Your sample line should normally be the widest line in your table. Before each `\=`, you should insert an additional space, for example with a `\qquad` instruction (space the width of two hyphens – see page 618). `\kill` deletes the sample line, so that it is only used as a sample, but is not output.

An example to conclude: the special character table on page 601 was produced with the following LaTeX instructions:

```
\begin{tabbing}
{\sm\verb?$formula$?}\qquad\=\kill
{\sm\verb?%?}
  \> starts comments\\
```

```
{\sm\verb?~?}
  \> fixed space (for example in {\sm\verb?5~cm?})\\
{\sm\verb?{..}?}
  \> encloses text areas (for example, for special formatting)\\
{\sm\verb?$formula$?}
  \> encloses formulae in flow text\\
{\sm\verb?_?}
  \> subscript (only in mathematical mode)\\
{\sm\verb?^?}
  \> superscript (only in mathematical mode)
\end{tabbing}
```

NOTE

If this simple table format is not sufficient for you, LaTeX provides the `tabular` environment which can be used to create tables with varying column width, frames, and so on. If in addition you also use the `table` environment, the table is automatically placed in the same way as an illustration, using the available space without creating gaps in the text.

Bulleted and numbered lists

LaTeX offers several possibilities for formatting lists of items. The simplest variation is constituted by the `itemize` environment.

Lists

```
\begin{itemize}
\item Text of the first item
\item Second item
\end{itemize}
```

The following example shows the visual layout of a bulleted list:

```
\begin{itemize}
\item \LaTeX\ marks the single items of a list with thick black
     bullets (special character \verb?$\bullet$?).
\item At the same time the entries are indented with respect
     to the normal text.
\end{itemize}
```

- LaTeX marks the single items of a list with thick black bullets (special character `$\bullet$`).
- At the same time the entries are indented with respect to the normal text.

If instead of `itemize` you use the environment name `enumerate`, LaTeX uses numbers (1., 2., and so on) instead of the bullets. Both environments can be embedded into each other. Depending on the level of embedding, different symbols are used for the bullets and different kinds of numbers for enumeration (lower case letters, roman numbers, and so on). In addition, the list items are indented by different amounts of space.

Multi-column text

We have already described on page 597 how the option `twocolumn` in the `documentclass` command can be used to arrange the entire text in two columns. In many cases, however, this solution is not suitable. Frequently, only small portions of text are to be arranged side by side, whereas the remaining text goes over the full page width in one column. For such occurrences, LaTeX again offers several variations, of which only the most important one is presented here: the `minipage` environment. The syntax looks as follows:

`minipage` environment

```
\begin{minipage}[t]{4cm}  % the first, 4 cm wide minipage
text ...                  % the text of the first minipage
\end{minipage}
\hfill                    % gutter between first and second minipage
\begin{minipage}[t]{4cm}  % the second minipage
text ...
\end{minipage}
\hfill
\begin{minipage}[t]{4cm}  % the third minipage
text ...
\end{minipage}
```

The total width of all specified `minipage` environments must not exceed the total text width. The optional parameter `t` (top) causes the upper edges of text blocks to be vertically aligned. Alternatively, you can specify `b` (bottom) to align the lower edges of the text blocks or you can omit the parameter to center the text blocks vertically. The command `\hfill` between the blocks causes the remaining horizontal free space between the blocks to be distributed equally between them.

```
\begin{minipage}[t]{6cm}
This is the first, 6 cm wide text block.
\end{minipage}
\hfill
\begin{minipage}[t]{6cm}
The second block is placed next to it and has the same width.
Both blocks are aligned with reference to their upper edges.
\end{minipage}
```

This is the first, 6 cm wide text block.	The second block is placed next to it and has the same width. Both blocks are aligned with reference to their upper edges.

Frames

Text can be highlighted by putting it into a frame. The command for this is `\fbox{text}` and produces results such as [this text]. When multi-line blocks are to be framed, a `minipage` environment must be defined within the `\fbox` command.

In the following example, a small text block is centered and framed with `\fbox`. When using `\hfill` it should be noted that a filling distance can only be specified between existing objects. Therefore, before and after `\hfill`, an empty text box must be specified with `\hbox{}`.

```
\hbox{}          % empty box on left-hand side
\hfill           % filling distance to minipage
\fbox{
\begin{minipage}{5cm}
Here, a 5 cm wide minipage has been centered by means of
one preceding and one following {\tt\char92}hfill command
and framed with {\tt\char92}fbox.
\end{minipage}}
\hfill           % filling distance to next box
\hbox{}          % empty box
```

Here, a 5 cm wide minipage has been centered by means of one preceding and one following \hfill command and framed with \fbox.

Inside `\fbox`, you are not allowed to use the `\verb_text_` command. In order to circumvent this restriction, LaTeX 2_ε has created the new environment `lrbox` with which (via some detours) a framed text containing `\verb_text_` can be realized (see page 629).

18.3 Typesetting scientific texts

In principle, you can set any text with LaTeX. However, the advantages of LaTeX over other typesetting and word processing programs really come to the fore in the layout of scientific texts, where the task is to create tables of contents, lists of illustrations, references and indices, to use cross-references, insert footnotes, and so on, with as little effort as possible. This section summarizes the LaTeX commands for the realization of such 'typically scientific' layout features.

Table of contents

The table of contents can be inserted at any point in the text by means of the `\tableofcontents` command. Usually, the table of contents is placed at the beginning of the text or after the preface.

In order to generate the table of contents, LaTeX processes the file `name.toc`. With the command `\tableofcontents`, each LaTeX run inserts into this file all information needed for the table of contents (chapter, section and subsection names, together with their page numbers). This procedure may cause a worst-case scenario of having to run LaTeX *three times* to obtain a correct table of contents.

In the first run, `name.toc` does not yet exist, that is, no table of contents can be created. In the second run, a table of contents can be generated, but since it will itself probably occupy several pages, all page numbers will shift. The page numbers in the table of contents will correspond to the actual page numbers in the text only after the third run.

The table of contents normally includes the texts of all `\part`, `\chapter`, `\section`, `\subsection` and `\subsubsection` commands. The number of structuring levels can be reduced with `\setcounter{tocdepth}{n}` (see page 622).

Formatting the table of contents is carried out automatically. LaTeX selects suitable type sizes, indents subordinate entries and fills the space between the entry and the page number with dots. The table of contents in this book is not a typical example, since the standard layout has been altered to comply with the publisher's house style for this series of computer books. A better idea of what a typical LaTeX table of contents looks like is given in Figure 18.1 on page 592.

Table of contents	
`\tableofcontents`	inserts the table of contents at this point in the text

Cross-references

Cross-references in a book are generated with the three commands `\label`, `\ref` and `\pageref`. The number supplied by `\ref` depends on the place where `\label` was executed: usually, it is a section number which denotes the current section. However, `\label` can also be executed in environments such as `equation`, `figure` or `tabbing`. In this case, `\ref` supplies the number of the formula, figure, table, and so on.

Cross-references are similar to page numbers in the table of contents: they are taken from the file `name.aux` which was generated during the last run of LaTeX. Therefore, after changes to a LaTeX text, two runs are needed in order to get all page numbers right again.

An example to conclude: if at this very point in the text a mark is set with `\label{sample-reference}` , then `\ref{sample-reference}` supplies the section number IV and `\pageref{sample-reference}` the page number 607.

Cross-references	
`\label{mark}`	defines a text mark
`\pageref{mark}`	supplies the page number of the mark
`\ref{mark}`	supplies section, figure or table number

Footnotes

Footnotes are created with `\footnote{text}`. LaTeX inserts a footnote reference in the form of a superscript number and places the footnote text at the bottom of the current page.

Footnotes are numbered automatically. In the text types `book` and `report`, numbering restarts with every chapter. The way footnotes appear is shown in Figure 18.1 on page 592.

Footnotes	
`\footnote{text}`	inserts a new footnote into the text

References or bibliography

Management of a reference list or bibliography is carried out in two steps: first, a list containing all entries must be created at the end of the book (where the bibliography is to appear). Subsequently, these entries can be referred to from any point in the entire text. The following syntax applies:

Bibliography

```
% in the flowing text
\cite{mark1}                    % reference to the entry `mark1'

% at the end of the article/book
\begin{thebibliography}{n}
\bibitem{mark1} Text1           % author, title, and so on
\bibitem{mark2} Text2
...
\end{thebibliography}
```

At the position of the `thebibliography` environment, LaTeX generates a list in which all entries are numbered in square brackets ([1], [2], and so on). The parameter `n` is the measure used for indenting the entries. For up to nine entries, `n` can be assigned the number 9, for up to 99 entries the number 99, and so on. The `\bibitem` entries are not sorted automatically – you must provide a suitable ordering yourself. Also, the entries are not formatted automatically. However, you can use all the commands for setting different letter types and thus format the author's name in bold, the publication title in italic, and so on.

In the flowing text you can now refer to a bibliographical entry with `\cite{mark}`. LaTeX inserts a square bracket with the corresponding number at this point in the text.

> **NOTE**
>
> While the `\bibitem` command is perfectly sufficient for occasional publications, LaTeX provides a much more powerful alternative with the `bibtex` utility program. The complete list of all references ever used (for example, in an entire department) is stored in a separate file. In the publication itself, this can be referred to by appropriate shortcuts. `bibtex` evaluates this information and automatically creates a bibliography which includes only the references actually used. This utility is extensively described in the LaTeX Companion by Michel Goossens *et al.*

The 'References' section at the end of this book has not been prepared with the above method, since there was no need to work with numbered bibliographical entries.

Figures

LaTeX provides the `figure` environment for integrating figures into the text. This environment's main task is to place the figure and give it a caption. The optional parameter after `\begin{figure}` determines how the figure is placed in the text. You can specify either `h` (here) or an arbitrary combination of the letters `t` (top), `b` (bottom) and `p` (page): the figure itself is generated by commands inside this environment (see below).

`figure` environment

```
\begin{figure}[h]
% commands for the generation of the illustration itself
\caption{\label{mark-for-crossreference}caption text}
\end{figure}
```

Positioning of the illustration

- h: the figure is shown at exactly this position in the text
- t: the figure is placed at the top of the current page
- b: the figure is placed at the bottom of the current page
- p: several figures are combined on a separate page

In two-column texts, the environment name `figure*` can be used instead of `figure`. In this case, the figure extends over both columns (instead of being restricted to the width of a single column). `figure*` cannot be combined with the option `h`.

`\caption` is used to give the figure a caption. In front of the caption text itself, LaTeX places 'Figure n:', where n is substituted either by a running number (text type `article`) or a chapter number (3.5 for the fifth figure in the third chapter). When a `\label` instruction is used inside `\caption`, `\ref` can be employed to refer to the figure number and `\pageref` to refer to the corresponding page number.

The caption text is automatically centered. When the figure is narrower than the caption text, the latter should be restricted to the width of the figure with `\parbox{7cm}{\caption{...}}` (here, 7 cm).

The figure itself is generated through commands in the `figure` environment. These commands also define the size of the figure. LaTeX has some graphics commands with which simple figures can be created directly in the LaTeX text. For reasons of space, these commands cannot be described in this book. In any case, in practice it is much more usual to place ready-made PostScript graphics, rather than create LaTeX figures.

Inserting PostScript graphics

```
\usepackage{epsf}    % must be executed immediately after
% ...                % \documentstyle
```

```
\epsfxsize=5cm      % specifies the width of the next figure
\epsfysize=4cm      % specifies the height of the next figure
\epsffile{file}     % inserts the specified PostScript file
```

Application of the three `\epsf...` commands is relatively easy: `\epsffile{file}` inserts a PostScript file into the document. If the size of the figure has not been previously specified by means of `\epsfx/ysize`, LaTeX leaves the illustration in its original size. If only one size was specified, LaTeX scales the other size in such a way that the proportions of the illustration remain as they originally were. Therefore, it is usually sufficient to execute only one of the two `\epsfx/y...` commands.

Generally, figures are neither centered nor framed. When these formatting features are required, centering can be achieved with `\centerline` and framing with `\fbox`.

The following table gives some examples for commands inside the `figure` environment. Commands are also shown which allow you to insert an empty (framed, if required) area, instead of a figure, into which an illustration can be glued at a later stage (admittedly a fairly old-fashioned method). Some new commands make their appearance: `\rule{b}{h}` generates a $b \times h$ black rectangle which is used here to make room for the illustration to be glued in later by means of an (invisible) vertical line. `\framebox` generates a framed rectangle of a given width and height.

```
\centerline{                              % centered PostScript graphic
  \epsfxsize=30mm                         %   no frame, 3 cm wide
  \epsffile{online.eps}}                  %
\centerline{\fbox{                        % centered PostScript graphic
  \epsfysize=40mm                         %   with frame, 4 cm high
  \epsffile{online.eps}}}                 %
\centerline{                              % empty centered frame
  \framebox[4cm]{\rule{0cm}{3cm}}}        %   4 cm wide, 3 cm high
\rule{0cm}{3cm}                           % unframed empty space,
                                          %   3 cm high
```

When several figures are to be placed side by side, several minipages must be placed inside the `figure` environment (see also page 605). The opposite case – the use of a `figure` environment inside a minipage – is not possible. Therefore it is not a trivial exercise to place a captioned figure alongside text. You can, however, place an unlabeled PostScript graphic into a minipage by directly using the `\epsf...` commands (without a `figure` environment.

```
\begin{figure}[h]
\begin{minipage[t]{6.1cm}
\centerline{\framebox[6cm]{\rule{0cm}{4.1cm}}}
\caption{\labellatex-b2} \textsl{An empty frame into which a picture
can be glued at a later stage.}}
\end{minipage}
\hfill
\begin{minipage}[t]{6cm}
```

```
\centerline{\epsfysize=4,1cm\epsffile{b-latex-kurven.ps}}
\caption{\label{latex-b3} \textsl{This diagram ... as a PostScript file.}}
\end{minipage}
\end{figure}
```

Figure 18.3: *An empty frame into which a picture can be glued at a later stage.*

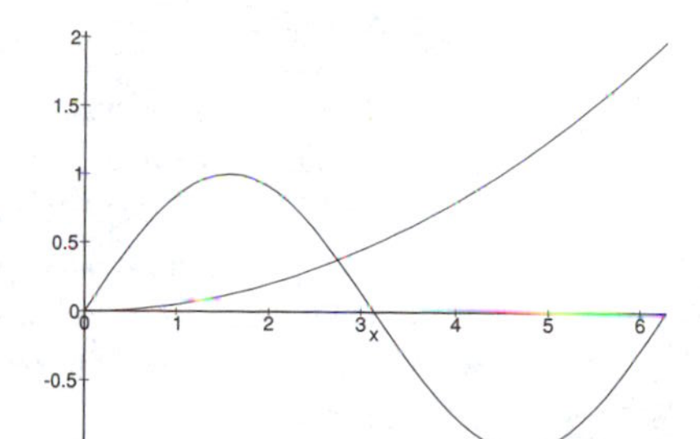

Figure 18.4: *This diagram has been calculated with the computer algebra program Maple and placed into the text as a PostScript file.*

The sample illustrations Figures 18.3 and 18.4 were generated with the above commands. The references to the figure numbers were created with `\ref{latex-b2}` and `\ref{latex-b3}`.

Index

If you want to equip your text with an index, several steps are necessary: first you must use `\usepackage` to load the `makeindex` package and execute the `\makeindex` command prior to `\begin{document}`. Index entries must be marked in the text with the `\index` command. And finally, the `\printindex` command must be specified at the point where the index is to appear in the text.

But this is not enough: after the text file prepared in this way has been processed with LaTeX a first time, the LINUX command `makeindex name.idx` must be executed. All index entries in the file `name.idx` generated by LaTeX are processed and sorted and the result is stored in the file `name.ind`. At the next LaTeX run this file is read during execution of `\printindex`.

Index entries

```
\usepackage{makeidx}             % after \documentclass
...
\makeindex                       % before \begin{document}
\newcommand{\ii}[1]{{\it #1}}  % for italic page numbers
...
\index{entry}                    % normal index entry
\index{main entry!subentry}      % subentry
\index{main!sub!subsub}          % subsubentry
```

```
\index{entry|(}                % entry from page
\index{entry|)}                % entry up to page
\index{entry|ii}               % italic page number
\index{Pi@$\pi$}               % sort formula as `Pi'
\index{entry@{\bf entry}}      % bold entry, sort correctly
...
\printindex                    % before \end{document}
```

The most important syntax variations of `\index{entry}` are obvious from the above table. The character combinations `|(` and `|)` are used to specify page ranges. The resulting index entry will, for example, look like this: entry 34-38. A command specified after `|` and *without* a prefixed `\` character can be used to format the page number. A sample for the specification of a suitable command has been indicated with `\ii`(see `newcommand` above). `@` can be used to place formulae or specially sorted entries at the correct position in the index. All formatting methods mentioned can also be combined, for example to highlight a particular subentry.

To conclude, here are some examples to illustrate the function of the `\index` command. The results can be seen in the index at the end of this book.

```
\index{index sample}
\index{index sample!subentry
\index{index sample!subentry@{\tt subentry courier}}
\index{index sample!special@{\verb?special chars % \?}}
\index{index sample!italic entry@{\it italic entry
\index{index sample!italic page number|ii}
\index{index@{\verb?\index?}}
\index{printindex@{\verb?\printindex?}}
\index{makeindex@{\verb?makeindex?}}
\index{usepackage@\verb?\usepackage?!makeidx@{\verb?\makeidx?}}
\index{index (\LaTeX)}
\index{index}
```

NOTE

A detailed description of the `makeindex` program exists as a `man` page. The only disadvantage of this text is that it is not LaTeX-specific. (`makeindex` can also be used to process index files generated by other programs.)

18.4 Mathematical formulae

In order to allow representation of mathematical formulae in LaTeX you must switch to mathematical mode. All of the commands presented here can only be executed in mathematical mode!

There are three ways to activate this mode: either the formula is enclosed inside the flowing text with two `$` characters, or the formula is started in a separate paragraph with `\[` and terminated with `\]`, or else the formula is written in an `equation` environment. In the last two variations, the formula is represented as centered in a separate paragraph; in the `equation` environment, it is also automatically numbered.

LaTeX formula modes

`$formula$`	formula in flow text
`\[ formula \]`	separate formula

`\begin{equation}`
`  formula`
`\end{equation}`
	separate formula with automatic numbering

Please note that formulae in the flowing text look slightly different from formulae in separate paragraphs: in `$` formulae, LaTeX uses a slightly smaller type size and tries to set the formula in such a way that it takes up as little vertical space as possible. In particular, superscripts and subscripts are positioned differently with some mathematical symbols (limits, integrals, sums).

In the following lines you will see the same formula, `\int_{i=1}^{n} x^i dx`, three times: in the flowing text, the formula enclosed in `$` looks like this: $\int_{i=1}^{n} x^i dx$. Enclosed in `\[ ... \]` or between `\begin{equation}` and `\end{equation}`, the following results are produced:

$$\int_{i=1}^{n} x^i dx$$

$$\int_{i=1}^{n} x^i dx \qquad (18.1)$$

If you prefer separate formulae not to be centered but ranged left, you can use the instruction `\usepackage{fleqno}` at the beginning of your LaTeX document. Subsequently, you can use `\mathindent2cm` to specify an indentation with respect to the left margin (here: 2 cm). Alternatively, you can use `\usepackage{leqno}` to ensure that the LaTeX numbers for formulae in the `equation` environment are ranged left instead of right.

Inside formulae, text is generally set in italics. For variables, this is the common mathematical notation. Function names, however, should usually be represented with upright characters. To achieve this, LaTeX provides its own commands such as `\sin`. $\sin(x^2)$ is generated through the text `$\sin(x^2)$`. LaTeX has the following commands for the output of functions:

Keywords for mathematical functions

```
\arccos, \arcsin, \arctan, \arg, \cos, \cosh, \cot, \coth, \csc,
\deg, \det, \dim, \exp, \gcd, \hom, \inf, \ker, \lg, \lim, \liminf,
\limsup, \ln, \log, \max, \min, \Pr, \sec, \sin, \sinh, \sup, \tan,
\tanh
```

If normal text or a function name not contained in the above list is to be used inside a formula, the text must be specified with `\mbox{...}`. Inside formulae, instructions such as `{\it varname}` or `{\bf X}` are allowed as well to output longer variable names or to highlight items of text.

In some cases, LaTeX uses spacing very sparingly. In the formula $\sin(xy)$ (`\sin(x y)`) you can hardly recognize that x and y are two separate variables to be multiplied by each other. To increase spacing, you can use the three commands `\,` (small distance), `\:` (average distance) and `\;` (wide distance): `\sin(x \: y)` thus becomes $\sin(x \: y)$.

Construction of mathematical formulae

`a^{b}`	a^b	`\sum_{a}^{b} c`	$\sum_{a}^{b} c$
`a_{b}`	a_b	`\prod_{a}^{b} c`	$\prod_{a}^{b} c$
`\frac{a}{b}`	$\frac{a}{b}$	`{a \choose b}`	${a \choose b}$
`\sqrt{a}`	$\sqrt{a}$	`\overline{abc}`	$\overline{abc}$
`\sqrt[n]{a}`	$\sqrt[n]{a}$	`\underline{abc}`	$\underline{abc}$
`\int_{a}^{b} c`	$\int_{a}^{b} c$	`\overbrace{abc}^{d}`	$\overbrace{abc}^{d}$
`\oint_{a}^{b} c`	$\oint_{a}^{b} c$	`\underbrace{abc}_{d}`	$\underbrace{abc}_{d}$

The above commands are used for the construction of fractions, roots, integrals, sums, and so on. The commands can be arbitrarily embedded to obtain roots in fractions or similar combinations. LaTeX automatically looks after suitable type size and other formatting details. Please remember when specifying superscripts or subscripts to enclose the relevant expressions in curly brackets – otherwise, `^` and `_` only apply to the first following character.

If you are not satisfied with the type sizes chosen automatically by LaTeX, you can influence them with the following four commands:

Type size in mathematical formulae

`\displaystyle`	normal
`\textstyle`	slightly smaller (type size used in `$` formulae)
`\scriptstyle`	still smaller (first order indices and exponents)
`\scriptscriptstyle`	tiny (second order indices and exponents)

The following formulae illustrate the interplay between some of the commands listed above. The formulae also contain some commands which will only be described in the following sections.

```
\[ \frac{ \frac{a+1}{b-1} }{ \frac{c+1}{d-1}}
   \qquad \mbox{and} \qquad
   \frac{\displaystyle \frac{a+1}{b-1}}
        {\displaystyle \frac{c+1}{d-1}}  \]
```

$$\frac{\frac{a+1}{b-1}}{\frac{c+1}{d-1}} \quad \text{and} \quad \dfrac{a+1}{\dfrac{b-1}{\dfrac{c+1}{d-1}}}$$

```
\[ \oint_C f(z) \, dz = \int_0^{2 \pi} f(z(t)) \,
   \frac{d \, z(t)}{dt} \, dt
   \qquad\mbox{with}\qquad
   z(t)= z0 + r\, (\cos(t) + I\, sin(t)) \]
```

$$\oint_C f(z)\,dz = \int_0^{2\pi} f(z(t))\,\frac{d\,z(t)}{dt}\,dt \qquad \text{with} \qquad z(t) = z0 + r\,(\cos(t) + I\,sin(t))$$

```
\[   \left[       {\begin{array}{c}
  {\displaystyle \frac {{\frac {{ \partial}}{{ \partial}{u}}}\,
    {\rm f}(\,{u}, {v}, {z}\,)}{{a}\,\sqrt {{\rm sin}(\,{v}\,)^{2} +
    {\rm sinh}(\,{u}\,)^{2}}}} \\[5mm]
  {\displaystyle \frac {{\frac {{ \partial}}{{ \partial}{v}}}\,
    {\rm f}(\,{u}, {v}, {z}\,)}{{a}\,\sqrt {{\rm sin}(\,{v}\,)^{2} +
    {\rm sinh}(\,{u}\,)^{2}}}} \\[5mm]
  {\frac {{ \partial}}{{ \partial}{z}}}\,{\rm f}(\,{u}, {v}, {z}\,)
\end{array}}     \right]    \]
```

$$\left[\begin{array}{c} \dfrac{\frac{\partial}{\partial u}\,\mathrm{f}(\,u, v, z\,)}{a\,\sqrt{\sin(\,v\,)^2 + \sinh(\,u\,)^2}} \\[5mm] \dfrac{\frac{\partial}{\partial v}\,\mathrm{f}(\,u, v, z\,)}{a\,\sqrt{\sin(\,v\,)^2 + \sinh(\,u\,)^2}} \\[5mm] \frac{\partial}{\partial z}\,\mathrm{f}(\,u, v, z\,) \end{array} \right]$$

Parentheses and brackets

Parentheses and brackets are mainly generated directly with `(..)` or `[...]`. Since curly brackets have a special meaning, they must be preceded by a backslash, thus, `\{...\}`.

In mathematical formulae, the size of parentheses and brackets should normally correspond to the size of the bracketed expression. As standard, this is not the case, but it can be achieved with the commands `\left` and `\right` put in front of the left and right parentheses or brackets. The previous example shows the application of the two commands. `\left` and `\right` can also be used in combination with several other mathematical symbols, for example with | for amounts.

Matrices

For the representation of matrices, the `array` environment is used. The general syntax is:

array environment

```
\begin{array}{ccc}          % one c (centered) for each column
term1 & term2 & term3\\ % separate terms with &, ends of line with \\
term4 & term5 & term6    % no \\ in the last line
\end{array}
```

The `array` environment produces unbracketed matrices. If the matrix is to be bracketed, the parentheses or the square brackets must be preceded with the commands `\left` and `\right`.

```
\[                              % start of formula
\left (                         % open large parenthesis
\begin{array}{cc}               % two-column matrix
x^y    & \frac{\alpha}{\beta}\\
a+b+c & \frac{a+b+c}{x^2
\end{array}                     % end of matrix
\right )                        % close large parenthesis
\]                              % end of formula
```

$$\left(\begin{array}{cc} x^y & \frac{\alpha}{\beta} \\ a+b+c & \frac{a+b+c}{x^2} \end{array} \right)$$

Special mathematical characters

The symbols `+ - / = ! ' | ( ) [ ]` can be directly used in formulae without any special effort. Moreover, there are countless other special characters (operators, arrows, mathematical symbols) which can be built with LaTeX commands. The following tables present (a choice of) commands for the most important special characters. When you want to use these characters in normal text (and not in a formula), you must place the command between two `$` characters.

Special characters

`\infty`	∞	`\cdot`	$\cdot$	`\pm`	$\pm$	`\neq`	$\neq$
`\partial`	∂	`\circ`	$\circ$	`\times`	$\times$	`\sim`	$\sim$
`\Re`	$\Re$	`\bullet`	$\bullet$	`\div`	$\div$	`\simeq`	$\simeq$
`\Im`	$\Im$	`\ldots`	$\ldots$	`\ast`	$\ast$	`\approx`	$\approx$
`\forall`	$\forall$	`\vdots`	$\vdots$	`|`	$\|$	`\equiv`	$\equiv$
`\exists`	$\exists$	`\cdots`	$\cdots$	`\vee`	$\vee$	`\le`	$\le$
				`\wedge`	$\wedge$	`\ge`	$\ge$
		`\ddots`	$\ddots$	`\nabla`	∇	`\ll`	$\ll$
				`\oplus`	$\oplus$	`\gg`	$\gg$
				`\ominus`	$\ominus$		
				`\otimes`	$\otimes$		

Arrows					
`\leftarrow`	$\leftarrow$	`\Leftarrow`	$\Leftarrow$	`\nearrow`	$\nearrow$
`\rightarrow`	$\rightarrow$	`\Rightarrow`	$\Rightarrow$	`\searrow`	$\searrow$
`\uparrow`	$\uparrow$	`\Uparrow`	$\Uparrow$	`\swarrow`	$\swarrow$
`\downarrow`	$\downarrow$	`\Downarrow`	$\Downarrow$	`\nwarrow`	$\nwarrow$
`\leftrightarrow`	$\leftrightarrow$	`\Leftrightarrow`	$\Leftrightarrow$		
`\updownarrow`	$\updownarrow$	`\Updownarrow`	$\Updownarrow$		
`\hookleftarrow`	$\hookleftarrow$				

In formulae, individual variables must often be marked with vector arrows, derivative dots or quotes or other additional symbols. The following table describes the most important marking commands. Please note that commands such as `\vec` can only be used for single letters (and not for groups of letters or even longer expressions).

Vectors, derivatives, etc.							
`\bar{x}`	$\bar{x}$	`\tilde{x}`	$\tilde{x}$	`x'`	x'	`x'''`	x'''
`\dot{x}`	$\dot{x}$	`\ddot{x}`	$\ddot{x}$	`\vec{x}`	$\vec{x}$		

Greek and calligraphic letters

Greek letters are also represented through LaTeX commands. The command name corresponds to the name of the letter, thus, for example, `\alpha` for a lower case α and `\Delta` for an upper case Δ.

Greek letters							
`\alpha`	α	`\kappa`	κ	`\Psi`	Ψ	`\Upsilon`	Υ
`\beta`	β	`\lambda`	λ	`\omega`	ω	`\varepsilon`	ε
`\chi`	χ	`\Lambda`	Λ	`\Omega`	Ω	`\varphi`	φ
`\delta`	δ	`\mu`	μ	`\rho`	ρ	`\varpi`	ϖ
`\Delta`	Δ	`\nu`	ν	`\sigma`	σ	`\varrho`	ϱ
`\epsilon`	ϵ	`\phi`	ϕ	`\Sigma`	Σ	`\varsigma`	ς
`\eta`	η	`\Phi`	Φ	`\tau`	τ	`\vartheta`	ϑ
`\gamma`	γ	`\pi`	π	`\theta`	θ	`\xi`	ξ
`\Gamma`	Γ	`\Pi`	Π	`\Theta`	Θ	`\Xi`	Ξ
`\iota`	ι	`\psi`	ψ	`\upsilon`	υ	`\zeta`	ζ

Calligraphic letters are only available in upper case. In order to represent these letters, the typeface must be changed by means of `\cal`, thus, for example, `{\cal A} \cup {\cal B}` for $\mathcal{A} \cup \mathcal{B}$.

18.5 Layout control

By and large, LaTeX carries out line and page breaking itself and achieves good results. There are, however, situations in which LaTeX fails. Sometimes (but not always), LaTeX signals line breaking problems with warnings such as 'over-/underfull hbox/vbox'. This means that LaTeX has placed text outside the page margin or that big gaps occur in the text. The most probable cause of such errors is a long word in which LaTeX has not identified any suitable hyphenation.

But even when LaTeX does not issue any warnings, you may be dissatisfied with the result – for example, when LaTeX has tried to use up all available space on a page and has placed one or two lines of a new paragraph at the bottom of the page even though, for the sake of clarity, starting a new page would have made much more sense. This section summarizes the most important commands that allow you to influence the line and page breaking process manually (that is, with additional commands).

Hyphenation

LaTeX always hyphenates automatically. The hyphenation rules applied are surprisingly reliable, that is, it rarely happens that LaTeX produces a really incorrect hyphenation. Much more often, LaTeX does not find a suitable hyphenation point, so it leaves the word intact and then gets into trouble when breaking the line (with either big gaps or text that goes well over the page margin). In these cases you can use `\-` to insert so-called soft hyphens into the word in question. Then LaTeX hyphenates the word – if necessary – at one of the points specified by yourself.

Sometimes, the opposite problem arises – you want to avoid LaTeX hyphenating a (maybe short) word. To prevent this, simply place the whole word into an `\mbox{}` command.

Influencing hyphenation	
`\-`	soft hyphenation
`\mbox{word}`	do not hyphenate the word

The LaTeX distributions NTeX and teTeX already contain built-in hyphenation files for British English, American English, German and several other languages. German hyphenation, for example, would be activated with the `german` package.

Word spacing and horizontal spacing

In order to justify the individual lines of a paragraph, LaTeX inserts the same amount of space between all words (in one line), with a slightly wider space after a full stop (end of a sentence). If only a normal space is to be used after a full stop (for example, after abbreviations), `\␣` must be specified after the full stop: `Prof.\␣Huber` for Prof. Huber. (␣ stands for a space.) When two words are not to be separated by a line break, a fixed space can be specified with `~`, for example, `3~cm`.

Additional space between two words can be inserted by means of `\quad`, `\qquad` or `\hspace{distance}`. Syntactically superfluous spaces before or after these commands should be avoided, because they might inadvertently cause wider spaces.

The three commands mentioned above generate spaces of exactly predefined width. The effect of `\hfill` is completely different. This command inserts all space available in a line at the current position. If `\hfill` is used several times in a line, the inserted space is reduced accordingly. If `\hfill` is used at the end of a line, the line must be terminated with `\hbox{}`. This creates an invisible LaTeX object which functions as a limit for `\hfill`. An example:

```
\hfill centered \hfill\hbox{}
```

centered

Additional vertical and horizontal spacing	
`\ `	word space after punctuation marks
`~`	fixed space; the line will not be broken at this point
`\quad`	additional space of 1 em width (see below)
`\qquad`	additional space of 2 em width (see below)
`\hspace{distance}`	insert space of specified width
`\hspace*{distance}`	as above, but also with line breaking
`\hfill`	insert so much space that the line is filled
`\dotfill`	as above, but dotted line instead of space
`\hrulefill`	as above, but continuous line
`\hbox{}`	invisible LaTeX object (as a limit for `\hfill`)

Numeric values in commands such as `\hspace` can be specified both with a decimal point and a decimal comma. The value must always be terminated with a measurement unit (even if it is 0). LaTeX allows the following measurement units:

Measurement units	
`mm`	millimeter
`cm`	centimeter
`pt`	point (1 point = 0.353 mm)
`ex`	the height of an 'x' in the current character set
`em`	the width of a dash (–) in the current character set

Line breaking and vertical spacing

Inside a paragraph, LaTeX only begins a new line when there is no space left in the current line. A premature line break can be obtained with `\\`. If after this you specify a distance enclosed in square brackets, LaTeX also inserts the corresponding vertical space: `\\[1cm]`. If a `*` is put between `\\` and the distance specification, the vertical space is also inserted when a page break is carried out. (This only makes sense in extremely rare cases!) `\vspace{distance}` can be used to insert additional space between two paragraphs. Negative values may be specified for all measurements.

Manual line breaking	
`\\`	line break without justification (line is ranged left)
`\\[distance]`	line break with increased space to next line
`\\*[distance]`	as above, but also applies in case of page break
`\linebreak`	line break with justification
`\vspace{distance}`	additional space between two paragraphs
`\vspace*{distance}`	as above, but also applies in case of page break

Forced page break

A forced page break can be obtained with the three commands `\newpage`, `\pagebreak` and `\clearpage`. The differences are shown in the following table:

Manual page breaking	
`\newpage`	begins a new page/column, rest of current page remains empty
`\pagebreak`	as above, but vertical justification (more space between paragraphs)
`\clearpage`	new page, even for two-column text

User-defined headers

Normally, LaTeX looks after running heads itself and sets them according to the text type. The most complex operations are carried out for the text type `book`: here, LaTeX differentiates between even and odd page numbers and incorporates chapter and section titles into the headers. If you are not satisfied with the standard headers and footers, you can use `\pagestyle` to deactivate the automatic headers and define your own via `\markright` or `\markboth`. LaTeX automatically integrates these user-defined headers with the current page number.

Headers	
`\pagestyle{headings}`	automatic layout of running heads (default setting)
`\pagestyle{empty}`	no header, no page number
`\pagestyle{plain}`	no header, page number centered in footer
`\pagestyle{myheadings}`	user-defined header, see `\markright` and `\markboth`
`\thispagestyle`	as `\pagestyle`, but only for one page
`\markright{header}`	header for single-sided texts
`\markboth{left}{right}`	header for double-sided texts

The above commands do not allow you to change the visual layout of the automatic LaTeX headers. As standard, LaTeX sets the titles in the headings in upper case letters and without rules. If you require a different layout, the setting must be changed with your own style file. A more elegant solution is to use the `fancyheadings.sty` style file. Unfortunately, this file for easy setting of headers and footers is not available in the NTeX distribution.

Global layout settings

The layout of a LaTeX text can be influenced not only through various commands mostly applied to small portions of text, but also through global settings. These settings are normally executed before the actual beginning of the text (that is, before `\begin{document}`) and apply to the whole text. Many of the commands listed on the following pages can also be used at any point in the text and become effective only from that point onward.

Most measure specifications can be changed with their own commands to which the following syntax applies: `\command`*measure* (without spaces between command and setting). Some settings must be carried out by direct assignments to LaTeX variables. In these cases, the syntax is: `\setcounter{name}{value}`.

The following table summarizes the measures for the setting of the printable area of a page. The commands are logically arranged from left to right and from top to bottom.

Page layout	
`\oddsidemargin`*measure*	distance left paper edge – text for odd pages
`\evensidemargin`*measure*	distance left paper edge – text for even pages
`\textwidth`*measure*	text width (printed page area)
`\topmargin`*measure*	distance top paper edge – header
`\headheight`*measure*	height of header
`\headsep`*measure*	distance header – text
`\textheight`*measure*	text height (for the text itself without headers and footers)
`\columnsep`*measure*	gutter (only for two-column text)
`\columnseprule`*measure*	width of rule between the columns (standard: 0)
`\footskip`*measure*	distance between text and lower (!) edge of footer
`\headheight`*measure*	height of footer

As standard, LaTeX does not insert vertical space between two paragraphs. Instead, beginning with the second paragraph of a section, the first line of each following paragraph is indented by a certain amount. If you want to obtain a different paragraph setting (for example, without the indent, but with a distinct spacing between paragraphs) you must set `\parindent` to 0 (not forgetting the unit – in spite of being 0) and set `\parskip` to a reasonable value – for example, `2ex`.

Some explanation is also needed for the `\flushbuttom` command: it causes LaTeX to carry out vertical justification of the text, by inserting as much space between paragraphs and headlines as is necessary to make all pages exactly the same length.

As standard, this formatting is only active for the text type `book` and can be switched off with `\raggedbottom`.

Paragraph layout	
`\parindent`*measure*	first line indent of the paragraph
`\parskip`*measure*	distance between two paragraphs
`\raggedright`	no justification, text ranged left
`\flushbottom`	vertical justification (equal page depth)
`\raggedbottom`	no vertical justification

The syntax for modifying line spacing differs from the above commands: With `\renewcommand{\baselinestretch`*factor*`}` the normal line spacing is reduced or increased by the specified factor. This slightly unusual definition is necessary because the line spacing depends on the current type size and should therefore not be set to a fixed value.

Normally, LaTeX automatically numbers all headlines down to and including `\subsubsection`, which generates section numbers such as 3.5.2.1. In this book, numbering has been reduced to two levels (chapter and section) by modifying the variable `secnumdepth`. Similarly, the number of levels for the table of contents can be controlled through the variable `tocdepth` (three levels in this book).

Numbering of headlines	
`\setcounter{secnumdepth}{n}`	numbers n+1 structuring levels
`\setcounter{tocdepth}{n}`	uses n+1 structuring levels in table of contents
`\setcounter{page}{n}`	changes the current page number
`\setcounter{chapter}{n}`	changes the current chapter number
`\setcounter{section}{n}`	changes the current section number

18.6 Metafont and PostScript fonts

The biggest comprehension problems when working with LaTeX are presumably caused by the handling of character sets. This section tries to clarify the situation. The two main topics in this section are the LaTeX utility program Metafont which generates LaTeX's own character sets (in most cases dynamically during output) and the use of true PostScript fonts instead of the original LaTeX fonts.

Metafont

When LaTeX was originally developed, the printer market was even more unstructured than it is today. An established standard such as PostScript with countless predefined fonts at a cost accessible to (nearly) everybody did not then exist. For this reason, the Metafont program was developed at the same time as LaTeX. This program is responsible for the calculation of character sets. The aim was to be able to support each and every possible printer with the highest possible quality. From this background it is also understandable why Metafont works with bitmap fonts (unlike PostScript which works with arbitrarily scalable vector fonts). Even today, LaTeX and Metafont constitute an integrated package, each program alone being practically useless.

How does Metafont work? The starting point for all character sets is the `name.mf` files. These text files contain commands for drawing the individual characters of a character set. Depending on the specified options, the Metafont program generates one or two files: in any case it generates a bitmap file `name.nnnpk` and sometimes (if this file does not yet exist) the metrics file `name.tfm`.

The bitmap files `*.nnnpk` contain the character set in compressed form. In these bitmap files, each letter is represented using thousands of single dots (pixels). `nnn` stands for a factor made up of the resolution in dpi (dots per inch) and the magnification. Typical dpi values are 300 or 600 dpi for laser printers and 1270 or 2540 dpi for image setters. The magnification factor comes into play when a character set is needed in a different size than the one in which it was developed (for example, for `\small` or `\large`). This results in values such as 720 (600 times 1.2).

The metrics files `*.tfm` contain the size specifications of the individual characters. Even if several `*.pk` files exist for a given character set, there is always only one metrics file (since the actual size of the characters depends on the printer resolution).

Now for the real meaning of the two file types: the metrics files `*.tfm` are needed by LaTeX while processing a text. From these files, LaTeX extracts the information of how large the individual letters are and uses this data to carry out line and page breaking. The result is a DVI file (*device independent*) which does not yet contain the actual character sets and which can be neither printed nor displayed in this form.

The `*pk` files are only needed for printing or for displaying the file on screen (`xdvi`). If the currently needed `*pk` file does not yet exist in the screen/printer resolution and the required magnification, Metafont is started automatically. This can lead to considerable delays during the first printing of a text with many type families and sizes. The next time, however, the required `*pk` files will be readily available.

As a rule, you will not have to concern yourself with character set files and you will never have to start the Metafont program (command name `mf`) yourself. All required `*.mf` and `*.tfm` files are already preinstalled, and the `*.nnnpk` files are automatically generated when needed.

Printing at a resolution higher than 300 dpi

`dvips` converts DVI files into PostScript files. When character set files are missing, the program automatically starts the Metafont program. `dvips` provides the option `-D` for changing the resolution. The default value is preset in the `dvips` configuration file `config.ps` in the `./dvips/config` directory (usually to 600 dpi).

However, modification of the resolution with `-D` does not work for all resolutions. This is because of the shell file `mktexpk` (which, via `MakeTeXPK`, is called by `dvips` for the generation of missing character sets). Corresponding printer modes are only preset for the listed resolution steps. The following listing shows the relevant section of `mktexpk`:

```
# /usr/bin/mktexpk
...
 if test -z "$MODE" || test "x$MODE" = xdefault; then
    case "$BDPI" in
      85) MODE=sun;;
     100) MODE=nextscrn;;
     180) MODE=toshiba;;
     300) MODE=cx;;
     400) MODE=nexthi;;
     600) MODE=ljfour;;
    1270) MODE=linoone;;
       *) echo "$progname: Can't guess mode for $BDPI dpi devices." >&2
          echo "$progname: Use a config file, or update me." >&2
          exit 1
    esac
  fi
...
```

The Metafont program expects not only the required resolution as a parameter for the generation of a character set, but also additional information about the printer type. If the printer type is known, Metafont can evaluate the `modes.mf` file in the `/usr/share/texmf/metafont/misc` directory. In this file, countless printers and image setters are listed, together with printer-specific data which allows the character sets to be optimally adapted to the printer's peculiarities. For example, for printers which make single pixels too big, thinner character sets are generated to compensate for this fault. A typical entry in `modes.mf` looks more or less like this (this is for a Canon ink jet printer with 360 dpi):

```
% /usr/share/texmf/metafont/misc/modes.mf
...
% From  sjwright@cix.compulink.co.uk, 9 February 1994.
mode_def bjtenex =                      % Canon BubbleJet 10ex
  mode_param (pixels_per_inch, 360);
  mode_param (blacker, .6);
  mode_param (fillin, 0);
  mode_param (o_correction, .6);
  mode_common_setup_;
enddef;
...
```

In order to generate a proper printout with this printer, you must insert the following line into the `case` statement in `mktexpk`:

```
# insert into /usr/bin/mktexpk
360) MODE=bjtenex;;
```

Now you can call `dvips` with the option `-D 360` and subsequently convert the resulting PostScript file with `gs` and the option `-sDEVICE=bj10e` into the format of the Canon printer. Please note that this yields satisfactory results only when using LaTeX fonts. PostScript fonts can only be converted into the format of another printer with acceptable quality when the necessary PostScript fonts are available.

NOTE Further information on PostScript fonts can be found on page 625. The `dvips` program is discussed in detail in Section 15.3 on page 507. This chapter also describes all other Linux programs for printing of texts of arbitrary origin.

Font files

If you want to know which font files are available to you, you can change to the `/usr/share/texmf` directory. There, you execute the command

```
user$ find -name '*.mf'
```

The result is a long list of font files (about 1500 on my computer). Out of all these fonts, you will normally only need very few, namely those of the `./fonts/source/public` subdirectories (in the NTeX distribution). The remaining character sets are designed for various TeX and LaTeX extensions (for example, AmsTeX) which are described in Lamport (1994) and Goossens *et al.* (1993).

The file names of the LaTeX standard fonts begin with the two letters 'cm', which stand for 'computer modern'. The cm fonts are still the *de facto* standard for all LaTeX documents. In parallel to these fonts, a new generation of fonts has been developed during the past few years; these are known as dc fonts. The dc fonts differ from the cm fonts in that they have an extended character set (more special characters). Their biggest disadvantage is that their character codes are partly different from the cm font codes and this creates compatibility problems. Thus, the use of dc fonts requires new hyphenation files, and so forth (see again the above-mentioned books).

Using PostScript fonts

The subject of this section is not simply how to print a LaTeX text on a PostScript printer – to do this, you only need the `dvips` program. The real subject of this section is actually how not to use the original LaTeX fonts for printing, but rather to use well-known PostScript fonts such as Courier, Helvetica, Times Roman or Palatino.

The main advantage of using PostScript fonts is that you have a much wider choice of fonts. A further argument in favor of PostScript fonts is their better scalability. Postscript fonts are always output at the highest possible quality and by every single PostScript printer. If you work with LaTeX fonts, on the other hand, you must generate a separate file for every printer in order to achieve optimum quality. (Printing with resolutions higher than 300 dpi has been discussed in the previous section.)

In principle, use of PostScript fonts is very easy: you must simply execute the `\usepackage` command at the beginning of your document, specifying one of the following package names:

PostScript font packages	
avant	AvantGarde instead of Sans Serif, other fonts original LaTeX
bookman	Bookman as Standard font, AvantGarde instead of Sans Serif, Courier instead of Typewriter
helvetica	Helvetica instead of Sans Serif, other fonts original LaTeX
newcentury	Standard font NewCenturySchoolbook, AvantGarde instead of Sans Serif, Courier instead of Typewriter
palatino	Standard font Palatino, Helvetica instead of Sans Serif, Courier instead of Typewriter
times	Standard font Times Roman, Helvetica instead of Sans Serif, Courier instead of Typewriter

Depending on the distribution, you will find additional packages in `.//tex/latex/psnfss/`.

Please note that even when using PostScript fonts you must still use the `dvips` option `-D` to set the required resolution for your printer. This is because special mathematical characters are still generated via LaTeX character sets (and are therefore resolution-dependent).

One particular feature in the use of PostScript fonts is that for most fonts (with the exception of Courier) the two quotation marks ’ and ‘ can only be distinguished with a magnifying glass.

18.7 LaTeX for advanced users

This section discusses some advanced subjects. It is really addressed to those users who need to plan the layout of long texts and wish to exploit the possibilities of LaTeX to their very limit. The subsections show how to define your own macros and how to split text across several files.

Macros

When creating longer LaTeX texts you will note that you need certain LaTeX commands over and over again. In order to minimize your typing effort, and also for the sake of better readability, you can define your own macros which then behave like LaTeX commands. The definition of macros must be carried out before `\begin{document}`.

There are three types of macro definition: simple commands without parameters, commands with parameters, and new environments. The syntax for the definition of new commands looks as follows:

User-defined macros and environments	
`\newcommand{\name}{code}`	command without parameters
`\newcommand{\name}[n]{code}`	command with *n* parameters
`\newenvironment{name}{code1}{code2}`	new environment

Parameters in commands with parameters can be used in the code area with `#1`, `#2`, and so on. Environments have two code areas: the first one is executed at the beginning of the environment, the second one at the end. Subsequently, new commands can be called with `\name` or `\name{para1}{para2}{...}`. New environments are used with `\begin{name}` and `\end{name}`.

The following lines show an example of new commands, one with and one without parameters, followed by an example for a new environment.

```
\newcommand{\dat}{\small\tt}                      % font to be used for
                                                  % file names

\newcommand{\pikkie}[3]{\begin{figure}[h]         % insert a picture
  \centerline{\epsfxsize=90mm\epsffile{#1}}       % with caption
  \caption{\label{#2} {\it #3}}
  \end{figure}}

\newenvironment{mycomment}{\begin{quote}          % set text small,
  \small\sl}                                      % italic and indented
  {\end{quote}}
```

Now to the application of these commands: `{\dat file name}` supplies the text `file name`. The instruction `\pikkie{file}{label}{caption}` inserts the specified PostScript file into the text, defines a label for cross-references and sets the specified text as a caption underneath the picture. The new environment `mycomment` sets the enclosed text small, italic and indented both left and right, as shown below.

> *Text set between* `\begin{mycomment}` *and* `\end{mycomment}` *looks like this paragraph.*

Processing long texts

When you want to produce longer texts with LaTeX, it is reasonable to split the text into several files. A well-proven method is a division into a central control file (`book.tex`), a file with global settings and macro definitions (`header.tex`) plus a separate file for each chapter. (By the way, even with documents put together in this way, LaTeX has no problems with tables of contents and indices. Cross-references can refer from one chapter to another without problems.)

The most important command for combining texts from several files is `\input{file}`. At the point of its occurrence, it reads the specified file and processes it as though the text contained in it had been entered at that point. `\input` can also occur embedded. When no file extension is specified, LaTeX automatically appends `.tex` to the file name.

Reading an external file	
`\input{file}`	inserts the specified LaTeX file at this point in the text

Splitting long texts into several files not only has the advantage of more clarity, but it also increases working speed. While working on one chapter, all other `\input` lines in `book.tex` can be commented out with a preceding `%` character. This considerably increases the LaTeX processing speed of that text. The files `book.tex` and `header.tex` usually look something like this:

```
% BOOK.TEX: central control file
\input{header}
\makeindex
\begin{document}
\tableofcontents        % insert table of contents
\input{preface}
\input{chapter1} \input{chapter2} \input{chapter3} % ...
% ...
\begin{appendix}
\input{appa}  \input{appb}  \input{appc}  % ...
\end{appendix}
\printindex             % insert index
\end{document}

% HEADER.TEX: global settings, macros
\documentclass{book}    % document type
\usepackage{german}     % various macro files
\usepackage{isolatin1}
\parindent0pt           % global settings
\parskip2ex             % and so on
\newcommand{\dat}[1]{{}\small\tt #1}   % macro definitions
```

Special typesetting features of this book

When you are leafing through this book, you will probably notice some particular layout features that are not entirely typical for LaTeX. This section reveals some of the tricks used to put these features into practice. A detailed explanation of how and why this works would, however, lead into the abysses of LaTeX and TeX and must be omitted for reasons of space.

In this book, keyboard symbols of the form Ctrl+C are represented by means of the `\keys{Ctrl}+\keys{C}` command. The keyboard symbols are generated with a macro which resorts to some elementary graphics commands of LaTeX. The large number of `%` characters at the end of each command serve the purpose of preventing unwanted insertion of spaces.

```
\newbox\mybox%                variable for LaTeX box
\newcount\length%             variable for integer number
\newcount\halflength%         another variable
\newcommand{\keys}[1]{%       text is passed as parameter
\setbox\mybox=%               store parameter in box
\hbox{\footnotesize #1}%
\length=\wd\mybox%            determine length of box
```

```
\advance\length by 370000%      increase length by 2 mm
\halflength=\length%            half of that
\divide \halflength by 2%
\unitlength1sp%                 all measurements in sp (1/65536 pt)
% picture environment for graphics commands
% \length wide, 600000 sp = 3.2 mm high
% horizontal offset 0,
% vertical offset 140000 sp (0.7 mm) below normal text
\begin{picture}(\length,600000)(0, 140000)%
% draw oval
\put(\halflength, 300000){\oval(\length, 600000)}%
% output stored box in this oval
% horiz. offset 1 mm, vert offset 0.7 mm
\put(185000, 140000){\unhbox\mybox}%
\end{picture}}
```

Relatively often, syntax boxes are used for various summaries. The standard `\fbox` command is not suitable for this purpose because it does not permit use of the `\verb` command. The following macro uses the new LaTeX 2_ε environment `lrbox`. The gray background is obtained with the `\fcolorbox` command defined in the `color` package.

```
\fboxsep1.36mm%                  space between syntax box and text
\definecolor{g1}{gray}{0.92}%    define grayshade
\newsavebox{\syntaxbox}%         as above
\newenvironment{sybox}%
{\begin{lrbox}{\syntaxbox}%
\begin{minipage}{12.5cm}}%
{\end{minipage}%
\end{lrbox}%                     output syntax box contents in a
{\fcolorbox{black}{g1}%          gray background \fcolorbox
{\parbox{12.5cm}{\usebox{\syntaxbox}\hfill\hbox{}}}}}
```

Application of the new environment looks as follows:

```
\begin{sybox}
Syntax box in in which special characters such as
\verb?%~^? can be represented
\end{sybox}
```

Syntax box in in which special characters such as %~^ can be represented

18.8 LaTeX2$_\varepsilon$ versus LaTeX 2.09

LaTeX 2_ε differs from the preceding version LaTeX 2.09 mainly in its improved handling of character sets. If you work on a computer on which LaTeX 2.09 is still installed, you must note the following points:

- Your LaTeX text begins with the instruction `\documentstyle[options]{type}` (instead of `\documentclass`). As options, you specify not only the options described on page 598, but also the names of additional files which in LaTeX 2_ε are loaded with `\usepackage`. An analogous command to `\usepackage` does not exist in LaTeX 2.09.
- For changing character sets, the only available commands are `\rm`, `\sf`, `\tt`, `\bf`, `\it`, `\sl`, `\sc` and `\em`. Combination of type attributes is only possible to a very limited extent. The commands for changing the type size (`\small`, `\large` etc.) automatically activate the standard font – if you want to change the type size for `\tt`, you must *first* specify the size command and then `\tt` (and not vice versa).
- The `lrbox` environment mentioned in in the previous section does not exist. Therefore, you cannot use the macro described above for the new `sybox` environment.

It is quite possible to live with these restrictions. The real functionality of LaTeX (setting of formulae, scientific layout elements, and so on) is not affected.

Compatibility problems with LaTeX2_ε

Totally different problems can occur when you try to process a text generated previously with LaTeX 2.09 with the new LaTeX 2_ε. LaTeX 2_ε automatically activates a compatibility mode when a document begins with `\documentstyle` instead of `\documentclass`. In this case, it tries to behave exactly in the same way as LaTeX 2.09. In principle, this compatibility mode works very well. The fact that problems still arise, in spite of this, has mainly two causes:

- The text uses macro files which are no longer available under LaTeX 2_ε or have a different name. This problem can be easily overcome by copying the file in question (usually `name.sty`) from your old LaTeX version into your current working directory. If you have already deleted LaTeX 2.09 on your computer (for example, during installation of a new LINUX distribution), you must try to obtain the file from another computer (if necessary, via the Internet).
- The text uses macro files in which additional character sets or type style commands are defined. These files are usually predecessor versions of the new type style commands of LaTeX 2_ε, which could already be used in LaTeX 2.09. In these predecessor versions, however, some different file names and a different syntax apply. Your best chance of processing such texts is to try to convert the files to LaTeX 2_ε. In many cases you will just have to modify the file header (that is, `\documentclass` and `\usepackage` instead of the old `\documentstyle`). You might also have to search for and replace some type style commands with their new counterparts or redefine these commands as new macros.

LyX – LaTeX made easy

The intention of LyX is to make the use of LaTeX so easy and user-friendly that even newcomers can cope with it right from the beginning. For this purpose, LyX provides a WYSIWYG editor in which the LaTeX document can be entered. The text is displayed in nearly the same form as it will later appear in printing. (WYSIWYG stands for *What you see is what you get*. True WYSIWYG in combination with LaTeX is practically impossible during interactive elaboration of texts. However, LyX comes surprisingly close to this ideal concept.)

Maybe you are wondering why this chapter comes after the LaTeX chapter and not before. LyX is certainly much easier to handle than LaTeX. Nevertheless, having some ideas of how LaTeX works is extremely useful for understanding LyX. Therefore, please read at least the introductory section of the LaTeX chapter before you begin working with LyX – it's well worth it!

Some words on the origin of LyX: both LyX (start 1995) and the KLyX port (1997) were initiated by Matthias Ettrich (who is also the initiator of KDE). A long list of co-developers can be displayed via the HELP menu. LyX and KLyX are free software in the sense of the GPL.

19.1 Introduction

What is LyX (and what is it not)?

LyX is a modern text editor. Different items of text can be formatted in different font sizes and attributes and are not only printed like that, but, within LyX, are also displayed on screen in the same way (WYSIWYG). Format templates are available

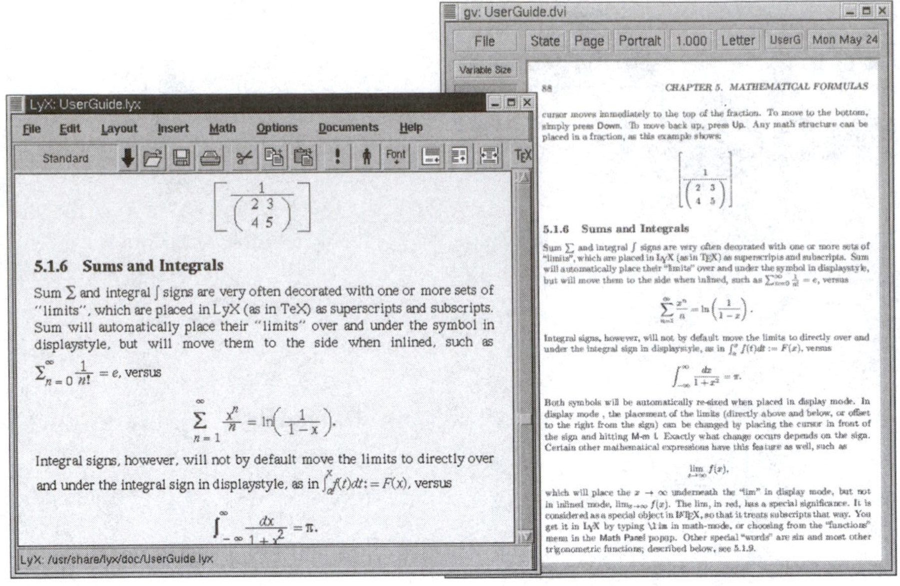

Figure 19.1 Left, WISIWYG in LyX; right, the page preview with `gv`.

for formatting different kinds of paragraphs (whose names will sound familiar to you if you have read the LaTeX chapter: *Itemize*, *List*, *Chapter*, *Section*, and so on.

In many details, the handling of this program resembles a traditional text processing program. Most keyboard shortcuts – such as cursor movement, selecting and copying of blocks, and so on – work in the same way as in Windows programs. (If this irritates you, you may as well select different keyboard assignments, for example with a greater resemblance to Emacs.)

LyX distinguishes itself through a number of professional features:

- In the documents, use can be made of tables, images, mathematical formulas, cross-references, and so forth.
- Input of mathematical formulas is supported by separate dialogs, symbol bars, and so on, and is very user-friendly.
- LyX helps with automatic generation of contents lists, indices, and lists of figures.
- Provided the `ispell` program is installed on the computer, LyX texts can be easily checked for correct spelling.
- LyX supports multi-level undo. In addition, at regular intervals automatic backup copies (with the file name `#name.lyx#`) are created of all LyX files that have been modified. Thus the risk of unwanted loss of data is very small.
- Menus and dialog texts are available in several languages. By default, LyX displays English language menus. If you prefer menus in another language, you need to set the environment variable `LANG` to `"xx"`, where *xx* is the two-character language code as defined in the ISO Standard 639 (for example, `de`

for German, `fr` for French, `it` for Italian, and so on). This variable needs to be set prior to starting LyX, for example in the `bash` with the instruction `export LANG="es"` (here, for Spanish language menus).

Layout restrictions

LyX is not a text processing program in the style of WinWord, WordPerfect, or StarWriter. In particular, formatting of LyX documents is limited by the possibilities of LaTeX. If you have previously worked with a traditional text processing program (such as WinWord), you need to rethink your approach. Here are some examples:

- It is not possible to enlarge the distance between two paragraphs by inserting additional empty lines – LaTeX ignores them. (You can, however, use Ctrl+↵ to insert 'hard' line breaks, which in LaTeX are generated by `\\`.)
- Equally, it is impossible to separate two words by more than one space. (You can, however, increase the space between two words by inserting LaTeX commands such as `\quad`, into the text. (In LyX texts, you can generally resort to all LaTeX commands.)
- You are also restricted in your selection of fonts – as usual in LaTeX documents, there is only one standard (default) font, plus two additional fonts (Sans Serif and `Typewriter`).
- LyX does not have tab stops. (There is a separate command for creating simple tables. Multi-column text can be realized by so-called minipages. In this regard, however, LyX cannot compete with traditional text processing programs.)

The above points represent a true restriction only if you put a great emphasis on a layout of your own – for example for designing a cover or a poster. For this kind of purpose, LyX is simply not suited. But for the vast majority of 'normal' texts – letters, masters theses, or articles – LyX is an obvious choice. In such cases, almost all of the layouts automatically generated by LyX look more professional than self-created ones.

TIP Reading the previous LaTeX chapter will be a great help in understanding the layout restrictions of LyX.

WYSIWYG limitations

It has already been mentioned that LyX can *nearly* handle WYSIWYG. So where are the restrictions?

- LyX can display neither line breaks nor page breaks. (To find out how the typeset document will finally look you need to convert the document into DVI or PostScript format to obtain a page preview.)
- No hyphenations are shown.
- Page numbers, headers, footers, and so on are also invisible.

A central feature of LyX is that text input is integrated into the program. Although the LyX text editor is excellent, Emacs fans (such as the author of this book) will miss their macros.

Other limitations

Obviously, LyX documents can be exported into LaTeX format without problems (LyX being simply a sort of user interface for LaTeX). Since version 1.0 the opposite, that is, import of LaTeX files into LyX, is also possible, although frequently a cause of problems. The relative command is FILE | IMPORT | LATEX. The file to be imported must, however, be a complete LaTeX document (not part of a group of several LaTeX files) and should preferably not use any LaTeX features not available under LyX. Even if all these conditions are met, import does not always work satisfactorily.

Behind the scenes, import is handled by the Perl script `relyx` which, by the way, is extremely well documented by a `man` text.

A further disadvantage is the fact that very long LyX documents cannot be subdivided into several smaller files without some difficulty.

LyX versus KLyX

Currently, there are two LyX versions which mainly differ from each other in their user interfaces. The standard version (that is LyX) is based on the Forms library, whereas KLyX uses the Qt library. KLyX is therefore particularly suitable for integration into a KDE system and gives a slightly more contemporary impression. Another decidedly useful feature is the possibility of opening several windows and of splitting windows. Thus the (partial) windows can be used to display several documents and/or different sections of a long document.

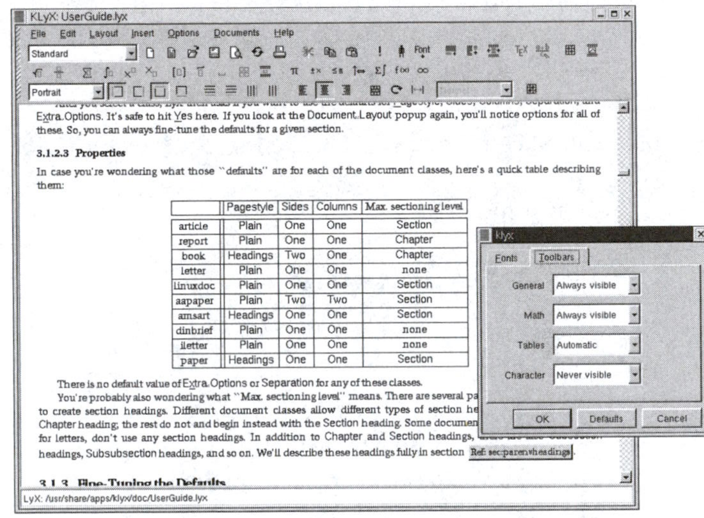

Figure 19.2 KLyX, the KDE variation of LyX.

Please note that, although KLyX is a derivation of LyX version 0.12, both versions are now maintained separately. For this reason, slight incompatibilities might occur here and there. (For the future, plans exist to reunite the two versions again and to separate the LyX code proper from the code for the user interface. Until then, both teams endeavor to keep the programs as synchronized as possible. In particular, the `*.lyx` files are to be compatible.)

At the time of writing this section, LyX was available in the stable version 1.0, while the corresponding KLyX version 0.9.9 still had beta status. During practical work, however, no difference could be noticed; both programs worked without problems.

> NOTE
> In this chapter, we do not continuously differentiate between LyX and KLyX. In short, everything that has been said about LyX also applies to KLyX. Only where the two versions differ noticeably is it explicitly stated which version is meant.

Online documentation

LyX comes with several online manuals which can be easily accessed via the help menu. These texts have mostly been written with LyX and are an excellent demonstration of the far-reaching possibilities. Obviously, they can also be printed. Unlike the menus, the help texts are currently only available in English; however, translations into other languages have already been started.

Another useful contribution for getting acquainted with LyX is provided by the sample files contained in the directories `/usr/share/lyx/examples` or `/opt/kde/share/apps/klyx/examples`.

> TIP
> To be able to work on your text and simultaneously view the help text, in KLyX you simply open a second window (FILE|WINDOWS|NEW WINDOW). In LyX this possibility does not exist – but nothing will prevent you from simply starting LyX a second time and using the second instance to display the help texts.
>
> Further information on LyX (including links to the KLyX project) can be found on the Internet:
>
> `http://www.lyx.org/`

19.2 Working techniques

Your first LyX document

To create a new, empty document, you execute FILE|NEW and specify a file name. LyX automatically completes the name with the extension `*.lyx`. Now you are ready to type your text. Help with formatting of the paragraphs – for example as title, enumeration, and so on – is mainly given by the paragraph format list field (at the left of the symbol bar). Many more details on formatting paragraphs, characters, and entire documents are discussed in the next three subsections.

As mentioned earlier, LyX only provides incomplete WYSIWYG. If you want to know what your page layout will actually look like, you need to call up a page preview by means of FILE|VIEW DVI or FILE|VIEW POSTSCRIPT. The difference between the two variations consists in the fact that in the first case, only a temporary `*.dvi` file is created, while in the second case, this temporary file is used to create a PostScript file. The contents of the two files – with regard to the page layout – is absolutely identical; however, different programs are used for display (`xdvi` / `ghostview` with `lyx` or `kdvi` / `kghostview` with `klyx`).

The variation you choose out of the two available is a matter of taste. The DVI variation is usually somewhat faster. However, if you use a large number of illustrations, you will probably prefer the PostScript variation.

NOTE

The first display of a LyX document – no matter whether in DVI or in PostScript format – may take some time while LaTeX character sets of the required sizes are created. However, this delay occurs only the first time (more precisely, every time you use a new character shape (font) or size for the first time).

TIP

You need not restart `xdvi` or `ghostview` for each page preview. Instead, you can use the commands FILE| UPDATE DVI or FILE|UPDATE POSTSCRIPT, which only update the current preview files. `xdvi` recognizes the changes automatically, while with `ghostview` you need to press [R] (for *reload*) to cause the file to be read again.

The quality of font display in `ghostview` increases sensibly if you activate the antialiasing function (see page 518).

Printing of LyX documents causes no problems, provided that the printer configuration was carried out correctly (see page 162). With FILE|PRINT, LyX generates the same PostScript file as for the page preview and passes it to the default printer `lp`by means of `lpr`.

Paragraph formatting

In most cases, you will use the list field at the left-hand side of the symbol bar to change the format type of one or more selected paragraphs. The choice of available format types depends on the selected document class (LAYOUT|DOCUMENT, see below).

Paragraph types	
standard	standard paragraph
verse	left-indented paragraph
list, description	left-indented paragraph, text ranged left with the first space character

quote, quotation	paragraph indented both left and right
part, chapter, section, subsection, subsubsection	numbered titles / document structure
part, chapter*, section*, subsection*, subsubsection**	as above, but without numbering
itemize, enumerate	enumerations with bullet points or numbers
caption	numbered captions above or below tables pictures, and so on)
lyx-code	program code (without vertical spacing), typewriter font
lyx-code-sans	as above, but sans serif font
comment	comment, will not be printed

Essentially, *lyx-code* corresponds to the `verbatim` environment of LaTeX. The advantage: inside the environment, font attributes can be changed (for example, bold or italic type). The disadvantage: the listings are indented, but the amount of indentation cannot be changed. Furthermore, empty lines are not accepted. (Remedy: simply enter a space in an empty line, or use Ctrl+↵.)

TIP

In the LAYOUT|PARAGRAPH dialogs you will search in vain for some frequently needed formatting features. If, for example, you wish to change the space between two paragraphs or the line spacing inside a paragraph, you need to make these modifications globally in the LAYOUT|DOCUMENT dialog (see below).

If you want to have two paragraphs follow each other without vertical spacing, indents, and so on, you should use Ctrl+↵ in stead of the simple ↵ to separate them. (In LaTeX this corresponds to the command \\.)

With Ctrl+Shift+C, you can copy the paragraph layout of the currently active paragraph. With Ctrl+Shift+V, you can apply this layout to another paragraph. In this way, you can continue to apply previously defined settings without great effort.

With Alt+↵, you can split a paragraph into two parts, applying the same old layout to both of the new paragraphs. (If you simply use ↵, the new paragraph will be of *standard* type.)

If these predefined format types are not sufficient, you can individually modify the formatting of paragraphs by means of LAYOUT|PARAGRAPH. This allows you to change justification (ranged left, ranged right, centered, justified), to insert rules above or below the paragraph, to increment or reduce the distance from the preceding or following paragraph, to force a page break before or after the end of the paragraph, and so on. The MORE button takes you to a further dialog which allows you to set paragraphs in `minipage` environments (see page 605).

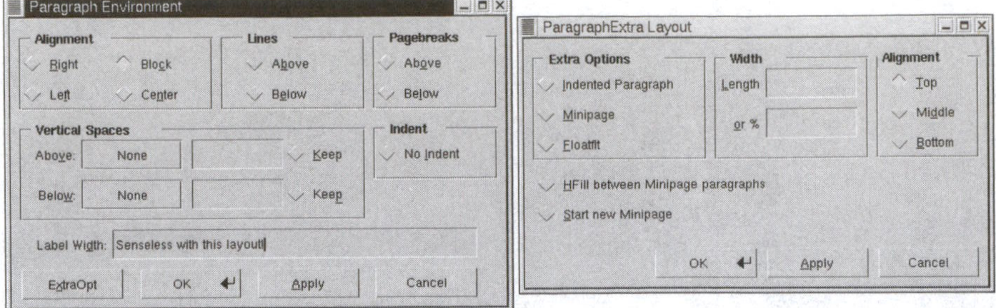

Figure 19.3 Individual paragraph formatting.

The definition of user-defined (additional) format types directly in LyX is not contemplated in the current version. The predefined formats are defined in the `/usr/share/lyx/layouts` or `/opt/kde/share/apps/klyx/layouts` directories. On the basis of these text files, you can create new document formats – but only if you have a clear understanding of LyX and LaTeX internals.

Character formatting

Handling the LAYOUT|CHARACTER dialog is so laborious that you will soon put a stop to excessive formatting of your documents. This may even have a positive effect on the overall layout of your document – however, from the pure point of view of user-friendly handling, LyX character formatting needs some improvement.

The idea in itself is simple: in several list fields of the CHARACTER dialog, you can set the font family (Standard, Sans Serif, Typewriter), the font series (bold), the font shape (italic, small capitals), the size, and the color. APPLY or the FONT button of the symbol bar apply the selected formatting to the currently selected text. The problem is that, whenever you need different formatting (for example, `Typewriter` font in one case, and a smaller standard font in the other), you must set all the attributes again.

> **TIP**
> Make use of keyboard shortcuts for character formatting! Ctrl+B for bold type (*bold*), Ctrl+E for italic type (*emphasized*), Ctrl+K for small capitals, and Shift+Ctrl+P for Typewriter (*program code*). Repeating the command resets the formatting.

Document layout

With LAYOUT|DOCUMENT, you can specify settings which affect the layout of the whole document. The following list describes the most important options:

- CLASS determines the type of the document (book, article, letter, and so on). Depending on the document class, different paragraph types are available.

- PAGESTYLE specifies the layout of headers and footers.
- SIDES specifies whether the position of section and page number is to be inverted on every second page (for a two-sided layout as in this book).
- COLUMNS specifies the number of columns. In two-column text, the columns are simply filled one after the other. This layout is not visible in LyX itself, but only in the page preview.
- FONTS specifies the default font. With *default*, LaTeX fonts are used; with *Times*, *Palatino*, and so on, PostScript fonts are used instead. (This book, for example, is set in Times.)
- FONT SIZE specifies the size of the default font in the range between 10 and 12 points. All other font sizes (for titles, and so on) are modified accordingly.
- LANGUAGE specifies the language to be used for the hyphenation rules and for some predefined text elements (such as *Figure/Abbildung* in figure captions).
- SEPARATION specifies whether paragraphs are to be separated by a first line indent (default, also used in this book) or by vertical spacing.
- DEFAULT SKIP specifies the vertical distance between two paragraphs.
- SPACING specifies the line spacing inside a paragraph.
- FLOAT PLACEMENT specifies where movable elements (tables, figures) should preferably be placed. Legal settings are `t` (*top*), `h` (*here*), and `b` (*bottom*).

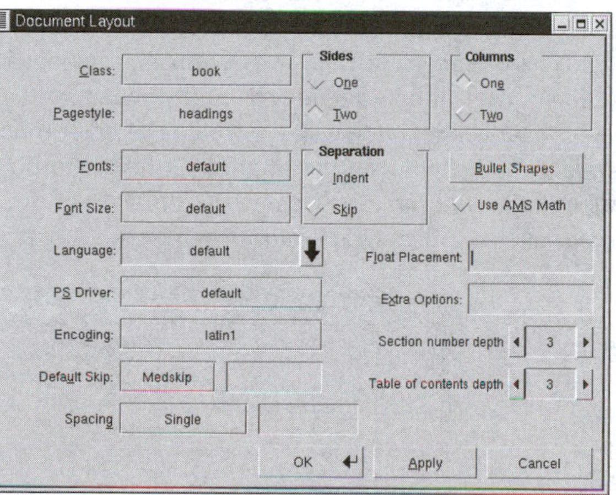

Figure 19.4 Document layout dialog.

CAUTION

During a later change of document class, information on the required paragraph format is lost if this format does not exist in the new document class (for example *chapter* in a letter). At the beginning of such paragraphs, an 'error' box indicates the problem. This box must be deleted and a new format selected for the paragraph. The change of document class cannot be undone.

TIP: Paper size and orientation (portrait or landscape) can be specified in the LAYOUT|PAPER dialog.

Templates

LyX comes with so-called templates. These are perfectly normal `*.lyx` files in which various layout settings are preset. In addition, these documents contain some sample text which simply needs to be replaced with the user's text. This is intended to provide LyX beginners with an easy way to make up their own documents. The templates are located in the `/usr/share/lyx/templates` or `/opt/kde/share/apps/klyx/templates` directories.

To open a template, you use FILE|NEW FROM TEMPLATE. In the file selection dialog, you click on the TEMPLATE button to change to the `templates` directory. (Why this directory is not used automatically as a default remains a mystery.) There, you select the required template – for example `a4letter` for a letter on A4-size paper.

When you try to save your document, LyX warns you that you are not allowed to modify the template file (to do this, you need `root` privileges). Therefore, save the document under a different name (and in your home directory).

Processing of large documents

With EDIT|TABLE OF CONTENTS, you activate a dialog in which the table of contents of the current document is displayed. The contents list is based on the paragraph types *part*, *chapter*, *section*, *subsection*, and so on, used in the text. This dialog allows efficient navigation even in very large documents.

The corresponding KLyX dialog is even more powerful: on the one hand, a slide ruler lets you set the number of levels to be shown in this structure; on the other hand, you can even change the structure of the document by shifting individual sections forward and backward, by changing the depth of structuring, and so forth.

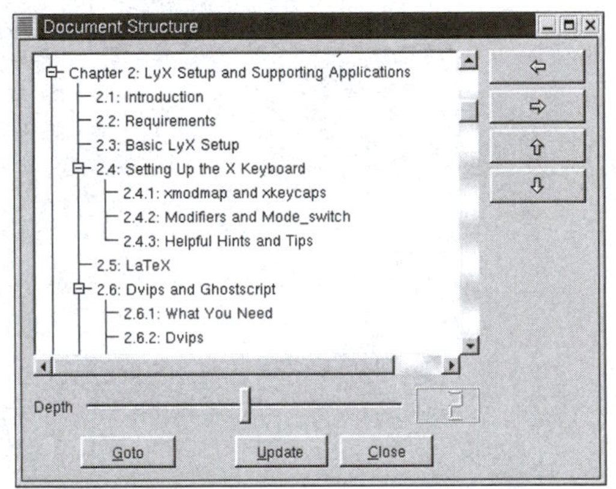

Figure 19.5 The structure of the User's Guide, shown in the KLyX dialog.

19.3 Scientific document layout

Figures

Like LaTeX, LyX too can only handle PostScript graphics. These can be inserted directly (at the position of the insertion point) – either as a separate paragraph or as a small graphic in the flowing text – by means of INSERT|FIGURE or by pressing the appropriate button on the symbol bar. Initially, LyX displays only an empty frame. As soon as you click on it, a dialog pops up which prompts you to select a file name and to set various options (including the quality in which LyX displays the preview of the figure).

> **TIP** Free-standing graphics can be formatted in the same way as paragraphs by means of LAYOUT|PARAGRAPH (and thus, for example, be centered).

> **NOTE** LyX displays a preview of the figure directly in the document (internally, `ghostview` is used for this purpose); however, the zoom factor is ignored, which frequently means that the size of the figure does not match the size of the text. Only the page preview (DVI/PostScript) shows the correct proportions.

Things become slightly more complicated when you want to place a caption above or below a figure. For this purpose, you first use INSERT|FLOATS|FIGURE FLOAT to insert a `figure` environment into the document. This environment provides a paragraph of the `caption` format for labeling the figure. In the final document, the text 'figure' is replaced with 'Figure *n*' – which means that LyX (or LaTeX) automatically look after the numbering.

To insert the figure itself into the `figure` environment, you use the commands described above. If the figure is to be placed below the caption, this works without problems. Placing the figure above the caption, however, requires some more effort – owing to the fact that the insertion point cannot be placed in front of the caption line. Therefore, you will need to position the insertion point at the beginning of the line and press ↵ to insert a new line.

> **TIP** Once you have succeeded in producing a figure together with its caption in the required formatting, you can reuse this figure any number of times by copying and pasting it; then you simply replace the graphics and the text of the caption.

> **NOTE** When LaTeX formats the document, the program may place the figure somewhat more towards the top or the bottom of the page to ensure optimum usage of print space. If you wish figures to remain as precisely as possible at the point of text where you specified them, you need to indicate the letter `h` (*here*) in the LAYOUT|DOCUMENT|FLOAT PLACEMENT dialog. Other alternatives are `t` (*top*, that is, at the beginning of the page) and `b` (*bottom*).

Tables

Producing clearly structured tables in LaTeX is not a very easy task. LyX facilitates this a bit thanks to its WYSIWYG features, but handling is still far from being really intuitive. (Here, the table symbol bar gives KLyX a clear advantage over LyX.) Furthermore, in comparison with true text processing programs, the layout possibilities are severely restricted. This, however, is not the fault of LyX, but rather of LaTeX.

CAUTION Tables belong to the very few features that may cause stability problems in both LyX and KLyX. The only crash that occurred during writing of (the German version of) this chapter concerned a table operation. (However, even in that situation, KLyX still succeeded in carrying out a complete emergency backup – wouldn't it be nice to see WinWord do the same?)

When you insert a new table into your document by means of INSERT|TABLE, it will look like this (initially, quite obviously, without contents).

Title 1	T2	T3	T4	T5
Line 1	A	B	C	D
Line 2	EE	FF	GG	HH
Line 3	III	JJJ	KKK	LLL

LyX treats the table as a whole as if it were a paragraph. Thus, if you wish to range the whole table left or right, you need to use LAYOUT|PARAGRAPH. (Before and after a table, LyX inserts a vertical space of 3 mm. This too can be changed or deleted in the PARAGRAPH dialog.)

Often it is useful to put tables into a float environment by means of INSERT|FLOATS|TABLE. This makes the table's position on the page variable, and LaTeX can avoid big holes when laying out the pages. (Labeling of tables in float environments works in the same way as with figures – see above.)

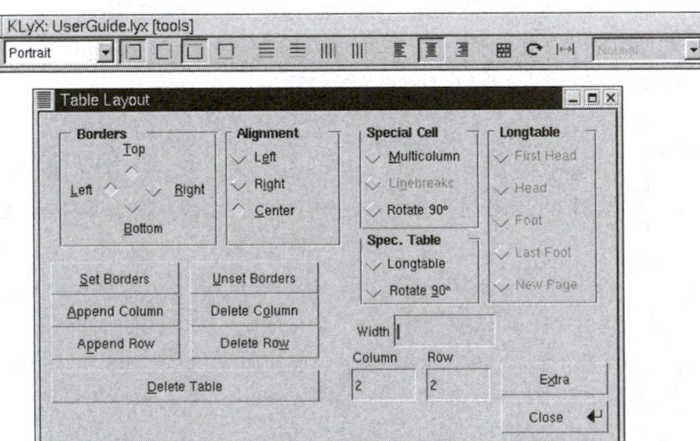

Figure 19.6 On top, the KLyX table symbol bar; below, the corresponding LyX dialog.

Table contents

Not only can normal text be entered in the cells of the table (including all character formatting alternatives), but it is also allowed to include figures and formulas integrated into the text. Not allowed, instead, are the use of paragraph formats (these apply to the whole table) and the insertion of floats or subtables.

Copying and pasting works in tables too, to a large extent. However, no columns can be selected or processed. Also, transfer of data between two tables only works without major problems if the number of columns is the same.

TIP: If you wish to copy an entire table (not just parts of the table's contents), you need to select the whole table, plus some characters of the preceding and of the subsequent paragraph.

Table structure:

For the purpose of changing the table structure – for example for inserting or deleting lines and columns, and so on – LyX provides a separate dialog (simply called by clicking the right mouse button), while KLyX provides a symbol bar. Some remarks:

- The ALIGNMENT (left / right / centered) applies to the entire column in which the cursor is currently positioned.
- SPECIAL CELL|MULTICOLUMN allows several fields of a row to be combined into one larger field.
- With SPECIAL CELL|ROTATE 90, the text of an individual field can be rotated by 90 degrees (for example, for column labeling).
- The column width is usually adjusted to the longest entry. The width of individual columns can, however, also be fixed (for example to 5 cm). In this case, the field contents are automatically distributed across several lines. However, this effect is not visible in LyX itself, but only in the preview. In a longer text, you can force a linebreak inside LyX by means of Ctrl+↩. However, this linebreak is valid only inside LyX and just helps to keep an overview of longer lines. LaTeX treats this linebreak as a space and breaks the contents of the table field itself. (Caution: once a linebreak has been inserted with Ctrl+↩, in the current version of LyX/KLyX it can only be removed by deleting the entire line!)
- Finally, the table dialog provides some possibilities for creating special tables in landscape format or tables that spread over several pages. However, these functions go beyond the scope of this chapter and are therefore not discussed.

TIP: Some special table features – such as the 90-degree rotation of individual fields or entire tables – are neither visible in LyX nor in the DVI preview. Please use the PostScript preview!

	Column 1	Column 2	Column 3
Text over several lines (the column width is set to a fixed 5 cm)	123	456	789
	Multicolumn text		
	100	200	300
Sum	**223**	**656**	**1089**

Frames

In the main, a line can be drawn left and/or right of each column and above and/or below each row. When *two* lines meet, a small space is inserted between the rows or columns. (Thus the double line above the sum row of the above table originates from the fact that lines have been drawn below the fourth row *and* above the fifth row.)

The buttons and symbols for handling frames apply mainly to all selected rows or columns. After many commands, however, the selection is automatically deselected, so that selections often need to be repeated several times.

NOTE

It is not possible to draw lines individually for single fields. All settings apply to entire rows or columns. (Obviously, this rule too has its exception – namely fields marked with the MULTICOLUMN attribute. A corresponding example can be found in the User Manual.)

TIP

During work on (the German version of) this book, several times table operations unwittingly brought the table into an incorrect state. (For example, a table field was missing in the last row. LaTeX failed in its attempt to set the table, because apparently `\end{tabular}` had got lost as well.) The only remedy was to create a new table and transfer it by copying and pasting into the correct parts. Subsequently, the defective table was completely deleted.

Table of Contents

Generation of a table of contents is a really simple operation: you just need to insert the contents list at the required place in your document (usually at the beginning or the end) by means of INSERT|LIST AND TOC|TABLE OF CONTENTS. Although in LyX you only see a small box, the whole list is visible in the preview.

To generate the contents list, LyX automatically considers all paragraphs of the types *chapter, section, subsection*, and so on, except for the homonymous types followed by an asterisk, that is *chapter**, *section**, and so on. The required depths of the table of contents (that is, the number of hierarchy levels) can be set via LAYOUT|DOCUMENT.

Index

Slightly more work is required to create an index. Here, you first need to insert the required entries into the text by means of INSERT|INDEX ENTRY. The syntax is the same as in LaTeX (see page 611). The Index itself is then inserted (usually at the end of the document) by means of INSERT|LIST AND TOC|INDEX LIST.

Cross references

If you wish to make use of cross references, you must first insert a text label with INSERT|LABEL and give it a name. Subsequently, you can insert a page or section number (reference) by means of INSERT|CROSS-REFERENCE. The LyX document only shows a small box at this position. Only the page preview displays the correct numbers. The following two references point to the beginning of this subsection: see page 645 in Section 19.3.

Bibliography, References

LyX can help to manage a simple reference section (bibliography). The entries in this list need to be made at the end of the document. For this purpose, you insert a new paragraph and select *bibliography* as its type. In this paragraph, you can now enter the references in the required format.

The peculiarity of the *bibliography* format is that a button with a running number appears to the left of the reference. When you click on this button, you can extend the number with two reference indications, the KEY and the LABEL. The KEY is required to be able to refer to the reference in the running text. The LABEL is the text that appears in the printed document. If you leave the label empty, all *bibliography* entries are simply numbered in the sequence in which they are quoted in the reference section.

To insert a reference to a bibliography entry into your text, you execute INSERT|CITATION REFERENCE and select the required entry from a selection list. (Caution: LyX displays the content of the KEY; the content of the LABEL is only shown in the final document!)

An example: a very compact introduction to LyX and in particular to KLyX is given by [Ett98]. The entry in the References section looks as follows:

[Ett98] *Ettrich, Matthias:* Schöner schreiben mit Linux. LyX – die etwas andere Textverarbeitung. In: PC Magazin Spezial 8/98, WEKU-Verlag 1998, S. 24-27.

NOTE

The method of creating a bibliography described above corresponds to the LaTeX commands `\cite` and `\bibitem` (see page 608). In future versions, LyX will probably also support the LaTeX utility program `bibtex`, which provides much more advanced features for managing bibliographic references.

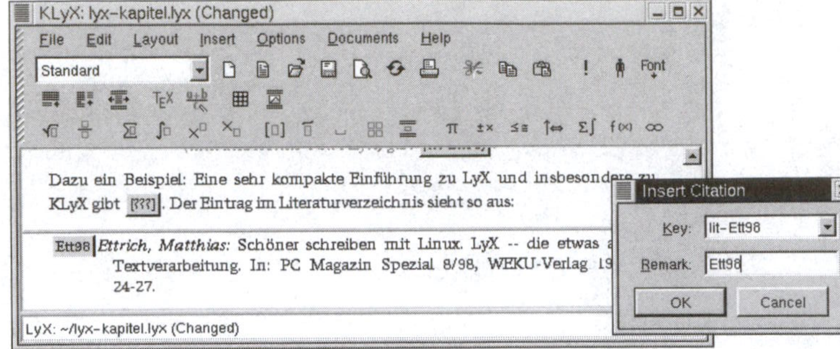

Figure 19.7 Reference list management with KLyX.

19.4 Maths

Input of maths is started via the commands of the MATH menu. By default, maths entries are integrated into the flowing text (such as the following x^2). With MATH|DISPLAY, however, a formula can also be highlighted and thus appears as a separate centered paragraph:

$$\int_\beta^\alpha \frac{\sqrt{x}}{n} dx$$

The elements of a formula (fractions, exponent and index, integral and sum, and so on) are assembled by means of MATH menu commands. Input of special math symbols can be carried out either via mouse click or via the keyboard. The first variation is more intuitive: with MATH|PANEL you open a small dialog which contains a lot of submenus for the majority of the special characters defined in LaTeX. Those who have already gained some experience with LyX will probably prefer keyboard input of math symbols (more about this on page 656).

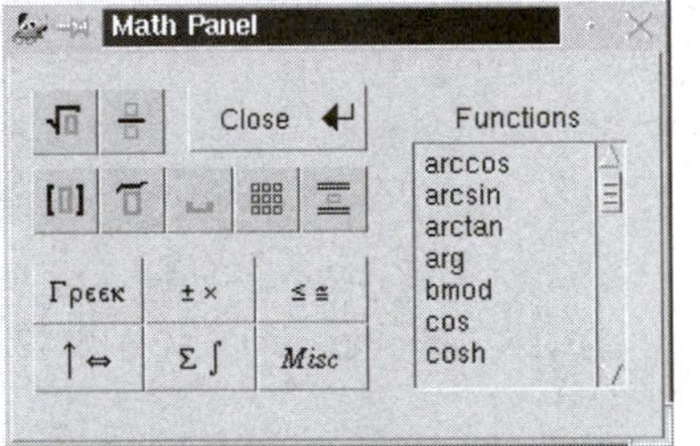

Figure 19.8 Input of math symbols.

NOTE

KLyX has neither a MATH menu nor a dialog such as the one mentioned above. Their functions are instead integrated into a single symbol bar. An essential advantage over LyX consists in the fact that the input focus always remains inside the document.

TIP

In LaTeX as in LyX, the limits of an integral or a summation variable are indicated as exponents or indices. Just place the insertion point after the corresponding symbol ($\int$, $\sum$, $\prod$, and so on), then enter the values with MATH|EXPONENT (or ^) or with MATH|INDEX (or _).

Brackets

LaTeX automatically adjusts the size of brackets to the contents of the enclosed elements (for example, a matrix). However, this works only if the brackets are entered either via the corresponding MATH|PANEL dialog or via the keyboard shortcuts Alt+M, (or Alt+M, [. Direct input of bracket characters from the keyboard, however, does not lead to the desired result.

Formula numbering

The easiest way to number free-standing formulas is to assign the formula a label (INSERT|LABEL). In LyX, this label is now displayed next to the formula; in the page preview the label is then replaced with a right-ranged number.

$$E = m\,c^2 \tag{19.1}$$

Spacing

LaTeX does not feature input of spaces in formulas – it takes care of correct spacing itself. A Spacebar in LyX does therefore not insert a space character, but leaves the currently active formula level. If you wish to insert a small space between two symbols (for example, to make clear that in a multiplication $a\,b$ is the product of two variables and not the variable ab), you simply use Ctrl+Spacebar. For fine adjustments of the layout, additional spacing elements are available (even a negative one, to put two elements closer to each other). In LyX, they can be entered via the SPACING dialog of the MATH panel.

Function names

To ensure that the names of mathematical standard functions are set upright (and not in italics, like variables), they must not be simply entered via the keyboard. Instead, you either select them from the function list of the MATH panel or you use the corresponding LaTeX code (for example `\sin` for the $\sin$ function).

Matrices

Empty matrices can be inserted via the appropriate button of the MATH panel or the symbol bar. Think about the size the matrix should have – it cannot be changed at a later stage! Matrices are not automatically enclosed in brackets. You can either enter the pair of brackets with Alt+M, (before you create the matrix, or you select all elements of an existing matrix and then execute the bracket command of the MATH panel or the symbol bar.

$$\begin{pmatrix} a & 1+b & \sqrt{c} \\ a^2 & 2+b^2 & c \\ a^3 & 3+b^3 & \sqrt{c^3} \end{pmatrix}$$

19.5 Hints and tricks

n-dashes

In LyX, as in LaTeX, en-dashes are entered as two consecutive normal minus signs, that is, `--`.

Word spacing

To extend the individual lines of a paragraph to the same length in justified typesetting, LaTeX inserts an equal amount of space between all words (of the same line). After a full stop (end of sentence), this space is a bit wider. If, for example after an abbreviation, a normal space is to be used after a full stop, a \ symbol must be inserted between the full stop and the space in LaTeX mode (input via Alt+C, T, \, Alt+C, T). In LyX this looks as follows: `Dr.\ Huber`. To prevent two words from being separated by a linebreak, a fixed space can be specified by means of Ctrl+Spacebar, for example 3 cm.

Hyphenation

LaTeX does not always recognize all possible hyphenations (or even hyphenates incorrectly). In such cases, you can use Ctrl+- to insert a soft hyphen which LaTeX will use if needed.

Quotation marks

Similarly to Emacs in LaTeX mode, LyX too tries to use typographic quotation marks of the "citation" form. (Although both quotation marks have been input with ", they have a different shape and constitute a group.) If you need normal (straight) quotes – for example when entering commands, program listings, and so on – you need to use Ctrl+".

Spell check

LyX has no spell check of its own, but resorts to the well-established `ispell` program of the Unix/Linux world. Once this program is installed together with the word tables for the desired language, you can start the spell check with EDIT|SPELLCHECKER or, still easier, with F7. (The spell check starts at the current cursor position.)

In non-English language documents (setting in LAYOUT|DOCUMENT), `ispell` usually does not find the dictionary. The reason: LyX passes, for example, 'german' as the required language; the name of the dictionary, however, is 'deutsch'. This problem can easily be solved: either you explicitly specify 'deutsch' as the required language in the spell check options dialog, or (as `root`) you establish links from `german.*` to `deutsch.*`:

```
root# cd /usr/lib/ispell
root# ln -s deutsch.aff german.aff
root# ln -s deutschlxg.hash german.hash
```

A second problem with non-English language documents is the coding of special characters: in any word containing a foreign language special character, the spell checker suspects an error. Here too, the remedy is simple: just activate the INPUT ENCODING FOR ISPELL option in the spell check options dialog.

A very disturbing peculiarity of the spell check in the current version of LyX/KLyX is that during replacement of incorrectly spelled words the character formatting (for example, italicized emphasis) is lost.

Inserting page breaks

LyX has no own command for inserting page breaks. Instead, you can force a page break before or after a paragraph in the LAYOUT|PARAGRAPH dialog.

Comments

With INSERT|NOTE, you can enter comments to your text which will not be printed. An alternative is paragraphs of the *comment* type.

Errors

Theoretically, LyX should always produce correct LaTeX code. In practice, however, sometimes errors may occur during translation. LaTeX errors are shown in LyX by a button. When you click on this button, you get some (mostly incomprehensible) information on the origin of the error. So what are we to do now? Generally, the most effective solution is to delete the corresponding LyX element (for example a figure) and to enter it again. Furthermore, you must remove the error button from the text. Then, you just try the translation again. LyX professionals might also want to use a text editor to look into the `*.lyx` file and try to correct the error directly. However, extreme caution is highly recommended. In any case, do not forget to create a backup copy of your `*.lyx` file!

In very rare cases LaTeX may also hang (for example, if the end of a LaTeX construction – such as a table – has got lost). You recognize this from the fact that the LaTeX translation just does not want to stop and LyX is blocked. In this case, you need to look for the `latex` process in a shell window with `ps` and terminate it with `kill`. (A decidedly more user-friendly solution is provided by KDE/GNOME with `ktop/gtop`.)

> **NOTE** As so often in this book, this chapter too can only give a first introduction. LyX obviously provides many more document layout possibilities, but the space is not sufficient to describe them all. Please consult the excellent online documentation!

19.6 Configuration

LyX and KLyX can be widely adapted to your own requirements. This section gives an overview of the configuration files and shows how, with little effort, work with LyX can be made even more comfortable. (More information can be obtained with HELP|CUSTOMIZATION.)

Configuration files

LyX and KLyX differentiate between global and local (that is user-specific) configuration files. The global configuration files can be found in the `LyXDir` directory. Where this directory is located can, at least in LyX, be easily determined by checking the HELP|VERSION dialog. On the author's computer, the directories were the following for LyX and KLyX:

```
/usr/share/lyx
/opt/kde/share/apps/klyx/
```

The central configuration file in this directory is `lyxrc` (and the rest of this section is exclusively dedicated to it). Further important files are contained in the subdirectories `bind` (keyboard shortcuts) and `kbd` (keyboard layout).

If homonymous local configuration files exist, they are automatically used instead of the global files. The local configuration directories for LyX and KLyX are:

```
~/.lyx
~/.kde/share/apps/klyx
```

NOTE

The configuration files for LyX and KLyX are stored in different locations but, fortunately enough, their format is identical. However, KLyX has an additional configuration file: `~/.kde/share/config/klyxrc` is used to store user-specific settings that can be adjusted directly in KLyX dialogs (such as the zoom factor in SETTINGS|SCREEN OPTIONS). These settings take precedence over the settings stored in `lyxrc`. In this regard, KLyX follows the KDE paradigm that programs should be configured directly via the user interface (and not through laborious modifications of configuration files).

Keyboard shortcuts

The keyboard shortcuts available under LyX/KLyX (as long as they do not concern the menu) are specified through the `*.bind` files in the `bind` directory. The two main files are `cua.bind` with the keyboard shortcuts common in the Windows world, together with `emacs.bind` and `xemacs.bind` with shortcuts as defined in (X)Emacs. In addition, all of these files resort to `menus.bind` and `math.bind`.

The choice of which keyboard scheme you wish to employ by default is made by means of the `\bind_file` command in `lyxrc`. The factory default is `cua`, the alternatives are `emacs` and `xemacs`.

```
# lyxrc configuration file; use Emacs keyboard shortcuts
bind_file emacs
```

If you so wish, you can modify a copy of the `*.bind` files and use it instead of the predefined files, or you can specify individual keyboard shortcuts directly in `lyxrc`. An example:

```
# F5: PostScript preview; Shift+F5: update preview
\bind "F5"    "buffer-view-ps"
\bind "S-F5"  "buffer-typeset-ps"
```

Toolbar

Changing the toolbar is only possible in LyX, but not in KLyX! If you want to modify the toolbar, you need to remove the comment characters in the `toolbar` section of `lyxrc`. These commands are now used at the start-up of LyX to replace the default toolbar with your own one. You can now easily modify the toolbar by removing individual `\add` commands and/or inserting your own commands.

```
\begin_toolbar
\layouts
\add buffer-open
\add buffer-write
...
\separator
\add buffer-view-ps
\add buffer-typeset-ps
\end_toolbar
```

Fonts

Optimization of font display can significantly increase working comfort in LyX. LyX uses three font families for representation of text. In the default setting, these are:

```
\screen_font_roman -*-times-*
\screen_font_sans -*-helvetica-*
\screen_font_typewriter -*-courier-*
```

Depending on which fonts your final document will use (set in LAYOUT|DOCUMENT|FONTS) and which fonts are installed on your computer (to find out, execute `xlsfonts | less`!), a different setting may achieve a better WYSIWYG effect. If, for example, you wish to display the default font in Palatino instead of Times, the setting is:

```
\screen_font_roman -*-palatino-*
```

Two parameters are responsible for the size in which the fonts are displayed: the dpi value of the graphics system and the zoom factor of LyX. XFree86 usually assumes a value of 75 dpi. Many computers with high-resolution screens, however, display about 100 pixels per inch, which makes the text look rather small. Instead of changing the dpi value of XFree86 (see page 255), it is often easier to set the dpi value just for LyX in `lyxrc`:

```
\screen_dpi 100
```

The zoom factor can be set both in OPTIONS|FONTS and in `lyxrc`.

```
\screen_zoom 133
```

> **TIP** Independently of which dpi factor you have set, you should install both the 75-dpi and the 100-dpi fonts of the X Window System and register them in `XF86Config`! (Often, only the 75-dpi fonts are installed for reasons of space.) After consideration of both dpi and zoom factor, LyX automatically uses the font that most closely matches the required size, no matter for which size the font was originally conceived.

A final measure to improve font quality may be to prevent LyX from scaling fonts. X fonts are usually available only in a few sizes (typically, in 8, 10, 12, 14, 18, and 24 points). When LyX needs a font in a different size, it asks the X system to scale an existing font accordingly. This functions without problems, but does not look very pretty. The fonts appear smudged and 'pixely'. The setting

```
\screen_font_scalable false
```

ensures that LyX only asks for fonts that are readily available. The advantage: the text looks much crispier. The disadvantage: since the choice of sizes is now rather limited, texts which are in reality set in different sizes may no longer look different on screen.

Colors

`lyxrc` only provides settings for the background and foreground colors of the text window. Practically all other colors (used for maths, LaTeX code, and so on) can be specified via options at the start-up of LyX. Possible settings are documented in the `man` text for LyX.

Unfortunately, there seems to be no way of setting the background color of LyX dialogs. These appear in such a dark shade of grey that the text they contain is very hard to read.

Auxiliary programs

Depending on whether you prefer `(k)ghostview` or `x/kdvi` for your page preview, you can enter the desired program in `lyxrc`:

```
\view_dvi_command "kdvi"
\view_ps_command "ghostview"
```

Miscellaneous

At regular intervals (by default, every 5 minutes), LyX carries out a backup copy. In `lyxrc` you may change this interval to your liking.

```
# Backup copy every 2 minutes
\autosave 120
```

19.7 Keyboard shortcuts

The following information applies to LyX version 1.0 and (with a few exceptions) to KLyX 0.9.*n* in the default setting. For reasons of space, not all shortcuts can be shown – see also the files `cua.bind`, `math.bind`, and `menus.bind` in the `/usr/share/lyx/bind/` or `/opt/kde/share/apps/klyx/bind` directory.

The cursor keys and Home and End work as in Microsoft Windows programs. When, in addition, Ctrl is pressed, whole words or paragraphs are included. If, in addition, Shift is pressed, the cursor movement is used to select an area of text.

Selected text can be copied with Ctrl+C, deleted with Del or Ctrl+X, and pasted with Ctrl+V or Shift+Ins. In contrast to many other programs, there is no possibility of toggling between an insert mode and an overtype mode. The Ins key has no effect: LyX does not have an overtype mode.

Menu commands can be entered with Alt, followed by the appropriate letter. While in KLyX the corresponding menu appears immediately, in LyX this needs to be forced by entering an additional space. (If you know the shortcuts by heart, you can obviously do without this.) Menu commands can also be initiated with F10 – this saves you the Alt key.

NOTE

When LyX is not used with the original English language menus (but, for example, with German language menus), problems arise with the keyboard entry of menu commands both with Alt and with F10. Furthermore, some keyboard shortcuts cause problems, in particular most of the Alt+S commands for changing the font size.

In this regard, KLyX is more robust. Independently from the chosen language, the menu can be controlled via the keyboard without great difficulty (although here too, the F10 key fails). Problems are instead caused by various keyboard shortcuts that do not work in the same way as in LyX (such as Alt+P, Spacebar for selection of a paragraph type).

Text mode

Elementary commands	
Ctrl + ↵	line break (\\ in LaTeX)
Alt + ↵	new paragraph with same layout
Ctrl + -	soft hyphen (\- in LaTeX)
Ctrl + "	straight quotes
Ctrl + Spacebar	insert hard space
Ctrl + C	copy text
Shift + Ctrl + C	copy paragraph layout
Ctrl + D	DVI preview
Shift + Ctrl + D	update DVI preview
Ctrl + F	search and replace (*find*)
Ctrl + I	open context dialog (*inset*)
Ctrl + L	LaTeX mode
Ctrl + M	Math mode
Ctrl + N	new document
Ctrl + O	open file
Ctrl + P	print file
Ctrl + Q	quit LyX
Ctrl + R	reload file (*reload*)
Ctrl + S	save file
Shift + Ctrl + S	save file as
Ctrl + T	PostScript preview
Shift + Ctrl + T	update PostScript preview
Ctrl + V	insert text
Shift + Ctrl + V	apply paragraph layout
Ctrl + W	close file
Ctrl + X	cut text
Ctrl + Z	Undo
Shift + Ctrl + Z	Redo
Alt + C	select font (see below)
Alt + M	math functions (see below)
Alt + P	select paragraph type (see below)
Alt + S	select font size (see below)
Alt + X	execute LyX command

F2	save file
F3	open file
Ctrl+F4	close file
Alt+F4	quit LyX
F7	spell check
F10, followed by letter	open menu (currently only with English menus)

Paragraph formatting	
Shift+Ctrl+C	copy paragraph layout
Shift+Ctrl+V	apply paragraph layout
Alt+P, Spacebar	Dropdown menu for paragraph types (sorry, not in KLyX)
Alt+P, 1-4	paragraph type *chapter, section, subsection, subsubsection*
Alt+P, Shift+1-4	paragraph type *chapter*, section*, subsection*, subsubsection**
Alt+P, I	paragraph type *itemized*
Alt+P, S	standard

Character formatting	
Ctrl+B	bold (**bold**)
Ctrl+E	italic (*emphasize*)
Ctrl+K	small capitals
Shift+Ctrl+P	Typewriter (*program code*)
Ctrl+U	underline
Alt+C, Spacebar	no formatting (default font)
Alt+C, B	bold (**bold**)
Alt+C, E	italic (*emphasize*)
Alt+C, M	formula (Math mode)
Alt+C, P	Typewriter (*program code*)
Alt+C, R	Roman
Alt+C, S	Sans Serif
Alt+C, T	LaTeX mode
Alt+C, U	underline

Alt+S, 1, 2, 3 - 0	tiny to huger (5 ... normal)
Alt+S, T	*tiny*
Alt+S, Shift+S	*smaller*
Alt+S, S	*small*
Alt+S, N	*normal*
Alt+S, L	*large*
Alt+S, Shift+L	*larger*
Alt+S, H	*huge*
Alt+S, Shift+H	*huger*
Alt+S, +	larger
Alt+S, -	smaller

Math mode

In one characteristic, LyX has a great advantage over many other formula editors (like that of Word): formulas can almost entirely be entered via the keyboard. LaTeX professionals in particular will heave a sigh of relief – nearly all LaTeX commands can be entered as usual. As soon as you press the Spacebar, LyX replaces the command with the corresponding symbol or construction. If, for example, you enter `\frac` and a space in Math mode, LyX generates a fraction stroke, and you can go on working in WYSIWYG mode.

Maths	
Ctrl+M	change to Math mode
Esc	quit Math mode, place insertion point at the end of the formula
Spacebar	quit math element (for example fraction or bracket level)
Ctrl+Spacebar	small space between two math elements
`\code` Spacebar	replace \code (see page 612) with the corresponding symbol
_	subscript
^	superscript
Alt+M, 8	infinity symbol (∞)
Alt+M, (or [and so on	insert pair of brackets
Alt+M, =	non-equal symbol ($\neq$)
Alt+M, +	plus/minus ($\pm$)
Alt+M, F	fraction
Alt+M, G, *letter*	Greek characters (for example Alt+M, G, B for β)

Alt+M, I	integral
Alt+M, P	symbol for partial derivation (∂)
Alt+M, S	(square) root
Alt+M, V	vector arrow over the next character ($\vec{v}$)

To conclude, two final examples:

$\int_{\alpha}^{\beta} x\,dx$	Ctrl+M, \int, Spacebar, ^, Spacebar, \beta, Spacebar, Spacebar, _, \alpha, Spacebar, x, Ctrl+Spacebar, dx, Esc
$\sin\left(\frac{\pi}{8}\right)$	Ctrl+M, \sin, Alt+M, (, \frac, Spacebar, \pi, cursor down, 8, Esc

Gimp – the Photoshop alternative

The acronym Gimp (*GNU Image Manipulation Program*) stands for an image processing program which in many respects offers similar and sometimes even better functions than the commercial program Adobe Photoshop. The essential difference: Gimp is free software (GPL). Its main authors are Peter Mattis and Spencer Kimball, supported by many others who have helped with debugging and optimization or who have written one of the numerous plug-ins (extension modules).

This chapter gives a first introduction to Gimp 1.0. Even though, for reasons of space, one cannot even attempt to describe the many features of Gimp to their full extent, the chapter will at least provide detailed information on all elementary functions.

> TIP
> Some smaller tools for simple conversion of graphics files, execution of elementary image processing functions, and production of screenshots are described in Chapter 15 from page 491 onward.

20.1 Introduction

What is Gimp?

Gimp is an image processing program – you know this from the introduction. If you have no experience with Adobe Photoshop or another comparable program, this term may still be somewhat vague. With Gimp you can:

- read and write bitmap files in the most disparate formats; supported formats include, amongst others, GIF, JPEG, PNG, and TIFF
- import PostScript files (EPS/PS) and Photoshop files (PSD)
- play the artist and paint pictures completely from scratch
- change the color and brightness distribution of images (for example, lighten the image, increase the contrast, and so on; such operations are mainly used to improve the quality of scanned images)
- apply various filters to the image, for example to detect and highlight edges, to achieve optical effects, and so on
- select and cut parts of the image, elaborate them separately, and combine them into new images (photo montage)
- integrate new graphical elements into the image (lines, patterns, graduated tints, text, and so on)
- create animated `*.gif` files (for example, to produce nerve-shattering Web pages)
- mechanize Gimp operations (to do this, however, you must familiarize yourself with the Script-Fu programming language integrated into Gimp)
- apply Gimp in batch operation to a whole collection of files
- print the resulting images or store them (as bitmaps, as PostScript files, or in the proprietary Gimp format XCF which, besides the image data as such, also stores processing information such as masks or layers). Gimp also contains printer drivers for a number of printers (not only for PostScript, like other Unix/Linux programs).

REFERENCE

Gimp does not include any image scanning functions. A rich function library for controlling your scanner under Linux is provided by the SANE (*Scanner Access Now Easy*) package which is part of most distributions. When installed correctly, SANE can be used directly from within Gimp via a plugin – see the `man` text for `xscanimage`. Up-to-date information on SANE can be found under `www.mostang.com/sane`.

Gimp does not include an import filter for photo CD files (extension PCD). If you wish to read images from photo CDs, you can resort to the very user-friendly `xpcd` program – see page 517.

Dream and reality

Gimp is an incredibly versatile and powerful program (and this chapter describes only about the first five percent!). Nevertheless, there is a great danger that, after your first experiments, you will lose all hope and delete the program from your hard disk. There are two main reasons for this:

- Gimp is a powerful tool, but you need very intensive familiarization with it before you can use it efficiently. Occasional messing about with a `*.gif` file on a homepage is a purpose for which the program is suited only to a very limited extent. (This is not only the fault of Gimp. Generally, professional image processing is an activity which is considerably more difficult than it appears.)
- Gimp makes considerable demands on your hardware. The same applies to the Gimp manual, which is usually read with `acroread`. As a reasonable working environment, you need enough RAM (at least 64 Mbytes, preferably more), a fast CPU, a big screen, a high-resolution mouse, and a graphics card supporting *Truecolor* (that is 2^{24} colors).

Wrong expectations also result from the fact that Gimp is often described as a free, but otherwise equivalent variation of Adobe Photoshop. This is somewhat of an exaggeration at the moment (but Gimp is being furiously developed further!). The following points summarize the most important restrictions and differences:

- The handling of Gimp differs considerably from that of Photoshop, at least in parts. True Gimp fans will obviously object that the handling of Gimp is much more intuitive and efficient. For some functions, this may be true; for others, however, one gets the impression that the program was written by technicians for technicians. Furthermore, for people changing over from Photoshop, it is often difficult to find the appropriate functions in the embedded levels of the context menu.
- Creation of (PostScript)files for professional print jobs is more difficult with Gimp than with other programs. Carrying out a CMY(K) color separation or production of images in special or ornamental colors (duplex image format) is possible, but the functions are all but easy to handle. Direct support of Pantone colors is lacking completely.
- If you create graphics with your own texts, you are tied to the character sets available under X. Although a considerable choice of freely scalable character sets is by now available, Unix/Linux can in no way compete with the multitude of fonts available in the Windows or Macintosh world. (Installation of new character sets is described on page 250).
- Gimp comes with an excellent manual, but provides no context-sensitive online help.
- Currently, menu and dialog texts are only available in English.

Online documentation

Although Gimp provides more than enough material for entire books, there is still surprisingly little printed documentation around. However, there is a 600-page manual (the *Gimp User Manual*, in short GUM), which is usually supplied together with Gimp. The GUM is available in several versions:

- as a `*.pdf` file (Adobe Acrobat document, 13 Mbytes)

- as a `*.ps.gz` file (PostScript, compressed, 43 Mbytes)
- as a `*.html.tar.bz2` file (HTML files, compressed, 16 Mbytes)
- as a `*.fm.tar.bz2` file (FrameMaker source files, compressed, 54 Mbytes).

The HTML version is also available online: `http://manual.gimp.org/`.

With most distributions, only the `*.pdf` version is supplied for reasons of space. The file can easily be read with the aid of `acroread`. (In principle, it could also be read with `xpdf`, `ghostview`, and `kghostview`; in practice, however, these programs have proven not to be very suitable: cut-off pages, no contents list, lower font quality, and so on.)

The page numbers of the GUM contents list and index do not correspond to `acroread`'s internal page counter. The reason: `acroread` begins page numbering with page 1, whereas the GUM starts with 4 unnumbered cover pages, followed by 48 Roman numbered pages – only then does the first part start with page (Arabic) 1.

With `acroread`, the manual can also be printed or exported into PostScript format – but note: a printout not only costs a lot of paper, but it also takes an endless time, because huge amounts of data (images!) must be transferred to and processed in the printer.

NOTE

Occasionally, the GUM describes Gimp features of plugins which do not belong to the standard installation. Information on available Gimp plugins and their installation can be found on the Internet under the following addresses:

`http://www.gimp.org/links.html`
`http://registry.gimp.org`

If you are overwhelmed by the extent of the Gimp manual, you might prefer the PostScript file `gimp_quick_reference.ps`. One single page presents a clear overview of all relevant Gimp keyboard shortcuts. If you have a PostScript printer, you can print the page straight away – otherwise you will need `gs` for printing (page 509).

Equally useful, but visually not as appealing, is `cheat_sheet.txt`, which summarizes the keyboard shortcuts corresponding to all toolbar buttons.

Finally, the mandatory reference to the Internet: `www.gimp.org` is the place where you can find the latest information on Gimp, lots of tips and tricks, a number of very useful, practice-oriented tutorials, and so on.

TIP

Learning the functions of Gimp is only the first step towards great results. Of at least equal importance is the understanding of how these functions can be sensibly employed in practice. Before you go and have your results printed in poster size in a print shop, you should furthermore get acquainted with the numerous problems of color representation on screen and in print (calibration). A Photoshop book which primarily discusses such fundamental issues of image processing (and not so much the software handling details) can also be a reasonable investment for Gimp users. The titles quoted in the Reference part of this book have been of great help to the author.

20.2 Examples

In this chapter, the main emphasis lies on a description of the most important functions of Gimp. To start with, this section gives two concrete examples, which represent a first approach, particularly for newcomers in the field of image processing. You will probably not be able to follow these examples at the first go – but fear not! Details on how to handle the many functions presented here will follow in the next sections.

Logos, buttons, and so on

A popular application of Gimp is to use it for drawing logos, buttons, and emblems, which can then be found on all sorts of Web pages. There are thousands of possibilities (I am certainly not exaggerating!), of which one has been selected as an example.

In order to reproduce the dotted outline shown in Figure 20.1, you insert some text in a sufficiently large size (here, 100 points were used). BORDER should be set to 10 to make the floating selection 10 pixels wider than the lettering itself. (This is necessary to ensure that the dots of the lettering are not cut off at the borders of the floating selection. You may, however, also resize the floating selection at a later time in the LAYER dialog.) Now, you fill the lettering with the background color (EDIT | FILL), so that only the selection is visible.

In the BRUSHES dialog, you now select a dot-shaped brush (for example Circle Fuzzy 9×9), and set SPACING to 100. With this, the brush is not applied continuously, but at specific intervals. (The unit used for the ruler is not known, but it is definitely not pixels.)

Now, you need to deactivate KEEP TRANSPARENCY in the LAYER dialog to make the round dots visible outside the outline as well. EDIT | STROKE completes the master piece. (Feel free to experiment with other brush shapes and SPACING settings!)

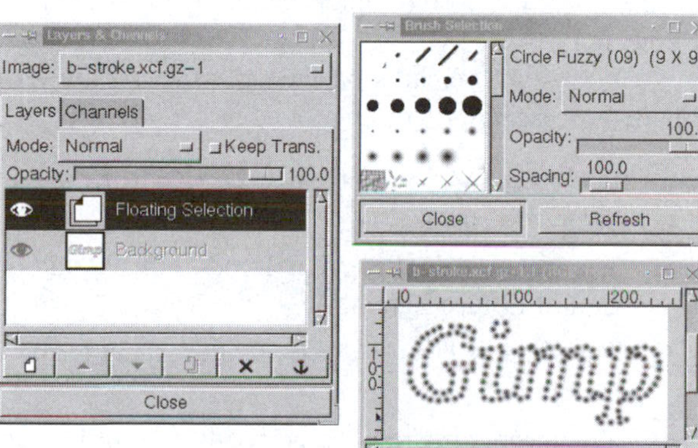

Figure 20.1 Dotted lettering achieved with the stroke command.

If you now wish to color the dots with a graduated tint, you cannot simply use the GRADIENT tool, because now the entire lettering including the dot-shaped dents is selected (not just the visible dots). Therefore, you need to deselect the floating selection on white background and use SELECT | BY COLOR with a THRESHOLD of 60 to select only the dots. Subsequently, the selection is slightly extended by means of SELECT | FEATHER with a value of 5. Now, you can apply the GRADIENT tool without problems.

If, on the other hand, you like things tridimensional, you can go and apply an additional filter to Figure 20.1: FILTER | MAP | BUMP MAP. The result is shown in Figure 20.2.

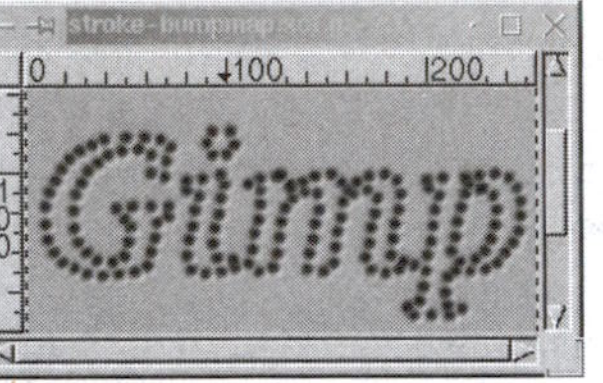

Figure 20.2 Lettering with 3D effect.

Shadows for a 3D object

The starting image for this example is three intertwined spirals computed (by the way, under Linux) with the aid of Mathematica. The image has the form of a TIF file of 1771×1713 pixels (about 9 Mbytes, left-hand side of Figure 20.3); the background is white. The aim is to provide the spirals with a shadow to make the image appear more spatial. (These spirals have indeed been used for the cover image of the author's book on Mathematica. The actual cover design, however, was carried out by the Hommer DesignProduction company – presumably not with Gimp, but with Photoshop.)

First some remarks on the principles of how shadows are produced with an image processing program:

- The object proper is separated (cut out) from its background and copied into a layer of its own.
- The object is duplicated, colored in black, and blurred. (This gives the impression of diffuse lighting.)
- The shadow layer is shifted with respect to the object layer and perspectively distorted.
- The layers are arranged correctly (the object on top, the shadow underneath, the background at the very bottom). The shadow can now be made a bit lighter.

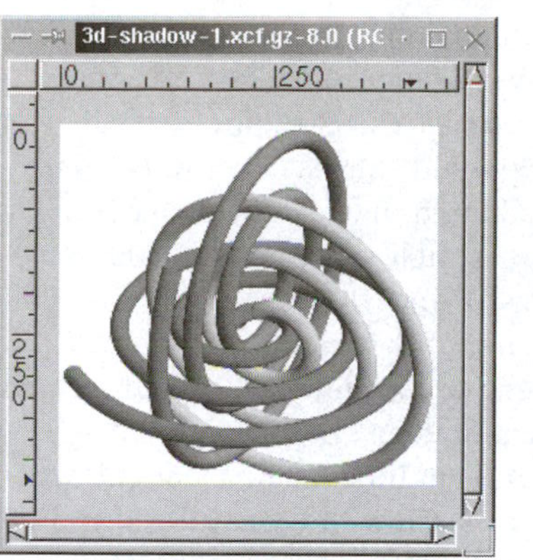

Figure 20.3 The starting image on the left, the final result on the right.

TIP

Working with very large bitmaps is quite laborious. Each Gimp command execution takes considerable time. If you do not yet know very precisely how to proceed, it is sensible first to carry out some experiments with a smaller bitmap. To reduce the bitmap's size, you can use the IMAGE | SCALE command.

NOTE

From the point of view of computer graphics, this way of calculating a shadow is obviously a hair-raising business. The effective shadow of these spirals would have to be determined through a projection of the 3D object on a surface – and this would be significantly different from the shadow we are producing here. Since the starting data is present as a flat image (not as a 3D object), two-dimensional image processing functions need to be employed. Fortunately enough, the eye is easy to deceive; only a very close look reveals that the shadow can in no way be correct.

Procedure

The first step consists in separating the 3D object from its background. Here, this is easy because the background is homogeneously white. With SELECT | BY COLOR, the entire background is selected with a single click of the mouse. Ctrl+I inverts the selection, so that it has now the exact shape of the spirals. To eliminate unwanted half-white border pixels, the selection is reduced by the width of one pixel with the aid of SELECT | SHRINK.

The selection obtained in this way is now transformed into a layer by means of SELECT | FLOAT. LAYERS | LAYERS & CHANNELS opens the dialog for handling layers. The new layer named 'Floating Selection' is renamed by means of a double click and receives the name '3D Object.' Ctrl+D duplicates the layer. The duplicate is named 'Shadow' and moved underneath the '3D Object' layer.

The subsequent operations refer to the 'Shadow' layer which is selected for this purpose with the mouse. In order to avoid confusion, all other layers are made invisible. The BUCKET FILL tool is used to color the shadow black. Subsequently, the LAYERS option KEEP TRANSPARENCY is deactivated so that the opaque part of the layer can be extended. In addition, the shadow layer is slightly enlarged by means of LAYER RESIZE to leave enough space for the additional fuzzy border. Finally, FILTER | BLUR | GAUSSIAN BLUR IIR with a radius of 10 blurs the shadow layer.

To get a first impression of the overall composition, the background layer is completely colored white, and the shadow layer is slightly shifted against the object layer. It turns out that the entire image needs to be enlarged (otherwise, the shadow would spill out of the image). Thus, first the image is enlarged with IMAGE | RESIZE, then the background layer is resized with LAYER RESIZE. After all three layers have been made visible, the resulting image is that of Figure 20.4.

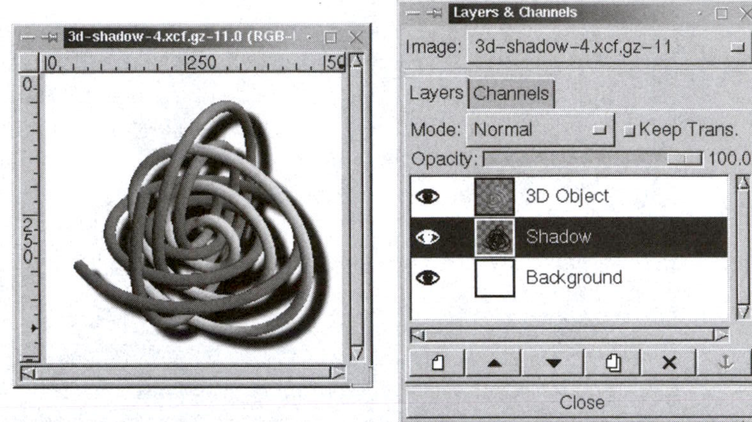

Figure 20.4 The intermediate result consists of three layers.

To make the shadow effect look more realistic, the shadow is perspectively distorted with the TRANSFORM tool (that is, the shadow gets bigger towards the back). In addition, the shadow is weakened by means of the OPACITY ruler of the LAYERS dialog, so that the contrast is not too strong. Finally, IMAGE | COLORS | LEVEL is used to give the shadow a light touch of blue to make the image fit better with the rest of the cover. A final flaw is that the cut-out spirals look so jagged. Here again, as with the shadow, the remedy is the BLUR filter, but with a much smaller radius (for example 2).

20.3 Basics

Survival rules

- **Menu handling:** Gimp has two main menus: a small toolbox menu, and a huge, multiply embedded context menu, which contains nearly all commands relevant for day-to-day work. (In addition, there are separate context menus in some dialogs.)

The context menu is controlled with the right mouse button in the image window. The GUM differentiates between the two main menus by means of <TOOLBOX> | MENU ... and <IMAGE> | MENU .... This chapter does without the specification of <IMAGE>. Thus, menu specifications without additional information always refer to the context menu of the image window.

- **Keyboard control:** Nearly all functions of Gimp can be selected and executed via the keyboard. Frequently, however, the problem arises that the keyboard focus still lies in the most recently used dialog and not, as required, in the image window. Try to set up your window manager (for example KDE) in such a way that the window underneath the mouse is automatically assigned the keyboard focus.
- **Aborting mouse actions:** If you want to abort an already initiated mouse action, all you need to do is press the right mouse button (in addition to the left button which you keep depressed); then you release first the left and then the right mouse button.
- **Guides:** Precise mouse positioning in Gimp is often rather difficult. Thus, make use of *guides*! The mouse locks in the immediate vicinity of these lines (as if it were magnetically attracted). To draw such guides, click on one of the two rulers and pull it out. To reposition existing guides, you first activate the MOVE button of the toolbox (quadruple arrow). You may use any number of guides, and you can easily hide them temporarily by means of VIEW | TOGGLE GUIDES.
- **Toolbox:** The elementary Gimp functions are selected via a mouse click in the toolbox. Many of these functions also provide an option dialog which is opened with a double click on the appropriate button.

  All toolbox tools can also be activated via keyboard commands, either by means of simple letters (such as R for RECTANGULAR SELECTION) or by letters in combination with Shift (such as Shift+M for ZOOM). In Figure 20.5, the relevant letters are underlined (and italicized if used together with Shift).
- **Colors:** All paint and draw commands work with the foreground and background colors set in the toolbox. The dialog for changing these colors is called up by a double click on the appropriate color field. The small symbol bottom left restores the default colors black and white, while the double arrow swaps background and foreground color.
- **Dialogs:** In addition, many elementary functions are influenced by the settings made in the BRUSHES (pencil and brush shapes) and PATTERN (fill patterns) dialogs. These dialogs are opened by means of the DIALOGS context menu command.

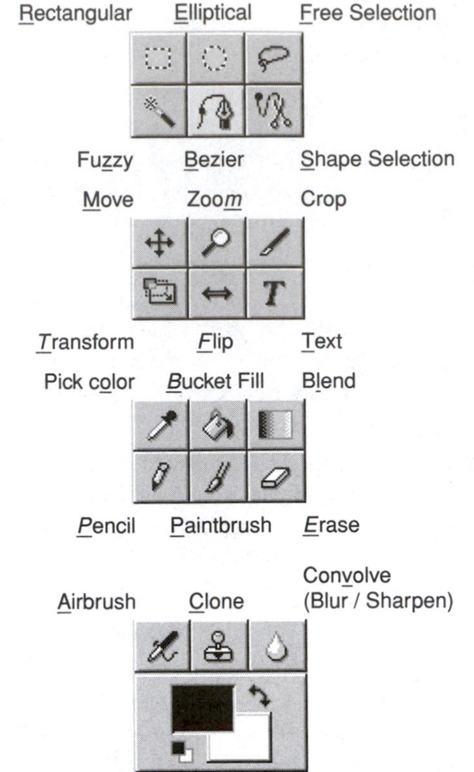

Figure 20.5 The Gimp toolbox and its keyboard shortcuts.

- **Undo and Redo:** With Ctrl+Z, you can undo the last five operations. Ctrl+R redoes the undone operations. The number of Undo levels can be set in FILE | PREFERENCES. (Caution: this may require a very large amount of memory.)
- **Save:** Save your work at regular intervals! In contrast to the statements made in the GUM, no autosave function is as yet implemented in Gimp 1.0. Crashes are rare, but they do occur. Also, during your first experiments , you may well involuntarily destroy your image. Make use of FILE | SAVE AS, using file names such as `name`*nn*`.xcf.gz`, where *nn* is a running number which allows you to access older versions of your masterpiece.

  The extension `*.xcf` indicates that you are using the proprietary Gimp format. (This is the only format in which definitely all information is stored. Formats such as GIF, TIFF, PNG, and so on should only be used for the final product!) The additional extension `*.gz` causes simultaneous compression of the file.
- **Zoom:** Obviously, you can arbitrarily resize the image to be processed. With the ZOOM function of the toolbox activated, a normal mouse click causes the

image to be enlarged, while a click in combination with Shift causes a reduction. Independently of the ZOOM tool, you can at any time restore a 1:1 scale by pressing 1.

- **Views:** It is often useful to display a second view in 1:1 scale in parallel to the enlarged or reduced image. Simply use VIEW | NEW VIEW to open a second window of the current image where you can, independently of the first window, set a different scale, and use Ctrl+T to hide the selection marker ('marching ants') and Shift+Ctrl+T to hide the guides. This will give you a good impression of how the final image will look.
- **Desktop:** Usually, at least half a dozen windows are simultaneously open in Gimp. To minimize the chaos on your screen, you should use a separate desktop for Gimp. (Practically any window manager for X can easily toggle between several desktops, which behave like virtual screens.)
- **Feedback:** Unfortunately, Gimp does not provide any feedback on whether a command has been accepted, is still being executed, or has terminated. (Nearly all other programs display an hourglass mouse cursor for this purpose.) With many operations, this lack of feedback is quite disturbing.

  As a remedy, you can start a small program that displays the current CPU load (for example `xosview`, `kcpumon`, and so on). If the CPU is fully occupied, this is usually an indication that Gimp is still busy with the last operation.
- **Character size:** In the default configuration, the lettering of Gimp menus and dialogs is so small that it is nearly unreadable. Check page 703 at the end of this chapter (*Configuration*) and set it to a larger size!

TIP

The processing speed of Gimp decreases (and its memory requirements increase) proportionally with the size of the bitmap to be processed. For your first experiments, you should therefore use smaller bitmaps (max. 500×500 pixels) – this will make your work quite a lot easier.

TIP

There are several ways to skin a cat! Don't let this book or other introductions to Gimp deter you from trying out your own experiments. Just use the operations that seem most intuitive to you!

File formats

Gimp supports quite a lot of file formats, both for loading and for saving images. This section provides a short overview of the most important formats and explains which format is suited for which purpose.

Important bitmap formats

BMP

This format is only needed for data exchange with the Microsoft Windows world.

GIF

This format is still the most popular Internet format for images and small animations. The bitmaps are compressed fairly efficiently and without losses, but the number of available colors is limited to 256. The format supports transparency (that is, a part of the rectangular bitmap is translucent). To save Gimp images as GIFs, you must first convert them to 256-color mode by means of IMAGE | INDEXED.

JPEG

The format excels through an extraordinarily efficient compression algorithm, which is particularly suitable for photographs (not so much for technical drawings or screenshots). However, JPEG compression is not lossless, that is, JPEG images differ from the original. The differences are mostly invisible to the naked eye, if the quality factor for saving is set to a sufficiently high value. The default setting of 75 per cent is usually a sensible compromise.

CAUTION

If a JPEG image is loaded, processed, and saved again several times, the quality decreases with each cycle. While JPEG losses are practically invisible after the first time the algorithm has been used (provided the quality factor for saving was not set too low), changes add up in a rather disturbing way with multiple application. Therefore, the JPEG format is absolutely unsuitable for working copies! Save only the final image in JPEG format (and archive an XCF copy)!

PNG

This format has been conceived as a successor for the GIF format and is better in every respect (no restriction to 256 colors, lossless in spite of better compression, and so on). As opposed to GIF, licensing problems no longer exist – the format (together with its source code) is freely available. However, PNG being a fairly recent format, older graphics programs and Web browsers are often incapable of handling PNG images.

TIFF

This format is surprisingly popular in professional image processing, although the reasons are more historical. Images are saved without loss; (a relatively weak) compression is optional. There are numerous variations of the TIFF format, which sometimes makes the exchange of TIFF images between different programs quite problematic.

CAUTION

If you work with layers, saving in bitmap formats only saves the currently active layer, not the complete image composition! Therefore, always use the XCF format for your working copies. To save the final bitmap, you must first combine the layers into a complete image by means of LAYERS | FLATTEN IMAGE. This hint also applies to saving images in PostScript format.

PostScript

The PostScript format (PS, EPS) has a good reputation as *the* format for professional exchange of images. However, this reputation only refers to text and vector graphics, not to bitmaps!

You should save images in PostScript format only if you want to use the file at a later time in a different program (for example a text processing or typesetting program). Here, two options are of interest:

ENCAPSULATED POSTSCRIPT means that a comment is stored at the beginning of the PostScript file, which specifies the coordinate range of the image. This information is required for correct incorporation of the image in another program. PostScript files intended for further use in other programs (and not just for printing) usually bear the extension `*.eps` (not simply `*.ps`).

PREVIEW means that, in addition to the PostScript commands, a bitmap is stored which allows a preview even in programs that have no access to a PostScript interpreter. This preview bitmap, however, increases the file size considerably without adding any information relevant for printing. You should therefore activate this option only if you want to use the PostScript file on Windows or Apple computers (where usually no `gs` is installed for an easy PostScript preview).

Gimp can also read PostScript and PDF files. (PDF is a format for document distribution defined by Adobe, which essentially consists of tightly compressed PostScript code. PDF documents are usually read with the aid of `acroread`.)

For the import, Gimp resorts to the `gs` PostScript interpreter. The attainable quality is influenced by two options: a high RESOLUTION yields very large bitmaps (which can the be optimized and reduced in Gimp), while the ANTIALIASING options cause `gs` itself to generate a high-resolution bitmap and subsequently reduce it. This allows the color of the individual pixels to be derived from several points, giving rise to grayscales and halftones which make the image appear more sharply defined.

XCF and PSD

XCF is Gimp's proprietary data format. It is the only format in which definitely all processing information (masks, layers, current selection, and so on) is stored. The file is not compressed. While an image is being elaborated, XCF is the only suitable format for working copies.

The PSD format is the Photoshop counterpart to XCF. Gimp can only read PSD files, but not write them (and it is rather improbable that Photoshop will get a Gimp import filter in the near future).

TIP

The following rules apply to all formats: if during saving you append the extensions `*.gz` or `*.bz2` to the file name, the file is automatically compressed. Obviously, this is only sensible if the file format does not already include compression itself (such as JPEG, GIF, and PNG). Quite obviously, files with these extensions are automatically decompressed again during loading. `bzip2` compresses slightly better than `gzip`, but is significantly slower. The following results were achieved with a test file: `.xzf` 250 Kbytes, `.xzf.gz` 100 Kbytes, `.xzf.bz2` 93 Kbytes.

20.4 Paint tools

With paint tools such as PENCIL, PAINTBRUSH, and AIRBRUSH, you can both create entirely new graphics or modify existing images. You should, however, always bear in mind that Gimp is a pixel-oriented image processing program, not a vector-oriented one: the result of a paint operation is a number of modified pixels. Gimps does not store any information about the drawn object; therefore, this object can no longer be manipulated at a later stage.

TIP

First experiments with paint tools are best carried out in an empty white image. This allows you to easily cancel unwanted results by means of [D] (default colors), [Ctrl]+[A] (select all), and [Ctrl]+[X] (cut). To experiment with colors, you can quickly create a colorful image with FILTERS | RENDER | PLASMA.

REFERENCE

Gimp lacks even the most trivial draw commands – for example to draw a rectangle or a circle. This does, however, not mean that this is impossible in Gimp! One alternative is to use selections – more about this from page 680 onwards. Another alternative is provided by the FILTERS | RENDER | GFIG tool which is, however, not described in this chapter.

The proper alternative, that is, to employ true vector-oriented drawing programs, is difficult under Linux. The choice is still limited. Probably the most powerful program is `tgif` – but its user interface makes you realize that the program is relatively old.

Pencil, Paintbrush, Airbrush, Erase

The paint tools PENCIL ([Shift]+[P]), PAINTBRUSH ([P]), and AIRBRUSH ([A]) are closely related to each other. All three tools use the shape set in the BRUSH dialog as a painting device. While the PENCIL interprets this as a black and white pattern and therefore yields very sharp edges, the PAINTBRUSH also considers grayscales.

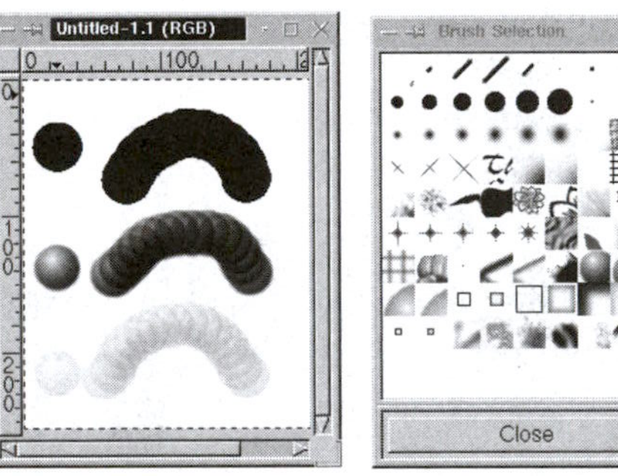

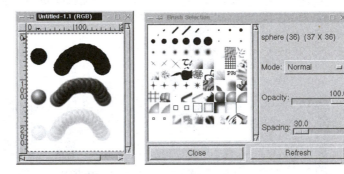

Figure 20.6 Examples of the application of Pencil (top), Paintbrush, and Airbrush (bottom).

With the AIRBRUSH, processing time comes into play: the longer the spraycan is applied or the more often it is moved over a point, the more intense the result. Intensity per time and per mouse movement can be controlled via options. Figure 20.6 shows all three tools, employing the same pattern.

At first sight, ERASE (Shift+E) seems to represent just the inverse function of PAINTBRUSH, employing the background color instead of the foreground color. However, the difference become visible when the tool is employed in so-called *floating selections* (see next section): here, the selected area is reduced by the tool shape.

TIP If you want to paint or delete a straight line with any of the four tools, quickly press the mouse button at the starting point. Then, move the mouse to the target point and briefly press the mouse button again, this time in combination with the Shift key.

Filling with colors and patterns (BUCKET FILL)

With BUCKET FILL (Shift+B), you can fill a color-delimited area with the foreground color or with a pattern set in the DIALOGS | PATTERNS dialog. If you click the mouse button in combination with Shift, the tool fills the area with the background color (only with COLOR FILL).

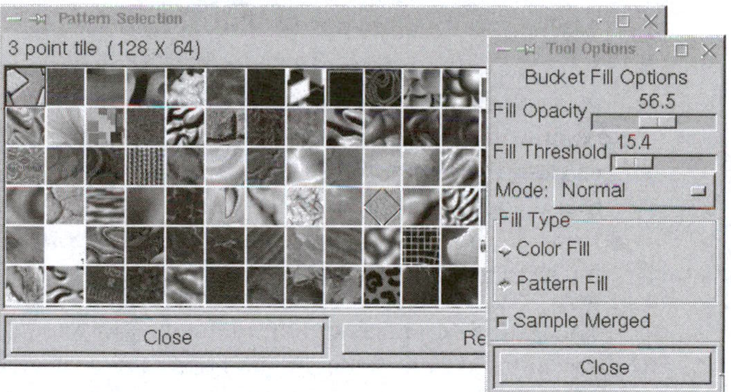

Figure 20.7 Fill patterns and options for BUCKET FILL.

In the default setting, the tool covers the contiguous area of all pixels whose colors differ by a maximum of 15 units from the starting pixel (on a unit scale from 0 to 255). The legal value range can be changed with FILL THRESHOLD in the options dialog. In Figure 20.8, FILL was applied with a tile-shaped pattern and a reduced OPACITY (50) to the medium grayshades.

TIP Limitation to a color area applies only if no selection is present! If a selection exists, it is filled completely, that is, without regard for the colors of its contents. To prevent this, you can either unmark the selection with Shift+Ctrl+A, or convert it into a floating selection with SELECT | FLOAT.

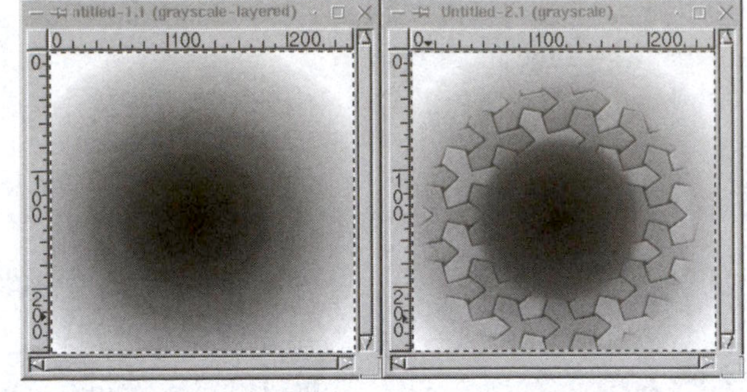

Figure 20.8 Sample application of BUCKET FILL.

Cloning without gene technology

The help text for the CLONE tool (C) in the toolbox states *paint using patterns or image regions*. This shows that CLONE has two rather different applications, depending on whether PATTERN or IMAGE is specified as the source in the toolbox dialog:

- PATTERN SOURCE: Here, CLONE functions similarly to PAINTBRUSH. The difference consists in the fact that a pattern is used for painting instead of a color. Pattern selection is carried out in the PATTERN dialog. Furthermore, you need to specify a pencil in the BRUSHES dialog.
- IMAGE SOURCE: Instead of a predefined pattern, you should use the current (or another) image as the source. For this purpose, you will mark the starting point of the source area with Ctrl and the mouse button. Subsequently, you can use the mouse button to copy areas of the source area. In practice, this tool is mostly used to hide flaws in the image (such as unwanted cover-ups). However, it also represents a simple way of copying an image area from one image to another (or from one layer to another).

The ALIGNED option specifies how the tool should behave with multiple application. In the default setting, this option is activated; when the mouse button is released during cloning and the process is subsequently continued at a different position, the overall pattern forms a seamless unit. If, on the other hand, the option is deactivated, the copying point is not moved relatively together with the mouse. (If you clone from an IMAGE SOURCE, the current position of the copying point is shown.)

Colors

Practically all tools that do not use fill patterns resort to the current background and foreground colors. The default setting is black and white and can be set or restored with D. The two colors can easily be swapped by pressing X. Various alternatives exist for setting the background and foreground colors:

- A double click on the background or foreground field in the toolbox activates the standard color selection dialog. It is worthwhile to experiment a little with this dialog! Six option buttons allow you to choose between different forms of representing the color layer. The six associated slide rulers change the *hue* (H), the *saturation* (S), and the brightness *value* (V), together with the intensity of the red (R), green (G), and blue (B) parts.
- With DIALOGS | PALETTE or Ctrl+P, you activate a dialog which provides a choice of several predefined color palettes.
- If you are working in the INDEXED color mode (see the following tip), you can use DIALOGS | INDEXED PALETTE to display the effectively available colors in a third color dialog.
- Finally, you can use the COLOR PICKER (O) to select the background or foreground color from the image with a click of the mouse.

NOTE

If you work with GIF images, a maximum of 256 colors are available. In the default setting, Gimp always works with RGB colors (2^{24} colors, that is, 256 tints each of red, green, and blue). IMAGE | RGB and IMAGE | INDEXED can be used to toggle between RGB mode and a limited number of colors. The third available mode is the GRAYSCALE mode with 256 shades of grey.

The color mode has no effect on the appearance of the color selection dialogs. The different paint operations automatically use the most nearly matching color. Please note that in the INDEXED color mode, a number of operations (particularly filters) are not available.

Blends

The BLEND tool (another name is GRADIENT FILL; keyboard shortcut L) fills a previously selected area with a continuous transition between two or more colors. For this purpose, the mouse is used to draw an invisible line either inside or outside the selection. The colors are applied following the course of this line, the foreground color being used for the starting point (and the preceding area) and the background color for the end point. In other words, the direction in which you draw the gradient line matters!

BLEND can only be sensibly employed with selections, which will be discussed only in the next section. Without a selection, the entire image is included, which can at best serve to create a background.

The blend can be controlled by numerous options that can be set in the BLEND toolbox dialog:

- The OFFSET ruler controls how soft (0) or hard the blends will look.
- The BLEND mode specifies how the colors for the blend are to be mixed. A particularly attractive mode is FG TO TRANSPARENT, in which the foreground color is mixed with a transparent color. If you feel that a blend between two

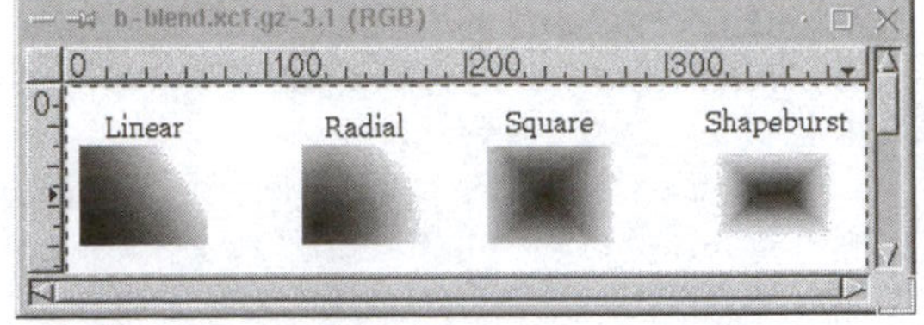

Figure 20.9 Sample application of Blend.

colors is not sufficient, you can set the CUSTOM mode and use DIALOGS | GRADIENT EDITOR to choose one of the various predefined blends with such euphonious names as *Burning Paper*, *Caribbean Blues*, *Sunrise*, or *Tropical Colors*. (Via the context menu of this dialog, you can also define your own blends.)

- The GRADIENT mode specifies whether the blend is to look linear, circular (radial), star-shaped, and so on. Figure 20.9 shows examples of the most important shapes. The differences between the modes become particularly evident with irregular shapes.
- Usually, the background and foreground colors are used in the areas before and after the gradient line. With the REPEAT option, you can also repeat the gradient fill. Figure 20.10 shows an example.

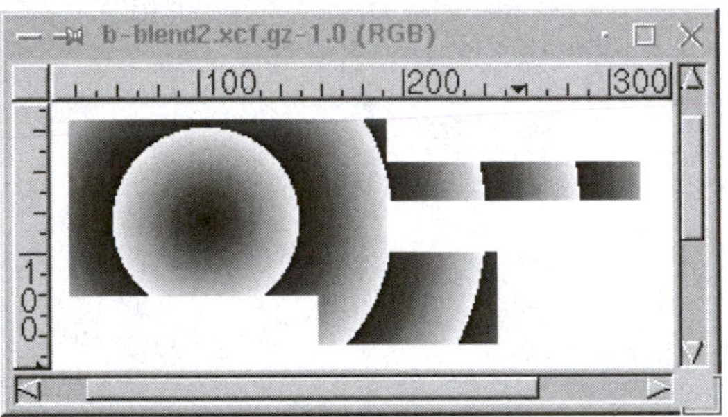

Figure 20.10 A radial, sawtooth-shaped repeated gradient fill.

- With ADAPTIVE SUPERSAMPLING, the blend is produced with the aid of a mathematically more sophisticated procedure. A visible difference is particularly noticeable where a blend is repeated (with REPEAT) a large number of times, thus, where very quick transitions take place (for example, to represent record grooves). Thanks to supersampling, such transitions look smoother (less 'dotty' or 'pixely'). However, this effect is in part annihilated through the printout, as can be seen in Figure 20.11 which renders the impression only approximately.

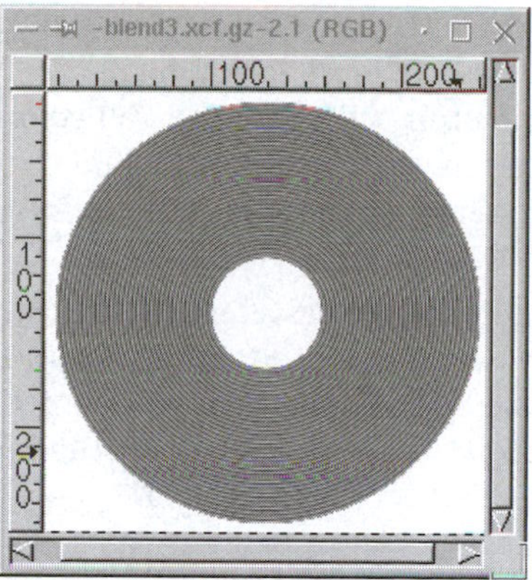

Figure 20.11 Thanks to supersampling, the circles look reasonably smooth.

Sharpen / Blur

Depending on the settings of the corresponding options dialog, you can use the CONVOLVER tool (V) to blur or to intensify (thus revealing the edges) the colors in the area of your brush. Caution: during blurring, the image becomes darker, because the operation favors the darkest color parts of the affected pixels.

TIP If you wish to change the sharpness in a larger area of the image, you should select this area and then apply a BLUR or an ENHANCE filter.

Additional options

Nearly all of the operations presented in this section can be controlled even more precisely by means of several options. Possibilities for setting these options are provided in the toolbox dialogs of the tools in question and in the BRUSHES and PATTERN dialogs. The following overview limits itself to a brief description which can obviously not replace your own experiments:

- MODE: Specifies in which way the previous and the new colors are to be combined, for example, by addition, subtraction, multiplication, or change of saturation. The effect of these modes is often quite difficult to guess in advance. The most intuitive modes are DARKEN ONLY and LIGHTEN ONLY.
- OPACITY: Specifies whether the operation is to be performed (100 per cent) opaque or transparent. In the second case, the previous image shows through the new pattern. The operation can be applied several times, with the intensity increasing every time.

- SAMPLE MERGED: This option is only of interest if you work with several layers. Then, all operations normally apply only to the active layer. When SAMPLE MERGED is active, however, all colors are considered that are actually visible on screen. (Independently of this option, however, only the active layer is *modified.* Thus, SAMPLE MERGED refers only to the reading of colors, not to their modification.)
- SPACING: Specifies after which extent of mouse movement (in pixels) a pattern is to be applied again. Thus, when SPACING is set to 25, you must move the mouse by 25 pixels (with a zoom factor of 1:1), before the pattern is applied a second time. Please note that the individual BRUSH shapes have different default settings for SPACING.

20.5 Text

To insert text into your image, you first activate the TEXT tool and then click with the mouse on the approximate position in the image where the text shall appear. This opens a dialog in which you select the desired character set and enter the text to be inserted. (Unfortunately, the dialog does not envisage multi-line text. Also, note that once the text has been inserted into the image, it can no longer be changed – Gimp is not a vector graphics program. Therefore, keep an eye on typing errors.)

After you have closed the dialog with OK, the text is now inserted at the previously clicked position. Now, the text can still be arbitrarily moved. To definitely amalgamate the text with the image, you can either activate a SELECT tool and click with the mouse outside the text, or you can press Ctrl+H. If, on the other hand, you are not happy with what you are doing, you can delete the text with Ctrl+X and start afresh.

> **NOTE** After the text has been inserted, it is considered as a so-called 'floating selection.' This is a variation of a normal selection, whose properties are described from page 686 onwards. You can now move the text, transform it, fill it with colors, and so on, without affecting the underlying image.

Font selection

The font selection dialog does not appear to be very intuitive – in particular not if you have previously worked under Windows or with an Apple Macintosh. The reason lies in the internal administration of characters sets in the X Window System. Each character set has a name of the following form (abridged):

```
-foundry-family-weight-slant-width-size-spacing-encoding
```

A concrete example illustrates the principle:

```
-adobe-helvetica-bold-o-normal--10-100-75-75-p-60-iso8859-1
```

- This is a character set of the Adobe company.
- The font name is Helvetica (*the* sans-serif font, model for Arial and the like).

- The character weight is bold. (Other alternative would be *normal*, *medium*, *black*, *extrabold* etc.).
- The slant is `o` (*oblique*, that is, inclined). (Other options are `r` (*roman*, that is, upright), or `i` (*italic*).)
- The width of the character set is not specified. (Some character sets use *condensed*, *extended*, and other widths.)
- The character size is 10 points.
- The spacing type is `p` (*proportional*). (Other alternatives are `c` or `m` for *character cell* or *monospaced*. Both mean that all characters of that font have equal width; an example for this is the Courier font.)
- The characters are coded according to Iso-Latin 1. (This coding covers all characters of the Western European language area.)

You can see from the above list that X provides many more possibilities for describing character sets than, for example, Windows. (It may well be the case that you have installed two Courier typefaces produced by different manufacturers. These typefaces also look different; you may decide to use the one that pleases you most.)

However, this multitude makes the dialog somewhat more laborious than one would wish. When you are looking for a suitable typeface, you should enter some characters of text in the text field at the bottom. Then you choose the desired size. Finally, you select the required typeface and, if necessary, change the remaining options. The * setting means that Gimp selects the first variation in alphabetical order.

TIP: Character sets are often shown by default in italics. Just set SLANT to `r` to obtain the upright variation.

After changing the type size, you need to press the Tab key to make Gimp accept the change. Please note that under X many character sets are only available in a series of predefined sizes (typically 10, 11, 12, 14, 17, 18, 20, 24, 25, and 34 points). Such character sets can also be represented in all other sizes, but will look rather ugly.

TIP: For representation of text, Gimp resorts to the character sets provided by the X Window System. Basic information and tips for the installation of additional character sets can be found on page 250. If you have installed only the common fonts and no font server, at least the *charter*, *courier*, and *utopia* typefaces should be available in all sizes and in a reasonable quality.

Antialiasing, border

Two Gimp-specific settings of the text dialog still need an explanation: ANTIALIASING and BORDER. The ANTIALIASING option causes the borders of the inserted text to be displayed in grayshades or colored tints. On screen, this makes the text look sharper and less pixely. This option should only be deactivated if you use very small character sizes and later want to print the resulting image.

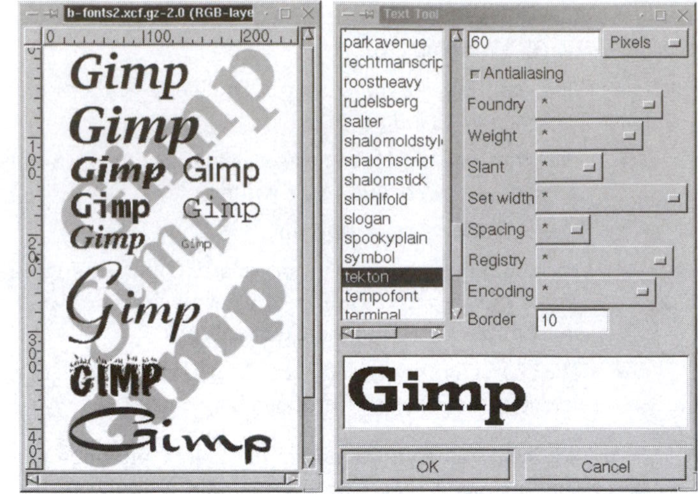

Figure 20.12 Gimp font selection.

If you specify a numeric value in the BORDER field, the border of the floating selection that surrounds the text is enlarged by this number of pixels. There are two reasons for this: without this option, text is cut off in some fonts (for example the first italicized letter, or descenders as in the letter `g`). Second, this makes it possible to enlarge the selected part of the floating selection in further processing steps. (The border of the floating selection can also be enlarged at a later stage with the aid of the LAYERS dialog.)

20.6 Selections

Application of paint tools to the entire image is an exception. Usually, most operations are to be applied only to well-defined parts of the image. The problem is now to select the required part of the image as precisely as possible. (This is particularly difficult in a photograph if, for example, a person or an object is to be separated from the background.)

The selected area is marked by a flashing border. (In the GUM, this border is called *marching ants*, for obvious reasons.) Before we really start, here are some indispensable keyboard shortcuts:

Processing selections	
Ctrl+T	toggles between showing and hiding the flashing selection border; the selection itself is preserved
Ctrl+I	inverts the selection, that is, everything that was outside is now inside
Ctrl+A	selects the whole image
Shift+Ctrl+A	deselects the selection

NOTE

There are two types of selection, normal ones and so-called floating selections. The difference is described on page 686. Just a brief remark in advance: some paint tools work differently depending on the type of selection. Thus, for example, in a normal selection BUCKET FILL no longer considers the pixel colors of the affected area, but fills the whole selection with a pattern or a color. Only in a floating selection does the tool work again as described on page 673.

TIP

Selections (with the exception of floating selections) can be permanently saved and later restored by means of SELECT | SAVE TO CHANNEL. Handling of channels is, however, only described on page 691. Channels are often an interesting alternative to selections.

Rectangular and elliptical selections

Rectangular, elliptical, and circular selections are drawn with the RECTANGULAR (R) and ELLIPTICAL SELECT (E) tools and the mouse. During the selection, the following keys can be pressed in addition to the left mouse button:

Influencing selection shapes	
Shift	constrain selection to square or circle
Ctrl	starting point is not a corner, but the center
Shift+Ctrl	square/circle around the center point

TIP

To make selections surround an object as closely as possible, you should draw guides beforehand.

If you want to select the border of a rectangle or an ellipse, you can either subtract two corresponding objects from one another (see below) or use the SELECT | BORDER command (page 686).

Combining selections

Sometimes you may wish to combine the selection of several parts – for example, a circle and two rectangles. Maybe you also wish to cut out a part of this shape. If a selection already exists, the Shift and Ctrl keys have the following meaning at the *beginning* of the selection:

Combining selections	
Shift	add to selection
Ctrl	subtract from selection
Shift+Ctrl	build intersection of previous and new selection

Maybe this looks to you as a contradiction of the previous table which described the meaning of Shift and Ctrl in the selection of rectangles and ellipses. However, the only thing that counts is the moment at which Shift and Ctrl are pressed!

If, for example, you want to produce the selection shown in Figure 20.13, you first select the rectangle. Then you press E, move the mouse to the center of the lower line of the rectangle, press Ctrl (subtraction), and begin the selection. While you are drawing the ellipse, you additionally press Shift. (The key combination Shift+Ctrl now causes selection of a circle around the starting point.) The change of Shift+Ctrl during the selection, that is, while the left mouse button is kept depressed, requires some practice, but then works out all right.

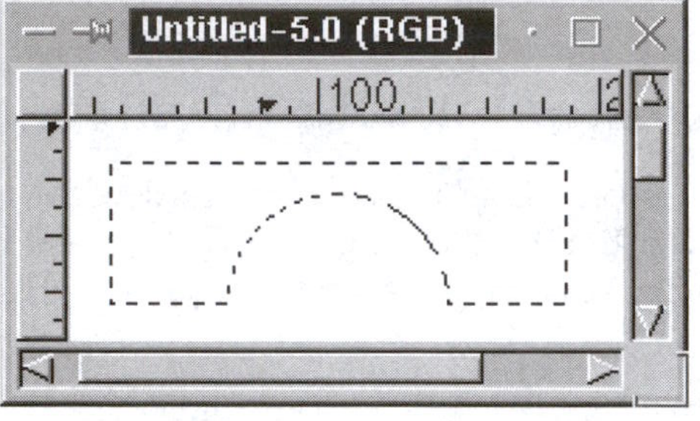

Figure 20.13 Combining selections.

> **TIP**
>
> To reiterate, another survival rule: if you want to abort an already started selection, you keep the left mouse button depressed and, in addition, press the right mouse button. Then you first release the left mouse button, followed by the right mouse button. Some hours of exercise with Gimp – and you have the dexterity of a pianist!

Lasso (Free / Shape Selection)

With the lasso function (FREE SELECTION, F), you simply select the area by surrounding it with the mouse with the mouse button kept depressed. (If the area is not entirely closed, Gimp joins the start and end points with a line.)

The SHAPE SELECTION (S) function goes one step further: as with FREE SELECTION, you draw the shape of the selection with the mouse. Gimp subsequently tries to improve the selection on the basis of the image contents. (For this reason, the tool is also called INTELLIGENT SCISSORS.) Several experiments with this function have, however, been deceptive: in none of the cases, Gimp was able to guess what should really have been selected. The numerous slide rulers of the corresponding dialog cannot change the selection *a posteriori*, which makes experimenting largely impossible. The most attractive alternative seems to be the possibility of subsequently converting the curve into Bezier form (which does not always work without problems, either).

Magic wand (Fuzzy / Color Selection)

The FUZZY SELECTION tool (Z) selects a contiguous area of similarly colored pixels (for example, the shining red car body in a picture). Simply click the mouse on a starting point whose color is most characteristic of the required area. With the mouse button still kept depressed, you can now increase (movement towards bottom right) or decrease (movement towards top left) the selection threshold.

A very similar task to FUZZY SELECT is fulfilled by SELECT | BY COLOR. This tool is controlled via its own dialog in which the current selection is shown as a black and white mask (Figure 20.14). The selection can very easily be extended or restricted by areas of a specific color. You can click both on the image and on the preview mask in the dialog.

The FUZZINESS slide ruler determines how large the color area shall be. However, the ruler does not apply to executed selections, but only to future operations. Unfortunately, there is no undo function for selections that have been constructed stepwise. (Try it out with SUBTRACT!) The BY COLOR tool has an option dialog (FEATHER, ANTIALIASING, and SAMPLE MERGED), which is automatically opened when a toolbox dialog was already present on screen.

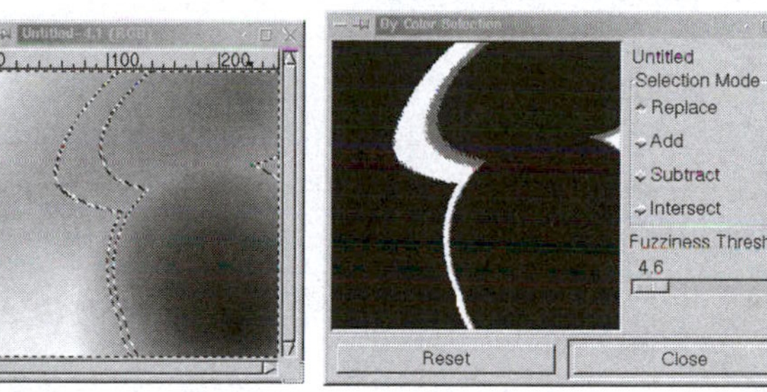

Figure 20.14 Selecting areas of the same color.

As fascinating as these two tools are, the selections carried out with their aid can seldom be used without further refinement. Thus, do not expect miracles!

> **TIP** SELECT | BY COLOR provides an easy way of making an object on a single-color background transparent: simply select the background and cut it with Ctrl+X! (Obviously, this only works without problems if the background color does not occur in the object as well.)

20.7 Bezier curves

Of all selection tools presented in this section, BEZIER SELECTIONS (B) are probably the hardest ones to handle; in return, you will mostly succeed in delimiting the required object with sufficient precision – which is where, in spite of all their ease of handling, all other tools fail.

First, a brief mathematical digression: Bezier curves are assembled out of pieces of lines each of which is described by a third-order polynomial. In practice, this means that for each piece of line, we can specify the start and end points, plus the tangents (that is, the direction) of the curves at these points. The BEZIER tool helps to determine these points together with their tangents.

A Bezier curve is assembled in several steps. Try to familiarize yourself with the tool before you have a go at an elaborate selection – most operations with Bezier curves cannot be undone, so that in case of an error, you have to start all over again.

- Set the anchor points of the curve with a series of single mouse clicks. You will need only one anchor point for each piece of curve (ideally where the flexure changes between concave and convex). You close the curve by clicking a second time on the first point.
- Once the (still angular) curve is closed, the left mouse button changes meaning. It now serves to pull the square tangents' control points out of the round anchor points and to modify them.
- Normally, two correlated tangent points lie on one line. However, using Shift together with the mouse button, you can also move the points separately, which gives you more room for creativity. In exchange, the curve gets a kink at the anchor point (whereas otherwise the transition is smooth).
- With Ctrl and the mouse, you can move the anchor points at any time.
- Finally, you click the mouse inside the curve. This converts the Bezier curve into a common selection.

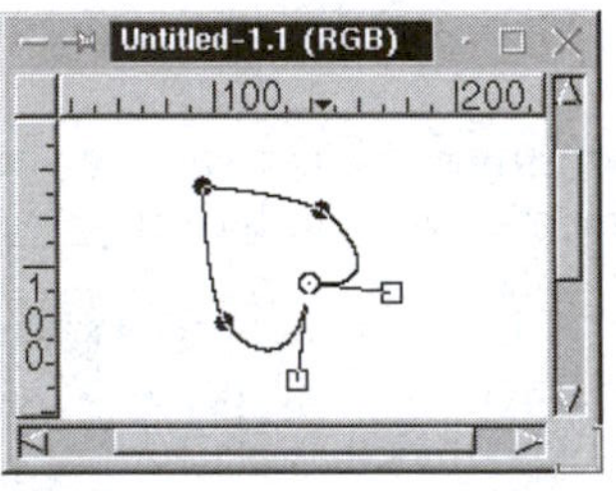

Figure 20.15 A simple Bezier curve.

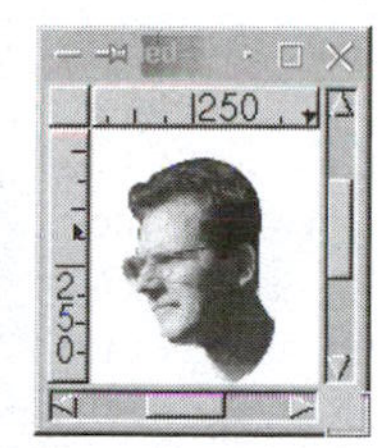

Figure 20.16 The author's head, cut out with a Bezier curve.

CAUTION

The number of anchor points of a Bezier curve can no longer be changed once the curve is closed. On the other hand, too many anchor points complicate your work unnecessarily – so do not overdo this!

During the selection process, the zoom factor of the image must not be changed – if you try to do that, all of your work is lost! Therefore, do not forget to enlarge the relevant area of your image as much as possible beforehand – this will greatly facilitate your work!

Once you click the mouse inside the curve, the curve is converted into a normal selection. This conversion cannot be undone.

Selection options

The following options are available in the toolbox dialogs of the tools discussed above. The options must be set *before* beginning the selection; later changes have no effect!

- FEATHER: This option causes the border of the selection to be a flowing transition instead of a sharp line. This transition zone only becomes noticeable when the selection is worked upon; there is no other visual feedback.
- ANTIALIASING: This option causes the greyshades or color tints at an oblique or rounded delimitation curve to be interpolated. This makes the selected shape look considerably smoother, the edges are less pronounced. ANTIALIASING is active by default. The effect can, however, only be noted when FEATHER is deactivated.
- SAMPLE MERGED: When this option is active, all colors actually visible on screen are taken into account (not just the colors of the active layer).

In Figure 20.17, a circle was selected and moved once without ANTIALIASING, once with ANTIALIASING, and a third time with FEATHER (Radius 15).

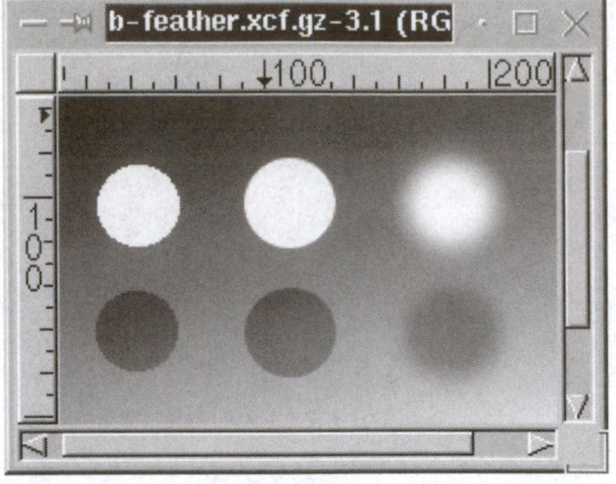

Figure 20.17 Selection without Antialiasing, with Antialiasing, and with Feather.

Enlarging and reducing selections

Even after a selection has been made, Gimp provides several possibilities for changing the shape at a later stage. Nearly all corresponding commands can be found in the SELECT menu.

SELECT | GROW and SELECT | SHRINK enlarge or reduce the selection by a specified number of pixels.

With SELECT | FEATHER, you can surround the selection with a transition zone (see above). Repeated application of this command can only increase this zone, but not reduce it. (The command can, however, be undone.)

SELECT | SHARPEN is a sort of inverse function to FEATHER and ANTIALIASING: a selection treated in this way precisely follows the pixel borders, thus looking sharp (but also pixely).

A very interesting function is SELECT | BORDER: this surrounds the former selection with an area of pixels outside and inside the selection edge boundary. Thus, for example, a circular selection is turned into an annulus (a kind of ring). The new selection automatically has a transition zone (FEATHER), which is intended to hide an essential flaw of this tool: the border is not of equal width in all directions, as can be clearly seen in Figure 20.18.

TIP

A similar effect as in Figure 20.18 can also be achieved with EDIT | STROKE. This command applies a pencil along a selection curve (see page 690).

Floating selections

Floating selections are probably the most confusing aspect in the handling of selections. At first sight, floating selections look like normal selections (that is, the famous *marching ants* are used to delimit the selection). Internally, however, they

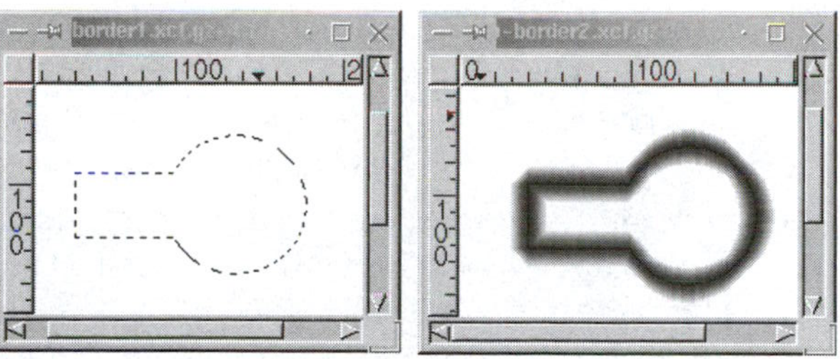

Figure 20.18 Left, the original selection, right, the filled border.

are represented in a different way (namely as layers) and provide some additional features (which, however, also entail some restrictions).

REFERENCE

A floating selection is a special form of a layer. Background information on this subject can be found in a separate section from page 691 onwards. Just one hint in advance: the layer management dialog is opened with IMAGE | LAYERS AND CHANNELS.

How do floating selections originate?

Floating selections often come into being quite involuntarily. The following list shows the most important possibilities:

- You select an image area and execute SELECT | FLOAT.
- You move a selection with the mouse.
- You transform a selection (TRANSFORM and FLIP tools).
- You copy a selection (CUT & PASTE).
- You insert text.

What are floating selections good for?

- Floating selections can easily be moved inside the image. (You must, however, use the MOVE tool for this purpose.)
- The outline of the floating selection can be reduced with the ERASE tool. (Thus, you use a pencil to delete parts of the floating selection. In this operation, the background color is ignored – in the deleted area, the floating selection simply becomes invisible.)
- Conversely, the floating selection can be enlarged with the paint tools (PENCIL, PAINTBRUSH, and AIRBRUSH). However, this works only if the KEEP TRANSPARENCY option is switched off in the LAYERS dialog. (This option usually prevents paint operations from having an effect beyond the selected area).

Paint operations are, however, restricted to a rectangular area that encloses the floating selection. If you want to enlarge the floating selection beyond this, you must first enlarge the corresponding layer. To do this, you click on the floating selection layer in the LAYERS dialog and execute RESIZE LAYER.

- In floating selections, the BUCKET FILL command functions differently than in normal selections (in the way described on page 673). If you want to fill the entire contents of a floating selection with the background color, you need to use the EDIT | FILL command instead of BUCKET FILL.
- The degree of transparency of the floating selection can be freely set in the LAYERS dialog (OPACITY ruler). This can be used to make a selection translucent.
- You can convert a floating selection into a normal layer. All you need to do is double click in the LAYERS dialog and give it a new name.

Normal selections versus floating selections

Many Gimp operations function the same way in floating selections and in normal selections, that is, their effect is limited to the selected area.

Even though floating selections look like selections, they are not selections. This is why the SELECT commands do not work, and this is why it is also not possible to invert a floating selection by simply pressing Ctrl+I.

NOTE

In addition to an existing floating selection, a normal selection can be made inside or outside. The floating selection is then only visible in the area of this selection. However, the location of the normal selection remains unchanged when the floating selection is moved. This can make simultaneous working with a floating selection *and* a normal selection quite confusing. Occasionally, however, this combination is a useful aid for restricting the scope of a movable floating selection.

Dissolving floating selections

Unless you have activated a paint tool in the toolbox, a simple mouse click on the floating selection is sufficient to integrate the floating selection back into the image. The same effect can also be achieved with the LAYERS | ANCHOR command or with Ctrl+H. Reconversion of a floating selection into a normal selection is unfortunately not possible.

Copying and pasting of selections

As in nearly all programs, a selected area can be copied into a buffer with Ctrl+C or cut with Ctrl+X. Ctrl+V pastes the selection into the image – evidently as a floating selection.

In addition, the EDIT menu provides some more exotic commands: PASTE INTO is a variation of PASTE where, prior to the pasting operation itself, a new selection must be created. With PASTE INTO, the content of the clipboard is inserted and cut off by the boundary of the selection. As with the normal PASTE, the floating selection can obviously still be moved after the command.

NAMED COPY or CUT can be used to give the copied or cut floating selection a name which can later be used to paste the selection. The advantage is that you can store several floating selections on the clipboard and access them when needed. (If you use the XCF format, this clipboard is even saved in the file!)

Moving and transforming selections

The Gimp User Manual states that 'moving selections in Gimp is not altogether intuitive' – and you will probably agree. After you have selected an area, you can easily move it *once* with the mouse. If you now try to move the area a second time, it is immediately glued to the image. (More precisely: the floating selection was amalgamated with the image.)

The reason for this strange behavior: selections can be moved without problems, but for this purpose, they are automatically converted into floating selections. (The same applies to all operations discussed in this section.) In floating selections, however, a normal mouse click has a different meaning from the one it has in simple selections – it corresponds to the LAYERS | ANCHOR LAYER command. Obviously, you can also move floating selections – but for doing so, you must first activate the MOVE tool of the toolbox!

CAUTION

MOVE is only designed for use with layers (including the special case of floating selections), but not with normal selections. If you have carried out a normal selection and employ MOVE, you move not only the selection, but the entire layer.

While MOVE is active, the floating selection can also be moved by means of the cursor keys. This often allows more precise positioning than the mouse. However, each keyboard input is counted as a separate operation, so that the few undo levels are quickly exhausted.

Selections and floating selections can be mirrored, rotated, distorted, and otherwise transformed by means of the two toolbox commands TRANSFORM and FLIP. Handling these tools is simple – just open the corresponding dialog with a double click on the toolbox.

TIP

When using perspective distortion with TRANSFORM, you should avoid excessive enlargement – otherwise the image will become visibly blurred. Also avoid carrying out too many transformations in sequence – with each of these, the image loses quality (definition).

Figure 20.19 Application sample of Flip, Rotation, and perspective distortion.

Creating a frame around a selection edge (Stroke)

With EDIT | STROKE, you can follow the edge of a selection with a pencil. Prior to carrying out this command, select an appropriate pencil (BRUSHES dialog), and experiment with the SPACING setting of this dialog. To paint the image shown in Figure 20.20, a circle was selected, and the 'Diagonal Star' pencil was applied with a SPACING of 100.

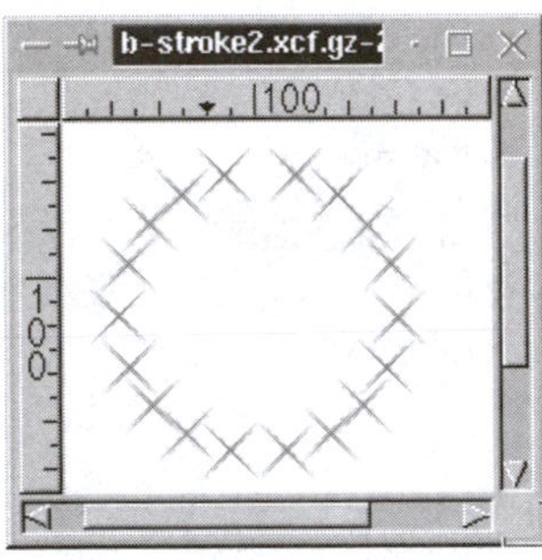

Figure 20.20 An aureole created with Gimp.

TIP

When you work with a floating selection, you should deactivate the KEEP TRANSPARENCY option in the LAYERS dialog to make the STROKE function work not only inside, but also outside the boundaries of the selection. In addition, you should enlarge the size of the floating selection's frame (RESIZE command in the context menu of the LAYERS dialog). An application sample of STROKE can be found on page 663 at the beginning of the chapter.

20.8 Layers, masks, and channels

Layers

A Gimp image may be composed of several layers. Imagine you want to build a fishtank by way of a photomontage: as a background layer, you use an image of water, maybe with some bubbles painted into it. On top of this, you put several layers of fish, and crown the whole thing with a layer that frames the whole fishtank. In the final image, the pixels of the higher layers cover the pixels of the lower layers. Obviously, the whole composition can only work if all non-relevant parts of all layers are transparent, not white (which would make the top layer cover up all other layers). The big advantage of layers is that each layer can be modified individually, without affecting the remaining image.

In practice, you will use layers to give a (previously cut-out) object a shadow, to make an image out of several photographs, and so on. (Often one layer controls to which extent an effect is applied to a second layer.) Once you have got used to working with layers (it's not that difficult!) they will quickly become so indispensable that you will no longer create or edit images without their help.

The Layers dialog

Manipulation of layers is carried out in a separate dialog which is opened by means of LAYERS | LAYERS & CHANNELS (Figure 20.21). Some operations can be executed directly, using the buttons at the bottom of the dialog; the remaining commands have a context menu. (All commands described in this section refer to this context menu. Some layer commands can, however, also be executed via the LAYERS menu of the image window.)

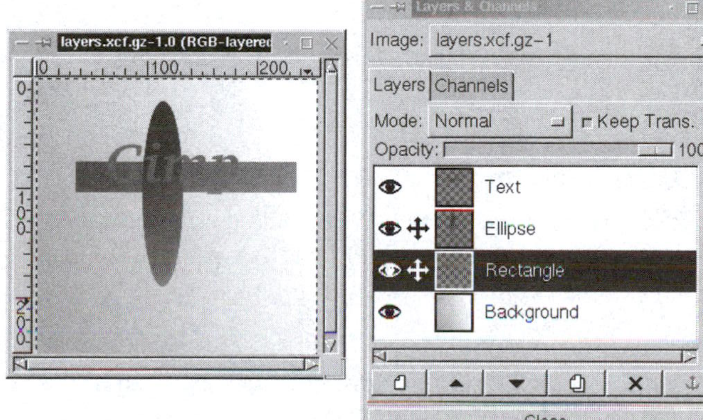

Figure 20.21 First experiments with the Layers dialog.

CAUTION

Please note that the layer dialog and the image window employ different keyboard shortcuts. For example, Ctrl+X definitely deletes the current layer (that is, the layer is not copied to the clipboard). Obviously, you can undo this command with Ctrl+Z – but to do so, you must first change to the image window.

CAUTION

If you save your image as a bitmap or in PostScript format, only the current layer is saved. If you want to save all layers, you need to employ Gimp's proprietary XCF format. If, instead, you wish to store a bitmap of the overall composition, you first need to unite the layers.

CAUTION

If you have several images opened simultaneously, for some mysterious reason the LAYERS dialog does *not* apply to the currently active image! The most probable cause for Gimp appearing to misunderstand your LAYERS commands is that the wrong image is selected in the list field at the very top of the dialog. This is dangerous in that the commands *are* executed, but on a different image. (To remedy the damage, click on the affected image and undo the command by pressing Ctrl+Z.)

Inserting new layers

Gimp asks whether the layer is to be transparent, white, or filled with the current background color. As a rule, TRANSPARENT is the best choice. In any case, you may still make parts of the layer transparent by using the ERASE tool or by cutting out a selection.

Visibility of layers

By clicking on the eye symbol in the LAYERS dialog, you can choose which layers are to be visible in the image window.

TIP

If you want to view only one layer, simply click on the eye symbol with the Shift key depressed – this makes all other layers invisible.

Layer hierarchy

The arrow buttons in the LAYERS dialog can be used to shift layers upwards or downwards. The topmost (visible) layer has priority. Non-transparent parts of this layer cover up all underlying layers.

Modifying layers

Independently of the visibility, only one layer can be worked on (modified) at a time. This layer is selected in the LAYERS dialog with a single click of the mouse, and is now highlighted with a blue bar. (Although in Figure 20.21 all layers are visible, only the 'Rectangle' layer is active.)

For your first experiments with layers, simply create a couple of new layers. Click on each of these layers and paint some patterns on them. Then use the LAYERS dialog to move the layers upwards and downwards, change the OPACITY of individual layers, and so on.

CAUTION

No matter which layers are *displayed*: all processing commands only apply to the currently active layer – even if it is momentarily invisible. You will inevitably change visibility of layers, and then nevertheless work on a still active, invisible layer. Therefore, please check that the correct layer is highlighted.

TIP

Selections are independent from layers. You may select something on one layer, then activate a different layer, and continue to use the selection there.

(Re)naming layers

All you need to give a layer a new name is a double click on the layer in the LAYERS dialog. (In this way, you can also turn a floating selection into a normal layer – simply give it a new name.)

Combining layers

Three commands are available for combining several layers into a new one. ANCHOR unites a floating selection with the last active layer. MERGE VISIBLE LAYERS combines all visible layers (that is, all layers for which the eye icon is shown). FLATTEN IMAGE unites all layers (no matter whether they are visible or not).

TIP

You should always store the image in an XCF backup file before you combine the layers. More often than not, you may need to modify an image you thought had been completed. If at that point you no longer have any layer information left, many changes become practically impossible.

Transparency (Keep Trans.)

The KEEP TRANS. option always refers to the currently active layer. It specifies whether paint or filter operations are restricted to the visible part of the layer. This is very useful in many cases. If, for example, a layer only contains a text, and you wish to change the color of this text, the option must be activated. If, instead, you wish to insert further texts, patterns, and so on, in this layer, you must switch the option off. (If your commands are ignored, one possible cause is an incorrect setting of the KEEP TRANS. option.)

TIP

The transparent part of a layer or a whole image is represented by a gray chessboard pattern. Both the grayshade and the size of the chessboard pattern can be set in the FILE | PREFERENCES dialog.

In the FILE | PREFERENCES dialog, you can also change the size of the layer preview icon displayed in the LAYERS dialog.

NOTE The lowest layer ('Background') occupies a special position. On the one hand, no part of this layer can be made invisible via a cutting operation (unless the layer was already defined as transparent in FILE | NEW). On the other hand, the 'Background' layer must always be the lowest layer. Both restrictions can easily be circumvented by executing ADD ALPHA CHANNEL and thus assigning transparency information to the background layer as well.

Image and layer size

In Gimp, the size of the layers and the size of the image are independent of each other. This saves memory and storage space (because many layers are significantly smaller than the whole image), but also causes much confusion. Layers that are smaller than the entire image are marked by a yellow and black border.

The size of a layer can be changed by means of the RESIZE and SCALE commands in the LAYERS context menu. However, these commands are by no means equivalent! RESIZE leaves the layer's contents unchanged and only adds an additional border, or cuts the edges of the layer (in case of reduction). SCALE, in contrast, reduces or enlarges the image contents (similarly to the TRANSFORM command). The analogous commands for the entire image are (now in the image context menu) IMAGE | RESIZE and IMAGE | SCALE.

TIP If you want to enlarge an image at a later stage, you must carry out RESIZE for both the image and all affected layers.

Moving layers

Layers can be moved relative to the entire image by means of the MOVE tool. (This will occasionally happen to you unwittingly when you try to move a selection with MOVE. As a reminder: MOVE can only be applied to layers and floating selections.)

A layer may be moved outside the limits of the overall image. The information situated outside is not lost – it is simply not displayed. (To make it visible, you need to enlarge the image – see above.)

Often several layers belong together from a contents point of view and should therefore be moved together. The MOVE command, however, works only on the currently active layer. The solution of the problem consists in activating the quadruple arrow in all affected layers, which is then shown in the column next to the eye icon. As soon as one of the layers marked with this arrow symbol is moved, all other equally marked layers are moved together with it. In Figure 20.21, the 'Ellipse' and 'Rectangle' layers are joined together in this way.

Reducing image and layers (Crop)

While the commands described above apply to one layer at a time or to the image, the CROP tool of the toolbox simultaneously crops the image together with all layers contained in it. After you have activated CROP in the toolbox, you can draw the new image size with the mouse. In the CROP information dialog you can adjust the borders to the current selection.

TIP: A useful variation of CROP is the IMAGE | TRANSFORMS | AUTOCROP command. This removes the white edges at the border of an image.

GIF animations

As already mentioned, when saving an image composed of several layers in a bitmap or PostScript format, only the current layer is saved. There is, however, one exception to this rule: the GIF format. Images with several layers are automatically saved as GIF animations.

Most of the parameters – such as the default display delay per image – can be specified in the GIF SAVE dialog. With image sequences where only relatively little information changes from frame to frame, the option MAKE FRAME FROM CUMULATIVE LAYERS results in a particularly compact storage.

TIP: If you wish to control the display time individually for each frame, you can specify this delay in parentheses in the comment text of the corresponding layer (that is, in the LAYERS dialog) – for example 'Starting frame (250 ms)'.

TIP: Gimp is not capable of displaying animations as such. For this purpose, your best bet is to start Netscape Navigator or Communicator and load the image.

Masks

Layers can be partially invisible, so that they give an impression of transparency when put on top of each other. Masks are another alternative for creating transparency.

A mask is an additional information layer (technically speaking: a grayscale bitmap; more technically speaking: an additional alpha channel), which can be created in parallel to each layer by means of the context menu command ADD LAYER MASK.

The brightness of the pixels in the mask indicates the degree of the mask's transparency at this point: white means that the mask is transparent, black means completely opaque, the grayshades in between specify the transition zone. (It is also possible to interpret the mask's colors the other way round from the point of view of the overall image, as in the dialog that belongs to the ADD MASK command: parts of the layer marked in black in the mask appear as transparent in the complete image.)

TIP: The background layer cannot normally be masked. If you wish to mask it, you need to execute ADD ALPHA CHANNEL, thus attributing transparency information to the background layer as well.

Processing masks

To process masks, you click on the mask icon in the LAYERS dialog. From now on, all Gimp commands you execute in the image window apply to the mask. Colors

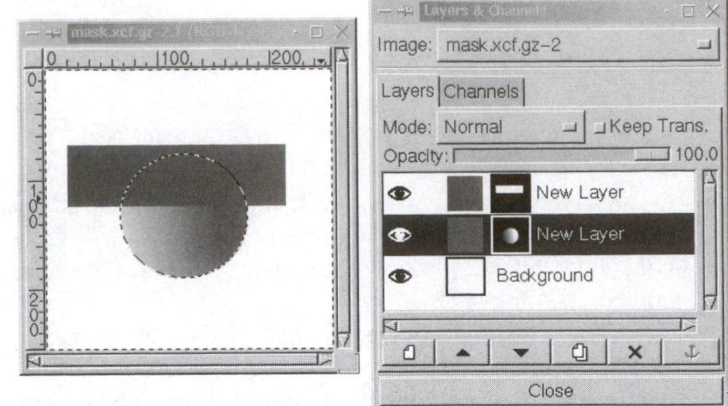

Figure 20.22 A simple application of masks.

are automatically converted into grayshades. However, the only visual feedback you get when you execute commands is a change of the mask icon – which is often not enough.

If you wish to view an exact picture of the mask in the image window instead of the layer contents, you need to click on the mask icon while keeping the Alt key depressed. This makes the mask visible; the mask icon is now lined with green. Another mouse click in combination with Alt deactivates this mode.

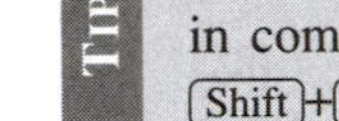

TIP

Some window managers – in particular that of KDE 1.0 – claim mouse clicks in combination with Alt for themselves. In Gimp, you then need to press Shift+Alt – this will make it work!

Unfortunately, it is quite difficult to tell from an additional line around the corresponding icon whether the layer itself or its mask is active at any given moment. You may therefore occasionally forget which of the two is currently active. Fortunately enough, undo with Ctrl+Z is once again there to help!

TIP

Often a mask is more suitable than a selection to cut out parts of an image. For this purpose, you make all layers except the current one invisible and add a white mask. Now you can process this mask with all available paint tools. If you paint or fill with black, parts of the image are masked out. With white, you can make them appear again. If you wish to use the BUCKET FILL tool, you must use the SAMPLE MERGE tool.

The big advantage of masks is that all Gimp commands are available without restriction and that the mask can be changed any number of times (whereas the shape of a selection can later be changed only with great difficulty). With MASK TO SELECTION, you can even convert a mask into a selection. The inverse command does not, however, exist – but you only need to apply white and black fill operations to the selection and its inversion to achieve the desired effect.

TIP Obviously, you can also use copy and paste to transfer image information between different layers or masks!

If you want to remove a mask, you need to carry out APPLY LAYER MASK, which opens a dialog that allows you either to apply the mask to the layer (thus making parts of the layer definitely transparent) or to simply delete it.

Channels

Color channels

With RGB images, the CHANNELS page of the LAYERS dialog displays three channels for the colors red, green, and blue. Usually, these channels are always selected and visible. To produce special effects, it may be sensible to work on individual color channels. Please note, however, that several Gimp operations (in particular, copying and pasting of image sections) always affect all channels.

Currently, Gimp does not provide any possibility of selecting a different channel separation (for example, for images in the CMY color model). Instead, Gimp has the special command IMAGE | CHANNEL OPS | DECOMPOSE, which allows a color image to be decomposed into several separate images each of which contains a grayscale image of the channels of different color models (RGB, HSV, CMY, CMYK). This is also useful when you need to create PostScript files for CMY imagesetting. (Prior to the DECOMPOSE command, the layers of the starting image must be merged by means of LAYERS | FLATTEN IMAGE.)

Each of these grayscale images can now be processed separately. IMAGE | CHANNEL OPS | COMPOSE merges the individual images back into one color image.

Alpha channels

While separate processing of individual color channels is rather intended to be used by experts, alpha channels are an indispensable tool for everyday work with Gimp. Besides the masks described earlier, channels represent yet another alternative to selections. Once a selection has been made, it can be saved as an alpha channel by means of SELECT | SAVE TO CHANNEL. All points lying inside the selection are assigned a brightness value of 255, all points lying outside are assigned 0. In the LAYER dialog, an alpha channel can at any time be reconverted into a selection. Thus alpha channels provide an ideal possibility for saving complex selections for later use.

Similar to masks, alpha channels can be inserted and deleted, activated and processed with all Gimp commands. As with masks, this provides numerous types of manipulation. (Visible channels are overlaid semi-transparently over the image and can therefore be processed very easily. The degree of transparency can be set by double clicks.)

TIP For some obscure reason, you cannot deactivate an alpha channel by clicking on an RGB channel. Instead, you need to click a second time on the active alpha channel.

NOTE When you work with layers, the transparency of each layer, too, is managed by an alpha channel. This channel does not, however, explicitly appear in the channel list of the LAYERS dialog. The alpha channel can, however, be made visible as a separate grayscale image by means of IMAGE | CHANNEL OPS | DECOMPOSE | ALPHA.

20.9 Gimp for advanced users

At this point, the chapter reaches its limits. A detailed treatment of Gimp's numerous special functions would require more space than we can afford in this book, together with the possibility of including sample color printouts. This chapter is therefore only intended to serve as a starting point for your own experiments. You should also consult the *Gimp User Manual*, which dedicates more than 150 pages just to the subject of filters.

Filters

The vast number of Gimp filters can be employed for the most varied tasks:

- Identification of specific features (such as edges) which are subsequently to be treated separately or in some special way.
- Achievement of a multitude of effects (such as smudging or sharpening the image, creating the impression of an oil painting, distorting the image as under a glass lens, making an image horizontally and vertically repeatable, and so on).
- Creation of entirely new color patterns (FILTERS | RENDER).

TIP Some filters do not merely process the current layer, but also consider information taken from a second layer. If a filter shows no effect at all, it may be that this second control layer is missing. Check the GUM!

TIP Before starting to try out filters, it is often useful to create a copy of the current image with Ctrl+D. The most recently used filter can be repeated with Alt+F. The corresponding dialog is displayed again with Shift+Alt+F.

Color manipulation

The commands for manipulating the color distribution are hidden in the IMAGE | COLORS submenu. They are particularly useful for optimizing scanned images and for creating bizarre color effects. The following table summarizes the most important commands:

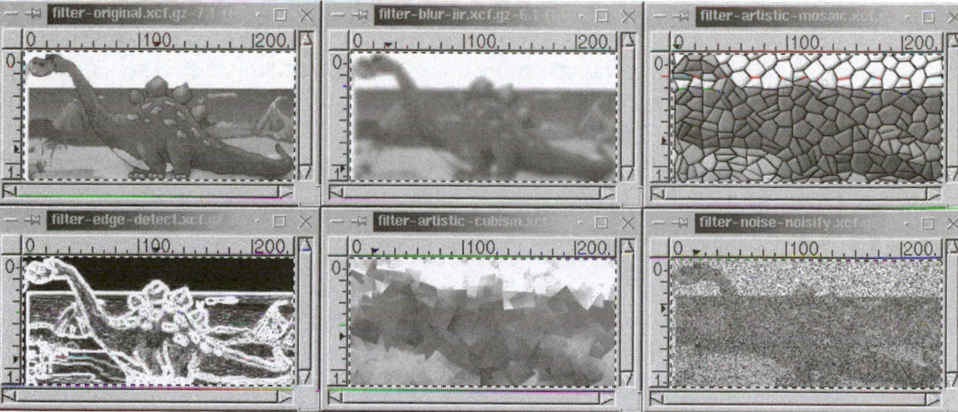

Figure 20.23 Some filters, applied to the image of a dinosaur.

Filters for color manipulation	
EQUALIZE	equal distribution of colors
INVERT	inversion of colors
POSTERIZE	reduction of number of colors
THRESHOLD	creation of a black and white image from brightness distribution
COLOR BALANCE	RGB color balance (for example for scanned photographs)
BRIGHTNESS – CONTRAST	setting brightness and contrast
HUE – SATURATION	setting color hue and saturation
CURVES	redistribute brightness by means of a separate curve
LEVELS	restrict color distribution
DESATURATE	convert colors into grayscales
AUTO-STRETCH HSV	optimize hue, saturation, and brightness
AUTO-STRETCH CONTRAST	optimize the contrast in all three RGB channels
NORMALIZE	optimze the overall contrast

NOTE As already mentioned, Gimp images can be created and processed in three different modes (256 levels of grey, 256^3 RGB levels or a limited number of colors for GIFs). The above color manipulation commands are, however, mostly available only for RGB images. If needed, simply execute IMAGE | RGB.

TIP Further color manipulation functions can be found in FILTERS | COLOR.

Script-Fu

Script-Fu is Gimp's own macro programming language. The language is a variation of Lisp; thus there are many similarities to Emacs-Lisp (see Chapter 17). Script-Fu is used for automation of frequently used command sequences. Gimp is supplied together with a whole range of ready-made scripts, which can be called via various SCRIPT-FU submenus.

Unfortunately, documentation for these scripts is fairly scarce. Even the GUM gives only a sort of overview. The problem is that the scripts place totally different demands on the current image. Thus, some scripts can only be applied to a selection or a floating selection. If these preconditions are not met, the script has no effect or leads to a (mostly cryptical) error message. Also the results look very different: some scripts modify the current layer, others create new layers, others create an entirely new image, and so on.

TIP In many cases, it is worthwhile checking the source code of the scripts, where you will often find a short description in the comments. The scripts are located in the Gimp subdirectory `scripts`, thus, for example, in `/usr/share/gimp/scripts`.

Figure 20.24 shows three examples of working with scripts. The two shadows were created with the SCRIPT-FU | SHADOW commands. The text was present in the form of a floating selection. For the bottom left image, the floating selection was dissolved; subsequently, SCRIPT-FU | ALCHEMY | UNSHARP MASK was applied. The original image layer was cut out; the two new layers pasted in. In addition, the image was given a new background (a graduated tint).

Figure 20.24 Some scripts applied to a short text.

Plugins

Plugins are extensions of Gimp. The essential difference from scripts is that plugins are compiled binary files. Many of the basic functions of Gimp are implemented as plugins. Furthermore, there are a number of optional extensions (such as the SANE scanner control package mentioned at the beginning of this chapter), which are usually called via the XTNS menu of the toolbox.

Standard plugins are normally located in the `/usr/lib/gimp/1.0/plug-ins` directory (see also FILE | PREFERENCES | DIRECTORIES). User-specific extensions are best accessed via a link from `~/.gimp/plug-ins/name` to the binary file.

Installation of additional components

Probably the most fascinating aspect of Gimp is that it can be nearly universally extended: additional color palettes, new brush shapes, scripts for easy creation of unbelievable effects, plugins for new file formats – all this is available on the Internet:

```
http://www.gimp.org/data.html
http://www.gimp.org/links.html
http://registry.gimp.org/
```

Installation usually causes no problems: you simply need to copy the relevant files into the appropriate directories. Gimp automatically recognizes the extensions at the next start-up. If extensions are to be made available only for specific users (to keep Gimp down to a reasonable extent for standard users), the `~/.gimp` directory provides the necessary features.

TIP

A particularly easy way of getting hold of a whole palette of fill patterns and brush shapes is to install the `gimp-data-extras` package. This package is an integral part of some distributions; otherwise, you can find it on the Internet.

Plugins are available on the Internet both as source text and in compiled form (at least for Intel systems). The second variation is easier to handle because compilation at the user's side becomes superfluous. The binary file just needs to be installed in a `plugin` directory.

NOTE

You can easily produce your own fill patterns and brush shapes. A new fill pattern is simply made out of a Gimp image that you store with the file name extension `*.pat`. (You need to make up the image in such a way that it can be [stepped and] repeated without a visible transition. A helpful function for this purpose is FILTERS | MAP | MAKE SEAMLESS.)

To create a new brush shape, you select a part of your image and execute SCRIPT-FU | SELECTION | TO BRUSH. The result is a `*.gbr` file in the `~/.gimp/brushes` directory.

Configuration

Gimp is largely configurable. As with many other programs, Gimp differentiates between global settings made in the Gimp installation directory, and local settings in the `~/.gimp` directory. (The local files always take precedence.)

Gimp configuration files	
`gimprc`	general configuration settings
`gtkrc`	configuration of the user interface library
`menurc`	user-defined keyboard shortcuts
`pluginrc`	information on plugins

Most of the general settings can be easily carried out in the FILES | PREFERENCES dialog. A direct modification of `gimprc` is only needed for a few special settings.

`pluginrc` is automatically updated at any start-up of Gimp. A direct modification should never become necessary. (If plugin problems occur, the GUM suggests simply deleting this file.)

Swap file, tile cache, undo layers

Particularly during processing of very large images, Gimp requires a lot of memory. In contrast to practically all other Linux programs, Gimp does not rely uniquely on the memory management functionality of the operating system, but in addition manages its own swap file which is, amongst other things, used to store undo information. (This has the advantage that excessive memory usage by Gimp does not affect the stability of the whole system.) The directory for the swap file is set in the DIRECTORIES sheet of the PREFERENCES dialog.

The so-called tile cache is another Gimp feature related to memory management. Tiles are parts of an image. Gimp is capable of processing images which require more space than is available as RAM. In this case, the image is processed in parts (that is, tiles). The TILE CACHE SIZE setting specifies the maximum RAM that can be used for storage of tiles. The smaller this value, the earlier Gimp begins to swap parts of large images to a file (which makes it significantly slower.)

TIP

The size of the tile cache should stand in a reasonable proportion to the available RAM. If you have plenty of RAM (for example, 128 Mbytes), you may without problems set the tile cache to 64 Mbytes. This will accelerate processing of very large images.

One of the most frequently used key combinations in the handling of Gimp is Ctrl+Z for the Undo function. In the default setting, however, this function is restricted to the last five operations. You can set a higher value in the INTERFACE page of the PREFERENCES dialog.

CAUTION

If you work with large images and allow many Undo levels, the space requirement of the Gimp swap file quickly rises to the stars! Several hundreds of megabytes are by no means rare. At the same time, the working speed slows down beyond endurance (unless you do not have a huge amount of RAM, that is, 256 Mbytes and more).

Please also note that in the event of a crash, Gimp does not remove the swap file. Thus, if your hard disk is unexpectedly full, check the Gimp swap file directory.

Redefining keyboard shortcuts

Many menu commands have their keyboard shortcuts which are displayed in the menu text. Nothing is easier than using a different shortcut instead, or assigning a new shortcut in the first place. Begin the menu selection with the mouse, letting the mouse point to the menu command, without concluding the selection with a mouse click. Then press the required key combination – done. It could not be simpler. (The modified keyboard shortcuts are stored in the local file `menurc`.)

Setting the menu font size

In the default configuration, Gimp displays its menus in a tiny font. This can be remedied by modifying `~/.gimp/gtkrc` (local) or `/usr/share/gimp/gtkrc` (global). The following lines help you to obtain a font size of 17 points in menus and dialogs.

```
# configuration file gktrc
style "ruler"
  { font = "-adobe-helvetica-medium-r-normal--17-*" }
style "default"
  { font = "-adobe-helvetica-medium-r-normal--17-*" }
widget_class "*Ruler*" style "ruler"
widget_class "*" style "default"
```

APPENDIX A

Debian GNU/ Linux 2.1

Unlike most other distributions the Debian distribution is not put together by a company which wants to make money out of it (which would be quite legitimate), but by a group of involved Linux users. The principal objectives of Debian are

- keeping the distribution as free as possible from commercial software and legal distribution problems,
- achieving maximum stability, and
- offering users maximum ease of maintenance (in particular with updates).

These aims generate a number of differences from the other distributions.

Package types

Packages are subdivided into several groups: *stable*, *contrib*, and *non-free*. The contents of the Debian distribution as such consists of the *stable* packages. Packages of the *contrib* and *non-free* groups are not officially supported by Debian. In spite of various restrictions (source code not available, commercial use only after registration, and so on) they are offered as a part of the distribution to allow problem-free use of as many programs as possible under Linux.

As well as these three main groups, there are some more: the *unstable* group contains new packages or new versions of existing packages which do not yet fulfill Debian's quality requirements. (As a rule, *unstable* packages are not supplied on CD-ROMs, but are available only via the Internet.) The *non-us* group includes various cryptographic software products which, due to US legislation, must not be exported from the USA. Therefore, this software is developed outside the USA and is only available on ftp servers or CDs outside the USA. The *local* group, finally, allows extension of a Debian distribution with additional packages.

Package format

Debian packages use a proprietary package format. (Before you start moaning – yet another package format! – you should consider that the Debian format was developed prior to the RPM format. In its development of the RPM format, RedHat has assimilated many original ideas of Debian.)

Topicality

Sometimes the Debian distribution does not appear as up-to-date as other distributions. This is because each package (and each new version of a program) must first pass a beta test cycle before it is incorporated into the distribution. This quality control, however, also affects topicality. (Thus, Debian 2.1 is the only distribution described in this appendix still based on kernel version 2.0.)

Updates

Usually, the Debian distribution can be updated during current operation by means of `dselect`. (In all other distributions, you need to restart your computer for an upgrade to a new version.)

Debian is a technically mature distribution – many other distributors could learn a lot from them – but it is very much behind when it comes to ease of operation. This applies in particular to the `dselect` package management program, whose handling is – to put it mildly – somewhat unconventional. The program is employed both for the first installation and for later system administration.

Insofar as packages are provided with configuration scripts, they are automatically started by `dselect`. Although in this way Debian can do without central configuration tools, this configuration approach is far from error-proof. Another irritating factor is that the endless screen output during installation is not logged anywhere.

Corel Linux

According to information circulating on the Internet, the envisaged Linux distribution of Corel Corporation will be based on Debian. For this distribution to be ready for the market, the installation in particular should be dramatically simplified.

Internet

Further information on Debian philosophy, internal organization, mailing lists, bug reports, and other forms of quality assurance can be found on the Internet:

```
http://www.debian.org
ftp://ftp.debian.org
```

Installation

NOTE

This section is based on Chapter 2, which gives general information on the installation of Linux, such as repartitioning the hard disk with `FIPS` or `FDISK`, creation of installation diskettes with `RAWRITE`, and so on.

Starting the installation

If you own a modern motherboard and/or BIOS, installation starts directly from the CD-ROM. If this is not the case, take a look at your BIOS settings: maybe booting from CD-ROM is deactivated.

If direct installation from CD-ROM does not work, you will need to create installation diskettes. Under DOS, or in a DOS window under Windows, you execute the following command (where `X:` stands for the drive letter of your CD-ROM drive).

```
> X:\TOOLS\RAWRITE2\RAWRITE2 -f X:\BOOT\RESC1440.BIN -d A:
```

If you already have a Linux system installed, you can obviously create the two diskettes under Linux:

```
root# dd if=/cdrom/boot/resc1440.bin of=/dev/fd0 bs=1440k
```

Basic installation

First a Linux kernel and then the installation program are automatically started. Subsequently, you work your way through all relevant items of the main menu, with the installation program automatically proposing the (presumably) most reasonable next item. However, you need not stick to these suggestions.

CONFIGURE KEYBOARD

Here you can select a keyboard table for support of a non-English keyboard (`xx-latin1`, where *xx* stands for the required language).

PARTITION HARDDISK

In contrast to most other distribution, Debian makes use of `cfdisk` instead of `fdisk` for partitioning the hard disk. Handling of this program is significantly easier than of `fdisk`. Do not forget to write down the device names of the new partition(s)!

```
                              cfdisk 0.8j

                          Disk Drive: /dev/hda
            Heads: 128   Sectors per Track: 63   Cylinders: 787

 Name        Flags      Part Type     FS Type                    Size (MB)
--------------------------------------------------------------------------
 /dev/hda1   Boot       Primary       DOS FAT16 [           ]       303.19
 /dev/hda5              Logical       DOS FAT16 [IDE-DATA   ]      1023.75
 /dev/hda6              Logical       Linux                         452.82
 /dev/hda7              Logical       Linux                         441.00
                        Pri/Log       Free Space                    878.07

    [Bootable]  [ Delete ]  [  Help  ]  [Maximize]  [ Print  ]
    [  Quit  ]  [  Type  ]  [ Units  ]  [ Write  ]
```

> **NOTE**
>
> If `cfdisk` laconically exits with a 'fatal error' the most probable cause is that the size of your hard disk exceeds 7.9 Gbytes, without Linux knowing this. Remedy: restart the installation and use `linux hda=c,h,s` as boot parameter, specifying the number of cylinders, heads, and sectors of your hard disk (without spaces) according to the BIOS information. See also page 48.
>
> Under Debian too, it is also possible to use `fdisk`. The program can be manually started in a second console (Alt+F2). However, if the number of cylinders assumed by Linux does not correspond to reality, `fdisk` will not help either.

INITIALIZE/ACTIVATE SWAP A PARTITION

If in the previous step you have created a Linux swap partition, you can now activate it.

INITIALIZE LINUX PARTITION

In this step, you format the previously created Linux partition with the ext2 file system.

MOUNT AS ROOT

The still empty file system is now mounted into the file system as the root system.

INSTALL OPERATING SYSTEM KERNEL AND MODULES

In this step, a Linux kernel is copied into the file system together with its associated modules. Only now do you need to specify the source from which the kernel should be read. (Usually, this is the CD-ROM drive, whose device file name – for example `/dev/cdrom` – must be indicated.)

As the path for the installation files, the program suggests `/debian` which, as a rule, is correct. Next, the installation program wants to know which version of `resc1440.bin` it should use. As a rule, only one version is provided anyway but, depending on the actual assembly of the Debian CDs, you may also have a choice of several variations. In this case, you should choose a path including 'current.'

CONFIGURE DEVICE DRIVER MODULES

Up to now, Linux runs only in a minimal configuration. If your installation requires a specific CD-ROM driver (only for very old devices; SCSI and EIDE drivers are automatically available), or if you want to use a specific network card, and so on, you can now activate the corresponding modules. (Additional modules can also be integrated into the running system at a later stage. The relevant file is `/etc/modules`, which is evaluated by `kerneld`.)

CONFIGURE THE NETWORK

In contrast to other distributions in which you can also configure the network at a later stage, Debian provides this possibility only at this point. If you forego it here, you will need to edit all required `/etc` files manually (see also page 171). If your computer is not connected to a local network, you only need to specify the domain name of the computer. (The installation program suggests 'debian.')

INSTALL THE BASE SYSTEM

Now the installation program installs a minimal set of programs which – together with the installed kernel – yield an operational Linux system. Once more you need to specify the CD-ROM as the installation source. The path is again `/debian`. Also the question for the correct file version – this time for `base2_1.tgz` – is repeated.

CONFIGURE THE BASE SYSTEM

To be more precise, only one thing is configured here: the time. To select the time zone, you first select the area (for example, Europe) in the 'Directories' list field on the right; then, in the list field on the left, you select a town (for example, Berlin). In addition, the installation program wants to know whether the local time of your computer is set to GMT. On most PCs with mixed Linux/Windows operation this is not the case; the time is set to the local time. Thus the answer is NO.

MAKE LINUX BOOTABLE FROM HARDDISK

At this point, the installation program would install LILO on the hard disk. As with all other distributions, the advice is to skip this point and go to the next menu item.

MAKE A BOOT FLOPPY

The installation program prompts you to insert an empty diskette which is then formatted. Onto this diskette, a Linux kernel is copied from which the just installed system can be booted.

This terminates the first part of the installation. The computer is restarted, and if all goes well, Debian should start up from the freshly created boot diskette. Why reading the kernel file in Debian takes about five minutes remains a mystery; in other distributions, this takes only a couple of seconds. To avoid this endless waiting time, you should create your own boot diskette at a later stage (see page 181).

Package selection

After this computer restart, you are prompted to specify a password for `root` and to create one or more new users (again with passwords). The question about shadow passwords should be answered with YES (more security, no disadvantages worth mentioning). If you have not installed Debian on a Laptop, the installation program asks whether it should deactivate the PCMCIA module – again the answer is YES.

Now the task is to select the packages to be installed. (Up to now, only a minimal Linux system has been installed. Usually, however, you will also want to have editors, network programs, and so on, available.) To relieve you from having to make a selection for every single package, several predefined profiles are available, amongst others:

- basic (28 Mbytes)
- standard without X (140 Mbytes)
- workstation standard (450 Mbytes)
- dialup – home machine (480 Mbytes)

- server standard with FTP, WWW, DNS, NIS, POP, no X (50 Mbytes)
- server complete, plus maillist, backup, news, samba, squid (70 Mbytes)

The optimal choice is not easy: the more packages you install, the more configuration questions you will need to answer (instantly). 'Standard without X' is quite attractive – in this way you obtain a running system relatively quickly, and just need to install any additional packages you require manually at a later stage. (This obviously requires a fairly advanced knowledge of Linux – but without this knowledge, you would despair with Debian anyway.) After the selection of the required profile, `dselect` is started automatically.

`dselect` during first installation

This section briefly describes the steps needed to conclude the installation. It is followed by more detailed information on the handling of this program (for example, for later installation of a specific package).

Essentially, you need to execute the three commands ACCESS, UPDATE, and INSTALL, with INSTALL probably having to be repeated several times (each with a change of CD-ROM).

In ACCESS several variations to access the installation data are available. If the data is to be found on one or more CD-ROMs, you should select `multi_cd`.

> **CAUTION**
>
> To make the installation program really find all required packages, it is mandatory that the last binary CD is currently present in the CD-ROM drive when you select `multi_cd`!
>
> Usually, a Debian 2.1 distribution consists of four CDs. CDs 1 and 2 contain the binary packages, while CDs 3 and 4 contain the source code. In this case, CD 2 must be present in the drive. (This also applies if you have a fifth `contrib` CD. During a first installation, its contents play no role.)

Subsequently, you need to specify the device name of your CD-ROM drive. As a rule, you can simply accept the default `/dev/cdrom`. This is a link to the actual device; this link has already been created during the earlier installation steps.

Now `dselect` tries to find the paths leading to the packages. The *main* and *contrib* package groups are recognized automatically. The *non-free*, *non-US*, and *local* package groups, however, are mostly sought for in vain – they are usually not included on the installation CDs. Just indicate 'none.'

The next command is UPDATE. With this, `dselect` reads the list of available packages (which takes only a few seconds).

Finally, INSTALL starts the installation as such. It will promptly come up with an error message – `dselect` does not find an essential package on CD 2 and asks you to insert CD 1. Subsequently, you execute INSTALL again. An endless list of screen output follows in which `dselect` reports on which packages it is installing. From time to time, you are prompted for configuration specifications of packages. If you feel overstressed with this, you can nearly always carry out the configuration at a later stage or simply accept the proposed default settings with ↵. An overview of the configuration scripts available after termination of the installation can be obtained with the following command:

```
root#  ls /usr/sbin/*config
```

After all packages of CD 1 have been installed, you once more insert CD 2 and execute INSTALL again. (In rare cases it is even necessary to repeat this procedure several times for CD 1 and CD 2 – namely when the installation of individual packages is dependent on packages that are to be found on the other CD. Installation is only terminated when INSTALL no longer leads to the installation of further packages from any of the CDs.)

QUIT terminates `dselect`. This concludes the installation, and you can start working straight away.

dselect

`dselect` is the package management program of the Debian distribution. You are confronted with this program for the first time during installation – see above. Later, you will always need it when you install additional packages, update existing packages, or remove packages. `dselect` makes sure that programs do not interfere with each other and that all packages needed for the execution of a program are installed together with it (that is, observation of package dependencies, as with RPM-based distributions).

TIP Documentation on `dselect` can be found on CD 1 in the `doc` directory.

The main menu

```
0. [A]ccess      Choose the access method to use.
1. [U]pdate      Update list of available packages, if possible.
2. [S]elect      Request which packages you want on your system.
3. [I]nstall     Install and upgrade wanted packages.
4. [C]onfig      Configure any packages that are unconfigured.
5. [R]emove      Remove unwanted software.
6. [Q]uit        Quit dselect.
```

ACCESS

At this point you specify from where the packages are to be read. Usually, only three of the numerous variations are relevant:

`multi_cd`

Installation from a group of CDs. (Because of the large number of packages, it is not possible to accommodate all packages of an installation on one CD.)

`multi_nfs, multi_mount`

This is a variation of `multi_cd`, in which the same installation files are located in a directory of the file system or on a network server.

`apt` This abbreviation for 'a package tool' is new in Debian 2.1. In the long run, `apt` is supposed to completely supplant the `dselect` program and, in combination with `gnome-apt`, allow intuitive management of packages. Unfortunately, it has not come to that yet: `apt` is only at development stage.

The functions already accessible via `dselect`, however, allow you even now to install or update individual packages fairly easily from an adequately setup http or ftp archive. After selecting the `apt` option, you must specify an http or ftp address. Predefined addresses are those of the central Debian server (`www.debian.org` or `ftp.debian.org`). However, it is usually more sensible to use a local mirror. Alternatively, you can also specify a directory of the file system which contains a properly prepared archive.

UPDATE

This step does not update the installed packages, but an internal list which holds the information on which packages are available where and in which version. `dselect` needs this information not only for package selection but also for automatically updating all installed packages (for example, if the installation medium contains more recent versions than those originally installed). This information is stored in `/var/lib/dpkg/available`.

SELECT

This menu entry first leads to a help text and subsequently (after pressing [Spacebar]) to a nearly endless list showing all available and installed packages. In this list, you can select packages for installation and/or mark already installed packages for uninstallation. A simple [↵] terminates the package selection. (Details follow in the next subsection.)

INSTALL

The previously selected packages are now installed. At the same time, all packages are updated whose versions on the CD-ROM are more recent than the installed versions. (In itself, this automatic update is a sensible feature and helps to keep the distribution up-to-date at any possible occasion. Nevertheless, it can be quite irritating when you are suddenly confronted with a new version of a program, the configuration files no longer work, and so on. If you wish to prevent automatic update, you must use [=] during the SELECT phase to set the corresponding package on 'hold.')

CONFIG

Normally, you are prompted for configuration (if required) immediately during package installation. If errors occur, or if you want to do without configuration for the time being, you can carry it out at a later stage by means of CONFIG. Already configured packages are not affected: if you want to reconfigure these, you must manually start the `*config` scripts in `/usr/sbin`.

REMOVE
: Packages marked for uninstallation during SELECT are now removed. The configuration files are kept unless the package has been marked for complete deletion ('purge').

QUIT
: Terminates `dselect`.

Package selection

The part of `dselect` which is probably most difficult to understand is the package list, whose top part looks more or less like this:

```
dselect - main package listing (avail., priority) mark:+/=/- verbose:v help:?
EIOM Pri Section  Package      Inst.ver     Avail.ver    Description
    --- Up to date installed packages ---
 *** Req base     adduser      3.2          3.2          Add users and groups
 *** Req base     ae           962-14       962-14       Anthony's Editor -- a
 *** Req base     base-files   1.3.5        1.3.5        Debian Base System
                  ...
    --- Available packages (not currently installed) ---
  __ Opt x11      9fonts       <none>       1-4          libXg UTF fonts for X
  __ Opt x11      9menu        <none>       1.4-6        Creates X menus from
```

Some brief information on the meanings of the individual columns: the letters EIOM stand for *error*, *installed*, *old mark*, and *marked for*. Differences between the O and M colums can occur if `dselect` detects a conflict in the dependencies and changes the setting in the M column (see below).

Column E (error)
Space: normal state.
`R` (for *reinstallation*): error during a previous installation attempt, the package needs to be reinstalled.

Column I (installed)
Space: neither the package nor any configuration files are installed.
`*` the package is installed.
`-` the package is not installed, but there are configuration files left from a previous installation.
U, C or I: the package is installed, but an error has occurred during installation.

Columns O (old mark), M (marked)
`*` the package is to be installed
`-` the package is to be removed, but configuration files are to be kept.
`_` the package is to be removed together with its configuration files.
`=` the package is to be left untouched ('hold', block automatic update).
`n` the package is new; no installation information is available.

Column Pri (priority)
This column specifies how important the package is for the system. Possible values are Req (*required*), Imp (*important*), Std (*standard*), Opt (*optional*), or Xtr (*extra*).

Column Section
This column assigns the package to a class. Possible classes are: admin, base, comm, contrib, doc, devel, editors, electronics, games, graphics, hamradio, interpreters, libs, mail, math, misc, net, news, non-free, otherosfs (tools or files systems for other operating systems), shells, sound, tex, text, utils, web, and x11.

The remaining columns are easier to describe: package name, currently installed version number, version number of the package on the CD-ROM, plus a brief description. A more extensive description can be found in the lower half of the screen. With [I] you toggle between the different modes of the info text, which you can leaf through (where possible) with [U] and [D].

`dselect` keyboard shortcuts	
[Cursor keys]	selection of packages or package groups
[Home], [End]	jump to beginning or end of the list
[N], [P]	if the cursor keys do not work (previous/next)
[Shift]+[B], [Shift]+[F]	scroll package text sideways
[/]	search for text
[\]	repeat search
[+], [Ins]	install package
[-], [Del]	uninstall package (delete)
[_]	uninstall package, also deleting modified configuration files
[=]	do not change state of installation
[V]	display state of installation extensively (verbose) or in short form
[O]	change sort order and grouping of displayed packages
[I]	change info text in the lower screen half (package info, installation state, dependencies)
[U], [D]	leaf through longer info texts (up/down)
[↵]	quit package list; back to main menu
[?]	display help text

Usually, package selection works in this way: you search for individual packages (mostly with [/], sometimes through appropriate sorting) and mark them with [+] for installation or with [-] for uninstallation. When you think that you have carried out all required settings you leave the package list with [↵] and carry out installation and uninstallation with the following two items of the main menu.

Package dependencies

As soon as you select a package that requires another package, a new screen appears with the list of all missing packages. This list shows all packages that should be installed as well. Required packages are already marked for installation, while packages which are only recommended are not marked. The following lines show unresolved package dependencies of the installation of `tkman`.

```
_* Xtr non-free  tkman   A graphical, hypertext, manual page browser.
_* Opt libs      tk42    The Tk toolkit for TCL and X11 v4.2 - Run-Time
_* Xtr non-free  rman    RosettaMan - Reverse compile man pages
_* Opt libs      tcl76   The Tool Command Language (TCL) v7.6 - Run-Time

tkman depends on tk42
tkman depends on rman
tk42 depends on tcl76 (>= 7.6-0)
```

In the simplest case, you leave the dependency page with [↵]. In this case, you simply accept all default settings suggested by `dselect`.

However, before you press [↵], you can also use [+] or [-] to select or deselect optional packages for installation, thus changing the defaults. It is, however, not possible to leave the dependency page as long as there are unresolved package dependencies. (You can force acceptance of your settings with [Q] if you really know what you are doing.)

If the extent of installation of the required packages is too large, and you wish to undo the selection of the package that caused the conflict, just press [X].

dpkg

While `dselect` provides a more or less user-friendly interface for package installation and management, the same tasks can also be achieved by means of the command option driven `dpkg` command.

As a Debian user, you usually manage with `dpkg`. `dpkg` is an efficient alternative to `dselect`, if you quickly want to install an individual package (for example, from an additional contrib CD). The different `dpkg-xyz` commands, instead, are mostly only of interest if you want to build your own packages.

Information on installed and available packages (no matter whether they were installed with `dselect` or `dpkg`) can be found in `/var/lib/dpkg`. Documentation on the installed packages that goes beyond the `man` and `info` texts can usually be found in `/usr/doc/`*`package_name`*.

```
dpkg --install package_file
```

This installs the specified package. If an older version is already installed, it is replaced with the new version. The following example shows the installation of the graphics program `xv`, which is included as a *non-free* package on the contrib CD.

```
#   dpkg --install /cdrom/debian/non-free/binary-i386/graphics/xv_3.10a-
20.deb
Selecting previously deselected package xv.
(Reading database ... 45374 files and directories currently installed.)
Unpacking xv (from .../graphics/xv_3.10a-20.deb) ...
Setting up xv (3.10a-20) ...
Update-menus: waiting for dpkg to finish(forking to background)
Update-menus: (checking /var/lib/dpkg/lock)
```

```
dpkg --configure package_name
```

This reconfigures an installed package. Please note that you need not specify the full file name (with the extension `*.deb`), but only the package name without path and extension.

```
dpkg --remove package_name
dpkg --purge package_name
```

These two commands remove the specified packages. In the second variation, the configuration files are deleted as well.

```
dpkg --list
dpkg --list 'pattern'
```

In the first syntax variation, `dpkg` displays all effectively installed packages. The second variation also considers all non-installed packages that had been registered as available during the last `dselect` in the menu item UPDATE.

```
dpkg --listfiles package_name
```

This command shows all files of a package. The command works only with installed packages. The contents of non-installed packages can be displayed by means of `dpkg-deb --contents file_name`.

```
dpkg --search file_name
```

In this syntax variation, `dpkg` searches for the package which contains the specified file. For example, `dpkg --search /etc/aliases` yields the package name `sendmail` (provided that `sendmail` is installed and the file `/etc/aliases` exists).

Peculiarities of Debian

Init-V process

Debian has the following Init levels:

```
0 - Halt                  2, 3, 4, 5 - Multi User
1 - Single User           6          - Reboot
```

Level 2 is considered the default level. Levels 2 to 5 do not differ from each other in the Debian default configuration. The `/etc/rc?.d` directories contain symbolic links to the corresponding Init scripts which are centrally stored in `/etc/init.d`.

The script `/etc/init.d/rcS`, which is executed immediately after system start-up, has a special significance. In it, all scripts of the `/etc/rcS.d` are executed. Thus, in contrast to most of the other distributions, Debian has no central initialization file. Instead, initialization is carried out, in the same way as a runlevel change, through a whole group of script files. This concept facilitates maintenance and makes later installation of additional components much easier.

RedHat 6.0

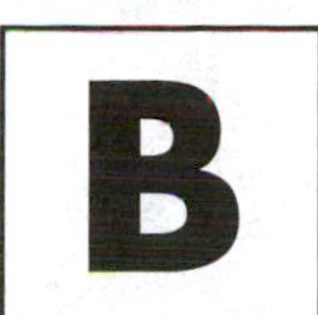

RedHat is probably the most popular and most widely available distribution in the English-speaking world. A whole range of other distributions are derived from RedHat. This appendix describes the installation and some of the features of the RedHat 6.0 distribution (such as `linuxconf` and `gnorpm`).

RedHat Linux comes out on top because of its easy installation and a number of modern tools for system administration. One of the strong points of this distribution is the transparent handling of bugs and security problems. As soon as problems with individual packages of the RedHat distribution become known, RedHat's Web site immediately shows warnings and advice and, as a rule, provides updates of the affected packages. This allows you to keep a RedHat system up-to-date with relatively little effort and without having to carry out a whole distribution update.

Internet

As usual, the most up-to-date information about the RedHat distribution can be found on the Internet:

```
http://www.redhat.com
  /support/                          (documentation)
  /support/docs/errata.html          (errata, bug fixes)
  /support/docs/hardware.html        (hardware compatibility)
http://archive.redhat.com            (mail archive)
ftp://ftp.redhat.com                 (FTP server)
http://www.redhat.com/mirrors.html   (mirror list)
```

Although the extent of RedHat has grown with every new version, the number of officially supplied packages is relatively low when compared with other distributions. If you think that program packages are missing, you should first take a look at the Linux Powertools, a collection of additional programs also maintained by RedHat. The Powertools are sold by RedHat as a separate product, but they are also available on the FTP server and are sometimes included on RedHat CDs from third-party distributors.

The `contrib` directory of the FTP server is a kind of second choice, because here you can find countless RPM packages with more or less exotic programs. The difference from the Powertools is that there is not such extensive quality control for the `contrib` directory – thus nobody guarantees that the programs actually work, and so forth (although, quite obviously, this is usually the case).

Installation

NOTE This section is based on Chapter 2, which gives you general information on the installation of Linux, such as repartitioning your hard disk with `FIPS` or `FDISK`, creation of installation diskettes with `RAWRITE`, usage of the Linux program `fdisk`, and so on.

TIP If you have no printed copy of the RedHat manual, you can also find it on the first CD-ROM, in an HTML version which you can also read under Windows prior to installation. The starting point is:

```
/cdrom/doc/rhmanual/manual/index.htm
```

Starting the installation

If you own a modern motherboard and/or BIOS, installation starts directly from the CD-ROM. If this is not the case, take a look at your BIOS settings: maybe booting from CD-ROM is deactivated.

If direct installation from CD-ROM does not work, you need to create one or two installation diskettes. Under DOS, or in a DOS window under Windows, you will need to execute the following command (where `X:` stands for the drive letter of your CD-ROM drive).

```
> X:\DOSUTILS\RAWRITE -f X:\IMAGES\BOOT.IMG -d A:
```

If you already have a Linux system installed, you can obviously create the two diskettes under Linux:

```
root# dd if=/cdrom/images/boot.img of=/dev/fd0 bs=1440k
```

If, during the installation, you want to access PCMCIA components of your notebook, or if installation data is to be read from a network server, you will need a second diskette. You can create it in the same way as the boot diskette, specifying `pcmcia.img` or `bootnet.img` as file names.

Types of installation

Independently of whether the installation is started from diskette or CD-ROM, you can now choose between three types of installation: *Expert*, *Kickstart*, or a normal installation (simply press ↵). The *Expert* variation allows individual specification of your hardware components; this becomes necessary when the automatic hardware recognition of the standard installation fails (thus, only rarely). The *Kickstart* variation allows an unsupervised installation in which all settings are read from an appropriate configuration file. This variation is particularly suited for carrying out the same RedHat installation on a number of computers. This appendix only describes the interactive standard installation.

The first questions of the standard installation concern the required language of the installation program and the selection of a (non-English) keyboard layout (`xx-latin1`, where `xx` stands for the required language). Subsequently, you can opt for one of several installation methods.

Installation methods

Properly speaking, this term refers only to the data source used for the installation. Once again, this appendix describes only the most widely used variation, namely the installation from a CD-ROM. As the data medium, you will select the local CD-ROM drive. The installation program automatically tries to recognize the CD-ROM drive; usually with success, even if it is connected to a SCSI card. Only if this does not work will you need to supply information on the drive type yourself.

A few words on the other variations (more information can be found in the online manual):

Hard disk

This variation is sensible if during installation no access to the CD-ROM drive is possible. In this case, prior to installation, the CD-ROM directories `RedHat/base` and `RedHat/RPMS` must be copied into a directory on the hard disk (the fact that the file names are truncated to 8+3 characters plays no role). The main problem of this installation variation is that you need a vast amount of additional space on your hard disk.

NFS

The installation data needs to be located on a Unix or Linux system which is addressed via a network. Thus, the variation assumes the existence of a local network. Furthermore, the computer must be configured in such a way that you can mount a network drive as a directory into the local file system. For this, you will need to know the IP number under which the computer containing the RedHat data can be addressed, and in which directory the installation data is located.

FTP/http

The preconditions for these two variations are similar to those of the NFS variation; however, different network protocols are used.

If you have already installed a RedHat version, you can now choose between a reinstallation or an update. Although an update should theoretically be possible, in practice it often creates more problems than it solves. Never take it for granted that an update attempt will end with a running system! Always make a complete backup of your personal data first. The following text assumes that you are installing RedHat from scratch.

Installation classes

From version 6, RedHat Linux supports three so-called installation classes: *Workstation*, *Server*, and *Custom*. If you are in doubt, you should choose *Custom*!

With the *Workstation* installation, all existing Linux partitions are deleted; with a *Server* installation, you also lose all other partitions (including Windows partitions). In both cases you have no influence on the size of the new Linux partitions. These two installation classes are mainly suited to a quick installation of Linux on new computers.

CAUTION

Let us repeat this: if you choose a *Workstation* or *Server* installation, all existing (Linux) partitions on all accessible hard disks are deleted! The installation program repartitions the hard disk(s) completely by itself. This takes away the burden of having to make some decisions, but you also lose a lot of control.

Hard disk partitioning (Disk Druid)

In the *Custom* installation, the next task is to create new Linux partitions in the free space of the hard disk. You have the choice between two programs: `fdisk` (see page 33) or the more user-friendly Disk Druid (a proprietary RedHat development). At this point, only the Disk Druid is described.

The program is controlled by means of [Tab] and/or function keys. The dialog for creation of a new partition is opened with [F1]. Here you must specify three details: the mount point (that is, the point at which the partition is integrated into the Linux file system), the required size of the partition, and the partition type (LINUX NATIVE or LINUX SWAP).

As options you can specify whether the partition should be GROWABLE, and on which hard disks the partition may be created (only if you have several hard disks). GROWABLE means that the Disk Druid automatically creates a larger partition if more space is available. If you select this option even with only one partition, the entire hard disk is filled. It is usually better to deactivate this option; when you need more space, you can still create additional Linux or Windows partitions at a later stage.

If there are partitions left over from a previous Linux installation which you would like to use, you can specify their mount points with [F3]. (Specifications of partitions to be formatted follow later.)

The Disk Druid is terminated with OK. Only now are you asked to confirm that you really want to carry out the changes. (Never modify any existing DOS or Windows partitions!)

In the following installation steps you are asked which partition marked as LINUX SWAP should effectively be used as the swap partition (just press [↵]), and which partitions are to be formatted. In a first installation, all partitions need to be indicated (selection by means of the [Spacebar]).

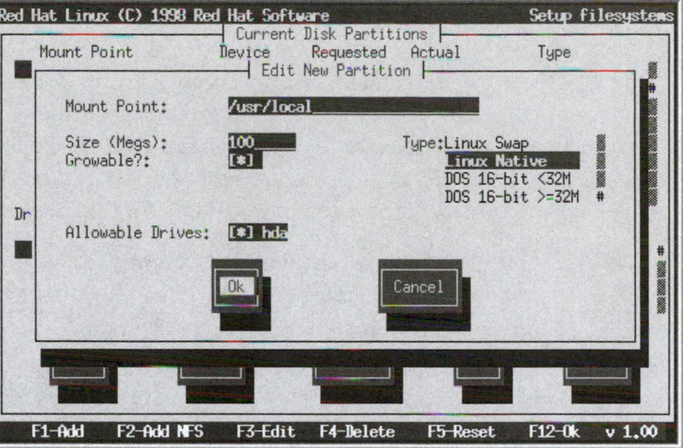

Figure B.1 Hard disk partitioning with the Disk Druid.

> **TIP** During installation, four screens (so-called text consoles) are shown between which you can switch: Alt+F2 allows direct input of Linux commands (for experts only), Alt+F3 displays various status messages, Alt+F4 shows error messages, and Alt+F1 takes you back to the installation program.

Package selection

Next, the components to be installed are selected. The following components are available:

```
* Printer Support               IPX/Netware(tm) Connectivity
X Window System                 Anonymous FTP Server
GNOME                           Web Server
KDE                             DNS Name Server
Mail/WWW/News Tools             Postgres (SQL) Server
DOS/Windows Connectivity        Network Management Workstation
File Managers                   TeX Document Formatting
Graphics Manipulation           Emacs
Console Games                   Emacs with X windows
X Games                         C Development
Console Multimedia              Development Libraries
X multimedia support            C++ Development
Networked Workstation           X Development
Dialup Workstation              GNOME Development
News Server                     Kernel Development
NFS Server                      Extra Documentation
SMB (Samba) Connectivity
```

If you select the components marked with `*` you will obtain a fairly solid base configuration (space requirement about 450 Mbytes). Unfortunately, it is not possible to specify the sizes of the individual components because they overlap considerably.

If during component selection you activate the option SETUP INDIVIDUAL PACKAGES, you can subsequently individually activate or deactivate single packages of the various components. Generally, however, it makes little sense to invest a lot of time in package selection during installation – once your installation has succeeded, you can always use the `rpm` or `gnorpm` tools for this purpose.

> **NOTE** Composition of the components is controlled by the file `RedHat/base/comps` on the installation CD-ROM. This text file contains a list of all packages that are installed per component. This file can be of valuable help if at a later stage you want to install additional packages: `gnorpm` does not recognize components but displays all available packages in a different hierarchy.

After selection of the required components and packages, these are installed into the previously created partitions. This process takes several minutes; progress is indicated with a bar diagram. (A log of all installed packages can be found after installation in `/tmp/install.log`.)

Basic configuration

In many cases, the mouse is recognized automatically – you only need to confirm the selection. If your computer is connected to a local network, you can next proceed with the configuration of network card and network parameters. Even if you do without this, the basic TCP/IP functions are initialized to enable Linux programs to use this protocol for local communication. Then, your computer simply receives the name `localhost.localdomain`.

When configuring the time, you need to specify whether the CMOS clock of your computer is set to GMT (Greenwich Mean Time) or local time. Local time will probably be the rule. Furthermore, you need to specify the required time zone (for example Europe / Berlin). In the system services configuration, you can simply confirm the default setting with ↵.

Printer set-up is of particular interest if you do not possess a PostScript printer. In this case, a filter is created which, by means of `gs`, converts PostScript files into the format of the relevant printer. This configuration step too can be carried out at a later time (using the `printtool` command under X).

Next, you are prompted to enter a password for `root`. In a further dialog you are asked whether you need NIS (common password management in a network), whether you want to use shadow passwords (this is more secure), and whether you want to use MD5 passwords (this allows passwords of up to 256 characters length instead of the usual restriction to 8 characters). By default, NIS is deactivated, while shadow and MD5 passwords are activated; as a rule, you should simply accept this setting.

The question about creation of a boot diskette should in any case be answered with YES. Subsequently, you can install LILO either into the Master Boot Record (MBR) of your hard disk or into the root partition. And once more the all-important warning: never ever trust an installation program to install LILO into the MBR! Use your freshly created boot diskette for your first tests with Linux and defer the LILO configuration until you have become more familiar with Linux.

X configuration (`Xconfigurator`)

As the last step, the setup program begins to configure the X Window system. (If this leads to a crash – which is improbable, but cannot be totally excluded – the remaining configuration remains valid; that is, you can start the newly installed Linux at least in text mode and make another attempt to configure X.)

For configuration of XFree86 (see also Chapter 7) the RedHat-specific `Xconfigurator` program is started. It tries to automatically recognize your graphics card on the basis of the PCI information. If this does not work, you will need to specify your type of graphics card yourself.

The monitor specifications that follow decide at which resolution and frequency the graphics mode will function. If you do not find your monitor in the list of predefined monitors, you need to select CUSTOM. Now you can select a menu item according to the technical specifications of your monitor (for example 1024×768 pixels at 70 Hz). Do not select too high a resolution or frequency, or you will risk the premature demise of your monitor. The allowed frequency range of your monitor is asked for again in an additional dialog (for example 50–100 Hz).

Recognition of the graphics card and its ratings (for example, the available video memory) is again carried out automatically. On the basis of this information and the monitor data, the configuration program automatically selects a suitable grahics mode. Alternatively, you can specify one or more graphics modes manually. (You can later toggle between these modes with Ctrl+(+) on the numeric keypad.)

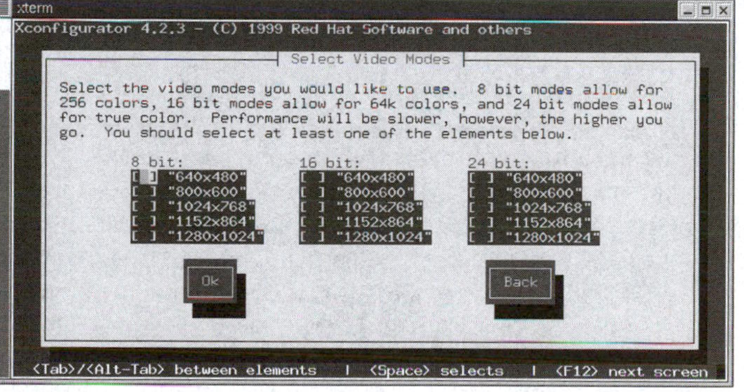

Figure B.2 Graphics mode selection with `Xconfigurator`.

> **TIP** If problems occur with the configuration, you can also execute `Xconfigurator` again at a later time, after termination of the installation. As an alternative, you can also employ the `XF86Setup` program described on page 230; however, before it can be used, it must first be installed by means of `rpm`.

This concludes the installation. After restarting your computer, Linux should come up with the login prompt – enter `root` and your password.

System optimization

Information on updates for fixing bugs and security gaps can be found on the Internet at the following address:

```
http://www.redhat.com/support/docs/errata.html
```

On many RedHat CDs, the update packages listed there are included with the distribution (usually in the `updates` directory) , provided they were available at the time of pressing the CD.

Obviously, you only need to carry out an update if you have installed the affected package. You can easily find this out with `rpm -q name`. The command for an update is simply `rpm -U file_name.rpm`.

Configuration details

In principle, you now have a functioning Linux system. To make it run perfectly, however, some minor modifications are needed. The following measures are recommendations which (in the author's opinion) significantly improve working comfort with RedHat Linux. However, the extent to which you want to follow these recommendations is obviously left to you. (Even more configuration hints and tips are included in Chapter 6.)

Default desktop

The default desktop system is GNOME. Alternatives are (provided they are installed) 'Another Level' known from earlier RedHat versions (a complex `fvwm` menu system) and KDE. To set the default system, you simply use the `switchdesk` program, which modifies the file `~/.Xclients` or `~/.Xclients-xxx`.

Keyboard focus in new windows

If you use GNOME in combination with the window manager Enlightenment (this is the default setting), you will probably be irritated by the fact that new windows do not automatically receive the keyboard focus. To remedy this nuisance, you start the GNOME control center `gnomecc` and click the button RUN CONFIGURATION TOOL FOR ENLIGHTENMENTin the dialog sheet DESKTOP|WINDOW MANAGER, where you need to activate the BEHAVIOUR option ALL NEW (POPUP) WINDOWS GET THE KEYBOARD FOCUS. In the Enlightenment configuration dialog you will also find a vast number of other practical setting options.

Emacs special keys

In GNU Emacs, Del functions in the same way as Backspace. The following file `~/.emacs` corrects this misbehavior:

```
; ~/.emacs
(global-set-key [delete]       'delete-char)
(global-set-key [home]         'beginning-of-line)
(global-set-key [end]          'end-of-line)
```

Colors and special keys in `xterm/nxterm`

RedHat developers have an inexplicable predilection for black `(n)xterm` windows with tiny writing. If you want to enjoy your eyesight a little bit longer, a first-aid recommendation is to delete or rename `.Xdefaults`. Even better results are achieved with the following `.Xdefaults` file, which at the same time looks after proper functioning of the special keys.

```
! ~/.Xdefaults
*VT100.Translations: #override \
        <KeyPress>BackSpace: string(0x7f)\n\
        <KeyPress>Delete: string(0x04)\n
*VT100*font:        9x15
*VT100*background: White
*VT100*foreground: Black
xterm*scrollBar:    true
```

Unfortunately, these setting have no validity for `gnome-terminal`. Here you can easily change the color scheme via a menu, but a configuration possibility for [Del] seems to be lacking. Use [Ctrl]+[D] instead.

Confirmation prompts with `mv` and `rm`

When you work as `root`, during execution of `mv` and `rm` continuous prompts appear for confirmation of whether you really want to carry out the operation. These confirmation prompts stop when you remove the `alias` instructions from `~/.bashrc`.

Display system messages at start-up

During start-up of Linux the kernel and various Init-V scripts display messages on screen. However, these messages are deleted as soon as the login prompt appears. Since these messages may under certain circumstance allow conclusions to be drawn on possible configuration problems, this behavior is not very smart. This can be remedied with a small modification in `/etc/inittab`: add the option `--noclear` at the start of `mingetty` for console 1.

```
# /etc/inittab
1:12345:respawn:/sbin/mingetty --noclear tty1
```

Control Panel

The `control-panel` program can be started by `root`. It allows an easy start of the RedHat configuration tools, which are described in the following subsections.

The individual tools can obviously also be started directly, without using `control-panel`. Despite the user-friendly interface, handling of these programs assumes a solid background knowledge. If in doubt, read the sections on manual configuration of the affected files (Chapter 6).

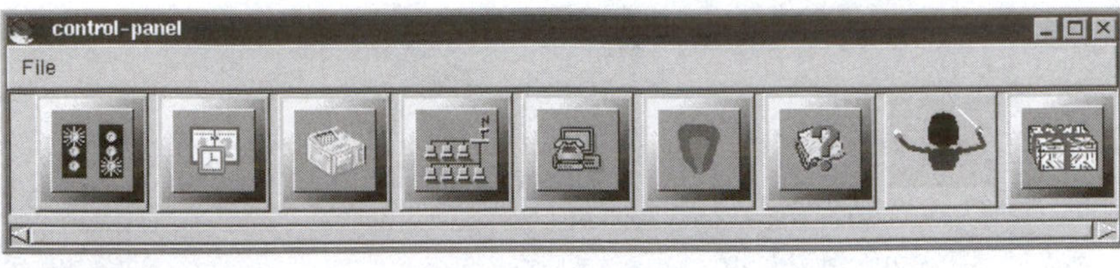

Figure B.3 The Control Panel.

NOTE

RedHat Linux is currently in a transition phase, moving away from RedHat-specific tools for each conceivable configuration task, towards `linuxconf` (see page 730). The problem is that `linuxconf` is not yet fully matured and still does not cover all areas of configuration. For this reason, there are *two* configuration programs for some aspects (for example network configuration) which are not really compatible neither in their handling nor in their function. In case of doubt, try `linuxconf` first!

Runlevel editor

`tksysv` is a user-friendly program for controlling the Init-V process. Via mouse click, you can determine which processes and daemons are to be started or stopped at which runlevel. But do not be blinded by the pretty interface: changing the Init process assumes some very solid background knowledge. A short description of the System V Init process can be obtained with the HELP command. More information can be found on page 124.

Printer configuration

Printers can be set up with `printtool` (also via network). This modifies the files `/etc/printcap` and `/var/spool/lpd/lp/filter`. If you do not have a PostScript printer, `gs` is called upon to convert the PostScript format into the format of the printer.

Network administration

With `netcfg` you can set the host name, create network interfaces (Ethernet, PPP, SLIP), and so on. Amongst others, `netcfg` modifies the files `/etc/HOSTNAME`, `/etc/hosts`, `/etc/resolv.conf`, `/etc/sysconfig/network`, and files in the `/etc/sysconfig/network-scripts` directory. Please note that a large part of the work carried out with `netcfg` can also be done with `linuxconf`.

Some more tips if you have manually changed the configuration files and nothing works any more: the name specified in `/etc/HOSTNAME` must in `/etc/hosts` be assigned an IP number of a running network. (Simply test `ping $HOSTNAME`.) With a non-networked computer, in `hosts` the loopback device must be assigned the name `localhost` and the computer name.

During system start-up a connection with the local network is only established if `/etc/sysconfig/network-scripts` contains the file `ifcfg-eth0` with the assignment of network parameters to various variables. (The file is created and/or deleted

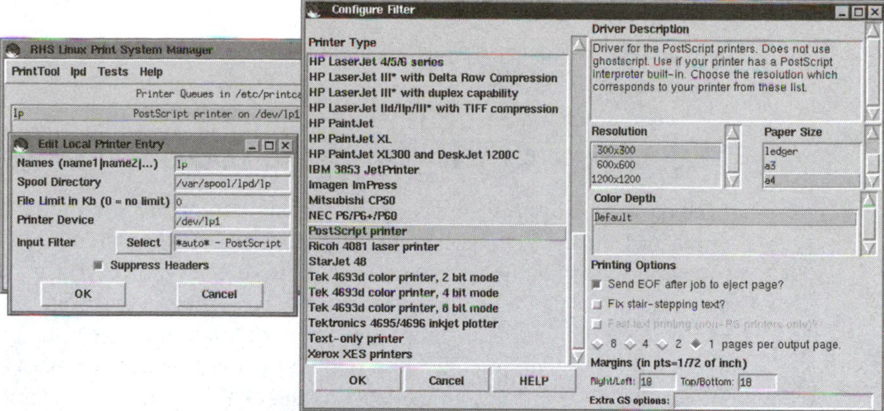

Figure B.4 Printer configuration with `printtool`.

by `netcfg` or `linuxconf`.) In the event of problems, take a look at the fundamentals section on the System V Init process (page 125) and the section on network configuration (page 171).

Setting up the modem interface

With `modemtool` you can select the serial interface for the modem. The program merely establishes a link from `/dev/modem` to the inteface (`/dev/ttyS`*n*). If you use `linuxconf` for PPP configuration, you can entirely do without `modemtool`.

Administration of the kernel daemon

`kernelcfg` is addressed to advanced Linux users. It is used to configure the kernel daemon, which cares for automatic loading of kernel modules as soon as they are needed. `kernelcfg` modifies the configuration file `/etc/conf.modules`.

Looking for online documentation

`helptool` helps with searching for online documentation. The program considers all `man` and `info` texts together with the files in the `/usr/doc` directory. However, the program does not carry out a full text search for `/usr/doc` and is therefore not able to find information in FAQs or READMEs.

> TIP
> A good cross-reference on RedHat info subjects is provided by the `*.html` file `/usr/doc/HTML/index.html`. This page contains links both to local files and to the RedHat Web server.

System configuration

Behind this icon we find the already mentioned `linuxconf` program. Details follow in the next section.

Package management

`gnorpm` (the successor of `glint`) allows user-friendly (de-)installation of packages (see page 732).

The Linux Configuration Tool (`linuxconf`)

`linuxconf` is a fascinating project. It attempts to create a unique configuration program for Linux which, on the one hand, has several user interfaces (command mode for Script programming, text mode, graphic mode, and control via a Web browser) and which, on the other hand, is suitable for different distributions. In contrast to many other configuration programs (in particular from the Windows world) `linuxconf` does not simply change a couple of files, but also ensures that the affected programs are started and stopped again (and all this without restarting the computer!).

In the present version, however, the program does not yet fully meet these goals. Probably the biggest problem is that the different Linux distributions widely differ in their configuration details (and that a lot of know-how and work has been invested in them). Therefore it is small wonder that, on the one hand, it is difficult for `linuxconf` to be compatible with all distributions and that, on the other hand, the individual distributors are reluctant to simply give up their own configuration concepts in favor of `linuxconf`. Furthermore, at this moment, `linuxconf` is not yet at all able to cover all aspects of configuration.

Currently `linuxconf` is reasonably well integrated only into the RedHat distribution (and even here many problems are still present). For this reason, the program is described in this appendix and not in Chapter 6 on configuration.

NOTE

Although help texts are available for most `linuxconf` dialogs, there is no introductory documentation. A good overview of the `linuxconf` project is given by the following Web site:

`http://www.solucorp.qc.ca/linuxconf/`

The currently most comprehensive instructions for use of `linuxconf`, however, are hidden in Chapter 8 of the RedHat manual, whose online installation is worthwhile for this reason alone.

Start

When you start `linuxconf` under X, a variation of `linuxconf` adapted to the GNOME project appears. If you do not start `linuxconf` as `root` you can use the program only after entering the `root` password.

If, however, you wish to use `linuxconf` in text mode, you must specify the option `--text` at start-up. Visually appealing results under X are only obtained when the program is executed in an `nxterm` window (not `xterm`). In the text console you should use `setfont` to activate a character set with outline characters prior to the start – otherwise the dialogs will look appalling. Suitable character sets are `lat1-16` or `lat1-08` of you work with 80×50 characters.

The third variation – control of `linuxconf` via a Web browser – is particularly attractive for administration of remote computers via a network connection. For security reasons, however, this variation is deactivated. To activate it, start `linuxconf` in text mode or under X and change the settings in the NETWORKING|MISC|LINUXCONF NETWORK ACCESS dialog . Subsequently you can access `linuxconf` with any Web browser (including `lynx`). The address is ***computer_name:98***, thus for example `http://localhost:98/`. However, before you can carry out any modifications, you will need to log in (`root` plus password).

Usage

The following description assumes that you work with the X variation of `linuxconf`. In the left-hand window area, a hierarchical list is displayed. Each entry in this list corresponds to one of the several configuration dialogs. As soon as you click on a list entry, the corresponding dialog appears in the right-hand window area. For many dialogs, HELP displays a (sometimes quite extensive) help text.

A slightly unconventional behavior of `linuxconf` comes to light when, after checking the dialog, you discard it as unfit and select another one: now both dialogs, the old one and the new one, are displayed on top of each other just like Windows dialog sheets. Because of the space requirement for the tab labeling, the `linuxconf` window quickly becomes wider. Remedy: you must close dialogs that are no longer needed explicitly by means of CANCEL, QUIT, or CLOSE.

Activation of changes

Usually, `linuxconf` carries out simple changes to configuration files directly with confirmation of the input via a dialog. Things look different when changes become effective only after the start of a new service (daemon). In this case, at the latest when you try to exit `linuxconf`, you are prompted for confirmation as to whether the change is really to be carried out. Only after you confirm the change at this point does the modified setting become active.

Users and groups (CONFIG|USER ACCOUNTS|NORMAL)

Creation of new users and groups creates no problems. At the same time, for each new user, a group of the same name is created automatically. Via the TASK button in the user dialog you can easily create `crontab` entries (which allow automatic execution of programs at regular intervals).

The dialogs of the SPECIAL ACCOUNTS subgroup allow creation of accounts for external users who log in via PPP. This is only sensible if the computer is configured as a PPP server (for example for an Internet service provider).

File system administration (CONFIG|FILE SYSTEMS)

In the ACCESS LOCAL DRIVE dialog you can mount partitions of the local hard disk into the directory tree. A particularly user-friendly feature is the many possibilities of setting options (including quotas). The ACCESS NFS VOLUME dialog fulfills the same task for NFS directories on remote computers. Both dialogs modify `/etc/fstab`.

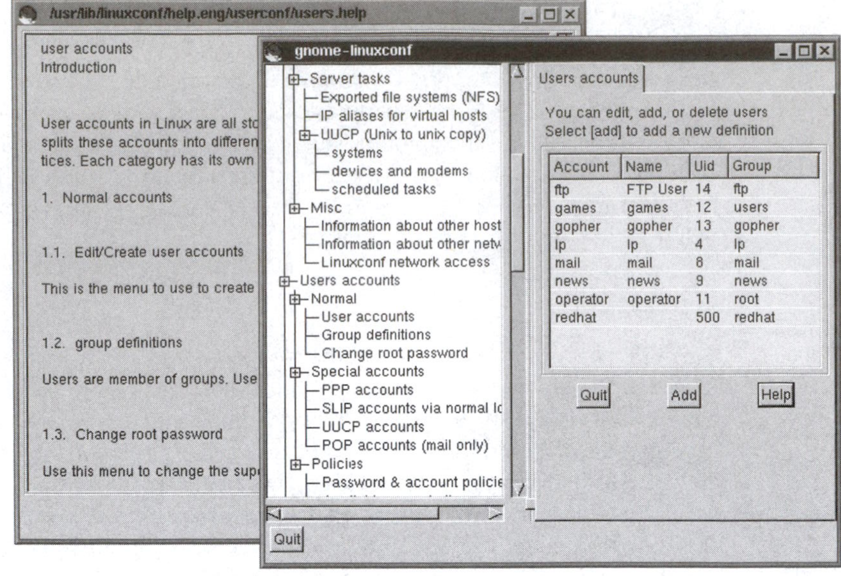

Figure B.5 User administration with `linuxconf`.

LILO configuration (CONFIG|BOOT MODE|LILO)

The dialogs for configuring LILO are not very convincing. They can only be used if you have enough knowledge to create `/etc/lilo.conf` yourself – and in this case you are better off with an editor.

Network configuration (CONFIG|NETWORKING)

This book cannot possibly cover all configuration possibilities for networks, for reasons of space. Elementary settings such as domain name and configuration of local network cards are carried out in BASIC HOST INFORMATION. For network cards, you must specify the required interface (usually `/dev/eth0`) and the required kernel module. In addition, you need to specify the IP number under which your computer can be reached in the local network, together with the complete network name (host and domain name). PPP configuration is carried out in the PPP/SLIP dialog and has already been described on page 320.

Date and time (CONTROL|DATE & TIME)

Here you can select the required time zone and specify whether your computer's CMOS is set to GMT or to local time (the normal case).

Package management with `gnorpm`

With RedHat version 6.0, the GNOME program `gnorpm` replaces `glint`, thus facilitating management of RedHat packages. The program can be handled more quickly and intuitively than `glint`. Compared with the installation tools of Debian or SuSE, however, the program has a long way to go before it can offer similar functionality. Thus it is RedHat of all companies (inventor and developer of the RPM package format) which is still incapable of resolving all unsatisfied package dependencies during the installation of new packages.

After the start, `gnorpm` displays all installed packages in a hierarchical order. (With RedHat 6.0 this hierarchy has been greatly simplified; it is now much clearer than before.)

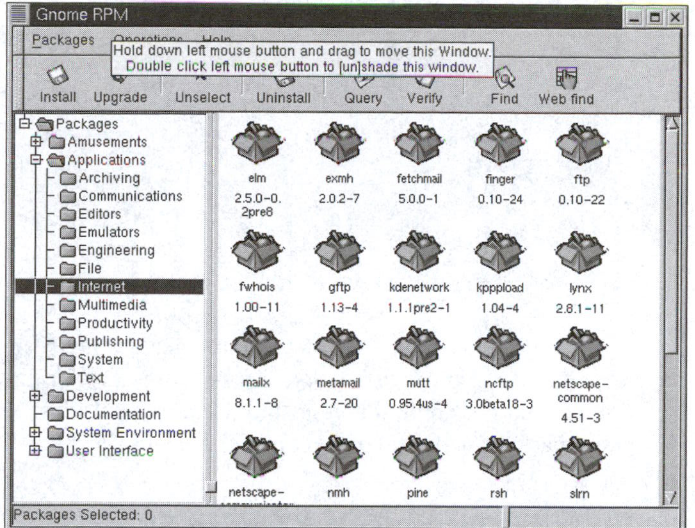

Figure B.6 `gnorpm` groups the packages by categories.

> **TIP**
> If you cannot find a package but are sure that it is installed you can also determine its place in the hierarchy by means of `rpm`. `rpm -qi perl`, for example, yields the short description of the installed Perl package. The `group` line gives information on where Perl is situated in the hierarchy (namely under Development/Languages). By the way, the hierarchy displayed in `gnorpm` has nothing to do with the components available during the first installation.

Individual packages can be selected with a click of the mouse. [Ctrl] or [Shift] plus mouse extends the selection as in common Windows usage. (You can even mark several packages which are located in different hierarchies at the same time. This often happens involuntarily – therefore be careful with uninstallation! Use UNSELECT to completely undo the selection carried out up to now.)

Three operations can be applied to selected packages: UNINSTALL, QUERY, and VERIFY.

UNINSTALL removes all files of the selected packages. (Files that are shared between several packages are only removed with the uninstallation of the last package.)

QUERY shows a list of all files of the selected package(s). Configuration files are marked with the letter C and files with online documentation with the letter D. (D mark-up is sometimes incomplete; `man` texts are often excluded.) What the letter S stands for is not documented. From the Query window, DETAILS takes you to another window which contains additional information about the package (space requirements, origin, version and release numbers, and so on).

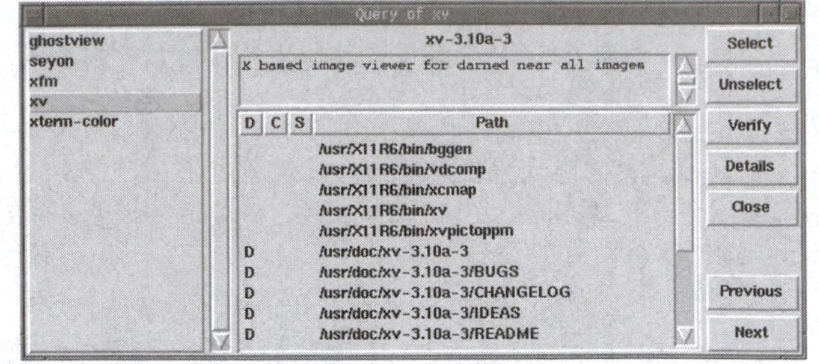

Figure B.7 The file list of the `emacs` package.

With VERIFY you can determine whether any files have been changed with respect to the original installation or may be missing. Unfortunately, however, `gnorpm` provides no possibility of (re)installing individual files. You can only uninstall the entire package and subsequently install it again.

Installation of new packages

Up to now, the description of `gnorpm` has referred only to already installed packages. Unfortunately, even in `gnorpm`, installation of new packages is not very intuitive. First, you need to use OPERATIONS|PREFERENCES|INTERFACE to specify the path where the RPM files are located. (With RedHat CDs this is usually `/cdrom/RedHat/RPMS` – but this obviously also depends on the point at which you have mounted the CD-ROM drive into your file system.)

Now you click the INSTALL button and, in the installation dialog, the button ADD. You can now select the required packages from an alphabetical file list. However, no hierarchy information is displayed, nor any hint as to whether the package is already installed. Thus, if you do not know the file name of the new package, you are practically lost. (Even `glint` offered more information in this regard.)

All selected packages are now displayed in a list of the installation dialog. With QUERY you can (only now!) show information regarding the contents of these packages.

INSTALL starts the installation. If the package is already installed, you now get an error message. An error message also occurs if the package is dependent on other packages. Unfortunately, however, `gnorpm` is not capable of simply installing the missing packages as well. You must therefore select the relevant packages yourself. With multi-level dependencies, this is often a laborious process.

Updating packages

A package update principally works in the same way as a new installation: you click the UPGRADE button and, as with a new installation, specify the required file names. (Against the UNINSTALL and INSTALL commands, UPGRADE has the advantage that copies (extension `*.rpmsave`) are created of all configuration files you modified.)

Finding packages

In already installed packages you can search for file names, dependencies, and so on, by means of the FIND command (for example to determine which package provides a specific file).

Provided you have an Internet connection, you can use WEBFIND to search even in non-installed packages. For this purpose, the program establishes a connection with an RPM database. (The location of the database is set with OPERATIONS|PREFERENCES|RPMFIND. The default setting is `http://www.redhat.com/RDF`.) After the required packages have been found there, they can be immediately downloaded and installed. (It would be nice if this worked also for packages on CD-ROMs.)

RedHat internals

PAM

Since version 4, RedHat is provided with PAM tools for authentication of users (login, and so on). PAM stands for *Pluggable Authentication Modules* and allows introduction of new and improved security systems. Configuration of PAM is carried out via the file `/etc/pam.conf`. Extensive documentation can be found in `/usr/doc/pam-`*n*.

Init-V process

RedHat recognizes the following Init levels:

```
0 - Halt                            3 - Multi-user (with network)
1 - Single User                     5 - X11 (xdm)
2 - Multi-user (without network)    6 - Reboot
```

Details of the Init process are described on page 125.

System kernel

RedHat generally installs a kernel without integrated SCSI support – even if RedHat has been installed on a SCSI hard disk. To make Linux bootable in spite of this, a RAM disk file is created (`/boot/initrd`) which, in the same way as the kernel, can be addressed by LILO. This RAM disk contains the modules used during installation.

To create this RAM disk, the RedHat-specific command `mkinitrd` is used. This command must be passed the file name of the `initrd` file to be created together with the kernel version number.

```
root# mkinitrd /boot/initrd 2.0.36-0.7
```

`mkinitrd` evaluates the information in `/etc/conf.modules`. If a SCSI adapter is required for booting, `conf.modules` must contain a line of the following form:

```
alias scsi_hostadapter aic7xxx
```

CAUTION

Because of this boot process, it is not possible in RedHat to simply copy `/boot/vmlinuz` onto a diskette and use this to boot a SCSI system. Instead, you must either use LILO with the option `initrd=/boot/initrd` or compile a new kernel in which SCSI support for your card is directly integrated.

Language settings

First a brief digression: at each start of a shell `/etc/profile` is executed. One peculiarity of RedHat is that in this script file all `*.sh` files in the `/etc/profile.d` directory are started. Out of these files, `lang.sh` is the one which is responsible for setting the required language (for example for GNOME menu texts).

However, the hide-and-seek game goes even further: `lang.sh` in turn resorts to `/etc/sysconfig/i18n`. (`i18n` is an abbreviation of 'internationalization' commonly used in the Unix world. Changes to this file must be carried out with an editor – currently neither the `control-panel` tools nor `linuxconf` can be used for this purpose. For the English language (US/UK) the following settings in `/etc/sysconfig/i18n` are of common use:

```
# /etc/sysconfig/i18n
LANG=C
LINGUAS=en
LC_ALL=en_US   or LC_ALL=en_UK
```

NOTE

Further information can be found in the `info` text about the GNU function `gettext` and on the Internet:

`http://www.vlsivie.tuwien.ac.at/mike/i18n.html`

SuSE 6.1

APPENDIX

The SuSE distribution is available in a German and in an international version (English menu commands, English manual). The main advantages of SuSE Linux include:

YaST (Yet another Setup Tool)
: This program is the central installation, configuration, and administration program of SuSE. It has now reached such a high degree of maturity that you will in most cases hardly ever need to modify a configuration file yourself.

Packages
: Many programs for which you otherwise would need to search the Internet or various other Linux CDs are an integral part of SuSE and can be installed at any time. The full version of the SuSE distribution currently consists of more than a thousand preconfigured software packages.

Manual
: The very practice-oriented manual has evidently profited from experience gained by the support department – seldom will you find so many hints and tips for the most disparate hardware and software problems.

SuSE on the Internet

SuSe's two Web sites have the following addresses:

```
http://www.suse.de
http://www.suse.com
```

A very valuable institution (even if you do not use SuSE) are the support and hardware databases which are currently available in several languages, but only on the German SuSE server.

```
http://www.suse.de/Support/sdb_e/
http://cdb.suse.de
```

An overview of known problems and bugs of SuSE 6.1 (obviously with solution suggestions) is given by the following text. (Similar articles are also available for earlier SuSE versions – and will hopefully be available for future versions as well.)

```
http://www.suse.de/Support/sdb_e/bugs61.html
```

If you miss a package (because you only have the trial version), or if you are looking for updates or want to take a look at the latest SuSE beta version, the SuSE FTP server and its numerous mirrors will help:

```
http://www.suse.de/ftp.html    (with mirror list)
ftp://ftp.suse.com
  /pub/contrib/i386/libc6/     (non-official extension packages)
  /pub/suse_update/            (updates/bugfixes)
  /pub/SuSE-Linux/             (current distributions)
  /pub/SuSE-Beta/              (beta versions)
```

If you are looking for an excellent SuSE manual, take a look at the `docu` directory in `SuSE-Linux` or `SuSE-Beta`.

Installation

REFERENCE

This section builds on Chapter 2 from page 17 onward, where general fundamentals of a Linux installation are described in great detail.

If you do not have a printed version of the SuSE manual, you can also find it on the first CD-ROM in the `docu` directory as DVI, compressed PostScript, PDF, and text files. While Linux is not yet up and running, the PDF variation is the most attractive one. In this format, you can read the manual for example under Windows and also print any pages you require. The only thing you need to do is install Adobe Acrobat Reader (which in many Windows systems is already the case anyway). You can find this program on the Internet at `www.adobe.com`.

Starting the installation

If you have a modern motherboard and/or BIOS, installation starts directly from the CD-ROM. If this is not the case, take a look at your BIOS settings: it may well be that booting from CD-ROMs is deactivated.

If a direct start is not possible, you will need to create a boot diskette. The easiest way to do this is by using the DOS program `SETUP.EXE`. The program can also be used under Windows 9x. If you want to write the boot diskette(s) manually (with `RAWRITE.EXE`), you will find the boot images in the `disks` directory of the first CD-ROM. Usually you would only need one diskette with the image `eide01`, but in rare cases you may need a second diskette `modules` with additional hardware modules.

`linuxrc`

To start the installation a minimal kernel is loaded which in turn starts the `linuxrc` program. This program allows a simple choice of kernel modules needed for the installation (SCSI, network, and CD-ROM drivers). By the way, if you use an EIDE or SCSI CD-ROM drive, you do not need any additional CD-ROM drivers. In the event of problems with linking kernel modules, the menu item SYSTEM INFORMATION displays information on the existing hardware and its resources.

`yast`

Once the hardware questions are cleared, the second phase of the installation begins, which is controlled by `yast`. The first decision to be made concerns the type of installation. Here we only deal with an INSTALL LINUX FROM SCRATCH installation. Other variations are UPDATE EXISTING LINUX SYSTEM or INSTALLATION USING EXPERT MODE.

Hard disk partitioning

The installation program asks whether it should simply use the whole disk for your Linux installation. In this case, `yast` looks after space assignment and partitioning itself. This may be easy, but it is usually more sensible to deny the question and carry out partitioning yourself. Here too, `yast` is of great help; that is, you will not be directly confronted with the user-unfriendly `fdisk` program.

Furthermore, you need to specify the mount point of partitions reserved for use with Linux. With this you decide which partition is to be mounted into the system and how/where it is to be mounted. Select the Linux partition with the cursor keys, press F4 and specify the mount point. For one partition, the mount point must be the root directory `/` (this is the system partition).

Finally, for a new installation, all Linux partitions need to be formatted. For this purpose you can select the relevant partitions with the cursor keys and press F6. (This only marks the partitions for later formatting; the actual formatting is only carried out after termination of the dialog and further prompts for confirmation.)

CAUTION

If `yast` does not find any free space on the hard disk, it ask whether it should simply use the entire hard disk for Linux (WHOLE HARD DISK). If you select this option (with a safety prompt requiring confirmation), you will lose all data stored on this hard disk! On page 23 you can find other alternatives for making room for a Linux installation.

Package selection

In the menu item LOAD CONFIGURATION you can choose between several preconfigured package collections. DEFAULT SYSTEM is usually the best choice. (This installs a 'Linux Base System (You need it!)' and a selection of important additional programs, such as KDE, Netscape, Emacs, and so on.)

Information on the required space can be obtained by executing the WHAT IF... command. In SuSE 6.1 the default variation requires a stately 730 Mbytes. If you want to save 150 Mbytes, you can execute CHANGE/CREATE CONFIGURATION and use D to deactivate all packages of the `aplx` group (demo version of ApplixWare Office). Pressing F10 twice takes you back to the main menu.

With START INSTALLATION the copy process begins, which may take several minutes. Subsequently, MAIN MENU takes you back to the installation program.

Basic configuration

Next you need to specify the boot kernel for the finished system. This is a modularized kernel, but what is important is that it includes all the parts needed for booting. Therefore SuSE presents several SCSI kernels for selection. Choose the kernel that matches your hard disk.

The question as to whether a boot diskette should be created should absolutely be answered with YES. As always, I strongly recommend against a LILO installation because of the risks connected with this – you can always do this later. (With a Windows 95 system, the chances that it will actually work are quite high for all distributions – but you never know. Anyway, the choice is yours...)

If your computer is not to be connected to a network, you can enter arbitrary character string for computer and domain names. If nothing better comes to mind, you can always use `myhost` and `mydomain`. In the TCP/IP configuration you will specify that you want to use the network only in loopback mode (that is locally). In this case, you can do without any further network configuration. In the `sendmail` configuration you can choose between several variations. The most sensible one is usually 'Name Server Access' (for example if at a later stage you establish Internet access via PPP and want to fetch email from your provider).

Now you need to enter a password for `root` twice. Selection of other screen fonts is rarely sensible. Instead, it is useful to create a sample user. As a name, you can, for example, use `suzy`.

The following mouse and modem configuration should create no problems. Mice connected to the PS/2 interface bear the cryptic name of 'C&T 82C710 or PS/2 mouse.' The correct interface for the modem is `/dev/ttyS0` (for COM1:) or `/dev/ttyS1` (for COM2:).

X configuration

At this point, the SuSE installation is finished and prompts you for login (first `root`, then the password). One point, however, is still open: the configuration of the XFree86 server. For this, you start `yast` and select the menu item ADMINISTRATION| XFREE86.

Here you have a choice between three configuration tools: SaX (SuSE advanced X Configuration), `xf86config` (a stone-age text-based tool), and `XF86Setup` (the standard configuration program of XFree86). At this point we only deal with SaX. Details on the other configuration programs (together with a lot of background information) can be found in Chapter 7. A clear statement on which is the 'best' configuration program is unfortunately impossible – depending on the hardware, sometimes one and sometimes another program works better.

Handling of SaX is very intuitive. The program tries to automatically recognize your hardware. Where this does not succeed, you need to supply the corresponding information yourself via mouse clicks. The program can also be entirely controlled via the keyboard (Alt together with a key, Tab), which is particularly important if the mouse is not immediately recognized.

If you do not find your monitor in the list, click on EXPERT and enter the ratings of your monitor (horizontal and vertical frequency range) directly.

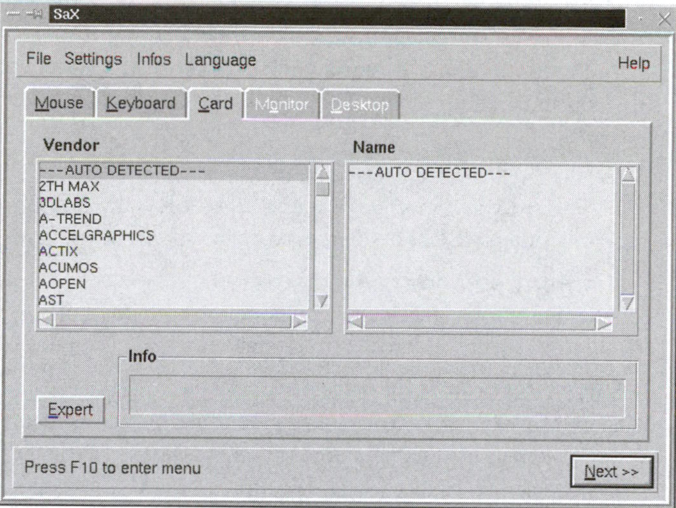

Figure C.1 Graphics card selection with SaX.

After selecting the graphics card, the program may signal that the corresponding X server is not yet installed. You then need to install this server with `yast` and start SaX once again. (If you already know which server you will be needing it is obviously much easier to install it prior to the first start of SaX.)

Start `yast`, select CHOOSE/INSTALL PACKAGES|CHANGE/CREATE CONFIGURATION, and select the appropriate server from the `xsrv` group. Pressing F10 twice takes you back to the Installation menu where you execute START INSTALLATION.

`yast`

`yast` is the acronym for *Yet another Setup Tool*, which is the central program of the SuSE distribution when it comes to system administration, integration of new hardware, and package management. Handling of `yast` with its multiply embedded menus and countless dialog levels reminds you of an adventure game, but apart from this the program has many advantages.

- `yast` is used both during and after the installation (whereas RedHat, for example, employs two different programs). No matter whether you configure your printer during the installation process or (re)configure it at a later stage – you are always faced with the same program.
- The program makes little requirements to the hardware.
- It is equipped with an excellent online help (F1).
- `yast` also takes on package management (Installation/Update/Deinstallation) and, as one of the few distributions discussed in this book, is capable of automatically resolving package dependencies.

Administration and configuration

You enter the administration part of `yast` via the SYSTEM ADMINISTRATION command in the main menu. The following list provides an overview of further alternatives:

INTEGRATE HARDWARE INTO SYSTEM
: Here you can change the settings of your mouse, modem, CD-ROM drives, printers, ISDN hardware, scanner, and network cards.

KERNEL AND BOOT CONFIGURATION
: Here you can select a new boot kernel (which in normal operation occurs rather infrequently), create a boot diskette, and configure LILO.

NETWORK CONFIGURATION
: Via submenu entries you can modify various aspects of the network connection, such as host name, name server, `sendmail`, network printers, ISDN, and PPP.

CONFIGURE LIVE-SYSTEM
: This command allows you to mount the Live file system of the last CD-ROM of the SuSE distribution into your system. This way you can try out a large part of the SuSE packages without installing them onto your (always too small) hard disk. Disadvantage: the CD-ROM is blocked by the Live CD and system start-up takes somewhat longer.

LOGIN CONFIGURATION
: Here you can set up your system in such a way that after system start-up a graphical login (either `xdm` or `kdm`) appears. However, please change the login only if both the base system and X are working reliably!

SETTINGS OF SUSEWM
: In this dialog you can set the default window manager for the entire system (that is, for all users). GNOME, however, is not among the alternatives presented in this dialog – more about the use of GNOME can be found on page 747.

  Obviously the window manager can also be set individually for each user, either by modifying the file `~/.xinitrc` or the environment variable `WINDOWMANAGER`.

  The `susewm` package is responsible for the fact that different X Window manager menus are available with which you can start (nearly) all installed programs. (In contrast to other distributions, these are not dummy menus most of whose entries lead to nothing because the programs are not installed.) These menus need to be updated at each software installation or uninstallation. This is the responsibility of the `SuSEconfig.wm` program. Since updating these menus takes some time, it can be completely switched off in the settings dialog, or at least restricted to a small number of window managers.

USER ADMINISTRATION and GROUP ADMINISTRATION
: These dialogs help with creation and assignment of new users and groups.

CREATE BACKUPS
: This menu item hosts a small backup program (see page 745).

SET THE CONSOLE FONT
: This allows you to change the character set used for the text console.

SET TIME ZONE
: If the time shown by `date` does not correspond to the actual time of day, you can select the correct time zone here.

CONFIGURE XFREE86
: This command selectively starts either SaX, `xf86config`, or `XF86Setup`.

CONFIGURE GPM
: `gpm` is the mouse server for the text console. The program is configured by means of the menu item HARDWARE|MOUSE. At this point, you can only specify whether the program should automatically be run at boot time. (If conflicts arise between `gpm` and XFree86, `gpm` should be deactivated.)

SECURITY SETTINGS
: Here you can specify several system security settings. As a rule, no change of the default values is needed. Background information is supplied by the online help via F1.

CHANGE CONFIGURATION FILE
: This menu item allows changing of the countless variables of the file `/etc/rc.config` or the files in the `/etc/rc.config.d` directory. It is, however, easier to use an editor for this purpose and subsequently execute the `SuSEconfig` program.

Package management

Before you can use the package functions of `yast` you need to tell the program in which drive the SuSE CD-ROMs are to be found. For this purpose you specify in ADJUSTMENTS OF INSTALLATION|SELECT INSTALLATION MEDIUM|INSTALLATION FROM CD-ROM via which interface (ATAPI EIDE, SCSI, or another specific interface) the drive is to be addressed.

> TIP
> Make sure at the start of `yast` that an arbitrary SuSE CD-ROM is present in the drive, but that the CD-ROM is not mounted into the file system. `yast` executes `mount` and `umount` on its own.

The package management component of `yast` is entered via the main menu entry CHOOSE/INSTALL PACKAGES. `yast` now reads a database of all available packages from the CD-ROM and displays a new menu. All commands described in the following paragraphs refer to this menu, not to the `yast` main menu.

The two menu items LOAD CONFIGURATION and SAVE CONFIGURATION allow you to mark a preselected choice of packages for installation and to save the current selection as a package profile. Both commands are of little importance during normal operation. (During installation, LOAD CONFIGURATION allows simple selection of a whole bundle of programs.)

Package selection

The most important command is without doubt CHANGE/CREATE CONFIGURATION. This takes you to a new dialog which contains several groups of packages (so-called series) (`a` for the base system, `kde` for KDE components, and so on). From each of these groups you can select individual programs and mark them for installation. The space required for the packages installed from each group is indicated in square brackets. F10 takes you back to the next higher level and finally back to the installation menu.

Detailed information on the individual packages (including a complete file list) can be obtained by pressing F2. The current installation status of each package is indicated by a letter and can be modified by means of the appropriate keys or with ↵.

`yast` shortcuts for the installation status

`X`	the package is marked for installation
`i`	already installed
`D`	already installed; to be removed (uninstall)
`R`	already installed; to be updated (replace)

```
xterm
 Series selection                    YaST Version 0.997 -- (c) 1994-99 SuSE GmbH
 Series
 a     Linux Base System (You need it!)                              [116.8 M] O
 ap    Programs that don't need X                                    [ 22.0 M] O
 aplx  ApplixWare Office                                             [    0 B] O
 beo   Extreme Linux (Beowulf)                                       [    0 B] O
 d     Development (C, C++, Lisp, etc.)                              [ 95.5 M] #
 doc   Documentation                                                 [ 59.6 M] #
 e     Emacs                                                         [ 55.9 M] #
 emu   Emulators                                                     [    0 B] #
 fun   Games and more                                                [225.1 K] #
 gnm   GNOME - GNU Network Object Model Environment                  [ 43.0 M] #
 gra   All about graphics                                            [ 22.6 M] #
 ham   Amateur Radio (AX.25, CW, Logs, etc.)                          [    0 B] #

 <F3>=Zoom
 device-name partition  total     used     free     free%  mount-point

 /dev/hda10   Linux      1.13 G  805.9 M  355.3 M   30%   /
 /dev/hdb     OTHER    637.9 M  637.9 M      0 B    0%   /var/adm/mount

          F1=Help   F4=Resorting   F5=Dependencies   F10=Esc=Exit
```

Figure C.2 `yast` during package selection.

With WHAT IF... you can find out what would happen in the event of installation. Basically, you are told how many packages would be (un)installed and how much space that would take up or free.

Package dependencies

Next, you can use CHECK DEPENDENCIES OF PACKAGES to find out whether your package selection is sensible. If you want to install a package that requires another package (which you have not (yet) selected) `yast` signals this fact. Although the results are not that clear, at least experienced programmers will be able to guess what this means.

In the following example, the X interface for the GNU debugger (`xxgdb`, included in the `xdev` series) is to be installed. `yast` has recognized that `xxgdb` can only be used if the GNU debugger (`gdb`, from the `d` series) is installed as well. If you terminate the dialog with the AUTO button, this package is automatically marked for installation. (You may well find that now another package is a precondition for `gdb` – in this case you have to go through the same process again.)

```
xxgdb (xdev):
  [AND]
   gdb      d

Packages which will be selected by <AUTO>
   gdb      d
```

Performing the installation

If you are sure that your selection is correct, the time has come for START INSTALLATION. If by chance the selected packages are not present on the currently inserted CD-ROM, `yast` prompts you for a change of CD.

During uninstallation of packages, `yast` asks whether a backup of all modified files of the affected directories is to be created. For this purpose, the backup component of `yast` described below is employed.

Finding packages

Fortunately, the SuSE series are not as entangled as those of RedHat, but in SuSE too it is often difficult to find a specific package. In such cases, the INDEX command, which creates an alphabetical list of all packages, is of great help. Already installed packages are marked with an asterisk. For each package, space requirements and series are indicated.

An even more powerful command is PACKAGE INFORMATION: here you can specify text which is searched for in the descriptions of all packages. In the list of results, you can then immediately mark the required package for installation.

The `yast` backup program

As well as the large number of configuration functions, `yast` also provides the possibility of creating backups. The backup program is called via SYSTEM ADMINISTRATION|CREATE BACKUPS. In the first step, you must specify the directories and file systems (usually DOS and CD-ROM) that you want to exclude from the backup. In the second step, the backup program determines which files have been changed with respect to the original installation from CD-ROM. The program now displays a list of all directories from which files would be backed up. At this point you have a second opportunity to exclude individual directories from being backed up.

In the last step, you can specify where the backup is to be stored. You may specify either the device file of a streamer or an ordinary file. The backup can also be compressed. Furthermore, a contents list can be created, that is, a list of all files included in the backup archive.

NOTE

Please note that what is created is not a full backup, but only a backup of files you have modified. The advantage is that in many cases the amount of data can still be handled without a streamer. Furthermore, creating a backup of files which are included on the SuSE CD-ROMs in the first place does not make much sense. You should, however, be aware that you cannot restore your system (for example after a loss of your hard disk) from the backup files alone. You would first need to reinstall the same packages that were present at backup time and could then use the backup to restore your own modifications.

The help system

One of the most attractive features of the SuSE distribution is certainly the help system. It consists of the following packages, all of which, for reasons of space, need not be installed. If not specified otherwise, all packages are located in the `doc` series.

`susehilf`	English and German starting page, script files `hilfe` and `susehelp`
`rman` (`ap` series)	`man` → HTML converter
`inf2htm`	`info` → HTML converter
`apache` (`n`)	http server (dynamic `info` texts, search function)
`gnuhtml`	HTML files for GNU programs
`howtoenh`	HTML version of the HOWTO documents
`ldp`	Linux Documentation Project (FAQs and several complete books)
`sdb_en`	texts of the support database
`sdb_cgi`	CGI scripts for searching the support database
`susepake`	short descriptions of all SuSE packages
`xf86html`	XFree86 documentation in HTML format

All of the documents mentioned above can be accessed via Netscape from a starting page. The help system can alternatively be started with `susehelp` (English version) or `hilfe` (German version). If Netscape is already running, the starting page is immediately displayed; otherwise Netscape is automatically started.

The support database contains an almost endless list of texts that have emerged from years of experience of the SuSE support department. (The version supplied with the distribution is obviously not entirely up-to-date. The current version can be found at SuSE's Web site.)

Depending on whether you have installed the CGI scripts and the Apache HTTP server, you can either use the comfortable keyword search or you will need to pick the help texts from an alphabetical keyword list. The search for 'ppp' in SuSE 6.1 yielded 52 entries in all!

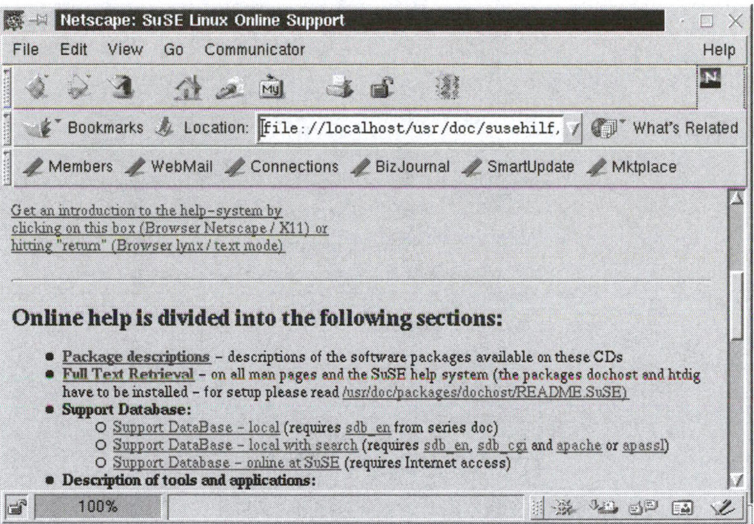

Figure C.3 The starting page of the help system.

NOTE

If several SuSE computers are linked together in a network, you have the possibility of storing the fairly massive documentation files on only one computer, which thus becomes the documentation server for all other computers. For this purpose, you need to install both the `htdig` and `dochost` packages of the `n` series on the server, whereas the clients only need `dochost`. Further information on this configuration is provided in `/usr/doc/packages/dochost/README.SuSE`. This method not only saves hard disk space, but also allows full text search across all HTML documents.

TIP

As well as the main HTML documentation described above there is quite a lot of package-specific documentation. The README files and other texts are usually installed in the `/usr/doc/packages/`*`name`* directories.

SuSE internals

GNOME

Although the SuSE 6.1 distribution includes GNOME 1.0, its use is rather difficult. In this respect, SuSE cannot keep up with RedHat 6.0.

The problems begin with the fact that after installation of all GNOME packages GNOME only comes up with error messages. For proper execution, you still need the `imlibdev` package of the `gra` series, which needs to be manually installed with `yast`. (Here the `yast` information on package dependencies is obviously not quite complete.)

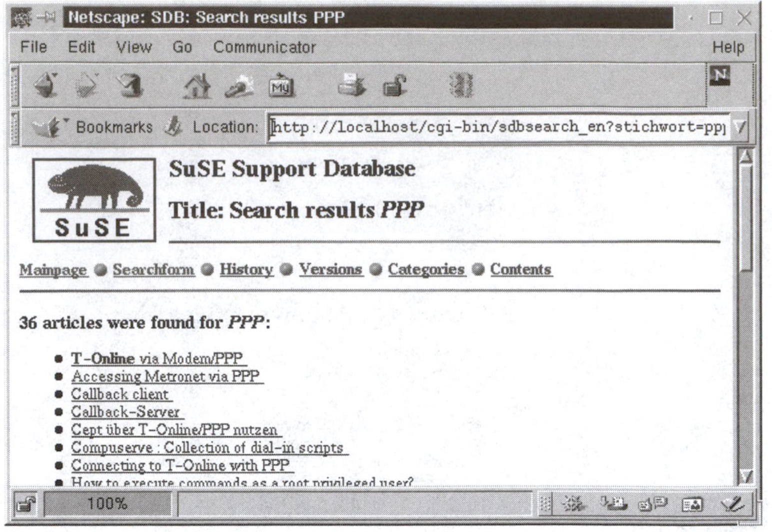

Figure C.4 The SuSe support database.

To start GNOME you can now execute the `panel` command in an arbitrary window manager. Currently, `yast` does not yet allow you to specify GNOME together with a window manager as the default desktop. If you want GNOME to be started automatically together with X, you will need to make the following changes to `~/.xintirc`:

```
# at the end of ~/.xinitrc, instead of: exec $WINDOWMANAGER
fvwm & exec panel
```

Instead of `fvwm` you can obviously also use any of the other window managers supplied (and installed) together with SuSE. Unfortunately, the window manager best suited to GNOME, namely Enlightenment, is supplied in an obsolete and poorly configured version. Only anoraks will get any joy out of this.

Shadow password system

SuSE uses the shadow password system. In this system, passwords are not stored directly in `/etc/passwd`, but in a separate file `/etc/shadow`, which can only be read by `root`. To register new users, you should use `yast`.

If you manually enter a new user into `passwd`, you also need to make a corresponding entry in `shadow` (leaving the password field empty). Subsequently, you log in with the new name and call `passwd` to assign the new user a password. Further information on the shadow password system can be found in the HOWTO text of the same name.

Init-V process

The Init-V process of SuSE also deviates slightly from that of other Linux systems (see also page 124). The numbering of runlevels looks as follows:

```
0 - Halt                                  3 - Multiuser with network and xdm
```

```
S - Single user                          4 - not used
1 - Multiuser without network            5 - not used
2 - Multiuser with network (default)     6 - Reboot
```

The `rc` scripts are located in `/sbin/init.d`. This has the advantage that the `/etc` directory effectively contains only configuration files, while all executable programs are located in `/sbin`.

`rc.config / SuSEconfig`

SuSE uses `/etc/rc.config` together with the files in the `/etc/rc.config.d` subdirectory as central configuration files. Both `yast` and the Init-V process access this file. The files are so well commented that in many cases even manual changes are possible. However, you must subsequently execute `SuSEconfig` to transfer the new settings to other system files as well. (If you modify `rc.config` via `yast`, `SuSEconfig` is executed automatically.)

libc compatibility

With version 6, SuSE was changed over to the new glibc library. If you still want to execute old libc programs, you need to install the optional libc compatibility package, which is well hidden in the `a` series under the name of `shlibs5`.

The libraries are installed in the `/usr/i486-linux-libc5/lib` directory and linked to `/etc/ld.so.conf`. (The space requirement of this package is quite considerable – more than 40 Mbytes! The reason is that it contains not only the base library but also the X libraries derived from it. Even the Qt library for old KDE programs is present.)

Problems with the Ctrl key

In the default configuration, SuSE swallows key combinations with the right-hand Ctrl key. If, for example, in XEmacs you enter Ctrl+← twice, the cursor is moved only by one word to the left.

The cause lies in `/usr/X11R6/lib/X11/Xmodmap` or in the local file `~/.Xmodmap`. Here, the Ctrl key (code 109 or hexadecimal 0x6D) is defined as the `Multi_key` symbol. If you want the Ctrl key to work without problems, you need to comment this instruction out by means of an exclamation mark and assign key 109 to `Control_R` instead.

```
! modification in /usr/X11R6/lib/X11/Xmodmap or in ~/.Xmodmap
! keycode  109  =  Multi_key
keycode 109  =  Control_R
```

The enclosed CD-ROMs

APPENDIX

The two CD-ROMs contain the Publisher's Edition of RedHat Linux 6.0 (CD-ROM 1) together with various supplements (CD-ROM 2). All programs are supplied together with their source code. As you know, 'free' refers not only to the price but also to the availability of the sources. The following sections provide more detailed information on contents and installation.

CD-ROM 1

CD-ROM 1 contains the Publisher's Edition of RedHat Linux 6.0 for PCs with Intel-compatible processors. The CD-ROM was made available for this book by RedHat Software, Inc. – a great many thanks! The official description of this CD according to the license agreement with RedHat is as follows:

> This book includes a copy of the Publisher's Edition of Red Hat Linux from Red Hat Software, Inc., which you may use in accordance with the GNU General Public License. The Official Red Hat Linux, which you may purchase from Red Hat Software, includes Red Hat Software's documentation and 30 days of free telephone and e-mail technical support regarding installation of Official Red Hat Linux. You also may purchase technical support from Red Hat Software on issues other than installation. You may purchase Official Red Hat Linux and technical support from Red Hat Software through the company's web site (www.redhat.com) or its toll-free number 1.888.REDHAT1.

As a complement to the above, the following points summarize the differences between the Publisher's Edition and the full version ('Official RedHat Linux') in less formal language:

- For reasons of space, some packages are left out in the Publisher's Edition – see the file `README.publishers-edition` on CD-ROM 1. All packages listed there can, however, be found on the enclosed second CD-ROM in the `publishers-edition` directory.
- For reasons of licensing, no commercial packages are included (that is, packages which are not freely available on the Internet or which cannot be redistributed on CD-ROM without appropriate licensing).
- Naturally the printed version of the RedHat manual is not supplied – but you do have this book, together with an online version of the RedHat manual which you can even read prior to installation (directory `/doc/manual` on CD 1).
- Finally, for understandable reasons, RedHat cannot provide support for this free-of-charge version of RedHat Linux.

Apart from this there are no restrictions as to the extent and application of the enclosed distribution – what you get is a complete and fully functional Linux distribution. Installation is performed as described in Appendix B, the only difference being that fewer packages (or series) are available for selection. The missing packages need to be installed manually at a later stage (see below).

CD-ROM 2

CD-ROM 2 contains sample files for the book, all RedHat 6.0 packages missing from the Publisher's Edition, all updates to RedHat Linux 6.0 that were available at the time of preparing this book, some additional packages for important programs described in this book, and the most recent kernel version 2.2.n available. This CD-ROM was assembled by the author of this book.

The `publishers-edition` directory

This directory contains a number of packages which normally belong to RedHat Linux 6.0 but could not be included on CD 1 for reasons of space. The `SRPMS` subdirectory contains the corresponding source code.

For installation of individual packages you best use `rpm`. It may happen that some packages require prior installation of other packages. The following example shows the installation of teTeX (that is, the LaTeX distribution). The first attempt fails:

```
#  rpm -i /cdrom/publishers-edition/tetex-0.9-17.i386
error: failed dependencies:
       dialog is needed by tetex-0.9-17
```

Thus you need to insert CD-ROM 1 (`umount`, `mount`) and install the `dialog` package first:

```
#  rpm -i /cdrom/RedHat/RPMS/dialog-0.6-14.i386.rpm
```

After another change of CD the `tetex` installation works without problems:

```
#  rpm -i /cdrom/publishers-edition/tetex-0.9-17.i386
```

The `updates` directory

If after completion of a new distribution problems or security gaps appear in individual packages, RedHat usually makes corrected packages available on its FTP server after a short time. The `updates` directory contains all the updates available by end of May, 1999. Information on the errors corrected by these updates can be found in the file `updates/README`.

To replace an already installed package with a more recent version, you use `rpm` with the `--upgrade` option. However, this does not always work straight away. Thus, for example, installation of Netscape Communicator 4.6 presumes the package `netscape-common-4.6`. This package can, however, not be updated because this would violate the package dependencies with the still installed previous Netscape version. The update function only when you update *both* packages with one single `rpm` command.

```
# rpm --upgrade netscape-communicator-4.6-1.i386.rpm
error: failed dependencies:
  netscape-common = 4.6 is needed by netscape-communicator-4.6-1
# rpm --upgrade netscape-common-4.6-1.i386.rpm
error: failed dependencies:
  netscape-common = 4.51 is needed by netscape-communicator-4.51-3
# rpm --upgrade netscape-common-4.6-1.i386.rpm \
    netscape-communicator-4.6-1.i386.rpm
```

NFS

For the first time, RedHat 6.0 uses the `knfsd` package as an NFS server which resorts directly to the new NFS functions in kernel 2.2. Although the brief info text of the `rpm` package promises better performance, this is obtained at the cost of considerable compatibility problems which in particular occur with computers running a different operating system. By the end of May 1999, no updates were available which would diminish these problems. However, by the time you hold this book in your hands you will probably find an improved version on RedHat's Web server:

`http://www.redhat.com/corp/support/errata/rh60-errata-general.html`

KDE

Unfortunately, the final version 1.1.1 is not supplied with RedHat 6.0, but the beta version 1.1.1pre2. In Linux Weekly News and in some newsgroups there have been reports about stability problems with this KDE version. At the time of presing the CD, no update was available. (By the way, the author has not experienced any difficulties during operation of KDE.)

The `contrib` directory

The `contrib` directory contains some packages which officially do not belong to RedHat 6.0 but are treated in this book: `leafnode`, LyX and KLyX, `xemacs`, and `xv`. These packages come from the `contrib` directory of the RedHat FTP server.

`leafnode`

This is a small news server which is particularly suited for private news archives that can be read via modem in offline mode. The following command is used for installation:

```
# rpm -i /cdrom/contrib/leafnode-1.9.2-1.i386.rpm
```

LyX

LyX is a WYSIWYG interface for LaTeX. The `xforms` package provides a library LyX is built on.

```
# rpm -i /cdrom/contrib/xforms-0.88-2.i386.rpm
# rpm -i /cdrom/contrib/lyx-1.0.1-2.i386.rpm
```

KLyX

KLyX is the KDE version of LyX. Installation is somewhat more complicated:

```
# cp /cdrom/contrib/libstdc++.so.2.9.0 /usr/lib
# ldconfig
# rpm -i --nodeps /cdrom/contrib/klyx-0.9.9-1.i686.rpm
# cp -rs /opt/kde/bin/* /usr/bin/
# cp -rs /opt/kde/share/* /usr/share/
```

Some remarks about the above: KLyX.9.9 presumes the library `libstdc++-2.9.0`. Although RedHat 6.0 supplies and installs the `libstdc++-2.9` package, this package actually provides only version 2.8 of the required library (you can easily verify this by means of `rpm -q --provides libstdc++`. It is unlikely that this confusion of versions was intentional.)

To install the required `libstdc++` version without messing up the RPM package management, the missing file is simply copied into the `/usr/lib` directory. `ldconfig` makes sure that this library is found.

The `--nodeps` option in the following `rpm` command forces the installation of `klyx` although `libstdc++-2.9` is still unknown in the RPM database.

The next problem is that under RedHat 6.0 all KDE files are found in the `/usr/share` directory. The KLyXpackage, however, is installed into `/opt/kde/share` instead. (This directory is the default directory which was taken over by many other distributions but not by RedHat.) To make KLyX find all required files, appropriate links are created by means of the two `cp -ls` commands.

NOTE

The KLyX package on CD-ROM 2 is optimized for i686 processors (Pentium Pro, Pentium II, and compatible processors). Installation and execution on older processors is not possible.

An i386 binary package which would run on all i386-compatible processors (although not as fast on the more advanced models) was unfortunately not available in RedHat's `contrib` directory. By the time you have this book, KLyX 1.0 will probably be completed – then, at the latest, you should find an appropriate i386 package in that `contrib` directory. Maybe RedHat will even decide to incorpate the program into the 6.0 Powertools, which were also unavailable at the time of writing.

The above problems with KLyX are in a way symptomatic: installation of packages that are not directly supplied together with (or optimized for) a distribution is practically impossible for the layperson (and not easy even for a Linux professional).

XEmacs

This alternative to GNU Emacs is subdivided into four packages. Normally you only need `xemacs` (the program files) and `xemacs-info` (the corresponding documentation). `xemacs-el` contains the Emacs Lisp source text of the countless Emacs extensions and is of interest only to programmers. `xemacs-extras` contains some files that are shared between GNU Emacs and XEmacs. This package can only be installed if the GNU Emacs is *not* installed.

```
# rpm -i /cdrom/contrib/xemacs-20.4-4.i386.rpm
# rpm -i /cdrom/contrib/xemacs-info-20.4-4.i386.rpm
```

xv

`xv` is a graphics program. Please note that it is shareware. The program may be employed free of charge only for private purposes. Commercial application is subject to registration. Please read the copyright information (button ABOUT XV)!

```
# rpm -i /cdrom/contrib/xv-3.10a-13+flmask.i386.rpm
```

The `kernel` directory

This directory contains the source code of the most recent kernel available (2.2.9) at the time of concluding work on this book. As a rule it is not necessary to carry out a kernel update (the kernel version 2.2.5 supplied together with RedHat 6.0 proves to be very stable in most cases).

The `samples` directory

This directory contains the sample files for the book (particularly configuration files). Many file names begin with a dot and are therefore invisible. Please use `ls -la`!

References

This book includes information gathered out of hundreds of `man`, `info`, `readme`, `faq` and `HOWTO` documents, together with countless usenet articles in `[de.]comp.os.linux.xxx`, articles from the German journals *ct* and *ix*, the German *Linux-Magazin*, and the American *Linux Journal*, and so on. It is therefore not possible to compile a precise and comprehensive reference list. I therefore limit myself to include a list of titles which were invaluable while I was working on this book:

Adobe Systems (1990). *PostScript Language Reference Manual* 2nd edn. Addison Wesley Publishing

Barnes D., Cosper K., Ewing M. and Troan E. (1998). *Red Hat Linux 5.2 – The Official Red Hat Linux User's Guide*. Red Hat Software, Inc.

Barnes D., Cosper K., Ewing M. and Troan E. (1996). *Red Hat Linux 4.1 – The Official Red Hat Linux User's Guide*. Red Hat Software, Inc.

Bauer B., Alexander Bisler, A, *et al.* (1998). *Installation, configuration and first steps with S.u.S.E Linux 6.0*. S.u.S.E. GmbH

Born G. (1991). *PostScript enträtselt.* Systhema-Verlag

Cameron D., Bill Rosenblatt B. (1991). *Learning GNU Emacs*. O'Reilly & Associates

Dayton, L., Davis, J. (1998). *Photoshop Wow!* Addison-Wesley-Longman

Garfinkel S., Spafford G. (1996). *Practical Unix & Internet Security.* O'Reilly & Associates

Gilly D. (1992). *UNIX in a Nutshell.* O'Reilly & Associates

Goossens M., Mittelbach F., Samarin A. (1994). *The LaTeX Companion*, Addison-Wesley

Hein J. (1999). *Linux Companion for System Administrators*, Addison-Wesley-Longman

Hetze S., Hohndel D., Kirch O., Müller M. (1995). *Linux Anwenderhandbuch* 5th edn., LunetIX

Kaufmann L., Matt Welsh M. (1995). *Running Linux.* O'Reilly & Associates

Olaf Kirch O. (1995). *Linux Network Administrator's Guide*. O'Reilly & Assosciates

Kopka H. (1992). LaTeX – *Eine Einführung*. Addison-Wesley Verlag

Kopka H. (1992). LaTeX – *Erweiterungsmöglichkeiten*. Addison-Wesley Verlag

Kopka H. (1995). LaTeX – *Ergänzungen* vol. 2. Addison-Wesley Verlag

Lamport, L (1994). LaTeX– *A Document Preparation System*. Addison Wesley Publishing

Kraus, H. (1998). *Photoshop 4*, Addison-Wesley-Longman

Kylander, K., Kylander, O. (1999). *The Gimp User Manual version 1.0.0.* (The book is freely available as an online document at `www.gimp.org`.)

Maier G., Wildberger A. (1994). *In 8 Sekunden um die Welt* 3rd edn. Addison-Wesley Verlag

Mattew, N., Stones, R. (1996). *Beginning Linux Programming*. Wrox Press

Microsoft (1996). *Microsoft Windows NT Workstation Resource Kit*. Microsoft Press

Ousterhout J. K. (1994). *Tcl and the Tk Toolkit*. Addison-Wesley Verlag

Peek J., O'Reilly T., Loukides M. (1993). *Unix Power Tools*. O'Reilly & Associates/ Random House

Röhrig, B. (1997). *Linux im Netz*. Computer & Literatur

Sobell, M. (1997). *A Practical Guide to Linux*. Addison Wesley Publishing

Strobel S., Thomas Uhl T. (1995). *Linux – Vom PC zur Workstation* 2nd edn. Springer Verlag

Termöllen, P. (1993). Shell-Programmierung im Alleingang, Springer Verlag

Trümper, W. (1998). *Intranetworking mit Linux*. Addison-Wesley-Longman

Uhl T., Haag R., Lotz C., Strobel S., Vogel D. (1994). *Chip Spezial: Linux – Unix für jedermann. Der PC als Workstation*. Vogel Verlag

Welch B. (1995). *Practical programming in Tcl and Tk*. Prentice Hall

Index

The index entries are ordered by their initial letters. Thus, the entries for the LaTeX command `\end`, the files in the `/etc` directory, and the configuration file `.emacs` are all found under the letter E.

The page references given below refer to the beginning of the section of text in which a term is discussed and not necessarily to the page where it physically occurs.

O

P